W9-DGE-373

OXFORD READINGS IN
THE ATTIC ORATORS

OXFORD READINGS IN CLASSICAL STUDIES

Greek Religion
Edited by Richard Buxton

Homer's *Iliad*
Edited by Douglas L. Cairns

Virgil's *Aeneid*
Edited by S. J. Harrison

The Roman Novel
Edited by S. J. Harrison

Ancient Literary Criticism
Edited by Andrew Laird

Euripides
Edited by Judith Mossman

Aristophanes
Edited by Erich Segal

Greek Tragedy
Edited by Erich Segal

Menander, Plautus, and Terence
Edited by Erich Segal

The Greek Novel
Edited by Simon Swain

Aeschylus
Edited by Michael Lloyd

Ovid
Edited by Peter E. Knox

All available in paperback

Oxford Readings in The Attic Orators

Edited by
EDWIN CARAWAN

LIBRARY
FRANKLIN PIERCE UNIVERSITY
RINDGE, NH 03461

OXFORD
UNIVERSITY PRESS

OXFORD

Great Clarendon Street, Oxford OX2 6DP

Oxford University Press is a department of the University of Oxford.
It furthers the University's objective of excellence in research, scholarship,
and education by publishing worldwide in

Oxford New York

Auckland Cape Town Dar es Salaam Hong Kong Karachi
Kuala Lumpur Madrid Melbourne Mexico City Nairobi
New Delhi Shanghai Taipei Toronto

With offices in

Argentina Austria Brazil Chile Czech Republic France Greece
Guatemala Hungary Italy Japan Poland Portugal Singapore
South Korea Switzerland Thailand Turkey Ukraine Vietnam

Oxford is a registered trade mark of Oxford University Press
in the UK and in certain other countries

Published in the United States
by Oxford University Press Inc., New York

© Oxford University Press 2007

The moral rights of the author have been asserted
Database right Oxford University Press (maker)

First published 2007

All rights reserved. No part of this publication may be reproduced,
stored in a retrieval system, or transmitted, in any form or by any means,
without the prior permission in writing of Oxford University Press,
or as expressly permitted by law, or under terms agreed with the appropriate
reprographics rights organization. Enquiries concerning reproduction
outside the scope of the above should be sent to the Rights Department,
Oxford University Press, at the address above

You must not circulate this book in any other binding or cover
and you must impose the same condition on any acquirer

British Library Cataloguing in Publication Data

Data available

Library of Congress Cataloging in Publication Data

Oxford readings in the Attic orators / edited by Edwin Carawan.
p. cm. – (Oxford readings in classical studies)
Includes bibliographical references and index.
ISBN-13: 978–0–19–927993–7 (alk. paper)
ISBN-10: 0–19–927993–4 (alk. paper)
ISBN-13: 978–0–19–927992–0 (alk. paper)
ISBN-10: 0–19–927992–6 (alk. paper)
1. Speeches, addresses, etc., Greek–History and criticism. 2. Athens
(Greece)–Intellectual life. 3. Athens (Greece)–Politics and government. 4. Political oratory–Greece–
Athens. 5. Rhetoric, Ancient. 6. Oratory, Ancient. I. Carawan, Edwin.
PA3264.094   2007
885'.0109–dc22   2006039353

Typeset by SPI Publisher Services, Pondicherry, India
Printed in Great Britain
on acid-free paper by
Biddles Ltd., King's Lynn, Norfolk

ISBN 978–0–19–927992–0
ISBN 978–0–19–927993–7 (Pbk.)

1 3 5 7 9 10 8 6 4 2

Preface

The Attic Orators present a large corpus and the scholarly work that informs our reading of it is far-ranging. For this volume I have set a rather narrow focus but one that should prove useful to scholars and students in a range of disciplines: *the intersection of rhetoric and law.* In choosing and presenting this material my aim was to make the collection interesting and accessible to a wide audience of informed readers, including those for whom long quotations in Greek would not be helpful. Therefore the Greek has been either translated or, for key phrases, transliterated. For the special terms of rhetoric and law a glossary is provided.

The aims of the series have shaped the content to some degree: I have not included any essay that can already be found in a recent collection of wide distribution; I preferred to revisit articles that have been influential but may not be easily available (not to overlook those that appeared in major journals). The references have been adapted to a concise format, eliminating many of the original footnotes. For a few of the articles, especially those translated or where the new format greatly altered the sequence of notes, the original page numbers are given in square brackets. Addenda by the editor or translator are also set in brackets.

To all the contributors and translators I am much indebted. But I owe special thanks: to Sally Humphreys for help with the citations in her chapter (which led to the lion's share of the References); and to Jess Miner for rendering Wolff's German (and Thür's) into an English version that faithfully captures both the sense and the spirit.

Contents

III. CASTING THE JURY

Abbreviations and Conventions

For ancient authors and their works and other persons and places mentioned in those works, spelling and abbreviations generally follow *the Oxford Classical Dictionary*, 3rd edn. (1996). For names lacking in *OCD* or where clarity seems to require, we retain the author's original, whether Latinized or Greek transliteration.

Relationships are sometimes abbreviated, according to a standard anthropological convention, as 'B' = brother, 'F' = father, 'M' = mother, 'S' = son, 'W' = wife, 'Z' = sister (e.g. ZS = sister's son).

For modern works, abbreviations are those used in the *Oxford Classical Dictionary* [3] and (where lacking in *OCD*) *L'Année Philologique*. Note also:

Agora XV	B. D. Meritt and J. S. Traill (eds.), *The Athenian Agora*, vol. XV, *Inscriptions. The Athenian Councillors*, Princeton, 1974
Agora XXVIII	A. Boegehold, *The Athenian Agora*, vol. XXVIII, *The Lawcourts at Athens: Sites, Buildings, Equipment, Procedure, and Testimonia*, Princeton, 1995
APF	J. K. Davies, *Athenian Propertied Families, 600–300 B.C.*, Oxford, 1971
Blass, *AB*	F. Blass, *Die attische Beredsamkeit*, 2nd edn., 3 vols. Leipzig, 1887–98 (3rd edn. Hildesheim, 1962; repr. New York, 1979)
CIG	A. Boeckh (ed.), *Corpus Inscriptionum Graecarum*, Berlin, 1827–77
FHG	K. Müller, *Fragmenta der griechischen Historiker*, 5 vols., Paris, 1841–70
FGrH	F. Jacoby, *Fragmenta der griechischen Historiker*, Leiden, 1923–
ICret	M. Guarducci (ed.), *Inscriptiones Creticae, opera et consilio Friderici Halbherr collectae*, Rome, 1935–50
IG	*Inscriptiones Graecae*, Berlin, 1873–

Kirchner, *PA*	J. Kirchner, *Prosopographia Attica*, 2 vols., Berlin, 1901–3 (repr. Chicago, 1981)
Lipsius, *AR*	J. H. Lipsius, *Das attische Recht und Rechtsverfahren*, 3 vols., Leipzig, 1905–15
Rabe	H. Rabe, *Prolegomenon Sylloge*, Leipzig, 1931
Radermacher, *AS*	L. Radermacher (ed.), *Artium scriptores. Reste der voraristotelischen Rhetorik*, Sitz. Wien 227.3, Vienna, 1951
RE	A. Pauly, G. Wissowa, and W. Kroll (eds.), *Real-encyclopädie der classischen Altertumswissenschaft*, Stuttgart, 1893–
Rhodes, *CAAP*	P. J. Rhodes, *A. Commentary on the Aristotelian Athenaion Politeia*, Oxford, 1981 (with addenda, 1993)
*SIG*³	W. Dittenberger, *Sylloge Inscriptionum Graecarum*, 3rd edn., Leipzig, 1915–24
Walz	C. Walz, *Rhetores Graeci*, Stuttgart–Tübingen, 1833–5
ZRG	*Zeitschrift der Savigny-Stiftung für Rechtsgeschichte, Romanistische Abteilung*

Introduction
The Speechwriter's Art and the Imagined Community

Edwin Carawan

Like the democracy that inspired it, the work of the Attic Orators was scorned for much of its history. The corpus is largely composed of three genres, all of which earned the contempt or suspicion of critics since Plato. There are the remains of a once prolific source, the *technē* or technical manual, the 'Art' itself. It was this material that Plato especially despised for replacing the truth with 'likenesses'. A large part of the corpus is composed of 'logographic' speeches; indeed, this was the main output of the early authors Antiphon, Lysias, and Isaeus. Here, typically, the artful ghostwriter crafts a case for the paying client, a practice rebuked even by the Orators themselves. And there are, of course, the speeches written *in propria persona* by a politician or social critic on some issue vital to the community—many of them obviously self-serving. Out of this mix it is not surprising that 'Rhetoric' became a dubious discipline in late antiquity: if it is not an exercise in deception, it is a study in style and form. The latter has served as the respectable Rhetoric for much of the modern era: this is Rhetoric as advanced Composition, focusing on figures of speech and syntax, devices of invention and arrangement. The great studies of the late nineteenth century—Blass's *Beredsamkeit*, Jebb's *Orators*, Navarre's *Essai*—show this preoccupation with formal features. And to this day it remains a productive approach, represented in Stephen Usher's very useful study, *Greek Oratory.*

But the last decades of the twentieth century saw a paradigm shift in the way scholars deal with this corpus, as they put aside Plato's prejudice to take a fresh look at the way the speech works in its formative setting. The focus moves from the literary circle to the courtroom, and the research revolves around practical questions: How and why does the speech find its way into text, as preparation for a particular trial or training for a litigious career? How does procedure affect the argument? What do witnesses and other means of proof really prove? And how does the speaker ally himself with the values and assumptions of those who will judge his case?

This approach leads to better understanding of rhetoric as a product of the social realities, especially the relationships that linked the speakers and the other participants. But it also helps us to understand how rhetoric shaped those realities. Much depends upon the speechmaker's skill in constructing an 'imagined community', articulating the shared morals and motivations that bound the citizen body together.[1] For modern nationalities that sense of 'who we are' is shaped largely at a distance, by print and other media. In ancient Athens that collective identity took shape in face-to-face gatherings of the community at large. And nowhere was that group identity more self-consciously invoked and interpreted than in the courts of the people.

That intersection of Law and Rhetoric is the focus of this collection. It leads back to the 'inventors' of the art in Sicily, as the earliest *technē* seems to have been largely devised for the courtroom. But the main area encompasses most of the work of the Attic Orators: speeches for trial or for demonstrating legal argument.

By taking this direction, we leave much important work aside (some represented in previous collections). There has been provocative work on theoretical issues, especially regarding the boundaries between rhetoric, sophistry, and philosophy, but without much reflection on how this overlap affected the actual arguments in

---

[1] The phrase 'imagined community' has made its way into the lexicon from Anderson's study of emerging nationalism (1991). 'Community' itself suggests a useful distinction between modern pluralist societies and the more cohesive bodies of the ancient world (as in Rawls 2001).

court.[2] For the workings of democracy, of course, council and assembly were as important as the courts;[3] but here that deliberative genre will be given less scope. There is a great store of new findings on the social dimension of the court speeches, what they tell us about the family, the predicament of women, children, and slaves, the price of honour, and the cost of doing business. These findings help us understand the issues at trial—and are much cited in the chapters of this collection—but most of these studies, in themselves, give little attention to our focus: the technique of writing speeches for a jury trial.

We begin, in Part I, with the origins of the Art, early *technai* and the emergence of logography as a strategy suited to the courts. In Part II, we turn to the elements of this legal argumentation, the means and methods available to the litigant for convincing a jury. And then, in Part III, we address the jury itself, as a committee of the democracy and a construct of the speechwriter.

The greater part of this collection derives from the last quarter of the twentieth century (eleven essays from 1976–2000), but I have included a few pieces that go back before that period because they are seminal, take stock of earlier scholarship, and serve to introduce the subsequent discussion (three essays, 1964–8). In all, they represent a wide range of approaches, involving the most influential work of the last half-century—especially work that has stirred wider interest. Some of the articles take issue with a particular predecessor but, rather than devote much of the volume to antilogies, it seems more useful to give one side of the debate that is particularly well reasoned, not to imply that the case is closed. Thus, for example, Usher's answer to Dover (Ch. 2), on the question of 'composite authorship', has convinced many of us, but, it is fair to say, Dover's thesis remains viable and instructive. Usher's essay is included here as much for the way it sets forth the problem as for its working solution. That aim is true of almost everything in the collection: there is little that

---

[2] Schiappa 1994 reprints 'Landmark' essays on rhetorical theory. Schiappa 1999 dismantles the division of rhetoric that has been standard since Kennedy's *Art of Persuasion* (1963).

[3] Rhodes 2004*b* includes formative articles on this dimension of the Orators and overlaps somewhat with the focus of this collection (with a cover illustration embracing the same theme).

is conclusive, much that disposes of old assumptions to open up the deeper difficulties. In each part the pieces are presented in chronological order (by date of publication, not of subject matter), with one exception: Part II, 'Tools of Argument', begins with Wolff's seminal essay on 'Demosthenes as Advocate', because that lecture introduces the legal dimension of speechwriting so well.

I. THE LOST ART AND THE FIRST WRITTEN SPEECHES

We shall let lie Tisias and Gorgias, who saw that 'likenesses' (*eikota*) must be preferred to the truth ...

(Plato, *Phaedrus* 267a)

These essays touch on two connected problems: the nature of early rhetorical handbooks, the *technai* proper; and the practical side of logography—especially how a speechwriter went about crafting an argument for a particular character.

We begin with a chapter from M. Lavency's dissertation on logography (here translated by George Kennedy). Introducing much of the key testimony on the speechwriter's practice and its limitations, Lavency emphasized the logographer's 'autonomy', his aim 'to construct a speech that would be an exposition of a thesis more than a reply', impervious to the arguments of his adversary. So, for instance, in the first speech of Antiphon, 'dramatic narrative ... takes the place of proof' and obviates any objections (see p. 17 at n. 51). In this profile Lavency anticipated much that scholars now generally suppose regarding the speechwriter's relationship with his client and the way he fashioned a fixed text for an interactive process.

But Lavency's dissertation was soon followed by Dover's *Lysias and the Corpus Lysiacum*, and with that provocative study, one could fairly say, the 'logographic problem' really begins. For Dover discovered significant disparities among the logographic speeches attributed to Lysias and, unhappy with the choice between 'genuine' and 'spurious', he suggested another alternative: composite authorship. The client, with his bought speech in hand, would naturally have added some material in his own words; after the trial, win or lose, he would treasure the text he had paid for so dearly; and that text, complete with whatever additions the client had made, might later find its way into circulation because it could be ascribed to the renowned Lysias. On practical considerations, perhaps, it is not an unlikely scenario; but the positive evidence amounts to little more than stylometrics (frequency of distinctive phrases, etc.). That quantifying of the text enjoyed a vogue in the 1950s and 1960s (and some applications are still useful) but it assumes that a writer sticks to his habits, whereas scholars now tend to regard the early speechwriters as remarkably free of such constraints. On this and other grounds Usher (Ch. 2) makes a case against composite authorship that many have found persuasive. The speechwriters seem reluctant to adapt material others have supplied, and awkward at it when they do so. What testimony we have suggests that they were protective of their intellectual property: if Isocrates 'succeeded in disowning a large number of forensic speeches which he wrote ... Lysias should have had an easier task' in disowning what was foisted upon him (p. 34).

Thomas Cole's article (Ch. 3) 'Who Was Corax', is valuable in many ways. It offers a persuasive theory about the 'inventor' of rhetoric: 'Corax' was not the teacher of Tisias but his epithet. That finding connects with Cole's thesis in *Origins of Rhetoric* (1991*b*): the earliest *technai* were largely 'practice and demonstration' texts; by contrast, explicitly theoretical instruction is first attested for Theodorus (about fifty years after Tisias). The inventor's 'Art' was especially devoted to the particular setting of jury trials in a democracy: for here the issue is clearly framed in advance, opening the door for experts to anticipate the adversary's claims and prepare an argument to answer them. Thus Tisias built his *technē* on the pairing of arguments and the tactic of reversing the most obvious advantages. Indeed, the figure of Corax, as the master who sued for payment from his famous disciple—only to meet with the argument that if the student lost the case it would prove that his teaching was worthless!—may have evolved from a textbook demonstration of such tactics. Cole's perspective is also invaluable for the way it situates the 'inventor' at the transition from oral culture to emerging literacy, probably before there was anything called 'Rhetoric'.[4]

One of the topics under-represented in recent work is *ēthopoeia*, the art of character portrayal so essential to logography. One might argue, there has been much reflection but little new direction since Ivo Bruns's classic study, *Das Literarisches Porträt der Griechen* (1896), whose last part shows that the Orators dealt largely in stereotypes and did little to capture the individual. Their characters are composed of the very 'likenesses' that so provoked Plato.

But John Porter's essay (Ch. 4) on Lysias 1, 'Adultery by the Book', shows where further study might lead. By thorough analysis of comparanda in comedy and elsewhere, Porter argues that Lysias' speech for the duped husband is likely to be an artificial piece based upon the stock characters of fiction. The point is well argued—I find it largely persuasive. But (as Porter acknowledges) it is certainly possible that the speech we have was based on an actual case but much fictionalized as a 'demonstration speech' (advertising the speechwriter's skill) or a 'teaching text' (illustrating the technique for others). Whether we are persuaded or not, Porter's study reminds us of basic problems in establishing the authenticity of a particular case and the purpose of the written speech. And it serves to illustrate in vivid detail how the Orators drew upon familiar 'likenesses' to construct the character most convincing to the layman jury (cf. Gagarin 2003).

For the next section it is important to put this foundational concept, *eikos*, in its original context. In modern translations we readily resort to 'probability'—and that rendering often serves well enough. But ordinarily *eikos* retains the literal sense of 'likeness' or 'resemblance'. This turn of thought is important in the 'imagined community': the audience must form their judgements from general characteristics of the group. When the Orators present 'probabilities' in order to reconstruct events, the implication is always that the participants conform to type and, thus considered, they are 'like(ly)'

---

[4] Schiappa 1990 argued persuasively that *rhetorikē* (*technē*) itself was a coinage no earlier than Plato; the fifth-century term of art was *logōn technē*. That distinction is important because when practitioners and critics began to call this craft *rhetorikē* it would signal a self-conscious division of categories that only arose with a wider and more analytical reading audience.

or 'unlike(ly)' actors in a certain role. To take a precocious example, in the *Hymn to Hermes* (377) the infant prince of thieves famously argued that a newborn is not 'like(ly)' a cattle-rustler.

The 'probabilities' of early rhetoric bear this typical character. There is none of the modern notion of statistical probability as an approximation to some objective reality. The Athenians seem more openly inclined to treat 'facts' as socially constructed. The way a character conforms to type, as others regard him, often seems more important than what actually happened. Indeed, the art of argument, as we find it in the speeches, seems largely devoted to combining law and evidence with the 'likenesses'. The next section focuses upon that combination of so-called 'artless' and 'artful' proofs.

II. THE TOOLS OF ARGUMENT: PROCEDURE AND PROOF

Before the 1960s scholars at work on the Orators usually discounted the legal issues. There was a general presumption that any hard questions of law or evidence were incidental to the argument and overshadowed by the Art. No one has done more to change that presumption than Hans Julius Wolff. And so it is fitting that this section begins with a seminal essay that appeared in 1968, on 'Demosthenes as Advocate' (here translated by Jess Miner, in collaboration with Gerhard Thür, as Ch. 5). Addressing a conference of German lawyers, Wolff takes his theme from a study of 'Cicero as Advocate', and he offers some interesting perspective comparing the Roman with the Athenian orator. The essay also provides a primer on legal proceedings at Athens, and thus serves well as an introduction to this section. But most valuable is the demonstration of how the constraints of procedure and demands for proof shaped the argumentation. Thus in Demosthenes 54, on a charge of assault, the whole arrangement is predicated on a weakness in the evidence: the plaintiff has no witness to affirm that the accused actually struck first, though the law sets that criterion; therefore the narrative and 'proof' produce a cloud of witnesses on every damning detail *except* the first blow. Thus the speechwriter's art can only be understood in the light or the shadow of the legal requirements. In a second example, from Dem. 38, the legal criteria are yet more crucial: here the defendants take advantage of the 'bar against litigation' for matters settled in arbitration, though it is clear from the argument that the case against them actually has to do with liabilities incurred *after* that binding settlement. And so it is only by a tenuous string of 'proofs' that the speechwriter bears his burden.

With the second piece in this part (Ch. 6), we turn back a few years before Wolff's 'Advocate' to a study that he relied upon and one that has shaped the way we understand the law itself as a source of 'proof': H. Meyer-Laurin's *Law and Equity* (as translated by David Mirhady). The so-called 'artless proofs', the *atechnoi pisteis*, included citations of the law itself. These uses of statute in argumentation remain puzzling, but Meyer-Laurin largely resolved some basic issues (cf. Harris 1994). I have included the first four chapters, the better half of the monograph, as it deals more directly with the Orators' argumentation than does the remainder (which is now translated elsewhere). It is exemplary in the way Meyer-Laurin analyses argument: he shows that what others had treated as *exceptio doli* (an exemption from liabilities incurred under false pretenses) was actually 'evidentiary' in nature, not in fact an argument on the law but on how the given evidence is to be weighed against circumstantial considerations. These arguments call for the jury to judge from 'likenesses' rather than documents or fixed rules. Thus, in Hyperides *Against Athenogenes* the plaintiff, who contends he was tricked into buying a bankrupt perfumery, can cite no law that specifically condemns the fraud but must argue from analogy, drawing on a litany of laws that have little to do with his case. As this selection concludes, the citations of law served essentially as material for 'artful proofs', *entechnoi pisteis*.

For the use of witnesses in argumentation, there follows the classic study by Sally Humphreys (Ch. 7). Her aim is to show how the relationships between witness and litigant often counted for more than the content of their testimony. The use of the testimony depends largely on a sort of 'proof by association': it is always telling that a family member, fellow demesman, public official, or even a personal enemy would testify for the speaker. This is a long and complex essay, dense with documentation. But it rewards the diligent reader with an invaluable perspective on the social construction of knowledge in ancient Athens and the difficulties it poses for us: the jurors tend to rely on 'second-hand representations' rather than direct observation (p. 201). 'They are trying to retain some of the qualities of village dispute-settlement procedures in an urban setting, and this leads to contradictions.'

Michael Gagarin's essay on 'Proofs in Antiphon' (Ch. 8) was originally addressed to a seminar at the University of Michigan Law School, and is especially important for its perspective on earlier theories. European scholars of the nineteenth and early twentieth centuries were preoccupied with an evolutionary model: rhetoric arose from certain formalistic and 'irrational' ways of deciding a dispute and developed into a more free and discerning evaluation of evidence and circumstance. Solmsen's brief monograph on Antiphon (1931) is a prime example. Gagarin's essay argues to the contrary: 'Greek culture is characterized by a thoroughly rational approach to debate and decision making' (223). 'The effect of Solmsen's study is to diminish [Antiphon's] accomplishment' (227).

For our understanding of the issue, it is important to be clear about terms of the debate: Solmsen and his predecessors did not mean that the speechmaker is 'irrational' in the usual sense, but that collective reasoning operates within fairly prescriptive conventions.[5] The artful arguments of 'probability' thus revolve around older forms of proof—oath, witness, etc.—what Aristotle and Anaximenes would call 'artless' or 'supplementary proofs'. Indeed, the probabilities (*eikota*) often deal with the likelihood of such evidence, not of the crime itself: is the testimony, oath, or challenge a plausible assertion for that actor in that situation? Of course one could always argue from such probabilities to the facts at issue. Indeed, it was a famous strategy—as old as Tisias—to argue that the accused would never have done the crime precisely because the probabilities would point to him. This principle Gagarin aptly calls 'reverse *eikos*', and it is a prime example of the rational and inventive freedom of even the earliest argumentation.

---

[5] This terminology was familiar in the early twentieth century, notably from Max Weber's 'ideal types': for a useful summary see Rheinstein 1954: pp. xxxix–lii.

In the closing paragraph of his 'update' Gagarin mentions my approach only to discount it, and so our disagreement warrants some explanation here. In *Rhetoric and the Law of Draco* (1998), I argued that the extant speeches for trial in the special courts for homicide, manned by Areopagites and *ephetai*, are organized on a distinctive principle (these cases include two of the court speeches of Antiphon): here the argument irresistibly revolves around the *atechnoi pisteis*—especially challenges to torture and oath. Before an ordinary jury the same speechwriter uses a more 'artful' arrangement—focusing on probabilities of motive and means. The disparity in technique has much to do with the conservatism or 'formal rationalism' of the ancient homicide court.[6] I saw this approach as a middle way, following Gagarin but guided by Solmsen's insight. Gagarin does not see it that way. He is right to insist upon the 'rationality' of early rhetoric, that the writers of speeches were not intellectually hobbled by superstitious baggage about ordeal—and, I have to admit, I did not always put things in the most helpful terms.[7] But I am not alone in finding that the homicide courts were manned by judges of some special competence who judged by their own standard.[8] And, as much of this collection illustrates, the developments in technique were geared to what the special audience—the jury in court—would understand and expect.

The next piece, 'Artless Proofs' by Christopher Carey (Ch. 9), complements Humphreys's (Ch. 7): it gives the other side of the speechmaker's witness strategy. Where Humphreys emphasized the significance that comes from social connections—and may have little to with content—Carey describes the technique by which the speechmaker coaxes or coerces the content that can do him the most good, the tricks of procedure and wording by which he crafts the deposition

---

[6] The term 'formal rationalism' is adapted from Weber (see n. 5) to describe systems in which legal reasoning is preoccupied with conventional forms of decision-making, by contrast to the 'substantive rationalism' that typifies modern democracies (guided by principles of justice or public interest).

[7] 'Primitive' was a poor choice of words. What I meant (and tried to explain) was that argumentation in the homicide courts adheres to conventions based on the original setting of the law, without reflecting social change or importing any 'secondary' rationalization from jurisprudents or outside influences. Perhaps 'primary' or 'pristine' would have been less troublesome.

[8] See esp. Lanni 2000 and 2006: ch. 4, 'The Homicide Courts'.

for the witness to affirm or deny. There is 'art of a sort' even in the handling of this 'artless material'.

This section closes with one particular form of proof that reflects upon the grim realities.[9] In the Orators and in the handbooks we have many references to the testimony of slaves under torture: how do these play into the argument? David Mirhady's article on 'Torture and Rhetoric' (Ch. 10) resurrects an old theory with some important corrections: challenges to slave torture (*basanoi*) were a regular alternative to trial (though not, as once supposed, a sort of vicarious ordeal); in the rare cases where such challenges were accepted, the procedure decides the dispute (and no further suit is viable on that particular issue); wherever such *basanoi* are treated as admissible at trial, the speaker is referring to the written *challenges* to torture (invariably rejected); the precise wording of these documents then becomes important material for argument. Mirhady's analysis has won acceptance not only among scholars who focus on law and rhetoric but also among those who study violence and social control.[10] For our purposes it is especially important for the way Mirhady has connected this practice with the developing theory of 'artless proofs': the formulation of these resources as a theoretical category does not go back to the ealiest *technai* but belongs to the era when such 'evidence' was regularly reduced to written text.

III. CASTING THE JURY

Beyond its use to test the claims of litigants, the 'likenesses' of early rhetoric could also be turned back like a mirror upon the judges, the better to persuade them who they are. The third section deals more directly with this ideological turn of argument, how rhetorical

---

[9] The realities of social control are well treated by V. Hunter 1994 and Allen 2000 (not dealing with argumentation). D. Cohen 1995 has more to say about the rhetorical implications: the trial is less about the merits of a particular claim than the zero–sum struggle for honour.

[10] e.g., by V. Hunter 1994: 93 (drawing on Mirhady's earlier presentation of this thesis). Gagarin 1996 argues effectively that the actual practice was rare: 'by the age of the orators evidentiary *basanos* had become a legal fiction' (16).

practice reflected democratic roles.[11] This process is well analysed in
a chapter from Josh Ober's important book, *Mass and Elite* (Ch. 11 in
this collection). The burden of Ober's book is that the popular
audience dictated the translation of aristocratic values into democratic terms: rhetoric was not an instrument of the 'iron law' drawing
democracies inevitably toward oligarchy but a way of subordinating
the elite to the imagined community.[12] Thus speakers in the courts
and assemblies are constantly negotiating their position as representatives of a code of values that the mass audience controls. This
precarious situation gives rise to certain fictions and paradoxes
based on the very 'wisdom of the people'. Such is the theme of this
chapter on the orator's special ability: the speechmaker must be
expert in some respect, if his voice is worth hearing; and yet he
must never challenge the idea that the common sense of his audience
is superior to all the experts.

   The character of the jury and its control of values is also the subject
of a much-cited article by Stephen Todd, '*Lady Chatterley's Lover* and
the Attic Orators' (Ch. 12). This essay is insightful in many respects:
for the way it draws a parallel to the modern lawyer's predicament,
guessing about the attitudes of an audience; for sorting out earlier
work on the make-up of the Athenian jury, with a persuasive
reckoning of the economic motives; and for its profile of the ancient
jury's most valued traits—native good sense, a healthy respect for
financial security, and a horror of litigiousness.

   The role of the citizen-judges in shaping their community is
treated most directly in an essay by Lene Rubinstein, 'Argument
from Precedent' (Ch. 13).[13] This 'argument from precedent' is not
to be confused with the rule familiar from common law (*stare
decisis*), that later courts are bound by prior judicial decisions on

----

[11] Influential in this regard is Loraux 1986 [1981], treating the annual praise of the
war-dead so powerfully recreated in Thucydides' speech of Pericles (2. 60–4) but also
well represented in the corpus of the Orators (Lyias, Demosthenes, Hyperides, and
adapted by Isocrates).

[12] Of course a chapter alone cannot convey all the connections it has in the book.
But this particular chapter stands alone quite well (with a new preface by Ober).

[13] The paper was originally presented in English at an APA meeting some years ago
(and remained unpublished); it was then translated into Danish (for a festschrift of
limited distribution). The author herself has rendered it back into English, now with
extensive revisions.

the same point of law. It is rather the argumentative principle that the jury should weigh their present verdict as a decision that will define or undermine the social order. In this regard, especially in public actions, 'the judges in effect act as the mouthpiece of the entire Athenian *dēmos*'. Rubinstein's study is important (*i.a.*) for showing how artful a technique this is and how extensive in the extant speeches (further investigation in Lanni 2004).

The last and latest of the essays in this volume (Ch. 14) establishes a new connection between the legal-rhetorical and the more trad-itional literary study of the orators. Demosthenes' speech *On the Crown* is perhaps the single most famous speech in the whole corpus of the Orators. It remains a problematic text on many points of law and history, not least of all how Demosthenes and Ctesiphon could have won their case on precarious legal ground and dubious merits.[14] Yunis succeeds in capturing an elusive aspect of the original recep-tion, how Demosthenes recast the image of the community in the mould of tragedy: their defiance was doomed by a higher power, but it would have been a betrayal of their character to do otherwise. It was a boldly unconventional way for the speaker to make his audi-ence see themselves, and that may have been the key to its success.

In this regard, touching the character of the jury, let me add a last point on translation. As we have noticed, a number of basic terms, crucial to this intersection of law and rhetoric, are problematic— 'proof' and 'probability', for instance. As these essays illustrate, it is not helpful to be doctrinaire or prescriptive. In the Glossary I have tried to represent the range of meanings. A good example is the term often used in this collection for the audience in court, the *dikastai*. Critics may insist that the root meaning and essential function require 'judges', and in many cases that rendering is best. But it is wrong to reject the familiar 'jurors' in every instance; for, aside from the obvious parallel to modern juries as committees of laymen, there is something essentially analogous in the source of their authority. It is ultimately the 'oath'—*jus jurandum*—that makes the 'juror'.

---

[14] Yunis deals here with the historical critique of Cawkwell 1969. On the legal issues, Harris 1994: 143–4, makes a good case that Ctesiphon's proposal was not so patently illegal as often supposed; but cf. Yunis 2001: 174–83.

At Athens that title is all the more apt, as there was no superior authority to restrict or overturn the jury's judgement by a more informed reading of the law. Empowered solely by their oath, these citizens must decide the fate of poor and powerful alike, judging largely from their 'likenesses'.

PART I

The Lost Art and the First Written Speeches

1

The Written Plea of the Logographer*

M. LAVENCY

Ancient texts, in particular those of Cicero and Plutarch, attest that a logographic plea was composed entirely by the writer before being given to the pleader. Fourth-century orators identified a particular style that characterizes the work of a logographer. To believe Alcidamas,[1] 'those who write speeches for the court avoid obscure expressions' that risk awakening the distrust of the judges: 'They imitate the manner of improvisers and their compositions have been considered perfectly successful when the speeches they produced did not at all resemble written works.'[2] However, this mode of composition, which conspicuously departs from the style of composition usual in grand-scale epideictic eloquence, this affected simplicity, did not at all exclude care in the choice of words, since Aristotle saw in judicial logography the model for oratorical precision.[3] Equally explicit [125] is a passage where Aeschines tries to stigmatize the dishonesty of Demosthenes, saying to his rival: 'You had written a speech for

---

* Ch. 6 of *Aspects de la logographie judiciaire attique* (1964), here translated by George A. Kennedy. Brackets indicate additions by the translator. Long quotations in the notes are omitted; the reader is referred to recent translations (esp. for Alcidamas, see now Muir 2001).

[1] [For the Greek text, see Radermacher, *AS* 135–41; Avezzù 1982; Muir 2001 (with English translation). In addition to works cited by Lavency, see also O'Sullivan 1992: 42–62.]

[2] Alcidamas, *On Those Who Write Written Speeches* (or *On the Sophists*), 13 [Muir 2001: 8–9]; see Isoc. 4. 11 and 15. 46; Plato, *Apology* 17b–c.

[3] *Rhetoric* 3. 12. 1413b13. Lipsius 1886: 5, compares this passage with 1414a10 to show that Aristotle intends to speak there of judicial logography; cf. Roberts 1904. One could add that Alcidamas 16 ties *akribeia* to composition revised in all details.

Phormio, the banker, and you had been paid for doing it; this speech you then handed over to Apollodorus who was initiating a capital action against Phormio.'[4] When then we hear one of Theophrastus' 'characters' complaining to his logographer even though the latter has just come to assure him of full success with the judges, we easily conclude that the litigants received from their advocate a carefully polished speech such that they would pay him well.[5]

Writing out a speech in advance poses many problems for us to examine in this chapter.

I. THE RHETORICAL THEORY

The method attributed to a logographer ought first to be situated, illustrated, and explicated in terms of oratorical technique. We have long known that the orators were normally able to have recourse to writing in preparation of their discourses. We also know that, although rhetoric supplied oratorical improvisation with the valuable aid of commonplaces, it had not banished from eloquence a technique of writing that numerous followers preserved. There is thus the question of how logographic methods compare with the rhetorical teaching of the time.

This study of the relation of school teachings to the preparation of a discourse deserves attention. Certainly it is a characteristic of an experienced orator not to let himself be enslaved by the school, and the schoolmaster's technique cannot completely dominate daily rhetorical practice. Nevertheless, the schools did impose certain limiting conventions, with the result that those who shook off the dust of the school unconsciously bear witness to the tradition that had formed them. On the other hand, although far from being in complete control of the usage of their time, the rhetors remained privileged witnesses and watchful stewards of it. The doctrine that

---

[4] Aeschines 2. 165; see also 3. 173, and, to worsen Demosthenes' conduct, Plut. *Dem.* 15. Other examples of such betrayal: Lysias 8. 12; perhaps Dem. 53. 14.

[5] [See Theophrastus, *Characters* 17. 8, describing a man who is always griping about something. The text only says, 'If he wins a court case, even receiving all the votes, he criticizes the writer of the speech for having left out many valid arguments.']

they professed and [126] the precepts the logographers collected from them and disseminated deserved to be firmly fixed in their values: for they had the prestige of a thing that had been instilled in them, the consecration of success, and the force of tradition.

This study is possible thanks to the evidence of Alcidamas. The short treatise that this author composed *against written eloquence* describes some rhetorical methods about which specialists of the fourth century were in dispute.[6]

The first method cited by the rhetor is that in which a speech was written in its entirety and learned by heart. Those who engage in this, Alcidamas says (§§ 1–2, 18), do not deserve to be called orators: they are only composers, writers, sophists. There is no need to be a specialist to write in quiet, to review a composition at one's ease, and [127] to take up in one's own name what others have invented (§ 4 [Muir 2001: 3–5]; cf. Isoc. *Letter* 6. 7). This is a method lacking distinction, and ineffective as well: it is incapable of responding to the needs of debate (§ 21); it leads only to an inert work, substituting for true eloquence an approximate image like the statues of a man (§ 27). It is a tedious method and full of pitfalls: it imposes on one who adopts it a process of memorization that is always laborious, without guarantees against the risk of losing in disgrace the fruit of such an effort (§ 18 [Muir 2001: 10–11]). Despite these limitations, the writer judges that writing out a speech in advance has its place in composing epideictic works and in school exercises (§ 31).

[128] Alongside integral preparation of a speech, Alcidamas briefly mentions the technique that consists of combining improvisation with short parts of a speech prepared in advance. He rejects it immediately: the combination of impromptu speech with prepared topics renders the speech uneven and offends the listener, who perceives very soon the discordance that separates the parts prepared at leisure and the improvised passages (§ 14).

---

6 *On Those Who Write Written Speeches* was apparently published before Isocrates' *Panegyricus* and in response to *On the Sophists*; it can thus be dated between 390 and 380; see Mathieu and Brémond 1950–62: i. 159–60. Isocrates seems to make Alcidamas his target in 13. 9–11, and Alcidamas doubtless responded (cf. §§3–4, 6–12). He is cited by Aristotle, *Rhetoric* 1. 1398b10, and listed with Isocrates by Dionysius of Halicarnassus, *Epistle to Ammaeus* i. 1 [Usher 1985: 309] (Radermacher, *AS* 132, n. 3); see also *Suda*, s.v. 'Alcidamas'. Plato cites him at least once without naming him: *Symp.* 196c; cf. Diès 1927: 417 n. 1.

The good method in the eyes of Alcidamas will be that which limits preparation to discovery of ideas and organization of the plan and leaves the choice of words to improvisation (§ 33). Schematic preparation of a speech freely arranged on the basis of memorized facts assures the orator complete autonomy and perfect mastery of his art. It permits him to adapt to the needs of debate and demands only minimal labour (§§ 18–21). Moreover, trained in this method, the orator will feel at ease in all genres: freed of every difficulty, he will be able, if he desires, to turn without difficulty to publication of a written speech (§ 6).

The division of methods on the basis of oratorical genres seems to have been firmly established. In the view of all, ceremonial discourse, destined to be read, [129] naturally ought to be written in advance (§ 31).[7] Aristotle so specifies, and adds: 'The style of epideictic oratory is that which is best suited to be written; for its proper objective is to be read; next to it, judicial style.'[8] Plato completes the classification: 'The art of speaking and of writing concerns, one would say, principally legal cases; the art of speaking concerns also political speeches.'[9]

The technique of writing a speech ahead of time thus has a well-assured place in classical rhetoric, which has approved it. As prototypes of written eloquence,[10] logographic speeches apply the procedures utilized in eloquence on the grand scale.[11]

---

[7] Cf. H. Brown 1914: 111–12, n. 193; Navarre 1900: 32 ff.; on *epideiknumi* in the sense of 'read', see Hudson-Williams 1949*b*: 67–8.

[8] *Rhet.* 3. 12. 5; note the word *dikographia* in Isocrates 15. 2.

[9] *Phaedrus* 261b: *alla malista men pōs peri tas dikas legetai te kai graphetai tekhnēi.* The passage has been interpreted in different ways. Robin 1926 (ad loc.) understands: 'It is, one would say, principally in legal cases that the art of speaking and of writing is applied, although speaking also has its place in the deliberations of the assembly of the people.' For Chambry 1964 (ad loc.) the translation should be: 'It is especially in courts of law that the art of speaking and writing reigns; the art of speaking is also practiced in the assemblies of the people;' Hudson-Williams 1951: 69, interprets it to mean: 'The political and judicial genre have their own system; judicial speeches are written in advance, but not the political speeches.' These translations, it seems to us, are not justified in the context and do not seem to render adequately the object of the preposition *peri*, 'concerning'. See Isocrates 15. 42.

[10] Plato, *Phaedrus* 257e, affirms that men in politics have been struck with love of logography: they long to leave some writings from their hand and they avidly search for admirers when they have 'written a speech'. This relates to political texts [i.e. to the texts of decrees including the name of the author of the motion]: the use of the word 'logography' in this special sense is all the more suggestive.

[11] See Plato, *Phaedrus* 227c: 'Lysias has written' (the discourse on love that Phaedrus is going to read aloud); see 228b, where there is a question of the scroll containing the discourse; cf. Alcidamas §1.

II. THE LOGOGRAPHER'S INFORMATION

Since the tradition that assigns to the logographer the entire composition ahead of time finds support in the rhetoric [**130**] of the times, there is the question of the quality and quantity of information that the writer has at his disposal at the moment when he elaborates his discourse.

One can certainly imagine that the logographer carefully collected, thanks to the confidences of his client, a good number of valuable suggestions, but such a task is in reality less simple than it seems at first glance. Advocates today, like those of yesterday (cf. Quintilian 12.8), know that all too often they have to overcome their client's reticence and correct or fill in the gaps before being able to construct a clear and complete view of the facts they can exploit. Certainly, the logographers deserve trust in this regard; their proverbial minute precision, abundantly revealed in the details of their work,[12] and their knowledge of the craft should have aided them to anticipate the value and the import of the assertions they receive. They were naturally attentive to exploit in the best way possible all the sources of information at their disposal, and one can believe that the Athenians did not lack informers, well disposed or self-interested—those unrepentant rogues who jabbered away in the Agora. A. P. Dorjahn (1935) was able to reconstruct for this purpose the multiplicity of means of information to which the pleaders could turn.[13] The texts candidly reveal some indiscretions, betrayals, and gossip from which the litigants profit. But whatever had been the richness of information that a man of experience could collect in these circumstances, a heavy debt encumbered the task of the logographer. It was essential for the writer to picture to himself, to know the position his adversary was going to adopt. More than the occasional sources which have just been mentioned, and of which there is hardly need to emphasize the uncertainty, what would interest us to know is to

[12] Lysias 1. 9 and Isaeus 5. 11, among others, cite details that give their narration the colour of sincerity.

[13] This information could be very extensive; see Dem. 28. 29; 46. 58; Isaeus 9. 18. On publication of lawsuits in progress see Isoc. 15. 37 and Dem. 21. 103; cf. Lipsius, *AR* 820.

what extent the procedure permitted the parties to be informed of the resources of the adversary. The problem was sharpened in the case of a pleader for the defence, who was the second to speak. Greek orators, moreover, do not fail [131] to stress their difficulties. They describe the agony that grips the defendant before the surprises that threaten him;[14] they love to depict the unfavourable situation created for the defence, and one of their commonplaces describes the embarrassment a speaker feels when he has to answer at once what the accuser has been able to concoct at leisure.[15] Accusers and accused utilize formulas of doubtful assertion to refute what the opponent may say (*prokatalēpsis*): the expressions 'Perhaps my adversary will say' and 'I learn that my adversary is going to say' lead one to think that the uncertainty, feigned or real, is probable. Alcidamas, for his part, attests as 'a proven fact that those who address the people, those who appear in the courts, and those who discuss something privately are forced to improvise' (§ 9). We should, consequently, ask ourselves if the unexpected was as menacing as the orators want to be believed, and if the logographers did not see themselves forced to give to their works a provisional structure that would permit the insertion of possible additions.

Our knowledge of the procedure owes much, in different ways, to the researches of R. G. Bonner and G. Smith, L. Gernet, L. Lämmli, and A. P. Dorjahn. Thanks to these scholars, the nature, scope, and limits of certain juridical paths, such as arbitration and preliminary hearing (*anakrisis*), can be recognized. Here again, the weakness of our knowledge lets more than one difficulty persist, of which not the least is uncertainty as to the sequence of proceedings.

We already know that quarrels were often settled on the private level thanks to the intervention of relatives or friends of the parties. Reconciliation was much valued and undoubtedly it was quite the usual recourse. If the parties refused to subject themselves [132] to private arbitrators, whose decision was definitive,[16] they were nonetheless able to draw from the preliminary negotiation a supply of useful information about the position of their adversaries.

---

[14] Andoc. 1. 1, 6 and 7; Lys. 7. 3; 19. 3–4; Isoc. 18. 54.

[15] Andoc. 1. 6–7; Lys. 7. 3 [Todd 2000: 80] and 19. 2–5; Isoc. 15. 18 and 18. 54. Cf. Schweizer 1936: 185.

[16] Gernet 1939: 400; Steinwenter 1925: 67 ff.; Lipsius *AR*, 230.

The transfer of litigation to the official level could be done in two ways: that of public arbitration, long employed for a good number of suits (Gernet 1939: 401), and that of the preliminary hearing. In the first case, the handing down—immediately—of the arbitrators' decision caused the passage of the case into the *sub iudice* phase, where only means of proof were admitted—laws, challenges, witnesses—collected during the arbitration and deposited at the end of the procedure in sealed urns. This handling of the case, known from Aristotle,[17] assured the parties extensive information about the evidence available to them.[18]

The procedure of the preliminary hearing (*anakrisis*), on the other hand, brought the antagonists before the instructing magistrate who had jurisdiction over the particular type of case. It is known today that by this route (distinct from the arbitration cases to which it was once mistakenly assimilated) the process did not recognize any legal limitation on the proof material.[19] The argument that has been built to support this thesis is not absolutely impeccable, for tactics of an advocate have sometimes been taken for obligations of procedure.[20] [133] The argument is based largely on the case—surprising[21] but quite probable—of a certain Cratinus, accused of murder. Isocrates tells us (18. 53–4):

---

[17] *Ath. Pol.* 53. 3; cf. Dem. 45. 57–8.

[18] Dem. 57. 14 causes less difficulty than it seems. The speaker confirms the rule stated by Aristotle: if he cites witesses, if he calls as witnesses those who have wronged him, it is by drawing the evidence from a document, doubtless official, that they have written, probably during the verbal process of a hearing when the litigant was excluded from a deme.

[19] Bonner and Smith 1930: 283 ff.; Lämmli 1938: 74–128; Gernet 1939: 400; Dorjahn 1941: 183–4; Bonner 1905: 50 ff.

[20] Bonner and Smith 1930: 285. Passages where the orators offer or demand during the hearing some new proofs, on the spot, result from rhetorical considerations. The writer hopes to draw moral advantage by a gesture that costs him nothing. We cannot in any case use these passages to affirm that the *anakrisis* was not exhaustive. That would be to forget that, from the ancient point of view, the litigant can abandon his legal ground and renounce what is owed him, after which he would be the only one to suffer from his move (Lämmli 1938: 84); cf. Dem. 54. 41. The formulas of doubtful anticipation employed by the pleaders belong more to rhetoric than to the legal procedure. See below, p. 14, at n. 39.

[21] Lämmli 1938: 96–7 emphasizes the unexpected character of this citation. We do not see why there would not be a question there of a witness. See Dem. 47. 10 and 53. 22.

[Cratinus] having grasped the plot of his adversaries, remained quiet for a long time.[22] He did not want his adversaries to change their plans and invent another story, but wanted to cause them to be caught in the act of committing a crime. The brother-in-law of his adversary had charged and the latter had testified that the woman was dead. Cratinus went to the house where the woman had been hidden, took her away, brought her into court, and showed all present that she was alive. Thus, before seven hundred judges, after fourteen witnesses had supported their claims, the accuser did not receive a single vote.

Such a theatrical act would not have been possible if Cratinus had been legally obliged to declare beforehand the nature of the proof—that the slave was alive—that he wanted so ingeniously to hold in reserve. Another pleader, on the eve of his trial, had been attacked by his opponent and before the court he did not refrain from listing all the misdeeds of his rival (Dem. 53. 17). It should not surprise us that the means of proof were not limited to those presented [134] at the preliminary hearing. There is obviously a risk that the manoeuvre might fail, and we may wonder why a rule in effect for public arbitration is not applied to a hearing that seems to have an identical role. The reason is that functional analogy does not signify procedural identity. The law of limitation assures the value of the arbitration as judgement. Certainly, when the action moves to the court, the pleader does not insist upon the arbitration decision—that would be improper,[23] an affront, doubtless, to the supreme authority of the dicast—but without a rule limiting new evidence at trial the arbitration procedure would be undermined in one of its key functions: to limit recourse to the court.[24]

The goal of an *anakrisis*, and the conditions under which it took place, were quite different. The instructing magistrate does not have the right to judge, which belongs to the citizen-dicast. He has no other duty than to introduce the case, to assess its admissibility,[25] and to watch over the formal regularity of the procedures; moreover,

---

[22] [They accused Cratinus of having killed a slave woman, who was alive and hidden.]

[23] See Dem. 40. 40; 27. 51; but also 41. 12, 21, and 24.

[24] See Gernet 1939: 394, in regard to deme judges. On limiting recourse to the courts, see Dem. 44. 59. On the congestion of the Athenian courts, see [Xen.], *Ath. Pol.* 3. 2.

[25] Bonner and Smith 1930: 292.

documents did not have, in Greek law, the same importance given them today.[26] On the other hand, the structure of public sessions of the courts—where the judges are called upon to pronounce judgement on the claims put to them without deliberating beforehand or discussing both sides—demands that the adversaries' respective positions be laid out clearly, if not defined in detail, at the first encounter. In this confrontation, the pleaders have the essential role. They submit to the *anakrisis* (*anakrinomai* in the middle voice) [135] under the oversight of the magistrate who instructs (*anakrinō* in the active; cf. Lipsius, *AR* 829). Without prejudging the matter of proof, the confrontation will take the form of a mutual interrogation by the parties themselves. Isaeus has described this in a suggestive fashion: 'When the *anakriseis* took place before the archon, our adversaries made their statement. ... When interrogated by us, they did not know what to say, while we protested and the archon told them to answer, as the law requires.'[27] In effect, the rule was that 'for the principals, there is an obligation to respond to the questions that they address each other, but there is no obligation to bear witness'.[28] Thereafter, Isaeus' client was able to say before the court: 'It does not suffice to provide some names at the *anakrisis*, but those present must attest to what truly happened.'[29] The *anakrisis* thus emerges as an important and delicate operation; it requires skill and prudence. Certainly, the procedure that characterizes it does not necessarily lead to false responses, for too much danger threatens the dishonest pleader (Plato, *Laws* 6. 766c), but we easily understand that to meet there with success and without harm to their case, the litigants would have recourse to the services of a specialist who 'all but lives in the lawcourts'.[30]

Despite everything, the situation as known to Athenian pleaders does not seem more dangerous than that which our litigants encounter. The rights of the parties seem reasonably protected. The city of

[26] Calhoun 1914: 134–6; cf. Dem. 34. 47, with the note of Gernet (1954–60), *ad loc.*
[27] Isaeus 6. 12 ff.; cf. Dem. 53. 22; Plato, *Laws* 6. 766d; Lämmli 1938: 77.
[28] Dem. 46. 10; see also 47. 10 and 27. 54 (arbitration).
[29] Isaeus 6. 15; cf. Dem. 47. 10.
[30] Isoc. 15. 38. On the oaths demanded by the parties during the trial, see Lipsius, *AR* 829–32; Bonner and Smith 1930: 162, 166–7; Gernet 1965 [1923]: 36–7 and 111 n. 3.

Athens afforded to litigants the assistance of its magistrates and one does not see why these men would [136] normally have failed in their duty of impartiality (Dem. 45. 58–9). Moreover, Athenian custom, if not the law,[31] prohibited speaking outside the case. The Areopagus, composed of former magistrates, better instructed about public matters than the citizens of the Heliaea, was particularly rigorous on this subject;[32] otherwise, 'when private cases are being judged, the parties involved promise under oath to limit their pleading to facts of the case' (Arist. *Ath. Pol.* 67. 1). Of course, the pleader can boldly turn up his nose at the obstacle and, under pretext of providing the judges complete information about his adversary, the litigant can indulge in a cruel game of accusation external to the case.[33]

It remains for the pleader and his adviser to investigate carefully, by a detailed study, the strengths and weaknesses of the case they undertake.

III. THE UNEXPECTED IN DEBATE
AND LOGOGRAPHIC PLEADING

However exhaustive the research and collection of means of proof could be, despite everything, the risk of the unexpected cannot be absolutely dispelled. Even during the hearing at the preliminary arbitration, a pleader could feel threatened by it. Demosthenes himself (27. 53) attacks the sly attitude that his adversary had adopted before the arbitrator in charge of the dispute [137] between himself and his guardians:

[31] Arist. *Rhet.* 1. 2. 5; cf. Lipsius, *AR* 149, 831 n. 9, 906, 918. On this interdiction, see Isoc. 15. 104 and Mathieu's note *ad loc.* [in Mathieu and Brémond 1950–62]. In cases of murder: Ant. 5. 11, 6. 9 (the pleader not hesitant to depart from the issue: 35 ff.)

[32] Aristotle, loc. cit; Bruns 1896, 486; Lipsius, *AR* 149, 831 n. 9. Lysias 7. 3 does not constitute an exception to this rule. The pleader complains of having to reply to a grievance that he has just heard at the trial. It seems evident that there is rhetorical exaggeration or at least brevity of expression. §2 bluntly cites events before the trial: a first citation and an extension of an inquiry are mentioned. The definitive citation is omitted. Imprecise legal vocabulary—regarding the term *apographē* in particular (Gernet, *ad loc.* [in Gernet and Bizos 1962–4: 111])—makes it easier.

[33] Lysias 19. 5; see Stobaeus 3. 42. 10. Antiphon 6. 35 ff. and Lys. 3. 44 show how illusory the interdiction of speaking outside the case can be.

He had the audacity to lie most shamefully, saying that my father left four talents in a hiding-place and made my mother responsible for them. He said this in order that, if expecting him to repeat it, I would waste time defending myself, having to make another accusation before you against him; but if I assumed he was not going to say it again and left the matter aside, he would say it now, in order that seeming to be rich I would be less pitied by you.

Nothing obliges us to believe that Demosthenes was so naive as he wishes to seem,[34] but granting that all the art of the litigant consists in planting a doubt about his intentions, although he had to arrange his pieces on the board in a way satisfying the procedure, the text proves that arbitration itself could let some doubt remain, or at least an embarrassment of choices about the argument of the adversary. That is only normal: one advocate will confer on certain facts and certain arguments an importance that another specialist would refuse them. This tactic is an art, and from appreciation of the way a practitioner uses the material at his disposal, quite various solutions could arise.[35]

Nothing indicates that ancient logographers were much worse off in this respect than their modern successors. We must not let ourselves be blinded by the complaints of Athenian pleaders: the distress of litigants is expressed too well and their rhetoric describes it with too much complacency; the accused will always find room to complain about what he should answer to his adversary.[36] Moreover, the formulas of doubtful anticipation that the logographers employ should not mislead us. Apropos of Eratosthenes, Lysias wrote that [138] the accused 'could perhaps say that he was driven by fear'.[37] The uncertainty of the author is fictional, for from all the evidence his adversary would have recourse to this argument, which he had not failed to use elsewhere to judge from the questioning to which Lysias had subjected him (12. 25; cf. 13. 52). Another pleader says to notice that his antagonist 'will reply briefly to the complaints lodged against him, glide over the facts, and conjure away the accusation in

[34] Not more than in 44. 26–7 and 45. 57.

[35] Cf. the arguments listed by Asconius Pedianus in his commentary on Cicero's *Pro Milone* 30; on theoretical possibilities in a particular case, see Antiphon 6. 17.

[36] On the commonplace: Andocides 1. 1, 6–7; Lys. 19. 2–5.

[37] Lysias 12. 50. An analogous tactic in the trial of his guardian: Dem. 38. 23 presents a topical argument as possible in a similar case.

his pleading. He will say on the other hand that he and his relatives have dispensed much money on behalf of the state, that they have zealously performed liturgies' (Lys. 26. 3; cf. Dem. 38. 25). Such a declaration could be made without fear of contradiction, for at the time of the restoration of the democracy litigants loved to make display of their patriotic merits.[38] Sometimes giving positive assertions, sometimes probabilities, the formulas should not be taken literally. They are part of the arsenal of stereotyped transitions put to good use by rhetors, and they express the reserved and simple attitude that Athenian litigants affect. The demands that the orators freely make to have some person or other appear in court unexpectedly or to make use of some means of proof are, also, most often made up. He who ventures them expects from them only a psychological effect.[39]

More puzzling seem to be those passages where the orator, one would say, recalls what his accuser has just said. [139] One client of Lysias declares (1. 27) that 'Eratosthenes was not dragged by force from the street nor did he take refuge at the hearth, as the accusers claim'. Another affirms: 'My adversary claims also that I am insolent, brutish, and ill-mannered, as if he could speak the truth only by employing some big words.'[40] If we could establish with certainty that these are direct references to what the accuser has said and if we could say with confidence that the logographer could in no way have had previous and precise knowledge, the assertion contained in the speech that we read would force us to admit that the edition of the speech departed from the original by adding improvised passages from the trial.[41] Or better, we could think that the author must have composed them by providing in his work a very flexible structure and, if the situation arose, some short bits for rebuttal.

In reality, the knowledge that we possess of debates and trials that the preserved pleadings report is too largely fragmentary to authorize

---

[38] Lysias 12. 38; 26. 3; see Ar. *Wasps* 281–2; cf. Clark 1929: 33–5. The argument of public services is still being used by Demosthenes, 38. 25.

[39] See Dem. 37. 44; Antiphon 5. 34. The same is true of passages where, after arbitration, the speaker offers to produce new witnesses: Dem. 57. 58, 61; Isaeus 12. 9, and even Dem. 57. 14 (see n. 18 above).

[40] Lysias 24. 15. See Dem. 54. 14 and Isaeus 6. 59.

[41] [On the possibility that logographic speeches may include the client's changes or additions, see Dover 1968: 148–74, and Usher's essay, Ch. 2 in this volume.]

definitive research. To understand a case, we have at our disposal only one of the speeches, and we are not at all clear about the conditions under which it was published. Sometimes there even survives only a speech pronounced by a supporting speaker and we are trying to reconstitute the whole case for the other side on the basis of information it furnishes and often in despite of that information. An effort of this sort can only lead to probabilities, all the less assured because not only the facts in the case but also the legal procedure and the law applicable to the trial are often only known to us through a faulty image that the pleader creates and which we are trying to refute. Moreover, in the present state of our knowledge, the study of the speeches does not permit us to establish that the alleged replies to the opposing speech contain literal citations. Very often, in evoking the arguments and propositions defended by his antagonist, the pleader may utilize precise terms, although the words that he employs may not be taken from the speaker whom he opposes. Some allusions to the manner adopted by the adversary or the material that he puts into his speech [140] may not be any more significant. An ancient advocate liked to attribute to his opponent arguments that would give him the advantage of showing their inanity, and the bold verbal fencing that such a tactic presupposes does not, in his eyes, have any limit other than the very uncertain vigilance of the judges.[42]

Everything suggests, on the other hand, that a logographer could without fear compose a coherent and 'autonomous' speech.[43] That was, in truth, the simplest solution and the one that most adequately suited the conditions in which logographic assistance was practised. The logographer had to justify his competence and the confidence that the pleader had in him[44] by delivering to his client a speech that expressed in the best way the argument that should lead to success. The pleader, unskilled as he might have been and as he wished to

---

[42] Lycurgus, *Against Leocrates* 68–74, 'attributes to the adversary an absurd argument in order to suggest to the judges that their intelligence is being mocked' (Durbach 1932, ad loc.). A false *katalēpsis* is found in the second hypothesis to Dem. 20, §10. Gernet 1954–60: ii. 180, shows that in Dem. 46 the speaker distorts the defence argument (cf. 45. 44 ff.).

[43] [By 'autonomous' Lavency means a text to be memorized and recited as written, not adapting to what is actually said by the opposition in court.]

[44] Aeschines 2. 165 designates the clients of Demosthenes' logographic work by the expression 'those who turned to you in all confidence'.

seem,[45] must have desired to make use of a text that he could follow
with complete assurance. It is hard to imagine how he would dare to
free himself from the written discourse to improvise or to rearrange
the material only to reply more or less adequately to the tactic of his
adversary, while in fear of exceeding or wasting the time for speaking
assigned to him. It would be difficult to demand of him what
Demosthenes seemed to require of himself in his political orations.
A. P. Dorjahn was able to show that the orator expected to improvise,
and comparing the speeches delivered at the time of the affair of the
Crown, he believed he could demonstrate that in order to reply
neatly to his adversaries, Demosthenes had improvised certain passages that he later inserted in his published works.[46] Is there any need
to observe that conditions are entirely different [141] in the case of
logography? Moreover, a political speech gains in value by being
edited so as to support the ideas of its author, who had every interest
in presenting a restatement, in finished form, of his case against his
adversaries. In the game Demosthenes plays, a talented orator risked
a great deal in losing the advantage of his preparation.[47] What is there
to say, then, of the effort that such improvising would demand of an
amateur speaker?

In addition, such an effort does not seem necessary or profitable
for the latter. The very structure of the trial did not demand it, for
delivery of the speech came as the final function required of the
litigant, and we know that the vote of the judges took place without
debate or deliberation among themselves. It was up to the pleaders to
propose their version of the case and advance their arguments, and
up to the judges to choose one or the other party. Nor did the tactic
of the advocate recommend [improvising an answer]. A slavish
response by the defence addressed point-by-point to the accuser
risked, moreover, arousing the judges' deep distrust in regard to a

[45] Cf. the commonplace in which the pleader deplores his inexperience; e.g. Plato,
Apology 17a; Antiphon 5. 1–3; Lys. 7. 1–3; 17. 1; 19. 1; etc.

[46] Dorjahn 1947. Some arguments advanced in this article and in those that
followed (1950 and 1952) are open to criticism. One cannot draw a conclusion
from passages 'in improvised style'. Moreover, Demosthenes does not respond to
Aeschines 3. 28.

[47] This is what Alcidamas observes, §24. On a similar disappointment experienced
by Demosthenes, see Aeschines 2. 35.

pleader who reveals himself incapable of giving a personal and convincing version of the facts and thus indirectly supports the account of his antagonists.

The autonomy of the pleaders is, moreover, an attested practice. Rhetorical teaching recognized it when it taught to glide over the facts,[48] and the practitioner does not fail to criticize such a tactic when he suspects his adversaries of employing it: 'There is here no possibility of doing what has become customary in Athens, that is, of not responding to the accusation but sometimes deceiving the judges by saying other things about themselves.'[49] [142]

Without going further, the pleaders on their own accord wish to be autonomous. They strongly object if, by chance, their adversary tries to dictate to them the plan of their speeches.[50] Logographers intended to construct a speech that would be an exposition of a thesis more than a reply. Notably in the first speech of the corpus of Antiphon, the author employs this tactic. A dramatic narrative of the facts takes the place of proof, and the affirmation, pure and simple, as well as the repetition replaces the demonstration.[51] In so far as one can judge, the first speech of the corpus of Lysias follows the same bent. To believe the speaker, the case is clear and the legal right of the accused not open to doubt. The pleader, an outraged husband who got justice by killing his rival, is accused of premeditated murder. The speech, beginning with the exordium, takes on the quality of an accusation. The speaker wants to make his judges share the indignation that moves him. He then announces a division of the speech (4): 'I have to prove that Eratosthenes was the lover of my wife, that he seduced her, that he dishonoured my children, that he came into my house to commit this outrage against me, that up until

---

[48] See Antiphon 5. 65 ff.: 'dodging a debate that he made seem necessary' (Gernet 1965, ad loc.); Aeschines 1. 173 and 178; Isaeus 6. 59. The orator shuffles the cards: Dem. 43. 59; 49. 53, and Ant. 5. 55; see Plato, *Protagoras* 336d and Aeschines 3. 202. Cf. H. Brown 1914: 60 n. 249, with Quintilian 5. 13. 3.

[49] Lysias 12. 38. See also 26. 3; Is. 6. 59; Dem. 25. 76; 38. 19; 43. 32. Cf. Gernet 1954–60: ii. 94, 105 n. 1, and 178 (on Dem. 35). Aeschines 1. 175, suggests a similar tactic. Finally, Dem. 57 is mute on a crucial legal point, the civic status of the mother.

[50] Isaeus 6. 62; Dem. 58. 69; 18. 1 in response to Aeschines, 3. 202 and 205. See the remark of Antiphon 3.4.1; Dem. 45. 49; 58. 69.

[51] Antiphon 1. 3 f.; in this paragraph it is affirmed that 'often' (*pollakis ēdē*) the mother of the accused made an attempt on the life of her husband, an assertion that is never proved.

then there existed no hostility between him and me, that I did not do these things for money to become rich instead of poor, and that I had no other interest than to secure justice in conformity with the laws.'[52] The propositions thus stated are not given equal scope in the speech,[53] where everything is used to establish that there was a seduction on the part of the adversary and that there was no entrapment on the part of the speaker. Lämmli believed he could reconstruct the accusation in an entirely different guise (1938: 59–68); the victim, [he argued,] would have been led on to commit adultery in order to fall [143] into the trap that Lysias' client was setting for him, desirous of ridding himself of an individual whom he hated. While defending himself in the confusion that followed the false discovery of the crime, Eratosthenes succeeded in escaping, but was brought back and put to death near the altar where he had believed he could find refuge. In accord with the subtle analysis of the facts that the German philologist proposes, we see that the actual adultery could not be contested by the relatives of Eratosthenes; only the conditions under which it had been brought about. In reading what Lysias says about it, and trying to read between the lines, while endeavouring to escape from the snares that the writer set for his audience, we touch the essential character of the speech, its bias. Points announced as equally important but not developed proportionally, and promises to reply in detail that are left unfulfilled—these are not uncommon in the works of the advocates (see n. 48). This is the place to recall that the fluency and self-confidence that the litigants affect does not suffice to establish that their case is well founded. To show what could not be true, to neglect to prove what must have been so, such are the cunning ways the ancient advocate does not disdain when the success of his client is at issue.[54]

The autonomy of the pleader was supported by the conditions under which judicial assistance was practised in Athens, implicated

[52] Antiphon 1. 3 also presents a false division of the argument.

[53] Hatred is only cited in one paragraph (§ 43), moreover in the midst of a commonplace. Lysias 9. 3 promises a detailed response to the accusation, but then gives nothing of the sort.

[54] Lysias 16. 8 treats haughtily the accuser who reproaches him with having been compliant under the Thirty. Such an imputation could have been very serious (26. 10), given the attitude of the time (Xen. *Hell.* 3. 1).

in the tactic proper to an advocate and manifested also in the inter-
rogatories that certain speeches preserve. The questions are organized
in such a way that the economy of the speech did not risk being
injured by responses of the adversary. The person questioned did not
in practice have a choice in his response; thus the questioner ran no
risk. Before the judges of the restored democracy, Eratosthenes was
only able to stress his opposition to the execution of Lysias' brother
and to claim he obeyed the orders given him (Lys. 12. 25). Interrogated in the course of another trial, a grain merchant was no more
able to shake the argument of his adversary (Lys. 22. 5): 'Tell me, are
you a metic?'—'Yes.'—'So as to obey the laws or do as you please?'—
'To obey the laws.'—[144] 'Don't you think you deserve death if you
committed a crime that the laws punish with death?'—'I do.'—'Tell
me, then: do you agree you bought fifty bushels of grain more than the
law permits?'—'I did so on order of the magistrates.'[55]

Related to this, it sometimes happens that a pleader envisions that a
witness can and will oppose him. The adversary of Stephanus declares:
'In support of my statements you are going to have first the evidence of
people who were present at the events, for I do not believe that they
will want to offer an oath of denial.'[56] He states immediately what
exposure he has in mind: 'If they have the impudence to act that way, a
challenge (*proklēsis*) will be read to you [judges] that will permit you to
catch them red-handed in perjury' (Dem. 45. 59). After the disposition
is read, the witnesses are summoned. The pleader, in triumph, states:
'It is not necessary, gentlemen of the jury, to be an expert to see what
they are going to do: promptly to abjure their testimony' (45. 61).
Examples are not lacking of parallel situations.[57] Moreover, it suffices
to state that a litigant could have avoided using an argument of this
sort if he had thought he would run some risk. And would he have
risked a situation where the person called on was well known to be on
the side of his adversary (e.g. Aeschin. 1. 69), or when he had refused
to give evidence at the earlier hearing (as in Isaeus 9. 18)? The
theatricality of the procedure seems evident, and in this scenario the

---

[55] The same tactic, with a youth responding to interrogation: Dem. 43. 49.
[56] Dem. 45. 58; cf. 24. 3. [On this tactic, see Carey's essay, Ch. 9 in this volume.]
[57] See Gernet's note, 1954–60, *ad loc.*; Isaeus 9. 18; Aeschines 1. 69.

litigant hopes to reap the psychological advantage in the eyes of the judges of a speaker who calmly seeks the truth. [145]

On the other hand, the few speeches-in-reply that we possess in private cases, where they have a special place,[58] do not indicate that the pleader was anxious about answering directly the assertions made by the opposing speaker. Insofar as we can judge, there was nothing new in a reply by Lysias when the accused had insisted at length on an argument that he must have presented in his first appearance.[59] The author furnishes less a reply to his adversary than a final repetition of his earlier arguments. The same impression results from the reading of two replies composed by Demosthenes. In the second speech against Aphobus (28. 2), the author affects to be taken by surprise by the tactic of his adversary who had waited until the last day to enter into the dossier a deposition that he would hold in reserve for his reply.[60] Demosthenes, however, could not have been duped, for he must have been alerted by the deposit of this important document. Moreover, he himself had kept in reserve for his reply an important and foreseeable argument that would reinforce his position in a unique way.[61] He utilizes the same tactic [146] in the second speech against Onetor. As Gernet describes it, he 'replies to

---

[58] Demosthenes' speeches 28, 31, and 46; cf. Lipsius, *AR* 910–11. [Ordinarily, in private cases both sides spoke twice, so that the plaintiff could respond to the defendant.]

[59] Lysias 4. The speech is not represented expressly as a reply. Here we follow the hypothesis of Bizos (Gernet and Bizos 1962–4), i. 78, based on 4. 18, where the pleader refers to some proofs utilized earlier. The orator passes half of his time drawing arguments from the refusal, opposed by his adversary, to put his slaves to torture (§§ 10ff.). In the rest, he insists on the enmity between himself and his accuser (§§ 1ff.).

[60] [Aphobus contended that Demosthenes' father had died indebted to the polis.] Gernet (1954–60: i. 53 n.), remarks rightly, '... he had put in the dossier a deposition to this effect. That was enough for Demosthenes to be warned. Naturally, to make his reply decisive, he plays the rôle of the pleader taken by surprise.' The hypothesis of Dem. 28 notes, moreover, that the second speech 'recalls also what had been said in the first speech'.

[61] Gernet 1954–60: i. 53: 'What seems especially bad in Aphobus's case is that he had not confirmed the size of the patrimony of his ward. Demosthenes will formally state (29. 29) that this was one of the major reasons for his condemnation. Aphobus had imagined he could defend himself on that score. And even before the arbitration, he had claimed that if he had not confirmed the amount, it was because the deceased

an argument that could have been advanced by Onetor at the time of the arbitration and refutes the allegation that … would be the essential point of the defence'.[62] Under these conditions, the reply was presented in the manner of certain supporting speeches (by *synē-goroi*), where, following a division of duties between the advocates, each speaker develops a separate line of argument (cf. Lys. 14. 3; Dem. 46. 1 with 45. 44).

It thus seems sure that a pleader could trust without fear to the instructions he had received from the logographer. The danger of having to answer some unexpected complaints should not burden his speech. On the other hand, his failure to reply to an argument used by his adversary would pass unnoticed as the speech went on.

To conclude, it is necessary to analyse certain special cases, the *dokimasiai*. We know that candidates for public offices had to undergo scrutiny of their character before taking up their duties. The procedure was, in general outline, the same in every case. The magistrate examined the candidate to know if he satisfied certain conditions and demanded that he produce his witnesses. After that, he posed the question: 'Who wishes to make an accusation?' If some accusations were forthcoming, the accused defended himself (Arist. *Ath. Pol.* 55; Lipsius *AR*, 269 ff.). We do not know what actions preceded such debates, but we observe that the adversaries were surprisingly well informed about what was being thought up against them. In any case, they could have had some contacts before the hearing,[63] and they would have known the names of the [147] advocates and witnesses who were going to intervene (Lys. 25. 33; 26. 21). On the other hand, if the number of accusers was not limited,

himself had advised him to "disguise" the size of his fortune because of a public debt for which the patrimony of Demosthenes remained liable. Demosthenes carefully held this back and had kept in reserve a reply to an allegation that gave him a good hand to play. He had a good hand, in fact, denouncing an ulterior motive for the deception and not only the absence of proofs, but the intrinsic improbability and the true character of a claim that, put in relief, would appear one of desperation'. Cf. 37. 23 [the defendant has learned of the allegations from another suit].

[62] Gernet, ibid. 89 n. 1, based on Dem. 31. 6, 12 ff. [Onetor valued the property no more than a talent, but Demosthenes cited mortgage markers (*horoi*) for an additional 1/3 talent.]

[63] Lysias 31. 32: 'I see some who are prepared to aid him and to plead with you, since they were not able to persuade me.' Cf. Lavency 1964: 76 n. 3.

each had only a single opportunity to speak and the candidate seems to have responded only after all his adversaries had spoken (Lys. 31. 4, 6; 30. 7). The defence, in such a case, is again easily autonomous. Lysias 25 illustrates this: it takes the form of a harangue where the orator cites recent history, preaches moderation, and develops some considerations of national politics in which one searches in vain for any direct refutation of specific complaints.[64]

The speech for Mantitheus (Lys. 16), on the other hand, seems organized in two clearly separate parts.[65] The second part, in a very usual way, describes the public services of the candidate. In the first part (16. 3), the orator tries to justify himself in reply to a very serious accusation (cf. 26. 10), the claim that under the Thirty he had belonged to a corps strongly suspected of Spartan sympathies, the cavalry (Xen. *Hell.* 3. 1). One can easily imagine that Mantitheus had to defend himself in any way he could, and nothing requires us to believe that his adversaries actually cited against him [148] the Spartan style of his long hair.[66] Many of the councillors could have formulated such an objection for themselves. The *dokimasiai* are in fact political processes, and it appears that very often what the interested party himself had done counted less than the political support at his disposal. Moreover, he could appeal to the court in case of rejection (Arist. *Ath. Pol.* 55. 2).

The plea *For the Disabled Man* (Lys. 24) involves the *dokimasia* of an invalid who wishes to continue receiving public support. There has been much discussion of this speech. Is it a school exercise,[67] of doubtful authenticity, or a genuine speech-for-trial?[68] One does not know. Whatever the case may be, the arguments denying the possibility that the logographer composed in advance certain passages that

---

[64] Lysias 25. 7, 21–32; cf. 20. 3–4; 21. 18; Aeschines 3. 168.

[65] The second part (9 ff.) is introduced in the manner of an autonomous discourse. Cf. Lys. 7. 3; 25. 7; 32. 3; Isaeus 7.4. [For the passages from Lysias see Todd 2000.]

[66] Lysias 16. 18. The reading *ou (chrē) ei tis komai dia touto misein* ('if one wears his hair long, it is no cause for resentment') rests on an ingenious conjecture by Hamaker and has been unanimously adopted. See Blass, *AB* i. 520–1 n. 6.

[67] Lämmli 1938: 72–3 ('Übungsrede', 'Kunstprodukt').

[68] Harpocration, s.v. *adunatos* ['disabled'], judges the speech 'doubtful'; but cf. Bizos (in Gernet and Bizos 1962–4), ii. 102.

we read in the speech are not decisive.[69] The man claiming disability is certainly very precise in his reply: 'My accuser says that it is not right that I receive money from the public treasury; for he claims I am strong of body, that I am not disabled, and that I practise a trade that permits me to live without the payment that I sollicit. His proof that I am strong of limb is that I ride a horse; the proof that my trade permits me to live without assistance is that I am able to associate with men who have money to spend' (24. 4–5). Another strange feature is that the speech lacks a narration and only deals with refutation of the adversary's claims (24. 4). Even if one admits that the presence of all beneficiaries was required on the day when the subsidies were distributed, and for that reason any *anakrisis* seems [149] excluded (Lämmli 1938: 70), there is no reason to believe that the applicant had to devise a defence in the terms that we have just read. The case defended by Lysias does not seem a strong one; indeed, the practice of a trade was incompatible with the grant of the desired subsidy,[70] and the trips on horseback were without any doubt what our modern legislators call 'external signs of wealth'.[71] The facts that are admitted, more serious than the casual reply leads one to believe, ought normally to provide the basis for opposition which the speaker ought to have anticipated. They would have furnished Lysias an occasion to exercise his talents brilliantly, and perhaps free of charge.[72]

IV. THE REPETITIONS IN ANTIPHON

Before concluding this chapter, it remains to study a question that Gernet has raised apropos of certain passages of Antiphon. Asking himself if the ancient author had given to all his speeches a final, definitive form, the eminent philologist observes (1965: 20):

[69] Lämmli 1938: 71, based on the absence of *anakrisis* and on what he regards as the unexpected mention of *hubris* in §§15–18.

[70] Arist. *Ath. Pol.* 49. 1. The allocation had been increased since Lys. 16. 26.

[71] Lys. 24. 11; cf. Dem. 37. 52 and 42. 24.

[72] Blass, *AB* i. 637. In this area, where all is guesswork, Bizos (Gernet and Bizos 1962–4), ii. 102 n. 2, thought he could establish that the disabled man 'could have paid for the help of a logographer'.

Publication in such a genre certainly does not entail this hypothesis which, after all, does not very well accord with the actual conditions under which the earliest of the Attic Orators must have written. But beyond that, there is something that needs notice. On several occasions our text offers some repetitions, such that one thinks immediately of a second recension [that has introduced doublets into the text] (1. 7; 6. 51). One would like to blame some copyist. But it is noteworthy that the speech *On the Murder of Herodes*, despite its length, presents nothing of the sort. It is also the most carefully worked and contrasts especially with the first oration, which is the earliest, the most inept, and one where these redundancies are most obvious. The case of the last speech [*On the Choreutes*] is also significant: at the end [§ 51] there is a repetition of the sort under discussion, and one that seems to have taken the place of the expected but lacking epilogue. [150] It has been established (by Blass) that a lacuna at this point—precisely at the end of the last speech in the collection—is hardly probable. Agreed. But it is all the same difficult to consider the speech finished as we have it. We would gain nothing, moreover, in rejecting such doublets as the work of a copyist. And if the epilogue had little chance of being lost, it probably never existed. There may be other lacunae, notably in the first speech, [*Against a Stepmother for Poisoning*], so let us admit that lacunas and repetitions go back to the primitive manuscript. In other words, Antiphon will have composed, in some cases, in a very free manner—one thinks (if the comparison is not too remote) of the *Sermons* of Bossuet [1627–1704] (1975). In other cases, and doubtless less often, he will have given his speech a finished form.

We are reluctant to subscribe to the French scholar's thesis. It is certain that logography must have taken tentative first steps, but the orators of this era seem to have perfectly mastered the composition of a speech. In our eyes, the repetitions that one observes in Antiphon's first speech can find a simpler explanation. After causing the pleader to say: 'How can my adversary conclude that he knows what he refused to find out?' (1. 7), the text continues: 'How, then, you who are judging the case, is it probable that he knows something of which he does not have exact knowledge?' One might, on Gernet's view, readily blame a copyist: the turn of phrase suggests a gloss, incorporated later into the manuscript tradition.[73] But there is more to say. In this speech, which one critic has warmly defended, the

---

[73] Schöll 1871 supposed a second recension. Manuscript N omits the repetition. *Dikazontes*, 'you who are judging the case', is not current in the language of the orators.

litigant must, in order to succeed, 'create a state of mind' and 'transform into a certitude what was only a vague suspicion' (Albini 1958: 41). Prolixity suits him very well. The second repetition noticed by Gernet (Ant. 1. 12), can, [151] like the first, be explained by the concern that the pleader had to impose his ideas on the judges. The case being of an embarrassing sort,[74] repetition will take the place of demonstration. The pleader constantly resorts to it. Speaking of his adversaries, he declares (1. 2): 'My adversaries should rightly have been the avengers of the dead man and allies of the accuser', and he continues repeating the same powerful idea (1. 4): 'These people ought to have been avengers of the dead and become my allies.' In Lysias, in the same kind of speech and doubtless for the same reasons, we find the formula repeated: 'All this came to mind and I was full of suspicion' (1. 7). As to Antiphon's sixth speech, the repetition at the end is certainly laboured. By the general character of the ideas that it expresses, it too draws on a commonplace and in its position it seems to provide a poor conclusion for the speech.[75] One will easily believe that the text has been padded, but nothing obliges us to conclude that the padding should be imputed to an editor and represents a rather free manner of revision. Some other speeches present passages stitched together without our putting the responsibility on a redactor of the written discourse.[76] [152]

In their present state, the rhetorical sources as well as the speeches attributed to orators thus teach us that the speech could, without any problem, be composed before the case came to court. The author has at his disposal sufficient documentation, varied and ample, the construction of which is legally protected. The speeches do not reveal any passages in which the speaker for the defence reacts literally and immediately to words pronounced by the prosecution. Everything that they offer us can be explained by the preliminaries of the process. The speech is completely autonomous. The very personality of the

[74] Gernet 1965: 45 n.1; Albini 1958: 39–40.

[75] Antiphon 6. 50. See Lys. 12. 100; Dem. 54. 44. There are some very maladroit conclusions in Demosthenes: 50. 68; 55. 35.

[76] e.g. Dem. 29. Gernet 1950–64: i. 68, thinks he sees in this speech 'a series of passages that Demosthenes utilizes for one or another of a number of speeches as needed. The work of the first editor, going beyond his mission—at least in the eyes of moderns—would consist in stitching these passages together.' Cf. Lysias 11.

speaker and the tactic of the advocate go best to certify this method, which remains applicable to replies and to *dokimasiai*.

It is quite evident that the written speech cannot respond to the unexpected turn of debate as can the method of improvisation recommended by Alcidamas. It will require the skill of the logographer to make up for that inadequacy.

2

Lysias and his Clients

S. Usher

In the eighth chapter of his book *Lysias and the Corpus Lysiacum*, Professor K. J. Dover argues (p. 152) that 'among the speeches ascribed to Lysias by the booksellers many, perhaps the majority, were to some degree or other his work, but not wholly his work'. The discussion which precedes this proposition is concerned chiefly with the relationship between a litigant and his *sumboulos* ('consultant'), a role which no ancient authority assigns to Lysias. It broadens thereafter to include the circumstances of ancient publication and the popular Athenian attitude to the profession of *logographos*, and Dover's treatment of these two subjects is lucid and convincing insofar as it is concerned with general conditions. It is to some extent vitiated, however, by the repeated assumption that clients, and even friends of clients, might have had strong motives for publishing forensic speeches after their use in trials (pp. 156, 159–60, 165). But far more serious is Dover's omission of the direct evidence for the independent composition of forensic speeches by the speechwriter. It is the purpose of the present article to re-examine this evidence, and to adduce fresh evidence and arguments in support of independent and against composite authorship.

We may usefully begin with the words employed in the fifth and fourth centuries BC to describe the function of the speechwriter. By far the commonest verb appears to be *graphein* ('write'). The others are *paraskeuazein, porizesthai, mēkhanasthai, poiein, ekdidonai* (lit. 'prepare, provide, devise, make, give out'). None of these implies cooperation, nor do the two compound verbs *sungraphein* and *suntattein* ('compose, arrange'), in which the prefix *sun*-bears the sense not of collaboration but of artistic composition (Lavency 1964: 124–9). Examination of the noun *logographos* confirms his literary pretensions. Nowhere is he found cooperating with anyone but works alone on his writings, whether they be history, forensic speeches, or epideictic discourses (ibid. 36–45).

[32] Contemporary evidence of a different kind arises from a comparison between Lysias and his older contemporary Antiphon. Dover refers to Thucydides' famous tribute (8. 68) and suggests, very reasonably, that the role here ascribed to Antiphon by the historian is that of *sumboulos* (1968: 149). This and the passage which Dover quotes from Aristophanes' *Clouds* (462–75) illustrate very well the confusion that existed in the fifth century between the nascent profession of speechwriter and the other activities that came within the purview of the sophists. There is good reason to suppose that Antiphon acted as consultant to litigants who shared his political beliefs, or whose cases might further his political aims by discrediting the democratic administration which he sought to overthrow. But he also wrote speeches for the lawcourts and subsequently published them, being the first to do so, according to tradition.[1] His three surviving speeches[2] show none of the stylistic inconsistencies noticed in the speeches of Lysias by Dover and adduced as evidence of composite authorship, and it has never been suggested that he collaborated with his client in the composition of a speech. He offered two distinct forms of legal assistance, and two only: advice and the complete speech, ready for delivery. If Dover's thesis is accepted, Lysias offered neither of these but something in between, and in so doing lost his individual identity as a writer and broke with the precedent established by Antiphon.

Such ready self-effacement is hardly consonant with the impression of the talents and reputation of Lysias which we receive from Plato in the *Phaedrus*. In this dialogue he is described as *deinotatos tōn nun graphein* ('cleverest at writing of those now'), sharply contrasted

---

[1] Diod. Sic. *apud* Clem. Alex. *Strom.* 1. 365 (1. 16. § 79.3 Stählin); [Plut.] *Vit. X Or.* 832c–d; Quint. 3. 1.11.

[2] *Murder of Herodes, On the Choreutes, Prosecution for Poisoning.* I regard the *Tetralogies* as rhetorical exercises of doubtful authorship.

with *idiōtēs*, the ordinary man (228a). He is a creative literary artist comparable with the poets (258d, 278c). Although the Lysianic speech which he analyses is epideictic, Plato acknowledges the breadth of Lysias' literary field by mentioning his activities as a forensic and political speechwriter, which had been the object of a jibe by a contemporary (257b–258e, esp. 257c). Ability to write in a variety of styles would be part of such a versatile author's stock-in-trade. While primarily a forensic speechwriter, Lysias was famous enough as an epideictic orator to have commanded an audience at Olympia in 388/7 BC for his remarkable invective against [33] Dionysius I of Syracuse.[3] In a writer of such protean talents stylistic variety is much more naturally explained in purely literary terms than by any assumption that he allowed an alien, uncultivated style to intrude into his compositions.

Plato, then, recognized Lysias' versatility, perhaps even as a talent kindred to his own. But he also must have thought that he could distinguish a Lysianic style, in order either to imitate it, if the *Eroticus* is by Plato, or to select an authentic work of the orator, if the *Eroticus* is by Lysias.[4] Assumption of Platonic authorship leads us to examine the piece for recurrent features which Plato may have regarded as Lysianic traits. The five occurrences of *kai men dē* ('and indeed') (twenty-six in the *Corpus Lysiacum*) and the two of *eti de* ('besides') (twenty-four in the *Corpus Lysiacum*), may be the result of Plato's study of a body of speeches and discourses which were, in his judgement, clearly stamped with one man's style.

Two generations after Plato, Theophrastus also thought he could identify the style of Lysias. It is interesting to note that he emphasized its artificiality, and included the orator among those who made excessive use of antithesis, symmetry, assonance, and related figures of language (Dion. Hal. *Lys.* 14). This is surely a surprising judgement

---

[3] Dion. Hal. *Lys.* 29; Diod. Sic. 14.109.

[4] Blass deduced Lysianic authorship from both style and method of argument (*AB* i. 428–30), and the case was argued at greater length by Vahlen 1903: 788–9. But since Weinstock's thorough investigation (1912), scholarly opinion has generally favoured Platonic authorship. See Darkow 1917: 90–4; Shorey 1933: 131–2; Dimock 1952: 392–6. Dover (1968: 194) considers the problem insoluble by means of 'technical criteria', but this excludes perhaps the strongest argument of all, that of literary unity and the convention that authors did not quote *verbatim* long passages from the works of others. This argument is not without relevance to the subject of this article.

if the speeches read by Theophrastus contained passages of any length written in the natural language of Lysias' clients. Dionysius, on the other hand, did see an element of apparent naturalness in Lysias' style, but considered that it was in reality as different as could be from the style of the ordinary man, and more carefully contrived than any work of art (*Lys.* 8). It was by these criteria that he, like his predecessors, identified an individual Lysianic style, and he saw in it too a certain indefinable *charis* (*Lys.* 10), absence of which he confidently took to be a sign of non-Lysianic authorship.

Contemporary evidence and subsequent critical opinion thus give [34] an impression of Lysias and his oratory which does not correspond with that suggested by Dover's thesis of a composer of hybrid works in which any literary distinction is diluted and obscured by the intrusion of *idiōtismoi*, the uncultivated speech of his clients. We shall have occasion to return to the question of Lysias' literary reputation, but turn now to two passages which describe the relationship between the speechwriter and his client in the fourth century BC. The first concerns Lysias himself, and though our source is Plutarch, there is no good reason to believe that he was not following a biographical tradition dating back at least to the third century BC (Hermippus of Smyrna?).[5] The passage runs as follows:

Lysias wrote a speech for a litigant and gave it to him, and the client, having read it many times, came to Lysias discouraged, saying that when he first went through the speech it seemed marvelous, but when he took it up a second and a third time it seemed absolutely dull and ineffective. But Lysias laughed and said, 'So what—aren't you going to read it just once to the jury?'[6]

This curious story seems to imply a lack of collaboration between speechwriter and client in the actual composition of the speech, however much prior consultation there may have been. Clearly the client received and read a speech written by the speechwriter. But his

---

[5] The unreliability of Hermippus and other sources of biographical material need not lead us to expect them to misrepresent a relationship such as that between speechwriter and client, which was a matter of recent, perhaps contemporary, experience for some of them. For purposes of the present argument it does not matter greatly whether Plutarch or his source introduced Lysias' name in order to colour the story.

[6] Plut. *De Garr.* 5 (*Mor.* 504c).

disappointment may suggest something more. If the speech had contained a number of passages in the client's own words, it would have been natural for his self-esteem to gain the better of his literary judgement, so that he might have enjoyed reading the speech simply because he saw his own words 'in print'. Again, if, as is reasonable, he is assumed to have reread the speech with the ultimate purpose of learning it off by heart (Dover 1968: 150, n. 4), part of his complaint may have arisen from finding its language totally foreign to his own, and therefore awkward and unnatural coming from the lips of a man with no experience of acting a part. At the very least, it is evident that the client recognized the speech as the work of the speechwriter, not as a collaborative composition.

[35] The second passage does not feature Lysias in person, but its author, Theophrastus, is closer in time than Plutarch to the heyday of the Attic speechwriters and was indeed a contemporary of the later ones. In *Characters* 17. 8 we read of a litigant who, on winning his suit with all the jury's votes, criticizes his speechwriter for omitting many legitimate points. A purely fictitious incident, no doubt; but hardly one which *could* not have happened, or its inclusion would have served the purpose neither of illustration nor of humour. If, as seems probable, Theophrastus is describing the habitual practice of the speechwriter, it may be supposed that in some cases consultation was minimal even on legal details, rendering it less likely still that matters of verbal presentation were discussed and agreed upon between speechwriter and client.

Nowhere in ancient literature does a contrary account of the speechwriter–client relationship appear. Indeed, there is a further passage which may seem to confirm what those of Theophrastus and Plutarch imply. Cicero tells us that Lysias composed a defence speech for Socrates and offered it to him 'to learn for use at his trial', *quam edisceret ut pro se in iudicio uteretur* (*De Oratore* 1. 231), but Socrates politely declined the offer on the ground that its elegant style did not suit his character. Here we have an exceptional case of a speechwriter volunteering his services gratuitously and writing a speech without prior consultation with the litigant. Dover (1968: 192) relates this story aetiologically to the subsequent existence of a Lysianic *Defence of Socrates*. It was apparently written in the orator's epideictic style, which no doubt gave rise to controversy as to whether it was actually delivered. Unscrupulous booksellers might affirm that it was, making it necessary for Socrates' adherents to invent the story in order to set the overall record straight and re-establish the tradition that Socrates conducted his own defence in his own unorthodox way. This is not the only possible explanation of the origin of the story, however. It should not have seemed necessary to fabricate it merely in order to explain the existence of an epideictic defence of Socrates in the fourth century, for his trial was the subject of numerous serious tracts, pamphlets and rhetorical exercises, not to mention the dialogues of Plato. It is therefore quite possible that an original story that Socrates was offered speech(es) for use at his trial by speechwriter(s) came into existence [36] independently of the appearance of a Lysianic[7] defence, which served to personalize the story and add to its colour. We may believe that there were exceptional cases when speechwriters offered their services to litigants, especially when their own political convictions or ambitions impelled them to do so. It is possible, without overrating Lysias' political pretensions, to envisage such a context for a number of his speeches, *e.g. Against Agoratus, Against Alcibiades i* and *ii*, and the *Defence on a Charge of Treason* (or. 25). In these, political flavour is combined with stylistic unity in a high degree.

With the aid of the foregoing evidence we may begin to form a coherent account of the probable procedure followed by Attic forensic orators when composing speeches for their clients. After initial consultation, which would vary in thoroughness according to the complexity or difficulty of the case, the actual composition of the speech was done by the speechwriter,[8] in his own words and with the exact degree of emphasis and emotional appeal that he considered necessary. The client then took the speech and learnt it off by heart[9] if he could, though it seems unlikely that a litigant who was unfortunate enough to have a poor memory and/or a nervous

---

[7] Tradition, and especially biographical tradition, abhors anonymity. Lysias' name could have been superscribed to the anonymous Defence any time after his epideictic style had become familiar through the publication of speeches like the *Olympiacus*. Cf. above, n. 5.

[8] There can be little doubt that forensic speeches were written out in full: see Isoc. *Paneg.* 188; *Antid.* 1, 46; *Panath.* 1–2, 271.

[9] See Ar. *Eq.* 347–50, and Hudson-Williams 1951: 68–9.

disposition was required to speak from memory and so place himself at a disadvantage.[10] However he chose to deliver his speech, the ordinary litigant was supplied by his speechwriter with various commonplace pleas, contrasting his own inexperience, innocent unpreparedness, and retiring character with the perverted cleverness, longstanding malice, and litigiousness of his opponent, and so pre-empting the sympathy and indulgence of a jury which contained many citizens like himself. For his part, a speechwriter with literary talents and consciousness of a reading public, like Lysias (below, pp. 34 with nn. 11–16), would naturally prefer to compose a [37] speech in a self-consistent style and to use his own judgement as to the form and degree of characterization demanded by the case.

Dover observes correctly that the needs and abilities of litigants varied (1968: 150), so that those with confidence or experience in legal matters or public speaking did not require the fullest available services of the speechwriter. But discussion of the *Corpus Lysiacum* centres around the *published* speeches, and even if Dover's thesis of collaborative composition is accepted, for some speeches the crucial *eikos*-question must still be asked: from the cases in which Lysias was consulted, which speeches is he likely to have prepared for publication as specimens of his professional and literary skill, those which he composed himself in their entirety or those which contained varying contributions from his clients? The answer should be obvious, but we cannot be sure that all the speeches in the corpus were chosen and prepared for publication by Lysias. It should be possible, however, to assert that 'probably the majority' were, if some evidence could be adduced to show that Lysias, or any other orator, was able to exercise effective supervision over the publication of speeches under his name. To this evidence we now turn.

If it is accepted, as I think it must be, that Lysias established himself as a writer on rhetorical theory, whether through the media

---

[10] Memorization played an important part in ancient education, and general standards were probably higher than they are today. But Alcidamas refers to it as a difficult and burdensome exercise (*Soph.* 18), and we know of one famous case in which a very experienced politician 'dried up' (Demosthenes on the first embassy to Philip, according to Aeschines 2. 34–5).

of technical treatises,[11] exercises,[12] or a wide range of display pieces,[13] it may be confidently assumed not only that readers would be anxious to obtain copies of his works and hence have a direct interest in their genuineness (Dover 1968: 153, 159) but that the orator, in order to increase his reputation and widen his clientele, would actively promote a market for his speeches, concentrating in the case of forensic speeches on those which were successful.[14] Epideictic speeches by famous orators of the period were certainly distributed among their pupils and admirers (Turner 1952: 19), and there is no evidence to suggest that forensic speeches were held in [38] lower esteem: on the contrary, those by reputable authors were considered desirable reading for any man who wished to make his mark in public life.[15] The same conditions obtained in the matter of distribution for forensic as for epideictic speeches, so that when Isocrates says of his own speech *Against the Sophists*, 'I wrote and distributed the speech' (*Antid.* 193: *logon diedōka grapsas*), Turner deduces very reasonably that 'The author in person supervises the circulation of his work' (1952: 20). We have no cause to believe that others who relied on their literary talents for their livelihood were less vigilant than he was in guarding their reputations.

An interesting illustration of the extent to which an author could influence opinion regarding his literary output is supplied, once more by Isocrates, who appears to have succeeded in disowning a large number of forensic speeches which he wrote early in his career.[16] If Isocrates could do this in the case of speeches which he may actually have written, Lysias should have had an easier task in disowning speeches which he did not compose. Another reason for

[11] [Plut.] *Vit. X Or.* 836b: 'there are also rhetorical treatises (*technai*) written by him.'

[12] Schol. Hermog. Walz iv. 352, 5. Blass, *AB* 382, points out that the topic here mentioned is treated by Lysias in 24. 15, and may therefore have been drawn by him from one of his already published *paraskeuai*.

[13] Dion. Hal. *Lys.* 1: 'he wrote a great many speeches well-conceived for court, council, and assembly, and, in addition to these, panegyrics, *erōtikoi*, and epistolary essays.'

[14] Lysias is said to have lost in only two of his published speeches ([Plut.] *Vit. X Or.* 836a).

[15] The fact is deplored by Isocrates (*Paneg.* 11). See Kennedy 1963: 34; Dover 1968: 182–3.

[16] *Antid.* 36. His attitude gave rise to the famous controversy involving Aristotle, described by Dion. Hal. *Isoc.* 18. See Dover 1968: 25.

supposing Isocrates' task to have been the more difficult is that we know he had many detractors, against whom he spoke at length in his early discourses and in the *Antidosis*, some of whom tried to discredit him by drawing attention to his early career as a speechwriter. We know nothing, however, about contemporary imitators of Lysias who tried to pass off their work as his, but we can be sure that their task would have been rendered the more difficult by his reputation and a discerning literary public.

As to his choice of speeches for publication, those which would display his art in its most favourable light would be speeches on difficult cases for obscure clients[17] who were inexperienced or diffident or both.[18] Examples of such speeches are easy to find in the *Corpus Lysiacum*. By publishing speeches of this kind Lysias might have expected to attract clients of all kinds.

A further consideration arises from the publication of forensic [39] speeches. To what extent were they revised and retouched before publication? An extreme view of this question was advanced by Darkow, who, in her examination of individual Lysianic speeches, emphasized the characteristics which rendered them unsuitable for delivery in court, and regarded the published speeches as purely epideictic in character. She even went so far as to suggest that 'Lysias and indeed all the orators of the canon were not *logopoioi* in the sense of professional speechwrights. They were the real representatives of a *technē* behind which all speech mongers sheltered themselves' (1917: 17). Although arrival at this conclusion entails an intolerably narrow and tendentious interpretation of the evidence, it is undoubtedly true that certain of the speeches contain strong epideictic elements, and it is arguable that the short fragments of speeches which found their way into the corpus did so because of their literary interest. If the orator revised his speeches before publication, his own part in their composition was thereby enhanced, and his client's, if he had any at all, diminished.

These arguments against composite authorship in the published speeches of Lysias receive internal confirmation from the passages of

---

[17] Dion. Hal. *Lys.* 16: 'he is more capable of speaking well on small, unexpected, or difficult matters.'

[18] It is an interesting question whether the large number of clients who claim inexperience or display diffidence are merely using commonplace pleas, or whether this large number is the result of the orator's choice of speeches for publication.

live speech which occur in them. In live speech, if anywhere, the orator might be expected to have allowed his clients to speak in their own words. The first fact which should surprise the proponents of composite authorship is that live speech, that is, the quotation of the actual words alleged to have been used in a conversation, argument, or harangue, is rare in Lysias, and this is one of the characteristics which makes him less of a 'natural' orator than, for example, Andocides and Aeschines. More interesting, however, is the fact that when live speech is used by Lysias, it tends to have a certain stiff formality, which may even contrast with the more relaxed style of the surrounding narrative. I have drawn attention to this peculiarity elsewhere (1965: 104–5) in reference to passages of *oratio recta* in *The Slaying of Eratosthenes*, where this strange formality is particularly striking. Another example, in which rhetorical resources are deployed most effectively, is the powerful harangue put into the mouth of Diodotus' widow in the speech *Against Diogeiton* (15–17), which must rank as one of the finest pieces of female Athenian oratory outside Aristophanes, though it is scarcely credible for its realism. Lysias, having no doubt received a verbal account of [40] the widow's harangue from his client, converted it into a highly polished tour de force which presents the 'rhetoric of the situation' with the maximum of emotional appeal. In this as in other aspects of our study of Lysias, we are impressed more by his conscious literary artistry than by his naturalism.

Dover's hypothesis would have surprised Dionysius and Plutarch and astounded Plato. Taking literary unity as a basic assumption, they would have explained the realism and variety of style which they found in the Lysianic speeches in terms not of composite authorship but of the writer's own talents, whether innate or cultivated. The foregoing investigation suggests that we should follow their example. It seems inconceivable that they could have misunderstood the literary habits of their own age. On the historical side of the question, it seems clear that the speechwriter–client relationship was more clear-cut than Dover requires us to believe, and that the publication and transmission of speeches was probably less haphazard. And finally, since it casts doubt upon the authenticity of all Attic oratory, not only the *Corpus Lysiacum*, the study is as yet incomplete and Lysias should not be singled out.

3

Who Was Corax?

Thomas Cole

Posed a thousand or so years ago, the question would have seemed easy, almost insultingly so. Any Byzantine schoolboy could have told you that Corax was a Sicilian from Syracuse, the man who invented rhetoric and defined it as the art of persuasion. He taught his discovery to another Sicilian, Tisias; and their doctrines (or textbooks) were later taken to Athens, perhaps through the activity of a fellow countryman, Gorgias of Leontini, during the course of a famous embassy there on behalf of his native city. The original discovery was a response to the challenges of the democratic politics after the popular revolution which deposed the last of the Syracusan tyrants, Hieron's brother Thrasybulus. Corax's art was a recipe for combining fact, argumentation, and appeals to audience sensibilities into an effective political discourse constructed in accordance with a canonical order that he was the first to devise: proem, demonstration (or narrative followed by demonstration), epilogue. Since the art of producing such discourses was teachable, its existence helped make public speaking a readily available as well as indispensable tool in the process of guiding and controlling popular deliberative bodies. (Guiding and controlling were Corax's specialties, since before the revolution he had been a counsellor and close associate of Hieron's.) The tool, however, like all tools, was subject to misuse, as Corax found out to his own cost. When he brought suit against Tisias for refusal to pay the prearranged fee for instruction in the new art, the latter impudently claimed that even if he lost the case he could not be held liable: losing his case would mean that Tisias had failed to persuade the jury, hence had not been taught the art of persuasion as per agreement. Corax responded by turning the argument around against his opponent: even a successful defence would require payment, since it would show that the defendant had in fact been taught the art—just as per agreement. At this point there were cries of 'Bad crow (*corax*), bad egg', on the part of jury and/or bystanders and the case had to be dropped.

The story, with minor variations, appears in six texts dating from the fifth century AD (Troilus' *Prolegomena to the Rhetoric of Hermogenes*) to the thirteenth or fourteenth (the *Prolegomena* of Maximus Planudes).[1] Since there is no strikingly different rival account from those ten centuries, we may conveniently call the one just presented the Byzantine answer to our initial question about Corax.

Most modern answers reveal in varying degrees the influence of this Byzantine prototype, but the question itself has come to seem much more problematic. If one looks for clear traces of the story in the millennium (roughly) between the time of Corax himself and that of his earliest biographers, the results[2] are disappointingly meagre. Plato (*Phdr.* 273c) is the first writer to mention Tisias by name; Aristotle the first to know of Corax (*Rh.* 2. 24, 1401a17); and Theophrastus the first to attribute to him the discovery of a new art (Radermacher, *AS* 18, A. V. 17). Dionysius of Halicarnassus is the first to connect him, via Tisias, with a prominent representative of the Athenian rhetorical tradition (Isocrates: cf. Radermacher, *AS* 29, B. II. 4). Sextus Empiricus (*Adv. Math.* 2. 96) or, conceivably, Cicero,[3] is

---

[1] Most fully in the Prolegomena printed as numbers 4 (anonymous) and 17 (Marcellinus?) in Rabe and in Walz vi. 4–30 and iv. 1–38. The best survey of the tradition is that of Wilcox 1943: 2 ff. For the versions of Troilus and Planudes, see, respectively, Rabe 5 = Walz vi. 52–4 and Rabe 7 = Walz v. 212–21. The six texts referred to here do not include Rabe 6a = Walz ii. 682–3, or the one from which it is abridged, Walz v. 5–8, a portion of Sopater's commentary to Hermogenes that contains the Corax–Tisias story but nothing about the content of Corax's teaching or the nature of his pre- and post-revolutionary political activities.

[2] Well summarized in Rabe viii–xi.

[3] *De Or.* 3. 81, *Coracem ... patiamur ... pullos suos excludere in nido, qui evolent clamatores odiosi et molesti* ('Let us allow the "Crow" to hatch out his nestlings and the hateful, ranting nuisances they fly away to become') is generally taken as an allusion to the 'Bad crow, bad egg' phrase. But Cicero need not be familiar with the Tisias story to apply the proverb in this context (cf. Radermacher, *AS* 29, ad B. II. 6).

the earliest source for the lawsuit over Corax's fee. The only notice, outside the Prolegomena and one late commentary,[4] that identifies Corax and Tisias as master and student is from the fifth-century Platonist Hermias (though there it is Tisias who is the master and Corax the student).[5] Ammianus Marcellinus (30. 4. 3) is the first to attribute a definition of rhetoric ('the artificer of persuasion') to Corax or Tisias.[6] Preoccupation with the politics of fledgling Syracusan democracy and the proper order of presentation (*dispositio, taxis*) in an oration comes only in the *Prolegomenon* of Troilus and the later works already mentioned.

Piecemeal attestation of the Byzantine tradition in earlier sources need not mean piecemeal origin over the course of the preceding millennium, but the possibility must obviously be reckoned with. And possibility begins to become probability once two further phenomena are taken into consideration: the frequency with which certain components of the traditional account are associated with figures other than Corax; and the contradiction between parts of the tradition and what is known from other, often better, sources about early writers on rhetoric. The dispute over payment of a fee (minus, obviously, the concluding dictum on crows and their eggs) appears first in connection with Protagoras and his student Euathlus,[7] and it may even have been familiar to Plato in a

---

Corax's chicks and the bad eggs that hatched them could be any or all of those speakers who claimed to owe something to the tradition of formal instruction in rhetoric thought to derive from him.

[4] Sopater (above, n. 1) on Hermogenes, usually dated, like Troilus, to the fifth century AD.

[5] *Ad Phaed.* 273c = p. 251. 8–9 Couvreur. Spengel's *kathēgētēs Tisiou* for the transmitted *mathētēs Tisiou* will 'correct' the text at this point—but need we assume that it was a copyist rather than Hermias himself who was unfamiliar with the details of the story in its Byzantine version?

[6] Several Prolegomena (Radermacher, *AS* 30, B. II. 13) offer the same formulation but attribute it to *hoi peri Tisian kai Koraka*, by which they may be referring in a vague way to the whole tradition which Corax and Tisias were thought to have founded. 'The power of persuasion' appears as Corax's definition in Athanasius' *Prolegomenon* to Hermogenes (p. 171. 19 Rabe = Radermacher, *AS* 30, B. II. 14).

[7] Apuleius, *Flor.* 18 = p. 30 K., Aulus Gellius 5. 10, Euathlus is already known to Aristotle (fr. 67 Rose) as someone involved in a prosecution of Protagoras; but it need not follow, as Radermacher 1897: 413, assumed, that the case involved payment of a fee (see Rabe xi).

Protagorean context.[8] 'Artificer of persuasion' is a definition of rhetoric attributed by Plato (*Gorg.* 453a) to Gorgias and considered by many[9] to be original with Plato himself; and the quadripartite oratorical *divisio* attributed to Corax in three Prolegomena[10] is associated alternatively with 'Isocrates and his followers' or his and Aristotle's friend Theodectes (Aristotle, fr. 133 Rose; Radermacher, *AS* 160, B. XXIV. 29).

The last-named bit of rhetorical doctrine is not only credited to figures other than the 'Byzantine' Corax but also—fairly clearly— much more plausibly credited to them. It is judicial oratory, not the political persuasion with which Corax is associated in the Byzantine tradition, that requires the Theodectean-Isocratean tetrad. *Diēgēsis,* the straightforward presentation of the speaker's view of what has happened, is, as theoreticians from Aristotle on down are in the habit of pointing out, likely to be unnecessary in a political case, where the audience is assumed to be well aware of the facts of the situation.[11] The one author who does attribute to Corax a *divisio* suited to political oratory (proem, argument, epilogue) writes as if he had begun with the judicial tetrad and then combined its second and third members into what counts as a single section dedicated to argument but whose

---

[8] Protagoras' statement, at the end of the long speech ascribed to him in the *Protagoras* (324b–c), that any student who feels the fee charged for his course of instruction to have been excessive can go to a temple and, upon swearing an oath, pay no more than what he declares the instruction to have been worth, suggests the possibility that disagreements over the payment and proper amount of fees was either a subject considered by Protagoras himself or one that provided the content of stories told about him—as would be natural in the case of the man who either was, or was thought to be (Diog. Laert. 9. 52), the first person to teach in return for pay.

[9] See Mutschmann 1918: 440–3, who cites the parallel Platonic formulations at *Charm.* 174e (medicine as an 'artificer of health', *hugieias dēmiourgos*) and *Symp.* 188d (prophecy as 'artificer of friendship between gods and men', *philias theōn kai anthrōpōn dēmiourgos*).

[10] The four-part arrangement—proem, narrative (*diēgēsis*), argument (*agōnes*), epilogue—is found in Rabe 7, p. 67. 6–7 = Walz v. 215. 22–3; Rabe 9, p. 126. 5– 15 = Walz ii. 119. 10–26; Rabe 13, p. 189. 16–17 = Walz vii. 6. 9–10.

[11] *Rh.* 3. 12, 1414a36–8. When narrative is included in the *divisio* of political orations (e.g. Anaximenes (?), *Rh. Al.* 30–1, and Syrianus, *In Hermogenem* 2. 170. 14–19 Rabe), it tends to be conceived as limited in scope, as in Anaximenes' rules for reporting an embassy, or tendentious in character (the *katastasis* of imperial rhetoricians; see below, n. 39).

purpose is narrative as well: 'to speak about matters on which one must advise the people *as in a narrative* (*hōs en diēgēsei*).'[12]

The same incompatibility exists between the Byzantine version of Corax's activity and Cicero's summary report[13] of what he claims to have been the account of Corax and Tisias that appeared in Aristotle's famous compendium of early writings on rhetoric—the *Synagōgē Technōn*. There the new art is linked in a totally different way to conditions at Syracuse following the fall of the tyrants. It is not the requirements of democratic debate that inspire Corax and Tisias, but lawsuits over property, once the original owners began to claim land confiscated by the tyrants and then given or sold by them to others (*cum sublatis... tyrannis res privatae longo intervallo iudiciis repeterentur*). This account (whether or not it corresponds to anything in Syracusan history) certainly accords better than the Byzantine one with the testimony of Isocrates, Plato, and Aristotle, who complain consistently that writers on public speaking concentrate on dicanic oratory to the total or nearly total exclusion of political oratory.[14] And the one Byzantine account of Corax that fails to assign him any role in politics (Walz v. 5–8, from Sopater's Hermogenes commentary),[15] is also the only one that contains a passage close enough in phraseology and organization of material to *Brutus* 46 to suggest the possibility of derivation from a common, Aristotelian source:

After this [the age of the tyrants] Corax became the first to develop a system of precepts (*didaskalia*) in rhetoric. For those who pursued	*tum primum* [after the fall of the Sicilian tyrants]... *artem et praecepta Siculos Coracem et Tisiam conscripsisse: nam antea neminem*

---

[12] Rabe 4, pp. 25. 17–26. 6 = Walz. vi. 13. 1–11 That tripartition in this passage derives in some sense from an original quadripartition is very likely even if, as Wilcox argues (1943: 15–16), its author here preserves the Byzantine tradition in its original form. In replacing the triad with a tetrad or some other scheme suitable only to judicial oratory, later writers would have been simply spelling out what was implicit in their model.

[13] *Brut.* 46–8 = Radermacher, *AS* 13–14, A. V. 9. On the general accuracy of the claim, see—against the doubts of Solmsen 1954: 218—Douglas 1955: 536–9.

[14] See Hamberger 1914: 12–16, with the concurring judgements of Hinks 1940: 62–3, and Stegemann 1934: 143–4.

[15] Corax's political role is also missing from Rabe 6a = Walz ii. 682–3, but that text is simply an abridgement of Sopater.

rhetoric **before him** were dependent on experience and **careful practice**, and so (*houtōs*)[16] **lacking in systematic method** and *aitia* **or art** (*technē*) of any sort. (Walz v. 6. 20–4)

solitum via nec arte, sed accurate tamen et de scripto plerosque dicere. (Cic. *Brut.* 46) [17]

The lists of fifth- and fourth-century rhetoricians that follow in both Sopater and Cicero again suggest a common derivation:[18]

Tisias was a student of this Corax... and **Gorgias** of Leontini, when he came on an embassy to Athens, brought Tisias' **written treatise** (*technē sungrapheisa*) with him, and produced another of his own; and after him **Antiphon** of Rhamnus, the teacher of **Thucydides**, is

[Protagoras is said to have provided the *scriptas disputationes* known as *loci communes*] *quod idem fecisse Gorgias... huic Antiphontem Rhamnusium similia quaedam habuisse conscripta quo neminem umquam melius oravisse capitis causam... scripsit Thucydides; nam Lysiam*

---

[16] 'So', *houtōs* (Radermacher), or 'they', *houtoi* (Gercke), seems a necessary emendation for the transmitted 'he' (*houtos*) which would make 'lacking in ... art' a description of Corax's own method and leave the nature of the contrast with earlier 'empirical' rhetoricians completely unclear.

[17] The parallel (first noted by Gercke 1897: 344–5) would of course be more compelling were it possible to get any sense out of Cicero's *de scripto* (often emended, not very satisfactorily, to *descripte*) or from the equally puzzling *aitias* in Sopater. In general, however, scholars have given it less attention than it deserves.

[18] Note that both lists end with Isocrates, as one would expect in Aristotle, not with the Hellenistic canon of Attic orators, as in the Prolegomena (Rabe 17, p. 273. 18–22 = Walz iv. 15. 17–20; Rabe 4, p. 28. 12–16 = Walz vi. 15. 19–16. 2). The value of the parallels is not lessened by the illegitimate conclusions which Hamberger sought to draw from them (below, n. 36). It would certainly be less if, as is generally assumed (e.g. Wilcox 1943: 9–10), the lines immediately following in Sopater (Walz v. 7. 15–18) maintained—against Aristotle and all other fourth-century sources—that the rhetorical works of Corax, Tisias, and their immediate successors were exclusively concerned with political oratory. But what the lines in fact say is that these works were *dēmagōgikai technai*, devoting no space to *stasis* theory but preoccupied instead with 'a certain persuasiveness' (*pithanotēs*) and 'how to influence the people'. Since there is, so far as I know, no parallel for *dēmagōgikos* as a synonym for *dēmēgorikos* or *symbouleutikos*, the normal adjectives used in reference to political oratory, it is perfectly possible that the word means nothing more here than 'popular' or 'calculated to appeal to a large audience' (*hupagōgimos tou dēmou*, as the phrase immediately following might suggest), whether in a popular lawcourt or a popular assembly. If so, there is a possible parallel (supporting derivation from the *Synagōgē*) to the contrast drawn in Arist. *Rh.* between the author's own conception of the discipline and that of his predecessors. Aristotelian rhetoric centres on the study of the enthymeme; that of his predecessors is directed at the 'listener' (*akroatēs*) and

said to have written an 'art'; and after this, Isocrates the *rhetor*... (Walz v. 6. 24–7. 14)

primo profiteri solitum artem esse...; similiter Isocrates... *se ad artes componendas transtulisse.*

(*Brut.* 47–8)

The difficulty of reconciling the 'non-Sopatran', political Corax with the rest of the ancient tradition relating to Corax and his activities poses the problems raised thus far in their acutest form. One has the choice of substantially recasting his role, or rejecting the testimony of the Prolegomena altogether. Scholars in this century have opted, by and large, for the first alternative. There is widespread agreement on jettisoning everything we are told about the biography of Corax: both his preoccupation, before and after the revolution, with political manipulation and persuasion,[19] and his lawsuit with Tisias.[20] The relationship between Corax and Tisias thereby becomes the purely generic one between two collaborators. The former is to be credited with a discussion of persuasive techniques organized in the order in which they would appear in a 'normal' dicanic speech of four parts (or more—see below); the latter with expanding and improving the collection of techniques, or perhaps, if Corax's teaching was purely oral, with setting it down for the first time in writing. The second hypothesis has the advantage of explaining a further inconsistency between the Byzantine Corax and his predecessors. There is no hint, at any point before Hermias and the Prolegomena,

framed with his shortcomings in mind ('incapacity' (*mochthēria*), 'vulgarity' (*phortikotēs*), 'worthlessness' (*phaulotēs*): *Rh.* 2. 21, 1395b1–2; 3. 1, 1404a8; 3. 14, 1415b5; 3. 18, 1419a18). What appears in Sopater may be nothing more than a 'Hermogenized' and simplified version of this contrast. Enthymeme study is Hermogenized into *stasis* theory (cf. *Rh.* 1. 1, 1354a14–15, 'they say nothing about ... enthymemes', with Sopater's 'having no space devoted to *staseis*', both in reference to the same body of texts); and Aristotle's intellectually limited audience (*akroatai phauloi*) is presented, more simply, as a lower-class one (*dēmos*).

[19] This political dimension is usually found incompatible with the *divisio* he is said to have devised and with fourth-century testimony about the overwhelmingly dicanic orientation of early writing on rhetoric. Kennedy 1963: 60–1, is virtually alone among contemporary writers in his inclination to make Corax 'a political speaker' and attribute to him 'a division of speech suitable to deliberative oratory'. [But see Kennedy's further considerations in the new edition of *Aristotle 'On Rhetoric'* (2006) 293–306.]

[20] This may be a floating story of indeterminate origin eventually attached to Corax because 'Bad crow, bad egg' provided such an effective piece of closure; cf. Kowalski 1937: 47.

of contrasting characters or separate achievements for Corax and Tisias. We are always told what Tisias did (and taught),[21] or what Corax did;[22] or, beginning with Cicero in the *De Oratore* (1. 91; cf. *Brut.* 46), what Tisias and Corax did without distinction; we are never told what Corax did unlike Tisias, or different things each of them did.[23] The two figures seem to have been interchangeable—so much so that, as pointed out earlier, they are in fact interchanged in Hermias' *Phaedrus* commentary, the only text (outside the Prolegomena) which refers to them explicitly as master and student. This suggests that the ultimate source of all our information was a single report or a single set of documents in which the contributions of the two men were not clearly distinguished from each other.

So far the new consensus. Tentative exploration of the second, more radical alternative suggested above has been limited thus far to a small minority of scholars—among them Friedrich Solmsen, to whose memory this essay was originally dedicated. In 1934 Solmsen drew attention[24] to a 'wichtiges, nicht genug ausgewertetes Zeugnis' of Aristotle concerning the character of 'the art [of rhetoric] before

[21] Plato, *Phdr.* 267a, 273c, Arist. *Soph. El.* 32, 183b29, Theophrastus (in Radermacher, *AS* 18, A. V. 17).

[22] Arist. *Rh.* 2. 24, 1402a17; cf. 'Aristotle' in the anonymous preface to the spurious *Rhetorica ad Alexandrum*; Cicero, *De Inv.* 2. 2. 6.

[23] 'Tisias after the first' (*meta tous prōtous*) heads Aristotle's list of contributors to the development at *Soph. El.* 32, 183b29 ff., and Corax is sometimes assumed (e.g. Hinks 1940: 65–6) to be included among, or identified with, the *prōtous*. If so, Aristotle may be implying some sort of contrast between Corax's achievements and the more solid or clearly identifiable ones of his successor. But it is much more likely that the *prōtoi* are Empedocles (called the inventor of the discipline in Aristotle's *Sophist* (fr. 65 Rose = Radermacher, *AS* 28, B. I. 1) and/or the divine patrons or mythical masters of effective speech—Hermes, Nestor, Odysseus—with whom the Prolegomena regularly begin and who probably played some role even in fourth-century accounts of the prehistory of the discipline (Wilcox 1943: 8, with n. 10): cf. *Crat.* 407e (Hermes), 398d (Greek *heroes* so called because they were *rhētores tines kai erōtētikoi*), *Phdr.* 261b (Nestor, Odysseus, Palamedes), and for what may be a distant echo of one of Aristotle's own formulations, Quintilian 3. 1. 8: *primus post eos quos poetae tradiderunt movisse aliqua circa rhetoricen dicitur Empedocles.* Kennedy (1957: 25) regards the last passage quoted as Quintilian's own attempt to strike a compromise between those who categorically affirmed, and those who categorically denied, the existence of rhetoric in the age of the heroes; but this sort of compromise is typically Aristotelian. If primitive maxims and proverbs can count as philosophy (fr. 13 Rose = *De Philos.* fr. 8 Ross), one would expect primitive eloquence and figures of speech to count as rhetoric.

[24] 'Theodorus', *RE* 5. A 2 (1934) 1842–4; cf. Hinks 1940: 68–9.

Theodorus'. According to *Rhetoric* 2. 24, 1400b15–16, a certain type of argument from probability constituted 'the entirety' of this art (*pasa hē proteron tou Theodōrou technē*). Since Theodorus was the second after Tisias in the canonical succession of early writers on rhetoric, the statement, if true, makes it highly unlikely that Corax or Tisias dealt with anything but the proofs section of the four-part oration. Any kind of argumentation from probability (*eikos*) is largely excluded from the narrative of a speech, and rarely if ever forms part of a proem or epilogue.[25] This, combined with Tisias' general addiction to *Eikostechnik*, well attested in Plato, and Theodorus' equally well-attested obsession with subdividing oratorical structures into their component parts (narrative, preparatory narrative, supplementary narrative, proof, supplementary proof, supplementary refutation, etc.), naturally points to the strong possibility that the entire topic of oratorical *divisio* was Theodorus' innovation.[26]

Solmsen's general doubts about the modern consensus—though not his views on Theodorus—were seconded several years later by Kroll,[27] and they have been carried a step further in two works of the early 1990s: E. Schiappa's 'The Beginnings of Greek Rhetorical Theory' (1993), and my own *The Origins of Rhetoric in Ancient Greece*

[25] Solmsen's own conclusion is more cautious, allowing for the possibility that there were pre-Theodoran discussions of other parts of the speech but that Aristotole chose to ignore them here because he is using *technē* to mean 'der eigentliche Inhalt der technēs'—i.e. enthymeme or *Argumentationstechnik*. But he cites no parallel for this use of *technē* when what is meant is merely *to entechnon tēs technēs*.

[26] *Phdr.* 267a, 272e, 273c–d (Tisias); *Phdr.* 266d; Arist. *Rh.* 3. 13, 1414b13–15 (Theodorus). Solmsen's conclusion follows for Corax and Tisias even if, as I think rather more likely, *hē proteron tou Theodōrou technē* is a reference not to 'the art of rhetoric before Theodorus', but to 'the earlier art of Theodorus', i.e. an earlier work of Theodorus written before the interest in *divisio* for which he was famous became apparent (cf. the variant reading *protera*, which would, of course, require that the phrase be so translated). This interpretation, unlike Solmsen's, does not eliminate the possibility that *divisio* was already a concern of Thrasymachus, Tisias' immediate follower in the sequence of early writers on rhetoric; but whatever the situation was with him, such concern is excluded for Corax by Aristotle's further observation (*Rh.* 2. 24, 1402a17) apropos of another type of argument from probability, that it was 'what the art of Corax is composed of' (*sunkeimenē*).

[27] 'Rhetorik', *RE* Suppl. 7 (1940) 1046. The general difficulty of reconciling Corax's *Eikostechnik* and his supposed preoccupation with *dispositio* was first pointed out, to my knowledge, by Süss 1910: 74.

(1991*b*).[28] The starting point for both investigations is the contention that the word 'rhetoric' (first attested in the *Gorgias*) is Plato's own term, coined or given currency sometime in the 380s, for a set of techniques not thitherto seen as constituting a separate definable discipline: this I advanced as a surmise (1991*b*: 2, 98–9), only to find it already proved—insofar as such things can ever be proved—by Schiappa (1990). Schiappa argues the unlikelihood of Tisias' having come up with anything like the systematic presentation of rhetorical techniques or theories which the notion of a definite art of *rhētorikē* suggests, and is inclined to doubt the tradition which credits him with a written rhetorical handbook. My own reconstruction accepts the existence of the handbook but posits a collection of model pieces, analogous to those found in the *Tetralogies* of Antiphon and based on the principle of *eikos*: pleadings pro and con (or, more likely, compressed summary versions of such pleadings) on topics likely to come up in court cases—not an analytic set of precepts. The famous pair of arguments associated with Tisias (*Phdr.* 273b3–c4) and Corax (*Rh.* 1402a18–21), in which a defendant's superior strength is adduced to establish first the likelihood and then the unlikelihood of his being guilty of having assaulted the plaintiff as charged, will have come from this collection. And the same may be true of the debate over non-payment of a teacher's fee recorded in the Prolegomena.[29] Though not based on probability, the latter illustrates a similar process of turning an argument around against its original propounder.

My own reconstruction is less radical than Schiappa's; and, unlike Schiappa's or the Byzantine tradition or the modified version of it which constitutes the modern consensus, it is compatible with all the

---

[28] See esp. ch. 5, with the works of the earlier scholars cited in nn. 11–12 (pp. 168–9): Gercke 1897; Radermacher, *AS*; Lesky (1963: 387); Barwick 1963; Koch 1970; Havelock (1982: 322). To that list add Kowalski 1933: 37–8 and 44; id. 1937: 85; and Solmsen's review of Radermacher (1954: 214–15). [The investigation continues in Schiappa 1999: 14–47.]

[29] Cf. Spengel 1828: 33–4, *Poterat in arte sua ... Tisias ... ingenii ostendendi causa meletas componere in quibus talia perlustrarent unde ad ipsum auctorem fabula translata videatur*; Kowalski 1933: 43.

ADDENDUM: That the earliest instruction in political and juridical eloquence took the form of such practice pieces (*meletas*) pro and con may be the view implied in Plutarch's story of how Themistocles was always indifferent, even as a boy, to

fifth- and fourth-century evidence.[30] But neither reconstruction addresses itself to the problem of how and why the Byzantine tradition came into being in the first place. A partial explanation has been suggested by some of the architects of the modern consensus, but their arguments must be carried further if the de-Byzantinization process under way here is really to work.

It is generally agreed that the transfer of the activity of Corax from the dicanic to the political sphere is a post-Aristotelian development in the tradition, and it is fairly easy to see why the transfer took place. Political rhetoric, in the view of Isocrates (*Antid.* 46, *Paneg.* 4), followed here by Aristotle (*Rh.* 1354b17 ff.), is a higher, more significant form than dicanic. That it should replace dicanic rhetoric in the discipline's foundation myth was almost inevitable once the view of Isocrates became authoritative, and once rhetoric itself had ceased to be, as it often was for Plato and Aristotle, a suspect discipline whose claims were to be disputed or curtailed, and had become, along with philosophy, the central ingredient in higher education. Its finest achievements were expected, quite naturally, to be present, at

---

'instructions given to teach him any pleasing or graceful accomplishment'. Instead he 'would be always inventing or arranging (*meletōn kai suntattomenos*) some oration or declamation to himself, the subject of which was generally the excusing (*apologia*) or accusing (*katēgoria*) of his companions, so that his master would often say to him, 'You my boy will be nothing small but great one way or other for good or else for bad' (*Life of Themistocles* 2.1–2, Clough trans.). The account may well be anachronistic so far as Themistocles himself is concerned—a by-product of the debate (cf. Thuc. 1. 138. 1–3; Xen. *Mem.* 4. 2. 2) which arose in the course of the next two generations as to whether he owed any of his extraordinary qualities as a leader to anything he learned from a teacher; but by indicating what were the first symptoms of his disdain for skills inculcated by 'pre-rhetorical' education (polite accomplishments such as playing the lyre and reciting or singing verses memorized from the poets), it does in effect point out where and how, in the view of its author, the break with the past began to occur.

[30] For those portions of the evidence that are usually taken (erroneously, I believe) to point to the existence of organized collections of rhetorical precepts before the handbook of Theodectes and the earliest version of Aristotle's *Rhetoric*, see T. Cole 1991*b*: 130–3. One possible testimony not discussed there is *POxy* 410 (Radermacher, *AS* 231–2, D), an analysis, in Doric, of stylistic *megaloprepeia*, which its first editor believed to be 'considerably influenced by Tisias' *technē*' or even taken from a summary of the 'productions of Tisias and his school' (cf. W. Roberts 1904: 18–21). But with the exception of Drerup (cf. Stegemann in 'Teisias', *RE* 5. A 1 [1934] 142), Roberts' view has found no followers.

least *in nucleo*, in the work of the 'first founder' (*prōtos heuretēs*) to whom it owed its existence. It is even possible that Corax's role in controlling and directing the passions of the Syracusan populace originally arose through a transfer into a particular historical situation of the civilizing, organizing role in the prehistory of the human race which certain laudatory texts assign either to eloquence (Isoc. 3. 6–9) or the first person to master it (Cicero, *De Inv.* 1. 2. 2, *De Or.* 1. 30 ff.).

A similar tendency to attribute everything that was basic in the discipline to its founder will explain why Corax came to be credited with the Gorgianic or Platonic definition of rhetoric as the power or artificer of persuasion, which ultimately became canonical. Having invented for the benefit of his contemporaries the art of rhetoric, it was inevitable that Corax should have told them in briefest possible compass what it was.

It is impossible to pinpoint the period(s) or author(s) in which Corax began undergoing this metamorphosis, though Timaeus of Tauromenium—our earliest authority for Gorgias' embassy to Athens—has often been suggested as its ultimate source.[31] The shifts involved, whether of scope (from minor achievement to major), venue (from courtroom to popular assembly), or narrative mode (from history to fiction), certainly point to the work of someone who, like Timaeus, was simultaneously Sicilian patriot, Sicilian 'democrat',[32] and, if Polybius is to be believed, congenital liar.

On the other hand, neither patriotism nor republicanism nor general mendacity will explain Timaeus' concern with the technicalities of *divisio*, and he does not in fact figure in the modern consensus in this connection. The assumption is, rather, that one at least of the various *divisiones* (four in all) attributed to the Byzantine Corax must be an isolated remnant of the real Corax, faithfully recorded

[31] Cf. Dion. Hal. *Lys.* 1 (p. 11.3 Us.-Rad.). Radermacher 1897: 412–19, followed by Hamberger 1914: 12–18, and Wilcox 1943: 20–3. Rabe, p. ix, and Schiappa 1993: n. 51, remain unconvinced, perhaps with good reason.

[32] i.e. anti-monarchist, as may be inferred from his hatred of Agathocles. Wilcox 1943: 21–2, draws attention to the close parallels between Rabe 4, p. 25. 3–8 = Walz vi. 12. 6–10 (the vowing of a cult in honour of *Zeus eleutherios* to be instituted once the dynasty of Hieron is expelled from Syracuse) and Diodorus' account, in a passage often thought to derive from Timaeus, of the actual institution of the cult after the expulsion had taken place (11. 72–3).

in Aristotle's *Synagōgē*, but later transferred inappropriately from its original dicanic context into a political one.

There is little justification, however, for the separation thus posited between one aspect of Corax's traditional role as a *prōtos heuretēs* and all the others. Like all the others, this aspect is missing from the one Byzantine text (above, at nn. 15–18) which shows a close verbal parallel to Cicero's summary of the *Synagōgē*. More important, the tetradic *divisio* encountered in three Prolegomena (above, at n. 10) is so canonical a feature of ancient rhetoric as a whole that it can, when linked to a listing of the presumed tasks (*erga*) or purposes of each of its four parts, function as a kind of alternative or supplementary definition. Rhetoric is the artificer of persuasion and, more particularly, the art of 'proemizing' for good will and attentiveness, narrating for clarity and believability, arguing for proof or refutation, and 'epilogizing' for summary and reminder (or perorating for pathos). To say that Corax invented rhetoric was tantamount to saying that he invented this fourfold way of conceiving his task and implementing its operation.

The ease with which definition can become foundation myth is particularly clear at Rabe 9, pp. 125. 22–126. 18 = Walz ii. 119. 18–29. The passage first describes how Corax went about producing his art of persuasion:

... they say that Corax became [rhetoric's] *heuretēs prōtos* ... when he found the people in turmoil and (1) devised the topics for proems so that he might stop their uproar and persuade them to pay attention; (2) he then devised the narrative so that he might instruct them in the business at hand with clarity and conviction, and (3) utilized 'arguments' (*agōnes*) in order to persuade and dissuade, and (4) added the epilogues to remind them and fill them with emotion.

It then goes on to enumerate the functions of rhetoric which Corax has in effect performed:

Some say the tasks of rhetoric are: (1) proemizing to create good will, attentiveness, and receptiveness; (2) narrative for clarity, (3) argument for credibility (*pistis*), and (4) epilogizing for reminding.

This précis is practically identical with the same author's formulation of the Theodectean or Isocratean tetrad (above at n. 10):

(1) proemizing for good will, (2) narrative for persuasiveness, (3) argument for demonstration (*apodeixis*), (4) summarizing for reminding.[33]

It is just conceivable that the reverse process has occurred, and the definition has been generated from a genuine tradition about Corax's *divisio*. But this is highly improbable, given that, though the *divisio* is basic to the organization of the third book of his *Rhetoric*, Aristotle never suggests that it is the work of any one writer from an earlier generation.

What applies to the 'historicization' of the Theodectean tetrad will also apply to the triadic *divisio* attributed to Corax in one of the Prolegomena. The latter, as was pointed out (above, at n. 12), seems to have arisen through the minimal change necessary to accommodate the tetrad to a political context. The same cannot be said, however, for the pentadic and heptadic *divisiones* found in two of the Prolegomena: the pentad consists of proem, narrative, *agōnes*, *parekbasis* (digression), and epilogue;[34] the heptad, which calls narrative *katastasis* instead of *diēgēsis*, inserts *proparaskeuē* (preliminary presentation) and *prokatastasis* (preliminary narrative) between it and the proem (Rabe 5 [Troilus], p. 52, 8–20 = Walz vi. 49, 1–20). It is clear that both Troilus' heptad and Marcellinus' pentad result from insertions into a tradition that elsewhere derives from the same source as do the Prolegomena with a briefer *divisio*. The extra parts required to produce them are simply named and defined, with no effort, as there is for the four parts shared with the other *divisio*, to indicate the purpose which they serve in the process of political

[33] Rabe 4, p. 32. 6–9 = Walz vi. 19. 5–8 = Aristotle, fr. 133 Rose. Cf. the alternative formulation in Rabe 13, p. 216. 1–4 = Walz vii. 33. 5–7: 'proemizing to create good will (1), narrating for credibility (2), producing proofs for persuasiveness (3), epilogizing to arouse indignation and pity (4).' The same definitional tetrad may be used equally well to produce an anti-foundation myth—cf. Cicero's contention (ascribed to the Academic philosopher Charmadas at *De Or.* 1. 90) that it is ridiculous to posit a *prōtos heuretēs* for rhetoric, since it was perfectly within the capacity of any one of us, as normal human beings, to *blandire* (1) *et rem gestam exponere* (2) *et id quod intenderemus confirmare et quod contra diceretur refellere* (3), *ad extremum deprecari et conqueri* (4), *quibus in rebus omnis oratorum versaretur facultas*. Quintilian makes the same point more briefly at 2. 17. 6.

[34] Rabe 17 [Marcellinus?], pp. 270. 22–271. 20 = Walz iv. 12. 17–13. 19. *Parekbasin* is the reading in all but one of the passages where this section is mentioned and presumably to be read there (Rabe p. 52. 14–15 = Walz vi. 49. 8) in place of the transmitted *parekthesin*.

persuasion (digression and *proparaskeuē* are assigned a purely dicanic function (see below), and *prokatastasis* has the merely formal one of preparing the way for the *katastasis* itself). But what is to guarantee that this different source is a later source? Since the pentad and heptad are so rarely encountered,[35] the most economical explanation for their presence in the Prolegomena is that one or the other of them derives from an isolated but genuine report or memory of the actual content of Corax's text.[36]

Though the possibility can obviously not be excluded, it seems to me to be, on balance, a fairly unlikely one. There is no reason to disbelieve Cicero when he says (*De Inv.* 2. 2. 6) that Aristotle's *Synagōgē* drove all the works it summarized out of circulation. Authentic notice of a five- or seven-part system of Corax would have had to be taken directly from some post-Aristotelian *Mittelquelle,* and then reinserted by Troilus and Marcellinus into an account derived indirectly—via Timaeus or whomever—from the same Aristotelian source. And it is hard to see any reason either for the original division of the two transmissions—direct and indirect—or their later reunification.

There are, moreover, clear difficulties in both the pentadic and heptadic *divisiones* which make it unlikely that either could ever have been intended as the basic organizing system for a course of practical instruction in public speaking. Digression (*parekbasis*) as defined by

---

[35] The heptad appears only in Troilus and the set of *confuse annexae ... definitiones, divisiones, interpretationes* (Rabe lxiii) adjoined in one set of manuscripts (cf. p. 212. 17–19 Rabe = Walz vii. 25. 8–10) to what now appears as Rabe 13. For the pentad, see below at n. 40.

[36] The seven parts of Troilus, in particular, 'are to a certain degree recommended by their singularity', whereas 'the four canonical ... *partes orationis* we suspect just because we should expect to find them referred back to the inventor of the Art' (Hinks 1940: 68). Hinks, like several others, seems unable either to accept, or find decisive considerations against, the authenticity (argued at length in Hamburger 1914: 31–8) of Troilus' heptad. Cf. Radermacher, *AS* 34, ad B. II. 23 (*ea ... fortasse ex Aristotele provenit memoria, scimus autem in terminis technicis inveniendis primos auctores quasi delirasse*) and Stegemann 1934: 146. Hamberger has, however, found no followers (cf. Hinks 1940: 68) in his attempt (pp. 7–8 and 31 ff.) to establish an Aristotelian origin for the immediate context within which the heptad appears. (The argument rests on supposed parallels with the remarks on the beginnings of rhetoric in Sopater's scholia to Hermogenes (Walz v. 5–8 ff.), the only late rhetorical text which has been thought (see at nn. 15–17) to contain close echoes of the *Synagōgē Technōn.*)

both Troilus and Marcellinus is an excursus on the prior life of the accused (*apodeixin . . . tou krinomenou biou* [Troilus] = *tēn proteran tou enagomenou diagōgēn* [Marcellinus]) designed to ensure conviction even if the case immediately at hand fails to do so. As such it is relevant to only half the judicial cases with which the student is likely to be confronted: those for the prosecution. As if to correct this fault, the longer *divisio* of Troilus balances *parekbasis* with an exact counterpart: the *proparaskeuē*, dedicated to removing a (presumably) pre-existing charge that is doing the speaker harm (*aitian lupousan auton*). The result, however, is a model oration plan which by virtue of including both *proparaskeuē* and *parekbasis* presupposes a speech that is simultaneously for the prosecution and for the defence. We seem to be dealing with a tradition that is Byzantine in more ways than one.[37]

Comparable difficulties attend the *katastasis* and *prokatastasis* in the heptadic *divisio*. Both terms are well attested in the imperial rhetoricians, but Troilus' definition of the former ('bare presentation of the events') makes it exactly what the imperial *katastasis* is not. Bare narrative is regularly *diēgēsis*, *katastasis* being the term used when some sort of slanting, or colouring, or skewing is called for.[38] Troilus' point of departure may have been the tradition, attested in a single source (Syrianus *in Hermogenem* 2, p. 127. 4 Rabe = Radermacher, *AS* 35, B. II. 24) that *katastasis* was Corax's word for 'proem'. He reconciles this with the usage with which he was more familiar by assuming that Corax must have recognized two subspecies: one was a 'proemic' or 'pro'-*katastasis*, which he defines as 'an entrance, beginning, or proem . . . to the *katastasis*'; the other, a *katastasis* 'proper', which he inaccurately identifies with the sort of narrative his contemporaries would have called a *diēgēsis*. Whether the tradition about Corax that inspired this subdivision was correct

---

[37] A section, toward the beginning of a speech for the defence, countering *aitiai* of the sort Troilus refers to is frequent enough, both in fourth-century oratory and in fourth-century rhetoric: cf. the suggestions for dealing with *diabolai* in Arist. *Rh.* 3.15 and Anaximenes (?), *Rh. Al.* 29, pp. 61. 11–64. 23 Fuhrmann. But Hamberger's attempt (1914: 105 ff.) to detect its presence in the three earliest surviving pieces of fifth-centry oratory (Antiphon 1, 5, and 6) seems to me to involve an artificial *Gliederung* which isolates from their surroundings sections that in two cases are better taken with the introduction, and in the third with the narrative.

[38] See Russell 1983: 88, with n. 6, and Kowalski 1933: 45–50.

or not, Troilus' use of it tells us nothing about the original organization of Corax's text.[39]

Even granting, however, that the *divisiones* including *prokatastasis, parekbasis,* and *proparaskeuē* are unlikely to be much older than the texts in which they are attested, one may still wonder what impelled their authors to seek out a five- or seven-part system in the first place. A possibility worth considering is that Troilus and Marcellinus were influenced here by another multipartite classification which they share, and which appears nowhere else in the Prolegomena. Both authors present their account of Corax's invention of rhetoric as an illustration of the way any act of creation can be described and accounted for in terms of the particular 'determining circumstances' (*peristatika*) that accompany it. These are five in number: the where, when, who, why, and how of its coming into being. In the case of rhetoric, the 'where' is Sicily, the 'when' the period following the fall of the tyrants, the 'who' Corax, the 'why' the desire to control the process of popular decision-making, the 'how' the five or seven parts of an oration. It is conceivable, therefore, that the number of subdivisions in the 'how' was regulated at some point in the development of the tradition in such a way as to make it equal to the number of *peristatika*. The suggestion is supported by the fact that Troilus actually mentions—though he does not accept—a variant list of seven *peristatika* (Rabe pp. 51. 26–52. 2 = Walz vi. 48. 22–5) which would match his own heptadic *divisio*, and refrains—as if seeking to

---

[39] If *katastasis* was in fact Corax's word for the first part of a speech, it may have been used, along with *agōnes* (the only other piece of terminology in the passages on *divisio* under examination here that has a fifth-century ring about it), to refer to the essential recurring components of the sort of collection of model pieces which, it was suggested above (at n. 29), Corax produced. Arguments pro and con (*agōnes*) would have to be preceded in every instance by a 'setting up' (*katastasis*) of the basic facts of the situation which the arguments presupposed. The results might have resembled the two- or three-line settings of the stage which introduce model rhetorical pieces in the most famous collection surviving from antiquity, the *Controversiae* of Seneca. For the fifth-century texts which support this meaning of *katastasis*, see T. Cole 1991*b*: 83, with n. 14. Later usage may derive from the meaning suggested here, normally identifying *katastasis* (as what precedes the arguments section of a speech) with the *diēgēsis*, but occasionally (as what begins a speech) with the proem (cf. *Rh. Al.* 29, pp. 64, 24 and 64. 9 Fuhrmann). Like Troilus, the author of Rabe 15, p. 247. 21–2 = Walz vii. 43. 1–2 ('we treat proems ... as setting up the argument', *prooimia katastatika tou agōnos lambanomen*) may be attempting to reconcile the two senses, but through elimination of the *diēgēsis* rather than addition of a proemic *katastasis*.

avoid a clash with the five *peristatika* he does accept—from ever explicitly mentioning the number of parts in that *divisio*.[40]

The longer list of *peristatika* is derived from the shorter by including, illogically, raw material (*hylē*) and final product (*pragma*) among the *peristatika* that attend the conversion of the one into the other. And the same may hold true, as was suggested earlier, for the longer list of speech parts: *proparaskeuē* is a *parekbasis* for the defence; and *prokatastasis* is produced by mating the *katastasis* attributed to Corax with its imperial counterpart. As for the shorter list, the addition of *parekbasis* may reflect in some fashion the influence of the five-part rhetorical *divisio* best known to Hellenistic and post-Hellenistic authors, that of Hermagoras of Temnos. Hermagoras introduces a *digressio*—in the form of an *orationem a causa atque iudicatione ipsa remotam*—between argument and conclusion (F 22a–d Matthes; cf. Cic. *De Inv.* 1.97 with Radermacher 1897: 414, n. 2). Other explanations are obviously possible, but their possibility does not in itself justify tracing the five- and seven-part oratorical models found in the Prolegomena back to Corax himself rather than some post-fourth-century epigone. If anything, the modern consensus is already too generous in allowing Corax to retain as many as two of the achievements with which earlier writers credited him: some sort of preoccupation with arguments based on probability and a handbook defining rhetoric and analysing the form of the juridical oration. He is better left in possession of nothing but the former. And Timaeus' role should be similarly reduced—to that of (at most) replacing Aristotle's dicanic context for Corax's invention of rhetoric with a political one: the situation following the fall of the Syracusan tyrants, when 'a throng of demagogues emerged . . . and the younger men were practicing clever speech' (*logou deinotēs*, Diod. Sic. 11. 87. 5). Diodorus may well derive at this point from a Timaean

---

Contrast the concluding reference to the 'how' in Marcellinus (*ta merē pente tou logou*, echoing *pente de eisi tina peristatika* five lines earlier (p. 271. 21–6 Rabe = Walz iv. 13. 19–25)) with its counterpart in Troilus (*dia tōn epinoēthentōn autōn merōn tou logou* taking up the earlier *dia tōn pente peristatikōn* (p. 52. 20–7 Rabe = Walz vi. 49. 15–20)). Note also that Troilus does not mention the six-part 'how' known to Syrianus (*In Hermogenem* 2, p. 39. 17–19 Rabe)—perhaps because it has no parallel in either of the *divisiones* found in the branch of the Prolegomena tradition to which he and Marcellinus belong.

account in which Corax was named as one of the throng or, more likely, as the first teacher of *logōn deinotēs* to the young; but his political pre-eminence, before and after the revolution, and his role as discoverer and definer of rhetoric and its basic parts, make far more sense as inseparable components of a coherent foundation myth than either does as the invention of a Sicilian historian.[41]

As for Corax himself, or what is left of him, it is natural to wonder whether continued existence in histories of ancient rhetoric is desirable at all, stripped as he has been of most of the *chorēgia*—offices, political status, pupils, progeny intellectual and literary—without which living, or at any rate living well, is impossible. Antiquity records, to my knowledge, only one other Corax from the historical period: the man who killed the poet Archilochus in a battle fought on the island of Naxos at some point toward the middle of the seventh century.[42] Plutarch, along with Aelian (fr. 80 Hercher) and, later, the *Suda* (s.v. 'Archilochos'), says that Corax was an epithet: the man's real name seems (*eoiken*) to have been Calandes.[43] One naturally wonders how Plutarch came to be informed so exactly on such a matter—probably not through independent research into the prosopography of seventh-century Naxos. Name as well as epithet may have been preserved on some document in the Archilocheum on

[41] Those inclined to go along with Farenga's deconstructionist reading of the myth (1979: 1033–53) will have even less reason to attribute any of it to Sicilian invention. Essential to Farenga's interpretation is the story—present in two Prolegomena (Rabe 4, pp. 24. 16–25. 3 and 17, pp. 269. 25–270. 3 = Walz vi. 11. 12–12. 5 and iv. 11. 18–24)—of how Hieron's suppression of free speech forced his subjects to communicate through gestures and dance steps; and this is surely too preposterous, even for Timaeus.

[42] Aristotle, fr. 611. 25 Rose = fr. viii (*FHG* II. 214) in the collection of excerpts from Aristotle's *Politeiai* erroneously transmitted under the name Heraclides Ponticus. The phrase mentioning Corax is missing in some manuscripts, and Rose prints it in his apparatus, evidently assuming that it has been added from elsewhere to fill a lacuna in the text of 'Heraclides' himself. Cf. *FHG* ad loc.
ADDENDUM: The list of Greek Coraxes should have included a Theran from the archaic period (*CIG* 12. 3, nr. 545), the original owner of a sixth-century Attic vase now in the Villa Giulia (no. 37 in Immerwahr 1990: 13), the Heracleot mentioned in a third-century soldier list from Tralles (*IG* ii. 2919b = no. 36 in Poljakov 1989: 47), and the (noisy?) infant mourned at *Anth. Pal.* 7. 632. Corax as a proper noun is encountered more frequently in Latin, but as a lower-class name or cognomen; cf. Petronius 117. 11 and 140. 7–9.

[43] *De sera num. vind.* 17. 560d–e.

Paros and available for consultation there. It is just as likely, however—since the real name merely 'seems' to have been Calandes—that Plutarch (or his source) found earlier accounts in disagreement on this point[44] and simply assumed on the basis of his own experience that Corax had to be the nickname: Greek parents were not in the habit of calling their children crows.

This rule may have admitted of exceptions in the Sicilian context with which we are concerned, but assuming an exception in the present case requires an additional, equally questionable assumption. Would any Greek named Crow—especially if he were a Siceliot (*acuta illa gens et controversa natura*)[45]—be ill-advised enough to try to make a living by teaching the art of public speaking? Even if it did not occur to his compatriots themselves to identify lessons in eloquence from the Crow with lessons in cawing and squawking, they had only to recollect Pindar's famous lines, from a poem premiered at Agrigentum in 476 BC, when Corax was a boy or young man, in which an unidentified group of lesson-takers—cacophonous rivals (or, perhaps, inept imitators and explicators) of the poet—are compared to a pair of crows (*korakes hōs*, *Ol.* 2. 86–8) who chatter fruitlessly against or about the eagle of Zeus.

That Pindar's simile is not irrelevant to the tradition about Corax was surmised over a century ago by A. W. Verrall (1889*a*: 130; 1889*b*: 197 ff). Verrall's own version of the connection—that the two crows are literally the 'two' Coraxes, Corax and his pupil Tisias—has the disadvantage of being incompatible with both the Pindaric context of the passage[46] and the tradition, at least as old as Aristotle, which places Corax's activity as teacher after the fall of Hieron and his dynasty (466/5). What the passage does show is how natural it would have been, in fifth-century Sicily, to associate loud and frequent, or inept and unwelcome, discourse with the chatter of

[44] Eusebius (*Praep. Ev.* 5. 93. 9) gives a third variant, Archias (usually assumed to be a corruption of *Kalandas*). In other passages mentioning the poet's death (listed in Lasserre's edition, pp. cvii–cviii) no name is given at all.

[45] Cicero's own explanation (*Brut.* 46) for why rhetoric should have arisen in Sicily rather than somewhere else.

[46] Whatever the exact point being made, it is clear that the crows in some sense want their cawing to be attended to along with, or instead of, the eagle's flight; and it is hard to see any comparable relationship between Pindaric song and the teachings of Corax and Tisias.

crows; and so, as a consequence, how unlikely it is that Corax was anything but a name bestowed after—not before—its bearer had started to teach people how to speak.

The epithet may have been totally derisive and contemptuous, or derisive and affectionate at the same time. The question cannot be answered. But if one asks what Corax was called before he got his new name, the answer is almost inevitable: Tisias. Much that is puzzling in the earlier stages of the tradition is thereby explained. No source earlier than Sextus Empiricus can distinguish the one figure from the other. The very name Corax often carries overtones of uncertainty or contempt: *Coracem istum veterem* (Cic. *De Or.* 3. 81); *usque a Corace nescioquo* (ibid. 1. 91); 'Tisias' Art ... the work of a damnable crow' (Lucian, *Pseudolog.* 30);[47] 'What wonder if the descendants of Corax, the inventor of rhetoric, are "crows" (*korakes*) themselves?'[48] Even more telling perhaps is the peculiar language in the earliest surviving reference to either man (Plato, *Phdr.* 273a): 'Tisias seems to have cleverly discovered a hidden art—or someone else, whoever he is and whatever he likes to be called (*hopothen chairei onomazomenos*).' In the light of the Byzantine tradition and its immediate forerunners, Socrates' reference at this point to 'Tisias ... or someone else' is usually taken, following Hermias,[49] as a way of indicating that credit for the 'art' of Tisias was disputed between him and another older, more obscure figure. But if the later tradition did not exist—and there is no independent evidence to suggest that it did exist in Plato's day—the most natural way of taking the passage would be as a reference to uncertainty about the identity of Tisias himself, not his collaborator: 'Tisias or whoever else he [the man sometimes known as Tisias] happens to be and whatever the source of the name he prefers to go by.' One would not necessarily suspect a further, malicious reference to the fact that anyone in his right mind would prefer

---

[47] Lucian's apparent equation of Tisias's art with the work of the Crow is even more suggestive of the view of Corax proposed here, as is Corax's appearance as an emblematic *corvus* atop a standard carried by Tisias at Martianus Capella 5. 433–4, p. 150 Willis. Both passages, however, are too vaguely allusive to allow any firm conclusions as to the form in which the story was familiar to their respective authors.

[48] Isocrates' supposed reply (*Apophthegmata* d 1, p. 278 Blass-Benseler) upon being asked why the populace is in the habit of being robbed and cheated by its rhetors.

[49] *ad loc.*, p. 251. 8–9 Couvreur.

not to have got a nickname in the way Tisias did; but if the nickname
was Corax and Plato knew it, the reference is almost certain to be
there. Onomastic precision is surely the last thing Socrates is aiming
at in the passage.[50]

That 'How to Speak as Taught by Tisias' (*hē tou Tisiou logōn
technē*) should become so widely known by the alternative title,
'How to Speak as Taught by the Crow' (*hē tou korakos logōn technē*),
as to lead to ignorance of the author's real name and later to positing
the existence of two authors would not be surprising, even today, in
certain parts of the Mediterranean world. And what applies there
now applies *a fortiori* to that world in antiquity: 'Anyone familiar
with the village life of central and southern Italy knows how difficult
it is to identify a person by his name but how easy it is to locate him
through the nickname known to the people of the area in which he
lives—' from which the author[51] rightly concludes, inferring ancient
practice from modern, that the appearance in archaic Greek poetry of
what are obviously *redende Namen* need not mean that the persons
who bear them are fictitious. Alessandro Manzoni had presumably
made the same observation about village life in the 1820s; and he,
too, drew inferences about an earlier period, when he came to write
his famous novel of seventeenth-century Lombardy:

Do what I tell you. [Agnese is launching Renzo on his ill-fated attempt to
seek out the services of a lawyer/*rhētōr* to counter the designs of Don
Rodrigo]... 'Go to Lecco... Ask for Doctor Azzecca-garbugli,[52] tell him
your story. But good heavens don't call him that. It's a nickname. You
have to say 'Signor Dottor...' What *is* his real name anyway? Curses,
I don't even know what it is. They all call him that. Never mind: just ask
for that tall, skinny, bald-headed doctor, the one with a raspberry spot on his
cheek. He's a prince of a man. Why, I've seen more than one case of someone
stuck worse than a fly in honey with nowhere in the world to turn and after

[50] Knowledge of the epithet may also have been one of the things that suggested to
Plato the prominent and contrasting role assigned in the *Phaedrus* to another famous
Tisias with an alias. Tisias the Chorus-Master—i.e. Stesichorus (cf. the *Suda*, s.v.)—is
as surely a patron saint of 'good' rhetoric in the first part of the dialogue as Tisias the
Crow is of 'bad' rhetoric in the second.

[51] Gentili 1988: 294–5.

[52] Dr Shystermeister (lit. 'Spy out the ploy') is surely—*hopothen chairei metaph-
razomenos*—a spiritual as well as onomastic analogue to Corax.

an hour in private with Dottor Azzecca-garbugli (mind you don't go calling him that) I swear they were just laughing it all off....[53]

A certain Uncle Nun-chaser (Buscabeatas) is the protagonist (never identified by his 'verdadero nombre') of a story of village life near Cádiz by a Spanish contemporary of Manzoni[54]—and the examples could doubtless be multiplied. Tisias was probably as powerless as Doctor Azzecca-garbugli to suppress the name to which local reaction to the infancy of rehearsed courtroom eloquence was condemning him and his fledglings. Only the published version of his model pieces, informing readers, at least down to Aristotle's day, of the author's identity and preserving some true memory of *hopothen chairei onomazomenos*, ultimately saved him from the fate of his Manzonian counterpart—though at the price of condemning historians of ancient rhetoric to a bimillenary case of seeing double.

Many of those historians will doubtless continue to prefer the double vision. But even if they do, they may well find that this 'antonomastic' accounting for Corax is at least *ben trovato*. What more appropriate fate for the putative founder of the entire rhetorical tradition, with the centuries-long study of figural speech it incorporates, than to be finally revealed as nothing more—or nothing less—than a figure of speech himself?

---

[53] *I promessi sposi*, ch. 3. 2.
[54] Pedro Antonio de Alarcón, *El libro talonario*.

4

Adultery by the Book: Lysias 1 (*On the Murder of Eratosthenes*) and Comic *Diēgēsis* *

JOHN R. PORTER

I

After years of relative neglect, particularly in the English-speaking world, Lysias' first speech has become one of the most widely read of the orator's works.[1] The reason for this rise in popularity is not far to seek: the very traits that made the speech mildly unpalatable to earlier generations of commentators—its less than uplifting subject matter and focus on the domestic world of the Athenian petty bourgeoisie— have led scholars and teachers alike to appreciate its importance in an age when social history, the status of women, and the appointments of the Athenian household have become not only legitimate but central matters of enquiry.

* An earlier version of this paper was presented at the annual meeting of the American Philological Association in December, 1994. I would like to thank the Center for Hellenic Studies, where I was able to complete much of the final research for this paper as a Summer Fellow in 1995. Thanks are also due to the anonymous reviewers for *EMC* for their helpful comments and criticisms.

[1] Annotated editions of the speech have appeared by Bizos (1967), Randazzo (1974), Vianello de Córdova (1980), Hansen (1982), Usher (in Edwards and Usher 1985), Carey (1989), Wöhrle (1995), and Edwards (1999), with school editions by Scodel (1986) and Domingo-Forasté (1994). See now Rydberg-Cox 2003. The frequent use of the speech in courses on women in antiquity has of late produced a large audience familiar with Lys. 1 in translation.

But perhaps equal credit for this rise in the speech's fortunes must be given to an increasing appreciation of its virtues as a piece of persuasive narrative. Through its cunning impression of an apparently unrehearsed simplicity, its selective focus, and its pointed use of repetition, the speech not only offers a superficially plausible account of the defendant's actions but conveys an engaging and believable impression of the speaker himself. Euphiletus emerges as a straightforward man of the earth, one whose sheer artlessness at first abets Eratosthenes' amorous intrigues, but is equally responsible for the austerity of the wronged husband's revenge once those intrigues come to light. Particularly effective in this regard are the artful shifts in perspective between the speaker's naive befuddlement at the time of the affair and his cynical and hard-won knowledge *post eventum*:[2] such a forthright character, we are made to feel, could never have devised the calculating schemes of which Euphiletus has been accused by the prosecution.[3]

These features of Euphiletus' speech have been studied in some detail.[4] What has not, perhaps, received the attention it deserves is the subtle fashion in which the speech exploits the motifs of the stereotypical adultery tale in achieving both its charm as a narrative and its effectiveness as a rhetorical appeal. The result is an account that manages simultaneously to inject a note of levity into what is at heart a very serious business (thereby implicitly lessening the gravity of Euphiletus' deed) and to evoke from the jury a sympathetic understanding of the outraged husband's response.

Euphiletus' account is replete with elements of what we might call the 'comic adultery scenario': the handsome young lover who catches sight of a woman on the occasion of a public rite (either a religious festival or, as here, a funeral: cf. Herodas 1. 56–7, Theocritus 2. 64–86, and Euripides' *Hippolytus* 24–8[5]); the slave go-between/accomplice (familiar from Eur. *Hipp.* 433–524 and 645–50, Ar. *Thesm.* 340–2, and Theoc. 2. 94–103); the elderly bawd (again, Herodas 1 provides

---

[2] On this aspect of Lys. 1, see Erbse 1958: 53–4.

[3] For an entertaining reconstruction of the heart of the prosecution's speech, see Desbordes 1990: 104–5.

[4] See, in particular, Erbse 1958, Usher 1965, Edwards and Usher 1985, Carey 1989.

[5] An ironic reversal? Cf. Halleran 1995, *ad loc.*

the best example);[6] the rejected former mistress (who appears as a stock figure at Ar. *Plutus* 959–1096 and in Theocritus' Simaitha); and, of course, the doltish husband and shamelessly ingenious wife, to whom we shall return.[7] Unfortunately, the only detailed treatment of this theme to survive in our fifth-century sources is found in Aristophanes' *Thesmophoriazusae*: the heyday of the comic adultery tale does not arrive until the Roman period. But the frequency and, often, the casualness with which Aristophanes refers to *moichoi*,[8] as well as the popularity of the theme in fourth-century comedy[9] and later mime,[10] suggest that characters of this sort would have been familiar to Lysias' contemporaries, in part at least, as literary types.

The stock elements in the speech have often been noted and the literary parallels duly cited,[11] but few scholars seem to have attached

---

[6] The similarities between Herodas' Gyllis and the Nurse in *Hipp.* demonstrate how closely the figure of the bawd resembles that of the slave go-between. Although the crone of Lys. 1 speaks as if closely allied to Eratosthenes' former mistress (§16), the vague terms employed by Euphiletus suggest that she is a former *hetaira* now earning her living as a bawd, a stock character familiar from comedy and mime: see Gernet and Bizos 1924: 33, n. 1; McKeown 1979: 78; Finnegan 1992: 24–5. See further Mastromarco 1990.

[7] Not all of the passages cited above deal with illicit affairs involving married women: e.g. Simaitha in Theoc. 2 does not seem to have a husband (Dover 1971: 95–6); Ussher 1985: 48–9, convincingly challenges the notion that Metriche is the wife of Mandris in Herod. 1. The same motifs and stereotypes are employed, however, in accounts of various types of amorous intrigues: what binds these accounts is the notion of women actively forming sexual liaisons independently of the will of a male *kyrios*. Cf. e.g. Segal 1985: 104–6, on Theoc. 2; on Metriche, di Gregorio 1995.

[8] See e.g. Murphy 1972: 184–6; Gardner 1989; cf. Trenkner 1958: 80–4. *Thesm.* 395–7, 410–13, and 498–501 are particularly significant for their casual allusion to several elements typical of the comic adultery scenario familiar from later sources: the adulterer hidden in the house upon the husband's unexpected return; the elderly husband who is at the mercy of his cunning young wife; the ingenious contrivance by which the wife effects her lover's escape.

[9] See e.g. Xenarchus 4 Kassel–Austin. Olivieri 1946–7: 49–50, notes that *Moichos* and *Moichoi* were titles of comedies by Amipsias (T 2 KA), Antiphanes (159 KA.), and Philemon (45 KA); cf. Plaut. *Bacch.* 916–18 and *Mil.* 460–1. (Olivieri also cites evidence of the theme's popularity in the so-called *phlyax* plays: cf. Murphy 1972: 178–9.) See also Trenkner 1958: 83 and 128–9.

[10] On the adultery mime, see esp. Reynolds 1946; Murphy 1972: 184–6; Kehoe 1984. Cf. Wüst 1932; Wiemken 1972: 146–8; McKeown 1979; Fantham 1986: 53–4; Panayotakis 1995: 130–5; Slater 1995: 151; Davidson 2000.

[11] See esp. Trenkner 1958: 155–60. (As befits her subject, however, Trenkner limits herself chiefly to parallels from later antiquity.) Cf. Carey 1989: 61–2.

much significance to their presence. Instead, the assumption seems
to be that such stereotypes have only entered the literary tradition in
the first place because they were so utterly common in real life:
their presence in an account such as that of Euphiletus should not,
according to this line of reasoning, occasion any surprise. Yet such
arguments from 'real life' often display a curious circularity. Ruth
Finnegan, for example (1992: 27 and n. 27), in examining the motif
of the chance meeting on the occasion of a public rite, notes that 'the
problems arising out of such unaccustomed meetings between
the sexes (i.e. adultery, seduction and rape) obviously occurred in
real life', but the passages she cites in order to substantiate the
occurrence of such meetings, apart from Lysias 1, come from works
by Euripides, Menander, Theocritus, and Plautus.[12] Similarly, Netta
Zagagi supports the statement that 'rape committed during religious
festivals was *not an infrequent occurrence*' (1995: 115; my emphasis),
with reference to various scholars who again cite Lysias 1 along
with texts by such authors as Euripides, Aristophanes, Antiphanes,
Menander, Callimachus, Theocritus, Plautus, Terence, Caecilius,
Aelian, and Xenophon of Ephesus.[13] One can imagine a variety of
reasons for the reticence displayed by our historical sources regarding
such matters, particularly in a society so concerned with matters of
face as was that of ancient Athens,[14] but it seems fair to point out that

---

[12] Similar arguments are presented by Roy 1997. Again, much of Roy's case entails
treating literary sources and political slander as mirroring common sociological
realities (see e.g. pp. 18–19). It would be foolish to deny any historical basis to such
accounts (see e.g. Richter 1971: 7, on the socio-historical background to the stereo-
type of the lusty young wife and the older husband). It is equally naive, however, to
assume that Athenian wives routinely engaged in sexual liaisons with young men on
whom they had never previously laid eyes, employing the ingenious contrivances of
their clever maids to sneak their lovers past their foolish husbands and into their
bedrooms: cf. Scodel 1993, §1: 'Obsession and Reality'.

[13] It is instructive that when Cicero wishes to establish that nocturnal religious
rites are notorious for such occurrences (*Leg.* 14. 36), he cites the *poëtae comici*. Din.
1. 23, sometimes cited as a historical instance of such an assault, probably did not
involve a case of rape: see S. Cole 1984: 104; D. Cohen 1991*b*: 180 (cf. 176–7); Fisher
1992: 39; Worthington 1992, *ad loc.*; Omitowoju 1997: 12.

[14] e.g. Roy 1997: 14–15; P. G. Brown 1993: 197, n. 29. Cf. S. Cole 1984: 104–6;
D. Cohen 1991*a*: 134, n. 1.

the assumption that such events were a common feature of everyday experience in ancient Greece is precisely that—an assumption.[15]

It is reasonable, therefore, to speculate whether the presence of these stock elements in Euphiletus' narrative, particularly in such profusion, might not indicate that we are dealing with something other than a forthright account of actual events. An analysis of the speech along these lines has been attempted by Sophie Trenkner in her study of the Greek novella. Trenkner offers a detailed catalogue of the stock character types and comic scenarios in Euphiletus' account, drawing her literary parallels mainly from the later novel. Unfortunately, the conclusions that she draws from these parallels are somewhat limited:

> Lysias . . . imitated the novella. In accordance with the tendency towards the use of stock characters and stock situations, which marked *ēthopoeia*, he stylized his characters and situations to conform with traditional types and motifs. The speech-writer chose from among the details provided by his client those which fitted the type best; probably he omitted certain more peculiar traits, and here and there added a small conventional detail to round out the whole picture. In this way the individual occurrence was transformed into a typical one. The novella of the unfaithful wife was well known in Athenian *gelōtopoeia*. Lysias' touching-up rendered the case clearer and more colourful; it must have aroused just those feelings and judgements which would come automatically to people familiar with novelle. (Trenkner 1958: 159–60)

There is little doubt that the similarities between Euphiletus' account and the comic adultery scenario (Trenkner's 'novella') would have made his narrative easier to assimilate while also encouraging sympathy for the wronged husband. The humorous element is important as well: Aristophanes attests to the use of humour to win the goodwill of Athenian juries (*Wasps* 566–7); the comic features of Euphiletus' narrative serve the additional function of distracting the jurors'

---

[15] As regards the issue of rape, in particular, critics often seem guilty of the unfounded supposition that patterns of sexual assault familiar in modern Western societies can be assumed for ancient Greece: cf. the admirably apt points raised by Kilmer 1997: 123–4. For the influence of socio-cultural factors on patterns and rates of sexual assault, see R. Porter 1986, and, for a useful overview, L. Ellis 1989: 6–7 and 12–14. S. Cole 1984 presents a judicious evaluation of the ancient sources.

attention from the more grisly realities of the case.[16] But Trenkner's analysis takes little account of the deeper structures of Euphiletus' tale—the less noticeable and therefore all the more significant ways in which the story of this domestic tragedy incorporates and adapts the themes, logic, and spirit of the traditional adultery narrative. One can argue that Lysias' invention goes beyond a matter of careful selection and the addition of the occasional conventional detail, that he has in fact introduced subtle yet telling variations on the traditional adultery tale in crafting Euphiletus' account. In what follows I indicate some of the finer touches of Lysias' speech that emerge when the speech is examined in light of comic adultery narratives.

The most striking feature of Euphiletus' account to emerge from such an examination is so obvious that it has never been considered in any detail: the fact that this particular tale of adultery must be told in the first person by the abused husband, and the subtle way in which this perspective is exploited by the logographer. The typical adultery narrative—whether in Homer, Aristophanes, Horace, Ovid, Apuleius, Boccaccio, or Chaucer[17]—is presented in the third person by an omniscient narrator or, as we shall find in Aristophanes' *Thesmophoriazusae*, in the first person by one of the culprits. The tale generally (but not invariably) follows a predictable pattern: an account of the marriage (generally between a frisky young wife and an older, rather dim-witted husband), followed by a description of the initial meeting between the wife and the young adulterer, their bamboozling of the husband, and (often, but not always) a final confrontation in which the guilty pair are caught in the act and either punished or, just as often, afforded the opportunity for a final triumph over the all-too gullible spouse. The narrative of Lysias 1 invokes this pattern, but works a subtle

---

[16] Cf. Trevett 1992: 88–9, on the use of such strategies by Apollodorus.

[17] Hom. *Od.* 8. 266–366; Hor. *Sat.* 1. 2. 37–46 and 64–134; 2. 7. 56–61; Ov. *Tr.* 2. 497–500 and 505–6 (cf. McKeown 1979: 80, n. 8); Apul. *Met.* 9. 5–7 and 14–28 (cf. Bechtle 1995, Mattiacci 1996, Lateiner 2000). For further parallels from later antiquity, see Trenkner 1958: 155–60. Cf. *Decameron* 5. 10; 6. 7; 7. 1–3, 5–9; 8. 2, 8, with Carey 1989: 61; and, for a useful overview of such tales in Boccaccio, Bonadeo 1981. For Chaucer's variations, see e.g. the *Miller's Tale*, the *Reeve's Tale*, the *Merchant's Tale*, and the fragmentary *Shipman's Tale*.

transformation in the crucial central scene, that of the bamboozling of the husband.

Euphiletus' account begins, as we would expect, with the story of his marriage, his conduct toward his new bride, and (with the aid of hindsight) the initial seduction: the lusty young Eratosthenes sees the wife at the funeral of Euphiletus' mother (a nicely pathetic touch) and wins her over through the agency of the wife's trusty maidservant. To this point Euphiletus' narrative is virtually indistinguishable from the typical adultery tale in Boccaccio. It is here, however, that the pattern is subtly altered. The account of the initial seduction concludes with the ominous statement (at the end of § 8), 'offering his proposals, Eratosthenes seduced her'. In the typical adultery scenario there would follow a description of the stratagem by which the guilty pair manage to consummate their passion. Generally speaking, this stratagem involves no more than waiting for the husband to depart on business (as at *Birds* 793–6) or somehow arranging to get him out of the way. The former is what seems to occur in Euphiletus' case: the couple merely wait for him to depart to work on the family farm. This fact is never stated, however; instead, Euphiletus immediately turns (in §§ 9 and 10 of the speech) to a detailed description of his house and the curious living arrangements necessitated by the arrival of a baby. Once these details have been laid out, Euphiletus then proceeds to the next stage in the narrative—his unexpected arrival home (some time after the affair has been initiated) and the guilty pair's comic triumph as they succeed in overcoming this apparent impediment to their illicit coupling. The lengthy aside in §§ 9 and 10 replaces the expected account of the adulterous affair's inception, creating a curiously pregnant ellipsis: the audience suspect that the odd living arrangements under discussion have been designed to serve a more devious purpose than merely protecting the wife from the danger of falling down stairs, but, like the naive Euphiletus, they are left in the dark, confronted by a seemingly innocent surface that conceals an uncertain substratum. This ambiguity is played upon by Euphiletus the narrator when, at the conclusion of this section, he voices, for the second time, his conviction that his wife was the most virtuous of women (10): 'I was so foolishly disposed that I used to think my own wife the most modest and chaste of all the wives in

Athens.'[18] These words present an ironic echo of Semonides' cynical reflections on seemingly loyal wives, that she who appears most to practice *sōphrosunē* is in fact guilty of the most flagrant offences:

For Zeus created this as the greatest evil of all: women. If indeed someone's wife seems an aid and comfort to the man who possesses her, for that man most of all does ruin arise.... I tell you, she who most seems modest and chaste, this is the one who is most thoroughly depraved. Her husband gapes complacently, and the neighbours delight in seeing how this one, too, is altogether without a clue. But each man will go out of his way to praise his own wife while finding fault with another's: we don't realize that we are all condemned to the same fate.[19]

For those who catch this echo Euphiletus' words are a signpost, confirming both the husband's complacent foolishness and the fact that foul deeds are afoot within the home. Just what the latter are, however, is left tantalizingly vague. Like the sadder-but-wiser Euphiletus, the audience momentarily confront the insidious deception of which women are capable and the sickening uncertainty as to what dire realities might underlie the apparently innocent façade that they present.

With §§ 11–14 (the comic triumph of the adulterous pair) we enter into the world of Aristophanic comedy, with its brazenly cunning adulteresses, its equally clever slave accomplices, and its sad-sack husbands. Again, however, comparison with comic accounts of adultery yields further insights into the artistry and the logic of Euphiletus' account. The first thing to note is the use of the baby.[20] It is the birth of the baby that first leads Euphiletus to leave his young bride to her own devices; the baby also is the excuse for the curious living arrangement that leaves the husband isolated in the women's quarters upstairs while the wife has the run of the main floor; the baby's cries provide the wife with a pretext for departing

---

[18] As the commentators note, the earlier reference to the fidelity of Euphiletus' wife (§ 7), prior to her chance encounter with Eratosthenes, both affirms the baby's legitimacy and highlights the enormity of Eratosthenes' crime. It also lays the ground for the embittered echoing of this evaluation by Euphiletus, § 10.

[19] Sem. 7. 96–8 and 108–14. Note the echoes of the well-known fable of Aesop: Lloyd-Jones 1975: 91 (on Sem. 7. 112–14) compares Phaed. 4. 10, Babr. 66, Men. 744 KA, and Catull. 22. 21.

[20] An interesting comparison is provided by Boccaccio, *Decameron* 7. 3.

from Euphiletus on the night described in §§ 11–14; and, finally, the need for a night-light provides a suitable excuse for the courtyard doors being opened during the night. Like the funeral of Euphiletus' mother in §§7–8, the exploitation of the baby adds pathos to the account and further motivates Euphiletus' outrage. But it also serves to associate the wife with the adulterous wives of Old Comedy and their seemingly boundless *ponēria* ('wickedness'). *Thesmophoriazusae* 476–89 is particularly useful in this regard:

Let me begin with my own case, so as not to mention anybody else. I've pulled many a wild stunt, but this was the wildest. I was a young bride of only three days and my husband was sleeping next to me. I had a certain 'friend' who had plucked my rose when I was only seven: he wanted me, you see, and came and scratched gently at our door. I knew what was up straight off and started to sneak downstairs when my husband asks me, 'What are you heading downstairs for?' 'What for?' says I, 'My stomach's making the most terrible fuss and hurts so bad that I'm off to the john.' 'Go on, then', he replied, and started grinding up a home remedy of juniper, dill, and sage. Meanwhile I poured water over the door hinges to keep them quiet and snuck out to my lover. Then I bent over and got a good screwing, right next to Apollo Agyieus, clinging for dear life to the laurel tree.

Here Euripides' relative, posing as a woman, boasts that 'her' first affair occurred when 'she' had been married only three days; Lysias presents the similarly brazen picture of a new mother exploiting her child in order to arrange an assignation with her lover. In the *Thesmophoriazusae* the wife's wanton betrayal of her husband's household is symbolized by her use of the shrine of Apollo Agyieus as a prop for her libidinous tryst, as she is mounted *a tergo* in a fashion more appropriate for a *pornē* than for the wife of an Athenian citizen.[21] The august shrine of Apollo, frequently invoked in solemn

---

[21] See Henderson 1991: 179–81. For the distinction between *pornē* and *gynē*, see Keuls 1985: esp. 204–28; Just 1989: 214–15; Wiles 1989; Carson 1990: 149–53; cf. Halperin 1990: 96. In addition to the well-known statement of Apollodorus regarding the distinction between *hetairai*, *pallakai*, and *gynaikes* ([Dem.] 59. 122), cf. e.g. Plut. *Mor.* 142b–c ('... a husband must be fair ... and reason as follows concerning a wife who is both chaste and severe: "I cannot consort with one and the same woman, employing her both as a lawful wife and as a *hetaira*" ', cited by Keuls) and Men. *Epit.* 793–6 ('it is difficult ... for a free woman to compete against a whore: the latter engages in more base cunning, knows more tricks, feels shame at nothing, fawns and wheedles more, and takes part in shameful deeds'); the humorous collapsing of such

familial contexts in tragedy,[22] here is reduced to a tawdry (and comic-ally phallic?) sexual aid. In our speech, the treatment of the child serves a similar function. The birth of children was, of course, a fundamental motive for marriage in Greek eyes.[23] Children represented the future, not only of the family name, but of its property and its religious traditions. Without legitimate children a man faced old age and death with no one to care for him and ran the risk of leaving his ancestral estate to strangers. The wife's exploitation of her child, then, is twofold: like Aristophanes' adulteress she wantonly abuses what should be an object of reverence; at the same time, the very act for which she employs the baby will lead to its legitimacy being called into question, thereby casting a pall over both its future and the future of Euphiletus' family line.[24]

Another feature of Euphiletus' account also deserves note: the curiously elaborate picture, in §§ 12–13, of his being locked away in the women's quarters while his wife proceeds downstairs to meet her lover:

I told my wife to go off and give the child the breast so that it might stop crying. At first she wasn't willing to leave, claiming that she was so happy to see me upon my return after such a long time, but when I became angry and told her to go she said, 'Oh yes, so that *you* can stay here and make a grab at the maid: you did it once before, you know, when you were drunk'. At this I laughed, but she got up and, in leaving, shut the door fast and drew the bolt, pretending it was in jest. I thought nothing of all this and hadn't a suspicion in the world, but gladly went to sleep since I'd just returned from the fields.

distinctions underlies jokes such as that at Ar. *Clouds* 1067–70. See, however, Kilmer 1993: 159–69, who challenges the assumption that women in overtly sexual scenes on Attic pottery must be slaves and/or professionals. Cf. D. Williams 1983, in general, and Fowler 1996, specifically on the Greek male's attitude toward sexual relations with his wife.

[22] See Mastronarde 1994 on Eur. *Phoen.* 631, and Gomme and Sandbach 1973 on Men. *Dys.* 659. On the image of Apollo Agyieus, see Mastronarde (loc. cit.) and di Filippo Balestrazzi 1984.

[23] Lacey 1968: 110–12; Just 1989: 89–95; Golden 1990: 164–5.

[24] Just 1989: 68–70; cf. Konstan 1994; Ogden 1996: 136–50, and 1997. For more on Greek social and legal attitudes to adultery, see Erdmann 1934: 286–99; Paoli 1950; Harrison 1968: 32–8; Lacey 1968: 113–16; Richter 1971; Cantarella 1972; S. Cole 1984; Gardner 1989; Harris 1990; Hoffmann 1990; D. Cohen 1991*a*: 98–170 and 1991*b*; Fisher 1992: 104–5; Carey 1993 and 1995; Kapparis 1995; Roy 1997; Schmitz 1997; Manthe 2000.

This picture is, of course, humiliating, and Euphiletus' burning resentment at this indignity will be presented as an important extenuating circumstance when it comes to explaining his decision to kill Eratosthenes, a step which was legal but, our sources suggest, not typical.[25] The scene is particularly humiliating in its sly suggestion that a reversal of roles has occurred, with the doltish husband locked helplessly away upstairs in the women's quarters while the wife proceeds downstairs to the men's quarters and a sexual liaison in which, rather than serving as the passive object, she operates as an active agent. Again, the influence of comedy can be seen here, both in the aggressive sexuality of the woman (a sure sign of feminine *ponēria*)[26] and in the motif of sexual role-reversal. The latter is common in comedy; it appears in a strikingly similar form in the *Thesmophoriazusae* passage discussed earlier, where the husband sits upstairs grinding together a remedy for his wife's supposed diarrhoea while the wife sneaks outside to partake in 'grinding' of another sort (ll. 483–9).[27] Again we find the man locked away in the women's sphere—here, engaged in the very feminine activity of grinding herbs—while the wife appropriates both the external world of the male and a decidedly 'masculine' sexual aggressiveness.[28]

A similar role-reversal is evident in Menander's *Samia*. Here the speaker Demeas tells how, in the course of helping to prepare his son's wedding banquet, he came to overhear comments from the household slaves suggesting that he had been cuckolded by his son

[25] Cf. Usher in Edwards and Usher 1985 (220 and on Lys. 1. 25 *ad loc.*); Carey 1989: 60–1; D. Cohen 1991*a*: 129–32; Herman 1993: 412; Carawan 1998: 282–99.

[26] In Athenian law, women are viewed as the passive object of the adulterer's wiles: see Cantarella 1972: 79; Sealey 1990: 28–9; and D. Cohen 1991*a*: 99–100, who notes that Attic Greek has no term for a female adulterer in common use (cf. J. Porter 1994: 143–7). The orators echo this view (in large part, one assumes, due to a desire to focus on the culpability of their opponents): note e.g. the compliant docility of even so experienced a professional as Apollodorus' Neaera. It is in comedy, by contrast, that the wily, sexually aggressive adulteress comes to the fore. See now Johnstone 1999: 53–4; Wolpert 2001.

[27] On the sexual overtones of *tribō* ('rub') and related words, see Henderson 1991: 176; cf. Latin *molere, permolere*.

[28] Garner 1987: 86–7, also notes the role-reversal in Lys. 1, but not the connection with comedy. The wife's brazen use of cosmetics (§§14, 17) further associates her with the bold adulteresses of comedy: for makeup as a sign of sexual wantonness in

Moschion and that the baby he supposed was his was Moschion's (225–34, 238–48):

The baby had been placed unceremoniously out of the way on a bed and was bawling, while the slave women shouted at each other all at once, 'Bring me some flour!' 'We need water over here!' 'Get some oil!' 'Bring the coals!' I joined in and helped fetch some things and happened to have gone into the pantry where I was retrieving some more items...and so didn't come out right away. While I was in there a slave woman came down from upstairs into the room just in front of the pantry....Seeing the baby bawling and neglected, and not having the slightest notion that I was in the house, she thought it safe to chatter away and so came up and started saying the usual things, 'Sweet little thing!' and 'You darling! Where's your mommy?' and kissed it and carried it about. When it stopped crying she says to herself, 'Dear me! Just a few days ago, it seems, I used to nurse Moschion and dandle him about when *he* was this size! Now, since he has a son of his own...'

Once again the cuckold figure is placed in a demeaning situation that suggests an inversion of the normal hierarchy.[29]

But the *Samia* is even more interesting for the further evidence it offers of a connection between characterization through first-person speech and comedy. Menander composes a narrative that is very similar to that of Euphiletus, but one that is employed to quite different ends. Demeas' monologue highlights his prudence, his care not to jump to unjustified conclusions about his adoptive son Moschion, whose character he knows and trusts. The speech skilfully elicits the older man's humane common sense, which is then further accentuated (through a technique common in New Comedy) by the comic excess of his neighbour Niceratus' response at 492–615.

It is possible that Menander's success in presenting such sympathetic portraits is based on a study of orators such as Lysias. A more promising

women, see the passages cited by Usher in Edwards and Usher 1985, on Lys. 1. 14; Dalby 2002: 114–15. Note, as well, how both the Aristophanic husband and Euphiletus are manipulated into actively urging the wife's departure: *Thesm.* 485 and Lys. 1. 12. Further touches of comic *ponēria* are added by the nurse's cunning provocation of the baby's cries in §11, the wife's brazen attribution of adulterous motives to Euphiletus in §12, and the wife's clever response in §14 to Euphiletus' enquiries about the door sounding during the night (a frequent motif in such contexts: cf. Ar. *Thesm.* 487–8, Plaut. *Curc.* 158–61, Tib. 1. 2. 10, and see Bader 1971: esp. 41–3).

[29] Cf. e.g. Boccaccio, *Decameron* 7. 7, where the husband, dressed in his wife's clothes, is soundly beaten by the adulterer.

hypothesis, however, is that both are working within a shared tradition
of what we might broadly term 'comic' first-person narrative,[30] characterized by a focus on distinctive features of the speaker's personality
(which in turn become the source of humorous insights of various
sorts) and by a down-to-earth realism. In Aristophanes such narratives
can present comic displays of *ponēria* (as in *Thesm.* 476–89, *Knights*
624–82, and, in a different vein, *Wasps* 1341–63) or offer a nostalgic
glimpse of the wholesome concerns of countryfolk, women, and other
groups opposed to the folly of the City (as at *Acharnians* 1–42, *Clouds*
41–77, *Lysistrata* 507–28). In Menander they provide moral insights
into various character types,[31] while in Lysias 1 the technique is
employed to enhance the impression of trustworthiness and win sympathy for the speaker.[32] All tend to be distinguished, however, from the
first-person narratives of epic, tragedy, and history both by their
homely realism and by their emphasis on *ēthos* over *dianoia*.

II

The above arguments suggest that Euphiletus' narrative presents
anything but a straightforward account of the events leading up to
Eratosthenes' death. Life often mirrors art, but the variety and
subtlety of the correspondences examined above seem to indicate
that Euphiletus' tale has been moulded by an author well versed in
the conventions of comic adultery narratives. The difficulty lies in
assessing the precise degree and significance of this authorial intervention. One could argue, with Trenkner, that Lysias merely 'edits'
Euphiletus' experiences in order to construct an account that will
appeal to an Athenian jury. In that case, one of the most striking
features of the speech is its imitation of literary models in the
description of the hapless Euphiletus being locked in the women's

---

[30] Cf. Fumarola 1965: 61–5; and see in general Albini 1952; Blundell 1980:
esp. 28–64.

[31] Cf. e.g. *Samia* 1–57, *Dysc.* 522–45, *Epit.* 908–31.

[32] Cf. Trevett 1992: 85–8, on the similar use of characterization in the narratives of
Apollodorus.

quarters, the women's exploitation of the baby, the wife's inappropriate use of cosmetics, and similar relatively peripheral details, none of which could be readily confirmed or denied by the prosecution. Kenneth Dover has observed (1968: 186) that 'the Athenian public's long habituation to the dramatization of events which they regarded as historical contributed to their acceptance of a written speech which did not purport to be a verbatim record of what was said in court but rather represented an artistically sophisticated version of what could or should have been said in court'; perhaps more interesting is the question of the degree to which this habituation permitted or even encouraged the stylization of forensic narratives to incorporate char-acter-types and patterns of action familiar from various literary genres.[33]

Trenkner's interpretation must assume a relatively limited degree of authorial intervention on Lysias' part or, at the very least, the willingness of witnesses to attest to the truth of the logographer's fictions, both reasonable hypotheses in the context of Athenian forensic contests.[34] But there are other features of the speech that point to a more fundamental question: can we be certain that Lysias 1 was in fact composed by the logographer Lysias for use in an actual trial, or might it be a fiction composed—either by Lysias or an unknown author—for some other purpose?

The authenticity of the speech—by which I mean its status as a forensic oration composed by Lysias for use in an actual case—is accepted by most editors, and for good reason. The speech as a whole observes the forms and conventions of the Athenian courtroom, while the lengthy series of *pisteis* that comprise §§ 29–46 scarcely seems the stuff of fiction. There is nothing in the style to lead one to question Lysias' authorship,[35] and § 9 is directly cited by Demetrius, *On Style* 190 as an example of the so-called 'plain' prose style in Lysias. Some curious features remain, however, that have not perhaps

---

[33] Cf. Pearson 1976: 40–3, on the possible influence of Euripidean prologues on Demosthenes' narratives. See also Devries 1892: 41, on a possible connection between Lys. 10 and the *Daitales* of Aristophanes; Fumarola 1965: 59–65; Carey 1989: 62, n. 8, on the portrayal of Euphiletus; Bers 1994: 189–91.

[34] On the agonistic aspects of Athenian litigation, see D. Cohen 1995, esp. ch. 5: 'Litigation as Feud.'

[35] See in particular Usher and Najock 1982: esp. 103; cf. Carey 1989: 11–12.

received due emphasis and that bear a direct relationship to the 'literary' qualities of Euphiletus' account noted above.[36]

Lysias 1 belongs to a subclass of speeches whose authenticity has been called into question at one time or another, including Lysias 3, Lysias 24, and Antiphon 1. They are all brief and relatively lacking in specifics; they deal with exceptional cases whose subject matter is melodramatic or, at the very least, colourful; they emphasize narrative and/or *ēthopoeia* over rhetorical argumentation and, in Lysias 1 and 24, evince a marked tendency to rely upon the performative aspects of the text as an integral part of their rhetorical strategy. In the case of Lysias 1, none of these features offers incontrovertible evidence that the speech does not derive from an oration delivered before the court at the Delphinion, but, taken together, they do suggest that a certain scepticism might well be in order.

We have no precise information regarding the amount of time allotted to speeches in murder trials in the early fourth century, but there is reason to consider Euphiletus' oration curiously brief. Antiphon 5 and 6, both of which pre-date Lysias 1 and involve charges of murder, are approximately 2.5 and 1.4 times the length of Lysias 1 respectively, while Lysias 12 and 13, where murder is again at issue, are each more than twice its length. The discussion of various time allotments at *Ath. Pol.* 67 reflects later practice, but it suggests that, as we would expect, the principal speeches in 'private' cases involving onerous penalties were lengthy:[37] the *dikē phonou* brought against Euphiletus very likely entailed the most extreme of penalties, death plus the confiscation of property (Harrison 1971: 178), yet his defence requires only some twenty-five to thirty minutes to deliver. Uncertainties regarding the origin and transmission of speeches in the corpus render any discussion of relative length difficult at best: we can never be altogether certain of the degree to which any speech in our manuscripts reflects what might have been said in court (Dover

[36] For a recent challenge to the authenticity of Lys. 1, see Perotti (1989–90), who argues that the speech offers an allegorical parable in which the ties between democracy (represented by Euphiletus) and the Athenian *polis* (Euphiletus' wife) are corrupted by the Thirty (represented by Eratosthenes, whose name, Perotti argues, deliberately recalls Lysias' notorious enemy).

[37] Cf. Rhodes 1981: 719–22; MacDowell 1985; M. Lang in *Agora XXVIII*: 77–8.

1968). The discrepancies noted above, however, must at least cast doubt upon the notion that Euphiletus' speech, despite its impression of completeness, represents the unedited transcript of an actual oration.

It is not simply the speech's brevity that is problematic, however, but its relative lack of detail and the omission of forensic *topoi* that we might expect to find in a typical oration of this sort. We learn very little about the various players in Euphiletus' domestic drama; instead, the speaker offers a collection of generic types: the randy young adulterer, the loyal and unscrupulous maid, the lusty young wife, the conniving bawd, and so forth. This use of stock figures is not, perhaps, remarkable in the case of the other characters—it would scarcely have been politic, for example, for Euphiletus to identify the woman on whose behalf the old bawd of §§ 15–17 was acting[38]—but the speaker's treatment of Eratosthenes certainly deserves comment. We learn nothing of this Eratosthenes other than: (a) he was young (37); (b) he first saw Euphiletus' wife at the funeral of Euphiletus' mother (8); (c) he managed to seduce the wife via the agency of her maid, whom he intercepted on her way to the market (8); (d) he was from the deme of Oe (16); and (e) he had much practice in the 'art' of adulterous liaisons (16). With the exception of the deme name, all of these details can be directly related to the comic adultery scenario, whose adulterers are regularly young (a) and lusty (e), and who routinely waylay servants in order to employ their services as intermediaries (c).[39] The role of Euphiletus' dead mother (b) is particularly interesting. As we have seen, her funeral provides a stock occasion on which the wife can be seen in public and adds a touching note of pathos to Euphiletus' account, but it also implies an additional reason for the success of Eratosthenes' schemes: not only was Euphiletus himself less keenly on guard once a child had been born (6), but his mother was no longer alive to oversee the wife's behaviour and provide guidance.[40]

[38] Schaps 1977. Cf. e.g. Andoc. 4. 10, Aeschin. 3. 172.

[39] A close parallel for Eratosthenes' strategy in Lys. 1. 8 is provided by Eub. 80 KA. Cf. the bawd's tactic at Lys. 1. 16.

[40] Wilamowitz 1923*a*: 59. Cf. Lys. 1. 20: the wife attended the Thesmophoria in the company of Eratosthenes' mother. This latter detail prepares for Euphiletus' argument at 1. 33 that adulterers, in corrupting other men's wives, render them more intimately

The detail of Eratosthenes' deme (d) also suits the speech's rhetorical ends. This information is provided by the elderly bawd when she informs the unsuspecting Euphiletus of what is occurring in his household: the fact that she must identify the young man in this quasi-formal manner supports Euphiletus' claim (43–5) that he knew nothing of Eratosthenes prior to this affair and had never even laid eyes upon him. But this isolated particular regarding Eratosthenes' origins merely highlights the fact that we learn nothing else of substance about him elsewhere in the speech. This lack of detail would be remarkable in any case: litigants in a Greek court-room regularly rely upon a good offence as the most effective form of defence, and one would expect Euphiletus to provide more evidence of the dead man's moral failings than the secondhand and relatively parenthetical accusation attributed to the unnamed bawd at § 16. But Euphiletus' reticence is still more remarkable if, as seems most likely, Eratosthenes the adulterer is a relation of the more famous Eratosthenes attacked by Lysias in his twelfth oration (*APF* 5035; Kapparis 1993: 364). That any Greek orator, but particularly Lysias, should neglect to exploit this connection is difficult to accept: the oligarch's infamous association with the Thirty offers too compelling a precedent for the adulterer's own 'tyrannical' contempt for law, too perfect an opportunity to generate further bias against the prosecution's case, for a competent logographer to have allowed it to pass in silence.[41]

This curious omission is compounded by the striking irony in the names of the two protagonists in this domestic drama: Euphiletus, the 'beloved' husband, and Eratosthenes, the lusty young adulterer

concerned with the adulterers' interests than with those of their own husbands. Again, it is the absence of Euphiletus' mother that allows this new attachment to arise. See further Roy 1997: 15; J. Porter 1994: 145–6.

[41] Cf. Whitehead 1980: 210 (cited by Avery 1991: 382, n. 8), and note e.g. the invidious references to Alcibiades *père* at Lys. 14. 26, 30, and 35–42 (cf. Isoc. 16. 1–2), with [Arist.] *Rh. Al.* 1445a12–17. (The reference to sycophancy at Lys. 1. 44 appears as part of a generic list of possible motives for murder and cannot (*pace* Kirchner, *PA* 5035) be taken as a reference to actual political activity on the adulterer's part.) My argument here assumes the traditional chronology, according to which Lysias' career as a logographer post-dates the fall of the Thirty: see e.g. Carey 1989: 2–3. The rule that forbade litigants in an Athenian homicide trial to raise irrelevant allegations (below, n. 45) is unlikely to have proved an effective bar against such invidious references: cf. e.g. Lys. 3. 44–5 and Lanni 2000: 321. Unfortunately, we possess little

who is 'vigorous in love'.[42] The name Euphiletus is certainly not rare in Attica,[43] but that of Eratosthenes is: other than the famous oligarch, only one homonym has been found, a *prytanis* from the deme Azenia in the middle of the first century BC.[44] To accept the speech as historical, we must suppose that two men with the peculiarly appropriate names Euphiletus and Eratosthenes, the latter extremely rare, should have chanced to become entangled in an adulterous love triangle and that the Eratosthenes in question was no relation to the well-known oligarch, although the two were very likely from the same deme and shared an exceptionally uncommon name. Stranger things have happened, but it seems equally conceivable that the curious appropriateness of the protagonists' names is of a piece with the other evidently fictional elements in Euphiletus' cleverly woven tale. The association of Eratosthenes the adulterer with Oe is then readily explained as a reminiscence of the well-known oligarch.

It is important to note that Euphiletus displays a similar reticence regarding his own situation. The speaker is characterized almost exclusively as the outraged cuckold. The only details offered that might identify him as a historical individual, rather than a stock character in a comic adultery tale, are the names of his friends Sostratus (22) and Harmodius (41), neither of whom are identified further. Nor are the customary rhetorical *topoi* invoked to create a

practical evidence on this point: as Lanni notes, only one speech composed for the prosecution in a trial before the homicide courts survives (Ant. 1, on the suspect nature of which see above), while our sources' claims regarding the elevated standards applied in such proceedings are themselves generally informed by rhetorical purposes. Rhodes 2004*a* employs the concept of what he calls the 'larger story' in assessing the relevance of such arguments, a rather slippery category that reveals just how subjective such judgements must be, but that also, by its very reasonableness, suggests how readily an ancient jury might have accepted such matters as relevant to a speaker's case.

[42] Cf. Perotti 1989–90: 45. Rosen 1988 offers some useful cautions, however, against assuming that all such potentially significant names are necessarily fictitious.

[43] e.g. *APF* 6057–69; men of that name are also to be found at Thuc. 3. 86, Andoc. 1. 35 (and *passim*), Isae. 12, and Dem. 35. 34 and 59. 25. Here and below, see Osborne and Byrne 1994.

[44] Avery 1991: 384. Cf., however, Kapparis 1993: 364; and, in general, Thompson 1974. The references in Harpocration (s.vv. *authentēs* ('perpetrator') and *metaulos* ('inner courtyard')) to a speech 'In Defense of Eratosthenes' are clearly erroneous: cf. Baiter and Sauppe 1845–50: 186–7; Carawan 2006: §v, at nn. 64–7.

general bias in the speaker's favour. Nothing is said, for example, of any past services to Athens: no liturgies are mentioned, nor is any prior military service. No reference is made to his avoidance of litigation or his inexperience in legal affairs. In short, no personal details are offered that would emphasize the speaker's status as a sound citizen and firm supporter of Athens' democracy. This is striking, in and of itself, but stands out all the more when one considers the emphasis placed on Euphiletus as a man who has enforced, and thereby preserved, the laws in the face of the outrages of a wanton hooligan.[45]

Instead, the speaker's focus throughout the speech remains fixed on the events narrated in the *diēgēsis* and the legal ramifications thereof. Nothing that would distract from that focus is admitted: no pleas for sympathy, no historical allusions or parallels, none of the forensic *topoi* outlined above (cf. Blass, *AB* i. 575). This gives the speech a pleasing formal unity and compactness, but literary merits of this sort are not usually sought by men compelled to plead for their lives before an Athenian jury. In fact, this focus is bought even at the expense of properly substantiating the facts of the case.

---

[45] e.g. Lys. 1. 26, 29, 34–6, 47–50. See now Lanni 2000 (esp. 317–25), who argues that such topics were precluded by the rigorous standards of the Athenian homicide courts, where it was forbidden for litigants to raise matters that lay outside of the point at issue (*exō tou pragmatos*). This question has potential implications as well for my arguments above concerning the length of Lys. 1. Lanni seems, however, to misinterpret the significance of the rule forbidding irrelevant statements, which appears to have been directed primarily against the use of slander (i.e. irrelevant allegations against one's opponent): Ant. 5. 11 and 6. 9; Lys. 3. 46; Lycurg. 1. 11–13 and 149, with Bearzot 1990. (Arist. *Rh*. 1354a implies that excessive appeals for pity were also forbidden: see, however, Bearzot 1990: 52–3.) Lys. 7. 42, which is commonly taken as an allusion to this rule, presents a common transitional formula, frequently found in the conclusion of Lysias' speeches (cf. 2. 77, 10. 31, 22. 22, 24. 21); its dismissive tone suggests rather that the defendant is flattering the jury via a particularly cunning form of *praeteritio*: the list of services begun at 7. 41 might, the speaker suggests, be useful in addressing one of the popular courts, but it is otiose in this venue (*enthade*), addressing the august court of the Areopagus who will judge the case on its merits. But there is little hint here of a legal prohibition against such tactics: cf. e.g. §§ 30–3 of the same speech; consider as well Lys. 3. 47 (also delivered before the Areopagus) and Ant. 2. 2.12 (a model speech for a case involving deliberate homicide). Much as the prosecution might deplore a defendant's attempts to win the jury's good opinion (e.g. Lys. 12. 38 and 26. 3), it would be difficult, in most instances, to establish that the question of the defendant's character was *exō tou pragmatos*. Cf. Rhodes 2004*a* and, more generally, Johnstone 1999: 93–108.

Euphiletus is surprisingly chary about calling witnesses, doing so only twice and only regarding the actual capture and killing of Eratosthenes: at the conclusion of § 29 witnesses are summoned to confirm that Eratosthenes admitted his guilt and offered to pay a monetary penalty; at the conclusion of § 42, that on the fateful night Euphiletus raced about gathering whatever witnesses he could on the spur of the moment. Sostratus—Euphiletus' dinner companion on the night in question (22)—is not specifically summoned;[46] no attempt is made to identify or call to witness the friend at whose house the maid was supposedly interrogated (18) or the old bawd who first enlightened Euphiletus about his wife's dalliance (15–17).[47] Most interesting of all is the lack of any reference to testimony from the wife's maid: the jury might expect, at the very least, some mention of the prosecution's failure to demand this testimony or an account of Euphiletus' failure to present the woman for interrogation.[48] Michael Gagarin has argued (1996: 9) that there is nothing odd about this omission since, generally speaking, the *proklēsis* was merely a rhetorical ploy, couched in terms designed to ensure that it would be rejected by one's opponent, and was therefore routinely ignored by the opposing litigant: if we assume that Euphiletus has reason to fear the maid's testimony, his failure to address this point would perhaps be understandable.[49] Even on this assumption, however, the prosecution's allegation that the maid enticed Eratosthenes

[46] Sostratus may have been included in the witnesses called in §42, but this is far from clear.

[47] If the crone is imagined to be a slave of the unnamed adulteress, Euphiletus' silence on this point is readily explained (cf. above at n. 38); see, however, above n. 6. Schaps (1977: 326) has shown that the usual reticence regarding the names of women and slaves did not apply in cases of 'women of low reputation' such as procuresses (see in particular [Dem.] 59. 18 and Hyp. 5. 2, 4, 5, and 34 [Jensen]): details of this sort offered a useful method for further blackening the character of one's opponent. For further doubts about the meeting with the elderly crone, see Weißenberger 1993: 61–2.

[48] Cf. Carey 1989: 63 and on Lys. 1. 37–42; Carawan 1998: 293–4. On the use of the challenge (*proklēsis*) to generate prejudice against one's opponent, see Bonner 1905: 67–9; Harrison 1971: 147–50 and 153; Thür 1977: 233–76 and 1996; Todd 1990*a*: 33–6; Carey 1989: 136–7, and 1994: 96–7; V. Hunter 1994: 89–94; Mirhady 1991*a*, *b*, and 1996.

[49] Gagarin's general thesis is opposed by Mirhady 1996 [Ch. 10 in this collection]. Cf. Thür 1977: 257–8, who notes only two cases in the orators of female slaves being offered for interrogation: he concludes that their age and sex made it risky (on the Greek view) to proffer them for torture. See now Johnstone 1999: 86–7.

into the house (37) seems to call for more than Euphiletus' rather feeble counter-assertions (37–42), nor does Euphiletus' promise that she would suffer no harm, reported in § 18, account sufficiently for the lack of any reference to her possible testimony.[50]

The result is a speech that has won critical praise for what are, in effect, the performative features of the text: its successful portrayal of the speaker as an unsophisticated man of the earth whose response to learning of his wife's affair, while excessive, was understandable, given both his personality and the outrageous wrongs he had suffered. The speaker is presented as blunt in both word and deed, the very sort of person who would take matters into his own hands and insist on confronting the adulterous pair in the act. But his most distinguishing characteristic is an outraged indignation, both at Eratosthenes' acts of *hubris* against him and, above all, at the fact that, having exacted a lawful punishment for those acts, he now finds himself placed on trial for his life. In this regard, Euphiletus' relentless focus upon the facts of the case and the legal justification for his deeds is effective. The speech is very much in character, displaying a strategy of deliberate bluntness as the speaker eschews the usual forensic *topoi* in order to drive home repeatedly both the legality of his actions and the folly of his now being compelled to stand trial. The question, again, is whether such a gambit is reasonable for a defendant pleading for his life before an Athenian jury: it would be the bold client who would risk his future on an effective 'performance' of Lysias' highly dramatic but brief and extremely selective oration.

A telling comparison is provided by the speeches of Apollodorus, another writer noted for his use of persuasive narratives.[51] As in

---

[50] Thür 1977: 258, n. 79, suggests that the description of Euphiletus' 'interrogation' of the maid at §§18–20 is intended to mask his failure to issue a *proklēsis*, or to undercut references to his failure to accept such a *proklēsis* from the prosecution: cf. Herman 1993: 409, on the use of language suggestive of a formal *basanos* at 1. 18–21. That Euphiletus does not refer to the possibility of testimony from his wife is not surprising, since, in addition to the expected alienation of affections, the law commanded divorce in cases of adultery ([Dem.] 59. 86–7: see Sealey 1990: 29; D. Cohen 1991*a*: 122 and n. 71; and, in general, Cohn-Haft 1995). On the general question of evidence provided by women in Athenian courts, see Todd 1990*a*: 25–6, 28, and 32–3; cf. MacDowell 1963: 105–6; Goldhill 1994: 357–60; V. Hunter 1994: 89–90.

[51] [Dem.] 49, 50, 52, 53, and 59; see Trevett 1992: 84–91, esp. 84, n. 26 on percentage of narrative. (I am indebted to one of the anonymous *EMC* reviewers for suggesting this line of investigation.)

Lysias 1, the *diēgēseis* of Apollodorus comprise, on average, approximately 50 per cent of the oration, and they are employed to lend credence to the speaker's case through their studied portrayal of the litigants' characters and their profusion of detail—not all of it, strictly speaking, relevant. The contrasts between these speeches and Lysias 1 are, however, as striking as the similarities. Two of the speeches in question ([Dem.] 49 and 50) are approximately twice the length of Lysias 1, while a third ([Dem.] 59) is more than three times as long: unlike Lysias 1, each affords the speaker ample opportunity to develop various arguments and *topoi* designed to support the narrative and lend credence to the speaker's case. Moreover, all of the speeches are profuse in specifics—names, places, dates, and sums of money are cited lavishly, at times to the point of tedium, and are amply supported by the testimony of witnesses.[52] Apollodorus' orations confirm the general observation, offered by Jeremy Trevett, that 'a detailed narrative supported by numerous witnesses could in certain situations speak for itself, so that additional arguments became otiose'.[53] This is not the case with Lysias 1, however, where the details offered are circumstantial, generic, and of doubtful relevance, where the testimony of witnesses is far from plentiful, and where the demonstration of the narrative's veracity consists largely of the speaker's reassertion of points raised in that narrative.

To be sure, none of the peculiarities noted above need indicate that Lysias 1 is not based on an actual forensic oration. Peter Krentz, for example, has noted some of these same peculiarities—a certain vagueness on crucial points of detail and the failure to document important allegations through the testimony of witnesses—in Lysias 12, the authenticity of which most scholars accept,[54] and few would argue that obfuscation or the failure to answer the opponents' allegations should be taken as proof of spuriousness. The use of

[52] Trevett 1992: 89–91. For example, [Dem.] 52 and 53, each of which is moderately shorter than Lys. 1, cite depositions from witnesses five and six times, respectively.

[53] Trevett 1992: 85; cf. 88: 'The accumulation of detail often serves to dispel any possible prejudice against the speaker, by lending credibility to a superficially unlikely story, or by demonstrating that the speaker was not acting from discreditable motives.'

[54] Krentz 1984: 25; cf., however, Carawan 1998: 376–7; Wolpert 2002: 59–60.

compelling narratives and vivid characterization for rhetorical ends is a hallmark of Lysias' style,[55] while the melodramatic and somewhat improbable content would make Lysias 1 an ideal sample to use in advertising the logographer's skill (cf. Usher 1976: 38). And, as Kenneth Dover suggests (1968: 188), we have no assurance that the 'published' version of a speech did not differ radically from that delivered before the jury, particularly as regards technical and potentially uninteresting matters of procedure.[56]

Yet a reasonable case remains for regarding Lysias 1 as a particularly sophisticated form of practical rhetorical exercise—a fictional speech based upon a fictional case, designed not only to instruct and delight but, quite probably, to advertise the logographer's skill.[57] That such display pieces were composed is evident from the *Tetralogies* ascribed to Antiphon, as well as such works as Gorgias' *Palamedes* and *Helen*, the *Ajax* and *Odysseus* of Antisthenes, and the *Odysseus* of ps.-Alcidamas.[58] While few would look upon the *Tetralogies* as popular entertainment, the other speeches in this list clearly do belong, at least in part, to such a category: the same people who could delight in Euripides' rhetorical *tours de force* and in the still more artificial rhetoric of the fourth-century tragic stage[59] would provide a ready audience for mythological set-pieces of this sort, as

[55] Cf. Dion. Hal. *Lys.* 18–19.

[56] See, however, Carey 1989, 63. The compact unity of Lys. 1, its skilful use of verbal echoes, its clever incorporation of motifs from the comic adultery scenario, and the masterly portrayal of the speaker's character all suggest, in this case at least, the improbability of Dover's theory of co-authorship between client and logographer: cf. Usher 1976 [Ch. 2 in this collection].

[57] Darkow 1917: 14, argues at length for 'the possibility that speeches were written as literature, or at least as "rhetorische Musterstücke" '. On fictitious speeches as a literary genre in antiquity, see Dover 1968: 190–3;Vianello de Córdova 1980: p. lii, n. 119; and Carawan 1998: 171–84, on the authorship of the *Tetralogies* attributed to Antiphon (esp. 182–4 on the fragmentary Lysianic speech against Mikines).

[58] The latter works are most readily available in Radermacher, *AS*; cf. Kennedy 1963: 167–73, and, on [Alcid.] *Od.*, Scodel 1980: 46–7, and Muir 2001. With the exception of the *Odysseus* attributed to Alcidamas, all of these works are securely dated to the late fifth or early fourth century. Following Kennedy, I accept a fourth-century date for the *Odysseus* (cf. Blass, *AB* ii. 359–63); but Kennedy's argument (173) that the attack on Nauplius (12–21) associates the speech with oratory of the latter part of the century is unconvincing: cf. above n. 41 and see Avezzù 1982: 79. For other views, see Brzoska in *RE* 1.2, s.v. 'Alkidamas' (1894), col. 1536; Zographou-Lyra 1991: 10–11.

[59] See e.g. Xanthakis-Karamanos 1979 and 1980: 59–70.

well as for such political, rhetorical, and philosophical works as ps.-Andocides 4, Polycrates' (lost) *Accusation of Socrates*, and the various *Apologies* of Socrates (one attributed to Lysias himself), all of which are cloaked in the guise of historical orations.[60] Thus, although Quintilian associates the practice of composing judicial and deliberative speeches on fictional cases with Demetrius of Phaleron (*Inst.* 2. 4. 41), it seems plausible that such speeches—similar to the those cited above but involving everyday characters caught in stereotypical yet outlandish situations—could have been composed in the early fourth century. In contrast to the *Tetralogies* ascribed to Antiphon, which focus on the development of opposing *pisteis*, such works would entail a broader range of rhetorical skills, including the construction of persuasive narratives and techniques of characterization.

Herodas' second *Mimiamb* demonstrates that, by the middle of the third century, a work of this sort could be produced solely for entertainment. There a *pornoboskos* ('brothel-keeper') named Battaros prosecutes a ship captain by the name of Thales for breaking into his establishment and attempting to make off with one of his girls. The speech offers a comic *tour de force*, particularly in its send-up of various conventions of forensic oratory. (Most notable is the 'pathetic' display, at 65–71, of the speaker's abused 'dependant' to evoke sympathy, as Battaros has the young prostitute in question strip before the jury, as if before her 'fathers or brothers', and display her *tilmata* (by implication, 'bruises', but more commonly used of depilation), 'both below and above'!) The piece is composed in a metre and dialect inspired by the poems of Hipponax and could never be mistaken for an actual courtroom oration; yet, despite its obvious artifice, it observes the procedures of the Athenian courtroom[61] and employs the language,[62] as well as the

---

[60] On [Andoc.] 4, see Edwards 1995: 131–6. On the various Socratic *logoi*, see Guthrie 1969: 330–3. For Lysias' defence of Socrates, see Baiter and Sauppe 1850: 203–4; Jebb 1893: i. 150–1.

[61] e.g. the appeal to the *grammateus* to read out the appropriate law, which is duly noted 'for the record' (41–2 and 46–8); the stopping of the *klepsudra* (42–5); the (comically distorted) *proklēsis eis basanon* (87–90, on which see Thür 1977: 172).

[62] The opening words (*andres dikastai*) present a common formula from the courtroom which immediately marks the piece as a forensic oration: cf. Perotti 1989–90: 46–7. The command to the *grammateus* at 41–2 recalls the frequent use

arguments,[63] of actual litigants. Above all, it is presented in dead earnest: humour abounds, but it is the humour inspired by the image of a *pornoboskos* who attempts to speak in the manner of a town worthy.[64]

That Herodas is working within a well-established tradition is suggested by Demetrius, *On Style* 153, where reference is made to Sophron's portrayal of the comic *rhētor* Boulias (Sophron, fr. 109 Kaibel): 'Incoherence of this sort is called *griphos* ['creel', used to designate something that is convoluted, enigmatic, or confused]—as, for example, Boulias when he delivers his oration in Sophron: for he says nothing that is at all coherent.'[65] Unfortunately, we possess little concrete evidence regarding fifth- and fourth-century mime.[66] Still, Demetrius' reference to the comic Boulias in action suggests a performance similar to that of Herodas' Battaros and not altogether unlike that of the speaker in Lysias 24, *For the Invalid*: in each case, we find a speech composed and, presumably, delivered in a manner that highlights the humorous *ēthos* of the speaker as much as the quality of his arguments.[67]

---

of such formulae by the orators (e.g. Dem. 27. 8). The address to the official in charge of regulating the *klepsudra* (42) recalls the formulae employed by the orators in such commands (Isae. 2. 34, 3. 12 and 76, Dem. 45. 8, 54. 36, 57. 21). Further echoes are provided by W. Headlam 1922: 70–107, *passim*.

[63] e.g. the reference to past services on behalf of the state (16–20, unfortunately mutilated), which recalls the frequent citation of past liturgies in the orators; emphasis on the opponent's contempt for law—contrasted with the attitude of sound-minded citizens (i.e. the jury: 25–7, 31–7, 55–6)—in combination with allegations of his barbaric origins (37–8; cf. 100–2) and alienation from the interests of the *polis* (57–9; cf. e.g. Hyp. 5. 29 [Jensen]). Also typical are: the speaker's explication of the law (50–6), supported by an appeal to the wise lawgiver of old (48); his expressed care not to annoy the jury with a lengthy and irrelevant diatribe (60–1; cf. Lys. 24. 21); the assertion that the issues at hand concern not simply the speaker but the larger community (92–8). For further parallels, see Hense 1900, W. Headlam 1922, Smotrytsch 1966: 68–70 and 73–5, and R. Hunter 1995: 167–9. I cannot agree with Ussher (1985: 52) that Battaros presents 'a farrago of *formulae* and *topoi* ... without order or coherence'.

[64] Massa Positano 1971: 5–8, detects parody of Demosthenes, who was given the nickname *Batalos* (Aeschin. 1. 126 and 131; Dem. 18. 180). Cf. Hense 1900, for possible mockery of Hyperides; Smotrytsch 1966: 64; Redondo Moyano 1994.

[65] Cf. Ussher 1985: 46; Smotrytsch 1966: 61–3. Murphy 1972: 174–5, suggests that such pieces can be traced back to Epicharmus. See now Sophr. 104 KA.

[66] See e.g. Fantham 1986: 52, n. 18.

[67] On the possibility of similar orations as part of trial scenes in the later 'Adultery Mime', see Reynolds 1946: 84; Kehoe 1984: 93–4 and 104–5; Slater 1995: 151; Schwartz 2000–1. The mock trial at *Wasps* 891–997 offers a precedent of sorts but,

Moreover, Aelius Theon, *Progymnasmata* 2. 69, suggests that display pieces something like this might have been associated with Lysias himself:

It is possible to take examples of exercises based upon hypothetical propositions from Aristotle and Theophrastus. For there are many books written on such propositions ascribed to them. Some hypothetical topics have been developed even by the orators, and, indeed, whole speeches might nearly be considered to be based upon hypothetical propositions, like the speech ascribed to Lysias concerning the rite of unveiling, and that concerning the abortion: for in the former the matter hinges on whether a woman ought to retain the gifts given to her as part of the bridal rite of unveiling, while in the latter it is a question of whether the foetus still in the womb is a human being and whether women can perform abortions without legal liability. They say that these speeches are not by Lysias; nevertheless, it is not out of place for the young to read even these for the sake of training.

As Blass indicates (*AB* i. 382–3), Theon himself notes doubt regarding the authenticity of these speeches, while his qualified introduction need only indicate that both displayed similarities to contemporary rhetorical exercises. Yet Radermacher, following Sauppe, argues that these works were indeed display pieces composed *in ficta causa theseos demonstrandae gratia*.[68]

We have already seen the dangers entailed in accepting Euphiletus' narrative at face value: scholars have tended to regard as simple fact matters that, considered in the light of comic adultery narratives, can be seen to be cunningly devised fictions. In the same way, the practical nature of the speech—its typical structure of *prooemion, diēgēsis, pisteis,* and *epilogos*; its use of laws, the testimony of witnesses, and arguments from probability (all common features of rhetorical argumentation in this period); the seemingly abundant circumstantial detail that it offers—has perhaps led commentators to accept its authenticity too readily. Many of these features are also found in the obviously fictitious speeches cited above: Herodas' Battaros has the

---

as befits the subject of Aristophanes' play and the general ethos of Old Comedy, the focus there is on public themes—political infighting in contemporary Athens, the malfeasance of public officials, Cleon's demagogic tactics—rather than on the character of the speakers.

[68] Radermacher, *AS* 149–50, no. 15, citing Baiter and Sauppe 1845–50: 175. Cf. in general Baiter and Sauppe 1850: 210–11; Blass, *AB* i. 381–3; Usher 1976: 37.

relevant laws read out to the court and explains their significance (Herod. 2. 41–54); ps.-Alcidamas' Odysseus calls upon the testimony of witnesses (7); both provide a wealth of circumstantial detail[69] in the course of developing various well-established forensic *topoi*, while ps.-Alcidamas provides his Odysseus with a carefully structured speech that includes *prooemion* (1–4), *diēgēsis* (5–7), *pisteis* (8–12), *diabolē* (12–28: a form of *refutatio*),[70] and *epilogos* (29).[71] Particularly noteworthy is the elaborate narrative of ps.-Alcidamas' Odysseus (5–7):

Diomedes and I happened to be stationed in the same place, near the gates, with Palamedes and Polypoites stationed nearby. When we engaged the enemy, one of their bowmen came running forward and, aiming at the defendant, missed him and struck near me. The defendant threw his spear at this man, and he, having picked up the spear, withdrew back amid the enemy forces. In the meanwhile, I picked up the arrow and gave it to Eurybates to give to Teucer, so that he might make use of it. A brief pause in the fighting arose and Eurybates indicated to me that the arrow had written characters on it underneath its quills. I was astonished at this, and, calling Sthenelus and Diomedes over, I showed them what was on the arrow. The inscription revealed the following: 'Alexander to Palamedes: You will receive all that was agreed upon between you and Telephus. My father gives you Cassandra as your wife, as you stipulated. Only let matters on your side be carried out with haste.'

The ingenuity displayed by the author here is impressive. Not only does he furnish his speaker with a convincing narrative, packed with convenient witnesses, persuasive detail, and an unbroken chain of evidence, but he goes on to manufacture a clever, and very un-Homeric, set of circumstances (a shortage of weapons among the Greek forces) to justify Odysseus' interest in retrieving the arrow in the first place.[72]

---

[69] In arguing against the likelihood that the speeches cited by Theon could be display pieces, Blass contends (*AB* i. 383) that it is 'ganz ohne Beispiel, daß solche Uebungen mit bestimmten Namen versehen wären'. The fictional speeches cited here demonstrate that this is not altogether the case.

[70] On the use of *diabolē*, see [Arist.] *Rh. Al.* 1445a12–29 and Arist. *Rh.* 1415a25–34.

[71] For a more detailed analysis of the speech's structure, see Avezzù 1982: 80; Zographou-Lyra 1991.

[72] The device of employing inscribed weapons to convey messages might well have been suggested by Euripides' *Palamedes*: see Ar. *Thesm.* 765–84 and Scodel 1980: 58–9; Jouan and Van Looy 2000; Collard 2004.

It seems reasonable to consider the possibility that Lysias 1 presents a similarly fictitious scenario. The author composes a defence speech for the cuckold figure in a typically elaborate tale of adultery, here one in which the wronged husband triumphs. The scenario offers ample opportunity for its author to display his skill in constructing an effective narrative and devising the appropriate arguments to support his 'client's' case; it also presents a tradition rich in colourful characters, comic incidents and devices, and (as we have seen in the discussion of Menander's *Samia* above) the potential for interesting psychological insights, all of which the author exploits in full. The attractiveness of this particular scenario for later rhetoricians is nicely illustrated by P. Rutilius Lupus, *De figuris sententiarum et elocutionis* 1. 21, where we find a fragment of a somewhat ham-handed variation on Euphiletus' narrative:

Lysias: As I was returning from my farm, gentlemen of the jury, a man of some years, in the searing afternoon heat, barely enduring the difficulty of my journey, still I consoled myself with these words: 'Bear up under your trials; you're awaited eagerly at home and you'll soon be there. Your attentive and loving wife will take you in, worn out as you are; she'll heal your weariness with her diligent and tender ministrations and will restore your aged spirits with her care.' This thought kept me going despite my fatigue. But then, when I got home, I found nothing of the sort, but rather an insidious plot against me laid out by my wife.

Although Rutilius cites Lysias as his authority for this passage, he clearly is not translating or even loosely paraphrasing Lysias 1: elements that are at best implied in Euphiletus' tale (the speaker's age; his hardworking, honest nature) here are presented more baldly and to much less effect, while the portrait of the wife plotting for her husband's return is altogether alien to Lysias' account. Rutilius has 'improved' upon his source in the interest of providing his students with a clearer, if less sophisticated, example of this particular rhetorical technique.[73] Yet the passage employs much the same strategy as that found in Euphiletus' narrative, encouraging a sympathetic response from the jury by having them enter into the mind of the all too unsuspecting cuckold, whose trusting naivety is viewed through the eyes of the cuckold/narrator himself. For the

---

[73] See, further, Barabino 1967: 98–100 and 133; J. Porter 2003: 85–6.

orator interested in trying his hand at *ēthopoeia*, the possibilities offered by such a narrator were clearly attractive.

To sum up: the reading of Lysias 1 as an elaborate fiction offers a plausible explanation for (a) the brevity of the speech, (b) the curiously generic treatment of the various characters and general lack of specifying detail, (c) the ironically appropriate names of the protagonists, (d) the numerous and systematic points of contact with the typical comic adultery tale, (e) the focus on the *diēgēsis*, and the resulting neglect of rhetorical *topoi* that we might otherwise expect to find. It also accounts for the wildly improbable daring of the adulterous couple (another point rarely considered by commentators on the speech): one can perhaps imagine that an Athenian adulteress might routinely welcome her lover into the house while her husband was in the upstairs bedroom (Euphiletus' wife does so twice in the space of what seem to have been a relatively few days), but this motif is such a regular element of the comic adultery scenario that doubts about Euphiletus' narrative must arise on this point as well (above, n. 12). At the very least, it seems reasonable to suspect that the prosecution's allegations of dire plottings on the part of Euphiletus (§§ 27, 37) contain real merit;[74] once this premise is accepted, however, the very weakness of Euphiletus' challenge to these allegations—the apparent hope that Lysias' compelling narrative alone would be sufficient to undermine the prosecution's various assertions—must raise doubts about whether the speech would have satisfied a client compelled to refute such charges before an Athenian jury. Practical matters of this sort need not concern the author of a display piece: the latter writes for an audience who have heard no case for the prosecution and one that, like today's commentators, is quite prepared to be won over by the speech's many aesthetic merits.

---

[74] Cf. e.g. Carey 1989: 62–4; Desbordes 1990: 103–4. For detailed consideration of various improbable features in Euphiletus' account, see Weißenberger 1993.

PART II

The Tools of Argument: Procedure and Proof

5

Demosthenes as Advocate: The Functions and Methods of Legal Consultants in Classical Athens*

Hans Julius Wolff

I

The title of my lecture today has been purposefully selected. It indicates my intention to offer a sequel of sorts to the lecture that my friend and colleague, Franz Wieacker, presented just over three years ago in this circle. Wieacker's topic was 'Cicero as Advocate' (1965). The main focus of his discussion was to present the method and general character of Cicero's art of advocacy, its political and intellectual premises, as well as its departures from patterns and views that are familiar to us.

It is my intention to head in a similar direction. I too will try to give you a description of the purpose, work method, and professional manner of the ancient advocate by using one of the most outstanding representatives of this group as an example. For the sake of simplicity, allow me to use the expression 'advocate', although it is only approximately applicable, as I will soon demonstrate. Let me take you back 300 years further and into a very different milieu. We will leave behind the aristocratically governed Roman Republic, which ruled the world but was torn apart by inner turmoil, and head into a realm that had

* Wolff's essay was originally presented as a lecture to the Berlin Juristic Society, 30 June 1967. It is here translated by Jess Miner, in consultation with Gerhard Thür.

regained a degree of prosperity and power after its downfall and was, for the most part, inwardly stable—the democratic middle-class world of Athens between the time of the Peloponnesian War and Alexander the Great.

It is obvious that a comparison between Demosthenes and Cicero, specifically in connection with their forensic occupations, is possible within narrow bounds at best. The vast differences in their surroundings, in fact, extended as far as the organization of the courts, judicial procedure, and the substantive legal system. What allows us, nonetheless, to place both [2] men side by side is the deeply rooted connection to *rhetoric* they both shared.[1] Wieacker vividly described for you the great degree to which Cicero's speeches, in both form and content, have been shaped by rhetorical art. Athens, however, during the fifth and fourth centuries BC, was the place where courtroom rhetoric first came to fruition, after being discovered in Syracuse somewhat earlier as a technique that could be learned. In the time of Demosthenes, whom Cicero so admired,[2] the original sociological and political premises of rhetoric still applied, yet its positive and negative characteristics were already fully developed. It is therefore justified to follow a presentation on Cicero's trial art with one on Demosthenes'.

Given that there is a practically symbolic ring to his name, no one will be surprised that I am placing Demosthenes at the centre of my present investigation and drawing examples primarily from speeches that he composed. But that is all the more reason to acknowledge that his forensic activity contributed the least to his fame. Demosthenes,

---

[1] A summary of scholarship on ancient rhetoric is beyond our scope. A brief but outstanding overview can be found in Hildebrecht Hommel's article, 'Rhetoric' in *Lexikon der Alten Welt* (Andresen *et al.* 1965): 2611–26. Kennedy 1963 provides a good introduction to the material; cf. Schottländer 1967: 125 ff.; and specifically in connection with the issues of interest here, see Erik Wolf's chapter, 'Fragwürdigkeit und Notwendigkeit der Rhetorik' (1956: 157–68). For further reference, consult the collection that William Calder is preparing, 'Attic Orators' (Wege der Forschung, 127). [Wege der Forschung vol. 127 would later appear (1977) as *Kleinere attische Redner*, edited by Anastassiou and Irmer.]

[2] e.g. Cic. *Brutus* 9. 35: *Nam plane quidem perfectum et cui nihil admodum desit Demosthenem facile dixeris* ('For one could easily say that Demosthenes is clearly perfect and in no way lacking anything').

just like his counterpart Cicero, achieved high rank as a stylist and in his role as a politician of undoubted effectiveness thanks to his outstanding talent at crafting rousing *political* speeches. In this respect, historians are by and large unanimous. However, they have tended [3] to view him according to their own political perspectives: in one instance he is a narrow-minded Athenian chauvinist, in another, an unscrupulous demagogue, and in another, a man who leads the fight for self-determination and freedom and is guided by the noblest ideals.[3] But, as a man who composed and delivered court speeches, there is no disputing his place among the highest tier of the orators in Athens at that time. Clearly we cannot say that he ever reached such unique heights with his speechwriting for civil cases as he did in some of his political speeches before the assembly or court.[4] But, in my opinion, which is of course subjective and admittedly oriented more toward a legal-historical rather than literary perspective, I would rank him in this particular area at least on par with his teacher Isaeus, for example.

Yet, even if we exercise a certain amount of reservation in our assessment, putting Demosthenes forth as the prototype of ancient 'advocates' is not unwarranted. The single fact that we do not have so rich and colourful a collection of speeches from any other Attic orator justifies this assessment;[5] in fact, our knowledge of Attic law from the classical period is based largely on this source. In addition, no one else gives us the same realistic view of trial practice at the time, a practice that was certainly not always admirable. Whether the situation demanded an explicit presentation, ethical tirades

---

[3] For an overview of the various opinions, see Jaeger 1939: 1 ff. [1938: 1–4]; Wolf 1956: 326–7.

[4] Cicero had the same opinion. As he once wrote to his friend Atticus (*Ad. Att.* 2. 1. 3): *quod in eis orationibus, quae Philippicae nominantur, enituerat tuus ille civis et quod se ab hoc refractariolo iudiciali dicendi genere abiunxerat, ut* semnoteros tis *et* polikoteros *videretur.* Helmut Kasten, a researcher for the Tusculum edition of the *Letters to Atticus*, paraphrased these words as follows: 'Your countryman Demosthenes reveals his powers in all their brilliance first in the so-called Philippics; there for the first time he rises above the artful blustering of the court speeches to appear more sublime and statesmanlike.'

[5] See Wolf 1956: 330, for a list of speeches by Demosthenes that are authentic; there are a total of 60 extant speeches attributed to him and approximately 20 of these are trial speeches.

performed with the highest pathos, or even dubious rhetorical tricks, in every respect Demosthenes was a master.

From the surviving court speeches written by Demosthenes, some are public criminal cases, [4] but the majority are either civil or private criminal cases. The first group is the better known and more admired, not least because these speeches dealt primarily with important political affairs that were decided by criminal trials, as was characteristic of political life in democratic Athens. For our purposes, and in general from the point of view of the legal historian, the private speeches are more important. Thus, I am going to confine myself to these. Naturally the speeches that are considered authentic according to philological criteria will remain at the forefront of my argument. But allow me an occasional side-glimpse at one or another of the rather numerous speeches that the ancient publishers were certainly or probably wrong to include in the *Corpus Demosthenicum*, for they come from contemporary authors and therefore are of the same value as the authentic speeches as sources for law and the nature of trials at the time.

II

Before we turn specifically to Demosthenes' forensic activity, allow me to familiarize you in broad terms with the legal and sociological world of the Athenian legal practitioner in the fourth century BC. The following questions arise: first, what was the framework of the legal system that he worked within—how were the courts and the trial procedure organized? Secondly, what sort of people were those whom I have described as 'advocates', and what was their intellectual background?

1. To begin, the legal system itself is relatively well known, and it is therefore neither possible nor necessary to give a detailed explanation here.[6] However, I wish to emphasize one point: Athenian material and procedural law certainly bore little similarity [5] to a rationally

---

[6] For a brief overview, see my article, 'Griechisches Recht', in Andresen *et al.* 1965: 2516 ff.

conceived system, as we understand it. But it is a mistake to think that it was nothing more than a simple collection of individual laws standing more or less in isolation, which, moreover, might be ignored by the courts if the laws seemed unjust in relation to the case at hand (as certain scholars have believed).[7] It was, in fact, a real legal system and it was consciously recognized and respected as such. Its core was formed by the laws (*nomoi*) that were chiselled in stone and erected in visually prominent locations. Solon was honoured as their creator, even if in some cases this was not true. In addition to the laws, there existed a set of traditional unwritten legal principles; they were considered even more sacred than the laws because they rested not only on human—and therefore changeable—'common law' (*Gewohnheitsrecht*—this term did not in fact exist), but they were ascribed to mythic or even divine lawgivers (Wolff 1962).

The structure of the Athenian legal system was based upon an individual's right to take a particular legal action (*aktionenrechtlich*). In other words, the laws provided for types of procedure (*dikai*) that were more or less clearly defined, and in accordance with these, both citizens and to a limited extent non-citizens prosecuted those who murdered their relatives or injured their persons or property. Furthermore, citizens could bring wrongdoers to justice publicly by means of a public suit, a privilege available to every citizen (public prosecutors of the sort that are common to us were unknown to the Greek city-states). For each type of *dikē*, the law governing it determined to which archon or other magistrate it should be brought. There were a few procedural differences of secondary importance among the different types of legal complaints. But, in fact, the defining characteristic of the *dikē* as a *central concept of legal procedure* was common to all individual *dikai*, and here I am speaking of the word only in its juristic [6] sense, not its philosophical or ethical sense:[8] the *dikē* was always a kind of lawful private seizure (*Zugriff*),

---

[7] Foremost among them, Vinogradoff 1922: ii. 71; 1928: ii. 15 ff.; Paoli 1933: 33 ff., 39 ff.; J. W. Jones 1956: 135. This opinion is laid out in detail by Meyer-Laurin 1965.

[8] On the juristic sense, cf. Andresen *et al.* 1965: 2517. On the philosophical sense, there is an abundance of scholarship; see e.g. Hirzel 1907; Ehrenberg 1921 [1966]: 54 ff.; J. W. Jones 1956: 24 ff.; Fränkel 1960: 162 ff.; Wolf 1950–68, *passim*. In the

especially in the fully developed system of litigation of the Classical *polis*, a request to be allowed such action, which the individual made by summoning his adversary to the official in charge and submitting a written accusation with a short explanation of the complaints. Accordingly, there was no functional or qualitative difference between the branches of judicial administration, particularly in a private case or public criminal case, despite their different objectives. Likewise, they do not fundamentally differ from one-another in terms of the trial procedure.[9]

In most circumstances,[10] the magistrate to whom the case was brought had to present it to a *dikastērion*, or *popular court*, in whose hands lay the decision about the legitimacy of a *dikē* and the penalty to be imposed, or the amount of the payment (a ransom, in the original sense). This payment was the goal of the 'seizure'. [7] The system of the *dikastēria* goes back to the time of Solon and reached its full development with the establishment of the radical democracy after the Persian wars. It was one of the most characteristic features of Athenian democracy, but also, for us, one of the most foreign. In its extreme form, it seems to have had no parallel even within the Greek world. It embodied the principle that the pronouncement of a verdict on someone's request for permission to infringe on the life, freedom, or property of a fellow citizen was a matter for the people itself (the *dēmos*) to decide.

---

scholarship just cited, however, the two connotations of the term are not kept sufficiently distinct from one another.

[9] It was indeed customary to distinguish the trial procedure as a *dikē* or as a *graphē* (lit. 'writing'), depending on whether it was geared toward private seizure or public punishment. It certainly would be a mistake, however, to conclude that this difference in terminology indicated either a far-reaching juridical distinction, or even a distinction in the form of procedure for each case. As far as juridical distinction is concerned, criminal procedure was also understood as a 'public' *dikē* (*dēmosia*), whereas, in regard to legal procedure, the civil suit or 'private' *dikē* (*idia*) likewise demanded the submission of a *written* accusation. *Dikē* was, therefore, a generic term that covered both objectives. It seems that the neutral term *graphē* was thus used for the criminal trial since in this case the prosecutor used the law for an action that was not on his own behalf, but on behalf of the entire polity, and was not entrusted to the self-help of the party involved, but to the authorities.

[10] With the exception of homicide cases (still a matter of private law even in the fourth century); the ancient aristocratic court of the Areopagos and the Ephetai held jurisdiction over these even in the democracy.

The idealist claim that it was really the entire people—described in this capacity as the 'Heliaia'—was, however, seldom achieved, and even then only approximately. This in fact happened when charges that were particularly serious and affected the core of the political system were brought before the entire Heliaia, a court assembly of no fewer than 6,000 men. For the everyday civil or criminal trial, they made do with sections of the Heliaia, which was divided into legally specified gradations of 201 up to 2,001 jurors determined by lot. A magistrate for each jurisdiction was assigned a *dikastērion* of this sort, and his assignment was determined anew daily. All citizens over the age of 30 were eligible, and they gladly volunteered because the activity offered satisfaction, amusement, and an easily earned daily wage.[11]

The role of the *dikastēria* was neither that of a jury whose only function was to pass judgement regarding the question of guilt, nor was it solely that of 'lay assessors' (*Schöffenbänke*) in our sense. Rather, the dicasts, *and they alone*, were judges in the full sense of the word; they used the secret ballot to determine the verdict by a majority decision. The responsibility of the magistrate was simply [8] to conduct the formal preliminary hearing of the *dikai* that were brought before him, then to submit the cases to the *dikastērion* and to preside at the trial; he did not participate in the vote.

Before a mass assembly of this sort, there was clearly no opportunity for any real dialogue between the parties such as might clarify questions of law and of fact through unstructured speech and response in an open presentation and evaluation of the evidence. The final hearing before the *dikastērion*, in fact, stood out because of its *rigid formality*. First, the presiding official read out the written complaint and the answer to the charges, both of which consisted of very brief written statements that simply named the compensation demanded, and summarized the affirmation or denial of the grounds for the accusation. The detailed presentations by each party

---

[11] In *Wasps*, Aristophanes makes fun of the typical dicast, whose sole concern was to feel important and to collect his juror's pay. Wolf attempts to grasp the political perspective particular to the jurors (1954: 256 ff.). The conservative faction at Athens condemned Pericles' introduction of jury pay on the grounds that the quality of juror performance would necessarily deteriorate since their interest in the job would now be material; cf. Bonner and Smith 1938: 294 ff. (with references).

immediately followed. Normally there were two presentations by each side, delivered in alternating order. A litigant was not allowed to interrupt during his opponent's presentation. The plaintiff went first, unless the defendant lodged what was called a *paragraphē* (an objection to the proceedings loosely similar to a special plea in bar of litigation, with speeches delivered in reverse order, addressing the admissibility of the trial itself). The length of each party's speech was limited; as a way of monitoring the time, a water-clock would drip until it ran out. The litigants wove the presentation of the evidence into their speeches. Any laws or documents that a litigant thought he could cite on his own behalf were read aloud (the principle of *iura novit curia* ('the court knows the laws') certainly could not have applied!). In the time of Demosthenes, even witness testimony generally consisted of merely reading back to the witness a record of his statement that was taken down before the trial on behalf of the litigant who was now presenting it as evidence. There was no further involvement or questioning of witnesses after the litigants delivered their speeches. Nor was there any deliberation among the jurors themselves; rather, the final decision by vote took place immediately.

Thus Athenian litigation, assuming it had not been previously concluded by arbitration or by some settlement (as often), found its resolution in a *combat of speeches before the dikastērion* that unfolded according to strict regulations. It was aptly called an *agōn*, a battle, or more precisely, a sporting contest, since that is in fact the concept [9] underlying this expression. And without a doubt, the exchange of speeches between opposing parties at Athens was very much like a sport.[12] When the decision-making body is an assembly of uneducated commoners who are easily riled up, as in fact it was at

---

[12] Burkhardt (1956–7: iv. 84 ff., 113 ff.) discovered and masterfully explained the ways in which the concept of the 'agonistic' mindset of the Greeks, i.e. a stereotypical enthusiasm for competition, played a role here; on this topic, see also Wieacker 1965: 23 f. (although perhaps somewhat exaggerated). At any rate, one must be warned against the fantastical assertions of Mannzmann 1962: 96 ff. In particular, it is wrong to derive the fact that the Athenian court was limited to the simple choice between the recommended verdicts of the parties (without the possibility of deviating from these after evaluating both petitions) from the agonistic principle, and then deem it a typical manifestation of the Greek spirit. Here we are simply dealing with one of many archaic formalities, and these characteristics are certainly not limited to Athenian trials of the classical period.

Athens, it is difficult to resist the temptation of demagogy. In Athens, moreover, it was also the case that there were actually very few weaknesses by which it was easier to enflame the average citizen than by his own aesthetic delight in polished speech and rhetorical fireworks, a passion shared by the whole nation. Even with the jurors' best intentions to remain objective—and if immediate political bias did not obscure their judgement, this good faith was demonstrably present[13]—it cannot be denied that the speaker's eloquence was largely responsible for determining his fortune. And yet, however much one views the trial as a contest between fine orations, and thinks that an oration could influence the jurors and possibly help elevate the weaker legal position to victory simply because it was skilfully conceived and delivered in a pleasing or entertaining manner, still, the famed *captatio benevolentiae* demonstrates with great clarity that the court could be lenient toward a speaker's inexperience and unfamiliarity with speaking, whether such modesty was real or feigned.[14]

[10]   2. I have dwelt at some length on the description of the typical Athenian court and the trial proper to it because a legal and sociological foundation is necessary for understanding the origin and character of an occupation similar to that of an advocate. Since a litigant's chance of success depended on the rhetorical quality of the argumentation, many litigants thought it advisable to secure the assistance of someone well versed in forensic rhetoric. A relative or friend might have been the one to assist a litigant in trouble, and often that was sufficient. Gradually, however, others also came forward who earned money for this service. Unfortunately, we cannot say exactly when the movement toward professionalization of this role began. In any case, we find 'professional' logographers (speechwriters [offering their services to others]; see below) no later than the last decades of the fifth century during the time of the Peloponnesian War.[15] This trade flourished during the fourth century after the

---

[13] Here again Meyer-Laurin 1965 should be consulted (esp. 32 ff.).

[14] An angry remark by Demosthenes (23. 206), to the effect that parties who were obviously guilty were acquitted if they made only one or two funny comments, indicates that the Athenians were always aware of these weaknesses of the courts (cf. also n. 19 below).

[15] According to Thucydides (8. 68.1), one of the first men, if not the first, to engage in this activity appears to have been Antiphon. We possess a few of his

violent regime of the Thirty Tyrants was ended and democracy was once again restored.

But who were these people? What did their job entail? What was expected of them and how were they trained?

First, I wish to say that my use of the term 'trade' (*Gewerbe*) is not a casual choice of words.[16] There cannot, of course, be any discussion of a true profession, and certainly not of a respected profession in today's sense. The occupation in question was available to anyone and required no qualifications, exams, or authorization. For some, it was a way to earn a living. But others devoted themselves to the job, as I just mentioned, occasionally and not for the sake of money. More important, however, is that as far as we can tell, the individuals for whom it provided a source of income were frequently *resident aliens*, known as metics. Two of the most famous, Lysias and Isaeus, fell into this category. Foreigners, however, did not have a monopoly on 'trial assistance', if I may call it that for the time being. [11] Athenian citizens, including even men who stemmed from the upper class, such as Antiphon, Isocrates, Hyperides, and Demosthenes, likewise devoted themselves to this occupation. Demosthenes, to be sure, gave up speaking for others after he entered into politics.[17] And Isocrates eventually stopped writing court speeches and later was displeased when anyone reminded him of this phase of his life.[18]

The facts just mentioned show that the 'profession' did not enjoy the highest level of respect in society—an impression confirmed by the disparaging comments that emerge here and there in the sources.[19] Upon first glance, the modern-day observer might find that strange.

speeches, some composed for actual use and some for the purpose of rhetorical training; cf. also Burkhardt 1956–7: iii. 310.

16 [I render *Gewerbe* loosely as 'trade', but only in the sense of an occupation that requires skill since logography was not always a commercial enterprise. (JM)]

17 Dem. 32. 32. [The text breaks off, but apparently Demosthenes agreed to assist his kinsman Demon in other ways but refused to appear as a supporting speaker in a private suit.]

18 Isoc. 15. 1; cf. Jaeger 1939: 30–1 [= 1938: 1–4].

19 Cf. [Dem.] 35. 41: 'This Lacritus, jurors, has not engaged in this trial believing in the justice of his case, but rather … in the belief that he is clever and that he could easily provide arguments for his unjust activities, he thinks that he can lead you astray at will. For it is this that he professes and he is clever at this in particular, and he charges a fee, gathers up students, and promises to instruct them precisely in these matters.' Further comments of this sort can be found in Bonner 1927: 22 ff.

Yet, it makes sense when we consider the *subordinate position* that procedural law imposed upon the profession, along with its peculiar working conditions. Athenian law, like many archaic laws, not only excluded *formal* trial advocacy but, beyond that, it fundamentally required each litigant to advocate his own case by speaking for himself in person. It goes without saying that a principle of this sort left no room for the figure of the brilliant lawyer to turn the trial into a public spectacle, and must have prevented the position of lawyer from ever becoming a true and respected profession. Admittedly, the courts allowed a substitute to speak on the litigant's behalf now and again for reasons of fairness. It is clear, however, that only those people were allowed to speak who had a close personal connection to the disadvantaged party or, at any rate, undertook the task out of generosity. In fact, generosity *must* have been the motive, since a *legal prohibition* against charging a fee ruled out the possibility that the professional advocate had a self-serving motive for speaking. [12] Metics, moreover, were in other ways denied access to trials designated for citizens before the citizen-run courts.

Accordingly, what remained for citizens and metics alike as work that was useful and not affected by the prohibition on charging a fee was the *composition* of speeches for those whose own talents were not adequate for the job but who still at least hoped to influence the court with the polished delivery of a speech that they had learned by heart. Unlike the active politician (a line of work that was open only to citizens, of course), the trial practitioner himself did not regularly step forward as a public speaker, but was content with drawing up speeches for others and giving his clients instruction— partly ad hoc, partly standard teaching—in the art of speaking and in the techniques of speech composition. The business often combined both functions [speech-writing and training]. Litigation was prevalent at Athens[20] and training in rhetoric not only paved the way for a career in politics, but was also more generally a mark of higher education. Since it was desired by many for this reason, offering this type of training could lead to a handsome profit and sometimes

---

[20] The Athenians themselves made fun of this fact. In Aristophanes' *Clouds*, someone is shown where Athens is located on the map and responds (207–8): 'What are you saying? I don't believe it, I don't see any jurors in session!'

even fame, particularly in the later fifth and fourth centuries when successful court speeches were sometimes published as literature. Evidently, this was done in order to make a name for oneself (Jaeger 1939: 36), and without necessarily connecting oneself to the political propaganda that was often disseminated in the same way. In the majority of cases, a 'ghost-writer' remained more or less anonymous, hidden behind the person delivering the speech. Indeed, in the case of a particularly good speech, no one could tell that it was not the speaker's own creation. So, despite all of the skill that a job of this sort clearly required, the subordinate nature that nevertheless remained associated with it explains the logographer's low social standing.

To conclude this general overview, a few words ought to be added about the profession's *intellectual basis*, [13] which arose out of its social function. Anyone who sees his own work as providing others with speeches that they could deliver themselves had to direct his attention above all else to shaping the arrangement, style, and content of the address so as to achieve the strongest possible rhetorical effect, as if the speaker himself had put forth a comparable oratorical effort. For this purpose, the *theory of rhetoric* developed specific models for instruction. This technique first appeared at Syracuse, and around the middle of the fifth century was transplanted to Athens, where it was adapted to the requirements of forensic practice. The speechwriters kept to these rules even as, depending of course on personal talents, one speechwriter could display more flexibility and originality, and another less.

Thus, as his first priority the logographer had to master the art of rhetoric. After that, he needed *legal expertise*, which, by comparison, took a distant second place. It is obvious that the preparation of a successful speech required a certain knowledge of the laws. It is likely that each Athenian possessed some familiarity with them, and greater knowledge could be gained in rhetorical schools and in practice. But the logographer was no jurist; he could not even be compared with Cicero, who himself was not a true legal expert (*iuris peritus*) in the Roman sense. Strangely enough, with respect to positive law, in contrast to legal philosophy, the ancient Greeks never progressed beyond a primitive knowledge of the law to true intellectual mastery of the material. I cannot go into an explanation here of the various reasons for this, but it should simply be noted that the structure of classical Athenian trials played a major role because it excluded any real discussion about law.[21] I readily admit that we, nonetheless, sometimes find in the speeches arguments that indicate considerable juristic understanding—or, should we say instead—juristic cleverness, especially since it was used for the purpose of distorting the law. I propose now to offer you one or two examples of this sort.

[14]   III

Such was the world to which Demosthenes belonged. Born in 384 BC, he earned his stripes as a speaker in court by the early age of 20 in trials against his disloyal guardian, Aphobos, and Aphobos' accomplice, Onetor. Because he was prosecuting these cases on his own behalf, he himself both wrote and delivered the accompanying speeches, which we still have today (Dem. 27–31). It seems that Demosthenes already won a reputation as a master of the art of oratory from his performance in these early trials.

How, then, is this world represented to us in general, and in the person of Demosthenes in particular? For every speechwriter, the first priority of course is to create a final product that satisfies all the requirements of the art of rhetoric. Thus, in addition to the common stylistic devices, handbook theories helped a speaker by giving him a template for devising the logical structure of a speech. Between the introduction (*prooimion*) and the concluding entreaty, the epilogue, the speaker had to cover the body of the speech proper. This, in turn, was divided into a narrative section (*diēgēsis*) and a section for laying out the arguments, in which the speaker attempted to demonstrate the justice of his perspective. The technical term for this section was *pistis*, a term that is difficult to grasp in its precise sense. Here perhaps it can be rendered approximately as 'making the case credible' or even 'persuading'.[22]

---

[21] Cf. Wolff 1964; Wolf 1956: 164 ff.

[22] [Wolff glosses *pistis* with *Glaubwurdigkeit* and *Glaubhaftmachung*, and for the latter cautions parenthetically, 'of course not in the technical sense in which our trial law uses the expression for bolstering weak proof'.]

Theoretically, then, we are confronted with a very strict organization whose usefulness no one even today would dispute. In actuality of course, this framework was wide enough to accommodate anything and everything, from the serious presentation and assessment of the facts, to tales designed to arouse or incite the jurors; from slandering an opponent and tallying one's own merits, to passionate appeals to lofty-sounding ethical principles. Since the speechwriters took full advantage of all of these possibilities, the presentation might or might not serve to set forth the litigants' rights in an objective way, but only when it seemed suitable for influencing the jurors in favour of their clients. A master of such methods, like [15] Demosthenes, knew these tricks so well that, even today, anyone who reads his speeches without submitting them to close juridical analysis is in danger of being blinded by them.

However high we may rate the efficacy of purely rhetorical devices, we must be careful to avoid the misconception that the salvation of a litigant lay in these tricks alone. As I have already indicated, there are grounds for the assumption that the jurors normally took seriously their oath to uphold the law and, in the absence of a relevant law, to judge in accordance with their most just opinion (*dikaiotatē gnōmē*). The logographer could therefore not simply be content to train his clients in rhetorical antics; he also had to strive to create a picture for the jurors that put them in the position to vote for the speaker based—at least subjectively—on their honest, legal convictions. The speechwriter was able to demonstrate real skill when he saw himself facing a desperate situation—whether his client could not bring him the evidence for which he (the client) was responsible, or his opponent had solid evidence in hand, or had a case that was unassailable on legal grounds, and therefore could not be overcome by outright lying (which was not avoided, if it were necessary) or by blatant rhetorical clichés.

IV

I wish now to present you with a few examples from the abundance of evidence available to us. These will show that Demosthenes understood his craft. In terms of ethics, from our perspective many of his methods justifiably invoke scepticism. We will be concerned later with how these tactics would have been judged during Demosthenes' own time. First, we will examine them in view of the objective possibilities that were available to a shrewd practitioner, given that the trial was confined to the agonistic conditions of a straightforward rhetorical duel before a crowd only narrowly capable of objective criticism.

1. One of the main tasks of the logographer was to keep the weaknesses of the actual position of his client [16] concealed from the court. He could, therefore, attempt to mislead the jurors by having an impressive number of witness testimonies about facts that were actually irrelevant read aloud, thus obscuring the fact that he still owed them proof of crucial assertions. As I already mentioned, the presentation of the evidence was woven into a purely oral speech, which created opportunities for psychologically influencing the audience just by speaking more quickly or slowly, fluctuating between a louder and softer tone of voice, using facial expressions, gestures, and the like. Moreover, any structural weakness of a speech could only be exposed, if at all, by the counter-speech, but not by discussion or critical interrogation on the part of the opponent or the judge. Still, one could expect more from mere rhetorical tactics than, for example, as in a civil case in Germany today, from a plethora of evidence that is vacuous, but subject to dispassionate examination on the part of the court.

In this somewhat primitive manner, the speaker of the pseudo-Demosthenic oration *Against Apaturios* (or. 33) tried, in fact, to cope with a hopeless situation (Wolff 1966: 25–35). And Demosthenes himself handled similar difficulties with greater subtlety in *Against Konon* (or. 54), a speech that he wrote for a young man named Ariston. Ariston charged Konon with assault (*aikeia*). He alleged that the sons of the defendant, who were malicious drunken brawlers (if we can believe him), had attacked him with the guidance and active participation of their father and had beaten him up so badly that he ended up on his sickbed for a long time, struggling to stay alive.

It sounds completely convincing. However, from an observant *reading* of the speech (of course the jurors would have only *heard it*

and certainly not read it carefully!), one notices first that the accuser knew how to speak at length about the beating and its unpleasant consequences for him, and that for all of this he had an impressive number of witnesses, but that he elegantly glided over the very point that the law required of his case—evidently because he lacked witnesses for it—namely, that the accused must have struck the *first*
[17] *blow.* Conversely, he could not avoid letting it show, even cautiously, that he was prepared for the defendant to charge him with precisely that allegation. This fear lurks unmistakably behind his pointedly contemptuous treatment of one piece of his opponent's evidence: Konon had challenged him, in the solemn formality called *proklēsis*, to interrogate under torture his (Konon's) slaves about the fight (54. 27).

That the whole matter revolves primarily around the *origin* of the fight is clear from Ariston's justification for refusing the formal challenge. In itself, this must have made the least favourable impression imaginable on the jurors since they would judge such an evasion as a concession to the opponent's allegation. In order to get away from the issue of interrogation under torture, Ariston quickly turns the tables (so to speak) and instead accuses Konon of delaying this challenge until the very last moment of the preliminary hearing, when the official arbitrator (*diaitētēs*) was at the point of pronouncing judgement. In this way, Ariston wanted Konon's tactic to be exposed as a blatant diversionary ploy. Then, the argument continues, if the defendant was serious about this line of defence, he would have responded immediately with all available means when Ariston himself was denouncing Konon as the attacker to everyone who visited him at his sickbed while he was expecting to die, especially since Konon would have been facing a murder charge if Ariston had actually died (54. 28). Even supposing that Konon was not aware of any of this, it is nonetheless evident that he would have offered to have his slaves interrogated right away in the *first* appointment before the arbitrator, if it were an honest challenge (54. 29).

As usual, the opposing arguments and the outcome of this case are unfortunately lost to us. Nevertheless, the speech about Konon is informative in many respects. In regard to Demosthenes' own artistry, it demonstrates that he was a keen-sighted legal practitioner, who recognized and understood how to use the opportunities available to his client—as the prosecutor and first speaker—to pre-emptively discredit the expected and potentially dangerous evidence of his opponent. If he succeeded with this strategy, he could even [18] expect the jurors to overlook his lack of strict evidence for the guilt of the accused party. Demosthenes' skill appears all the more clearly in the way he exploits the bad reputation of Konon and his sons, who were possibly—indeed, in their relatively small community *probably*—well known as hooligans.

But this speech does not just bear witness to Demosthenes' personal talent. In general terms, it can also be viewed as one example among very many of how ancient rhetoric developed as a craft (*technē*) of high art: in the absence of real evidence, such as witnesses, documents, and the like, rhetorical theory advocated working with indirect forms of proof, such as arguments from *probability* (called *eikos*) and *circumstantial evidence* (*tekmēria*). The former were described by ancient theory as *atechnoi pisteis*, 'non-technical proofs', in opposition to the latter, which were called *entechnoi pisteis*, 'technical proofs' (ancient terminology used the term 'technical' in precisely the opposite sense from ours).

Still another, even more important, characteristic of Athenian oratory from the fourth century that can also be confirmed in numerous other speeches emerges in exemplary fashion from the Konon speech; the pleading *never* aims to entice the jurors toward an open disregard of the law. To the Athenians, still deeply entrenched in archaic formalism, it would appear to be a perversion of justice to treat fairness as a corrective to the all-too-rigid rule of law, as in *exceptio doli* (Meyer-Laurin 1965). The fact that the contemporary philosophy of Plato and Aristotle recognized the conflict between legal justice and true justice changes nothing.[23] In an actual trial, this means that the speaker had to try [19] to configure the *facts of the case* in such a way that the jurors could in good conscience apply a law that was favourable to the litigant and decide that an unfavourable law did not apply.

To serve this purpose, the most effective ploy (at least in a civil case), along with a suitably colourful narrative, was the *play on emotions*—a very typical feature of forensic oratory at that time, for

[23] Cf. Michelakis 1953; Stoffels 1954.

which we have little sympathy. Demosthenes was outstanding at this, particularly at using it in just the right dosage. Blackening an opponent's character raised doubts about *his trustworthiness*, while focusing on oneself or arousing pity was aimed primarily at increasing *one's own trustworthiness*.

2. Sometimes the law was so clearly on the side of an opponent that even this approach was of no use. In this situation, only one possibility remained: to set the heads of the jurors spinning by concealing the true situation from them to such an extent that they are no longer capable of reaching a correct verdict. The following example will demonstrate that Demosthenes was not above such methods.

The speech I have in mind is one that Demosthenes wrote against two brothers, *Nausimachos and Xeinopeithes* (or. 38), on behalf of four clients whose names are not known, but who were also brothers. Four parallel cases had been brought by the opponents against his clients. Formally, each case would presumably be handled as a separate trial, but the cases might have been treated together and the extant speech could have been delivered by one of the four defendants on behalf of all of them.

The background to the case is as follows:[24] Aristaichmos, the father of the four accused, had been the guardian of the two plaintiffs. At the conclusion of his guardianship, a conflict broke out concerning the settlement of the guardianship accounts. Eight years later the conflict was resolved through a release [20] and discharge (*aphesis kai apallagē*) granted to Aristaichmos by the prosecutors. At this point, after no fewer than fourteen years, the former wards suddenly alleged that either Aristaichmos or, after his death, the guardian of his sons had collected payment on a debt that was owed to the wards' estate; this debt was listed as outstanding in the final settlement which was approved as part of the release. The amount, however, had neither been paid out by Aristaichmos himself nor by his sons

---

[24] I need not hide the fact that the reconstruction of events offered above is hypothetical. It is based on a critical assessment of the procedural steps taken by the litigants according to the speech itself, steps that would only make sense under the premises assumed here. For details, consult my exhaustive analysis in Wolff 1963: 95 ff.; cf. 1966: 57 ff.

and heirs after he died. The plaintiffs considered this to be an *ongoing injury*, an unjustified withholding (*aposterein;* lit. 'stripping away') of property rightly belonging to them. Thus, they brought charges against all of Aristaichmos' sons, since his estate was still undivided. They brought a civil action called a 'suit for damages' (*dikē blabēs*) for double the amount that was taken away from them; moreover, it was *cumulative* against each of the four defendants. The plaintiffs were entitled to this action (though it seems at first astonishing to the modern observer) since the doubled amount was not simply under-stood as lump-sum compensation for the actual loss but, in keeping with archaic thought, as strictly punitive damages and therefore rightly assessed against each offender.

As a result, the defendants were charged *eight times* the amount that they had allegedly never paid! If this alone made their situation unenviable, it also happened that they had no defence on points of law and against the factual claims of their accusers, as the speech reveals (38. 9 ff.), they had little more than flimsy arguments from probability. Nevertheless, their adviser, Demosthenes, came up with an alternative approach that bears witness not only to his complete mastery of the tactical possibilities that existed in the legal process and in the psychology of the popular courts, but also to his audacity. He does not engage in a hopeless attempt at directly confronting the prosecution's claim; rather, he chooses an alternate route.

In particular, he makes use of the fact that the charge, though actually based on a wrong that was still current, was a repercussion of Aristaichmos' guardianship. [21] By this device he distorts the accusers' claim unexpectedly into one against Aristaichmos' conduct in the guardianship [rather than against his estate]. He then repre-sents the claim as long ago resolved and now legally inadmissible (*ouk eisagōgimos*) by referring to the release that was previously granted, and to the legal limitation imposed on guardianship cases after five years. The entire speech was directed at leading the jurors down this wrong path, a task made easier for the speechwriter by the circumstance that the counter-attack demanded the procedure of *paragraphē*, which resulted in his client having the advantage of giving the opening speech. Speaking first made it possible for him to arrange the arguments in such a way that he could create the impression from the beginning that this case still concerned the issue of the guardianship, which in fact was no longer relevant. By such a tactic, as well as by deliberately distorting the sense of the previous and present grounds for the prosecution's claim in a way that, even upon the closest scrutiny, was scarcely apparent to the casual listeners of the spoken oration, he attempted to distract the jurors from the main point of the case.[25]

Once again we do not know whether or not he was successful. However, we should consider the fact that modern scholars, including even Louis Gernet, philologist, jurist, and one of the most influential experts on Demosthenes of our time, did not recognize that Nausimachos and Xeinopeithes actually no longer derived their current legal claim in this case from Aristaichmos' conduct of the guardianship.[26]

[22]   V

The late time prohibits me from introducing further examples (which do exist) of deceptive,[27] or even misleading, citations of

----

[25] At the time of the account settlement with Aristaichmos, the prosecutors had accused him of not having settled the debt that was still outstanding; now, they referred to the itemization of the debt in the final account that had been drawn up in the meantime and approved by them, and expressed this in their prosecution speech: 'inasmuch as Aristaichmos transferred the debt items to me in the guardianship account.' Out of this, Demosthenes argues: 'at one time they appeal to the settlement of the debt, at another time they complain because no account has been given'; in other words, they give different reasons but always ask for the same exact thing (38. 15, 16)!

[26] Cf. Gernet 1954: 250, 252, n. 2. Earlier philologists and lawyers came to conclusions similar to Gernet's (citations in Wolff 1963: 97, n. 24).

[27] It was up to the speaker in Demosthenes' speech *Against Spudias* (Dem. 41) to give the impression that his opponent, his brother-in-law, received a dowry from their father-in-law for approximately the same amount as he himself did. For this purpose, he made an accounting in which he included personal items for both women that did not actually belong in the dowry and he practically passed over the cash sum that he had agreed on but not yet paid (41. 27 f.). If this complicated summary were delivered aloud quickly, then the scam [*Schwindel*] would be scarcely discernible. But if it were delivered in an ordinary voice, it would be shown to be, if not a bald lie, then a calculated attempt at confusion. For a more detailed analysis, cf. Wolff 1961: 175 ff. A similar trick of confusion can be found in [Dem.] 34. 25–6; cf. Wolff 1966: 68, n. 90.

irrelevant laws.[28] Nevertheless, allow me to conclude with a few general observations.

First, I would like to counter a false impression that my remarks might have evoked: the tactics that I discussed, which are somewhat objectionable according to our own perceptions, and the examples that I offered should not mislead us into envisioning Demosthenes as a shabby hack lawyer! In the Konon case, he did nothing, in my opinion, that any lawyer today would find unconscionable. The speech [23] against Nausimachos and Xeinopeithes demonstrates that, when he had to, he was ready to take crooked paths (a point that is confirmed by some of his other speeches). But here certainly we must take into consideration that the eightfold penalty that threatened his clients truly represented a disproportional hardship, as much as it may have been completely in compliance with formal law. One might wonder in a case such as this if it was not the archaic stiffness of the law that left no room for the *overt* concerns for fairness (of course no one could control the secret vote of individual jurors) that practically forced a litigant into using the tricks of the trade, as we have observed. And examples that are entirely parallel are readily found in the speeches.[29]

---

[28] In the speech against Spudias just mentioned, the speaker defended himself, so it seems, against his opponent's attempt to include a house that was under the administration of their father-in-law but 'mortgaged'—i.e. handed over as a deposit, and if necessary, as security—to him (the speaker) allegedly because of the remaining dowry that the father-in-law had not yet paid. In order to prove that no legal claims could be raised regarding the house, he introduced a law (41. 7) that explicitly excluded claims, so long as an *apotimēma* (mortgage) was in place. In reality, however, this law meant that there should be no suit for the return of a dowry after the marriage ended, as long as dowry items or a piece of property of comparable value belonging to the husband had been given as *apotimēma* to the *kyrios* (legal guardian) of the woman as security on the dowry. The speaker took advantage of the fact that his own case also had something to do with a dowry, and of the version of the regulation that was generally upheld, in order to dispute claims that were not at all governed by this regulation. Cf. Wolff 1954: 308 f., 331.

[29] A similarity (admittedly somewhat distant) exists in *Against Zenothemis* (or. 32). It is possible that Demosthenes was the author of this speech since he was related to the speaker, a certain Demon, but the authenticity is disputed by scholars. Demon made use of arguments that were skilfully devised, but unusually flimsy and hair-splitting in an attempt to thwart the introduction of a trial brought against him by Zenothemis. Although he was perhaps not responsible, Demon found himself in an evidentiary situation so hopeless when it came to the main issue of the case that his only chance lay in blocking the trial altogether (detailed analysis in Wolff 1966: 35 ff).

Given the nature of our sources, such questions related to individual cases must remain open. More important, however, is the main observation that one is guilty of a completely unhistorical approach if one measures Demosthenes and his colleagues against today's ethical standards. And this mistake has in fact been made: Schaeffer (1858: 177–8) practically based his argument against the authenticity of the speech *Against Stephanus I* (Dem. 45) on the fact that Demosthenes had first worked for one side of the case in *For Phormio* (Dem. 36), and then, in the later speech, for the opposing side, when Phormio's witness Stephanus was charged with false testimony; and on top of that, Demosthenes covered each client with insults when he was working for the opposition. This scholar honestly believed that such treachery was not even conceivable for so noble a man! Others,[30] including even the ancient moralist Plutarch, have [24] taken the opposing point of view and either turned their noses up at Demosthenes, or sought out excuses for him.

The first of these opinions has not been accepted at all; the majority of philologists have long been in agreement that Demosthenes is the author of both speeches. But aside from the problem of authenticity, any moralizing critique is also inappropriate because it tends to be guided by abstract considerations that have no relation to the working conditions of the logographers. Let us have a look at the actual situation!

It would be an exaggeration to claim that questions about what is ethically permitted played no role at all for the logographers. Betrayal was considered disgraceful in their time as well, only the boundaries were drawn far more narrowly than now. A remark by Aeschines (2. 165) sheds light on where they lay: in connection with the above-mentioned case, Aeschines accuses Demosthenes of *betraying the confidence* of his client (Phormio) in the first case, but not of composing speeches for both sides. If that had been frowned on, Aeschines certainly would not have passed up the opportunity to hold this too against his mortal enemy.[31]

[30] Cf. Wolff 1966: 50, n. 66. [Trevett 1992: 50–76, reviews the evidence and reaches the same conclusion as Wolff (73).]

[31] Jaeger (1939: 212, n. 34) believes that Aeschines' silence ought to make it clear that he did not have adequate information about the facts. It is hardly imaginable, however, that the machinations of two politicians as well known as Demosthenes and Apollodorus (his opponent in the first trial and client in the second) would have remained hidden from Demosthenes' sworn enemy.

We can conclude, therefore, that the logographer had only a limited responsibility toward his client to abide by 'professional ethics'—if I may use this anachronistic expression here. So it is hardly surprising that we find nothing at all about ethical scruples with regard to an opponent. Certainly the logographer did not consider himself an 'officer of the court'! One expected much the same of him as we do today of an American lawyer, namely that he leave no stone unturned if it would help his client win. It is in [25] this light that we must view not only the shady and unscrupulous manoeuvres, but also attacks that are at times unrestrained against the character of an opponent. Since Demosthenes understood such tactics particularly well, scholars have wished to see them as signs of his supposedly irritable nature (cf. Bruns 1896: 545–6). In no way, however, was he the only one who used these methods, and in this regard we should agree with Werner Jaeger (1939: 41), who characterizes such barrages of insults as simply, from the logographer's perspective, impersonal and in the interest of one's client.

On this subject, it should also be mentioned that the ancients, for whom the general notion of personal rights was still foreign, had an entirely different attitude toward personal invective than we do. To be sure, Athenian law sanctioned a special suit for damages against slander called a *dikē kakēgorias*, but it appears that the conditions for this type of suit were narrowly limited to a fixed catalogue of slanderous expressions.[32]

The general characteristics that I have compiled above make perfect sense when we once again recall the type of person the logographer was, his position within the social structure of the *polis*, and his function. We are dealing with people who were distinguished by no regulated qualifications at all. They did not enjoy any special reputation in the community, and they most likely accomplished their work behind the scenes in the majority of cases. They must have remained anonymous to the masses; and the fact that a few individuals among them achieved fame and political importance changed nothing. They were not a professional group, and obviously could not have developed a professional code of ethics. They did not work for the law but for the interests of their clients. Thus, their only guiding principles were necessarily those of *rhetoric*, that is, the rules

---

[32] The problem requires closer analysis. In the meantime, cf. Lipsius, *AR* 646 ff.

of a craft that lacked any ethical foundation[33] and whose clear purpose, as Wieacker (1965: 22) emphasized, was not to convey objective truths, but simply to *persuade* the audience.

VI

With that, I have reached the end of my contribution. If I may go back to Wieacker's lecture one last time, Wieacker stressed that Cicero's 'effect on later antiquity and on the rest of the European world could not be overrated' (1965: 26). Cicero, however, is inconceivable without Attic oratory of the fifth and fourth centuries. The Athenian logographers, including Demosthenes, were a long way from what the civilized world today associates with the profession of lawyer. In the legal history of antiquity, however, as far as we can tell, they were the first to be concerned professionally with providing some support to litigants.[34] At the very least, the tradition of this profession that still exists today began with them. In this sense, we are justified in concluding that the history of European advocacy started with them, and above all, with Demosthenes, as the one among them who had the strongest influence on posterity. Therein lies their importance, and the importance of Demosthenes, for the world history of law.

Epilogue

Gerhard Thür

Hans Julius Wolff gave his famous Berlin lecture, 'Demosthenes als Advokat', in the summer of 1967, when he was at the high point of his

---

[33] As scholars have often observed; see e.g. Wolf 1956: 159.

[34] Even though the practice of rhetoric as an art form originated in Sicily, we do not have a record of anything similar from there.

work on Athenian law of procedure. Just one year earlier his book on the *paragraphē* ('special plea') was published, and in the fall of 1967 he spoke in Venice about the significance of Athenian court speeches for the study of legal history (Wolff 1971). His strength lay in his 'wide-angle analysis' of the speeches—*Gesamtinterpretation*—an approach that he himself developed. In Wolff's view, the law of Athens cannot be understood from individual passages observed in isolation, but rather from the everyday practices of the *dikastēria*, as large juries of laymen. Wolff recognized that the original legal aim of a suit could only be explained in modern times by carefully peeling away the rhetorical layers of the case. He thus arrived at new insights regarding Greek family, contract, and procedural law.

His lecture itself leads us into a world of trial procedure that is foreign to us. Wolff emphasizes the external conditions, in particular the strict rules of the competition (*agōn*) that took place between litigants in front of the lay-judges. The implicit rules of conduct before the court are thereby also determined. What Athenian litigants needed most of all, in addition to legal advice, was a rhetorical strategy. The orators offered both. These experts are roughly described as 'advocates'; 'speechwriters' is more fitting (*logographoi*; see Wolff 1964). With Demosthenes as a paradigm, Wolff explores the working conditions and mindset of the Athenian legal expert without modern prejudice. His overall assessment is still valid today.[35]

Wolff was also an astute scholar of Roman and late antique law. After 1970 he devoted himself to legal papyrology (Wolff 1978–2002), a study that he had begun in his youth. Thus, this version of his 1967 lecture, newly published here in English, has the ring of a parting tribute to the discipline that he brought to maturity.

A comprehensive bibliography of Wolff's scholarship can be found in *Symposion 1977* (Modrzejewski and Liebs 1982), pp. xiii–xxviii. A supplement, covering publications that appeared until Wolff's death in 1983, is provided in the obituary that I wrote in *Zeitschrift der Savigny Stiftung* in 1984 (*ZRG* 101: 476–92, esp. 491–2).

---

[35] For a more recent appraisal of rhetoric and law in ancient Athens, see *The Cambridge Companion to Ancient Greek Law* (Gagarin and Cohen 2005), Part 2: Law in Athens I: Procedure.

6

Law and Equity in the Attic Trial*

HARALD MEYER-LAURIN

I. THE PROBLEM AND THE APPROACH

The following work will investigate whether there was regard for equity in Athenian positive law. The question has already been repeatedly posed in the literature. Particular thanks are due to Vinogradoff for fundamental investigations on the topic.[1] He came to the conclusion that equity was a fixed element of legal discourse. *Epieikeia*, which he translated as 'fairness' and 'justice in the highest sense', was for him 'the central term of legal discourse' (1922: ii. 71) and 'the most characteristic contribution of Greece to the treatment of legal problems' (1928: ii. 15). Among more recent authors, Gernet (1955a: 67), J. W. Jones (1956: 64 ff.), and in particular Stoffels, in his dissertation (1954), have argued that judgement among the Greeks was not strictly according to the laws but according to equity. Paoli also saw in the laws only a guideline, from which it was possible to diverge on grounds of higher justice.[2]

---

* David Mirhady translates the main text for the first four chapters of Meyer-Laurin's *Gesetz und Billigkeit im attischen Prozess* (1965). The notes are somewhat condensed (largely at the hand of the editor). In this part of the study Meyer-Laurin makes his case against what were then conventional views on argument from fairness or 'equity' in the Attic Orators. For the remaining chapters a translation can be found at http://www.sfu.ca/nomoi/ml5-7.htm.

[1] Vinogradoff 1922: ii. 63 ff.; 1928: ii. 15 ff. Cf. Hirzel 1900: 57 ff.; Weiss 1923: 75; Kübler 1934: 94–5.

[2] Paoli 1933: 33 ff., 39 ff. To the contrary, esp. Arangio-Ruiz 1946: 242, n. 1; Wolff 1962: 17–18.

These authors concern themselves largely with the considerations of the Greek legal thinkers, especially Plato and Aristotle, and believe in a strong influence of theoretical speculation on practical law. Above all Vinogradoff (1928: ii. 19) starts from the observation that Aristotle, in teaching concerning *epieikeia* developed in *NE* 5 and *Rhetoric* 1. 13, created for the Athenian judges 'a mechanism for the free interpretation of law'.

[2] Other researchers, however, starting from the perspective of positive law, have always argued that there is a big difference between Greek law and Greek legal philosophy. In his review of Maschke's *Willenslehre*, Kunkel gave a warning that must be noted:[3] 'Philosophical speculation is far ahead of actual legal practice, the techniques of legislation and trials . . . The ethical ideal that speaks from the abstract thought processes of Aristotle and the concrete descriptions of Plato may be impressive, but life deals with ordinary measures, not with the high ideals the philosopher poses for himself and others. There is here a great divide between positive law and philosophy that necessarily precludes equating them.'

In his *Willenslehre*, Maschke showed the difference between theory and practice with the example of the moment of decision and guilt. Wolff (1961: 254, n. 15) expressed the concern that even Aristotle's attempt to portray a doctrine of *epieikeia* as a corrective to *ius strictum* appears to have had no impact on the positive law of Athens.

For this reason, in what follows the question of whether litigants appeal to equity arguments and the courts react to equity considerations will be considered exclusively on the basis of the surviving forensic speeches. In this we are concerned only with the principles of jurisprudence. Rhetorical appeals to equity and the common argumentation *ad personam*, even when they are carried on in detail, have nothing to do with the basic principles of jurisprudence according to which the dicasts were to judge. It certainly cannot be ruled out that in the legal reality of Athens all sorts of points, including such [equity] arguments, were occasionally considered emotionally and that the heliasts thus unknowingly broke their judicial oath.

---

[3] Kunkel 1928: 710; cf. Wolff 1961: 250 ff.

However, given the nature of the subject, such circumstances are imponderable and do not lend themselves to systematic study. [...]

[3]   II. FRAUD AS A DEFENCE CLAIM

Kübler (1934: 87) argued that in Athenian law there was for a long time a formal objection (*Einrede*) similar to the *exceptio doli* ('exception for fraud'). His idea, that the existence of such an argument could be shown from Hyperides' *Against Athenogenes*, has already been rejected on compelling grounds in the literature. However, it remains to be investigated whether, in general, such a formal objection is even conceivable in Attic law. [Two procedural parallels are considered, (1) *diamarturia* and (2) *paragraphē*.]

1. The *diamarturia* was certainly not a suitable legal mechanism for this purpose. As a form of decisive formal evidence, it entailed that there was no longer a trial over the matter before judges. The inadmissibility of the opponent's case, or the admissibility of one's own case, was demonstrated simply through the statement of a witness.[4] If the opposing party wanted to pursue his demands further, he had to prosecute the witness for his statement through a *dikē pseudomarturiōn*. If he won this case, he could take up the latent main issue anew.

[4]   2. But could the *paragraphē* perhaps be proposed as an *exceptio doli*? In the form common in the forensic speeches of the fourth century it had existed only since the law of Archinus in 403 (cf. Isoc. 18. 2; Lys. 23. 5, 10). In contrast to the *diamarturia*, with the *paragraphē* the assertion that the opponent's suit was inadmissible was offered by the defendant before the *hēgemon* ('presiding magistrate')

----

[4] There is some dispute whether by law the *diamarturia* was exclusively applicable in inheritance cases and the *paragraphē* unavailable in this area (Beauchet 1897: iii. 596, n. 2; Leisi 1908: 29) or whether it was simply more appropriate in inheritance disputes than the *paragraphē* (Calhoun 1918: 173–8; Bonner and Smith 1938: 76, 79). It is also disputed whether *diamarturia* was also available outside inheritance cases. These questions can be left aside here.

of the appropriate heliastic court. However, the suit was not set aside entirely on this basis; it was instead passed on to the heliasts, who simply had to decide first the question of the admissibility of the complaint that was posed through the *paragraphē*.[5]

This procedure certainly recalls the *exceptio* of the Roman formulary procedure in a certain way. For this reason the *paragraphē* became known as an 'exception' and was placed in parallel with the Roman *exceptio*.[6] In fact, however, it involves circumstances specified in Athenian legislation in which 'there were to be no suits' (*mē einai dikas*), whereby it was left up to the accused party to dispute as 'inadmissible' (*mē eisagōgimos*) the 'suit' (*dikē*) that had been brought.[7]

Our main source for these legal cases is Pollux 8. 57, although his listing is in no way exhaustive:

Paragraphē—whenever someone claims that the suit is inadmissible, either as having been already decided, or on the grounds that there had been an arbitration, or that he had been released, or that the time had run out in which it had to have been tried (or that this suit was not to be tried...)

Several of the grounds named by Pollux, like those in certain legal citations in the orators, correspond to *exceptiones* in [5] Roman law (e.g. lack of jurisdiction by the particular court, [questionable] validity of the law, expiration of time-limit).[8] However, none corresponds to the *exceptio doli*. This circumstance alone of course in no way proves the absence of such grounds for a *paragraphē*, for the survival of Athenian legal provisions is very incomplete.

The pseudo-Demosthenic speech *Against Zenothemis* ([Dem.] 32), which involves a *paragraphē*, indicates that a case for *paragraphē* comparable to the *exceptio doli* really seems as yet unknown. According

---

[5] Cf. Calhoun 1918: 169; 1919: 344 ff.; Paoli 1933: 97 ff.; Steinwenter 1934: 87, n. 5, 384; Hellebrand, *RE* 18. 3 (s.v. *Paragraphē*) 1176–7; Wolff 1963: 102, n. 38.

[6] Dareste 1875: i. xx; Lipsius, *AR* 845 ff.; Gernet 1955a: 86, n. 4.

[7] Against the comparison with *exceptio doli*, see esp. Paoli 1933: 119–20; Hellebrand, *RE* 18.3, 1173; Wolff 1963: 102.

[8] Wolff 1963: 108 showed that the perspective of equity played no role in the application of *prothesmia* ('statute of limitations').

to the defendant's narrative, here was a typical case in which, by our terminology, an appeal to *exceptio doli* would have been made.[9]

The importer Protos took out a loan from Athenian lenders, one of whom was the defendant, Demon, using as collateral the grain that was to be bought with the money. He used the ship of the Massilian Hegestratos, who had for his part also received money on the collateral of the ship and cargo for shipping grain to Athens. The prosecutor Zenothemis, a compatriot of Hegestratos, travelled along with them.

In Syracuse the ship was loaded only with the grain purchased by Protos.[10] Hegestratos and Zenothemis exploited this fact for their deceitful plan. They took out a maritime loan from Massilian lenders for which they used the ship's [6] cargo as security as if it were their own property.[11] In order to escape the obligation to pay it back, they intended to sink the ship during the voyage to Athens. This trickery went amiss. Hegestratos was caught in the act and threw himself into the sea in fear of the angered crew.

The already damaged ship had to make for the harbor at Kephallenia, where it was repaired. During this time Zenothemis made efforts to get a ruling from the harbour authorities in Kephallenia according to which the ship would have to continue travelling not to Athens, but to Massilia. Since the plan cooked up with Hegestratos had gone amiss, he intended to disappear in his home city in order at least to escape the grasp of the Athenian lenders (8). However, Protos successfully objected, and by order of the harbour authorities the ship had to travel to Athens. Once reaching Athens, Protos at first appeared to have possession of the landed grain shipment; Zenothemis

[9] Research into the actual situation does not concern us here; of interest are simply the one-sided presentation that the speaker gives and the legal conclusions that he draws from it. [Meyer-Laurin lists various treatments and then analyses them in the succeeding notes (partly abridged in this translation): Blass, *AB* iii. 492 ff.; Leist 1896: 54 ff.; Mitteis 1902: 288 ff.; Rabel 1915: 367 ff.; Pringsheim 1916: 10 ff.; Vinogradoff 1928: ii. 24 ff.; Photiades 1925; Gernet 1954: 110 ff.]

[10] Gernet 1955*a* (among others): 113–16, treats Protos as the crook, as he had not used the money he received to buy the grain. But Gernet cannot then explain Hegestratos' attempt to scuttle the boat as anything other than an obscure incident.

[11] Mitteis 1902: 289, and Vinogradoff 1928: ii. 25, wrongly suppose that (both) ship and cargo are pledged (as collateral); for a clear explanation see Pringsheim 1916: 12; cf. Gernet 1954: 114.

protested this and put in a demand for the grain, claiming that it was not Protos but Hegestratos who had bought it and pledged it to him (Zenothemis) as security for a loan (14, 'he "made a dispute", *ēmphesbētei*, over the grain, claiming he had made a loan to Hegestratos'). That was a lie, but led to an *embateusis* ('assumption of control') of the cargo without there being need for proof of his claims.[12] Zenothemis [7] took control by asserting his claim to the cargo as security; this was an especially strong position legally, similar to ownership, to which he held fast from then on (17).

For this reason Protos conducted a 'removal', an *exagōgē*, against him (17). Zenothemis responded, however, that he would not submit to such treatment unless it were carried out by Demon ('this man... said specifically that he would not be removed by anyone but me', 17). He apparently meant by this that no one, other than Demon at best, had any right to the cargo that was better than his own. Mitteis pointed out Zenothemis' goal in this:[13] he could never hope to win a suit against Protos, who had all the evidence on his side, so he had to try to get Protos onto his side and have Demon as his opponent, who had no direct evidence without Protos. He initiated this plan by portraying Demon as the actual importer and Protos simply as his agent.

The trick worked. When the price of grain suddenly fell in Athens, Protos had to fear that if he continued to represent himself, as he had, as an independent importer (25), he would become personally responsible not for a profit but for the shortfall (*ekdeia*) between the amount of the loan and the proceeds from the security (30). He therefore adopted Zenothemis' thesis and claimed from then on that he had merely acquired the grain as an agent of Demon and on his (Demon's) account (25). Therefore, a dispute over the cargo did not concern him and it would be no concern of his if Demon relinquished the grain (19).

In order not to lose everything, both the loan and the security, without a fight, there remained no alternative for Demon other than

---

[12] Rabel 1915: 369, Pringsheim 1916: 13, and Vinogradoff 1928: ii. 31, point to the expression *ēmphesbētei* as indicating a *diadiakasia*.

[13] Mitteis 1902: 290 f. [Meyer-Laurin (nn. 25–7) cites further discussion in *ZRG* 36–9: Rabel 1915: 369–70; 1917: 311–12; Lipsius 1916: 11–12; 1918: 49–50.]

to take over the [8] *exagōgē* himself against Zenothemis (18, 'I had to choose either to put Zenothemis out, or to lose my property which had been brought safe to port and was there before my eyes'; 20, 'the only course left... was to remove this man'). Thereupon Zenothemis brought suit on the basis of a *sungraphē* ('written agreement') which Demon did not dispute (16), in which Hegestratos had pledged to him the grain cargo as security for a loan.[14]

Demon clearly regarded the conduct of Zenothemis as malicious: 'the man, whom no one would have thought audacious enough to come here, after having plotted and done such deeds—this man, Athenians, has so surpassed all in shamelessness and boldness, that he has not only come, but has actually laid claim to my grain and brought suit against me' (9).

Since most of the speech consists of a portrayal of Zenothemis' behaviour as deceitful, one would expect that he would also make this the grounds for his *paragraphē*. In fact, he does begin his remarks with the claim that he will show that the suit is inadmissible with reference to the lies and intrigues of the accuser (2, 'the same speech will suffice to prove to you that his action is not maintainable and to make you see the whole of his plot and his rascality'; 3, 'you will hear of a man's audacity and uncommon villainy').

It is all the more striking that the *paragraphē* is clearly based on different grounds. Demon makes use of the purely formal distinction that Zenothemis brought the charge as a *dikē emporikē* ('maritime suit'). He is of the opinion that a *dikē emporikē* is inadmissible because no contract exists between him and the plaintiff. He appeals to the following law: 'actions for shippers and merchants shall be upon obligations for shipments to or from Athens and concerning which there shall be written agreements' (1; cf. Dem. 33. 1 and 34. 42). The grounding of the *paragraphē* scarcely goes beyond [9] this

---

[14] In the literature it is generally assumed that the suit was a *dikē exoulēs* ('suit for ejectment'): cf. Rabel 1915: 367; Lipsius 1916: 12; Gernet 1954: 116. Some have misgivings, as the *dikē exoulēs* is the remedy of an executor against a possessor who will not relinquish the property and the latter is precisely the role of Zenothemis. Lipsius had supposed a *dikē blabēs* ('suit for damage'): AR 656 f. with n. 77. Mitteis 1902: 291, considered the whole matter of a *sungraphē* 'obviously invented'; Pringsheim 1916: 13, to the contrary; cf. Vinogradoff 1928: ii. 28.

plain reading of the law (1, 23).[15] It is not only exceedingly short and meagre in comparison with the portrayal of the fraudulent machinations of the accuser, but also doubtful in legal terms.

It is crucial what meaning is given to the wording of the law. If one interprets it to the effect that, of contractual obligations (*sumbolaia*) that have been undertaken for the purpose of sea trade concerning Athens, *only* those under a written agreement (*sungraphē*) can be the basis for a *dikē emporikē*,[16] then, to this extent, Demon's *paragraphē* is well grounded; for between him and Zenothemis no written agreement existed. But if one separates the two half-sentences from each other, so that 'concerning which' does not refer restrictively to 'the obligations', then the law means, for *all* obligations that are undertaken for the purpose of maritime commerce and concern the city of Athens and, *in addition*, in *all* commerce for which a *sungraphē* exists, a *dikē emporikē* is admissible'.[17] As Gernet (1954: 122) has shown, this second meaning not only corresponds better than the first to the spirit of the legislation, which is supposed to facilitate maritime trade, but also to the letter of the text, in which, significantly, not the term *sunthēkē* ('contract') but rather the more inclusive *sumbolaion* ('obligation') is used. If one follows this view, one arrives at the conclusion that in this dispute a *dikē emporikē* is admissible since it concerns a transaction of maritime trade between merchants. Demon would then have tried to foist the narrow meaning of *sunthēkē* upon the word *sumbolaion*.

Even if he is successful in the *paragraphē* (the result of the trial is not known), since it was based on the claim that the commercial court did not have jurisdiction, Demon must have expected the same charge to be brought against him again before the proper court. In any case he had to expect this [10] if Zenothemis was an Athenian metic.[18] If the prosecutor belonged to the class of *epidēmountes*

---

[15] Blass, *AB* iii. 495, and Gernet 1954: 116, n. 2, emphasized the inadequacy of the grounds.

[16] Blass, *AB* iii. 495; Lipsius, *AR* 632, n. 18; Weiss 1923: 437 with n. 31 and *ZRG* 52 (1932), 443.

[17] Hitzig 1907: 227 ff.; Partsch 1909: 153; Gernet 1954: 111–12, and 1955*a*: 187.

[18] On litigation rights of metics, cf. Meier-Schömann 1883–7: ii. 753; Lipsius, *AR* 369 ff.; Hitzig 1907: 218–24; Weiss 1923: 178; Busolt 1920: 292–8; Hommel, *RE* 15.2 [1932], 1443 ff.; on rights of aliens, Hitzig 1907: 227–31; Busolt-Swoboda 1926: 1243; Vinogradoff 1928: ii. 29; Photiades 1925: 132; Gernet 1954: 117.

('visitors'), who stayed in Athens exclusively to transact business until their cargoes were landed or otherwise for a short visit, then he was, as a *xenos* ('foreigner') largely without rights and legally incompetent. The 'foreigners' were apparently allowed access to 'commercial suits' but otherwise only to those disputes that came about through contracts (*sumbola*) regulated by treaty between Athens and the home city of the 'foreigner'.

On the other hand, a successful claim of fraud would have entirely ruled out the possibility for a further charge. According to the defendant's narrative, that would not only have been expected, but it would have been the surest means of meeting the charge. Since Demon, despite describing Zenothemis' behaviour as fraudulent, used a formal objection against the admissibility of the suit, it seems clear that no criterion comparable to the *exceptio doli* was available to him for the *paragraphē*.

It remains unclear why he describes the substantive legal position so fully, if it was not required to ground the *paragraphē*. This observation can be made, more or less, with regard to all the *paragraphē* speeches. In addition, the speakers almost excuse themselves for having proceeded with a *paragraphē*, insisting that they could have refuted the claims of their accusers even without this means of defence (Dem. 36. 2). Conversely, from the prosecutor's point of view, a defence by means of a *paragraphē* is automatically suspect (Dem. 35. 1–2), as is a *diamarturia* (Dem. 44. 57; Isae. 3. 3–4; 6. 3, 43).

[11]   One might conclude that this legal mechanism often served as a last resort, in order to prolong the dispute, and for this reason provoked an unfavourable prejudice among the dicasts (Dem. 36. 2). However, it must be pointed out that in fact only a small, scarcely discernible, prejudice could have existed against 'special pleas', for in the trial of Apollodorus against his stepfather Phormio over four-fifths of the judges voted for Phormio, who had defended himself with a *paragraphē*.[19] That does not explain, of course, why the substantive issue [as opposed to the legal question] is always set forth in the *paragraphē* speeches.

---

[19] With Dem. 36 and 45.6, cf. Lipsius, *AR* 856; Bonner and Smith 1938: 85–8.

Scholars have tried to solve this problem by pointing out that the heliasts, because of their 'limited formal legal understanding, wanted to decide on the "real" question' (Lämmli 1938: 16; Paoli 1933: 40–1). This supposition seems to ignore the formalistic traits of Attic law. It is incompatible with the apparent attempt in the Zenothemis speech, and in the other *paragraphē* speeches, to justify the *paragraphē* by giving conclusive evidence, that a legal condition hinders the bringing of what is, in itself, a possibly admissible 'suit'.

The Pantainetos speech (Dem. 37. 32–6) seems to show how seriously litigants adhered to the *paragraphē* criteria. Pantainetos charged Nikobolos for 'damages' (*blabē*) by means of a *dikē metallikē* (22). The 'charge' (*enklēma*) must also have entailed other allegations, such as 'assault' (*aikeia*), 'hybris', 'violence' (*biaia*), and 'injustices towards heiresses' (33, *pros epiklērous adikēmata*). The accused defended himself by means of a *paragraphē*. Against the claim of 'damages' he appealed to a 'release and discharge' (*aphesis kai apallagē*: 1, 17, 19). Against the other allegations he objected that they could not properly be made part of the current 'suit', since there were special suits and separate jurisdictions for them. This part of the *paragraphē* had been erased by the Thesmothetae [who presided over the case] (34). That could only have taken place because it was inadmissible, for [12] the heliasts would have had to decide the question of their own authority.[20] It seems clear that the Thesmothetae erased the questionable passage for this reason, because the special plea—that it was inadmissible to make multiple claims together before one court that was not responsible for them all—was based not on an explicit legal requirement but on an inference from the laws.

Paoli has given one plausible explanation why not only the special pleas contained in the *paragraphai* are brought forward in the *paragraphē* speeches but also the entire legal and substantive arguments against the suit itself.[21] He tried to show that in the same session,

---

[20] See Hellebrand, *RE* 18.3, 1177; cf. Calhoun 1919: 344 ff.; Paoli 1933: 97 ff.; Steinwenter 1934: 384; [on the competence of the archons] Lipsius, *AR* 874–5; Busolt-Swoboda 1926: 1100.

[21] Paoli 1933: 75–173 speaks of 'the indivisibility' of the issues at trial in Attic law. [With works cited in the previous notes,] cf. Wolff 1963: 102, n. 38; [and Wolff 1966, against Paoli's model (EC)].

before the same judges, there was a vote first on the admissibility of the *paragraphē* and then, if necessary, on the suit. For this reason arguments on the issue itself were brought forward right from the beginning.

3. Are equity arguments apparent in other cases? Vinogradoff claims that in the dispute against Dionysodoros (Dem. 56) the accused clearly pleads *vis maior* and that, it follows, he could expect the clemency of the jurors.[22]

Dionysodoros and Parmeniskos had taken out a maritime loan in the amount of 3,000 drachmas on the security [13] of their ship. In the *sungraphē* it stated that the money was only allotted for a trip from Athens to Egypt and directly back; otherwise there would be a double penalty. As always in a maritime loan the contract contained the clause that the capital was only to be paid back if the ship returned safely to the Piraeus. Parmeniskos had gone to Egypt and bought grain and other goods. On the return trip the ship became disabled and was only able to reach the harbour at Rhodes badly damaged.

Dionysodoros now asked the lenders, in view of the non-culpable shipping accident,[23] whether he might pay back the loaned capital as well as interest for the stretch of the journey actually completed by the ship, from Athens to Egypt and from there back to Rhodes (12, 13, 33, 34, 38, 41). Other lenders agreed to this (22). Dareios and Pamphilos, however, stood by their demand for payment of the entire interest agreed upon, since the contract did not foresee any different rule for capital and interest (35). They were only ready to

[22] Vinogradoff 1922: ii. 28; 1928: ii. 19–20. Dareste 1875: 337 also supposed that the defendant has appealed to equity.

[23] Beauchet 1897: iv. 284 took it as self-evident that the cargo was also pledged (though not expressly set forth in the contract). This is unconvincing; in Dem. 32. 14 a maritime loan is mentioned in which clearly it is only the ship that is pledged as security. In favour of Beauchet's assumption is simply the fact that the borrowers were barred from offloading and selling the cargo en route (Dem. 56. 10); but the only security expressly mentioned is the ship. Cf. Pringsheim 1916: 14–15. Beauchet believed (306) that the creditor must relinquish part of the interest in view of the debtor's claim of *force majeur*, limiting his liability. But the plaintiff's rigid posture towards Dionysodoros at least suggests that no such obligation was clear. In Dem. 34. 32 another contract is mentioned where capital and accumulated interest can be paid after the voyage out, but it envisions no part-payment of the interest if the return voyage is cut short.

accept the money offered as partial payment, but reserved the right to pursue the remaining interest through litigation (14–15). [14] On this basis Dionysodoros paid them nothing at all, and he was unwilling to submit the dispute to a private arbitrator (18).

Since they were unable to obtain payment, the creditors sued Dionysodoros as sole debtor, for double the amount, on the grounds that the ship, although not sunk, had travelled not to the Piraeus but to Rhodes (20, 27, 38, 41, 44).[24] But the accused, like the accusers, cited the wording of the contract, according to which the money only became due if the ship reached the agreed port safely. He did not appeal to *vis maior* (as the speaker's charges show). He was instead concerned with the question whether, because the ship became disabled, even if it did not sink, already the negative condition of the contract—if the ship did not return safely—had been fulfilled (31–2, and esp. 41, 'you have the insolence to declare that the vessel did not arrive safe at the Piraeus'). Therefore both sides dispute in formal terms over interpretation of this clause of the contract.

One case, in which the accused could have pleaded the unreasonableness [of the charge], pertains to the pseudo-Demosthenic speech against Polycles ([Dem.] 50). In the literature it has not yet, it seems, been discussed from this aspect.

Apollodorus had as trierarch spent lavishly on the equipping of a trireme. He had not, as was the usual practice, taken the ship's equipment supplied by the state authorities, but instead provided his own equipment which was especially ostentatious. He also chose to forgo employing the Athenians who had been drafted for military service and assigned to him and hired a mercenary crew at his own cost.

After his appointment had run out, his successor Polycles was supposed to take over the trireme. Polycles appeared with the fleet at Thasos and put himself under the command of the general Timomachos. However, he refused to take the ship over from Apollodorus on the grounds that it [15] was unreasonable for him to have to carry

---

[24] Beauchet 1897: iv. 396, Lipsius, *AR* 633, 657, and Gernet 1955*a*: 217, treat the suit as a *dikē blabēs*; Blass, *AB* iii.2, 521, and Pringsheim 1950: 53, as *dikē daneiou*. Gernet doubts that a *dikē daneiou* was available. Probably the plaintiffs base their charge simply on the *sungraphē*, since for them, as for the defendant, so much depends on the interpretation of the contract. This insight I owe to Prof. Wolff.

on the high expense, since he would have to take over the private ship equipment and the expensive crew (10, 34–6).

As a result Apollodorus had to remain in service for over five months longer and was only able to return home when the whole fleet was ordered back to Athens. There he sued Polycles for 'damages' to recoup the expenses he had incurred during the time in which Polycles was supposed to have been in command of the trireme. He cited the decree according to which Polycles had had to report to the ship (29) and take it over.

In the speech there is no mention of the grounds for defence (Blass, *AB* iii.1: 527). Apparently Polycles did not plead that the charge was unreasonable. For if that had been a legally valid objection, the speaker would not have admitted plainly that the accused had refused for this reason to take over the ship (10). His only recourse was to appeal to the wording of the decree and claim that by travelling to the fleet and being present with the general he had fulfilled the decree. The dispute was thus solely over interpretation of the decree.

III. EQUITY ARGUMENTS ON THE PROSECUTION SIDE

1. The most important source for our subject is Hyperides' speech *Against Athenogenes*, in which the speaker tries to get free of a contract that came about through fraud. As Partsch put it, the case concerns 'a challenge similar to an *actio de dolo*' (1909: 172, n. 6; cf. Pringsheim 1950: 24, n. 2).

[16] The speaker Epicrates fell in love with a slave who was employed, together with his father and brother, in a perfume business belonging to the metic Athenogenes. Athenogenes learned of the relationship and saw in it the possibility to get rid of the perfumery, which was heavily indebted. He forbade Epicrates further access to the youth, but suggested to him at the same time to purchase all three slaves for 40 minas. In the ensuing negotiations he hypocritically advised him not just to purchase the slaves' freedom but to acquire

them for himself, together with the shop in which they were employed and all its assets and liabilities.[25] He gave assurance, contrary to the truth, that only small debts encumbered the shop, which would be more than offset by its stock. As soon as he had won Epicrates over to this suggestion, he took out a prepared draft of the contract and insisted that the document be immediately sealed and deposited.

Then the parties went to the perfume business, where the transfer of the shop took place upon payment of the purchase price.[26] That had scarcely taken place when the shop's first creditors were demanding their money from Epicrates. After three months the demands ran to 5 talents altogether.

When Epicrates read through his copy of the contract in greater detail he realized that he had not only taken over the small business debts specified, but that he had also agreed, through a seemingly innocuous clause, to assume liability for all obligations that the manager Midas had incurred in running the business (10). He felt himself deceived and complained to Athenogenes, who, however, appealed to the wording of the contract. He denied having known the extent of the debts that had not been indicated in detail.

[17] Epicrates brought a suit for damages. The damages consisted of the 40 minas that he had paid.[27] Through the contract Athenogenes had caused him 'injurious disposition of goods'.[28] On this basis the speaker tried to demonstrate the invalidity of the contract.

The speech shows that there was no general rule according to which a contract could be cancelled because of malicious deception. The speaker would otherwise have mentioned the relevant law

---

[25] Taking over the business [together with the slaves] must have been included in the contract, although it is not specified [in the surviving speech]. If the textual supplement is right at § 18, the 40 mina sale price expressly included the shop. See Hitzig 1897: 168–9; Partsch 1909: 69–70, 322; Pringsheim 1950: 192, n. 1.

[26] Only at this stage was the sale complete; cf. Pringsheim 1916: 52; 1950: 173, 192.

[27] Blass, *AB* iii.2, 83, and Maschke 1926: 104, 166–7, see the damage (*blabē*) in the loss that Epicrates incurred by assuming the business's debts when he was deceived as to their magnitude. Maschke, however, admits to being unable to explain why the speaker attempts to prove the invalidity of the contract because of deceit.

[28] The concept of *blabē* as 'injurious disposition of goods' (*schädigende Vermögensverfügung*) is developed by Wolff 1957: 63.

instead of deriving the contract's invalidity by analogy from various statutes specific to other matters.[29]

Some authors assume that he was appealing to equity.[30] They refer to § 13, where the absolute validity of contracts is rejected: 'only just (agreements), my good man; (contracts) that are not (just) it renounces as invalid.' This sentence is supposed to show the legal possibility of voiding a contract that has come about through malicious deception.

That the accuser was actually unable to refer back simply to the evident deceit of the accused shows again that he had to use statutory provisions of more limited application [18] to prove the contract invalid. Even the first rule cited by him makes clear that dealings negotiated through tricks were not generally invalid. It involves regulations for officials keeping order in the market, which prohibited malicious deceit specifically in small transactions (*kapeleia*) in the agora (14). In order to apply this specific regulation to his case, the speaker speaks as if he had been deceived in the middle of the marketplace and passes silently over the fact that it had nothing to do with a market sale ('Yet you lied in the middle of the market when you made the agreement to defraud me', 14).

The second rule was also apparently only a market regulation, through which a further special case of deceit was supposed to be prevented. It prohibited the selling of slaves while concealing their injuries and diseases (15). The laws cited subsequently do not involve any cases of fraud at all. There are rules about the requirements for a legally valid marriage (16) and the clause of the inheritance law concerning volition (17). Finally, there is a law, which is not otherwise preserved, according to which that person is liable to whom a slave belonged when he caused any 'damages and losses' (22). This law probably regulated a kind of liability for a case where the seller

---

[29] Beauchet 1897: iv. 35 ff.; Hitzig 1897: 184; Lipsius, *AR* 685; Partsch 1909: 172 with n. 6; Maschke 1926: 170; Pringsheim 1950: 498 with n. 1. To the contrary, Sieveking 1893: 30, n. 3, supposes that there was certainly a law that the speaker invokes.

[30] Vinogradoff 1922: ii. 68; 1928: ii. 20–1; Gernet 1955: 80, n. 3; Stoffels 1954: 33. Kübler's view (1934: 87–8) of an objection corresponding to Roman *exceptio doli* is incorrect for the very reason that here we have no 'objection' but rather a charge to be debated.

did not pay and the slave is seized by an injured third party, but it certainly does not entail any rules that might best apply here, about reparation for non-performance or poor compliance.

[19]   In sum, the argumentation of the speaker consists of an arbitrary listing of laws in which certain acts are declared invalid, but none fits his case. However, he applies these proscriptions in order to prove the nullity of his contract with Athenogenes. His approach can only be explained, not as an explicit appeal to equity, but as an attempt to bring his suit into conformity with legal provisions.

2. Dareste (1875: iv. 70–1) and Vinogradoff (1922: ii. 61; 1928: ii. 21–2) also see a suit for fraud based on equity in the dispute of Demosthenes *Against Onetor* (Dem. 30–1). As a result of a suit of Demosthenes, Aphobus had been sentenced to a payment of 10 talents because of his poorly conducted guardianship (Dem. 29. 60). In fulfilment of this, Demosthenes wanted to seize, among other things, a property worth 1 talent. Aphobus had, however, purportedly given it to his brother-in-law Onetor as security for the return of his wife's dowry. Onetor had placed *horoi* ('markers') on the property even before the end of the guardianship trial and taken it into his possession as *kyrios* for the wife when, after Aphobus' conviction, the marriage was dissolved. When Demosthenes also laid claim to it, Onetor executed a 'removal' (*exagōgē*) against him. Against this Demosthenes brought suit by means of a 'suit for ejectment' (*dikē exoulēs*).

Dareste and Vinogradoff suppose Demosthenes to be trying to assert with this suit that protection of a ward from deceitful guardians demands priority over security for a dowry. Such a supposition is in no way justified by Demosthenes' argumentation. His principal argument against the legal admissibility of the 'removal' is precisely that there is no security for a dowry at all, since the dowry to be secured had never been paid to Aphobus (30. 4, 7–24). His ancillary argument is just as formal: that the marriage between Aphobus and Onetor's sister had never been dissolved, so there had been no legitimate claim for the dowry that would have required security (Dem. 30. 25 ff., 33 ff.). Demosthenes would best have made an appeal [to equity] [20] if he had conceded the formal legality of the security arrangement, but nevertheless laid claim to the property based on the deception.

3. Isaeus' speech *On the Estate of Cleonymus* (Isae. 1) has often been presented as an example of a challenge against a will based on equity. The speaker tried, as it is argued, to construe his clients' precedence with respect to the estate from their closer blood relationship.[31] Long before his death, purportedly out of enmity against the guardian of his nearest relatives (who were then still under age), Cleonymus had decided that after his death not these but more distant relatives should receive his estate. He left the document about these matters with an *astynomos* ('city supervisor') for official safekeeping. In the literature it is mostly accepted as Cleonymus' will, which he apparently had left with the authorities out of special concern that his bequest should reach his appointed heirs.[32]

Immediately before his death he wanted to make another modification and authorized one of his appointed heirs to get the document. He died, however, before the change could be made. At this point the intestate heirs put in a claim for the estate. They cited their nearer relationship, as well as the good understanding they shared with the testator (4, 17, 37, 38, 41–4), and claimed that he had only had the will fetched in order to abrogate it in their favour (3, 14). In formal, juristic terms this argument was very weak in comparison with the claim of the appointed heirs, who could point to the document.[33] If the speaker had really appealed only to this, there would be a true equity claim. It must not escape notice, however, that he challenged the will at the same time as 'invalid'. He claims the testator [21] had composed it when 'disturbed' (*paraphronōn* 11, 20, 21, 43, 50).[34] Despite the

---

[31] Blass, *AB* ii.2, 529; Vinogradoff 1922: ii. 67, 79 f.; Wolf 1956: 204.

[32] Wyse 1904: 177; Meier-Schömann 1883–7: i. 52, 108; Beauchet 1897: iii. 644; Hitzig 1897: 179.

[33] Wyse 1904: 177; Bruck 1909: 133; Vinogradoff 1922: ii. 67.

[34] Blass, *AB* ii.2, 529, seems to see grounds to invalidate a will in insanity, yet the clause on volition does not allow that inference. Cf. Hyp. *Against Athenogenes* 17 [partly restored]: 'for [the law] makes it possible for a man to dispose of his property as he wishes except on account of senility or disease or insanity or if subject to a woman's influence, physical restraint, or coercion'; Dem. 48. 56; Isae. 4. 19; 6. 9; Dem 46. 14 adding, after 'senility', also 'or drugs'. See Bruck 1909: 55 with n. 2; Weiss 1923: 235–6. Wyse 1904: 223, § 41 nn. 7–8, supposes that the speaker asserted grounds to invalidate the will on the basis of equity, on the consideration that the testator had not seriously intended to disinherit his nephews. Such a criterion is unlikely, for the testator kept the supposedly frivolous will in force for years.

claimed nearer relationship, Isaeus still thought it necessary to make use of the clause in the inheritance law dealing with volition [requiring that the testator be of sound mind, without constraint or improper influence]. That indicates not an appeal to equity, but rather, 'this legal provision was the last recourse of desperate advocates in legal challenges, who otherwise had little chance of success'.[35] It even seems that the speaker only discussed the closer relationship and the good understanding with the testator in order to demonstrate his 'insanity'. In that case, the argument would have nothing to do with equity.

This becomes clearer if the document was not a will but rather, as Bruck (1909: 125–33) has made probable, a 'gift in case of death'. [22] In this case it would be an intentional misdirection by the speaker to claim that there was a will. Such a deception of the judges was possible because of the informality of wills and the similarity of gifts and bequests. The purpose of this tactic is clear. For one thing, the argument of the opposing party, that the testator did not want to abrogate his allocation but to confirm it (24), was reduced to absurdity, since one will could hardly be confirmed by a second. Above all, however, the clause concerning volition was only applicable to wills, not to gifts, for which the kinds of dealings that existed among living persons applied. To apply testamentary rules seemed so important to the speaker that he tried to pass off the deed of gift falsely as a will.

4. One further indication that equity considerations did not emerge is the speech of Isocrates *Against Callimachus* (18), which involves a *paragraphē*. During the civil war, when the oligarchic party was ruling Athens, Callimachus was apprehended and denounced on the street by the speaker and two others for possessing money that belonged to an exiled member of the Piraeus party. The Ten had subsequently ordered the confiscation of the money. After the end of

---

[35] Hitzig 1897: 180–1. Surprisingly Wyse (1904: 177–8), who himself assumes a criterion of fairness, takes the contrary position: 'It should be noted as a curiosity of criticism, that K. Seeliger (1876: 637 ff.), with a simplicity worthy of Tom Pinch, finds ... that Isaeus was "*a champion of equity against strict law*".' Wolf 1956: 204 posed as an advocate of Seeliger's view, but then expressly qualified his support, p. 218, n. 8.

the civil war, Callimachus sued the speaker for 'damage',[36] demanding 100 minas as a penalty—perhaps including 'assault'. The claim
that he had been bodily mistreated during the arrest (9) and the size
of the demanded penalty would support the idea of 'assault'. It is
unclear from the speech how much money had been confiscated.

The speaker brings a *paragraphē* in defence against the suit. He
appeals to the law of Archinus. This law was created for the purpose
of clamping down on the sort of private legal disputes that were
stirred up by the disturbances of the civil war. According to this law,
and also for other reasons, the suit was clearly inadmissible: the
speaker had already declared himself ready to pay [23] 200 drachmas,
if Callimachus would give up the suit. The contents of the agreement
were announced as an 'arbitration on fixed terms' (10, *diaita epi
rhētois*). The accuser had already instituted the same suit previously,
and when the speaker blocked the suit with a witness's sworn statement (*diamarturia*) [that the matter was settled in arbitration], he
[Callimachus] failed to prosecute for 'false testimony' (11–12).[37]
That the presiding magistrate had not rejected the new suit suggests
that the official was not authorized to do this, even if the inadmissibility of the suit was evident.[38] This is explained by the fact that, in
the meantime—through the law of Archinus—the *paragraphē* had
been introduced, under which it was always for the *dikastērion* to
decide admissibility.

Significantly, the speaker seems not to be so sure of his position. He
apparently feared a decision according to extra-legal considerations
(34): 'Consequently, it is not fitting that your votes should be based

[36] Steinwenter 1925: 128; Maschke 1926: 102. [The alternative explanation, that
the claim of 100 minas included a charge of assault, is now generally discounted. For
English translation of this speech with explanatory notes, see Mirhady and Too 2000
(EC).]
[37] On the arbitration, see Steinwenter 1925: 133. It is often asserted that the
paragraphē must have been based on the fact that the *diamarturia* had not been
challenged for false testimony: cf. Lipsius, *AR* 857, n. 41; Calhoun 1918: 179 with n. 2;
Bonner and Smith 1938: 77; Lämmli 1938: 149. To the contrary, one might object that
the speaker bases his *paragraphē* not on these [formal] grounds but on the Amnesty.
[See, however, Carawan 2001: 23–8; 2002: 10–12.]
[38] Whether and in which cases the authorities could reject a suit at their own
discretion is much disputed. Cf. Lipsius, *AR* 818–19, 845, 854; Calhoun 1919: 344 ff.;
Paoli 1933: 97 ff.; Steinwenter 1934: 384, 386, n.1; Hellebrand, *RE* 18.3, 1176–7.

upon favour (*charis*), or upon mere fairness (*epieikeia*), nor upon anything other than upon the oaths you took when you made the covenant of Amnesty.' The words 'favour' and 'fairness' suggest that Callimachus had appealed to equity (cf. Stoffels 1954: 24). If his prosecution speech were preserved and an appeal to *epieikeia* found in it, the case would be unambiguous. However, the prosecutor's arguments are portrayed by the defendant as an appeal to equity in such a way as to weaken them and thus to render them unworthy of consideration. In clear opposition to this, the speaker's own argument for dismissal of the suit is based on the entirely formal grounds that [24] judgement may only be passed according to the oaths of amnesty. Moreover, the speaker's discussion indicates that he had far less fear of an equity judgement than concerns of another kind. Mention of political trials in which the defendants had been convicted but released because of the amnesty agreements, or where a suit had simply not been brought because of the agreements (22–4), as well as ongoing references to the peace treaty between the parties of the civil war (19, 21, 25–7, 34, 42, 47), show that as a supporter of the discredited oligarchic party he had to fear the political prejudice of the judges. In order not to reveal his suspicions too clearly, he seems to refer to the dicasts' possible bias as *epieikeia*. So true equity considerations played no role.

IV. EQUITY ARGUMENTS AS *ENTECHNOI PISTEIS*

The selection of speeches discussed so far has been dictated by whether they have been cited in the literature as examples of speakers having recourse to equity argumentation. Added to these were two speeches (Isoc. 18 and Dem. 50) in which possible equity arguments might have been seen from the opposing party.

Analysis of the speeches has shown that equity considerations have not played a role. Instead, the disputes followed precisely formal lines over interpretation of a contract provision (Dem. 56), a decree (Dem. 50), a document (Isae. 1), or over the existence or nonexistence of security for a dowry (Dem. 30 and 31). In the speech *Against Callimachus* (Isoc. 18) there was no thought of an equity judgement, but rather fear of the political bias of the judges.

Only in the case of the pseudo-Demosthenic speech *Against Zenothemis* (or. 32) and Hyperides' speech *Against Athenogenes* could the substance of the case have had something to do with equity. However, here it appeared that in order to strengthen his position with regard to the particular statute, the speaker [25] had recourse to provisions that were legally doubtful and even irrelevant before addressing the obvious deception of his opponent. That allows the conclusion that equity considerations had no legal significance.

However, the question arises why so often in the speeches we find what looks like equity argumentation. It is striking in this regard that such discussions are not limited to speeches in which no other arguments are available to the speakers on substantive or legal grounds. They are found as a typical element in almost all forensic speeches. This strengthens the impression that they achieved no special significance. But it is also true that their enduring place in the composition of forensic speeches assures that they were not just idle talk. Pringsheim expressed the suspicion that 'perhaps what Vinogradoff calls equitable arguments would be best brought under the heading *logoi* (*entechnoi pisteis*)'.[39]

At the time of the orators two kinds of proofs were distinguished, the *atechnoi* and *entechnoi pisteis*. To the former, according to Aristotle, belonged laws, witness testimony, contracts, slaves' admissions from torture, and oaths (*Rh.* 1375a23; cf. 1355b35 ff.). These 'artless' proofs belonged to archaic legal procedure, when the decision of a legal dispute was bound by strict evidentiary rules, under the assumption that these 'proofs' were by themselves decisive when carried out in the prescribed forms.[40] During the classical period this stage of evidentiary theory was eclipsed in Athens' courts. Free evaluation of evidence ruled; that is, the dicasts could freely decide each legal dispute in view of the evidence.[41] As a result, the significance of the *entechnoi pisteis*, the *logoi*, increased. This 'logical' reasoning served to upset the opponent's presentation of proof,

[39] Pringsheim 1950: 24, n.5. [That is, arguments from equity belong rather to rhetorical invention than properly to legal reasoning.]

[40] Cf. Lipsius, *AR* 866 ff.; Latte 1920: 3, 21 ff.; Leisi 1908: 107; Solmsen 1931: 5 ff., 56; Gernet 1955a: 63.

[41] Cf. Latte 1920: 26–7, 38; Leisi 1908: 108–9; Bonner 1927: 187; Weiss 1923: 232–3; Pringsheim 1950: 23.

which was no longer undisputable, [26] and to firm up or fill out one's own, especially when the *atechnoi pisteis* offered no unequivocal evidence. This was the hour of birth for forensic rhetoric.⁴² It was essentially, in Gernet's formulation, the art of finding and examining probabilities (*vraisemblances*), which by definition were something other than evidence in the original sense. They were technical means of persuasion (*moyens de persuasion*) that were employed against the evidence or in its absence.

It is known that the orators had recourse to all psychological means and methods that were suitable for improving one's own position or harming the opponent's. Like an appeal to sympathy for oneself and the personal abuse of the opponent, raising the particular justice of one's own demands seems simply to have been one of these *entechnoi pisteis*.

In Dem. 44. 8 the speaker says that the judges should vote for the opponent even if he does not have the law on his side but his demands seem 'just and humane' (*dikaia kai philanthrōpa*). J. W. Jones (1956: 35) inferred from this a common tendency to push for a decision according to *dikaiōtatē gnōmē* ('most just understanding'), not only when there was a gap in the statutory law but also when there was a conflict between law and right. He misunderstood the sense of this clever argumentation, which does not involve any possible recognition of the opponent's claim but is directed at weakening it. The expression in Dem. 44. 8 is a deliberate *contradictio in adiecto* [contradiction in terms]: He is saying that the opponent's claim cannot be right if it does not conform to the statute, since only he who abides by the statute himself can at the same time have justice on his side.⁴³

[27] If one examines once more the rhetoric of the speeches that seem to indicate equity arguments, aside from questions of interpretation, one notices that unambiguous evidence is missing. The speaker of the pseudo-Demosthenic speech *Against Zenothemis*

⁴² Cf. Wolf 1950–68: ii. 47–8; Gernet 1955a: 66. On psychological tactics, cf. Lipsius, *AR* 919–20; Leisi 1908: 108–9; Bonner 1927: 78–9; Bonner and Smith 1938: 123; Solmsen 1931: 69–71.

⁴³ [The passage is an implied contrary-to-fact in the form of a general condition: 'if there is no argument from the laws (as surely there is), but their claims appear "just and humane" (as they are obviously not), then we concede' (EC).] Cf. Paoli 1933: 40–1.

(or. 32) was deprived of any possibility of proving his right to the grain from the moment that Protos went over to Zenothemis' side (29–30). He could not make a formal appeal against the deception as such, but by pointing out the fraudulent dealing he could explain his own lack of evidence and weaken the credibility of the prosecutor, though the latter could point to a written agreement.

The Demosthenic speeches *Against Onetor* (Dem. 30–1) are similar. Demosthenes tried to oppose the legal admissibility of the 'removal' (*exagōgē*) with the claim that the dowry security could never have been granted since the dowry to be secured had never been paid to Aphobus. As evidence he offered the testimony of the first husband Timocrates, in which he revealed that, according to a contract, he owed a sum that was once a dowry now as a loan at an interest rate of 10 per cent, which he was to pay to Aphobus (30. 9). Here it is significant that the interest was not payable to Onetor [the woman's *kyrios*] but to Aphobus [her second husband], and that the rate of 10 per cent was not the ordinary 18 per cent that a divorced husband usually had to pay for an unreturned dowry. So it appears that the money was not owed to Onetor as a dowry but to Aphobus as a loan.[44] In that case Aphobus would have held the dowry simply in the form of a loan to Timocrates, just as Onetor claimed (Dem. 30. 18–20) and wished to prove through the witness [28] statements of Aphobus and Timocrates ('providing Aphobus and Timocrates as witnesses, the one that he has paid the dowry, and the other that he has received it', 38). If, as Demosthenes claimed (Dem. 30. 3, 5, 18, 39), everything had been arranged by Onetor and Aphobus for fraudulent purposes in order to disadvantage him, the mention of this was necessary simply in order to weaken the credibility of the opposing argument, even if the orator had not grounded his suit on the deception per se.

---

[44] That rationale would explain the odd rate of 10%. Wolff (*RE* 13.1 [1957]: 154–5) apparently did not consider this possibility. For it would support his view that the high interest of 18% [was the ordinary rate on repaying the dowry to the woman's family] (as opposed to Beauchet 1897: i. 325, and Lipsius, *AR* 482, n. 39, 498 [suggesting the higher rate was punitive]), since in this case the 10% rate applies not to a dowry but rather to a loan [a debt owed by the first husband to the second; cf. Harrison 1968: 55–9 (EC)].

Finally, the speaker in the speech *Against Athenogenes* was missing a relevant law as an *atechnos pistis*. Even if he could not appeal against the defendant's fraud, mention of the deception was at least a psychological means of influencing the judges.

Protagoras portrayed the goal of forensic rhetoric as 'making the weaker argument the stronger' (Arist. *Rh.* 2. 24 1402a23–5; cf. Plato, *Tht.* 166d). By this he understood a fully value-neutral ability 'to make the side prevail that was difficult to defend and supplied with little evidence, whether in a legal dispute or a political debate' (Wolf 1950–68: ii. 45–6; iii.2 [1956] 160). In other words, the orator had no real problem with *epieikeia*, but with *pisteis*. Arguments that have the appearance of general appeals to equity actually involve provability and are connected with the principle of the free evaluation of evidence.

7

Social Relations on Stage: Witnesses in Classical Athens*

S. C. HUMPHREYS

The study of witness testimony raises questions which are fundamental for the student of other cultures, whether past or contemporary. What are the standards expected of a reliable informant and how is reliability to be recognized? How is reliable knowledge about the past established?

The aim of this paper is to analyse the use of witnesses in classical Athenian lawcourts both for its epistemological implications—what does it tell us about Athenian ideas of 'expert witnesses', of reliability, of truthfulness and bias—and for the information it gives us about Athenian society and court practice. What kind of men did Athenian litigants select to act as witnesses for them, and what effect did they hope their witnesses' testimonies would have on the jury?

If we start out from the assumption of modern courts that witnesses are called to 'establish the facts of the case' we shall misunderstand the Athenian data. What witnesses actually testified often was not very important: their testimonies might be insignificant, irrelevant, or repetitive. To understand their role it is necessary to see them as minor characters in a drama, whose presence provides the backdrop against which the litigant wishes his own actions and character to be seen. Respectable witnesses—officials, members of the 'professions', reputable politicians—establish his own respectability. The support of neighbours, associates, and kin shows that those who

* Originally published in Humphreys (ed.), *The Discourse of Law* (1985): 313–69.

know the milieu in which the dispute arose are on the litigant's side. Denigration of the opponent's witnesses, kin, and associates presents him as a vicious and unreliable character. In the construction of a character-portrait in court, witnesses had an important role to play.

Surprisingly little work has been done on the comparative study of witnesses and witness testimony in different societies. The pervasive doctrine of modern Anglo-American legal theory, that witnesses are called 'to establish the facts', has created an impression even among anthropologists and historians that the functions and activities of witnesses do not vary much from one culture to another. When lawyers have studied witness testimony in past societies their questions have been shaped by the Anglo-American law of evidence: they establish who is debarred from testifying, either by social status or by relationship to the litigants, and discuss rules of relevance and of hearsay, perjury procedure, and ways of compelling witnesses to testify (e.g. Bonner 1905). Students of the evolution of law have pointed out that in some early legal systems witnesses act as 'oath-helpers' whose support for the litigant is more active and committed than that of the modern witness (below, n. 33), and students of communist legal systems have noted that these take a broader view of the defendant's character, record, and standing in the community than that presented to the Anglo-American jury (e.g. Feifer 1964; cf., however, Shapland 1981). But I know of no general study which relates the act of bearing witness in court to the two central issues which it raises: how is a particular account of past events legitimated as a valid representation of 'the facts', and how is the complex web of interactions which make up social experience related to the selective representations of the person and of actions which are offered in court?

The first of these two themes—testifying as the construction of socially accepted knowledge—leads directly to enquiries into the bases of authority and the social factors influencing perception, questions which our own culture has until recently been very unwilling to face (cf. Kuhn 1962; Chalmers 1976). It is not enough merely to note that in many cultures women, children, the mentally sick, or members of 'inferior races'[1] have been debarred from testifying,

---

[1] In California in the mid-19th century blacks, Indians, and immigrant Chinese were not allowed to testify: Doo 1973.

that members of certain occupations may have a privileged status
as 'expert witnesses', or that in some cases those with especially close
ties to defendants in criminal cases cannot be compelled to testify
against them. Such categories are far too crude for a sociological
analysis of the cognitive processes involved in selecting, preparing,
and evaluating testimony given by witnesses. Even in daily life we
are all constantly involved in assessing the reliability of what we
are told, taking into account not only the informant's access to
relevant information but also his or her character, qualifications,
possible biases, and general standing in the community. Historians
and anthropologists should be particularly aware of this, since assessment of the reliability of sources and informants is fundamental to their research (cf. G. Lewis 1852: 185–97; 1849: 21–43;
Malinowski 1913: ch. 1, part 2). Some legal codes explicitly specify
that witnesses must be of a certain jural status or social standing
(cf. W. Davies 1985); it would be extremely naive to assume that in
modern legal systems which set no such formal limits to the capacity
to testify, except those related to undeveloped or impaired mental
powers, judges and jurors are not influenced by their perception of
the social class, sex, age, and probable politico-cultural orientation of
witnesses.

In the view of modern Anglo-American legal textbooks (e.g.
Mauet 1980: 98) the typical witness is the 'occurrence witness', a
stranger who just happened to be present when a car accident or
similar incident took place. Witnesses who are to appear in court
are selected partly on the basis of impartiality; it is quite possible
that kin, friends, and neighbours may be questioned during
the preparation of a case but not called as witnesses (cf. Twining
1983). The fact that most witnesses in Athenian lawsuits are overtly
partisan has surprised modern commentators, but in comparative
perspective this is far from unusual. Among the Tiv of Nigeria, no
one will act as witness for a man with whom he has no social
relationship because this would be an act of aggressive mischief-
making (cf. Kurczewski and Frieske 1978: 182). When a stranger is
needed as a witness, a relationship is created by paying him to testify
(Bohannan 1957: 39–40). Witnesses reluctant to testify against those
with whom they are closely associated may be compelled by the
court to testify on oath—which gives them an acceptable excuse

for speaking out.[2] In small village communities any expression of opinion concerning a dispute involves taking up a position about how it should be settled; no sharp distinction can be drawn between testifying, mediating, and judging. The formal hearing of a dispute essentially dramatizes power relations between opposing groups within the society, although it also allows the demonstration or withdrawal of support to be expressed in the impersonal terms of an argument about justice (cf. Gulliver 1963; P. R. Brown 1975; Moore 1977). It is understood by all that the significance of what is said depends on the speaker's status and relationship with the contending parties.[3]

An ideal lawcourt would have perfect knowledge of all the circumstances of the disputes brought to it, and perfect impartiality. But these two ideals stand in opposition to each other—not merely for practical, operational reasons but because the notion of impartiality implies a detachment from the immediate social process. Institutionalized arrangements for impartial judging[4] have to rely on 'outside' (objectivist) rather than 'inside' knowledge; the court sets itself and its judgement outside the temporal process of social life (cf. Bourdieu 1977: 3–9; Gernet 1956); it selects only a limited segment of that process for its attention.[5] It is faced with the problem of obtaining information: whose responsibility is it to do this, and what powers are they to be given? As soon as the court is in any way detached from the ongoing social process of the community, these become crucial

[2] Bohannan 1957: 44–5. Tiv distinguish two forms of right speaking: speaking *mimi* is speaking in conformity with social relationships, speaking *vough* is truthtelling. When Bohannan says: 'It is generally conceded … that for a witness to speak *vough* is *ipso facto* to speak *mimi*. From the standpoint of the witness the "right" thing to do is to smooth over social relationships and hence to report what actually occurred so that judges will have a way of knowing what the rights of the matter are', he is reporting court ideology rather than the views of litigants.

[3] Note the use made of Bernstein's concepts 'restricted code' and 'elaborated code' in the field of law by Perry 1977.

[4] Impartial judgements can be given in a local court without institutionalized safeguards against bias, if a substantial sector of the community is neutral or if judges' class interests are not involved, but the only safeguard against bias in local courts is the fact that all parties concerned have to continue to live together.

[5] Cf. Gernet 1951, on early legal formalism as an extreme example of this process of selection. See Udovitch 1985 for another analysis of the relation between law and local knowledge.

questions. At some point there must be communication between the inside knowledge of the local community and the outsider's perspective adopted by the court. Our own culture has elaborated a fantasy world round this point of interaction: the amateur detective immerses himself or herself, like an anthropological 'participant observer', in the local community and discovers the truth which the plodding policeman's routine methods of investigation would have missed. The detective story was invented in China, where it was the duty of the judge (appointed to a district in which he was a stranger) to find his way through the labyrinth of local relationships (Van Gulik 1956; cf. J. Cohen 1968: 461–3, 466–8, 502–3 for modern parallels). Continental courts, where police investigators work under a *juge d'instruction*, and continental detective stories (Simenon, Freeling) remain closer to the Chinese pattern.

Legal process can be thought of as having three elements: gathering information, the representation of that information, and passing judgement on it. Different aspects of the process are emphasized in different systems. In Athenian courts the collection of information was left to litigants, and at least after 378/7 BC, when the use of written witness testimonies became compulsory, witnesses could not be cross-questioned.[6] Judgement was expressed only by the jury's vote; the presiding magistrate did not sum up the case. The process in court therefore consisted of two contrasting representations of the litigants' behaviour and rights. The work of investigation is rarely emphasized;[7] litigants wished to give the impression that they were

---

[6] Cf. Calhoun 1919*a*. It is difficult to tell how much cross-questioning was ever used. In Ar. *Wasps* 962–6 and Andoc. 1 *Myst.* 14 (399 BC) witnesses are led through their testimony by questions from the litigant for whom they are testifying. In Isae. 3 *Pyrrh.* 79 (*c*.370?) the speaker urges the jury to question his opponent; I see this as an invitation to heckle rather than a reference to cross-questioning. On the other hand the case in Aesch. *Eumenides* 585–673 is conducted entirely by questions directed by the plaintiff to the defendant and his witness, and questioning was certainly a well-known method of attacking an argument in non-legal contexts. Aristotle's discussion of the use of questions in forensic oratory (*Rh.* 1418a 40–1419a 18) makes no mention of witnesses.

[7] There was no office of public prosecutor in Athens and no official machinery for making investigations except in matters of public finance (the *logistai*). The Council could appoint a committee of investigators (*zētētai*) to examine cases in which a public denunciation (*eisangelia*) was made (Rhodes 1972: 158, 186–7). The right to torture slaves to obtain evidence pertains to their owners, not to the court;

stating truths obvious to all. The function of witnesses, I shall argue, is to bring the inside knowledge of the local community into the court process. A similar employment of witnesses can be observed in the local courts of communist Russia and China (cf. esp. Feifer 1964); as in ancient Greece, the court is presented with stereotypes rather than the complex web of real-life interactions, but there is the same attempt to show what kind of person the litigant is by locating him or her in a social milieu whose consensus of opinion is—supposedly—represented by the witnesses.

I have argued elsewhere (Humphreys 1983*c*) that the legal process in ancient Athens evolved between *c*.750 and 450 BC from the kind of small community moot which anthropologists have described and which is depicted in Homer's description of the trial scene on the shield of Achilles (*Il.* 18. 497–509)[8] to trial before a mass jury of 200 or more in a city court. Awareness that the transfer from local community to urban court meant a loss of knowledge even if it increased impartiality was shown at various points in the process of evolution by the creation of supplementary institutions: the boards of local judges (*dikastai kata dēmous*) to deal with minor cases, and the public arbitrators who had to hear most types of suit before the disputants (if dissatisfied with the arbitrator's verdict) took their case to court. Specialist speechwriters used their skills in presenting juries with a favourable picture of the litigant's character, past behaviour, and social milieu. The purpose of the present paper is to

---

cf. Menander, *Samia* 305–25 for the use of torture threats to obtain confessions from slaves in a domestic context. The rule that slaves' evidence could only be admitted in court if obtained by torture (a) represented a continuation and formalization of domestic practice, (b) provided the slave with a legitimate excuse for testifying against his or her owner (cf. Soubie 1974: 127, and the parallel use of oaths to 'compel' reluctant witnesses to testify among the Tiv, Bohannan 1957), (c) mitigates the contradiction between the slave's cognitive capacity as a human being and his lack of legal capacity qua slave. Extant speeches contain arguments both in favour of the use of torture and against it, depending on the speaker's circumstances, but though challenges and offers to hand over slaves for torture are common, only *P Oxy.* 2686 (Hyperides) refers to an actual instance of slave torture (Thür 1977: 19, 23 thinks this passage refers to torture of non-Athenian free witnesses, as in Antiphon 5 *Herod.*). Plato abandoned torture in the *Laws*. For other problems posed by the slave's lack of legal capacity, cf. Cunha 1985.

[8] For parallels to the judgement in turn by elders in the 'Shield' scene see Gluckman 1955.

show how the selection and presentation of witnesses was designed to re-create in court the social context from which the litigant had been detached.

THE EVIDENCE

Before considering what we know about witnesses in Athenian courts, it is necessary to say something about the texts of lawcourt speeches from which this knowledge is derived, and the processes which influenced their circulation and transmission. It has at times in the past been argued that all the witness testimonies in extant speeches are forgeries, 'restored' in the text by pedantic editors (esp. A. Westermann 1850). On this view it was necessary to assume either that witness testimonies and texts of laws were not included in the original published versions of speeches, or else that they were later omitted by copyists; in either case, it was assumed that speeches were published and read only as specimens of the art of rhetoric, narrowly defined as skill in prose composition. There are, it is true, examples of speeches in which most scholars consider the extant witness testimonies and documents to be forged: Demosthenes 18 *De Corona* and Aeschines 1 *Timarchus*.[9] There are also many speeches which lack witness testimonies. In at least some of the speeches put into circulation before 378/7 this will be due to the fact that witnesses could give their testimony orally until that date (thereafter, they appeared in court to affirm a written testimony: Calhoun 1919*a*; Harrison 1971: 139). However, there is no reason to assume that none of the extant witness testimonies are genuine. Epigraphic evidence has been slowly building up over the years to confirm the historicity of persons and details mentioned only in witness testi-

---

[9] On Dem. 18 see Treves 1940; on Aeschin. 1 (with conflicts between text and witness testimony in §§ 41/50 and 63/68), Drerup 1898. Drerup also suspects the documents and testimonies in Dem. 21 *Meid.*, except for the laws in §§ 8, 10 and 94. Doubts have also been expressed about the documents in Andoc. 1 *Myst.* and Dem. 23 *Aristocr.*, but cf. Dover 1968, 4, n. 4; 36–7. I have dealt with the question of the archon-date in the witness testimony of [Dem.] 43 *Macart.* 31 in Humphreys 1983*b*.

monies;[10] and in any case the argument that speeches either lacked *ab initio*, or soon lost, their witness testimonies because readers were only interested in 'rhetoric' stems from a much oversimplified view of a complex process of transmission in which a variety of interests and motives were involved.

The use of mass juries of 200 or more to try legal cases was very much extended in Athens after 461 BC (Humphreys 1983c). Even though appearance before a court of law was always restricted to those who had sufficient property for litigation to be worthwhile,[11] this change meant that men who had not hitherto had much experience of addressing large audiences had to do so in the courts. In the assembly, too, increasing attention was being paid at this period to the way in which opposing views were argued rather than the status and achievements of their proponents (Connor 1971; Lanza 1979: 37–49). Teachers of the art of argument came forward to offer their services both to the politically ambitious and to litigants. Antiphon, the earliest of these experts whose speeches have survived, does not seem to have taken money for his services but gave advice to friends both on political matters and on litigation (Thuc. 8. 68); he published, probably in the 440s–430s,[12] sets of four speeches (*Tetralogies*) in which both sides of an imaginary case were argued, and he wrote

---

[10] Since Drerup's discussion (1898), epigraphic evidence has confirmed information given only in witness testimonies on the following persons: [Dem.] 43 *Macart.* 36, 44, the sons of Straton (*APF* 2921); ibid. 42, Phanostratus father of Stratius (Humphreys 1983b); [Dem.] 45 *Steph. i.* 55, deme of Deinias (*IG* ii² 1641; *APF* 11672, X); [Dem.] 59 *Neaera* 40, Aristocrates of Phaleron (*APF* 1926); ibid. 61, Eualces of Phaleron (read Eualcos: *PA* 5264), Euphranor of Aigilia (or Angele?: Kirchner, *PA* 6091; *Agora XV* 32. 32), Nicippus of Kephale (*APF* 10833); ibid. 71, deme of Nausiphilus (*PA* 10601; *Agora XV* 8.1); ibid. 123, Diophanes son of Diophanes of Alopeke (*PA* 4406; cf. *Agora XV* 155.43). Drerup was already able to report epigraphical confirmation on Phormio son of Ctesiphon of Piraeus ([Dem.] 35 *Lacr.* 13–14; *APF* 11672, IX), Endius of Lamptrai ([Dem.] 45.8; *APF* 4810), Philostratus son of Dionysius of Kolone ([Dem.] 59.23; *APF* 14734), Glaucetes of Kephisia ([Dem.] 59.40; *APF* 2954), Deinomenes son of Archelaus of Kydathenaion ([Dem.] 59.123, *APF* 3188), and Deinias son of Phormus of Kydantidai ([Dem.] 59.123; *IG* ii² 6609). On Dem. 21 *Meid.* 82 and 168, see Vanderpool 1966.

[11] Cases involving less than ten drachmas (approximately ten days' wages) were dealt with by tribal judges, the *dikastai kata dēmous* (see Humphreys 1983c). Magistrates had summary powers to arrest lower-class criminals (*kakourgoi*) and those caught *in flagrante*: see Harrison 1971, 221–32; Hansen 1976.

[12] On the date of the *Tetralogies* see Zuntz 1949; Dover 1950.

speeches for others to deliver in court—a practice which was already becoming established by the end of the fifth century.

It might be considered surprising that no profession of advocacy developed. An Athenian litigant was permitted to share his allotted speaking time with one or more supporting speakers (*synēgoroi*). In a few cases known to us the *synēgoros* carried the main burden of presenting the case: Demosthenes[13] or some other client did so for the ex-slave banker Phormio in Dem. 36; Apollodorus son of Pasion of Acharnai, for his wife's brother and daughter's husband, Theomnestus, in [Dem.] 59 *Neaera* 16 ff.; Demosthenes may also have spoken for his cousin Demon in the Zenothemis case (Dem. 32). The absence of personal ties between litigant and *synēgoros* in the first example is rather unusual; more commonly, as in the two latter instances, *synēgoroi* play an extensive part in the presentation of a case only when they can represent themselves as kin or long-standing friends.[14] But normally *synēgoroi* only appeared briefly to praise the litigant's character. It seems likely that the emergence in Athens in the later fifth century of quasi-professional prosecutors (sycophants) who made a living by bringing charges in cases where 'anyone who wished' could prosecute, and got a reward if the defendant was convicted, made Athenians suspicious of those who spoke in the courts for money (cf. Plato, *Laws* 937e–938c). Instead of becoming advocates, experts in presenting legal cases became *logographoi*, who composed or helped to compose speeches to be delivered in court by litigants or by their supporters.

As Dover has pointed out in his study of Lysias (1968),[15] what an expert speechwriter did for his client could vary widely, from outlining a few key points to composing an entire speech for the litigant to learn by heart. It is important to bear in mind that the client expected advice on all aspects of his case: what laws to cite, what

[13] In § 1 the speaker says that 'we, Phormio's *epitēdeioi*' will speak for him; at the end of the speech (62) he tells the court officials to pour away the rest of the water in the clock. Either he decided that supporting speeches were superfluous (cf. [Dem.] 45 *Steph. i.* 6) or the plural in § 1 is rhetorical. It is far from certain that the speaker was Demosthenes himself (Schaefer 1858: 292–6).

[14] On *synēgoroi* see Lavency 1964; Kennedy 1968; Dover 1968, ch. 8.

[15] Usher 1976 disagrees with Dover but proves only that in some instances speechwriters supplied complete speeches and used them afterwards in teaching and for advertisement—which was not in doubt.

witnesses to call and what their testimony should say (cf. Aeschin. 1 *Tim.* 45, 67); what arguments the opponent was likely to use (cf. Dorjahn 1935); how to divide the presentation of the case between the first and second speeches allowed to the litigant, and between the litigant and his supporters. Rhetorical handbooks have little to say on these practical points because it was difficult to generalize about them, and handbooks therefore give a misleading impression of the speechwriter's functions. An adviser who merely supplied the litigant with suitable examples from a selection of stock proemia and exordia would not have been worth much.[16]

Occasionally a speechwriter would indulge in a virtuoso display of specialized knowledge: for example, in Lys. 10 *Against Theomnestus* 15–19 a number of early laws are cited and their archaic terms explained (cf. also Dem. 23 *Aristocr.* 22–62). It might sometimes be necessary to make clear (or unclear) to the jury a complicated financial transaction or genealogy, or to argue an abstruse point of law: Isaeus 11 *Hagnias* illustrates all three points. But in most cases the litigants did not wish to sound too clever. The speechwriter had to practice the *ars celandi artem*, to use his skill and ingenuity on the task of presenting the speaker as the honest, innocent, sympathetic victim of villainy and intrigue (cf. Dover 1974: 25–8; Carter 1986).

The speeches which have reached us had to survive three crucial tests. In the first place either speechwriter or speaker had to consider it worthwhile to begin to circulate copies of the speech in Athens. Secondly, a bookseller had to consider the speech interesting enough to export to Alexandria. Thirdly, it had to find its way into a collection of speeches attributed to one of a small number of famous orators.[17] The motives of those responsible for having copies made, and of readers, were different at each stage; understanding of the process has been impeded by telescoping all three stages together and

---

[16] Kennedy (1963: 57–8) suggests that the earliest rhetorical handbooks were substitutes for the services of the speechwriter. If one takes Dover's view of the speechwriter's advisory functions, a training in rhetoric would be complementary; it would have given the litigant a basic structural frame for his argument and a repertoire of *topoi* which would help him to deliver it with confidence. Cf. Yates 1966, on the technique of memorization involved. On the practical orientation of rhetorical education Johnson 1959 has useful remarks.

[17] Turner 1951: 19–21. On the formation of the Demosthenic corpus, see Canfora 1974.

assuming that the whole process was uniformly dominated by 'interest in rhetoric'. The common view is that speeches were put into circulation by speechwriters as a means of attracting further clients, and that they remained in circulation because they were used as rhetorical models. Exceptions to this rule are recognized only in the case of certain speeches which admittedly also aroused 'political' interest, such as Demosthenes' *De Corona*.

It is, however, impossible to draw a sharp line between 'political' and 'non-political' speeches. For the man with political ambitions such as Apollodorus son of Pasion of Acharnai, author of speeches 45[18]–6, 49–50, 52–3, and 59 in the Demosthenic corpus, any occasion for public speaking was a political opportunity. Apollodorus, who was clearly both conceited and insensitive to the opinions of others, may have considered his speeches rhetorical masterpieces; but he certainly also wanted as many Athenians as possible to hear his side of any dispute in which he was involved. The cases for which his speeches were composed show a mixture of 'political' and 'private' elements which is characteristic of the Athenian courts. [Dem.] 50 *Polycles* comes from a private suit for damages but is concerned with Apollodorus' zealous performance of the public role of trierarch. [Dem.] 59 *Neaera* (in which Apollodorus acted as *synēgoros* for his wife's brother and son-in-law Theomnestus: *APF* 11672, X) was written for a 'public' charge (*graphē*)[19] concerning civic status; the accusation was motivated by Apollodorus' desire to get revenge for his own trial after his one moment of political importance, when he acted as fall-guy for Demosthenes' proposal to spend the theatre fund (*theōrikon*) on military purposes; but the main theme of the speech was the sex-life of the prostitute Neaera. One of the earliest speeches preserved, Antiphon 6 *Choreutes* (419/18) was written for a member of the Council of 500 who had been accused of homicide—a 'private' suit in Attic law—in order to prevent him from charging a public official with corruption.

[18] Plutarch's statement (*Moralia* 852e–f) that this speech was written by Demosthenes for Apollodorus is accepted by e.g. Wolff 1968. But the story was apparently unknown to Aeschines (Gernet 1957: 153–4).

[19] On the distinction between *dikē* and *graphē*—which does not fully correspond either to the civil/criminal or to the private/public law distinction—see Harrison 1971: 75–8.

The two latter examples illustrate another point relevant to the motives of those who published speeches: in Athenian courts one case often led to another. The laws prohibiting reopening of issues already settled in court were ineffective (Harrison 1971: 119–20, 190–9); witnesses might be sued for perjury either as a way of preparing the ground for reopening a case (ibid. 192–7) or—so speakers allege—merely from a desire for revenge; 'private' cases were often brought as part of a complex of political manoeuvres. Furthermore, a man who had won his case might still have difficulty in exacting restitution or reparation from his adversary. It is only reasonable to assume that speeches were often initially put into circulation because the speakers viewed them as part of an ongoing conflict.

'Publication' in the ancient world was not necessarily aimed at a large audience. Before the invention of printing there were no economies of scale to be considered.[20] Dover (1968: 170) defines the reading public for speeches as 'the partisan, the floating voter, the would-be politician and the connoisseur'. The interest of the two latter types of reader would keep a speech in circulation for longer than those of the former two. But even politicians and connoisseurs of the art of speaking, in the Greek world of the fourth-to-third centuries BC, did not think of oratorical expertise in narrowly scholastic terms. What the would-be politician wanted to learn was 'how to manage public affairs' and 'how to win cases'. He had to be familiar with the technicalities of court procedure and the art of drafting testimonies acceptable to reluctant witnesses (Aeschin. 1 *Tim.* 45, 67; Harrison 1971: 144; below at nn. 64–5) as well as with the niceties of prose rhythm. Connoisseurs must have relished the conversational tone of Demosthenes' private speeches (e.g. 36 *Phormio* 52–62), the dramatic outburst of the reported speech of Diogiton's daughter in Lys. 32 *Diogiton* 12–17, and the rueful description of his folly by Hyperides' client in Hyp. 3 *Athenogenes* 1–12 at least as much as the more stilted eloquence of Isocrates. Court speeches were—in the company of dramatic texts and mimes, with which they had much

---

[20] The speaker of Dem. 57 *Eub.* was presumably primarily interested in persuading his 80 fellow demesmen. Bystanders could attend trials (Dover 1968: 182) but speakers might well wish to reach a wider, though still restricted, public. For interest in major cases among non-Athenians see Dorjahn and Cronin 1938.

in common (Humphreys 1983*a*: 7–9; Dover 1968: 185–6)—the light reading of the period: real-life stories hot from the popular press (cf. Wilamowitz 1923*b*). Familiarity with Attic law was widespread, owing to the jury system; Athenian readers could appreciate better than we can a speechwriter's skilful concealment of the weaknesses in his client's case, selective quotation of laws, or adroit deployment of witnesses (cf. Wolff 1971).

Many of the speeches launched into circulation in Athens will have attracted only limited, local and ephemeral interest. The wider reading public outside Athens preferred—or was thought to prefer—works by orators whose names were well known. But even within these limits the export trade reached amazing proportions. The library of Alexandria contained 425 speeches attributed to Lysias alone, of which 233 were still regarded as genuine by the critics of the Augustan period[21] (Dover 1968: 15, 21). Such a massive production was not the result of the occasional publication of speeches by professional speechwriters for purposes of advertisement, but of widespread general interest in courtroom dramas. It was only in the later Hellenistic and Roman periods, when the legal system was very different and other forms of light literature had developed, that interest became more narrowly stylistic.

The variability of the interests involved in the transmission of speeches also affected the form in which they survived. In some cases the author may have decided from the beginning only to publish part of a speech (Dover 1968: 160).[22] At the opposite end of the spectrum, some speeches are only known to us from fragments selected by Dionysius of Halicarnassus in the first century BC to

---

[21] Attributions were often based on very slender grounds. Apollodorus' speeches found their way into the Demosthenic corpus at least partly because [Dem.] 45–6 *Steph. i–ii* arose from Demosthenes' successful speech for Phormio (Dem. 36) and [Dem.] 50 *Polycles* was linked in theme to Dem. 51 *Trier. Crown*. [Dem.] 58 *Theocr.* entered the corpus because of its references to Demosthenes (35–44, cf. 23), although the hostile tone of these clearly excludes Demosthenic authorship. In some cases, as Dover suggests (1968: ch. 8) attributions may have been based on informed gossip. Cf. Drerup 1899. The number of surviving classical forensic speeches and substantial fragments (excluding some which were clearly not intended for delivery in court) is just over 100, divided between ten orators.

[22] On modification of speeches between delivery and publication see Wilamowitz 1923*a*; Dorjahn, 1935; Dover 1968: 168–72, 187–93.

illustrate points of style. The history of the documents included in speeches—witness testimonies, quotations of laws,[23] and other citations—has been, as indicated above, the subject of controversy. But in my view there is every reason to suppose that contemporary readers were—and were expected to be—interested in knowing what witnesses had attested. It was only later, when speeches were copied for readers no longer familiar with Athenian prosopography or law, that copyists tended to omit such material.

COURT PRACTICE[24]

In the classical period, from which our evidence comes, all court cases were tried by juries of 200 or more members. Before reaching court the litigants would have had to present their cases either to one of the city's annual magistrates or to one of the public arbitrators (men in their sixtieth year). The magistrate's function was merely to determine whether the plea lay within the competence of the court over which he presided;[25] the arbitrator, if he could not persuade the parties to compromise, had to pass judgement, but his verdict could be rejected (Gernet 1939). After 378/7, written pleas and texts of witness testimonies and other documents produced at these preliminary hearings were, at least in the case of hearings by arbitrators, sealed and passed to the officers of the court in which the trial was to be held[26] (Calhoun 1919*a*). Each witness had to appear in court at the trial and formally confirm his acceptance of the testimony drafted for him—or else take an oath disclaiming knowledge of the facts concerned (Harrison 1971: 143–4, and n. 55 below). If a witness was going to be absent from the city at the time of trial

[23] Quotations of laws are often selective and do not necessarily follow the original text verbatim: see Bonner 1927: 177. This aspect of the speech-writer's technique deserves further study.

[24] For a more detailed treatment see Harrison 1971.

[25] In practice, in the 4th-century magistrates were probably little inclined to use their powers to reject questionable suits (cf. Calhoun 1919*b*). Possibly they had employed them more energetically in earlier periods.

[26] On the differences between arbitrators' hearings and *anakrisis* (preliminary examination) by magistrates see Bonner 1905: ch. 8; Lämmli 1938: ch. 2; Dorjahn 1941; Harrison 1971: 94–105.

he could testify formally in the presence of other witnesses who appeared in court on his behalf. A witness who failed to appear could be sued for damages by the litigant, but there was no effective way to compel a reluctant witness to testify.[27]

Each speaker was entitled to make two speeches, for which time was allotted, and a third speech in the *timēma* (in which the penalty to be paid by the defendant was assessed) if there was one (cf. Harrison 1971: 80 ff., 152–62). Witness testimonies and citations of laws were not included in the time-allowance; the court's water-clock was stopped while they were read. However, supporting speakers (*synēgoroi*) shared the litigant's time-allowance. He could divide it as he wished between himself and his supporters.[28] *Synēgoroi* often served more or less as character witnesses but, unlike witnesses, were not exposed to the risk of perjury charges (Aeschin. 2 *Emb*. 170). They could speak in the *timēma* as well as, or instead of, contributing to the presentation of the case.

At least after written testimony was made compulsory in 378/7, witnesses could not be cross-questioned. It seems likely that this rule was introduced to simplify the trial of perjury charges against witnesses, which were common: seven extant speeches derive from perjury cases.[29] It was the litigant's responsibility to summon his

[27] Ruschenbusch (1968: 61–2) argues that in early times magistrates judging *eisangeliai* or *graphai* could summons witnesses by *klēteusis* and impose summary fines on those who failed to appear. Aeschin. 1. *Tim*. 46 seems to refer to such a fine, but the procedure was in all likelihood obsolete by the 4th century, though its use is still threatened, rhetorically, in Lyc. 1 *Leocr*. 20, [Dem.] 59 *Neaera* 28, Aeschin. 2 *Emb*. 68, and Dem. 32 *Zen*. 30. The last case was a *dikē*; we have to assume, on Ruschenbusch's theory, that the precise conditions for using *klēteusis* had by this time been forgotten—which is not unlikely. In practice litigants had to provide themselves with witnesses who could be trusted to appear (see [Dem.] 58 *Theocr*. on alleged attempts by opponents to persuade witnesses to default). It is not clear to me whether Plato, *Laws* 936e–937a proposes stronger powers to compel witnesses to attend than were available in Athens (Morrow 1960: 285 thinks not). References in texts to compelling reluctant witnesses to testify or take an oath of disclaimer refer to witnesses already present in court (see below, n. 30).

[28] Cf. above, n. 14. Brief remarks by *synēgoroi* at end of speech, [Dem.] 58 *Theocr*. 70; cf. Dem. 19 *Emb*. 290.

[29] Isae. 2 *Men.*, 3 *Pyrrh.*, 6 *Philoct.*; [Dem.] 44–7 (*Leoch., Steph. i–ii, Euerg*); [Dem.] 29 *Aph. iii*, if genuine (below, n. 70). The procedure for suing witnesses for perjury may have developed in the context of *diamarturia*, in which the content of the testimony was not in doubt (cf. Gernet 1927; Harrison 1971: 124–31; below, n. 33). For an example of a very casuistic attack on a witness testimony, see [Dem.] 45–6 *Steph. i–ii*.

witnesses, and he could sue them for non-appearance if they failed to present themselves in court after being formally summoned. In court, a witness could refuse to accept the testimony drafted for him, but only by taking an oath disclaiming all knowledge of the facts in question, which in many cases was liable to make him look foolish and perhaps lay him open to a subsequent perjury charge. In practice this tactic seems to have been most commonly used as a way of discrediting the adversary or his witnesses by trying to make them testify against their own case.[30] Most witnesses were friends or kinsmen of the litigant, whose willingness to support him and consent to the testimony as drafted had already been established.

WITNESSES AS SUPPORTERS: ATTIC LAW AND ITS SOCIAL CONTEXT

The fact that witnesses in Athenian lawsuits appear as supporters of the litigant rather than offering independent corroboration of his account of the facts of the case[31] has often been noticed, but has usually been treated as a survival of the use in earlier periods of 'oath-helpers' who supported the litigant by taking an oath attesting to his version of the facts of the case. This practice is attested in the Law of Gortyn in Crete, *c*.450 (Kohler and Ziebarth 1912: 36, no. 6, 82–3) but parallels from small medieval communities or from the Cretan countryside are not relevant to the courts of classical Athens, with jurors drawn from an urban population which is likely to have included 10,000–15,000 adult male citizens.[32] Oath-helping and the use of friends and kin as witnesses and supporting speakers in

---

[30] Aeschin. 1 *Tim.* 67; [Dem.] 45 *Steph. i* 59–60; Dem. 54 *Conon* 26; Isae. 9 *Asty.* 18; cf. [Dem.] 29 *Aph. iii* 16, if genuine. For refusal to testify (apparently without oath) as a way of getting testimony 'in the record' without risk of perjury suits, see Anaximenes, *Ars Rhetorica* ([Arist.] *Rh. Al.*) 15.7.

[31] On 'bystander' witnesses see below at nn. 51–4.

[32] The total city population within the Long Walls linking Athens and Piraeus may have been as high as 200,000 during the Peloponnesian War, but is not likely to have exceeded 70,000 in the 4th century (cf. Gomme 1933; Osborne 1985). The proportion of slaves and resident aliens in the population was higher in the city than in the countryside.

Athenian courts should, in my opinion, be viewed as two alternative ways of formalizing the influence of interested members of the community in dispute settlement, which by now is ethnographically well documented (Gulliver 1963; cf. P. R. Brown 1975); there is no reason to suppose that oath-helpers had ever been used in Athens.[33] In fact we find oath-helping formalized in codes which dictate to courts how they are to reach decisions. Attic laws were concerned, in the procedural sphere, with the distribution of cases to different courts, with specifying who was entitled to accuse, and with the specification in some cases of penalties, rather than with defining what constituted decisive proof. The evolution of law in Athens followed its own path; the key factors in explaining the role of witnesses as supporters in Athenian courts are the non-technical approach of Athenian juries and the rarity and marginality, even in the fourth century, of the use of written documents as evidence.

In the last thirty years of the fifth century—not long after the generalization of trial by jury—many Athenians had hurriedly uprooted themselves from their villages and moved into the walled area between Athens and Piraeus to escape the dangers of Spartan invasion. The sources of wealth changed; land, during the war, lost

[33] Shack 1979 provides a recent comparative study of oath-helping; W. Davies 1985 shows how closely interrelated the activities of testifying, oath-helping, and judging can be. For the view that oath-helping left its traces in Attic procedure see Meister 1908; Gernet 1927; Pringsheim 1951; Sautel 1964; Soubie 1974: 125. Cf. also (with caution) Glotz 1904: 288–98. Gernet's paper, which linked oath-helping and *diamarturia*, has had a considerable influence (cf. also Lämmli 1938: ch. 4; Wolff 1966: 121–31); but on a close examination the introduction of the idea of oath-helping turns out not to be essential to his reconstruction of the history of *diamarturia*, and seems to me to be out of place. Oath-helping is essentially a means of reaching a decision in court, while *diamarturia* is designed for use outside courts. Gernet rightly stresses that uses of *diamarturein* and *diamarturesthai* must be studied together; both refer to formal protestations in public—the former before a magistrate, the latter in the presence of witnesses—which supposedly become immediately effective by virtue of their publicity (or are opposed by an equally public counterclaim which leads to adjudication). *Diamarturesthai* is always, and *diamarturein* sometimes, used of the person whose claim is being asserted (or his or her legal representative); understandably, there were circumstances in which use of a patron or person of more substance to make a *diamarturia* was preferred (e.g. when a *graphē aprostasiou* was being brought against a metic, cf. Harpocr. s.v. *diamarturia*; the speaker of Isae. 2 *Men.* used an older man, his father-in-law), but basically the term seems to be used of affirmation *before* witnesses rather than *by* a witness. The man who makes a *diamarturia* does not give evidence, he makes a formal statement to a magistrate, who is obliged to take note of it.

much of its value, while riches could be made from political office at home or in the subject cities, from attacking wealthy men in the courts, from financing urban trade, or from owning urban property and slave workshops. The restraining effects of local community opinion in village or urban neighbourhood were lessened by the general sense of social upheaval and uncertainty, which had been exacerbated by the experience of the plague of 430–429 (Thuc. 2. 53). The jury-courts were faced with an increasing flood of business. Jurors were paid; Aristophanes in the *Wasps* portrays the typical juror as elderly, in need of ready cash, and somewhat boorish,[34] and it is likely enough that the older refugees from the countryside would have taken up jury service as an easy source of cash payments (cf. Humphreys 1978: 71, 147). Hence many of the jurors of the Peloponnesian War period, when the profession of speechwriting was developing and the pattern of presentation of cases to juries was crystallizing, were men who had experience of life in a stable village community in which judgements on the behaviour of neighbours were based on detailed knowledge of the social context (cf. Moore 1977). In an Athenian court jurors got no instruction in law. The presiding magistrate did not sum up the arguments made by the two parties or give authoritative rulings on legal issues. Litigants quoted laws selectively and incompletely, subject to no control except the production of counter-quotations by the opposing side. The move to the city did not therefore introduce jurors to a new and different type of legal culture. What it did was to complement the ideas of equity and morality formed in the social milieu of the village (or pre-war city neighbourhood) with the experience of two urban institutions: the assembly and the theatre. Both put the audience in the position of judge; both made extensive use of competitions in argument. The assembly, however, had a greater tendency to depersonalize the issue under discussion; although, to judge from Thucydides' report of the debate over the Sicilian expedition, references to the *ēthos* of

---

[34] The social status of Philocleon and Bdelycleon in the *Wasps* is somewhat ambiguous: the father needs his juror's pay but the son is a smart young-man-about-town. A comic poet cannot be pressed too far for consistency, but the discrepancies are lessened if we assume that the father has had to leave his land and that the son has been earning a cash income in town, perhaps as a soldier. On the social status of 4th-century jurors see Kroll 1972: 261–7: about two-fifths of the attested jurors are also known from other sources.

competing speakers were not excluded, the assembly had to decide between alternative future policies for a collectivity, the city. The theatre, on the other hand, represented the past actions (or in the case of comedy, actions in a fictional present) of individuals. In the theatre, therefore, action inevitably became, as Aristotle said, 'coloured' by *ēthos* or 'moral style' (cf. J. Jones 1962: 37).

The litigant in court also had to give an account of his past actions, and to represent them as proceeding from an *ēthos* which the jury would find sympathetic. His witnesses had an important role to play in showing what kind of man he was. One of the characters in Euripides' *Phoenix* (fr. 812 Nauck[2]) says: I've already been chosen to judge many disputes and have heard witnesses competing against each other with opposing accounts of the same event. And like any wise man I work out the truth by looking at a man's nature and the life he leads... I never question[35] a man who likes bad company. I reckon you can tell what a man's like by the company he keeps.'

The theory—though perhaps not the practice—in modern Western courts is that what matters about a witness is not who he is but what he says. As we shall see, this theory does not apply to Athenian courts, where the content of witness testimonies is often unimportant or irrelevant. For example, the father-in-law of the egregious Apollodorus, Deinias son of Theomnestus of Athmonon (*APF* 11672, X), appeared as witness for Apollodorus when he was suing Deinias' nephew (ZS) Stephanus for perjury ([Dem.] 45. 55). Deinias' testimony said only that he had married his daughter to Apollodorus according to law, and that he had not been present when Apollodorus released his father's ex-slave Phormio from alleged debts, nor had he heard of such a release being given. As factual testimony this counted for little; but it was significant that Deinias was prepared to support his son-in-law against another member of his own family.[36] In [Dem.] 43 *Macartatus* and Dem. 57 *Eubulides*

---

[35] The speaker seems to represent himself as an arbitrator rather than a juror. Cf. also Isoc. 8 *Peace* 53 (character of metics judged by their *prostatai*) and Herodas, *Mimiambi* ii. 10–12.

[36] Sandys and Paley (1896: 101) think that Apollodorus offered Deinias the testimony given in § 55 and Deinias took an oath of disclaimer, but Deinias was not a hostile witness (cf. above, nn. 27, 30); when Apollodorus says that Deinias was not prepared to swear to the truth because he did not wish to injure his nephew (56) he means that Deinias was not prepared to give a positive testimony in his own favour.

the litigants produce numerous witnesses to testify to the same facts (not always relevant) again and again. What matters to them is to show that they are solidly supported by a large body of kin. The aim of every litigant was to represent himself as surrounded by a sub-stantial group of respectable and law-abiding kin, friends, and asso-ciates, and conversely to accuse his opponent of relying on the dubious services of professional *rhētores*, bribed witnesses, and dis-reputable drinking companions.

The choice of witnesses was also, as I have said, conditioned by the limited use made of written documents as evidence (cf. Pringsheim 1955). Official procedures for registering and authenticating written documents did not exist. In cases where a business contract, marriage settlement, or will was felt to be potentially controversial the parties concerned might indeed put its provisions in writing and deposit the document with a trusted third party. But the document would have to be written and deposited in the presence of witnesses prepared to appear in court and testify to its validity; it was not sufficient merely to have a contract signed by witnesses.

In [Dem.] 35 *Lacritus* 10–14 the speaker successively presents (1) the text of a loan contract concluding with the names of three witnesses, (2) the testimony of the man with whom the contract was deposited, and (3) the testimony of the three witnesses to the contract and two other persons that they were present when the loan was made and knew that the contract had been deposited with the previous witness. Written wills were made in the presence of the testator's kin and often other witnesses as well. (Harrison 1968: 153–4; cf. Thompson 1981; Humphreys 1983a: 84–5).

Even where transactions with the state are in question, documents are not produced.[37] Since the actual text of witness testimonies is not preserved in any of these cases we cannot be absolutely certain that documents were not mentioned, but in only one case is the witness a secretary with specific responsibilities for record-keeping: here, in

---

[37] Citizens paid neither poll-tax nor land-tax, so the state had no reason to keep a census or tax register; most taxes were collected by tax-farmers working as independ-ent entrepreneurs. It is very doubtful whether formal land registers were kept (Finley 1952: 14, 207–8; Thompson 1971). Demes kept lists of their members and of resident aliens domiciled in their area, and were certainly well informed about land-ownership, but their records were not above suspicion (Dem. 57 *Eub.*; Haussoullier 1883: 32–55).

[Dem.] 58 *Theocrines* 8–9 (cf. 26), the secretary to the supervisors of the port (*epimelētai tou emporiou*) witnesses that he received a denunciation, and other witnesses testify that they saw it posted outside the supervisors' office; the port supervisors also testify. No reference is made to the preservation of a copy of the denunciation in the records of the office. In general, when testimony is required on transactions with the state in past years it is the man who held office in the relevant year who is called; there is no request to men currently in office to consult the records for past years and testify to what they find, or reference to the production of certified copies of records.

In [Dem.] 59 *Neaera* 40 and perhaps also in Isoc. 17 *Trap.* 12 and 14, former polemarchs testify concerning cases brought before them; in Lys. 17 *Eraton* 8–9 the archons of the previous year and the *nautodikai* of the current year witness to the speaker's attempts to claim land owed to him; in Aeschin. 2 *Embassy* 84–5 and Andoc. 1 *Myst.* 46 men who had been members of the presiding board of *prytaneis* in the assembly give testimony concerning events which had taken place under their presidency. Officials responsible for various aspects of taxation are called to testify to amounts demanded, collected, or paid out in Lys. 31 *Philo* 16, Isoc. 17 *Trap.* 40–1, [Dem.] 47 *Euerg.* 22–4, [Dem.] 50 *Polycles* 10, and perhaps also Dem. 27 *Aphobus i* 46, but no reference is made to the production of written records. In [Dem.] 42 *Phaen.* 16 officials perhaps testify to the date on which the speaker had handed in a property declaration, but again there is no suggestion that written evidence was produced.[38]

THE CHOICE OF WITNESSES

The marginal status of written documentation meant that witnesses were recruited in Athens well before any question of legal proceedings arose. For any transaction which might conceivably give rise to

[38] Officials probably also gave evidence in Lys. 30 *Nicomachus* 20 (city finances), Dem. 19 *Emb.* 211–14 (scrutiny of magistrates), [Dem.] 42 *Phaen.* 3, 9 and possibly Isae. 3 *Pyrrh.* 43 (courts), although the identity of the witnesses in these passages is not stated.

a legal dispute in the future, an Athenian had to provide himself with witnesses who could be relied upon to support him if the need arose. Kinsmen, fellow members of deme and phratry, and neighbours were often essential for establishing family relationships, legitimacy, and ownership of property; but even outside these fields it was natural to turn to kin and close associates. Even in the new types of urban business transaction which were developing in the late fifth and fourth centuries, such as banking and loans for sea trade, contacts remained personal. A man had to trust to his own assessment of the reliability of a lender or borrower; one did business with friends, or with friends of friends. For example, in [Dem.] 35 *Lacritus* 6–7, Aristocles of Sphettos says that he lent money for a trading voyage on the basis of an introduction by a pair of brothers, his fellow demesmen and friends (*epitēdeioi*), with whom he regularly associated. Admittedly, to be supported only by close kin as witnesses could be a weakness; the opponent would suggest that they were lying out of family loyalty. Witnesses who looked independent were desirable—but they were not always available. In the following analysis I shall proceed, roughly speaking, from more independent to less independent categories of witness as I think an Athenian jury would assess them, discussing first city officials and members of 'respectable' professions (doctors, teachers, bankers); then business associates, who often had their own motives for publicizing transactions in which they had been involved; then witnesses chosen because they were present when particular events took place—bystanders, fellow voyagers and fellow soldiers, witnesses from abroad; then the use of well-known politicians and of the opponent's enemies as witnesses; then the outer circle of the litigant's associates—neighbours, fellow members of cult groups, fellow clansmen—and finally those identified as kin and friends.

OFFICIALS

An Athenian magistrate had to pass scrutiny before entering an office and submit to a strict process of accounting at the end of his period of tenure (Piérart 1971); the need for impartiality in public roles was in some instances stressed in oaths taken before assuming office. The fact that one of the guarantors and private arbitrators who testifies had held office as *thesmothetēs* and that the father of another had been elected eponymous archon is cited, apparently as an indication of respectability, in [Dem.] 59 *Neaera* 65. It is perhaps in the use of office-holders as witnesses that Athenian courts came closest to the modern idea that the witness has a civic duty to tell the court what he knows.

Court officials testify to earlier indictments in [Dem.] 58 *Theocr.* 8–9 (cf. 26) and 32, and in [Dem.] 25 *Aristog. i* 58 (if genuine); in [Dem.] 47 *Euerg.* 27 and 41–4 magistrates and members of the Council of 500 testify to previous condemnations of Theophemus, whose brother and brother-in-law the speaker was suing for perjury as witnesses for Theophemus in a previous suit. In Andocides 1 *Myst.* 112 the council's herald testifies to events which took place in a meeting of the council held at the Eleusinion. Members of the Areopagus council (who held office for life) testified for Dinarchus (1 *Dem.* 51–2) that he had not been denounced by the Areopagus, and for Demosthenes (18 *Crown* 134) that when his opponent Aeschines was elected to plead a case against the Delians at Delphi the Areopagus rejected him and substituted Hyperides. In Lys. 22 *Corn-dealers* 8–9 one of the archons witnessed to instructions which he had given to corn merchants; in Lys. 16 *Mantitheus* 13 Orthobulus, commander of the cavalry squadron of the speaker's tribe, testified that he had called up the speaker to serve in the cavalry and that he had asked to serve on foot as a hoplite instead, which was considered more dangerous.

It is likely enough that in some of these cases the magistrates and ex-magistrates who testified were also personal friends or acquaintances of the litigant, and in some cases this is explicitly stated. In Dem. 51 *On the Trierarchic Crown*, the general Cephisodotus, a family friend, acted as supporting speaker (*synēgoros*) for Demosthenes while at the same time functioning *de facto* as an official witnessing to the events of the campaign in which he had commanded (cf. APF 3597, XXII B). In an exceptional instance which is rather revealing, the speaker of Isocrates 18 *Callimachus* (8) calls Rhinon and his colleagues in the government of Ten which had briefly ruled Athens in 403 after the tyranny of the Thirty oligarchs, together with members of the council, to testify that he had not been responsible for the confiscation of his opponent's property. Those who had held office under this oligarchic regime had a very dubious reputation, and the speaker was probably heavily compromised already by association with them; Patrocles, the man who had held the religious office of king-archon at the time, was his friend (*epitēdeios*) and probably one of the witnesses. But some idea of the authority of office-holders as witnesses seems to survive even in this case.

THE 'PROFESSIONS' AND THE WORLD OF BUSINESS RELATIONS

There were certain other occupational groups at Athens whose members, not necessarily holding official positions,[39] relied for their success on a reputation for honesty, and were therefore unlikely to compromise themselves by perjury in court. Doctors are the most notable example. They are also, in a sense, expert witnesses; they do not give technical medical reports, but their assessment of the seriousness of a wound is considered more authoritative than that of laymen.

The speaker of Dem. 54 *Conon* calls a doctor to witness to his critical condition after being beaten up by his opponents (10, 12) and points out that although they claim he started the fight, they have not found a doctor to testify for them (36). In [Dem.] 40 *Boeot. ii* 32–3 we are told that the speaker's half-brother Boeotus had accused him before the Areopagus of having wounded him, and he was only saved by Euthydicus the doctor who testified that Boeotus had asked him to fake a convincing head-wound. Euthydicus may have repeated this testimony—which highlighted his own honesty—in § 33.[40] Demosthenes

---

[39] Doctors and teachers received stipends from the state in some cities, but we have no evidence of this in classical Athens; the city was large and prosperous enough to attract doctors and teachers without such inducements. Cf. Cohn-Haft 1956; on the doctor's need to make himself known, and his methods of doing so, see also Edelstein 1967: 87–90 [1931].

[40] Euthydicus is mentioned again in Aeschin. 1 *Tim.* 40; Timarchus is said to have pretended to be a student in his clinic (*iatreion*) in Piraeus, while actually living as a male prostitute.

in his suit against Onetor called a doctor, Pasiphon, to testify that when he had attended Onetor's sister in an illness Aphobus, supposedly divorced from her, was present at her bedside (Dem. 30. 34). A doctor's word was not, however, always accepted as sufficient in itself. In [Dem.] 47 *Euerg.* 67 the speaker reports that he summoned a doctor to examine a freedwoman who had been attacked on his premises and other witnesses to testify to what the doctor said. The only doctor on whom suspicions are cast in the extant speeches is Execestus, who came with Aeschines' brother to swear that Aeschines was too ill to go on an embassy to Philip of Macedon in 346 (Dem. 19 *Emb.* 124).

It is noteworthy that in three out of these five cases the doctor's name is given in the text of the speech, perhaps suggesting that these men were already well known to the general public.[41]

Whether teachers enjoyed a similar reputation among the general public is more difficult to say, but it certainly would not improve a teacher's chances of attracting pupils if he appeared in court in obviously suspect company. Demosthenes' teachers witnessed for him that his guardian Aphobus had failed to pay them (27. 46), a fact which it was in their interest to publicize; and in Isae. 9 *Astyphilus* 28 the speaker's teachers testified that he had been educated together with his matrilateral half-brother Astyphilus, whose estate he was claiming.

Another profession in which success depended heavily on maintaining a reputation for honesty was banking (Isoc. 17 *Trap.* 2). Bankers had to keep careful records of transactions. Apollodorus, as a banker's son, recorded in his trierarchy 'not only my expenses, but where the money was paid out, and what we were doing at the time, and the price and in what currency it was paid and what the exchange rate was' ([Dem.] 50 *Polycles* 30).

In his suit against the general Timotheus for money borrowed from the bank of his father Pasion, Apollodorus called Phormio, the manager of the bank, to testify ([Dem.] 49 *Tim.* 18, 33, 43), and

---

[41] A doctor who appeared as a witness would of course name himself when giving evidence, but speechwriters on the whole seem to avoid loading their texts with names unless these are likely to be familiar to the public. However, this question needs further investigation. Doctors are more explicitly recognized as 'experts' in Plato, *Laws* 916a–c and in Roman Egypt (Nanetti 1941; Cohn-Haft 1956: 70–1).

referred to the bank's records and to Pasion's oral statement concerning money owed to him, made to his two sons in his last illness (42–3). In [Dem.] 34 *Ag. Phorm.*, a bottomry-loan contract is deposited with the banker Cittus, who may have appeared in court to witness to this (6–7). The banker Blepaeus probably acted as witness in [Dem.] 40 *Boeot. ii* 52, and the witness who testified to a purchase of gold coin in Isoc. 17 *Trap.* 40–1 was presumably a banker or moneychanger.

There were, however, some problems involved in calling bankers as witnesses. In the first place, they were often involved in litigation themselves; bank clients might need others to testify for them to their transactions with the bank, as is probably the case in Isoc. 17 *Trapeziticus* 40–1, or the bank might need to draw on supplementary witnesses to substantiate its own case (ibid. 38). In [Dem.] 52 *Callippus* Apollodorus called not only Phormio but also two witnesses who had vouched for the identity of the recipient of a payment, and others (presumably clients of the bank) who had been present when it was made (7, 18–19). Furthermore, banks were largely staffed by slaves, who could only give evidence under torture,[42] and bank owners would scarcely be willing to hand over valuable slaves to be tortured to provide evidence for a client's case (cf. Isoc. 17 *Trap.* 11–17).

Witness testimonies concerning monetary transactions occur in many types of case, not only in suits arising out of the quasi-professional world of banking and business deals.[43] Lessees of land testify for their landlords in Lys. 7 *Sacred Olive* 9–10 that the estate

---

[42] After the introduction of special procedures for suits concerning sea trade, in which distinctions of status were effectively disregarded, slaves could testify and indeed even appear as litigants in such suits (Gernet 1950), but it is not clear whether the same was true of suits concerning mining, banking, and tax-farming, for which revised procedures were also introduced in the middle of the 4th century (Gernet 1938). On the challenge to deliver a slave for torture in Dem. 37 *Pant.* 40–2, a mining suit in one party's view of the case, dated in or after 346/5, see Thür 1977: 214–32. The statement in Isoc. 17 *Trap.* 2 that banking transactions took place without witnesses should not be taken too literally, *pace* Pringsheim 1955 (cf. Bogaert 1968: 382–3); the speaker had reasons for keeping his dealings with Pasion's bank secret.

[43] In several of the passages referred to the witness testimonies have not survived, and it is not therefore certain that every transaction listed in the text was confirmed by witnesses.

contained no sacred olive trees, and in Lysias 17 *Eraton* 8–9 (cf. 5) that the land was not liable to confiscation as part of Erasistratus' property, having been awarded by a court to the speaker's father. In such cases the tenant shared the landlord's interest in proving that the property was free from liabilities; such common interests can normally be perceived where witnesses testify to business transactions which are not directly involved in litigation.

In Isae. 11 *Hagn.* 40–3 lessees of properties belonging to Theopompus' brother Stratocles may have corroborated Theopompus' statement of the extent of his wealth. Several witnesses testify to having bought land or other items from litigants. The speaker of Isae. 6 *Philoct.*, accusing his opponents of having persuaded the elderly Euctemon to convert 'visible' into 'invisible' property so that they could more easily gain control of it, produces witnesses who have bought land, and perhaps also livestock, and slave craftsmen, from Euctemon (33–4); Aeschines, to show that his opponent Timarchus had squandered away his inheritance, produces two witnesses who had bought land from him, a third witness who had purchased a house resold by one of these two, and a fellow demesman who had borrowed money from Timarchus' father and repaid part of the loan to Timarchus (Aeschin. 1 *Tim.* 98–100). Demosthenes, while detailing the sums of which his guardians had defrauded him, brings witnesses to testify that they had purchased ivory from both his father and his guardians (Dem. 27 *Aph. i* 30–3).

In [Dem.] 40 *Boeotus ii* 58, the speaker says that his opponents have produced testimony that he sold or mortgaged to one of their witnesses, Crito, a one-third share in the house which he is claiming as due to him in lieu of his mother's dowry. His arguments are interesting. First he claims that Crito is too profligate to be able to buy a house—thereby implying also that he is just the type of irresponsible young man who would bear false witness for a companion. Secondly, he says this is not a witness testimony but a counter-claim in law: 'As you all know, witnesses are people who have no interest in the matter under dispute, while interested parties appear as opponents.' This is somewhat tendentious; everyone must have been aware that witnesses frequently had an interest of some kind (cf. Bonner 1905: 29). It was true, however, that a procedure existed by which Crito could have put in a counter-claim for his share of the property.[44] Finally, the speaker stresses the fact that only one further witness to the transaction has been produced, an age-mate (*hēlikiōtēs*) of the plaintiff who has already brought suspicion on himself by claiming knowledge of a naming ceremony held for the plaintiff when he was ten days old (59).

A number of witnesses testify either to loans made in the past which have been repaid, or to debts still outstanding. A creditor who was prepared to bear witness that he had been repaid would obviously be believed; he would only have made difficulties for himself if he had been lying.

Satisfied creditors testify in Isae. 2 *Menecles* 34 (cf. §§ 9, 29) that the speaker's adoptive father repaid a debt, and in Lyc. 1 *Leocr.* 24 that the opponent's debts had been paid by his elder sister's husband while he was in Megara. The witnesses in [Dem.] 40 *Boeot. ii* 52—a banker, Blepaeus, and a fellow demesman, Lysistratus of Thorikos, who had lent money for funeral expenses (cf. Finley 1952: 83–7)— will also have testified that they had been repaid.[45] However, Apollodorus son of Pasion failed to get testimony from the steward of Philip the shipowner that Pasion had repaid a debt to Philip on behalf of Apollodorus' opponent Timotheus. The steward, Antiphanes of Lamptrai, failed to appear when the case came up before the public arbitrator ([Dem.] 49 *Tim.* 18–20);[46] he and his employer may have been reluctant to offend Timotheus, a powerful general, especially if selling supplies to the fleet was part of their business.

Other creditors of Timotheus, who presumably had not yet been repaid, were quite ready to testify for Apollodorus on the same occasion that the general had been borrowing from them without giving security ([Dem.] 49. 61).[47] Apollodorus' own creditors may

[44] By *diadikasia* (Harrison 1971: 214–17) or, if he claimed to be a mortgagee, by a *dikē exoulēs* (ibid. 217–21). The term *oneisthai* used in [Dem.] 40. 58 can refer to mortgage as well as sale and the fact that only a part share is claimed suggests mortgage.

[45] The witnesses in Isoc. 17 *Trap.* 37 may have testified that Stratocles had been repaid.

[46] Apollodorus intended to sue this delinquent witness for damages (*blabē*, not *lipomartyria*), but the procedural situation is far from clear: see Harrison 1971: 141–3, and n. 27 above.

[47] In such circumstances one would expect Timotheus to have been borrowing from personal friends (cf. Finley 1952: 83–5) who would remain loyal to him; but the seriousness of his financial difficulties in the late 370s (*APF* 13700, pp. 509–10) has to be taken into account.

have testified on his behalf to the loans they had made him while serving as trierarch ([Dem.] 50 *Polycl.* 13, 56?) and on another occasion ([Dem.] 53 *Nicostr.* 18, cf. 13). In two of these cases Apollodorus had mortgaged land, that is, had 'sold' property on the understanding that he could repurchase it by repaying the debt (Finley 1952); his creditors were personal friends.

Those who had borrowed money and repaid it were also happy to publicize the fact. The speaker of Dem. 37 *Pant.* (54) calls ex-creditors and ex-debtors as character witnesses. In Demosthenes' suit against his guardian Aphobus, Moeriades testified that he had borrowed money from Aphobus and repaid it (Dem. 27. 27–8).[48] The witnesses in [Dem.] 33 *Apat.*, [Dem.] 35 *Lacr.*, and Dem. 37 *Pant.* were involved in more complex business transactions. In [Dem.] 35. 23 the witness had lent money against the security of property which had already—unknown to him—been mortgaged to the speaker. Possibly the latter offered to him, in return for his testimony, support in his own proceedings against the debtor. In [Dem.] 33 the speaker had lent money for a trading voyage and had been repaid, as his witnesses testify (8, 12), but had been drawn into a subsequent dispute involving his ex-debtor. In Dem. 37 Pantainetus had borrowed money from the speaker, putting up his mining works and slaves as security (4), and had subsequently borrowed money from others in order to repay the first loan; witnesses testified that the speaker and another man who shared in the loan with him had transferred the workshop to the second set of creditors and had been freed from all liability towards Pantainetus (13, 17). Witnesses were also called to testify that the workshop had subsequently changed hands again (31).

---

[48] The same witness may, however, have given evidence for Aphobus that others had a claim on the bedmaking establishment which Demosthenes' father had acquired from him (Dem. 27. 25); his transactions with Aphobus seem to have been rather complex. In [Dem.] 52 *Callipp.* 20–1 the speaker calls a witness who had been involved in a legal dispute with *de cuius*, Lycon [the deceased whose property is claimed], to testify that Lycon had no dealings with the speaker's adversary Callippus. As an ex-opponent of Lycon this deponent looks like an impartial witness—but we have no means of knowing what his relations with the speaker or with Callippus may have been.

The relationship of employer to employee rarely forms the subject of witness testimonies,[49] since most employees were slaves, but there are two examples. In [Dem.] 53 *Nicostratus* 21 men who had hired slave harvesters from the speaker's opponent, Arethusius, testified that he acted as the slaves' owner, and in Dem. 57 *Eubulides* 44–5 a family which had employed the speaker's mother as a wet-nurse testified on his behalf that she was a free citizen. Cases such as this last, in which one citizen appears almost in the relation of patron to another, are rare; though it should be noted that resident aliens and freedmen had to be supported in court by citizen patrons in some circumstances.[50]

There are a few cases in which 'clients' provide aid in legal cases for patrons. In Dem. 27 *Aphobus i* 19–22 it is just possible that the freedman manager of the workshop Demosthenes had inherited testified for him. In [Dem.] 49 *Timotheus* 43 we learn that Timotheus had sent Phrasierides of Anaphlystos, who had been granted citizenship on his proposal and enrolled in his deme (Dem. 23 *Aristocr.* 202; *APF* 14976), to copy bank records which Timotheus needed for his defence against Apollodorus. In this case Apollodorus got Phrasierides to witness on his own behalf that he had been given full facilities, a testimony which had little strict bearing on the case but which, like the testimonies of Timotheus' creditors in § 61, was probably designed to give the jury the impression that all Timotheus' supporters were deserting him and aiding his opponent.

Rich men who were generous with gifts and loans to the impecunious expected to be repaid by help in court when needed. In Lys. 19 *Aristophanes* 59 those who had been given, or lent, money by the speaker's father for dowries, funeral expenses, or ransoms testify to

---

[49] Similarly, the institution of partnership was not well developed, and we have no instances of testimony from business partners. The only example of testimony arising from an economic 'partnership' is Nicocles' testimony for his co-guardian Phormio in [Dem.] 45 *Steph. i* 37; clearly it was in Nicocles' interest to testify that the two guardians had behaved correctly.

[50] Harrison 1968: 189–99; Gauthier 1972: 126–7, 132–56 (cf. D. Lewis 1959); Whitehead 1977: 89–97. The main function of the patron was to guarantee that his client was entitled to metic status, which by the late 5th century could also be established in other ways (proof of tax-payment). Metics continued to need citizen patrons for other reasons (e.g. as guarantors, cf. Plut. *Alc.* 5), but did not necessarily maintain a permanent relationship with one 'officially' recognized *prostatēs*.

his generosity, and in Dem. 19 *Embassy* 169–70 (cf. 166–8) prisoners-of-war to whom Demosthenes had lent money support him. The speaker of Lys. 16 *Mantitheus* was supported by witnesses from his deme to whom he had given money to help them equip themselves for campaign (14).

BYSTANDERS

As has already been indicated, in small-scale societies disinterested bystanders are hardly to be found; the impartial witness is not one who has no ties with the litigants, but one who has ties with both parties of approximately equal weight. Though fourth-century Athens was no village, members of the litigating class would probably be able to find an acquaintance or two in most urban gatherings. The fact that a witness is presented as a bystander does not necessarily imply that he was a total stranger.

Since, as we have seen, it was a normal precaution for an Athenian to provide himself with witnesses while going about his lawful business on many different occasions, it was the man who wished to present himself as the victim of unprovoked and unexpected aggression who called on 'bystanders' to act as witnesses. This is the case in Lys. 3 *Simon* 14 and 20, Dem. 54 *Conon* 9, and probably also in [Dem.] 53 *Nicostratus* 17–18 and Isoc. 18 *Callimachus* 8.[51]

In Demosthenes 54 the speaker, Ariston, claimed to have been seriously wounded by his opponent, Conon, in a fight in the agora one evening. Conon, for his part, maintained that the incident had been an insignificant scuffle between young men—his son, Ariston, and others—in which he himself had not taken part. Ariston introduced his own witnesses in § 9. The exact words of their testimony are not preserved, nor are their full names. It is clear, however, that one was a well-known member of a distinguished family, Niceratus

---

[51] In [Dem.] 53 *Nicostr.* 17–18 the speaker relates that he was attacked near the stone-quarries while returning to the city from Piraeus and rescued by passers-by who heard his cries for help; presumably they were among the witnesses who gave evidence in § 18. In Isoc. 18 *Callim.* 8 it is not clear who gave evidence about the seizure of Callimachus' money by the speaker's friend (*epitēdeios*) Patrocles.

III son of Nicias II of Kydantidai (*APF* 10808). His great-grandfather Nicias I had been a respected general in the Peloponnesian War, his paternal grandfather Niceratus II had been killed by the Thirty Tyrants, his maternal grandfather Thrasybulus of Steiria was another noted democrat of the late fifth century. Niceratus III, born in 389/8 (D. Lewis 1955: 30), was at the time of this case in his mid-forties, suffered from weak health, and had served as trierarch and treasurer of military funds; he was later to figure as one of the elder statesmen associated with the conservative reforms of Lycurgus. Demosthenes (21 *Meidias* 165) calls him *ho agapētos*, 'dear old Niceratus'. He was an ideal example of the respectable witness and was hardly picked out of the crowd at random; he must almost certainly have been known at least by sight, if not personally, to Ariston and his companion.[52]

Ariston gives only the first names of his witnesses, so the other three cannot be identified with confidence. Lysistratus might be the son of Polyeuctus of Bate, councillor in 341/0 and member of a rich and distinguished priestly family (*APF* 4549); if so, he was another respectable supporter, somewhat younger than Niceratus—but the name is common and the identification highly conjectural. The other two, Paseas and Diodorus, are unidentifiable.

In §§ 31–2 the speaker contrasts his own witnesses with those of his opponent. Conon, he tells the jury:

> put in a false testimony in the name of men whose reputation even you, I think, will recognize when you hear them: 'Diotimus son of Diotimus of Ikarion, Archebiades son of Demoteles of Halai, Chaeretius son of Chaerimenes of Pithos testify that they were going away from a dinner party together with Conon and met Ariston and Conon's son fighting in the agora, and that Conon did not strike Ariston'—as if you would immediately believe that, and not reason out the truth, namely that, in the first place, Lysistratus, Paseas, Niceratus, and Diodorus, who have explicitly testified that they saw me being beaten by Conon and being ill-treated in all these other ways, being strangers to me who arrived on the scene purely by accident, would not have been willing to bear false witness, and so would not have testified as they did unless they had actually seen that I had suffered these things.

[52] The companion was 'held back' by one of Conon's group during the fight (8) but apparently was not personally injured; it was probably he who looked about, when released, to collect witnesses. As Mensching 1963 points out, it is suspicious that Ariston did not call him as a witness.

The testimony which Ariston quotes had not yet been heard by the jury (Conon, as defendant, had not yet spoken) but was known to Ariston from the preliminary hearing of the case by one of the public arbitrators. We should not assume without question that he is quoting the testimony either of Conon's or of his own witnesses verbatim (cf. Mensching 1963). He carefully includes the detail that Conon's witnesses were leaving a dinner-party (*deipnon*), which fits in with his own earlier assertion that they had been drinking (7); apart from this, he tells us only that Conon's witnesses explicitly testified that Conon took no part in the fight—a damaging testimony which he had to weaken as far as he could. The fact that he called his own witnesses at an earlier point in the speech (9) strongly suggests that their testimony did not formally contradict that of Conon's witnesses; if Niceratus and the others had explicitly stated that they saw Conon strike Ariston (as he claims in his summary of their testimony in § 31), one would expect him to have called them to testify immediately after his quotation of Conon's witness statement. Instead, he vaguely insinuates that Conon's witnesses are notoriously disreputable, without, however, being able to cite any specific incidents to their discredit. We know that Archebiades (*APF* 819) came of a wealthy trierarchic family and had a nephew (BS) who held the office of polemarch c.330, so Archebiades is likely to have been in his forties at the time of this speech.[53] Probably Conon's witnesses were just as well-to-do and reputable as those of the speaker; the latter's witnesses included Demosthenes' enemy Meidias (§ 10; *APF* 9719), and it is easy to imagine what Demosthenes would have said against him had he been writing his speech for the other side—though to an unprejudiced eye Meidias was respectable enough.

A similar attack on the opponent's witnesses occurs in Isae. 3 *Pyrrhus* 23, where the speaker says of the witnesses to a formal deposition (*ekmarturia*, Harrison 1971: 146–7) made by an absent witness, Pyretiades, which he had subsequently repudiated, that they were 'none of his intimate associates (*oikeioi*), but Dionysius of

---

[53] The Anaschetus whose testimony is impugned in Hyp. 2 *Lyc. ii* fr. v (*POxy.* 1607) may be the brother of this Archebiades (*APF* 819). Another witness, Chaeretimus, appears in a tribal list of the middle of the 4th century (*IG* ii² 2385: 104), but its purpose is unknown.

Erchia and Aristolochus of Aithalidai. With these two men they say they took the deposition in the city—these men, for such an important deposition! Men whom no one else would trust on any matter whatsoever.' Here the implication is that the deposition was forged and the witnesses bribed; but note that again the speaker produces no specific evidence of their unreliability.

The speaker of [Dem.] 47 *Euerg.* also had to face attacks on the credibility of his witnesses (39). He had gone to the house of Theophemos, one of his opponents, with a slave from the office of the port supervisors (*epimelētai tou emporiou*),[54] to collect trireme gear for which he was responsible. When Theophemos refused to allow them to enter, the speaker sent the slave to collect passers-by to testify to his refusal (36), and they testify in §§ 38–40 to this and to the fight which took place when he tried to enter the house.

In [Dem.] 58 *Theocr.* 9, 26 the speaker presents his witnesses as if they were picked at random, but actually he can have had no difficulty in calling on persons known to him; the witnesses merely testify that a denunciation had been posted in front of the office of the port supervisors.

The witness presented as bystander or passer-by, then, was often subject to suspicion, either because this description could be used to conceal personal ties with the litigant or because it was felt that witnesses who lacked personal ties were likely to be testifying for payment or out of an irresponsible pleasure in making trouble.

FELLOW VOYAGERS AND FELLOW SOLDIERS

Other witnesses were thrown together with the litigant by chance, but remained associated with him for long enough to develop a closer relationship. Owing to the celebrated case between Demosthenes and Aeschines over the embassy to Philip of Macedon in 346 BC, those

---

[54] Pringsheim 1961 [1949], 267, notes that it was more permissible for a magistrate to enter a private house and take possession of goods than for an ordinary citizen to do so. Possibly the speaker had asked for a magistrate to accompany him and had been given a slave instead. Whether public slaves could testify without being tortured is uncertain: Harrison 1968: 177; 1971: 150; Thür 1977: 162.

who served as fellow ambassadors figure prominently in the data. Boards of ambassadors were partly self-recruiting—those nominated could themselves suggest additional names—and might therefore be divided into cliques even before setting out.

Aeschines calls fellow ambassadors to testify for him about Demosthenes' behaviour, and his own in 2 *Embassy* 19, 46, 55, 107, and 127; the ambassador Dercylus son of Autocles of Hagnous also testified for him (to events which had taken place in Athens) in 2. 155.

Demosthenes probably called a fellow ambassador in Dem. 19 *Emb.* 163–5, to bear witness to the time taken over journeys, and challenged his fellow ambassadors in 19. 175–6 to give testimony against Aeschines or take an oath disclaiming knowledge.[55] In 19. 129–30 he calls fellow ambassadors of Aeschines to testify about another embassy in which he himself did not take part. None of these ambassadors gave testimony on controversial matters except for Dercylus son of Autocles of Hagnous—named by Demosthenes in 19. 175 as an ally set by him to watch Aeschines' movements—who testified in Aeschin. 2. 154–5 that he had heard Aristophanes of Olynthus relating that Demosthenes had tried to bribe him. The main purpose of summoning fellow ambassadors to testify was apparently to show the jury where the sympathies of the board of ambassadors predominantly lay—which was, on this criterion, with Aeschines. Note that two of his witnesses, the ambassador Iatrocles and Aglaocreon of Tenedus, representing Athens' allies, are said to have shared his tent (Aeschin. 2. 126).

In a less controversial situation Eunomus, who had gone to Sicily on an embassy in 393 with Aristophanes son of Nicophemus, witnessed for the speaker of Lys. 19 *Aristoph.* (23) that Aristophanes had borrowed money on this occasion.

---

[55] The origins of the oath of disclaimer in Athenian process are obscure, but there is no reason to regard it, as Harrison does (1971: 143–4) as a survival of oath-helping. Witness testimonies were normally agreed with witnesses before they came to court; the option of taking this oath protected the witness from a litigant's attempt to manipulate his testimony, and offered litigants some safeguard against changes of testimony by witnesses (cf. Lyc. 1 *Leocr.* 20; [Dem.] 58 *Theocr.* 7). References in court speeches (above, n. 30) are to the rhetorical use of challenges to opponents to give testimony damaging to their own case or swear ignorance; the oath was actually administered to a hostile witness in Isae. 9 *Astyph.* 18, Aeschin. 1 *Tim.* 67.

Those whose suits concerned events which had happened on campaign naturally had to call on fellow soldiers or on trireme crews and their commanders, the trierarchs. Isae. 4 *Nicostratus* concerns the estate of a mercenary soldier who died on campaign. The speaker delivered the second speech in the case on behalf of Hagnon and Hagnotheus, who claimed that they ought to inherit as next-of-kin; the other side produced a will in favour of Chariades, who had been with the deceased on campaign, witnessed by fellow soldiers. Hagnon and Hagnotheus had brought forward other soldiers to testify that the dead man, Nicostratus, and Chariades were not friends or members of the same unit (*taxis*) and did not mess together (18), and that Chariades and his supporters did not conduct Nicostratus' funeral (19–20). They claimed that Chariades' witnesses were friends of his own and not friends of Nicostratus (23). Astyphilus son of Euthycrates of Araphen (*APF* 7252) died on campaign in Mytilene;[56] fellow soldiers brought his bones home and aided his kin in making arrangements for burial, and probably testified to this in Isaeus 9 *Astyphilus* 4. Those who testified in Dem. 57 *Eubulides* 18–19, in 346–5, that the speaker's father had been taken prisoner in the Peloponnesian War, can hardly have included fellow soldiers, but might have included their sons.

Fellow soldiers were often also called as character witnesses. The speaker of Lys. 20 *Polystratus*, defending his father on a charge of helping the oligarchic government in 411, calls witnesses to testify to his own and his brothers' conduct on campaign (24–9); some of these witnesses may have been ransomed by him (24). The speaker of Lys. 16 *Mantitheus*, calling witnesses to testify to his bravery in war, states explicitly that he fought boldly in order to get a reputation which would help him if he found himself in danger in the lawcourts (cf. Adkins 1960: 201–8). Conversely, the speaker of Dem. 54 *Conon* calls fellow soldiers and perhaps officers to testify that when his opponent's sons had camped near him on guard duty two years earlier they had behaved in such a disorderly and aggressive manner that he and his messmates had reported them to the general, after which the two parties had come to blows (3–6).

---

[56] Possibly Astyphilus did not die in battle, since the funeral was private.

Trierarchs, being members of the wealthy class, were quite often called upon to bear witness to events which took place during their period of service. Demosthenes' ally Euthycles called trierarchs as witnesses in Dem. 23 *Aristocrates* 168 to Charidemus' attacks on Athenian forces in Perinthus and the Thracian Chersonese; Demosthenes' witnesses 'who were in the Hellespont' in Dem. 19 *Embassy* 162 may also have been trierarchs, though alternatively they may have been traders. Apollodorus son of Pasion called fellow trierarchs to witness to his attempts to get his successor Polycles to take over his ship ([Dem.] 50, 33–42; cf. [Dem.] 47 *Euergus* 77–8); he also called the officers and some of the crew of his own ships (10, 24–31, 37). In Lys. 21 *Bribery*, the concluding part of a defence in which the speaker dilated on his character and services to the city, a fellow trierarch who had served with him at the battle of Arginusae gave evidence that the speaker had rescued his trireme (9–10). In [Dem.] 47 *Euergus* 48 fellow trierarchs are called to testify that they, like the speaker, had seized property from men who had failed to hand over trireme gear: a clear example of the way in which members of the upper class call on their peers for testimony which has little direct bearing on the case, but indicates solidarity with the litigant and legitimizes his behaviour.

When disputes arose as a result of trading voyages, ships' captains, crew, and fellow passengers might be called as witnesses, as in Dem. 34 *Against Phormio* 9–10 and 37, [Dem.] 35 *Lacritus* 20 and 34, Lys. fr. XL.8 Gernet (1926) and probably in Dem. 32 *Zenothemis* 13 and 19.[57] In a more unusual case, the Lesbian speaker of Antiph. 5 *Herodes* was accused of having murdered an Athenian fellow passenger on a voyage round Lesbos; the witnesses who testified for him in §§ 22 and 24 must have been fellow passengers, and those who testified in §§ 20 and 28 may also have been on the vessel. The prosecution tortured a witness who had been a fellow passenger and had explicitly corroborated the defendant's story (42).[58] All these witnesses are likely to have been Lesbians rather than Athenians; those called by the defendant had to travel to Athens to support him and may have been

---

[57] In Isoc. 17 *Trap.* 19–20 an agreement concerning arrangements for the end of a voyage is deposited with a fellow-traveller.

[58] On torture of free non-Athenians see Thür 1977: 15–25.

personal friends. Alternatively, they may have been motivated by opposition to the Athenian empire; the victim was an Athenian colonist (cleruch) settled on Lesbian land.

This may be an appropriate place to collect together other evidence for the use of witnesses from abroad in Athenian courts.

The speaker of [Dem.] 40 *Boeot. ii* apparently calls Mytileneans in §§ 36–7 to rebut his half-brother's assertion that he had used money owed to their father when recruiting mercenaries in Mytilene. Their father was *persona grata* in that city and the witnesses are described to the jury as 'your friends', that is, pro-Athenian. The orator Lycurgus called witnesses from Rhodes, probably traders, to describe the scene when his opponent Leocrates arrived there with the news of the Greek defeat at the battle of Chaeronea (Lyc. 1 *Leocr.* 19–20). The speaker of Hyperides 3 *Athenog.* called Troezenian witnesses to testify that his opponent Athenogenes, an Egyptian resident in Athens, had been made a citizen of Troezen (31–3). Witnesses from Plataea and Thebes testified for the speaker of Lys. 23 *Pancl.* that his opponent (who claimed to be a Plataean citizen) was not known in Plataea and had been living in Thebes, a city for which the Plataeans felt deep enmity (5–8, 15; some of the Plataean witnesses may have lived in Athens). Foreigners were also, from time to time, drawn into Athenian political disputes. Aeschines in his speech *On the False Embassy* (2. 86) calls on representatives of Athens' allies, and on Phocian and Boeotian ambassadors (2. 143). Demosthenes calls Olynthians to testify that Philip of Macedon had given grants of Olynthian land to Aeschines and Philocrates for their role in negotiating peace between him and Athens (Dem. 19 *Emb.* 145–6); being grateful to Demosthenes for his championship of their city and bitterly hostile to Philip, these will have been eager witnesses.

POLITICIANS (*RHĒTORES*)

As has already been indicated, it is impossible to make a sharp distinction in Athens between 'political' and non-political cases, and similarly it is somewhat arbitrary to distinguish between calling 'politicians' as witnesses and calling on friends. Nevertheless,

Athenians were aware of a distinction between those who regularly spoke in courts and in the assembly and those who did not (Dover 1974: 25–8), and litigants who called on the services of experienced speakers, *rhētores*, had to balance the advantages of their skills and the fact that they were well known to the jury against the risk that the opponent would accuse them of insincerity, inconsistency (cf. Dem. 51 *Trierarchic Crown* 16), and self-interest.

Such accusations are directed particularly against supporting speakers (*synēgoroi*), since ordinary witnessing gave no scope to rhetorical talents; but witnesses and *synēgoroi* supplied similar kinds of support. Aeschines remarks that he might have asked the general Phocion to act as *synēgoros* but prefers to call him as witness so that he will be liable to perjury charges if he deviates from the truth (2 *Emb.* 170); the statement is disingenuous, since Phocion might not have been willing to identify himself with Aeschines to the point of acting as *synēgoros*, but illustrates the functional similarity of the two roles. The speech of the general Cephisodotus in support of Demosthenes' claim to the trierarchic crown (Dem. 51. 1), and those of his opponents' supporters (ibid. 16) presumably took the form of testimony about their activities on campaign. The speaker of Isaeus 3 *Pyrrhus* says that Diophantus of Sphettos, a well-known politician (Kirchner, *PA* 4438),[59] both defended the opponent, Xenocles, on a perjury charge and was taken by him as a witness when he tried to take possession of disputed property (22). Hyperides in two speeches (1 *Lycophron* 10, 19–20; 4 *Euxenippus* 11–13) makes the point that because the speaker's friends are skilful orators his opponent will complain and warn the jury against listening to them, even though he too calls on politicians to act as his *synēgoroi*. The speaker of Dem. 48 *Olympiodorus* accuses his opponent of collecting *rhētores* to speak against him (36). Hyperides 4 *Eux.* 11–13 mentions the custom of asking one's tribe to provide ten *synēgoroi* to support one's defence in court (cf. below n. 83); we have another example in Andocides' defence against the charge of profaning the Eleusinian Mysteries (1.150). This speech also provides an instance in which we can measure more precisely than usual the significance of a politician's appearance in court as a supporter; one of Andocides' other *synēgoroi*

---

[59] He was challenged to testify in Dem. 19 *Emb.* 198–200.

(ibid.) was Anytus, who in the same year acted as one of the accusers of Socrates.[60] His support for Andocides was intended to symbolize Andocides' complete dissociation from the milieu of Alcibiades and his friends, who had been responsible for the profanation of the Mysteries and for whose misdeeds Socrates was in effect being brought to trial.

In most cases we do not know enough about the details of Athenian political life to understand the precise implications of support by well-known public figures; we can catch only a faint whiff of the aura of importance, respectability, or glamour imparted by the appearance of Moerocles (Ampolo 1981) as *synēgoros* for the speaker of [Dem.] 58 *Theocrines* (53–4), by the testimony of Demosthenes and others for Apollodorus in [Dem.] 59 *Neaera* 123, of Glaucon of Cholargos (*andri kai mala chrēstōi*, 'a very worthy man') for Aeschines in 1 *Timarchus* 62–5, or the possible testimony of Demos son of Pyrilampes—a colourful character who owned peacocks and was a personal friend of the Persian king[61]—for the speaker of Lys. 19 *Aristophanes* (27).

Sometimes the enhancement of prestige was mutual; I suspect that the men who witnessed for Apollodorus that they had known Neaera as a prostitute, who included the *rhētor* Philostratus son of Dionysius of Kolone (*APF* 14734; [Dem.] 59. 23), the statesman Eubulus of Probalinthus ([Dem.] 59. 48), a former *thesmothetēs*, and the son of an archon (ibid. 71),[62] got a certain kick and even kudos out of making it publicly known that they had—long ago—had connections with such a notorious lady. Aeschines had a more difficult time,

---

[60] According to scandal, Anytus himself had been one of Alcibiades' lovers (Plut. *Alc.* 4; *APF* 1324). He and Andocides were in the same situation, both trying to escape the backlash of hostility which threatened (despite the amnesty law of 403, the efficacy of which has been much exaggerated) to strike anyone who had been connected with the oligarchic coups of the late 5th century. Andocides was also supported by Cephalus (Kirchner, *PA* 8277), who had taken his side in the Council when he was first accused (Andoc. 1 *Myst.* 115–16).

[61] *APF* 8792, VIII. There is no particular reason to assume with Davies that Demos had died in Cyprus. The witnesses who gave evidence in [Dem.] 50 *Polycles* 13 about the honours which Apollodorus had received from the *dēmos* for his services as trierarch, and those who testified in Din. 1 *Dem.* 27 about the misdeeds of Demosthenes, were presumably also significant public figures.

[62] For other witnesses in this case see [Dem.] 59. 25 (two members of wealthy families, *APF* 1969 and 9574), ibid. § 28 (an actor), §§ 32, 34, 48 (two more wealthy men, *APF* 4322, 8908).

naturally, in persuading witnesses in 346 to substantiate his case that Timarchus had had a career as a male prostitute in his youth. He had witnesses who knew that Timarchus had lived in the house of Misgolas (Aesch. 1. 50) and with their testimonies in hand was able to persuade Misgolas—a man of 54 (*APF* 14625 II) who was quite possibly still unmarried and making no secret of his sexual preferences[63]—to subscribe to a tactfully worded testimony (45–50).[64] Phaedrus son of Callias of Sphettos (*APF* 139647), general in 347/6, testified that he took part in a procession at the city festival of Dionysus with Misgolas and Timarchus (43, 50), a fairly harmless testimony; and Philemon, an actor, testified that he had bribed Timarchus to accuse Philotades of Kydathenaion of not being a citizen (115). Aeschines also proffered an insulting challenge to the politician Hegesandrus of Souniom (*APF* 6351) to testify that he had slept with Timarchus (67); since Hegesandrus and his brother were among Timarchus' supporters (71), Aeschines did not expect him to testify but was merely trying to prejudice the jury against him.[65]

As can be seen, politicians who appear as witnesses are not necessarily asked to testify on strictly political business, though a few instances of this can be found.

Aeschines in his speech *On the False Embassy* hoped to get Amyntor of Erchia to testify against Demosthenes that the latter had tried to get him to propose peace with Philip (67–8); in the same speech (84–5) he called Aleximachus of Pelekes and those who had served on the presiding committee of *proedroi* in the assembly with Demosthenes to witness that Demosthenes had tried to prevent a decree proposed by Aleximachus from being put to the vote; he also called various Athenians officially concerned in relations between Athens and Phocis to testify to the roles they had played (134).[66] Demosthenes in the

---

[63] He and his brother jointly manumitted two slaves *c.*330 at the age of about 70 (D. Lewis 1959 = *SEG* 18.36 B 335–42); it was unusual for brothers to keep property undivided unless one was childless (cf. [Dem.] 44 *Leoch.* and the case of Timarchus' blind uncle, Aeschin. 1 *Tim.* 102–4).

[64] The wording of the testimony is lost; the testimonies in our present text are late insertions.

[65] Cf. above, at n. 30. For attitudes to homosexuality and male prostitution see Dover 1978.

[66] One of these witnesses, Callicrates, may have been the son of the well-known politician Callistratus of Aphidna (*APF* 8157, IV).

same case (19 *Emb.* 31–2) summoned a witness to testify that he (the witness) had proposed a motion in the council implicitly censuring the members of the embassy to Philip. Finally, Aristomachus son of Critodemus of Alopeke (*APF* 1969) testified *c.*340 for the speaker of [Dem.] 58 *Theocr.* that the latter's opponent Theocrines had received $1\frac{1}{2}$ minas (about 150 days' wages) in the witness's house about three years earlier 'for the decree which Antimedon was proposing on behalf of the Tenedians' (35). Aristomachus was also one of those who testified for Apollodorus in the Neaera case ([Dem.] 59.25); he seems to have had a taste for notoriety.

Authoritative figures from political life were sought after as witnesses for all kinds of transactions. The banker Pasion, whose position as an extremely rich ex-slave who had been granted citizenship was inevitably precarious, deposited his will with Cephalion of Aphidna (*APF* 8410), whose son, the well-known politician Cephisophon, testified to this on behalf of Phormio when Pasion's son Apollodorus tried to dispute the will ([Dem.] 45 *Steph. i* 19). Pasion had used another prominent politician, Agyrrhius, as mediator earlier in a banking dispute (Isoc. 17 *Trap.* 31–2);[67] his profession gave him contacts in the highest circles. The speaker of [Dem.] 42 and his adversary Phaenippus made an agreement to delay filing property statements in the presence of Polyeuctus of Crioa, another well-known public figure (*APF* 13772), and other witnesses, who testified to this in court (11, 16). Xenocles, opponent of the speaker of Isaeus 3 *Pyrrhus*, took well-known men as witnesses when trying to take possession of disputed property (22).

THE OPPONENT'S ENEMIES

One obvious way to score over an opponent was to persuade his close associates or supporters to testify against him.[68] Aeschines' challenge

---

[67] He testified for Pasion's opponent; we do not know if he also gave evidence for Pasion.

[68] Cf. the *topos*: 'My enemies are bearing witness against themselves', used in pointing out damaging admissions by an adversary (Dem. 28 *Aph. ii* 14), and the use of testimony from the opponent's witnesses on non-controversial points in Dem. 57 *Eub.* 14.

to Hegesandrus (1 *Tim.* 67) and the substantially innocuous and irrelevant testimony extracted from Timotheus' client Phrasierides by Apollodorus ([Dem.] 49. 43) have already been mentioned. The author of [Dem.] 25 *Aristogiton i,* a speech which is likely to be a rhetorical exercise or pamphlet even if fourth-century (Treves 1936; cf. Sealey 1967) offers as witnesses: (1) a man who had buried the opponent's father and had been unable to recover his expenses from the son; (2) the arbitrator responsible for the case which the opponent's half-brother had brought against him for trying to sell his half-sister into slavery; (3) the patron (*prostatēs*) of Zobia, a freedwoman prostitute who had helped the opponent when he had escaped from prison and whom he had later denounced for failing to pay the resident alien's tax (the officials responsible, the *polētai,* also appear as witnesses); and (4) a man whose nose the opponent had bitten off while in prison (54–8, 62).[69] It is also stated that witnesses in an earlier speech in the same case had testified that Aristogiton had sexually attacked his mother and had deserted his father when the latter was in prison (54–5).

In another suspect speech, Demosthenes is represented as having forced Aphobus' brother Aesius in a previous suit to give a testimony against Aphobus which he is now disclaiming ([Dem.] 29 *Aph. iii* 15–18, cf. 23, 55).[70] These probably fictional examples throw into high relief the aim of many more realistic and reliable testimonies, to portray the opponent as a man whose behaviour was such that he had gone through life making enemies rather than friends. Seeking out the opponent's enemies was a routine tactic for the speechwriter (cf. Dorjahn 1935).

[69] See Schaefer 1858: 113–29; Treves 1936: 252–8; Sealey 1967. The *hypothesis* to [Dem.] 25 is probably based on the speech of Lycurgus which this piece supposedly followed. Dinarchus 2 *Aristogiton* 8–10 (cf. 18) says that when Aristogiton was allotted the office of port superintendent, witnesses testified at his scrutiny that he had not looked after or buried his father and had stolen from his fellow prisoners; Treves thinks that Dinarchus' speech depends on [Dem.] 25, but the reverse relation seems more likely. Aristogiton's half-brother is said to be standing ready to speak in his defence despite their quarrel (55); the dilemma of the brother expected to show family solidarity in an unworthy cause attracted composers of rhetorical exercises.

[70] [Dem.] 29 is supposedly a defence of Phanus, a friend and fellow tribesman of Aphobus who had testified for Demosthenes and whom Aphobus had indicted for perjury. Gernet (1954: 68–70) considers it a collection of genuine Demosthenic fragments which were never used in court; but see Harrison 1968: 105–6, n. 5.

The commonest type of enemy is one who has previously been involved in a lawsuit against the opponent. In Dem. 36 *Phormio* 21, those who had been sued by Apollodorus for debts to his father's bank testified that his claim that the bank accounts had been destroyed was false, and in §§ 53, 56 witnesses testify that Apollodorus was constantly bringing lawsuits. The speaker of [Dem.] 58 similarly accused his opponent Theocrines of being a sycophant, promising to bring witnesses including the orators Hyperides and Demosthenes to testify that he took bribes for his activities (35; but cf. 4). He accused Demosthenes of having bribed Theocrines to drop a charge (*graphē*) against him (42–3) and in consequence breaking his promise to support the speaker in his suit; he called Micon of Cholleidai[71] and officials to witness that Theocrines had denounced Micon for taking corn to a port other than Athens and had been bribed to drop the charge (9, 26); and he introduced Cephisodorus to testify that Theocrines' father had illegitimately tried to claim his slave-girl as free (19). Further examples of witnesses who had been concerned in lawsuits of various kinds against the speaker's opponent can be found in Isoc. 18 *Callim.* 52–4; Aeschin. 1 *Tim.* 115; Lyc. 1 *Leocr.* 19–20; Lys. 23 *Pancl.* 3–4 and (?) 13–14; Dem. 39 *Boeot. i* 19; and [Dem.] 53 *Nicostr.* 20. In [Dem.] 47 *Euerg.* 32 and [Dem.] 50 *Polycl.* 68 witnesses testify to disputes with the opponent over trierarchic obligations;[72] in Lys. fr. XXXVIII G. 4–5, [Dem.] 42 *Phaen.* 29, [Dem.] 53 *Nicostr.* 20, and probably Dem. 41 *Spud.* 11, to conflicts over debts. In Lys. 13. 66 witnesses testify that they had convicted the opponent, Agoratus, on adultery charges (cf. Lys. fr. XXXVIII G. 5).

Other conflicts had not reached the courts. In [Dem.] 59 *Neaera* Phrastor of Aegilia (50–4) and Theagenes of the *genos* Koironidai (who had held office as king-archon: 72–84) testified, with some signs of embarrassment,[73] that they had successively married Neaera's

---

[71] On the possibility that Micon was a kinsman of the speaker see *APF* 1904.

[72] Cf. [Dem.] 47 *Euerg.* 48, where trierarchs testify that they, like the speaker, have had to seize property from defaulting fellow trierarchs—ostensibly a display of solidarity and approval of the speaker's behaviour, but also an opportunity to air old grudges.

[73] The speaker says that Stephanus sued Phrastor for the return of the girl's dowry when he divorced her, and Phrastor in retaliation brought a *graphē* charging him with passing a non-citizen woman as his legitimate daughter, in order to force Stephanus to drop his suit; Phrastor's testimony reverses the order of the two suits so that the

illegitimate daughter Phano, accepting the assurances of the defendant that she was his legitimate child. The speaker of Isae. 8 *Ciron* (46) says he will call a witness to prove that his opponent's main supporter, Diocles, had been caught in adultery. The speaker of Isae. 5 called witnesses to testify to the miserliness of his opponent Dicaeogenes (35–8). In Lys. 31 *Philo* the plaintiff calls witnesses to testify that they had been robbed by the defendant during the rule of the Thirty Tyrants, when he was living at Oropos and raiding across the border (18–19, cf. 14). The witnesses who testified to the misdeeds of Eratosthenes in the same period and said that they had heard him admit to being an 'ephor' under the Thirty (Lys. 12. 43–7, cf. 61) probably also had personal grudges, and the same is likely to be true of some of the witnesses who testified against Agoratus (Lys. 13. 23–8, 67–8, 79, 81). The speaker of [Dem.] 47 *Euergus* describes his witnesses as those 'wronged' (*ēdikēmenoi*) by his opponents (82).[74]

In other cases the hostility of witnesses arose out of more intimate ties. In Lys. 23 *Pancleon* one of the speaker's witnesses claims that the opponent is not, as he alleges, a Plataean, but the witness's slave (7–8). Even after a slave had been freed his former master might testify against him or his descendants; if a freedman became too successful, his position could give rise to resentment. In Lys. 13. 64 the ex-owners of the father of the defendant, Agoratus, testify to his slave origin and in Dem. 36 *Phormio* 45–8 the ex-owners of Apollodorus' father Pasion did the same; since Apollodorus was a particularly arrogant, graceless, and ostentatious *nouveau riche* citizen, their hostility is scarcely surprising. Similar resentments may have motivated the witnesses who made statements for Demosthenes (19 *Emb.* 200) about the early upbringing and menial occupations of Aeschines.

Kin also could feel resentment, either as a result of disputes over property or merely from jealousy of others' success. In Isae. 8 *Ciron*

graphē (which he admits he dropped) appears to have been motivated by righteous indignation. The speaker furthermore promises that Phrastor will give evidence that after he had expelled Phano, being ill and childless and on bad terms with his kin, he tried to introduce the child she had borne him to his *genos* and phratry; but in the upshot, not surprisingly, it is only the *gennētai* who testify to this (55–61).

[74] In Dem. 54 *Conon* 36–7 Ariston seems to imply that his witnesses testified that Conon's associates and witnesses had been involved in house-breaking, but we do not have the text of their testimony. Another hostile testimony, with no indication of motive, in Dem. 18 *Crown* 137.

40–2 the speaker says that he will call the victims, 'or if they are afraid to speak, others who know the facts',[75] to testify that his opponent's supporter Diocles imprisoned the husband of one of his sisters and had the husband of a second sister murdered, subsequently defrauding her son of his property.

In [Dem.] 48 *Olymp.* 34–5 witnesses who had initially put in a successful claim for the estate of Comon, which had subsequently been awarded to the speaker's opponent, testified that the speaker had duly handed property over to them (a testimony of little relevance serving mainly to suggest that the speaker had the support of his kindred). In [Dem.] 42 *Phaen.* 23 the witnesses who testified that the defendant Phaenippus had inherited two large estates, one from his father and one from his mother's father, may well have been resentful kin. In Isae. 7 *Apoll.* 31–2 witnesses testify that the opponent and her sister had sold up the property of their deceased brother and divided the proceeds, instead of posthumously adopting a son to him to 'continue his *oikos*', and in §§ 23–5 witnesses testify that the son of this sister, Thrasybulus son of Aeschines of Lousia, did not wish to put in a claim against the speaker for the estate of his mother's cousin (MFBS)—a testimony implying that the opponent, who stood in the same relation to *de cuius* as Thrasybulus, had equally little right to claim.[76] Very probably the division had left the families of the two sisters on bad terms.

NEIGHBOURS, CULT ASSOCIATES, AND CLANSMEN

From enmity to friendship is a short step; a man's personal network of associates included both enemies and friends. With most of them

---

[75] This would presumably have been hearsay evidence even by Athenian standards, which differed from those of Anglo-American law (Bonner 1905: ch. 3).

[76] Thrasybulus had been adopted, presumably after his father's death, by Hippolochides of Lousia, probably a patrilateral kinsman (*APF* 1395); he had inherited his father's estate and half that of his MB, and stood to inherit from his adoptive father too. The adoption did not affect his legal claim to inherit from Apollodorus, traced through his mother, but the accumulation of estates would have put him morally in a weak position. The division of his MB's estate may have left him on bad terms with the speaker's opponent, his MZ (represented by her husband).

association was due to circumstance rather than choice, even though choice could partly determine alignments and alliances within ascribed groupings: villages, city neighbourhoods, cult groups, and the patriclans which mingled elements of co-residence, shared cult, and kinship in their organization—tribes, trittyes, demes, and phratries. Interest in maintaining good relations and potential sources of conflict and friction mingled in all these relationships.

Neighbours

It is taken for granted that neighbours know all about each other's affairs (cf. Lys. 7 *Olive Tree* 18–19, 29). In [Dem.] 55 *Callicles* the speaker's neighbour was suing him for damages allegedly caused by his having diverted a rain-gully so that it inundated the plaintiff's land. The speaker claims that this suit was part of a campaign of harassment aimed at getting him to cede or sell his land to the plaintiff's family; a cousin had contested his title, and the plaintiff and his brother had previously brought other suits (1–2). The parents of the two parties were on good terms (23); relations apparently became bad after their fathers died. It is not impossible that there was some kind of kinship between the two parties and some dispute about inheritance underlying the whole quarrel. Neighbours of both parties testify on the speaker's behalf in §§ 12–15, 21, and 27; but his opponent no doubt had his local supporters, too. In [Dem.] 47 *Euergus* the speaker was supported by neighbours who bore witness that they had seen his opponents taking property from his house and had protested at the seizure of his son, whom the opponents had taken to be a slave; they had come to Piraeus to inform the speaker of all this (60–2). A stonemason who had been working on a funerary monument near the speaker's house—again, probably, a local man—seems to have testified about a second seizure of property (65–6). In Isae. 3 *Pyrrhus* 12–15, Pyrrhus' neighbours bore witness for the speaker, who was claiming his estate, that the woman alleged by the opponent to have been Pyrrhus' wife had behaved like a prostitute—noisy parties, male visitors at all hours (these are presumably city neighbours).

The speaker of Lys. 17 *Eraton* brought neighbours to testify that he had been trying unsuccessfully to get possession of property in

Kikynna (in the plain east of Hymettus?) awarded to his father by a court judgement (8–9). In Lycurgus 1 *Leocrates* 22–3 'those who know', who testify that the husband of the elder sister of the defendant, Leocrates, bought his house when he had gone to Megara, were probably also neighbours; neighbours also witnessed in §§ 19–20 that Leocrates left Athens after the defeat at Chaeronea. In Dem. 31 *Onetor ii* 4 the witnesses who testified that Onetor had put up notices (*horoi*) on his house stating that it stood as security for a dowry of 2,000 drachmai, and had subsequently removed them, were again probably neighbours; so probably were the witnesses who stated on Demosthenes' behalf in Dem. 30 *Onetor i* 26–30 that Aphobus had continued to farm and harvest crops from land supposedly ceded to Onetor as surety for dowry repayments. Similarly, it will probably have been neighbours who testified for Apollodorus in [Dem.] 53 *Nicostratus* 19–20 that the slave Cerdon belonged to the household of Arethusius, from whom Apollodorus was claiming damages, and who testified in §§ 16–18 of the same speech to the damage caused by the opponents to Apollodorus' property.

Cult Associates (Thiasōtai and Gennētai)

Thiasoi were groups founded solely for performance of cult and membership was voluntary. However, no element of conversion was involved (Nock 1933) and one does not have the impression that the choice of one cult or another usually carried much significance in terms of the worshipper's conception of his or her identity; a *thiasos* would overlap in membership with the other groupings discussed in this section and would not form a significantly different reference group.

In Isae. 9 *Astyphilus* 30 members of a *thiasos* of Heracles testify that the speaker's father had introduced his stepson, Astyphilus, to it; the speaker was no doubt a member himself, and the purport of the testimony was to show that his father and his stepbrother, whose estate he hoped to inherit, were on close terms (cf. Isae. 8 *Ciron* 15–17).

A *genos* was both a cult association and a clan, a subdivision of a phratry. Not all phratry members were members of a *genos* (*gennētai*), but *genos* membership automatically conferred phratry membership

(Andrewes 1961). Only legitimate children of members were eligible for admission, and therefore *genos* members may be called as witnesses where legitimacy is in question. In [Dem.] 59 *Neaera* 61 (cf. 56–60) Apollodorus called members of the *genos* Brytidai to testify that they had refused to accept the daughter of Phrastor of Aegilia by Neaera as legitimate; when Phrastor objected, they had challenged him to take an oath and he had withdrawn his claim.[77] Similarly, members of the *genos* Kerykes gave evidence for Andocides (1 *Myst.* 126–7) that Callias III son of Hipponicus of Alopeke had presented to them as legitimate a child which he was known previously to have repudiated. Objections were raised, but Callias took an oath that the child was legitimate and was allowed to register it. Callias was a controversial figure, belonging to a very rich family which had held the leading position in the *genos*, the office of Torchbearer in the Eleusinian Mysteries, for at least three generations; he failed to pass the office on to his son, and was said to have dissipated much of the family fortune (*APF* 7826, VIII); he can hardly have been universally popular in the *genos*.[78]

Genos witnesses may also have been called to testify that the speaker of Dem. 57 *Eubulides* was selected 'among those of noble birth' (*en tois eugenestatois*, 46) as one of those from whom the priest of Heracles in the deme Halimous was to be selected by lot.

Phratry

Since *genos*, phratry, and deme were all recruited by patrifiliation, a man's fellow *phratores* always included kin. If he lived in the place where the phratry had its cult centre, they also included neighbours and allies and rivals in local politics—as was the case for those who resided in the deme to which they belonged. The testimony of *genos* and phratry members was particularly important in questions of

[77] Rules on presentation of female children may have varied from one phratry to another (cf. Isae. 3 *Pyrrh.* 76). On marriage a woman was introduced to her husband's phratry with the sacrifice of *gamēlia*.

[78] Priestly offices held by *genē* were often *de facto* hereditary, though not *de jure*. According to Ps.-Plutarch, *Lives of the Ten Orators* 834b, Andocides himself was a member of the Kerykes; but Jacoby (*FGrH* 323a F 24) has shown that this is a mistake.

marriage, legitimate filiation, and adoption because phratry rituals were carried out at marriage (*gamēlia*) and soon after the birth of children (*meion*), and because the formal introduction of a boy to his father's phratry (*koureion*) took place two years before the admission to the deme by which citizenship was officially conferred (Labarbe 1953). In the phratry Demotionidai (*IG* ii² 1237) each candidate had to be supported by three witnesses from his introducer's subsection of the phratry (*thiasos*) who took an oath attesting his legitimacy and could be subjected to cross-questioning (1. 74)—an interesting variation from practice in the city courts.

Phratores testified to the introduction of boys to their phratries in Dem. 39 *Boeot. i* 4–5 (cf. 20), *POxy.* 2538 col. iii. 23–8 (cf. Thompson 1968), and Isae. 12 *Euphil.* 3, 8. In Isae. 6 *Philoct.* 26 *phratores* testified to the elderly Euctemon's unsuccessful attempt to introduce a freed-woman's child to his phratry (22–4), and possibly to the boy's subsequent admission.[79] In the same speech, §§ 10–11, Euctemon's *phratores* attested that he had had only one wife, and five children. In Isae. 3 *Pyrrh.* 76 *phratores* of the speaker's uncle (MB), Pyrrhus, testified that he did not sacrifice *gamēlia* in the phratry for his alleged marriage to the mother of Phile, the counter-claimant to his estate, nor present Phile to the phratry as his daughter. The speaker's deceased brother Endius had been adopted into Pyrrhus's phratry, which no doubt helped him to find allies there. In Isae. 8 *Ciron* 18–20 *phratores* of the speaker testified to the celebration of *gamēlia* for the marriage of his mother, and to the introduction of the speaker and his brother.[80] In Isae. 2 *Menecles* 16 *phratores* and *orgeōnes* (members of a sub-group within the phratry with privileges like those of a *genos*) testify to an adoption; so do *phratores* and *genos* members in Isae. 7 *Apoll.* 13–17. *Phratores* in Isae. 9 *Astyph.* 33 testify that the opponent, Cleon, had been adopted out of their phratry into another (cf. ibid. 8) and in [Dem.] 44 *Leoch.* 44 *phratores* testify concerning a series of adoptions and associated manoeuvres.

[79] Cf. the similar case of Callias and the Kerykes, discussed above; no doubt the witnesses claimed to have voted against these illegal manoeuvres.

[80] This refers to the celebration of the *meion* when the boys were young and their father was still alive. One of the weak points in their case, which they are trying to gloss over, is that after the death of his sons Ciron had made no attempt to introduce these grandsons to his own phratry and deme as his heirs (for other weaknesses see Wyse 1904: 586–7).

In Dem. 57 *Eub.* 19 the speaker's *phratores* testified that his father had never been accused of lacking the qualifications for citizenship; in § 23 they testified again to his father's membership of the phratry and of the citizen body; in § 43 his kin and family friends (*oikeioi*) in the phratry testified that his father had sacrificed *gamēlia* for his mother when he married her; in § 46 *phratores* bore witness to his own introduction to the phratry, and perhaps also testified that he had been a candidate for the priesthood of Heracles (cf. above, at n. 78); in § 40 the *phratores* of his mother's family testified that she was of citizen parentage. The speaker was a rich and locally influential man; his mobilization of supporting witnesses in his appeal against his deme's vote that he was not entitled to citizenship will be considered in more detail in a separate analysis of kin as witnesses (Humphreys 1986).

Deme Members

The deme was the smallest unit in the series of segmentary patriclans into which the citizen body was divided: deme, trittys, tribe. There were 139 demes, of very unequal size, thirty trittyes, and ten tribes. A boy was admitted to his father's deme, if accepted as the legitimate child of citizen parents, in his eighteenth year, and thereby acquired citizenship. Each deme had a local base and its own religious rituals, although not all members lived in the deme centre.

Testimonies of deme members often concern matters similar to those attested by *phratores.* They might appear as *synēgoroi*: in Lys. 27 *Epicrates* 12 the speaker says that fellow demesmen of his opponent, the ambassador Epicrates (*APF* 4859) will probably come to speak in his defence. In Dem. 39 *Boeotus i* 4–5 demesmen testify that the opponent had sought registration under the name Mantitheus, and in Dem. 44 *Leochares* 44 they bear witness to the manoeuvres by which the opponent tried to transfer himself and his sons from one deme to another in order to maintain a claim to the estate of a deceased kinsman, Archiades. In Isae. 2 *Menecles* 16 and 7 *Apollodorus* 27–8 demesmen testify to the registration of adopted sons (cf. Isae. 9 *Asty.* 8). In Lys. 23 *Pancleon* 3–4 demesmen of Dekeleia, to which the opponent claimed to belong, testify that they do not know him.

Their competence extended to knowledge about female members of deme families. In Isae. 8 *Ciron* 18–20 members of the speaker's deme testify that his mother had acted as archon at the Thesmophoria, a ritual performed by demesmen's wives (cf. Detienne 1979: 199), and in Isae. 3 *Pyrrhus* 80 they testify that Pyrrhus had never paid for a feast at the Thesmophoria—evidence that the mother of the speaker of Isae. 8 was lawfully married and Pyrrhus' alleged 'wife' was not. In Isae. 6 *Philoctemon* 10–11 demesmen testified that Euctemon, father of *de cuius*, had only one wife and family; in Dem. 57 *Eubulides* 40 fellow demesmen of the speaker's matrikin testify to his mother's legitimacy;[81] in [Dem.] 43 *Macartatus* 35 fellow demesmen of Polemon, the father of *de cuius* (Hagnias), and of his cousin (FBS) Philagrus, ancestor of the speaker's wife, testified that Philagrus' wife Phylomache I was considered to be the full sister of Polemon and that he had no brother (cf. Humphreys 1986).

In some cases we can be fairly sure that the persons concerned lived in the territory of the deme, under the eye of its resident members. In Isae. 9 *Astyphilus* 17–18 the speaker claims that his opponent's fellow demesmen know of the fight over land-division in which the speaker's stepfather Euthycrates was allegedly killed by his brother Thudippus of Araphen, the opponent's father, but they are unwilling to testify. The fight presumably took place near Araphen (modern Rafina, on the east coast of Attica), even though Thudippus had something of a career as a politician in the city, being son-in-law of the demagogue Cleon (*APF* 7252, 8674). Though understandably reluctant to commit themselves on the question of Euthycrates' death, the demesmen were prepared to support the speaker (whose own deme is unknown) with testimony that they did not know of a will of his matrilateral half-brother, Astyphilus, in favour of the opponent, Cleon II (8–9), and that Astyphilus and Cleon II had never attended deme sacrifices together. This is a typical case where the content of the witnesses' testimony is of little significance, but their presence in court is intended to convey to the jury that the speaker has the opinion of the local community on his side. Possibly the city interests of Thudippus and his son had aroused

---

[81] Cf. Humphreys 1986. Some of Euxitheus' own fellow demesmen (perhaps kin) testify in § 46 that he had been admitted to the deme—not a controversial point.

some resentment against them in the deme; but Cleon II probably had his own faction of supporting witnesses.

In Isae. 2 *Menecles* 29–33 the speaker gives an account of a private arbitration between his adoptive father Menecles and his opponent, Menecles' brother, which ended with an oath of reconciliation at the altar of Aphrodite (cf. Croissant and Salviat 1966) at Kephale in south-east Attica. He claims that the arbitrators, an affine (*kēdestēs*) of his opponent and friends (*philoi*) of both parties, were biased against Menecles; if they are unwilling to testify he will call 'those who were present', *hoi paragenomenoi*. This expression probably refers to friends whom Menecles invited to the arbitration as witnesses, as would normally be the practice; but if, as seems likely, the altar at Kephale was chosen because this was the brothers' deme, these witnesses may well have been—or have included—fellow demesmen. In the same speech fellow demesmen testify that the speaker had performed all the burial rites for his adoptive father in a sumptuous manner (36–7).

Military call-up was also organized through demes, and fellow demesmen probably often messed together on campaign. In Lys. 20 *Polystratus* 23 we are told that 'the demesmen, who know' could testify that the speaker's father Polystratus had never missed a campaign. But no witness appears. Polystratus was over 70 (9–10) and many of his coevals will have died; but the main reason for this lack of support was probably his involvement with the oligarchic governments of 411–410 as a registrar of those eligible for citizenship. Those whom he had not registered would be resentful, while those whom he had listed would not be over-keen to have the fact remembered.

The speaker of Lys. 16 *Mantitheus* had better relations with his fellow demesmen, who testified (14) that in the 390s, when there was much poverty in Attica, he had called on the richer hoplites in his deme to help poorer men outfit themselves for the Corinthian war, and had himself given two men 30 drachmas each for this purpose.[82]

If we had fuller information on deme affairs such examples of local patronage and the appearance of demesmen in court as supporters of rival deme factions would be multiplied. Eubulides and Euxitheus of

---

[82] The money was to supply *epitēdeia*, either armour or provisions; the sum seems rather large for the latter purpose.

Halimous, deme rivals and opponents in the case for which Dem. 57 was written, had already clashed in court on a previous occasion when Euxitheus had testified against Eubulides (8); Euxitheus calls deme witnesses, who he says are hostile to him, in § 14 to testify to points of marginal relevance. These groups were small worlds in which paths inevitably crossed, in an interlacing network of often competitive relationships.

Fellow Tribesmen

The tribe was a much larger, less intimate unit than phratry or deme, and probably met less often. Where fellow tribesmen are called as witnesses or act as supporters the significance of their presence belongs to the level of city politics and administration rather than community affairs. There are references in Andoc. 1 *Mysteries* 150 and Dem. 23 *Aristocrates* 206 to tribes appointing a commission of members to act as *synēgoroi* supporting a defendant; clearly a man had to be well known in the tribe for his political activities or his wealth, and involved in a charge of some public significance, to be able to request such support.[83]

Wealth was, in fact, an important consideration. Many of the 'liturgies' in which the rich were induced to spend money in the service of the city were organized on a tribal basis, and this was a likely subject for testimony. In Isae. 7 *Apollodorus* 36 fellow tribesmen testified that the speaker had acted as gymnasiarch for the tribe at the festival of Prometheus, undertaking the expenses of training the tribal relay team for the torch-race. In Dem. 39 *Boeotus i* 23–4 the speaker, Mantitheus (*APF* 9667) called witnesses from the tribe Hippothontis, which was that of his opponent's mother's family, to testify that the opponent, Boeotus, his half-brother, had taken part in boys' choruses for Hippothontis and not for Akamantis, the tribe of their father—an indication that their father did not recognize Boeotus as legitimate. Other testimonies arise from the functions of tribes in the organization of the *polis*, and their mechanisms for running

---

[83] Cf. Hyp. 4 *Euxen.* 12. The decision to provide tribal support for an individual would presumably be made by a tribal assembly or authorized by tribal officials.

their own affairs. In Lys. 16 *Mantitheus* 13 the commander of a tribal cavalry squadron testified that the speaker[84] had transferred himself voluntarily from the cavalry to the riskier infantry; in [Dem.] 58 *Theocrines* 14–15 fellow tribesmen of the opponent were called by the speaker to testify that the opponent had been convicted of embezzling money belonging to the eponymous heroes of the tribe.

KIN

It is not possible here to analyse in detail the appearances of kin as witnesses in Athenian courts (see Humphreys 1986). For obvious reasons, they were called on especially when testimony on questions of legitimacy and inheritance was required, both because they could appear as well-informed witnesses on such matters and because it was important to a litigant to give the impression that his claims were considered valid by his kin group. [Dem.] 43 *Macartatus* is a particularly clear case of the mobilization of a large number of kin to testify repeatedly to the same facts, with the aim of showing that family opinion, in an inheritance dispute which had lasted about twenty years (Humphreys 1983*b*), was now firmly on the speaker's side. The speakers of Dem. 57 *Eubulides* and Isae. 12 *Euphiletus* also call on numerous kin, to help them defend their entitlement to citizenship; in these cases solidarity was probably in the whole group's interest, since defeat of the speaker would leave his relatives in an embarrassing or perhaps even dangerous position.

Athenians who needed witnesses to their actions and transactions might naturally turn to kin for help, but to be supported only by close kin in dubious circumstances put the litigant in a weak position; his opponent would claim that the witness was lying, due to family loyalty. Even testators often call in an unrelated family friend as well as those kin who have an interest in the estate.

Except in cases directly concerned with inheritance or legitimacy, such as the three mentioned above, the range of kinsmen whose relation to the parties to the case is precisely identified is narrow.

---

[84] Probably no relation to the family of Dem. 39–40 *Boeot. i-ii* (*APF* 9667).

Parents and their siblings, step-parents, own siblings and half-siblings, first cousins, children and stepchildren, wife's parents and siblings, and sister's and daughter's husbands appear quite frequently with precise identification, but outside this circle the number of references falls off rapidly and we are often left with vague references to 'kinsmen'—*syngeneis, prosēkontes*—or terms which can cover both kin and family friends (*philoi, oikeioi, anankaioi, epitēdeioi*). Within the narrower circle of positively identified relationships affines are strongly represented, an indication of the enduring ties which women maintained with their fathers and brothers after marriage and their ability to exert influence behind the scenes, though they could not appear in court to testify. Often, too, a woman's second husband will help her sons by her first marriage, or they will support him. The importance of links through women in the networks of solidarity which can be traced through witness testimonies thus provides one of our few indications of the role which women could play in Athenians' private affairs. Their influence may often have been at work too in relations between neighbours, and perhaps in fostering ties with family friends, but here it is less easy to detect.

FRIENDS

Friendship is stressed particularly in the case of supporting speakers. When they could, litigants called on *synēgoroi* who were influential and skilled in public speaking, but such support was represented as a pure response to the claims of friendship. (The opposite side, as we shall see, might present a different interpretation: cf. Kennedy 1968). It is often emphasized that the friendship has lasted for more than a generation. The general Cephisodotus who supported Demosthenes' claim to a trierarchs' prize (Dem. 51 *Trier. Crown*, cf. *APF* 3597, XXII B) had been a friend of his father (*patrikos philos*, Aeschin. 3 *Ctes.* 52). Isae. 4 *Nicostratus* is a supporting speech in an inheritance case delivered by an *epitēdeios* of the claimants and of their father. Lys. 5 *Callias* is a supporting speech by a friend of the defendant; the speaker's father had been friendly with the family too. Isae. 6

Philoctemon was spoken by a friend of the claimant, who had sailed to Sicily and been imprisoned there with him.[85]

A speaker might also represent his appearance in court as motivated by an inherited enmity, or the desire to avenge a wrong done to a friend. Lys. 14–15 (*Alcibiades i–ii*), probably rhetorical exercises but nevertheless indicative of Athenian conventions, are supposedly supporting speeches in a suit against Alcibiades IV (*APF* 600, IX–X)— the first made by a speaker whose father had been at enmity with the defendant's father Alcibiades III, the second by a friend of the plaintiff (15. 12). Lys. 26 *Euandrus* belongs to a suit brought against Euandrus, a protégé of the politician Thrasybulus of Kollytos, by a friend of Leodamas (15) who had been prevented from holding office as archon by Thrasybulus.

As has already been said, the line between supporting speakers and witnesses was not sharply drawn. Acting as witness could lead to involvement in a subsequent perjury charge. The speaker of Lys. 10 *Theomnestus* was in danger of being prosecuted for perjury for having testified in an earlier (unsuccessful) suit that Theomnestus had lost his civic rights. Theomnestus in this previous suit had called the speaker a parricide, and he was consequently bringing a counter-suit for libel (*kakēgoria*). Litigants who wish to suggest that their opponents' witnesses are lying sometimes stress the closeness of the ties between witness and litigant ([Dem.] 48 *Olymp.* 24–5), most noticeably in the case of kin witnesses. The long-standing character of friendship between litigant and witness was likely to be stressed when a defendant called witnesses to testify to his character and his generosity in performing liturgies (e.g. Lys. 19 *Aristophanes* 58, Dem. 18 *Crown* 267, Dem. 36 *For Phormio* 55, Isoc. 17 *Trap.* 40–41?).[86] In *POxy.* 2538 the speaker's friendship with his witnesses goes back to his schooldays; they testify that he and his half-brother were educated together (frag. 2 col. iv 9 ff.). The speaker of Lys. 17 *Eraton* calls witnesses to testify to a loan made by his grandfather to the father of the man whose property he is claiming (2) and to attest that his

---

[85] § 1; some editors emend Chaerestratus to Phanostratus, making the speaker a friend of the claimant's father.

[86] Some of these testimonies may come from officials or well-known public figures, as is perhaps the case in [Dem.] 34 *Ag. Phorm.* 38–9.

father had secured judgement against the debtor's son in a suit four years previously (3). Family friends may also be called to give evidence on patterns of solidarity or hostility within a kin group, as probably in Isae. 1 *Cleonymus* 15–16 and 31–2. The speaker of Isae. 8 *Ciron* calls friends of his maternal grandfather to testify that he regularly invited the speaker and his brother to attend sacrifices with him (15–17).

In some cases business associates were also family friends. Therippides of Paiania, one of Demosthenes' guardians, who gave testimony for him in Dem. 27 *Aphobus i* 19–22 and Dem. 28 *Aphobus ii* 12, had three slaves employed in the workshop owned by Demosthenes' father from whom he received a regular income; he was a friend whom Demosthenes had known from his childhood (*philos ek paidos*; Dem. 27. 4). The speaker of Isoc. 17 *Trapeziticus* calls friends to testify about his financial affairs (40–1). Pythodorus of Acharnae (*APF* 12413), who tried to help his fellow demesman Apollodorus son of Pasion in his difficulties as trierarch by offering to guarantee the lease of Apollodorus' equipment to his successor Polycles, and subsequently testified to having done so ([Dem.] 50 *Polycl.* 27–8), was probably the grandson of Pythodorus the stallholder (*ho skēnitēs*) who had acted as agent for Apollodorus' father thirty years earlier (*APF* 11672, IV).

The friends of one's opponent are of course described in very different terms. Ariston, the speaker of Dem. 54 *Conon*, describes the witnesses who support his opponent as Conon's 'fellow drinkers' (*sympotai*, 33; cf. above at nn. 52–3). The speaker of Dem. 39 *Boeotus i* maintains that his half-brother, the opponent, is surrounded by a gang (literally 'workshop', *ergastērion*, 2, cf. [Dem.] 40 *Boeot. ii* 9) of sycophants; in [Dem.] 40. 28 he reiterates the point, rejecting their testimony concerning Boeotus' naming ceremony: they were not kin or *philoi* of Boeotus' father, and one was the same age as Boeotus and could therefore have had no knowledge of the matter (cf. 58). The same image of a 'workshop' for manufacturing false testimony is used[87] in Dem. 37 *Pantainetus* 39 of the witnesses who came with the opponent to challenge the speaker to hand over his slaves for torture

---

[87] Perhaps even of the same man: one of the accomplices is called Mnesicles in both instances (*PA* 10307 [the second reference should read XL. 9] and 10314).

(*tous meth' heautou, to ergastērion tōn synestōtōn*). The speaker of
[Dem.] 48 *Olympiodorus* accuses his opponent of collecting professional speakers, *rhētores*, to support him.

Another popular tactic was to represent witnesses as friends both
of the speaker and of the opponent, therefore structurally impartial
and motivated only by a commitment to truth and justice. The
speaker of [Dem.] 48 calls *oikeioi* both of himself and of his
brother-in-law (WB) Olympiodorus to testify about Olympiodorus'
loose morals and the amount of money he spends on his mistress
(*hetaira*, 55). It may well be the same witnesses who testify in §§ 3–4
that the speaker wanted to submit his dispute with Olympiodorus
to private arbitration, but that the latter would not agree to this,
and who in § 33 testify that the two brothers-in-law had divided
Comon's estate equally between them while it was in their possession.
It was important for the speaker to show that common kinsmen
were on his side. It was even better if it could be shown—or suggested—that common friends had broken with the opponent while
maintaining good relations with the speaker. The speaker of Dem. 37
Pantainetus points out that his associate Euergus, who had been a
particular friend (*philos... ta malista*, 15) of the opponent Pantainetus, had subsequently been sued by him. The speaker of Isae. 1
Cleonymus calls an acquaintance of his opponent, Pherenicus, to
testify that *de cuius* was on bad terms with Pherenicus shortly
before his death (31–2). The speaker of Dem. 57 *Eubulides* calls
supporters of his opponent to testify for him on non-controversial
points (14).

A great many witness testimonies, for which no indication of the
relation between witness and litigant is provided, concern the types
of transaction for which any prudent Athenian would provide himself with reliable friends as witnesses (Isae. 3 *Pyrrhus* 19–21): sum-
monses ([Dem.] 34 *Ag. Phorm.* 12–15); formal challenges of offers to
hand over slaves for torture (Isoc. 17 *Trap.* 14–16; Isae. 6 *Philoct.*
15–16, 41–2; Dem. 30 *Onetor i* 26–30; 37 *Pant.* 39–42; [Dem.] 45
Steph. i 61; 46 *Steph. ii* 21; 47 *Euerg.* 10, 17; 53 *Nicostr.* 25; Dem. 54
Conon 28); challenges concerning other matters such as oaths, wills,
exchange of property, etc. (Dem. 27 *Aph. i* 41; [Dem.] 42 *Phaen.* 5–9;
45 *Steph. i* 8; 47 *Euerg.* 51, 66, cf. 62; 48 *Olymp.* 34, 48–9; Dem.
55 *Callicl.* 35); statements made by opponents when formally

questioned before witnesses (Dem. 30 *Onetor i* 19–20, 24; [Dem.] 47
Euerg. 34); payments and admissions of receipt and release from
liability (Lys. 17 *Eraton* 2; Dem. 36 *Phorm.* 10, 24; [Dem.] 38 *Nausim.*
3, cf. 12–13; 47 *Euerg.* 64–6, 77; cf. [Dem.] 45 *Steph. i* 37); division of
an estate between heirs (Dem. 36 *Phorm.* 10, 35, 40; [Dem.] 40 *Boeot.
ii* 14–15); the contents of a household at the time of its owner's
decease (Isae. 6 *Philoct.* 41–2); inspection and evaluation of opponents' estates ([Dem.] 42 *Phaen.* 5–9, *oikeioi* and *philoi*; 43 *Macart.* 70)
and of injuries to victims of attack ([Dem.] 47 *Euerg.* 67); disputes
over the status of a slave (Lys. 23 *Pancleon* 9–11); deposit of documents ([Dem.] 48 *Olymp.* 8–11, 32, 47; cf. Dem. 36 *Phorm.* 4, 7). The
speaker of Lys. 1 *Eratosthenes* was claiming to have killed a man
justifiably because he had caught him *in flagrante* sleeping with his
wife; to prove that the act was unpremeditated he called as witnesses
one friend (*epitēdeios* and *philos*) who had dined with him and left
before the intruder was discovered (22–9), others whom he had
roused at night to accompany him when he broke in on the guilty
couple (23–4), and others whom he had tried to summon but who
had not been at home (41–2; note that this is hearsay evidence by
modern criteria).

Witnesses are often called to testify to the outcome of earlier legal
proeeedings (Lys. 17 *Eraton* 3; Isoc. 17 *Trap.* 12, 14; Isae. 5 *Dicaeog.* 2,
4, 18, 20, 22–4; Dem. 30 *Onetor i* 17–18, 32; Dem. 39 *Boeot. i* 2–5;
[Dem.] 40 *Boeot. ii* 35; 43 *Macart.* 31; Dem. 55 *Callicl.* 34) or to
judgements given by the public arbitrators ([Dem.] 40 *Boeot. ii* 17–18,
cf. 39; Dem. 41 *Spud.* 28) or by private arbitrators (testimony by
arbitrators: Isoc. 18 *Callim.* 10; Isae. 12 *Euphil.* 11; [Dem.] 34 *Ag.
Phorm.* 18, 20; 59 *Neaera* 45–7;[88] testimony by persons present at the
arbitration, Isae. 5 *Dicaeog.* 31–3; Dem. 36 *Phorm.* 16 and 24; [Dem.]
52 *Callipp.* 15–17, 30–1). Witnesses might also be called for testimony
about occurrences during arbitration hearings ([Dem.] 52 *Callipp.*
15–17), about offers to settle disputes by private arbitration which

---

[88] Arbitrators were usually friends, or at least acquaintances, of both parties. In
[Dem.] 59. 45 there are three arbitrators, a friend of each of the two men competing
for Neaera's favours, Stephanus and Phrynion, and a common friend of both. Very
likely all belonged to the circle of Neaera's clients; Phrynion's arbitrator, Satyrus of
Alopeke, married his daughter to Phrastor of Aigilia after the latter's abortive
'marriage' to Neaera's daughter.

were rejected ([Dem.] 40 *Boeot. ii* 44, [Dem.] 48 *Olymp.* 3–4), attempts at compromise (Andoc. 1 *Myst.* 122–3, Callias asks three friends of Andocides to act as mediators; [Dem.] 58 *Theocr.* 33, offer to withdraw a suit for a payment of 1,000 drachmas), compromise settlements ([Dem.] 58. 42–3), or other conflicts (Dem. 39 *Boeot. i* 19, [Dem.] 40 *Boeot. ii* 34–5).

CONCLUSIONS

As I indicated at the beginning of this paper, study of witness testimonies can tell us something about a society's theory of knowledge.[89] It can also tell us about theories of the person and of action: the relation of a deviant action to the offender's past lifestyle and future relationships, and of the individual to his associates and social milieu.

We can see that Athenians still expected to be able to rely on face-to-face knowledge of persons in judging situations. Speakers quite often appeal to jurors' personal knowledge of the parties and their doings; even when jurors did not know litigants personally they knew by sight or reputation the public figures who appeared in court—politicians, officials, doctors, bankers, trierarchs—and they were expected to perceive other witnesses as representing the social networks in which litigants were personally known. The support and good opinion of such social networks was very important for the litigant; an Athenian could not even imagine relying on official registration procedures, written documents, and the interpretation by legal experts of an unambiguous body of written rules to define his status and secure him his rights. Questions of identity were phrased in relation to persons, living and dead: who are your kin, where are your ancestors' tombs?[90] The reliability of witnesses is

---

[89] Twining (1983, 1984) has pointed out that the Anglo-American theory of evidence currently rests on an empiricist epistemology which has long been rejected by philosophers. I should like to take this opportunity of thanking Professor Twining for helpful discussion and bibliographical advice; he is not responsible for the use I have made of it.

[90] For the opposite extreme in conceptions of personal identity see Venezis 1931.

judged in personal terms even where questions of professional qualification might come into play; a doctor is a useful witness because he is known to the jurors as a trustworthy man, not because he has been certified as professionally competent. On the other hand—and this is a point to which we shall return—the jurors now have to rely to a considerable extent on second-hand representations of interaction rather than on direct experience. They are trying to retain some of the qualities of village dispute-settlement procedures in an urban setting, and this leads to contradictions.

What kind of results did the system deliver? We are in a poor position to judge, because the speeches we have represent only litigants whose disputes were not settled by arbitration and who were, or employed, ambitious speechwriters. Nevertheless, these speeches do have some features worth noting. A reader accustomed to Anglo-American law will obviously be surprised at the absence of any opportunity to cross-question witnesses, which often makes it possible for litigants to present as supporters witnesses whose testimony deliberately avoids the main point at issue.[91] As I have suggested above, the reasons for this limitation may have been largely practical; before the invention of shorthand, it was difficult to obtain reliable evidence about witnesses' testimony for use in perjury suits except by prescribing that the witness should confine himself to a previously prepared written text. Other attitudes may, however, have contributed. A modern textbook on trial techniques (Mauet 1980) notes that jurors tend to identify with witnesses and resent aggressive cross-questioning by advocates; jurors' dislike of seeing litigants and witnesses tied in knots by sophists may have led to a reaction against

---

[91] Lord Devlin (foreword to Shepherd *et al.* 1982) states categorically: 'There is only one forensic weapon for testing the reliability of evidence and that is cross-examination. When that weapon is blunted, the advocate has no other to use.' Morrow 1960 believes that Plato introduces cross-questioning into his courts in the *Laws*, citing 766d and 855e–856a, but neither of these passages singles out the need to cross-question witnesses as a special problem; Plato wants courts to scrutinize the cases put to them more carefully (cf. *Apology* 37a–b), but he does not specify how such a scrutiny is to be carried out; he might well have considered cross-examination undesirably sophistic. On the possibility that Athenians used cross-examination before 378/7 BC see above, n. 6. *Eisangelia* trials at Athens could take two days (Rhodes 1972: 164; [Dem.] 47 *Euerg.* 41–3), but we do not know how the extra time was used. Cf. Morrow 1960: 282.

cross-examination, if it was ever used. The organization of the Athenian courts also depended increasingly, as their workload grew, on the allocation of a fixed time for each case; lengthy cross-examination of witnesses could have upset calculations. The use of speeches prepared in advance by speechwriters, and the fact that each court case had previously been heard by an arbitrator or reviewed in outline by a magistrate (*anakrisis*), meant that surprise was not an important element in trial technique. The theatrical skills of the speechwriter lay in narrative and the depiction of character, the art of representing the litigant and his claims as part of a just and harmonious pattern disrupted by the adversary, rather than in engineering dramatic confrontations; the excitement came from the jury's task of choosing between two alternative versions of the same scenario rather than from direct clashes between the protagonists. And finally, the jury's attitude to witnesses was less past-oriented than that of modern Anglo-American courts.[92] The jury's task was not merely to 'find facts', but to find a just solution to an ongoing conflict; the witnesses were there not merely to reproduce past experiences stored in memory, but to indicate how the groups in which the litigants lived were reacting to their behaviour and would react to alternative settlements. Witnesses were expected to be partisan; on these assumptions cross-examination becomes less relevant.

Criticism of the way the courts functioned certainly existed in Athens; it is expressed in considered form in Plato's *Laws*, written probably in the 360s–350s. Strict penalties are laid down for those who speak on behalf of others, give advice on influencing courts, or sue too freely (937d–938). Civil cases are to be heard first by a panel of arbitrators chosen from the neighbours and friends of the disputing parties, since they are best informed about the facts at issue. Litigants dissatisfied with the arbitrators' decision may appeal to a tribal court of jurors selected by lot, and those dissatisfied with this court's decision may appeal to a supreme court in which the judges are a small body of ex-magistrates. Penalties for unsuccessful appeal are increased at each stage. The supreme court also has jurisdiction in

---

[92] On the range of variation possible in courts' attitudes to time see Gernet 1951 and 1956. Note that the distinction between character and 'fact' witnesses is introduced in Arist. *Rh.* 1376a 24–5.

capital cases. Accusations of damaging the interests of the state are made before the assembly, handed over to a committee of three senior magistrates for investigation, and returned to the assembly for sentencing if the charge is found to be substantiated.[93] Plato's system thus minimizes the importance of trial by large juries selected by lot, although he recognizes the value of making jury duty part of the experience of every citizen (766d–768d). Plato attempts to make judicial decisions more final by penalties for appeal, by making more effective provision for the execution of sentences (958a–c) and by specifying that conviction of witnesses for perjury does not justify retrial unless at least half of the testimonies are thus invalidated. He recognizes the need for expertise in some cases: those involving medical injury are to be tried by doctors (916a–c). He objects to the use of oaths by litigants,[94] but not to the disclaimer oath taken by witnesses as an alternative to testifying (948b–949b; 936e); it is not clear whether he tries to provide stronger sanctions against witnesses who fail to appear (936e–937a; cf. above, n. 27). He eliminates the use of torture in securing evidence from slaves (Morrow 1939: 80–1). Slaves and children are permitted to testify in homicide cases only; women over 40 can testify and act as *synēgoroi* in any case, and can sue on their own behalf (937a). Conditions to be fulfilled if documents are to be accepted as valid evidence are laid down (953e).

Plato sees law as essentially repressive. In an ideal society courts would be unnecessary because citizens would be perfectly socialized and would never engage in the kind of behaviour forbidden by law (853b–c). He believed (unlike Aristotle) that conflicts of interest in society could be eliminated. He admits that laws sufficiently detailed to cover every possible contingency and aspect of behaviour would be ridiculous (788a–b, 789d–790a), but one feels that the prospect nevertheless attracts him; the looseness and ambiguity of the Athenian legal code, which democrats claimed was due to deliberate choice on Solon's part, to give greater power to the courts ([Aristotle], *Constitution of Athens* 9. 2), was not in his eyes a virtue. He is more

---

[93] The procedure is not dissimilar to that of *eisangelia* in Athens, cf. n. 7 above; Morrow 1960. Plato's supreme court is to consider its verdict on each case in three separate sittings.

[94] Doubts are already expressed about this oath in Aesch. *Eumenides* 429–32.

confident in the educational value of a law-code, provided each set of laws is prefaced by an explanation of its rationale (718b–723d) than in the educational value of courts.[95] Though justice is a social skill which all can practise, law-making requires specialized knowledge. Problem cases are to be dealt with by legal specialists, not by jurors' discretion as in Athens.

Plato was articulating a hostility to the jury courts and those who made money out of litigation which can be more widely recognized among the Athenian upper class (Carter 1986). This class increased its power in the Greek cities after the Macedonian victories of the late fourth century, and speechwriting as an art addressed to a public of readers as well as jurors seems to have died out, although forensic oratory continued to be taught, advocacy became more common, and the speeches of the classical orators continued to be widely read (cf. R. Smith 1974, for a recent survey). Judges tended to replace jury courts, at least in the Hellenistic kingdoms, as the proportion of laws concerned with taxation and other administrative matters increased; the use of written documentation grew (Pringsheim 1955; Préaux 1964). But there is still a considerable gap between pointing out that these changes follow directions sketched out by Plato in the *Laws*, and concluding that they result from any general dissatisfaction with the Athenian system in the fourth century. Such general trends in the development of Hellenistic law resulted from the new political regimes of the period rather than from conscious programmes for reform, and in many places they may represent continuity rather than change; the use of jury courts may well have been confined to Athens and the democratic regimes which were introduced under her influence in the fifth century.

Legal institutions varied from one Greek city to another, and we cannot reconstruct the history of this variation by arranging practices documented in different places and periods along an evolutionary continuum whose trajectory is determined by the values and ideology of our own legal system. I have already argued that the

---

[95] In general, the gap between the abstract concept of justice and perceptions of legal institutions was wider in ancient Greece than in the rhetoric of our own legal tradition. Judges were not idealized (Humphreys 1983c. appendix); Antiphon the Sophist claimed that lawcourts were unjust because they produced hostility (Sprague 1972, fr. B 92; 44 D–K).

record with the long-term evolutionary trends which can also be discerned in it if we recognize that both in the unconscious drift of praxis and in moments of conscious reform societies are trying to maintain a balance between contradictory ideals.[96] In the case of legal process one ideal is perfect knowledge and the other is absence of bias. The Athenians preferred witnesses who had had many dealings with the litigants, in the course of which they had developed feelings of loyalty or hostility, to impartial witnesses who had only encountered the litigants occasionally. They also preferred a witness who had been deliberately invited to a meeting to observe and remember what took place, to the casual passer-by who arrives *in medias res* and puts his own interpretation on what he sees. Put this way, there is nothing very 'primitive' or archaic about their preferences.

If we compare the use of witnesses in Athenian lawcourts with the modern Anglo-American system, using this perspective of the contradiction between full local knowledge and impartiality, we can see that Anglo-American law has gone particularly far in the direction of trying to ensure impartiality and thereby restricting the kinds of knowledge of which the court officially takes cognisance. Jurors are asked to decide whether the defendant has committed a particular act in the past, without considering the implications of their decision for the future relations of the parties concerned, without knowing whether the defendant has previous convictions, often without any evidence on character.[97] Witnesses introduced in court may well be chosen because they appear independent, lacking close ties to the defendant;[98] hearsay evidence is not allowed, except in closely specified circumstances. To see how artificial these limitations are we have only to look at what happens before and after the presentation of evidence to the jury. Police do not observe these restrictions while making investigations (McBarnet 1981), and it is significant that detective novels go even further in the pursuit of complete knowledge; the amateur detective is valued for being able to penetrate

[96] Leach 1954 uses a somewhat similar idea but attributes more clearly structured models to his actors than I would wish to hypothesize.

[97] Character evidence can only be presented by the prosecution if it is also offered by the defence. In practice juries do not completely close their eyes to the relation between verdict and sentence (Kalven and Zeisel 1966).

[98] Practising lawyers note, however, that even 'independent' witnesses tend to identify with the side for which they are testifying (E. Smith 1944).

unquestioned Athenian assumption that witnesses are suppor
those for whom they testify—'une procession d'amis, un dé
connaissances ou de relations qui viennent apporter leur sc
(Soubie 1974: 182–3)—is not a survival from the use of oath-h
documented in Gortyn, but a response to the increased use c
jury courts from *c.*450 BC onwards. It is related to the Ath
decision in 461 to eliminate judges (Humphreys 1983*c*); the ve
of Athenian courts are legitimated as the expression of comm
opinion, not as the rulings of an individual to whom auth
has been delegated, and in forming their opinions jurors not ur
urally looked for evidence of the opinion of the more limited l
communities to which litigants belonged.

In any case, the difference between Athenian and contempo
Anglo-American conceptions of witnesses is not as great as sc
scholars have imagined. In both instances only a selection of
evidence potentially available is presented in court; perhaps one
the main differences is that this selectivity was more obvious to
jury in the Athenian system. Unilinear theories of evolution exagg
ate differences between archaic or 'primitive' and 'modern' instit
tions, and conceal similarities. They too often take ideology f
reality at the 'modern' end of the evolutionary continuum ar
construct the 'primitive' end eclectically out of decontextualize
scraps of historical and/or ethnographic evidence chosen to provic
a suitably 'irrational' contrast to the supposedly rational institution
of modern society (cf. Van Velsen 1969). Certainly there has been ar
overall trend in human history towards larger urban settlements
more rapid means of communication, greater spatial and socia
mobility, occupational diversification, divergences in social experience, and increasing impersonality in social interaction. But this
evolution has not abolished intimacy; it has merely made the contrast between *Gemeinschaft* and *Gesellschaft* more pointed and more
accessible to conscious reflection. Theories of evolution have all too
often derived their plausibility from representing as opposite ends of
the evolutionary continuum contradictory ideals simultaneously
present in the theorist's own culture: stability and opportunity,
continuity and change, group solidarity and freedom from intimidation. I have suggested elsewhere (Humphreys 1983*c*) that we may
be better able to integrate the diversity of the detailed historical

into the local community like an anthropologist doing participant observation, and the world created by the novelist must be seen to be capable of reforming and continuing to function after the denouement. Courts, too, change their rules when they turn from verdict to sentencing; the offender's character, circumstances, and previous convictions are taken into account, the effects of different penalties on family and associates are considered, relatives and employers or fellow employees are often called as witnesses, and a much more holistic view of the person is taken (Shapland 1981).

Those who have expressed surprise at the way in which witnesses were used in Athenian lawcourts have thus been misled by comparing ancient practice with modern theory. We might, instead, ask what questions this analysis of ancient practice could suggest to the student of the practice of modern courts. Remarkably little has been done so far in assessing the social factors which influence jurors' estimations of the credibility of witnesses. Lawyers have their 'folk models' of the effects of the social characteristics of jurors and witnesses (E. Smith 1944; Simon 1967: ch. 6; 1980: 15, 32–6; Erlanger 1970; Saks and Hastie 1978: ch. 3), but these are kept out of academic discussions, partly because of the narrow definition of the role of witnesses in legal theory and partly because such judgements belong to the kind of 'common-sense' knowledge of society, embedded in practice, which operates without conscious formulation (Bourdieu 1977). Most studies of jurors and their reactions to witnesses rely on experiments using psychology students, and therefore start with a narrower sociological range than one would find in a court case (Erlanger 1970; Saks and Hastie 1978; Lloyd-Bostock and Clifford 1983). Experiments show that jurors are influenced by witnesses' 'confidence' in giving testimony, and this has been correlated with studies of witnesses' speech patterns (Lind and O'Barr 1979; cf. Scherer 1979), but obvious questions about the relation of confidence and its linguistic correlates to education, social class, and age are not being directly tackled.[99]

[99] Cf. Simon 1975: 116. More work has been done on the effects of the witness's sex. It may be noted that although the law of hearsay is justified by reference to the importance to the jury of being able to observe witnesses' demeanour, 'demeanour' is currently defined in narrowly psychological terms (confidence/hesitation, etc.), while its sociological dimensions are ignored. Textbook advice on witnesses' 'character' is largely restricted to the question of previous criminal convictions (McCormick 1972: ch. 17).

The Athenian experience is also relevant to another question currently of interest to lawyers, the advantages of 'neighbourhood courts' (cf. Sander and Snyder 1979). It is clear from the Athenian evidence that a distinction has to be made—not always presented with sufficient clarity in modern discussions (e.g. Conn and Hippler 1974)—between village courts in which judges and audience know the litigants intimately and have to continue living with them, and urban courts with lay judges, assessors, or jurors who can be considered typical representatives of the disputants' milieu and speak in the name of a moral community (esp. Yaffe 1972), but are not usually directly involved in social interaction with those who appear before them. Communist countries have courts at both levels; I have, however, been unable to find any detailed ethnographic analysis of the relation between court proceedings and social interaction at the most local level of village, factory, and apartment-block courts. In Moscow City courts (Feifer 1964), where the area served is considerably larger, community involvement mainly seems to take the form of witness testimony about litigants' characters (verdict and sentence are combined, and a holistic view is taken of the persons being judged), although community members in the audience may also express opinions.[100] As in classical Athens and in modern English sentencing procedure (Shapland 1981), the character portraits presented seem stereotyped, and the court is unlikely to get any detailed view of local networks and power structures.

Courts, in all societies which have them, form one of a range of alternative mechanisms for dealing with disputes and deviance which includes friendly discussion between the parties concerned, gossip, mediation, violence, public confrontation of various kinds, reports in mass media, and a whole range of literary and dramatic genres from shadow puppets to soap operas. Courts are inherently rhetorical and theatrical (Ball 1975; Bennett and Feldman 1981; Humphreys 1983a: 7–9); their sittings are public performances in which the audience has a part to play as well as the actors, re-presentations of action and of

---

[100] Cf. Greene 1962: 181–200, for similar points about Chinese courts. The effect of the presence of supporters in court is worth studying in modern England also; in one case I observed, in which a white boy was accused of knifing a West Indian, the defence lawyer pointed out the presence of his client's black girlfriend and her family in court, to prove that there was no racial prejudice involved.

social responses to action in which idealized pictures of social behaviour are presented and tried out (cf. Peacock 1968 on *ludruk*). At the same time, court verdicts have real results (cf. Redfield 1975: 162–5), and so the element of idealization has to be concealed. Court practice both reflects and helps to shape conceptions of the person and of action; we should not allow the view presented by legal theorists of a succession of sociologically naked witnesses observing an equally isolated set of occurrences to obscure our everyday realization that actions and persons can only be understood in context.[101]

POSTSCRIPT

The aim of this note is to situate the article reprinted here in its context in the 1980s, to provide a brief summary of subsequent developments, and to identify some areas where further research might be fruitful.

The article belongs to a series of papers arising from my research on Athenian kinship, and was written in close conjunction with two companion pieces, the introduction to the volume in which it appeared (Humphreys 1985) and a more detailed study of kin and affines as witnesses (Humphreys 1986; the question of the use of women as intermediaries in affinal relations was followed up in Humphreys 1998). At the time, although K. J. Dover had used forensic speeches extensively for his work on popular morality (1974; cf. Dover 1994: 156–8), they were not otherwise much read or discussed. The study of Greek law was for the most part left to lawyers, trained in Roman and modern law, who judged it by the standards of that training. Aspects of Greek law that seemed defective

---

[101] On the need for a comparative study of concepts of the person see Carrithers, Collins, and Lukes 1985, and the discussion of concepts of the person and of character in Greek tragedy and later dramatic theory in J. Jones 1962. Another fruitful field of enquiry would be Western medicine, in which the patient is normally treated without much consideration of his or her social milieu, and there is a tendency to focus on one organ or part of the body in isolation from the rest.

from this point of view were considered primitive.[102] In these circumstances I found I had to rethink the question of the evolution of
Athenian law (Humphreys 1983c), to look at litigation in its social
context, and to ask what conceptions of personhood and knowledge
were suggested by the data. The approach was anthropological not so
much because I tried to approximate the fieldworker's view of court
practice and drew on comparative reading, but above all because
I tried to question unstated assumptions about identity, knowledge,
and the aims and outcomes of litigation.

Similar work was subsequently produced by Stephen Todd (especially the paper reprinted as Ch. 12 in this volume) and Lene Rubinstein (2000); Messick 1993, on Yemen, is also very pertinent. More
generally, expressions of sympathy for anthropological approaches
are now commonplace, though there is still some tension between
lawyers and historians (e.g. Maffi 2001).[103] Such polarization seems
to me particularly misplaced because some of the newest work on
anthropological issues, in the sense of critical examination of categories, is produced by lawyers (Nedelsky 1990 on the self; Scheppele
1990 on 'law' and 'fact'; cf. White 1990), while the social historians
who restrict their comparative reading to studies of ancient societies,
the Middle Ages, or 'traditional' Mediterranean rural communities
are reintroducing in modified form the evolutionist perspective they
claim to reject.[104] This selectivity rests, implicitly or explicitly, on the
assumption that the purpose of comparative reading is to help us fill
gaps in our data by examining practices similar to those of ancient
Greece. If, however, the aim of comparison is to make us aware of
unexamined presuppositions (disciplinary or cultural), a wide, eclec-
tic range of reading may be more useful. For example, it is precisely
because Messick (1993) presents Islamic law as a textual culture that

---

[102] This may seem unfair to Gernet and Paoli, but Gernet did not leave students
who continued his work on Greek law; Momigliano's view in 1964 that the separation
between lawyers' and historians' approaches had disappeared seems to me now to
have been over-optimistic even for Italy. Thomas 1984 is valuable on the 19th-century
background.

[103] It should, however, be stressed that David Cohen, who reads relatively widely
in anthropology (e.g. 1995), began his work with a technical analysis (1983).

[104] See the claim of Foxhall and Lewis (1996: 2) that 'law in Greek cities was pre-
Roman and yet not primitive'.

his analysis can sharpen our questions about the relations between oral presentation and written law in Athens.

There are some valuable new studies of the relations between lawcourts and theatre,[105] but there may still be more to say about the relationships between 'character', self, memory, and social situatedness.[106] The standard legal category-distinction between persons and things may be an obstacle to understanding litigation over land and houses.

Speakers who constructed character in court also tried to destroy it. Earlier scholars (especially Wyse 1904) devoted much effort to reconstructing the lost legal arguments of opponents in cases from which speeches survive, but were not interested in questions of character, or strategies dependent on the historical context; this situation is changing only slowly.[107] Androcles (Isaeus 6) does not seem to have been a tactical genius, but he could present his opponents as wealthy men only interested in further acquisitions and insensitive to the claims of the old (Euctemon as Lear?), women, and orphans. Historians regularly discuss the influence of reaction against oligarchy on the trial of Socrates, but there is less recognition of such historical influences on other lawsuits of the 390s (cf. Loening 1987).

The class relations of 'Athenian democracy' did not persist unchanged from 461 to 322. Antagonisms were sharpened in the 390s by the effect on the poor of loss of pay for military service, as well as political divisions within the elite. Return to the countryside, repairs to damaged property, and restocking farms with animals and trees will have been easier for the rich than for smallholders. By the same token, the disruption of the move into the city during the Peloponnesian War will also have been a greater hardship for the poor; this may explain the impression conveyed by sources of the war period that the rich felt terrorized by sycophants (cf. Xenophon, *Memorabilia* 2.9 on Crito and Archedemus). Conversely, in periods of normal peacetime activity poorer citizens may have been readier

---

[105] See esp. Hall 1995 for the material aspects of self-presentation, Scafuro 1997 for 'plot', and Lape 2004 for a nuanced discussion of 'reproduction'.
[106] See e.g. Luhmann 1982, Hacking 1995; more bibliography in Humphreys 2002.
[107] Russell 1990 is one of the better examples.

to appreciate the generosity of the rich (exercised in demes and other small-scale associations as well as city liturgies), and to view their appearances in court as an enjoyable spectacle.

Several scholars have discussed the social composition of the jury (see Todd, this volume), but less has been said about the social class of litigants. Speeches that were circulated in writing and have survived to be read today were mostly composed for the wealthy, but even though there was a large reading public for forensic speeches (see Dover 1968 on the library of Alexandria), the written corpus must have represented only a fraction of the number of speeches heard by jurors. On the other hand, cases involving less than 10 drachmas were settled by the Forty, while others were resolved by the public arbitrators. More time, in private cases, was allocated to those involving more than 500 drachmas (Rhodes 1981: 720; cf. Rubinstein 2000), which may therefore have made more impression on jurors. The question is not whether the values expressed in speeches appealed to jurors,[108] but what kinds of engagement or detachment were at work in the confrontation between spectator/judge and actor/pleader. Media studies, both of the press and of film and drama, may be useful here. Athenians were used to watching the extraordinary experiences of kings and heroes on stage, and this may have shaped their expectations in court. While litigants no doubt hoped to persuade jurors into some kind of sympathetic identification with their sufferings, and written texts of speeches may have been circulated at least partly because further litigation was contemplated, there are also signs that both jurors and readers enjoyed scandal and the spectacle of rich or powerful men in difficulties.[109] We need more work on the reception of forensic speeches (and the related genre of 'political pamphlets') both in antiquity and later.

The question of access to legal process has been explored in work on the rights and activities of upper-class women, and on the business operations of slaves (E. Cohen 1992); the topic is also raised, implicitly, by studies of the alternatives available to those who were

---

[108] On values and rhetoric see Humphreys 2002: 318–24. Krastev 2003 is an excellent case study of value-discourse in operation.

[109] *Pace* Trevett 1992, Apollodorus son of Pasion is an obvious example. The social control exerted by use of gossip in litigation (V. Hunter 1994) may be more like that of the modern gutter press than the 'anthropological' small community.

excluded from or shy of formal legal institutions. Violence and intimidation are well attested even in the litigating class;[110] slaves and freedmen, socialized into a culture of violence and threats by their owners, presumably used the same tactics on rivals in their own class. Curses, used by upper-class litigants hoping to paralyse opponents and their supporters, were also used by clients of small businesses (tavernas and workshops) seeking revenge, and perhaps in the rivalries of this market-level milieu.[111] Curse-tablets, in turn, are related to 'judicial prayers' (Versnel 1991), used especially where the identity of the wrongdoer was unknown, and to 'confession inscriptions' (Chaniotis 2004) erected when an appeal to the gods had been successful. Prayers (like confession stelae, and unlike curses) were sometimes publicly exhibited; in these cases (as in recourse to asylum in public places, Chaniotis 1996) the victim—quite often female, in the written documents—is seeking public recognition that she has been wronged, as well as hoping to bring social pressure to bear on the offender (cf. Boltanski 1990 on the aims of victims who write letters to newspapers today). This is a reminder that litigants too may have wanted public recognition of the justice of their claims, and not only 'dispute settlement'. The strategic timing of appeals to publicity (cf. Humphreys 1989), and the contours of individuality shaped by such uses of the public domain, need further examination.

To include curses, judicial prayers, and confession stelae in the background that generates questions about forensic speeches brings us back to the issue of knowledge. Boundaries of class and gender impeded access to knowledge as well as to courts. The client of Hyperides 3 *Athenogenes*, who fell for a slave-boy and found himself liable for the debts of a perfume-stall, lacked local knowledge of market gossip. It is revealing that Athenians did not think the knowledge of women or slaves worth hearing in court; for a different perspective see Messick 1993: 176–82.

---

[110] Rhodes 1998, cf. Scafuro 1997; it should be noted that violence was more acceptable for young men who were not yet formally engaged in performing political roles.

[111] Faraone 1999, 2002; like Versnel (1991: 62), I do not think all 'commercial' curses were linked to rivalry.

8

The Nature of Proofs in Antiphon*

Michael Gagarin

In discussing the revolution of the Four Hundred in 411 BC, Thucydides (8. 68) gives us a brief description of one of its leaders, Antiphon of Rhamnus:

Of all the Athenians of his day Antiphon was second to none in virtue and had the greatest power both in intellect and in the expression of his thoughts. He did not come forward in public or willingly enter any dispute, being regarded with suspicion by the multitude because of his reputation for cleverness (*dia doxan deinotētos*). Nevertheless, for those involved in a dispute, whether legal or political, he alone was most able to help whoever consulted him for advice.

When the Four Hundred were overthrown, Antiphon was tried, convicted, and sentenced to death, but (Thucydides continues) 'of all the men up to my time who were accused on this charge of subversion he seems to me to have made the best defence in a capital case'.

In the centuries since Thucydides recorded this opinion Antiphon's reputation has suffered, and in terms of rhetorical ability he is usually ranked behind the fourth-century masters, Lysias, Isocrates, and Demosthenes.[1] This evaluation of Antiphon, though perhaps

---

* An earlier version of this paper was presented at a seminar at the University of Michigan Law School. I should like to thank the organizers, James Boyd White, Sally Humphreys, and GailAnn Rickert, and the other members of the seminar for their many helpful comments.

[1] George Kennedy, for example, compares Antiphon unfavorably with Lysias and Isaeus, though he does acknowledge that Antiphon's speeches 'have certain virtues, which were sometimes to be lost later' (1963: 131–3). J. de Romilly asserts that, in contrast to Antiphon and Andocides, 'with [Lysias], forensic oratory becomes more than a technique; henceforth it is a literary art' (1985: 114).

valid in some respects, is in part the result of a slim but influential volume published in 1931, *Antiphonstudien*, in which Friedrich Solmsen examined Antiphon's three courtroom speeches (1, 5, and 6) from the perspective of Aristotle's distinction, in the *Rhetoric*, between 'non-artistic proofs' (*pisteis atechnoi*) and 'artistic proofs' (*pisteis entechnoi*). Claiming that early Greek legal procedure knew only non-artistic proofs (e.g. oaths), which were automatically decisive, Solmsen placed Antiphon at a point of transition between this archaic system and fourth-century procedure, in which artistic proofs dominate. Antiphon makes much use of the newer artistic proofs, but (Solmsen argued) the archaic, [23] non-artistic proofs still influence his speeches, determining to some extent the nature of his arguments and the arrangement of his material.[2]

Solmsen's thesis is brilliant in many respects, and has the undeniable merit of situating Antiphon within a legal and intellectual tradition; but however desirable such a perspective may be, it is a mistake, in my view, to portray Antiphon as dominated or even strongly influenced by the kind of archaic legal tradition described by Solmsen. The legal tradition, I suggest, put no such constraints on Antiphon's argumentation or use of proofs; rather, we must understand that the construction of his arguments was determined essentially by the facts of the case (in a broad sense) and by his own rhetorical ability.

One way of refuting Solmsen's views is to examine the speeches of Antiphon and demonstrate that non-artistic proofs do not in fact play the role that Solmsen alleges. This approach would require a thorough study of all the arguments of each speech, a task I shall not undertake here.[3] Rather, I should like to raise more basic questions, concerning two points: first, Solmsen's use of Aristotle's distinction

---

[2] Solmsen's conclusions (1931) have not necessarily been adopted in detail, but he has set the terms for discussion of Antiphon. This is especially clear in the work of Kennedy, the most important contemporary scholar of Greek rhetoric writing in English; see Kennedy 1963: 131–2, and in Knox and Easterling 1986: 501, where Kennedy writes: 'In terms of content and technique the most significant aspect of Antiphon's speeches is the conflict evident in them between direct evidence and argumentation, what Aristotle was later to call non-artistic and artistic proof,' citing Solmsen. See also J. W. Jones 1956: 143.

[3] Some work along these lines has been done by Vollmer 1958, Due 1980, and Goebel 1983: 49–55. For the arguments of Ant. 5 see Gagarin 1989*b*.

between 'artistic proofs' and 'non-artistic proofs'; second, the question of proofs in early Greek legal procedure. I shall argue that Solmsen's thesis is grounded on a mistaken understanding of early Greek legal procedure compounded by a mistaken application of Aristotle's categories of proofs, and that he thus situates Antiphon in a falsely conceived legal tradition.

I. PROOFS IN ARISTOTLE

The terms *pisteis atechnoi* and *pisteis entechnoi* were created by Aristotle.[4] A similar distinction is made by Anaximenes in the *Rhetorica ad Alexandrum* (7, 1428a16–26), which may be slightly earlier,[5] but since Solmsen bases his thesis on Aristotle, I shall concern myself only with the discussion in his *Rhetoric*. Near the beginning of Book 1, after defining rhetoric as the 'ability to discover the available means of [24] persuasion (*to endechomenon pithanon*) for any subject', Aristotle introduces a fundamental distinction (1. 2. 2, 1355b35–9):

Proofs [as *pisteis* is usually translated] are either non-artistic (*atechnoi*) or artistic (*entechnoi*). By non-artistic I mean those that are not provided by us but are already at hand, such as witnesses (*martures*), interrogations (*basanoi*),[6] contracts (*sungraphai*), and the like; by artistic I mean those that can be constructed systematically by us. Thus we have only to make use of the former, but we must discover the latter.

Most of Book 1 is concerned with artistic proofs, but in 1. 15 Aristotle returns to the non-artistic proofs, adding laws and the

---

[4] So Quint. *Inst.* 5. 1. 1, which agrees with the evidence of the surviving texts. I have searched the data for base *Thesaurus Linguae Graecae* (on their Pilot CD ROM #C) for the expressions *atechnoi pisteis* and *entechnoi pisteis*; they are not uncommon in later writers on rhetoric, all of whom are directly or indirectly influenced by Aristotle.

[5] Anaximenes uses the term 'supplementary' (*epithetoi*) proofs, which includes witnesses, interrogations, oaths, and the opinion (*doxa*) of the speaker.

[6] I use 'interrogation' to translate *basanos*, which designates both the process of questioning slaves (whose testimony was admissible in Athens only if obtained by torture, *basanos*) and the testimony that results. In *Rh.* 1. 15 interrogations are treated as a special category of witnesses.

oath to the three already mentioned (witnesses, interrogations, and contracts) and examining each of these in turn.

Regarding laws, he advises the orator (much as a modern law professor might advise his students) that if the relevant law favours his opponent, he must argue for the priority of unwritten laws or equity, whereas if the written law favours his side, he must argue that the jurors have an obligation to uphold the law. Next, witnesses from the past, such as poets, should be enlisted where they are needed. As for contemporary witnesses who are familiar with the facts of the case, if such witnesses are available to testify in his favour, he should stress the superiority of their testimony over general arguments; but if he has no such witnesses, he should argue that the jurors must judge on the basis of probability, since arguments from probability cannot be bribed, and so forth. Aristotle continues in a similar vein, showing how to use the available evidence of contracts, interrogations, and oaths. For instance, if the interrogation supports your case, you argue that this is the only sort of reliable testimony; but if it goes against you, you argue that testimony gained through torture is not reliable.

To understand the nature and function of these 'non-artistic proofs', we must begin by noting that *pistis*, at least when modified by *atechnos* or *entechnos*, does not mean 'proof', or even 'evidence', but (in Grimaldi's words) 'evidentiary material', that is, the material on which the speaker draws in constructing his arguments.[7] For Aristotle, the testimony of a witness is not in itself proof, nor even necessarily evidence, but material the speaker may use as it suits the needs of his case. In this respect the non-artistic *pisteis* serve much the same function for the speaker as the artistic *pisteis*, the main difference being that the latter are general considerations whereas the former are specific to a particular case. The testimony of a witness, for example, may be used in the same [25] sort of argument from

---

[7] Grimaldi 1980: 20. This meaning is confirmed by the opening words of *Rhetoric*, Book 2: 'These [i.e. the proofs discussed in Book 1] are the things from which (*ek tinōn*) one must' construct the argument. The German translation of *pistis* is usually *Beweis* ('proof, evidence'), which is broader than any single English word but still suggests material that is decisive in itself rather than a source of or basis for argument. *Beweismittel* is better. For the meaning of *pistis* in other contexts in the *Rhetoric*, see Grimaldi 1980: 19–20, 349–56.

probability as the analysis of criminal mentality (1. 12), and Aristotle's
analysis of just and unjust acts (1. 13) begins with a discussion of laws,
to which he returns in 1. 15.

None of these non-artistic *pisteis* is automatically decisive. Aristotle occasionally hints that an oath may decide a case; for example,
one justification he suggests for refusing to swear an oath is that this
refusal is virtuous because one knows that one would win the case by
swearing the oath, but not by refusing it (1377a17–19). But throughout the discussion of oaths Aristotle clearly envisions the swearing of
an oath by one party or the other as an action requiring discussion
and argument by the speaker in court; in such cases, plainly, the oath
is not decisive per se. He is particularly interested in oath-challenges,
where a litigant either offers to take an oath himself or asks his
opponent to take one, and he provides justification for issuing either
kind of challenge, and for the acceptance or refusal of a challenge
issued by one's opponent. In each instance, however, he assumes that
the challenge has or has not been made before the case comes to
court, and that if made, it has or has not been accepted. Thus the
oath-challenges, like the other *pisteis*, are material for the speaker to
manipulate in whatever way suits his case. And as with the other
pisteis, artistic and non-artistic alike, that manipulation takes the
form of rational argument.

There is no hint, moreover, that the non-artistic *pisteis* are logically
or historically prior to the artistic *pisteis*. Aristotle devotes less time
to the non-artistic *pisteis* because they are limited in number and are
used only in forensic oratory, whereas the artistic *pisteis* have a
broader scope and are relevant to all three branches of oratory. But
the logical status or force of the non-artistic *pisteis* is indistinguishable from that of the artistic *pisteis*. The distinction between the two
in the *Rhetoric* is a useful tool for Aristotle's systematic analysis of the
art of rhetoric, nothing more.

I must emphasize that although Aristotle often presents general
arguments to be used in challenging the evidence of non-artistic
pisteis, he does not value these general arguments more highly than
the direct evidence. In the whole section about witnesses (1375b26–
76a32), for example, there is one short passage (1376a17–23) about
pistōmata (the means of confirming the testimony of witnesses),
where we are given arguments both for and against their testimony:

Someone who has no witnesses can say that one must decide from probabilities and that this is the meaning of [the oath] 'according to my best judgement', and that probabilities cannot be bribed or convicted of bearing false witness; but someone who has witnesses when his opponent does not can say that probability arguments have no responsibility and that there would be no need for witnesses if [the truth] could be sufficiently determined by arguments.

Throughout this section Aristotle clearly implies that the evidence of witnesses is indeed valuable and should be depreciated only when it favours one's opponent; and yet it is sometimes claimed (in an evident [26] echo of this passage) that 'in practice probability appeared safer than witnesses who were only too easily corrupted, for probabilities could not be bought'.[8] Any unbiased reading of Aristotle or of the surviving Greek orations shows otherwise.[9]

In sum, Aristotle's conceptual distinction between the two kinds of *pisteis* does not imply the kind of distinction between automatic, so-called 'irrational' proofs and logical arguments that underlies Solmsen's analysis of early Greek legal procedure and its development in the fifth and fourth centuries. It does not necessarily follow that this kind of distinction was not present in the law, but we can find no evidence for it in Aristotle. Thus, if we wish to understand the nature of Greek law before Antiphon, we must turn away from the *Rhetoric* and look at the evidence for law itself.

II. PROOFS IN EARLY GREEK LAW

In his discussion of the nature of early Greek law Solmsen relies fundamentally and exclusively on the work of Kurt Latte.[10] As his title

---

[8] Kennedy 1963: 32, and similarly 1980: 21. (I single out Kennedy because of his wide influence and because Solmsen's thesis so clearly colours his views. It is only fair to add that I, like all who study Greek oratory, have learned a great deal from his many books and articles.)

[9] The bias goes back to Plato, whose antipathy to rhetoric is well known; see esp. *Phdr.* 267a, where Socrates says that Tisias and Gorgias 'saw that probabilities were more to be honoured than the truth' (cf. 272d–73a).

[10] Latte 1920, esp. part 1, 'Das Verfahren' (pp. 5–47), discussed by Solmsen 1931: 6–8. Sautel 1965 provides a more comprehensive statement of the traditional view, but is generally superficial and uninformative.

(*Heiliges Recht*) implies, Latte traces the 'religious' element in Greek law, particularly the use of oaths and witnesses, which (he argues) was especially important in early procedure. These methods of proof (*Beweis*) operated automatically: a litigant who swore a specified oath or produced a specified number of witnesses would win his case without further ado. In this formal theory of proof (*formale Beweistheorie*) early Greek law resembled early Germanic law, with its procedures for deciding cases by ordeal (which Latte discusses briefly), oath, or formal witnesses. This picture of an automatic, irrational, formalistic legal process is wholeheartedly accepted by Solmsen, who adds interrogations to Latte's list of archaic methods of proof.[11] However, although we may find traces of some of these procedures in early Greek law, the evidence does not support Latte's overall picture of archaic legal procedure or the parallel with early Germanic law. I shall consider each of the procedures separately, beginning with interrogation.

[27]   Latte never discusses interrogation in early procedure, for the simple reason that *basanos* is not used in the sense 'examination by torture' before the last third of the fifth century.[12] Solmsen includes interrogation in his summary because it is important for his discussion of Antiphon, but we have no evidence that it played a role in earlier procedure. It seems clear, moreover, that the primary motivation for the common challenge to an interrogation (*proklēsis eis basanon*), whereby one litigant challenges the other either to interrogate the challenger's slaves or to hand over his own slaves for interrogation by the challenger, is rhetorical. The challenger normally does not expect his challenge to produce a statement from the tortured slave; rather, he expects to use his opponent's refusal of the challenge as evidence that he is trying to avoid the truth (Thür 1977: 233–61). Many such challenges are mentioned in the surviving

---

[11] Solmsen 1931: 6–7 summarizes Latte's conclusions as follows: 'daß im *arch-aischen* Gerichtsverfahren jenen untechnischen, vorrhetorischen, ja man darf sagen: *logos*-fremden Bestandteilen des Prozesses die eigentlich entscheidende Rolle zufällt und das richterliche Urteil durch den Befund der *martures* und *horkoi* weitgehend festgelegt ist. Die *martures, basanoi, horkoi* sind ursprünglich durchaus vollwertige und autarke *pisteis*, ja sogar die eigentlichen *pisteis*, neben denen der *logos* gar keinen Erweiswert hat.'

[12] Thür 1977: 14–15, cites Antiphon and Aristophanes for 5th-century examples of this meaning. I would add Hdt. 8. 110.

speeches, but none appears to have been accepted. In this and other respects the procedure remained essentially unchanged from the late fifth to the late fourth century. As Aristotle's advice in *Rhetoric* 1. 15 shows, an interrogation provides the evidentiary material for rhetorical arguments; it is not in itself an automatic or definitive proof.[13]

The evidence for ordeal as a legal procedure in Greece at any time is so meagre as to be virtually non-existent. Latte (1920: 5–6) cites only the statement of the watchman in *Antigone*, who before reporting to Creon the burial of Polyneices asserts (264–67), 'I am ready to hold molten iron in my hands and walk through fire and swear to the gods that I neither did the deed nor have any knowledge of anyone who planned or did the deed'. Latte may be correct in thinking that this recalls an ancient procedure of ordeal, which in various forms is known in medieval Europe and elsewhere, and one can find a few other scraps of evidence for the ordeal in Greece, especially if one defines ordeal broadly enough to include such things as the exposure of children in the wilds.[14] But nothing points to its use in a legal context. Slaves may have been subjected to ordeal by their masters, or children by their parents, but there is no evidence that a legal case might be so decided. I might add [28] that much the same is true of trial by combat, which some have proposed as an early Greek legal procedure (Armstrong 1950), though Latte and Solmsen do not mention it. Such examples as the duel between Paris and Menelaus in the *Iliad* show only that single combat could be used to settle a war, not that it was ever used for deciding a legal case.

With regard to witnesses, it has been argued that witnesses at Gortyn were always 'formal witnesses'—that is, witnesses who were formally summoned to witness a particular event and later testified in court, where their testimony was automatically decisive—and that

[13] Thür 1977: 205–32 demonstrates that the orators always speak of *basanos* as a means of certifying the truth of a slave's testimony and not as an automatic, decisive procedure (as was argued by J. Headlam 1893). Thür (1977: 287–312) argues that the procedures of the *basanos* made it very difficult for jurors independently to evaluate the truthfulness of the tortured slave's testimony; as a result, they tended to accept the evidence of the interrogation as incontrovertible. Even if this is correct (and I am not fully persuaded), it is not evidence for an archaic procedure of interrogation operating automatically. [See Gagarin 1996 and Mirhady 1996 (= Ch. 10 below).]

[14] So Glotz 1904. For a different view of ordeal, as a flexible tool for dispute-settlement, see P. R. Brown 1982: 306–17, 'Society and the Supernatural' (repr. from *Daedalus*, 104 (1975): 133–51).

at Gortyn, as in early Germanic law, the testimony of an accidental witness who happened to know the facts of the case was not admissible.[15] It can be shown, however, that although in certain cases a person was required formally to summon a specific number of witnesses, whose testimony could later be decisive in court, accidental witnesses were certainly permitted to testify in at least some cases and could probably testify in many other cases where their testimony is not mentioned explicitly.[16] We have a few possible indications (e.g. Arist. *Pol.* 1269a1–3) that in some cases the testimony of a specific number of witnesses might automatically decide a legal case, but these examples do not establish that witnesses were in general automatically decisive in early Greek law. And there is no certain Greek parallel to the 'oath-helpers' of early Germanic law, who swore in support of someone's case regardless of their knowledge of the facts, and whose sworn statements were decisive. Moreover, although witnesses in Athenian courts regularly were relatives or associates of the litigant and swore to the truth of his entire case, they were certainly expected to know the facts to which they swore.[17] This is clear as early as Antiphon's fifth speech (*The Murder of Herodes*), in which witnesses are called nine times;[18] in each case they testify to facts they happen to know from their own experience. Moreover, their testimony is clearly not decisive in itself, but is subject to examination and argument just like other sorts of evidence.

Most of Latte's study is devoted to oaths. At Gortyn, the law could direct one litigant to swear an oath that would decide the matter, but such laws normally regulated situations where there probably would not be any other relevant evidence;[19] it does not appear that automatic, [29] decisive oaths were used in other cases. We also find occasional oath-challenges in literature, where one litigant either challenges the

---

[15] See J. Headlam 1892–3, followed by Willetts 1967: 33.

[16] See Gagarin 1989*a*. For accidental witnesses the clearest example is *ICret.* iv 41. 5. 4–11, discussed by Gagarin 1984.

[17] See Humphreys 1985: 313–69; her objections (p. 353) to certain studies of the 'primitive' nature of Athenian witnesses apply equally well to the study of early Greek procedure. [See Ch. 7 above, 'Conclusions', esp. 205–6.]

[18] Ant. 5. 20, 22, 24, 28, 30, 35, 56, 61, 83.

[19] See e.g. *ICret.* iv 72. 3. 5–9: in a divorce, the wife is allowed to keep her own property and half of the income it has produced; a wife accused of taking more can swear an oath of denial, which is decisive.

other to swear an oath or offers to swear one himself: for example, Menelaus challenges Antilochus, after the chariot race in *Iliad* 23, to swear an oath that he did not use trickery to gain second place, and the Furies challenge Orestes, in Aeschylus' *Eumenides*, to swear an oath that he did not kill his mother. In neither case is the challenge accepted, though the implication may be that if it were, the oath would be decisive. But in both passages, as in Aristotle, the oath-challenge (like the challenge to an interrogation in legal speeches) is more a rhetorical strategy than a means of proof: it is primarily intended to provide material for argument after the challenge has been refused, not to settle the case automatically when the challenge has been accepted.

We may conclude that, despite isolated cases, there is no evidence for the general use of automatic, 'irrational' procedures for settling legal disputes in early Greece. Moreover, the literary evidence from Homer to the fifth century consistently depicts legal procedure as largely consisting of rational debate by the litigants before a judge or judges empowered to render a decision (Gagarin 1986: 19–50), and this picture is utterly at odds with the picture drawn by Latte and accepted by Solmsen. Indeed, the 'irrational' procedures of medieval Germanic law, which have often been introduced as parallels for early Greek law, were crucially dependent on the general belief in, or at least acceptance of, an almighty divinity, whose hand would guide the procedure to a just outcome. In contrast, at no stage of Greek culture evident to us did a similarly authoritative divine force exist. From the Homeric epics on, Greek culture is characterized by a thoroughly rational approach to debate and decision-making, in which omens, prophecies, and even the direct commands of the gods are discussed, debated, and sometimes, but by no means always, followed. It would be contrary to everything we know to ascribe fundamentally 'irrational' procedures to early Greek law.

III. PROOFS IN ANTIPHON

Let us now return to Antiphon and his place in the legal and rhetorical tradition. Much of the early history of Greek oratory is obscure (cf. Kennedy 1963: 52–70), but there is little doubt that the formal study of rhetoric began about the middle of the fifth century, probably in Sicily with Tisias and Corax. At this time rhetoric also became an important concern of the sophists Gorgias, Protagoras, and later Thrasymachus and others. The ideas of these thinkers found a particularly receptive audience in Athens, where the reforms of Ephialtes and Pericles in the middle of the fifth century led to greatly increased use of the popular lawcourts. The most obvious effect of this new interest in rhetoric was an increased use of logical argument, in particular the argument from probability, or *eikos*.

[30] The argument from *eikos* was not invented by Tisias or Corax. The earliest explicit example is in the *Hymn to Hermes*, where Hermes argues that he, a mere babe, is not like a cattle thief (265, *oude... eoika*) and thus did not steal Apollo's cattle. The date of the *Hymn* is uncertain, but almost all scholars date it before 450.[20] The earliest explicit argument from *eikos* in tragedy is probably Pasiphaë's speech in Euripides' lost play the *Cretans*, usually dated to the 430s (Goebel 1983: 290–301); and Herodotus is fond of arguments from *eikos* (e.g. 3. 38. 2). But if Tisias and Corax did not invent this kind of argument, they almost certainly developed new forms of it, including what I call the reverse argument from *eikos*. The classic example concerns a fight between a weak man and a strong man. The weak man gives the expected argument: it is not likely that he, a weak man, assaulted a strong man. The other counters with a 'reverse *eikos*': he is not likely to have assaulted a weak man, since he would immediately be suspected of the crime.[21] The reverse argument is sophistic (in both senses), and was seldom used, though it is introduced by the defendant in Antiphon's *First Tetralogy* (2. 2. 6), which is certainly a product of the intellectual ferment of this period.[22]

The second half of the fifth century saw an increasing use of arguments from *eikos* and other rhetorical techniques, but this development did not mark any move away from non-artistic *pisteis*,

[20] Most date it around 500; see Janko 1982: 140–3.

[21] Arist. *Rh.* 2. 24.11 1402a17–28 attributes this example of a fallacious argument to Corax. Its relation to a similar example (attributed to Tisias) in Plato, *Phdr.* 273b–c is not clear; cf. Goebel 1983: 117–35.

[22] *Pace* Sealey 1984, I accept the *Tetralogies* as 5th-century works, probably by Antiphon. [See now Gagarin 2002: 52–62, 103–34.]

since these (as I have argued) had no special value before this time. The development may be seen in the speeches of Antiphon's younger contemporary Andocides, where the use of logical arguments increases over a twenty-year period (*c.*410–390).[23] Andocides' earliest speech, *On His Own Return*, shows little interest in rhetorical argument, but also no significant use of non-artistic *pisteis*. One decree is cited during a historical account, but no law is cited, no witness is called, and *basanos* (25) is used only in the sense of 'test of character'. Thus Andocides' earliest speech is 'non-artistic' in that it lacks rhetorical and logical sophistication, but not because it uses non-artistic *pisteis* of the sort discussed by Solmsen. Other contemporary evidence, moreover, such as the parody of a trial in the *Wasps* (produced in 422), also provides no evidence for the use of non-artistic *pisteis* in legal cases. Particularly significant for our purposes is the testimony of the cheese-grater (962–6), who is an impartial witness and testifies to the facts as he happens to know them.

Consider, finally, Antiphon's courtroom speeches. From among the four kinds of non-artistic *pisteis* mentioned by Aristotle (other than [31] written contracts), no law is cited, and the occasional references to oaths concern only those normally sworn by litigants or witnesses in the course of a trial. True, the importance of oaths in an ordinary homicide trial (as opposed to the procedure of *apagōgē*) is emphasized in Antiphon 5, but the reference to oaths does not control or dominate the arguments on this point and there is no hint that the oaths would ever be automatically decisive. Nor does Antiphon place any special emphasis on witnesses. None is called in Antiphon 1, one is called in 6, and only in 5 are witnesses called about as frequently as they are in later oratory. As far as we can tell, all these witnesses testify to facts they happen to know, as narrated by the speaker. This leaves the interrogation. It is only here that Antiphon seems out of step with the practice of later oratory, and this is the topic to which Solmsen devotes most of his attention. There are references to *basanos* in all three speeches, but it plays a prominent role only in *The Murder of Herodes* (Antiphon 5), for reasons

---

[23] Kennedy 1958 cites Latte and Solmsen on the use of proofs in early procedure (p. 34), but says nothing about such proofs in his analysis of Andocides.

that become clear when we examine the case against the speaker, Euxitheus.[24]

Herodes' relatives have clearly based their case primarily on the testimony extracted from a slave by torture. He admitted being Euxitheus' accomplice in the murder and gave a detailed account of the crime. Euxitheus' defence includes both facts, which he narrates and calls witnesses to support, and arguments from probability, which cast doubt on the slave's account. He also tries to discredit the slave's testimony by repeatedly questioning the propriety of the prosecution's interrogation of the slave and the value of any evidence obtained by it (30–51). For this purpose, in addition to arguments from probability (37), Euxitheus employs general arguments against the validity of such evidence (32), just as Aristotle recommends (cf. *Rh.* 1.15.26 1377a1–5). But in all this there is nothing automatically decisive or 'irrational' about the interrogation, nor does it have any special value or force different from that of the other evidence he introduces. The interrogation is particularly important to Euxitheus because the prosecution's argument in this particular case depends so heavily on the testimony obtained by *basanos*. But if the argument about the interrogation is developed at greater length here than in other surviving speeches, this is attributable to the nature of the case and the lack of other kinds of evidence, not to any particular *Beweistheorie* or lack thereof.

In sum, the interrogation in Antiphon 5 is not an archaic, 'irrational' means of proof but is material for rational argument of the kind developed and fostered by the sophists and rhetoricians of Antiphon's day. Its prominent role in this speech can be explained by the special facts of this case. This is not to deny that in general the use of and interest in arguments about interrogation seem to have declined after Antiphon; perhaps such arguments were so frequently introduced by Antiphon and his contemporaries that they came to be considered commonplace and [32] ineffective. In *Rhetoric* 1.15 Aristotle devotes less space to the interrogation than to any other non-artistic *pistis*, claiming that it is not a difficult subject to handle.[25] But the diminished role of the *basanos* in later oratory is a sign of the

---

[24] For a detailed examination of the case, see Gagarin 1989*b*.

[25] Interrogation is discussed in eleven lines (1376b31–1377a7); the other four *pisteis* each receive about three times as much space.

increased sophistication of rhetorical argument, rather than of a new theory of proof.

I have tried to show that Antiphon was not controlled or even influenced by a tradition of 'irrational' proofs from which he was trying to free himself. He was an innovator, testing new kinds of arguments and using whatever material he had available in each particular case. The effect of Solmsen's study is to diminish his accomplishment by introducing a dominant theory of proof to explain the presence or absence of certain arguments. We ought rather to look for explanations in the material itself. Once we understand the legal tradition correctly, we may still think that Antiphon's rhetorical skill is less developed than his successors', but we will be able more accurately to understand and evaluate the nature of his argumentation. Antiphon was the first Athenian to apply the new rhetorical techniques to actual cases, or at least the first to make extensive use of them, and his impact on his fellow citizens is well attested by Thucydides. It is time modern scholars appreciated his accomplishment.

BIBLIOGRAPHICAL UPDATE

In this paper I tried to refute Solmsen's influential view that Antiphon's methods of argument were constrained by earlier, formalistic judicial procedures that depended on 'irrational' or automatic 'proofs' (*pisteis*), proofs later classified as 'non-artistic' (*atechnoi*) by Aristotle. Solmsen's view of Antiphon's argumentation was already under attack (e.g. Vollmer 1958); I argue further that non-artistic proofs in general require rhetorical art, and that, although automatic proofs are found in early Greek law, they were never the dominant means of proof. During the past fifteen years there has been continued interest in (I) the rhetorical use of proofs, (II) automatic proofs in early law, and (III) proofs in classical homicide pleadings.

I. Carey's 1994 article (reprinted as Chapter 9 in this volume) explores more fully the art of 'non-artistic' proofs (cf. Mirhady

1991*a*), and many scholars have studied the art of individual proofs—oaths (Mirhady 1991*b*; Thür 1996a; Gagarin 1997), *basanos* or the interrogation of slaves under torture (Mirhady 1996, 2001; Thür 1996*b*; Gagarin 1996), and law or *nomos* (Carey 1996; De Brauw 2001–2).

II. Thür 1996*a* and Gagarin 1997 also discuss automatic proofs in early law, and Parker 2005 gives a wide-ranging assessment of Latte 1920, the work on which Solmsen drew.

III. Carawan (1998) tries to resurrect a modified form of Solmsen's theory, arguing that pleadings in traditional homicide cases (Antiphon 1, 6, Lysias 1) reflect the primitive use of automatic proofs, but those in homicide cases brought by *apagōgē* (Antiphon 5, Lysias 13) show more developed methods of argument. Reviewers (e.g. Wallace 2000) have been sceptical, questioning, for example, why litigants felt constrained in their use of advanced methods of argument in some homicide cases but not others. And other, more plausible explanations exist for the rhetorical features Carawan explains as primitive (Gagarin 2002).

9

'Artless' Proofs in Aristotle and the Orators*

Christopher Carey

In the *Rhetoric* Aristotle distinguishes two varieties of proof in oratory. These categories are 'artless' or 'inartificial' proofs, *atechnoi pisteis*, and 'artful' or 'artificial' proofs, *entechnoi pisteis* (1355b35–56a4). The definition is justified as follows: 'By "inartificial" I mean all those which have not been provided by means of ourselves but were there at the outset, such as witnesses, tortures, contracts, and the like, and by "artificial" all those which can be provided by technique and by ourselves; the former must be employed, the latter devised.' Aristotle goes on to define the 'artificial' proofs as moral character, emotion, and argument. The distinction drawn by Aristotle is real and inescapable. There is a clear difference both in form and in employment between documents such as wills and contracts which were read out by the clerk of the court at intervals during a forensic speech and elements of the speech itself, be they arguments presented by the speaker as a means of proving his factual case, the moral character projected by the speaker in order to establish himself as a credible source of information and opinion, and the emotion induced in the hearer as a means of creating in him a state of mind favourable to the speaker and unfavourable to his opponent. The distinction is especially clear in the light of the limited role allocated

* An embryonic version of this paper was delivered at the University of Minnesota in May 1988, and subsequent versions at the University of Keele in 1990 and the Classical Association meeting at the University of Warwick in 1991. I am grateful to all who commented on those occasions, particularly Betty Belfiore, Lin Foxhall, and Stephen Todd.

to evidence in Athenian courts. Whereas in a modern British court evidence plays a prominent part in the presentation as well as the proof of the case, in the Athenian courts much of the information which in contemporary courts would be provided by witnesses is actually provided by the litigant in the narrative section of the speech, so that evidence plays a confirmatory role only. As Kennedy has noted (1963: 88), the same distinction is drawn in the roughly contemporary *Rhetorica ad Alexandrum* commonly ascribed to Anaximenes of Lampsacus (1428a17 ff.), and also less systematically in the orators. Anaximenes uses different terms from Aristotle; the 'artificial' proofs he describes as 'direct' (his actual wording is 'drawn from the words and actions and persons themselves'), while 'inartificial' proofs are termed 'supplementary' (*epithetoi*). However, despite the different terminology, his categories coincide almost exactly with Aristotle's.

Aristotle and Anaximenes also agree in their treatment of the use of 'inartificial' (Aristotle) or 'supplementary' (Anaximenes) proofs. Although Anaximenes gives advice on ways to sneak in evidence without rendering a witness liable to an action for false witness (1432a3 ff.), in general both writers see the orator's task as essentially to utilize arguments to exploit the strength and palliate the weakness caused by the presence or absence of such proofs,[1] for instance, the contradictory positions to be adopted on the issue of evidence by torture accordingly as the speaker needs to exploit his own or his opponent's willingness or unwillingness to obtain evidence by the torture of slaves. Thus even when dealing with 'inartificial' proofs, both writers have in mind the exploitation of their presence or absence by means of 'artificial' proof. This is in accordance with the development of Greek rhetoric in the fifth and fourth centuries BC. As Kennedy notes (1963: 89), pre-rhetoric oratory relied heavily on evidence (witnesses, etc.) rather than argument. But during the fifth century the development of argument from probability enabled litigants to undermine cases based on such evidence. The old practice can be seen in Andocides, who makes little use of argument from probability, while the new practice can be seen in Antiphon, who applies it extensively, if on occasion a little mechanically. The rhetoricians

---

[1] *Rhetoric* 1375a22–77b12; *Rh. Al.* 1431b9–32b4.

are clearly right to view the main business of rhetoric as being the speech itself. But it is a mistake to suppose that these elements are something inert and inevitable. Aristotle's description of 'artless' proofs as something which 'was there at the outset' (*prouperchen*) fails to take note of the fact that from the outset, when considering the use of such evidence, the litigant or speechwriter had a number of choices to make: to draft or not to draft, how to formulate documents which might be used in the trial, how to deploy them within the speech. Even 'artless' proofs allow scope for ingenuity, and we find this scope exploited in practice in Greek oratory in the fifth and fourth centuries, even if it is not enshrined in theory.

One area open to exploitation was the wording of documents ultimately intended for use as evidence. An example of this can be seen in the formal challenge preserved at [Dem.] 59. 124. Such challenges played a major role in Greek litigation. They could be issued at any time prior to the summons in an attempt to avoid litigation, or once litigation had commenced in order to achieve an out-of-court settlement, though in cases which came before public arbitrators, they could be cited in court only if they were issued before the process of formal arbitration had been completed, since the rule in such cases was that only evidence which had been submitted at arbitration was admissible in court (*Ath. Pol.* 53. 2). Ostensibly they are intended to prevent litigation or to provide fresh evidence. Their real aim, however, is to give the challenger a moral advantage in court, since the challenge is always issued in the confident expectation that the opponent will refuse it. The challenge therefore has two purposes, and two audiences. As evidence to be introduced in court, it must be so worded as to satisfy the jurors of the litigant's good faith. On the other hand, it must never be so attractive that the opponent is tempted to accept it. How this balancing act could be done is seen in the text in question, the only challenge text to survive:[2]

This challenge was issued by Apollodorus to Stephanus concerning the charge on which he has indicted Neaera, that she is living in marriage with a citizen although she is a foreigner: Apollodorus was ready to take Neaera's

---

[2] The text of this challenge is disputed. For a brief discussion of the problems see Carey 1992: 149–50.

maidservants whom she brought with her from Megara—Thratta and Kokkaline—and those whom she acquired later when living with Stephanus—Xennis and Drosis—who possess accurate knowledge about Stephanus' children, that they are by Neaera—Proxenos, who is dead, and Ariston, who is still alive, Antidorides the sprinter, and Phano—for examination. And if they should admit that these are the children of Stephanus and Neaera, Neaera was to be sold in accordance with the laws and the children were to be aliens; but if they did not admit that these children were by this woman but by another wife of citizen birth, I was ready to withdraw from the case against Neaera, and, if the slaves had suffered any damage from the examination, to pay for any damage suffered.

The challenger Apollodorus is prosecuting the ex-slave prostitute Neaera for living in marriage with an Athenian citizen, Stephanus. Here he challenges Stephanus to surrender Neaera's slaves for torture to prove that the children claimed as legitimate by Stephanus are really Neaera's, not, as Stephanus claims, his children by an Athenian wife. If Stephanus accepts the challenge and the slaves support the prosecution under torture, Neaera is to be sold as a slave and the children are to lose their citizenship. If the evidence favours Neaera, Stephanus will abandon his suit. The challenge is clearly unacceptable to Stephanus, since the risks are uneven for the opposing parties. But Apollodorus adds a veneer of reasonableness to his challenge by offering to pay for any damage done to the slaves. That this was a common practice is suggested by a passage in Lycurgus (*Leocr.* 30; cf. Ar. *Frogs* 623–4). Another way in which the challenge could be rendered unacceptable to the recipient was to demand a format for the process which placed the recipient at a disadvantage, for instance, by suggesting a questioner for the torture whom the opponent would not trust (cf. Dem. 37. 42).

Interestingly, the importance of the wording of a challenge became more significant at the same time as 'artificial' proof assumed a dominant role in Athenian litigation. The works of Antiphon and Lysias suggest that procedure for challenges in the fifth century was relatively informal, neither the challenge nor witnesses to its issue being introduced in court.[3] As a result the precise terms of the challenge were not revealed to the jurors. Fourth-century practice

---

[3] See Bonner 1905: 67; cf. Lys. 4. 12 ff., 7. 34; Ant. 1. 6, 5. 38, 6. 23.

was more formal; the challenge was introduced in court, either as a separate document or incorporated in the testimony of witnesses.

Depositions are another area in which the scope for effective drafting increased rather than decreased in the classical period, despite the increased emphasis on 'artificial' proofs. In the fifth century witnesses deposed in person. At some stage early in the fourth century, this practice was replaced by one in which the litigant drafted a deposition, which was read out by the clerk of the court (Bonner 1905: 46–7). The witness could not query details in court. Unless he was prepared to take an oath of disclaimer asserting that he had not been present or that he knew nothing of the matter, he could merely attest the facts as stated (Harrison 1971: 143–4).

The net effect of the procedural changes was to give the litigant greater control over the testimony. However, from passages in the orators where witnesses opt for the oath of disclaimer, it is clear that depositions which deviated wildly from what the witness was prepared to attest would not be acceptable to the witness. Moreover, the witness might simply refuse to appear. Although the litigant had remedies at his disposal, in the process of *klēteusis* and the action for failure to give evidence (*dikē lipomarturiou*),[4] a possible consequence for him was the loss of the case with uncertain prospect of redress. So the litigant was not free to attribute any statement to the potential witness at will. Clearly the best course was to secure the compliance of potential witnesses. Again the litigant engages in a balancing act. He requires a drafting which will simultaneously satisfy the potential witnesses and strengthen his case. This was especially important with hostile or neutral witnesses. Where possible, an Athenian litigant would take friendly witnesses with him when approaching a matter which might lead to litigation.[5] When caught unprepared, he might have to use neutral or even hostile witnesses, like the speaker in Dem. 57, Euxitheos, who claims he was the victim of a plot by his enemies, who contrived to have him ejected by a trick during the scrutiny of deme members under the

---

[4] The *dikē blabēs* may also have been available. For these processes see Harrison 1971: 139–43. For a more recent discussion of *klēteusis*, see Todd 1990a: 24 ff., with my demurrer, Carey 1992: 25, n. 38.

[5] Cf. Dem. 57. 14 (quoted below), Isae. 3. 19.

Demophilos decree of 346. Euxitheos alleges that his opponent
Euboulides postponed the vote on Euxitheos until late, when many
of the demesmen had left, and that Euboulides' associates used the
cover of darkness to cast more than one vote each. The witnesses in
this instance are the alleged offenders (14):

To prove I am telling the truth in this, that the voting did not take place
among the full membership and that the votes outnumbered the voters,
I shall provide witnesses for you. It happens that no witness from among my
friends or the rest of the Athenians is available to me because of the lateness
of the hour and the fact that I had not asked anyone, but I am using as
witnesses the actual men who have wronged me. So I have written down for
them statements which they will not be able to deny.

Clearly, the witnesses concerned will not support his allegations of
malpractice, in particular his claim that they all voted more than
once. His task, therefore, is to draft the deposition in order to secure
maximum agreement. Under the circumstances it is especially
unfortunate that the deposition is lost.

Another possible example of the deposition drafted to achieve
maximum support from a reluctant witness is the testimony of the
officials at [Dem.] 58. 9. These officials are called to attest that
Theokrines prosecuted a certain Mikon by *phasis*. Part of the case
against Theokrines is that he failed to carry through this prosecution,
and has therefore exposed himself to the appropriate penalties under
the law. This testimony was given reluctantly (26). There is no means
of determining why the officials were unenthusiastic. It is conceivable
that, as the speaker claims (7), Theokrines and his associates have
interfered with the witnesses. Possibly, however, there was more to
the incident than the prosecutor tells us. We are badly informed as to
the circumstances under which a public action might be retracted
without incurring any penalty.[6] It may be that the reluctance of the
officials stemmed from the fact that the speaker has omitted or
distorted the precise context of Theokrines' failure to proceed. The
facts which they are called upon to attest may be the truth but not the
whole truth.

---

[6] From the use of the verb *anaireisthai* at [Dem.] 59. 53 and 68, which suggests
formal withdrawal rather than failure to proceed, it would appear that there were in
existence arrangements for termination of a public action; cf. Calhoun 1913: 58–9.

Two further examples may be cited of depositions drafted in such a way to secure the compliance of a reluctant witness.[7] At Aeschines 1.67 a witness is called to attest to a homosexual liaison with Timarchus, the defendant: 'Now I shall call Hegesandros in person. I have written for him a deposition which is more decorous than his character, but somewhat more explicit than that for Misgolas. I am well aware that he will disclaim on oath and swear falsely.' The testimony of Misgolas on his own relationship with Timarchus (adduced in § 50) was evidently less explicit than the speaker would have liked, owing to the need to secure Misgolas' compliance. At Dem. 54. 26 the defendant is described as drafting depositions at the arbitration hearing, evidently for confirmation by his opponent's witnesses. Again the aim is to secure the maximum possible support from an unhelpful quarter.

In theory, friendly witnesses should cause fewer problems. Friends may be asked, and may agree, to lie. But they are taking a risk (in ancient Athens as in modern Britain), since the opponent may prosecute them for false testimony. One obvious way round this problem is to draft the deposition in an ambiguous fashion which leaves my friends feeling secure but gives a spurious air of authority to my case. A possible example of this occurs in Dem. 54. The case concerns an alleged assault by Konon on Ariston. Ariston claims that while walking in the agora one evening he was brutally assaulted by Konon and his associates. Probably the decision at arbitration went to Konon, who was able to amass a substantial number of witnesses to the effect that he had not in fact beaten Ariston, who could adduce only a single witness to the actual assault.[8] It is, however, likely that Konon was guilty of the assault.[9] The testimony quoted here is therefore probably misleading. However, it is clear from Dem. 54. 31 that Konon submitted to the deposition only at the very end of the arbitration process, when his case looked hopeless. Ariston has to discredit these witnesses in court, which he does by representing them as habitual criminals (Dem. 54. 36–7). But Konon's friends

---

[7] So Harrison 1971: 144 with n. 2.

[8] Dem. 54. 7. His other witnesses appear to have arrived too late to be able to identify the perpetrator (9).

[9] See Carey and Reid 1985: 72.

evidently did not have a cavalier attitude to the truth. They did not want to lie for him. Why did they agree to in the end? Part of the answer may lie in the drafting of the deposition: 'Diotimos son of Diotimos of Ikarion, Archebiades son of Demomeles of Halai, Chairetios son of Chairimenes of Pithos attest that they were returning from dinner with Konon and came upon Ariston and the son of Konon fighting in the agora, and that Konon did not strike Ariston.' Perhaps the most striking feature of the document is its syntactical ambiguity. The use of the infinitive construction, with subject and object both in the accusative, leaves unclear who struck and who was struck. The jury would understand *mē pataxai Konōna Aristōna* to mean: 'that Konon did not strike Ariston', which is probably untrue. But the witnesses may have agreed to the deposition because it could also mean: 'that Ariston did not strike Konon', which is probably true. The syntax allows Konon's friends to tell the truth while offering specious support for Konon's lie. This is, of course, conjectural. It does, however, gain in plausibility if one examines Anaximenes' discussion of style (*Rh. Al.* 1435b6 ff.), where the ambiguity of precisely this construction is discussed. 'The construction of words should be neither confused nor transposed. Confused construction is, for instance, when you say: "it is intolerable that this man should strike this man" (*touton touton tuptein*); for it is unclear which did the striking. If you state it as follows, you will make it clear: "it is intolerable that this man should be struck by this man" (*touton hupo toutou*).' We can conclude, at least, that a Greek litigant could be aware of the ambiguity of certain syntactical forms.[10] A more secure case is presented by [Dem.] 59. 54:

Phrastor of Aigilia deposes that when he realized that Stephanus had betrothed Neaera's daughter to him, representing her as his own daughter, he indicted him before the Thesmothetae according to the law, and ejected the woman from his house and stopped living with her; and when Stephanus brought a suit for maintenance against him at the Odeion, he came to terms with him with the result that the indictment was withdrawn from the Thesmothetae and the suit for maintenance which Stephanus brought against me.

---

[10] An alternative possibility is that the ambiguity lies in the verb *pataxai*, i.e. Konon's part in the assault may have consisted in tripping Ariston up, kicking him, or jumping on him, but not striking a blow with the hand.

It has been noted since the nineteenth century that there are significant discrepancies between Phrastor's deposition and the narrative which it is meant to substantiate. The speaker Apollodorus states that Phrastor ejected the female in question and refused to return the dowry. In response, Stephanus brought the suit to recover the dowry, whereupon Phrastor indicted Stephanus under the law forbidding an Athenian citizen to betroth an alien to another Athenian under false pretences. The impression conveyed is that Phrastor's indictment is a response to the attempt to extract the dowry, which he was not entitled to keep. Phrastor's deposition does not mention the dowry; it also represents his indictment of Stephanus as a direct response to Stephanus' breach of the law. Although we are dealing here with concern for reputation rather than fear of penalty, what we appear to have is a deposition drafted to secure the maximum factual support for the litigant's version while still remaining broadly acceptable to the witness.

Even where the speaker anticipates rejection by the witness, it is evidently felt to be worthwhile under certain circumstances to draft a deposition for him. At Dem. 45. 60 allegations against the opponent are supported by a deposition which the witnesses reject, using the oath of disclaimer. The speaker adds, 'it was quite clear, jurymen, that this is what they would do, emphatically disclaim on oath' (*prothumōs exomeisthai*). Thus (in private cases where the water-clock stops for the reading of documents) the speaker can devote extra time to the allegation, without reducing his time-allowance, and also turn the refusal to his own rhetorical advantage, by using it as evidence of the duplicity of those ranged against him. In public cases, one effect is to associate an enemy with dishonourable activities in full view, on the principle that some mud will always stick.[11] The choice between a compromise wording and one which was unacceptable to the witness probably depends on the likelihood of an agreement being reached in any given case and a consideration of the relative advantages of an acceptable but limited deposition and one which, while unacceptable, is explicitly favourable to the speaker.

[11] Cf. Aeschin. 1. 67, quoted above. For the deposition offered but declined on oath, see also Isae. 9. 18, with Harrison 1971: 140, n. 1, who points out the modern device of having a statement made only to have it struck from the record (though not, of course, from the mind of the juror).

Just as the litigant must decide on the number and content of depositions which will serve his case, so he must decide on the laws which it will be useful to cite, and produce extracts. Here, too, the issue is not straightforward. Obviously, the litigant will copy clauses from laws relevant to the dispute. But the decision to extract does not turn solely on the issue of relevance. Laws, irrespective of their relevance to the main issue, may be used to add moral authority, sometimes dubious, to the case. For instance, [Dem.] 46 is full of citations of laws, often of doubtful relevance to the case. The speaker's intention in collecting these gems was clearly to impress the jurors with a spurious display of legal knowledge and give a veneer of authority to his arguments. In the same way, in [Dem.] 43 the lengthy citation of the law limiting the removal of olive trees allegedly breached by the opponent, which has no direct bearing on the speaker's case, helps both to raise a question about the opponent's commitment to the estate which is the subject of the dispute and to create a prejudice in the minds of the jurors.

The requirement under the Athenian system that the litigant assemble for himself copies of laws which may assist his case means that the potential for astute drafting could on occasion extend even to laws, though how often this was possible it is difficult to say. In Lysias 1 the law on adultery[12] is cited to prove that the speaker was justified in killing a man taken in adultery with his wife (28). Since the speech as a whole consistently suppresses the fact that Athenian law allowed the aggrieved husband a variety of remedies in these circumstances and insists throughout on the legality, indeed the inevitability, of a single remedy, summary execution, it is unlikely that he will have cited the whole of the law. Probably what was cited was the clause granting the right to kill. What we have then, in all probability, is selective quotation. How often the laws were susceptible to manipulation in this way is difficult to say. There was nothing illegal about such a practice. The penalty for citing a non-existent law

---

[12] Since the law on homicide which is cited at § 30 is not the law cited at the end of § 28 (at § 30 the speaker says *kai touton ton nomon*), it is difficult to see what law can be intended at § 28 other than that on adultery. The suggestion of D. Cohen 1991*a*: 111 ff., that the clause in question dealt with the liability of *moichoi* to *kakourgōn apagōgē* is unlikely to be correct, since Harris 1990 has argued cogently against the view that *moichoi* were classed *kakourgoi* and therefore liable to *apagōgē*.

was death ([Dem.] 26. 24); but anyone who excerpted from a law was still citing a genuine law.

The other and more important way in which documents may be manipulated is by deployment. Unlike the exploitation of the drafting process, which requires no more than Autolycan cunning, the deployment of 'artless' proofs impinges directly upon the art of rhetoric, since the positioning of documents is part of the architecture of the speech. This positioning is by no means inevitable. Dionysius of Halicarnassus, in his essay on Isaeus (§ 14), sees some skill in the deployment of depositions. He notes that Isaeus sometimes provides a continuous narrative but sometimes breaks it up with documentary proofs.[13] In this way Isaeus avoids the confusion which would come from the presentation of too much information in one block of narrative followed by one block of documentation. This effect is further assisted, of course, by the slower pace created by stopping at intervals for the clerk of the court to read out the documents. The change of speakers, combined with the brief interval while the correct document is located, involves some delay,[14] and this allows the jury to assimilate the narrative more successfully. This is a minor but significant point, when we recall that each litigant had only a limited amount of time to present his case, but (in private cases at least) no specified limit on the time-allowance for the reading of documents. Documents can thus be used to gain time. Moreover, this type of precisely demonstrated narrative structure contributes to the speaker's credibility by creating an impression of confidence.

The question of deployment becomes particularly important when the litigant has only limited documentary support for his version of the facts. One solution to this problem is offered by Lysias, who shows great skill in sneaking past his audience cases or statements for which there is little objective support. He has a tendency to place his best-attested item last, and then, by demonstrating this item convincingly with witnesses, he uses his well-attested item to bolster up earlier items for which no evidence is available. Since I have discussed this technique elsewhere (1989: 77, 96, 211), I shall confine myself to a single example. Lys. 32 was written for the prosecution of a certain

---

[13] As an example of the latter technique one might cite Isae. 8, *On the Estate of Kiron*.
[14] For the delay involved, see Dem. 21. 108.

Diogeiton for defrauding his wards. In his attempt to refute Diogeiton's balance-sheet for the eight years of his guardianship (19–27), Lysias picks a number of items rather than seeking to refute the whole calculation in detail. He deals with the alleged maintenance cost (20), which he argues (with justification) is exaggerated. He then claims (21) that Diogeiton claimed a cost of 5,000 drachmas for the tomb of the boys' father, half of which he charged to his wards, though in fact the real cost was only 2,500. Thus Diogeiton charged the whole cost to the boys and contributed nothing. He played a similar trick with a sacrificial lamb, and by devices such as this contrived to charge the wards a preposterously high figure for participation in festivals. Worst of all, when selected as joint trierarch under the liturgy system along with a certain Alexis, he claimed a total cost of 5,000 drachmas and charged half to the orphans. This was anyway illegal, since orphans were not liable to recurring public services. But what made it worse was that the speaker was able to ascertain from Alexis' surviving brother, Aristodikos, that Diogeiton's contribution was only 2,500 drachmas. At the end of this section of the speech (27), witnesses are summoned. It is difficult to see who these witnesses can be other than those who were present at the interview with Aristodikos. If so, the evidence here relates to the last item in the allegation against Diogeiton. This is also suggested by the fullness of this section of the narrative in comparison with the allegations concerning the tomb and the sacrifices. The account in general achieves plausibility by the internal consistency of the behaviour attributed to Diogeiton. But this plausibility is further increased by the deft use of limited evidence; the best-attested item is held back till last, and the convincing demonstration of the truth of this allegation creates an impression that more has been substantiated than is actually the case.

Two passages in the first speech in the Lysianic corpus show us another way of deploying depositions deftly. This, arguably Lysias' finest speech, is a defence of a man accused of murder. The defence is that the dead man was caught in adultery with the wife in question. The circumstantial narrative ends with an account of events on the night in question. The speaker, Euphiletus, tells how he was awakened by the maid and informed that the adulterer was in the house, how he slipped out and with great difficulty succeeded in rounding up a posse from among his friends, returned, and killed the adulterer. The reason for the difficulty in collecting the posse was that some of them were out of town. This point is important, since the dead man's relatives claim that he was the victim of a plot. Accordingly, the speaker returns to it later on, using the difficulty he experienced in collecting his friends as the basis for an argument from probability against the existence of any plot. If he had been plotting against the dead man, he would have made adequate preparations in advance (42):

And yet if I had known in advance, don't you think I would have got my servants ready and sent word to my friends, so that I could have entered with the utmost safety myself (for how could I know if he, too, had a weapon?) and taken my revenge amid the greatest possible number of witnesses? As it is, in complete ignorance of what was to take place that night, I brought those I could. I bid the witnesses to this to take the stand.

At the end of the narrative section (29) witnesses were introduced. From the absence of any indication in § 42 that the depositions read out there have already been presented, it would appear that the speaker does not introduce all his evidence relating to the night of the killing at the close of the narrative, which at first sight would seem to be the most obvious place for its introduction. Evidently the testimony there relates to the discovery of Eratosthenes with the speaker's wife, his confession and pleas for mercy, and his death. Lysias saves the evidence relating to Euphiletus' behaviour on the night in question for the argument section, where it will have most effect.[15] The postponement also avoids complicating the narrative, and prevents the dilution of the carefully crafted presentation of the speaker as a guileless individual[16] which would result from raising prematurely the possibility of deception and exposing a degree of calculation in the presentation of the case.

My final example of careful deployment comes from Dem. 57. The speaker's enemy Euboulides has questioned the citizenship of both

---

[15] For another effective postponement, see Dem. 39. 19, where, after a long list of potential confusion threatened by the possession of the same name by two brothers (6–19), the speaker scotches any suspicion in the minds of the jurors that all this is merely the hypothetical ramblings of a man with an obsession by providing testimony to real damage caused by the situation.

[16] For the characterization of the speaker, Usher 1965: 101 ff.; Carey 1989: 61 f.

his parents. These allegations are based at least in part (as presented by Euxitheos) on trifling details, his father's foreign accent, and the fact that his mother had performed tasks unworthy of a woman of citizen status. Euxitheos rebuts these charges and adduces a wealth of testimony from relatives to prove that his mother and father were of unquestionable citizen status. He then proceeds to prove that his own birth qualifications have been tested satisfactorily. However, the mode of demonstration at this point is strikingly different. In the case of his parents, Euxitheos proceeds very slowly, itemizing all the proofs of citizenship. In the case of his father, depositions are adduced on several points: first from those who can prove that his father was captured in war and sold into slavery, that he returned and was accepted by family, deme, and phratry as a rightful member of all these bodies (19); next from the extended family, the cousins of this paternal grandparents (21) and his father's maternal relatives (22);[17] then from members of his father's phratry, genos, and deme (23, 25, 27), to prove first that his father was accepted as a deme member, second that the father held deme office after successfully passing his *dokimasia*, third that his father's citizenship qualifications were tested and accepted during an extraordinary scrutiny of the deme; and finally witnesses to prove that his parents had four children whose burial in the family resting-place went unchallenged. In the case of his mother, Euxitheos begins by adducing paternal and maternal relatives (38) to attest her parentage, her brother's sons (39), members of the phratry and deme of his mother's relatives, and those who share the family burial-place (40); he then calls the sons of his mother's first husband, Protomachos, the husband of his half-sister (that is, the mother's daughter by Protomachos), and the half-sister's son, all of whom can attest that Euxitheos' mother had been married to another Athenian citizen before she married his father, those who were present at the formal bethrothal when Euxitheos' father formally agreed to the marriage, and those among his phratry who attended the feast which was normally given to phratry members on the occasion of a marriage (43); finally he calls members of the family for whom his mother had served as a wet-nurse (45).

---

[17] I follow the characterization of this branch of the family tree by Thompson 1971*a*: 89 f.

Thus, with reference to his parents there is a slow and painstaking demonstration of the possession of the necessary qualifications for citizenship. When he comes to his own qualifications his approach is different. He calls en bloc witnesses to his introduction to the phratry and enrolment in the deme, to the fact that he was put forward for sortition as priest of Heracles and held deme offices after undergoing the *dokimasia*. The slow and detailed demonstration is replaced by one which lumps together and hurries through the individual items. This haste was not caused by lack of time; this is the last set of depositions introduced, and the speech is only two-thirds completed. It is, of course, possible that Euxitheos feels that most of his task has already been accomplished through the proof of his parents' citizenship. However, this is really only half the task, since it is important for him to demonstrate that these are his real parents. The reader in the study is struck by the fact that this important point is dealt with so briskly.

The suspicion that Euxitheos' case is not as strong as it appears at first sight is increased by a number of details both here and elsewhere in the speech. One or two omissions in § 46 raise doubts. One might have expected a reference to the *dekatē*, the ceremony at which the newborn infant received a name, which is commonly cited in cases where parentage is at issue.[18] As evidence of legitimacy, this ceremony offered *a fortiori* proof of citizen status. Equally striking is the fact that, though mention is made of introduction to the phratry, there is no reference to admission to his father's *genos*,[19] where qualifications for membership were probably tougher. Moreover, Euxitheos is evidently rich, while his parents were by his own admission paupers.[20] A further question is raised by the failure of his male

---

[18] Cf. Dem. 39. 20, 40. 28 f.; Isae. 3. 30.

[19] Andrewes 1961: 6 f. suggests that the father, Thoukritos, did not belong to a genos. He sees the *gennētai* of §§ 23–4 as simply the genos which formed the elite of Thoukritos' phratry. But in context the word could only mean 'members of the same genos'. The odd reference to these people in § 67 as *Apollōnos patrōiou kai Dios herkeiou gennētai*, rather than by name, is occasioned solely by the desire to imitate the dokimasia of the thesmothetai.

[20] His wealth: §§ 64–5 (his claims there may be untrue, but they are not the claims a pauper would make) and the allegations of his opponents, § 52; the family poverty: §§ 25, 31, 35, 36, 42. However, since we are badly informed about the economics of market trading in Athens, we cannot rule out the possibility that Euxitheos increased the family wealth by his work in the market.

relatives on his father's side, members of the same deme, to support him for scrutiny when he was rejected by the deme.[21] Unfortunately, it is easier to note problems than to arrive at an acceptable solution. We are as usual hampered by the loss of the case for the opposition. As Euxitheos presents it, his opponent's case against him does not seem particularly strong; the allegations against Euxitheos' parents are easily rebutted. However, we must admit the possibility that Euxitheos is distorting the case against him. It may be that the allegations against Euxitheos' parents were supplementary accusations rather than the main thrust of the case, that Euboulides had more to say about Euxitheos himself. It is possible, for instance, that he claims that Euxitheos is a rich metic who has bought his way into a family poor enough to be receptive to bribes and obscure enough to afford concealment (Gernet 1960: 11). The Athenians at least believed that such frauds were possible (Isae. 12. 2). Alternatively, he may be arguing that Euxitheos joined the family in infancy. Euxitheos states that his mother lost four children.[22] A childless couple, eager to preserve the family unit and in need of money, might agree to present an alien child as their own; the mother's trade as wet-nurse might well introduce her to a rich metic family with ambitions for their son. A less exotic conjecture is simply that Euxitheos is a bastard.[23] Whether the illegitimate son of two Athenian

[21] It should be noted, however, that three of the four belonged to his father's generation, and might be among the 'older members' (10) who set off early to walk to Halimous from the city before dark, no doubt to avoid dangers from the poor country roads and possible attacks from *lōpodutai* ('muggers').

[22] A possibility suggested to me by Dr R. A. Reid.

[23] That might explain why Euxitheos' mother, Nikarete, was forced to serve as wet-nurse during his father's absence on military service (41); one might have expected her to support herself from her husband's property or to receive support from his family; as mistress, however, she would have no claim on them (on the other hand, the economic climate at the close of the Peloponnesian War might have made it difficult for her husband's relatives to do more than support themselves). On this hypothesis, those who testify to the marriage (43) are lying. Those who attest his admission to the phratry (46) may be lying; but equally his father, Thoukritos, could simply have sworn falsely to the phratry that the son was legitimate. It is perhaps also worth mentioning here that the claim that Euxitheos was chosen as phratriarch (23) is probably false. Since depositions from members of the phratry have been read out only minutes before (23), and these could as easily have included a reference to his service as phratriarch, it is exceedingly suspicious that he calls upon his relatives, not phratry members, to confirm this point.

parents was entitled to citizen rights is controversial.[24] But even if (as I suppose) bastards were entitled to citizenship, such people would find it difficult to defend their status under an extraordinary scrutiny, since bastards lacked the proofs of paternity bestowed on legitimate issue.

It is difficult to choose between these alternatives in the absence of the speech made by Euboulides. But doubts about the strength of Euxitheos' case remain. Not unnaturally, what he elects to do is lump together the evidence for his own qualifications, in the hope that volume and speed will divert the jurors from one or two odd omissions, and to rely on the air of authority generated by the detailed presentation of the case for his parents' citizenship earlier.

Inevitably much of what has been said is conjectural. In most disputes from ancient Athens we have only one side of the case surviving. We are therefore compelled to resort to conjecture in order to reconstruct the opponent's case and to formulate an opinion on the rights and wrongs. Conjecture is also forced on us by the large and numerous holes in the arguments which have survived. The speeches themselves are usually complete, but documentation is sporadic in the Demosthenic corpus and non-existent in most other orators. Often all we have is an indication in the text, in the form of a title, of what once stood in the gap. Confronted with the word MARTYRIA or NOMOS in the text, all we can do is attempt to reconstruct the probable scope of the lost evidence on the basis of the surrounding text. In any court case we must accept the possibility that witnesses are lying. But if the above remarks about the opportunities for litigants to exploit the drafting process have any validity, then we must accept in some cases at least the possibility that seemingly well-attested features of a case are actually less securely supported than it would seem even on a moderately pessimistic estimate.

Clearly, Aristotle was correct to regard the more obviously rhetorical means of proof as the more important. The type of ingenuity I have sought to illustrate is inadequate to sustain a case on its own. However, he and Anaximenes err in restricting their treatment of artless proofs to the appropriate means for confirming or refuting

---

[24] For a recent discussion, with bibliography of the issue, see Patterson 1990: 40–73.

them. The Athenian litigant, when assembling his evidence had in mind the impact of that evidence in court from the outset. The speechwriter, when approaching a brief, took the amount and scope of documentary evidence into consideration as well as the type of argument which might support his client's case and weaken his opponent's. The architecture of the speech paid attention to the disposition of documentary proof as well as, and in relation to, the disposition and economy of argumentation. The degree of art involved in the formulation and deployment of 'artless' proofs probably varies from animal cunning to astute and sensitive expertise. But art of a sort there is, and the reader must take it into consideration as part of his overall evaluation of a speech.

10

Torture and Rhetoric in Athens*

David C. Mirhady

In a short article published over a hundred years ago, J. W. Headlam (1893) presented the thesis that in Athenian law the function of the challenge to torture slaves was to propose an alternative method of trial outside the *dikastērion*, a kind of ordeal. The thesis met immediate opposition and, despite a brief rejoinder by Headlam to his first critic,[1] it has been rejected by those writing on Athenian law up to the present time,[2] including Gerhard Thür, whose monograph (1977) is by far the most important work on the subject.[3] However, the significance of the issue compels us not to let it drop. For it touches not only upon the use of torture, which affects our understanding of the position of slaves, but also upon the Athenian rules of evidence, indeed, their entire method of dispute resolution. The purpose of the present paper is first (I) to revive Headlam's thesis in a modified form, and then (II) to answer the criticisms against it. I shall argue that Headlam was essentially correct with regard to the judicial function of the challenge, but his association of it with the trial by ordeal is misplaced. Finally (III), I shall touch upon the influence of

* For financial support in this project I am indebted to the Social Sciences and Humanities Research Council of Canada and the Killam Memorial Trust. For helpful comments on earlier drafts, thanks are due to P. Harding, P. Kussmaul, E. M. Harris, and, not least, to Gerhard Thür, as well as the readers for *JHS*.

[1] Cf. Thompson 1894: 136; J. Headlam 1894: 136–7.

[2] See e.g. Bonner 1905: 72; Lipsius, *AR* 889, n. 91; Harrison 1971: 147–50.

[3] Thür's conclusions have been followed by Gagarin 1990: 22–32, and Todd 1990*a*, esp. 34–5.

rhetoricians in Athens, for they appear responsible for some of the disagreement.

I

In the surviving speeches of the Athenian orators there are many reports of challenges (*proklēseis*) to torture (*basanos*). The challenges were made generally before the dispute reached the *dikastērion*, in which the speeches are delivered. According to the usual procedure, a litigant proposed to his opponent to have a slave interrogated by torture: the owner would have brought the slave to his opponent for torture, but would have maintained a control over how it was done. The slave, the speaker argues, knows the truth of the disputed point, and torture, had it been applied, would have secured that truth.[4]

However, in almost all of the reports the challenge was refused, and in no reported case has a *basanos* actually been completed as the result of a challenge. In view of this evidence, Headlam asks: 'What happened if the challenge was accepted... [and] the torture really came off?' His answer is that a torture that was performed in these circumstances would resolve the dispute and that there would be no recourse then to a *dikastērion*. In fact, as Headlam knew, he was not the first to propose the thesis: in the second century AD the lexicographer Pollux (8. 62) also said that the function of a challenge, whether 'to some defined oath or testimony or *basanos* or to something else of that sort', was 'the resolution of the suit'.[5] Many cases were not so straightforward, for the statement of a slave might render only circumstantial evidence. Here the Athenian legal process gave protection to the slave (even if not intentionally). If a litigant wished to torture a slave with credibility, he had to make an agreement with his opponent and be willing to let the point, even the whole case, rest on the outcome. Sometimes this decision was a close call

---

[4] I am in complete agreement with Thür 1977: 181, where he argues that it was the function of the *basanos* either to affirm or to deny a statement formulated in the challenge.

[5] The *Suda*, s.v. *proklēsis*, mentions private arbitration as well; cf. Dem. 45. 15–16.

(see Dem. 37. 41). The mistake of many scholars, including Headlam, has been to emphasize the torture itself, while ignoring the challenge. Few would dispute that the Athenians reached agreement through challenges, to end disputes by private arbitration or the swearing of prescribed oaths (cf. Mirhady 1991*a*). But the irrationality of resolving a dispute by torturing a third party, as well as some obfuscated passages in the orators, has prevented Headlam's view from receiving wider acceptance.

The *basanos*-challenge functioned only for private disputes. Where state security was threatened, for instance, in a case of treason, no private settlement was possible. On the other hand, in private disputes where exile or the death penalty was possible—for a homicide, for instance—despite Thür's concerns (1977: 211–14), it does not seem problematic that after privately surrendering the dispute through a *basanos* procedure an accused party would go into exile and leave the case judicially uncontested. Alternatively, if through the *basanos* he were shown to be innocent, the prosecutor would have little ground for continuing the prosecution. In either case, the validity of the *basanos* as a dispute-ending procedure would be guaranteed by sufficient witnesses from both sides.

Headlam offers several passages in support of his thesis; in each the *basanos* is portrayed as an alternative method of dispute resolution. In Isocrates' *Trapeziticus* 17. 55, *basanos* and 'being put on trial' are pitted as alternatives: 'he submitted both to being put on trial and to having the other accusations (made against him), so that there would be no *basanos* concerning this matter.' In Lycurgus 1. 32 the *basanos* is contrasted with the dicasts and so with the court, where, it is claimed, it is possible to mislead: 'What people was it impossible to lead astray through cleverness and the devices of the speech? According to nature, as you know, those tortured, the male and female slaves, were going to tell the entire truth concerning all the injustices.' In [Dem.] 47. 5, a suit for false testimony, acceptance of the *basanos* would bring an end to the suit and the 'risk' of facing the dicasts: 'for while it was possible for them to be released from the matter and not run the risk of coming before you, by certifying in deed that the testimony was true, they have not been willing to surrender the person.' In the *Tetralogies* 1. 4. 8 there is an informal challenge made before the court to let the case stand on an alibi that is to be supported by *basanoi*: 'for I surrender all of my male and female slaves for torture; and if I appear [as a result of the torture] on that night not to have been at home asleep or to have gone out somewhere, then I agree that I am a murderer.'

Dem. 37. 40–2 reports an accepted challenge to torture that then broke down. But initially (§ 40) the purpose of the *basanos*, to end the dispute, is clear: 'he read to me a great challenge demanding to have a slave tortured who, he claimed, knew these things and if they were true, I should pay the statutory debt, and if they were false, the torturer Mnesicles would assess the value of the slave.' In [Dem.] 59. 121 a challenge expressly includes the condition that the litigant, Apollodorus, discontinue litigation if the *basanos* goes against him: 'and if it should appear from the torture that this man Stephanus had married a citizen wife, and that these children are his by another wife, and not by Neaera, then I was willing to withdraw from the contest and not to pursue this charge.'[6] In Lysias 7. 37 the litigant indicates that whichever way the interrogation had turned out, the dispute would have been decided: 'for if [the slaves] said what this man wanted concerning me, it would not have been possible for me to make a defence, but if they did not agree with him, he was liable to no penalty.' In *On the Embassy* Aeschines (2. 127) challenges Demosthenes before the court and demands that the entire dispute be resolved by *basanoi*: 'if the slaves when tortured say that I slept away from my messmates, don't spare me, men of Athens, but rise up and kill me. But if you are disproved and lying, Demosthenes, then pay this sort of penalty.' (It is a mock challenge, like *Tetr.* 1. 4. 8, because the *basanos* cannot take place before the dicasts.)[7] In Dem. 29. 11, although many witnesses are offered on circumstantial points, the *basanos*-challenge relates to the point on which the whole case depends: 'since I knew that you would cast your votes concerning

---

[6] The challenge is made so explicit because formally, as a *graphē*, the charge should not have been settled privately.

[7] Thus Harrison 1971: 149, n. 4. Thür 1977: 190–2, is inclined to accept the legal, if not the practical, possibility of a *basanos* before the dicasts in private disputes. In public disputes, moreover, where a whole day was allocated to the disputing positions, he sees the completion of Aeschines' challenge as more practically possible. I am more persuaded by Demosthenes' simple denial of the possibility in 45. 16. The rhetorical flash of Aeschines' challenge seems little diminished by the fact that its fulfillment was a legal impossibility.

this issue, I thought it necessary to do nothing else before testing this man through a challenge.'[8] It could have carried the weight of the entire suit.

Thür (1977: 211–13) raises the concern that in several speeches (e.g. Lys. 4. 10–11; Isae. 8. 9, 17; Dem. 30. 26–7, 35) the challenge deals with several questions and not simply the one that would decide the dispute. But in each passage, it seems to me, any one of the questions could have decided the case, *if the adversary once accepted the challenge*. The fact that certain points in the challenge seem circumstantial, irrelevant, or pure bluff does not prove that a challenge accepted would be inconclusive. Indeed, the strategy that played out in the preliminaries (as Thür himself makes clear, pp. 152–8), aimed at embarrassing the adversary by his admissions (*homologiai*) on matters that are largely circumstantial, sometimes even irrelevant to the central issue (e.g. in Dem. 37. 27). Challenges that the adversary dare not contest contribute to this strategy. The challenger who knew that his opponent would refuse the challenge had nothing to lose in making it.

Headlam bolsters his thesis by comparing the *basanos*-challenge to the oath-challenge, whose function as an extra-judicial means of settling a dispute is supported by strong evidence.[9] But he also makes other remarks, and it is with them that I wish to take issue. First, he suggests that the *basanos* procedure was very rarely, if ever, completed during the age of the orators.[10] About this view we do not have sufficient evidence. If it was used and if it always led to resolution of the dispute, we would not expect to see it mentioned in speeches before the *dikastērion*, which was the court of last resort. (We do hear of one case, Dem. 39–40, in which an oath-challenge was accepted and thus resolved the dispute.) Certainly the arguments we see concerning *basanos*, for and against, do not suggest that it is moribund or obsolete. Rather, they suggest the opposite: the great number of speeches that mention the possibility of slave torture

---

[8] See also Dem. 29. 38, 51–3 and 30. 35.

[9] See Mirhady 1991*a* and Thür 1977: 205–6.

[10] Thür 1977 shares the assumption that the *basanos* procedure was not actually carried out in this period (i.e. leading to the torture of slaves for evidence); indeed, he makes this assumption the basis of his sixth chapter.

suggests that its employment continued to be an actual possibility in many disputes. If the dicasts had not heard of its use in private disputes in fifty or more years, the challenge would have become a very transparent and thus ineffective tactic. I imagine that some forms of torture were used to settle disputes within an *oikos* with some regularity (see e.g. Lys. 1. 16, 18–19; Dem. 48. 16–18), and certainly torture continued in use where state security was in jeopardy (cf. Dem. 18. 133; Din. 1. 63; Thalheim, *RE* 3 (1899) s.v. *basanoi*).

Headlam also wishes to liken the *basanos* to an 'ordeal'. He argues: 'if we knew more about the early history of Attic law, we should find that the effectiveness of the *basanos* depended very little on whether or not the man who was subjected to it knew anything at all about the matter on which he was questioned, and that it is really a vicarious ordeal, altered and wrested until it has become little distinguishable from ordinary evidence' (1893: 5). Headlam is right that we know little of the early history of Attic law, but it is an integral part of the arguments that favour the *basanos* that they say the slave 'knows the truth' of the matter—his knowledge is direct, not based on hearsay.[11] It always appears as a way of eliciting truthful information, or, more precisely, of affirming or denying a proposed statement.[12]

II

Critics of Headlam want to make a distinction between those challenges that are to lead to resolution of a dispute—which all admit that there are—and those that simply have an evidentiary purpose. My view, like that of Pollux (above at n. 5), is that they are all meant to lead to resolution, since that is the nature of the formal challenge.

---

[11] Thür 1977: 111–31: the verb *(sun)eidenai* is integral to the formal phrasing.

[12] [In *basanoi* there is no suggestion that divine forces will magically intervene, unlike medieval ordeal.] There are several passages in literature in which a speaker expresses a willingness to undergo fire, voluntarily, in order to demonstrate good faith: Soph. *Ant.* 265–6; Xen. *Symp.* 4. 16; Ar. *Lys.* 133 (cf. Dem. 54. 40). But in these situations the pain is not meant to elicit specific information or to test a particular proposition.

Criticism has centred on three points (cf. Thür 1977: 207–11). First, there are texts that appear to indicate that the results of *basanoi* could be employed before the *dikastērion*. The *basanos*-challenge would then not be an alternative means of settling a dispute, but only a means for securing a piece of non-binding evidence. Second, there are texts in which the *basanos* is compared to other forms of evidence that come before the courts, such as the testimony of free witnesses, with the implication that they share a similar status. Finally, there are texts according to which, it is claimed, a statement under torture, had it taken place, would have come to court. All of these objections can be met.

In the first group there are nine texts. The first is Lys. 7. 37: 'mind you, I was so solicitous because I thought that it was to my benefit that you learn the truth about the matter from *basanoi*, from testimonies, and from sure signs.' Here, as elsewhere, despite the most natural reading, the litigant means not that he would produce the *basanoi* themselves for the dicasts. Rather, he means only that he will produce the challenge to *basanoi* that he presented to his opponent. Since the opponent refused the challenge, the litigant feels justified in mentioning *basanoi* as if they had taken place and as if they had been in his favour, as is suggested by the reversal argument in 7. 36: 'if I did not submit the people when Nicomachus was demanding them, I would appear to be conscious of my own guilt; accordingly, since he was not willing to accept [them] when I was submitting, it is right to form the same thought about him.'[13] Isocrates 17. 54 suggests that the dicasts should have the results of a *basanos* read before them: 'Pasio, since he knew these things, wished you to conjecture about the matter rather than to know clearly' (cf. Thür 1977: 294–6). The nature of this *basanos*-challenge as an alternative proposal is made clear in 17. 55 (above, § I). The emphasis in 17. 54 is that the dicasts decide by conjecture, not with clear knowledge. The words 'rather than to know clearly' reveal a conceit: since they have no direct knowledge of a dispute, dicasts always decide by conjecture. The 'clear knowledge' stemming from a *basanos*—clear to both disputing parties as well as to other witnesses to the torture—would have

---

[13] The 'reversal argument' (*hypothetische Rollentausch*) is common; it is discussed by Solmsen 1931: 10–14, and Thür 1977: 269–71.

obviated the need for the dicasts' decision. The more literal verb for
the second-hand knowledge of the dicasts, as in Lys. 7. 37, is 'learn'
(*puthesthai*).

[Dem.] 47. 35 provides what might seem the strongest evidence
against Headlam: 'although I have demanded [this slave], I am not
able to get her, so that you may learn the truth.' However, in §§ 7–8 it
appears the *basanos* could have 'released' (*apēllachthai*) the allegedly
false witnesses from trial. Again, the speaker makes a presumptive
point, as if the results of the *basanos* would have come before the
dicasts, when in fact he can only refer to his own willingness for the
procedure with the assumption—based on his opponents' refusal
of the challenge—that the *basanos* would have been in his favour.
Dem. 29. 11 (quoted above at n. 8) provides a clearer sense of how this
presumptive argument is made. There the *elenchos*, the test, is
achieved not by the *basanos* but by the challenge and its refusal. The
implication is that through the refusal the opponent reveals that he
knows he is in the wrong. In Dem. 30. 27 a similar scenario is
described: 'since I wished to make these things clear to all of you,
I deemed it right to disprove him' (cf. Dem. 45. 62). Demosthenes goes
on to reveal that he challenged Onetor before witnesses, whereupon
Onetor refused the *basanos* on one point and admitted to the other.[14]

In [Dem.] 49 *Tim.* 57 there is mention of a *basanos*-challenge over
one of several points. Disagreement arises over what the significance
of this point would have been had the *basanos* occurred. The key
phrase is the following: 'and to exploit this sure sign before you that
I am lying also with respect to the other matters.' The 'sure sign'
(*tekmērion*) is the unrealized eventuality that the *basanos* had gone
against him. Thür (1977: 208, n. 12) argues that the passage can only
be understood to mean that the *basanos* should serve both as evidence concerning the one point and as the basis for further conclusions, that is, whether or not the speaker is lying about other matters
as well. But 'that I am lying *also* with respect to other matters' can
only mean that the speaker would have had to admit lying on the
point tested by the *basanos*, if it had gone against him.

---

[14] On such partial admissions and the procedural consequences, see Thür 1977:
152–8.

In [Dem.] 59. 120 there is again reference to a challenge: 'I tendered him a challenge ... through which you might have known all the true facts.' Thür puts emphasis on *humin* ('you') and argues that the *basanos* would come before the dicasts. But it is through the challenge, not the *basanos*, that Apollodorus proceeds to argue (125): 'and he himself will disprove himself because he is saying nothing sound after being unwilling to surrender the servants for torture.' Lycurgus 1. 28 also speaks of the dicasts' knowing the truth: 'I think that it is necessary that about such great matters you do not vote by conjecture, but by knowing the truth.'[15] In § 29 the source of 'the truth' is again revealed as his opponent's refusal of the challenge: 'for by fleeing the test by those who know, he has agreed that the charges are true.'[16] Finally, there is Lys. 4. 11: 'Each of these points, as well as others, would have been nothing but easy to make clear in other ways and especially by these means' (*toutois*). Thür interprets *toutois*, as many do, as *die Geschworenen*, the sworn judges: 'make [it] clear *to these men*.' But elsewhere in the speech the Areopagites, who are acting as judges, are always referred to in the second person. For this reason it seems better to translate the word as an instrumental dative referring to the *elenchoi*, that is, the *basanoi*: 'make [it] clear *by these means*.' In § 14 the test of the *basanos* and argumentation before the Areopagites appear as alternatives: 'he thought that after putting aside so accurate a test, it would be easy to deceive you.' The text does not say explicitly that the *basanos*, if accepted and carried out, would have obviated an appearance before the Areopagus, but that is clearly the suggestion; §§ 12 and 17 give further indications that such a test would have been decisive.

The second group of texts shows the *basanos* compared to other forms of evidence, either as confirming them or opposing them (Thür 1977: 209; cf. 178–81). In the first three the *basanos* is to serve as an *elenchos* ('refutation-test') for witnesses. First, Isaeus 8. 10: 'since I wished in addition to the existing witnesses to have an *elenchos* done concerning them from *basanoi*—in order that you

---

[15] Here the verb for the judges' 'knowing' is *eidenai*, since they can have direct knowledge of the refused challenge, which can be removed from the evidence jar and read aloud.

[16] Cf. Lyc. 1. 35–6; Thür 1977: 268–9.

might believe them not as [witnesses] who were yet to undergo an *elenchos* but as having already undergone it concerning the matters about which they are testifying—I thought it right that they hand over their slave women and men.' As in several other passages, it is consistent with this text that the *elenchos* that was intended and that actually occurred derived not from *basanoi* but from the challenge. The speaker goes on to note that his opponent has witnesses also, so the two groups of witnesses cancel each other out. Whichever side loses could bring a *dikē pseudomarturiōn* against his opponent's witnesses, which would supply an *elenchos*, but only after the dicasts' decision. What the speaker argues in § 11 is that the dicasts must conclude from his opponent's refusal of the *basanos* that his witnesses are lying. The speaker's own witnesses have then, in a sense, already passed an *elenchos*, even if it is not in fact the one he implies. Lycurgus 1. 28, discussed above, presents a similar picture. According to the argument, the opponent who refuses to test the testimony of his witness through *basanos* admits that it is untrue. Isaeus 8. 28 and fr. 23 Thalheim (= Dion. Hal. *Isaeus* 12) illustrate the commonplace character of this argumentation. In both passages the *basanos* is initially mentioned as a support for witnesses that is purportedly analogous to the witnesses' support for the litigant's original state-ments. But when the speaker goes on to argue against the credibility of his opponent's statements, he can mention only the *refusal* of the *basanos*-challenge.[17]

Thür presents Dem. 45. 59 and 52. 22 as similarly showing the speakers planning to refute a witness through a *basanos*. But in 45. 59 it is again not the *basanos* but the challenge that provides the refutation: '[the clerk] will read to you the challenge, from which you will catch them in the very act of false swearing.' In Dem. 52 *Callippus* 22 the refutation of witnesses through the *basanos* is a purely hypothetical response to testimony that was never given [viz., that Lycon had stayed with Callippus]: they gave no such

---

[17] Dem. 29 *Aph. iii.* 21 also presents such a situation, but the argumentation is slightly different. In § III, below, I shall discuss how Isae. 8 is notable for its confusion of the functions of *marturia* and *basanos*. [There is no comparing the content of the challenge-to-torture with the content of testimony; it is only *refusing* the challenge that is compared to testimony (and not compared with a witness's refusal to testify as in e.g. Aeschin. 1. 67 discussed by Carey in Ch. 9 above)].

testimony because 'they knew very well that there would be a test through torture of the slaves, if they told any such lie as this'. The speaker claims that the risk of a *basanos*-challenge dissuaded them.[18]

Two texts suggest that *basanoi* should buttress speeches. Demosthenes 30. 35 seems at first a clear case: 'so that there would be not only *logoi*, but also *basanoi* concerning these matters.' But the *logoi* are not the speeches to be delivered before the court, but only preliminary discussions held before witnesses. Onetor, it is explained in the next section, was not willing 'to have recourse' (*kataphugein*) to the precision of the *basanos*. Antiphon 1. 7 demonstrates how selective quotation can mislead. In Thür's (admittedly very rapid) critique of Headlam, only the following is quoted: 'if the slaves did not agree [that she is a murderer], he would have defended her with good knowledge.' So much certainly speaks against the Headlam thesis, since the Greek word for 'defending' (*apologeomai*) is the term used for making a defence in court. But what follows is left out: 'and his mother would have been released from this charge.' This subsequent wording clearly supports Headlam: if the tortured slaves had disagreed, the stepmother would have been off the hook legally. The prosecuting son could have continued to carry a grudge but against that grudge, his stepbrother would have had a vigorous reply.[19] A reason for confusion seems partly to be that two possibilities for torture are suggested: the defending son could have had the torture performed within the context of the challenge, or he could have performed it unilaterally, since he owned the slaves. If he had performed the torture unilaterally, the case might have proceeded, although he might have claimed 'good knowledge'. But if the torture

---

[18] Thür 1977: 212 mentions three other passages that he says are predicated on the *Beweisfunktion* of the *basanos*: Isoc. 17. 54, Isae. 8. 10, and Dem. 30. 37. None of these affects Headlam's thesis in any way that has not already been dealt with. The parallel employment of the *basanos*-challenge and the oath-challenge in Dem. 29. 25 ff. reaffirms that the function of both challenges is the same, to propose an alternative means of settlement.

[19] This text suggests an interesting complication. The fact that there is more than one slave, as well as the fact that the verb used of the slaves' statements under torture is 'to agree' (*homologeo*), allows either that the slaves as a group would not have agreed with the prosecutor or that they would not have agreed with each other. Although in this case the first alternative is the only one possible, the second would clearly present difficulty for the Athenian view of torture.

resulted from the challenge, his mother might have been freed of the trial.[20]

Lastly, there are texts in which it appears that evidence adduced in a *basanos* would come to a *dikastērion*. In [Dem.] 53. 22–4 there are counter-challenges to *basanoi*. The defendant in the *apographē*, Nicostratus, wishes the prosecutor, Apollodorus, to conduct *basanoi* on two slaves. But Apollodorus claims that the state owns the slaves and that he, as a private individual, cannot take responsibility for torturing them. According to his challenge, the *basanos* should be conducted 'publicly', by the Eleven. The evidence derived would then be produced before a *dikastērion*. Headlam points out that what is suggested by Apollodorus is not the usual challenge, but the procedure to be followed where the state is itself one of the parties. However, Thür rejects the argumentation as highly suspect. Nicostratus, he argues, by agreeing to the public *basanos* would admit that the slaves belonged to the state and so concede the case. Perhaps that is true. Certainly Nicostratus might have argued along these lines, and Apollodorus was in no mood to achieve an extra-judicial settlement. But we really cannot say what rules there were regarding such situations, so that Thür's outright dismissal of Headlam's reading is not justified. What matters for the present is whether *basanoi* resulting from challenges resolved disputes or merely served as evidence. This text shows at most that *basanoi* conducted by the Eleven could serve as evidence. Headlam's thesis, which concerns private disputes, remains to that extent unshaken. Moreover, the text does not say that the *dikastērion* would have evaluated the veracity of the *basanoi* or that it would have 'judged' (*dikazein*) the case, but only that, on hearing the results of the *basanos*, it would have voted on *what seemed best to do*. The language used is political rather than forensic, for the dicasts would, it seems, be voting not on the veracity of the *basanos*, but on how best to use state property (the slaves). Apparently they would accept the evidence of the *basanoi* as true.

---

[20] Thür 1977: 210 also mentions three texts in which he understands the terminological distinction between *marturia* and *basanos* to be blurred: [Dem.] 47. 8, 53. 22, and 59. 122. [Dem.] 53. 22 is not problematic: the *marturia* is not identified with the *basanos*. I discuss the other instances in § III.

Dem. 54. 27 is introduced with the suggestion that statements of slaves also here are to be put into the evidence jars (*echinoi*): 'they make a challenge—with a view to delay and preventing the evidence jars from being sealed—that they are willing to hand over their slaves concerning the assaults.' Again, it is not the slaves' statements under torture that are to go into the evidence jars. Only the challenges, whose wording would have to be worked out in a time-consuming process, went into the collection. It appears that the slaves were not present at the arbitration and immediately available to be tortured, since, as the speaker alleges, time is taken even to write down their names.[21]

The result of the foregoing is that the criticisms levelled against Headlam's thesis are not successful. It still appears the most economical way of dealing with the evidence, and there are no texts that cannot be adequately explained through it. On the other hand, a key objection of scholars such as Thür, that the dicasts had the ability independently to evaluate the credibility of all forms of evidence that came before them (*freie Beweiswürdigung*), is also answered. A *basanos* that is actually carried out (rather than rejected) does not bind the dicasts since it never comes before them.[22]

In Antiphon 5 a slave is tortured privately by the family of the murder victim and then killed. Euxitheos, the defendant, says to the prosecutors: 'you thought it right that [the dicasts] become judges of his words [under torture], while you yourselves became dicasts of his actions.' The implication is that the prosecutors reversed their roles with the dicasts. Just as it was not the place of the prosecutors to judge and execute the slave for the murder of Herodes, it was not normally the place of the dicasts to assess the statements of a slave under torture. A master was always free to torture his own slaves and to report what was revealed in court, but such reports could scarcely

---

[21] In [Dem.] 47. 13–15 the speaker uses as evidence against the good faith of his opponent that, despite allegedly offering his slave for torture, he did not have her available immediately to hand over.

[22] It should also be stressed that much of Thür's analysis of the tactical use of the *basanos*-challenge is unaffected by the correctness of Headlam's thesis. However, his hypotheses that in every case the challenge was only a trick and that the speeches we possess contain an unrepresentatively high number of *basanos*-challenges seem unnecessary.

have persuaded anyone but the master himself. They would have been almost useless in court.

The requirement of the Athenian court that dicasts decide a case after only hearing brief presentations from the opposing sides entails that their judgements could only ever be based on opinion and conjecture, on at best second-hand information (Thür 1977: 294–5). The litigants recognize that it would have been far better had they themselves—who had direct knowledge—resolved their dispute, or, alternatively, had they resolved it with the help of a private arbitrator, who would have had more intimate knowledge of the circumstances than the dicasts can achieve. Demosthenes 27. 1 makes just this point: 'this man has fled those who have clear insight into our affairs determining anything about them, but has come to you, who have no accurate knowledge of our affairs.'[23] According to the Athenians, the *basanos*-challenge, like the private arbitration, afforded the opportunity to resolve the dispute based on 'accurate knowledge' or 'the entire truth'.[24] However, this view is not based on any division between 'technical' and 'non-technical' modes or argumentation (to which I turn in § III), or on a division between archaic and classical Athenian law. It is based on a recognition of the imperfect quality of the democratic *dikastērion*, which lacked powers of independent investigation. A resolution of a dispute based on accurate knowledge had to stem from the resources of the parties themselves. The *basanos*, conducted through the agreement of both parties, represented one such resource.

III

> Now of course this is all rhetoric and the Orators were not serious in it.

Many legal scholars are tempted to dismiss the role of rhetoric as something extrinsic and bothersome to their study of legal procedures.

---

[23] Cf. Dem. 47. 40 and 55. 35. On the role of the private arbitrators, see Thür 1977: 33, n. 36 and 228–31.

[24] Thür 1977: 294 gathers the relevant passages: Ant. *Tetr.* 1. 4. 8, 6. 18; Lys. 7. 43; Isoc. 17. 54; Dem. 30. 35; Lyc. 1. 28–9.

Statements like Headlam's, above, are common in the literature. But it is my view that rhetoric is an integral part of ancient legal discourse and that an appreciation of it can be extremely helpful, even essential, for dealing with legal questions. In the period from which we have Athenian forensic writings, the late fifth and fourth centuries BC, there were developments in two areas that affected the rhetorical strategies used in litigation, including those directed toward the torture of slaves.

The first was the increasing use of written documents in court, which replaced the use of direct oral testimony. It is generally agreed that the transition to the use of written testimony was completed before Isaeus, perhaps by about 390 and at any rate not later than 378.[25] Accordingly, while the speeches of the earlier orators, Antiphon, Andocides, Lysias, and Isocrates, employ oral testimony, those of Isaeus, Demosthenes, Lycurgus, Dinarchus, Demades, and Hyperides use only written testimony. In the speeches themselves this transition is most noticeable in that, in general, the speakers no longer say 'call the witnesses' but 'read the testimony'. In private suits, those which came before a public arbitrator, written testimony may have been used right from the inception of public arbitration, about 403.[26] Certainly writing was used earlier, as is indicated at Ant. 1. 10, and the formulas by which evidence of various sorts was used did not change substantially. But the procedural changes made c.380 must have forced a new examination of writing and written documents by those who were composing speeches to be used in court (cf. Dem. 45. 44–5).

The second development that affected rhetorical strategies resulted from the prodigious activity of the professional rhetoricians, both as speechwriters and teachers. These rhetoricians served to canonize lines of argumentation in new ways. However, the process by which they did so could result in arguments based on an incomplete understanding of the legal procedure. As sophists, theirs was not a mode of thought that was informed simply by traditional conceptions or even by the law. The freedom with which they approached problems of law and legal procedure allowed them to see rationality

[25] See Bonner 1906: 46–54, and Calhoun 1919a; cf. Pringsheim 1955; Thür 1977: 89–90.
[26] See Bonner 1916 and Harrell 1936: 27–8.

in procedures where none existed, or where a quite different reasoning was at work. Our most direct evidence for the role of professional rhetoricians in categorizing forensic arguments consists of the accounts of Aristotle (*Rh.* 1. 15) and Anaximenes (*Rh. Al.* 14–17) on the *atechnoi pisteis*, the documentary evidence used in court. Rather than *atechnoi*, Anaximenes uses the term *epithetoi* ('supplementary') *pisteis*, which indicates that, like Aristotle, he sees them as somewhat extrinsic to the speech and the rhetorician's *technē*. These were the documents that would, for the most part, be read aloud by the court secretary at the request of the speaker. Aristotle includes five sorts, laws, testimony of witnesses, contracts, *basanoi*, and oaths, while Anaximenes has what he calls 'the opinion of the speaker' and then witnesses, *basanoi*, and oaths.

Despite their superficial differences, both handbooks rely on a common precursor (Mirhady 1991*b*). Although there are times when they differ in specific language, the arguments they recommend are essentially the same, the similarity being especially striking in regard to the *basanoi*. Aristotle and Anaximenes composed their handbooks in the period 350–330 BC. If, as seems likely, the common precursor was composed specifically as a result of the changes made in judicial procedure that required the use of written testimony, about 378 BC, then it was probably written sometime between 378 and 360. That would put it one generation before those of Aristotle and Anaximenes.

However, the sequence in the handbooks 'laws, witnesses, *basanoi*, and oaths' reveals an important difference between legal categories and rhetorical ones. In *Ath. Pol.* 53. 2–3 it is said that the documents placed in the evidence jar after a public arbitration—which are the only ones that can be used before the court—are the 'laws, challenges (*proklēseis*), and testimonies (of witnesses)'.[27] The rhetorical handbooks follow this judicial scheme, by including laws and witnesses,

---

[27] No particular weight should be put on the order. In *Ath. Pol.* 53. 2 'laws' and 'testimonies' are reversed. Cf. Harpocration, s.v. *diaitētai* and *SIG*³ 953. 20–3. Thür 1977: 132–48 argues in great detail against identifying the challenge as an *atechnos pistis* on the grounds that since its authenticity must be supported by *marturiai*, its evidentiary force is reducible to the *marturiai*. Aristotle, however, supports the authenticity of contracts through *marturiai* and yet recognizes them as *atechnoi pisteis* (1376b2–5).

but they replace the general 'challenges' with the more specific '*basanoi*' and 'oaths'. The phrasing in *Ath. Pol.* perhaps reflects the procedural economy of the law itself, dealing generally with 'challenges' and not distinguishing by type. In rhetorical treatment, however, the distinction is important: the hypothetical testimony becomes more useful than the actual procedure. Thus, though there is perhaps an idea of the challenge preserved in Aristotle's handling of oath, in their treatments of the *basanos* neither Aristotle nor Anaximenes explores the procedural implications of the challenge itself; rather, they emphasize the probative value of slave-torture. Similarly (as observed in § II), the orators commonly speak of the *basanos* as if it had taken place, when in fact they can refer only to a challenge.

The consequences of the substitution, whatever its rationale, are more than superficial, for the handbooks take one further and very misleading step: with the procedural distinction of the challenge seemingly forgotten, they identify the *basanos* as a form of testimony (*marturia*). Aristotle calls *basanoi* a kind of testimony (*marturiai tines*, 1376b31), while Anaximenes 16. 1 calls a *basanos* 'an agreement of someone who knows but is involuntary'; for him the only difference between a *marturia* and a *basanos* is whether the 'agreement' is voluntary or not.[28] Through this identification the rhetoricians put the *basanos* on a par with the testimony of free males. The identification comes easily to the modern perspective, as it must have to a sophist. Since we live in a slaveless society, we see little difference between the statement of a slave and that of a free person. Moreover, our difficulty in translating *basanos* adds to the confusion: the word is often rendered as 'the testimony of a slave under torture', and so the word 'testimony' is used of both *marturia* and *basanos*. The sophist must likewise have emphasized the parallel between the statements of free and slave in involving 'those who know' the truth (*hoi suneidotes*). In Antiphon 6. 22–5, where the speaker is emphasizing how he sought to settle his dispute amicably, there is a close connection made between the two. But in Antiphon, unlike the handbooks, there is no confusion of *marturia* and *basanos*. In fact, in 6. 25 Antiphon is at pains to emphasize the close parallel between *basanos* and oath.

[28] Cf. *Rh. Al.* 36. 18 and 31.

If in the first part of this paper I had argued that Thür and the other legal scholars who have rejected Headlam's thesis are right and that the results of a *basanos* could come before a court which would evaluate its credibility, then it would hardly matter that the handbooks identify it as a form of testimony. But if the *basanos* is actually an out-of-court means of settling a dispute, then what the handbooks say is quite misleading. The *marturia* and the *basanos* are in no way similar from a judicial point of view.[29] The *marturia* is the statement of a free male that is made in order to support the credibility of something said by the litigant in court. By making the statement, the man takes a share in the risk run by the litigant (cf. Arist. *Rh.* 1. 15, 1376a8). The *basanos*, on the other hand, is an extra-judicial means of securing 'the truth' concerning a disputed point. Its function is to decide a dispute, just as would the decision of a private arbitrator or the agreed-upon swearing of an oath.

As was mentioned in § II, there are several texts in which speakers compare the *basanos* to the *marturia* (Thür 1977: 209–10). Some understand the texts to be an indication of their judicially parallel status. However, they appear instead to indicate that the orators briefly took over a misleading step from the rhetoricians. In the speeches of Antiphon, Andocides, and Lysias there is no suggestion that the *basanos* and the *marturia* are parallel. But Isocrates 17. 54 (*c.*393 BC) argues that '[while the judges believe that] it is possible to suborn witnesses of things that have not occurred, *basanoi* demonstrate clearly which side is telling the truth'. He actually preserves the judicial distinction between the *basanos* and *marturia*, since he does not quite suggest that they are parallel. At the same time he intimates a point of comparison. Isaeus 8. 12 (before 364) and Demosthenes 30. 37 (*c.*363), following Isaeus verbatim, take this point further. They connect another argument, which also appears in the handbooks, that the existence of a suit against false testimony (*dikē pseudomarturiōn*) implies the suspect nature of the *marturia* (cf. *Rh.*

---

[29] See Thür 1977: 210, and Todd 1990a: 27–31. See also Morrow 1939: 82, n. 48, on *Laws* 11. 937B: 'Plato uses the word *marturein* ... in its precise legal sense ... In the strict sense of the word neither the slave-informer nor the slave put to the torture could be called a *martus*.' Cf. Ant. *Tetr.* 1. 2. 7, 1. 3. 4 and 1. 4. 7; Lys. 7. 37; Isoc., 21. 4; Dem. 30. 36; Hyperides, fr. 5 Jensen.

1. 15, 1376a20–1, *Rh. Al.* 15. 6), and argue as follows: 'you know that of those who have testified in the past some appeared not to testify truly, but none of those tortured has ever been proven to have said what was not true as a result of the tortures.' This comparison is absurd from a judicial point of view, since slaves were tortured partly because they were not liable to prosecution for false testimony.[30] It was procedurally impossible for them to be caught saying what was untrue. One of the conditions necessary for an accepted *basanos*-challenge was that both parties believed the slave would tell the truth under torture.[31]

Another commonplace linking Isocrates, the rhetorical handbooks, and Isaeus and Demosthenes is found in an argument used together with the identification of *basanos* and *marturia*. Isocrates 17. 54 says to the judges: 'I see that you think that concerning both private and public matters there is nothing more credible or truer than the *basanos*.' Aristotle, *Rh.* 1376b30–1 abbreviates the argument, but Anaximenes, *Rh. Al.* 16.1 gives it in full: 'private people concerning the most serious matters and cities concerning the most important affairs take credence from *basanoi*' (cf. Lyc. 1. 29). Isaeus (8. 12) and Demosthenes (30. 37) rehearse nearly the same argument. Demosthenes' verbatim copying of Isaeus may reflect a lack of intellectual commitment on the part of the young orator. It seems likely that Isocrates inspired this part of the original handbook, even if he did not have a role in writing it himself.[32] The comparison between the *basanos* and the *marturia*, which was irrelevant in terms of the law, was useful rhetorically. Isaeus and his student Demosthenes, who compose speeches only after all testimony is being committed to writing, appear to be influenced by the sort of handbook that inspired Aristotle. The chronology fits this pattern.

---

[30] Plato, *Laws* 11. 937a–b, allows slaves to testify and to speak in court only at trials for murder and only on the condition that they be made accountable through the *dikē pseudomarturiōn*. Attic law had no such provisions. Thür 1977: 309 calls the comparison of *basanos* and *marturia* hollow.

[31] Cf. Ant.1.8, 6.25; Lyc. 1.29. Thür 1977: 227–4 points out that in those disputes that refer explicitly to the dispute-ending quality of the *basanos* the references to *aphesis* and *apallagē* correspond to the other methods of mutually ending disputes.

[32] See Plut. *Dem.* 5. 5 and Mirhady 1991*b*: 6–7.

Basanos and *marturia* are directly identified in only two speeches. The first, [Dem.] 47, was composed *c.*355, but the thrust of the argument, a paraphrase of the opponent, closely follows Isoc. 17. 54, with its suggestion of suborning witnesses (8): 'for [my opponent] said in the suit for assault that the witnesses who had been present and were testifying about what had happened—in writing according to the law—were false and had been suborned by me, but that the [slave] woman who had been present would speak the truth, testifying not in writing, but from the strongest testimony, while being tortured.' The speaker reports a stock argument from the handbooks that his opponent (mis)used in order to deceive the judges in a previous suit (cf. 47. 40). He treats the opponent's identification of the *basanos* as *marturia* ironically, since, even if this argument were persuasive at one time, it now appears a transparent deception, as more importance is placed upon writing and conformity to the law. The irony suggests that this particular influence of the rhetoricians on the orators was short-lived. As influential (and misleading) as the passages that identify *basanos* as *marturia* have been for modern scholarship, they did not catch on among the orators. The only other occurrence, [Dem.] 59. 122, is equivocal: '[Stephanus] might have made a demonstration from the most accurate testimony, by handing over these servants.' Apollodorus is certainly referring to the *basanos*, but he also refers, metaphorically, to Stephanus' virtual 'testimony' in simply acceding to the challenge and producing the servants (cf. Isae. 8. 14 for this metaphor of *marturia*).

Since the rhetorical handbooks that we possess from the fourth century were composed after most of the speeches that survive, or at any rate after those who wrote the speeches were mature and unlikely to rely on handbooks, it is often difficult to discern where systematic rhetorical thought has directly influenced the orators. But in the case of the *atechnoi pisteis*, where the general structure of what appears in our handbooks was likely already in circulation a generation before Aristotle composed his *Rhetoric*, it is plausible to search for such influences. Because the status accorded the *basanos* in the handbooks, as a form of *marturia*, differs so markedly from its judicial status, the influence of the handbooks becomes clear.

EPILOGUE

Interest in Athenian torture has continued unabated since the publication of this paper in 1996 and the reply by Gerhard Thür that accompanied it in *JHS*. Professor Thür makes several points. First, he insists on the necessity for witnesses to support the 'probative force' both of the challenge, that it was made, and so on, and of *basanos*, that it was correctly done. While I agree on the enormous importance of witness testimony (see Mirhady 2002), I believe a qualification is necessary. 'Probative force' needs to be understood in two ways, first in terms of credibility, what Aristotle calls *to piston*, and second in terms of persuasiveness, *to pithanon*, the former clearly being necessary for the latter, but not sufficient. Witnesses are necessary for the credibility of challenges—that the challenge was actually made, and so on—but they cannot support their persuasiveness beyond that. A second point made by Professor Thür in reply to my paper was that I had passed over a group of texts (Isoc. 17. 15–16; Dem. 29. 51–2, 37. 40–1, 59. 124; and Aeschin. 2. 127), which he discusses in his book (1977: 214–32) and which offer expressly drawn up *basanos*-challenges that were to regulate how the slave's testimony would terminate litigation. Thür argues that only such explicit wording allows us the conclusion that the *basanos* would end the litigation, whereas a 'simple' *basanos* was used as a piece of evidence in court. Since these texts all portray the fulfilled *basanos*-challenge as a dispute-ending procedure, they do not seem to weaken the Headlam hypothesis. On a third point, whether *toutois* in Lys. 4. 11 refers to the Areopagites or to the *basanos* procedures (§ II, following n. 16), there seems no way to resolve our different readings of the evidence. While Ant. 5. 47, which he mentions, would seem to me to support the Headlam view over his, it also seems to me that in Lys. 4. 10–12 the repeated wording *ek tēs anthrōpou basanistheisēs ton elenchon poiēsasthai* ('to prove from the woman under torture') seems a parallel rendering of *emphanes kai toutois poiēsai* ('make plain by these means', *toutois* being instrumental dative) that would again support the Headlam reading over his, although either reading seems entirely possible. Dem. 54. 27–31 is raised by Professor Thür in a fifth point, but I do not see where he finds in it evidence that the *basanos* goes into the *echinos*.

In the same year in which I published my paper in *JHS*, Michael Gagarin published a stimulating paper on the strategy of the *basanos*-challenge, in which he employs the notion of the *basanos* as a 'legal fiction'. The *basanos*-challenge, he argues, allowed the evidence of slaves to be brought before the court while necessitating little phys-ical harm to slaves. While I agree wholeheartedly with many of Gagarin's interpretations of individual passages, I worry that a uni-versal 'fiction' involved in the *basanos*-challenge would have been too transparent, that unless there really was a possibility of the torture taking place, the challenge and argumentation based on it would have been useless as hearsay evidence.

After hearing drafts of my 1996 *JHS* paper (which was a long time in press), as well as reading previous papers, Virginia Hunter (1994) found that she had reached similar conclusions in accepting the Headlam thesis. As a social historian she has done much to explain the social status and role of slaves within the Athenian household and society, and I (2000) have tried to honour her work by exploring the Athenian attitudes towards slave psychology that allowed them to believe that slave torture was a rational activity. Steven Johnstone (1999) has written an interesting chapter in his book on the *proklēsis*, what he calls a 'dare'. In order to understand the function of the *basanos*-challenge it does seem necessary to understand the function of challenges generally.

The close reading and analysis of particular passages that has been pursued by Thür, Gagarin, Hunter, and, to some extent, Johnstone, has revealed a great deal about torture in ancient Athens. When I was writing the paper 'Torture and Rhetoric', Page Dubois' book *Torture and Truth* (1991) had recently been published. I thought it mis-guided, an unfruitful approach. I decided that I wouldn't cite the book, but only refer to it elliptically in my title. Such can be the vanities of young scholars. I still believe, however, that closely reading their rhetoric offers us the most fruitful guide to the Athenians and their role in our cultural tradition.

PART III

Casting the Jury

11

Ability and Education: The Power of Persuasion*

Josiah Ober

[These pages are excerpted from a book that seeks to make sense of public oratory in democratic Athens in terms of dynamic social relations between elite speakers and mass audiences. Like much of my subsequent work, the book attempted to answer a simple question: how could a highly participatory democracy have worked—featuring, as it did, frequent and direct decision-making on justice and state policy by mass audiences of ordinary people? That democracy at Athens did work is matter of historical record: when compared to its *polis* rivals over time, on measures of wealth, power, or cultural influence, democratic Athens was an astonishingly successful *polis*. It was not, of course, consistently successful: focusing on high-profile mistakes by public bodies (e.g. the invasion of Sicily in 415, the execution of Socrates in 399) can obscure the fact of overall Athenian success. It is, of course, easy to show that Athens loses in comparison to an ideal state, like Plato's Kallipolis, or a counterfactual 'mistake-free Athens'. But historians are for the most part concerned with the real world, and so we need to explain why democratic Athens fared so well in continuous and fierce competition with rival states.

The book's primary argument is that Athenian success was predicated on the development of effective communication between a mass of ordinary citizens and various sociologically and ideologically definable elites: the rich, the well-born, and—the focus of this

* Originally published as chapter 4 of *Mass and Elite in Democratic Athens* (1989).

section—the highly educated. Public oratory, especially in assembly and lawcourt, provided fora in which elite speakers were judged by a mass audience. The performance context of Athenian oratory therefore juxtaposed authoritative mass judgement and elite attempts at persuasion. Moreover, the speeches themselves often contain passages that directly or indirectly address the issue of mass and elite. Whether the ostensible topic of a speech was a dispute over property, a charge of treason, or public policy, each speech was also, I argued, a site for negotiation over values, interests, and aspirations by ordinary and elite Athenians. The conclusion of the book, which is anticipated in these pages, is that the system of public communication worked well in that it allowed individual elite Athenians to play a variety of highly productive roles in the community (including those of benefactor and political leader), while preventing the elite as a body from developing into a ruling oligarchy.

Oratorical ability, as Robert Michels points out, is a prerequisite for political leadership in a democracy.[1] Athenian politicians invariably possessed great public-speaking ability, and their natural rhetorical skills had often been refined through formal education in schools of rhetoric.

The political orators were, collectively, the most visible sector of the Athenian 'educated elite', but they never became a ruling elite. Analysing how the topics of ability and education are treated in public discourse reveals both continuities and discontinuities between Athenian political experience and the functioning of modern democracy. How did the Athenians regard those who possessed superior ability to communicate ideas to large audiences, and who had been educated in the arts of persuasion? How did the masses control the ambitions of the educated elite and so combat the drift toward oligarchy, which Michels considered the inevitable fate of democratic organizations?

I. GROUP DECISIONS AND COLLECTIVE WISDOM

Athenian procedures for making important political decisions, both at the level of legislation (in the assembly and by boards of *nomothetai*)

[1] Michels 1915: 98–100; cf. Marger 1981: 196–8. See also Ober 1989: 11–7, 112–21.

and at the level of the judiciary, always involved public discussion before a large group of citizens, followed by a group vote. The decision reached was typically binding on the society as a whole. Thus Athenian decision-making was explicitly predicated on the belief that group decisions were likely to be right decisions. The political implications of that conclusion, and of the assumptions that underpinned it, were far-reaching.

(I. 1) Natural Ability and Formal Education of Ordinary Athenians

Part of the Athenians' faith in the wisdom of collective decisions made by the masses rested upon their conviction that Athenians were by nature more intelligent than other people. Aeschines (1. 178), for example, avowed that in his opinion Athenians were naturally more clever (*epidexioi*) than other people and so naturally made better laws. Demosthenes (3. 15) noted that the Athenians were quicker (*oxutatoi*) than other men to grasp the meaning of speeches. Isaeus' client (11. 19) stated that he need say no more concerning the subject at hand, since the jurors were intelligent men (*eu phronousi humin*), able to judge well for themselves the rights and wrongs of the matter (cf. Eur. *Medea* 826–7, 844–5).

The Athenians' image of themselves as a shrewd lot was sometimes exploited by a public speaker in an attempt to shame the audience into voting in his favour. Demosthenes (23. 109) notes that the Olynthians had demonstrated that they were able to plan ahead against Philip, and he claimed that it would surely be shameful (*aischron*) if the Athenians, 'who have a reputation for having superior ability in political deliberations', should prove inferior to mere Olynthians. Elsewhere (18. 149), Demosthenes remarks that Aeschines had been able to fool the non-Athenian members of the Amphictionic council, since they were 'men unused to speeches'; Demosthenes implies that his current audience of experienced Athenians will not be misled so easily. Dinarchus (1. 93) wondered which of the jurors was so blindly hopeful, so ignorant (*alogistos*), or so unaware of affairs (*apeiros*) as to vote for Demosthenes, and he suggested (1. 104) that Demosthenes himself had too much faith in his power of speech and in the jurors' simplemindedness (*euētheias*). Hyperides (3. 23) claimed that his opponent regarded the jurors as fools (*ēlithious*) who would not recognize his effrontery.

The native intelligence of the common Athenian may have been reinforced by at least some formal schooling. The excellence of Athenian education was a *topos* of funeral orations.[2] But in fact we know regrettably little about primary education in the Greek *poleis* before the Hellenistic period and virtually nothing about the education of the non-elite.[3] Basic literacy—the ability to read and to write some words—seems to have been general among the citizen population of Athens, at least by the fourth century and perhaps well before.[4] In order to function as a citizen, and certainly in order to carry out the responsibilities of many of the magistracies, the Athenian citizen needed a basic command of letters. On the other hand, it seems unlikely that many Athenians were fully literate in the sense that they read easily and frequently, for pleasure and instruction. Books were, relatively speaking, rare and expensive. Although books were no longer exotic by the later fifth century, they were probably still, for the most part, the possessions of the educated elite, and Athenian political culture remained at its heart an oral culture.[5] Thus, in the Funeral Oration (Thuc. 2. 40. 2) Pericles emphasized that the Athenians made good political decisions because they believed that speeches (*logoi*) were not a hindrance to action, but rather they regarded it as a disgrace not to be well instructed by public debate before engaging in action.[6]

Even if the common Athenian citizen was not fully literate, he was widely exposed to the products of literary culture. The state-subsidized performances at the Panathenaic festival and the

---

[2] Thuc. 2. 40–1; Lys. 2. 69; Dem. 60. 16; Hyp. 6. 8; contrast Loraux 1986: 151.

[3] See esp. Plato, *Protagoras* 325e–26a; cf. Marrou 1964: 63–146, esp. 65; Pélékidis 1962: 31–2, 62.

[4] See esp. Harvey 1966; Burns 1981; Davison 1962; Woodbury 1976, esp. 355–7. For the even more difficult question of female literacy, see S. Cole 1981.

[5] On the interrelations among literacy, citizenship, and literature, see Harvey 1966; Burns 1981, esp. 384–5; Whitehead 1986: 139 (literate demarchs); Finley 1982: 9–10; Davison 1962: 219–21.

[6] Cf. similar sentiments in Lys. 2. 19. Contrast Thucydides' discussion (3. 83) of the atmosphere of distrust of speeches and cleverness generally in the Corcyraean civil war, where he contrasts those who think ahead with those who act immediately; see also Connor 1984: 14–15, on this passage.

festival of Dionysus exposed the average citizen to poetry, music, and dance (Ober 1989: 152–5). He might also attend various public readings, such as the ones Herodotus reputedly gave of his *Histories*.[7] The average Athenian had, no doubt, gained at least a passing acquaintance with the stories of Homer and the myths and legends associated with Athenian antiquity. Much would have been learned from his parents and relatives, much picked up casually in the course of listening to others, perhaps especially to the elders of his deme.

Attendance at assemblies and participation in the lawcourts as a juror gave the citizen considerable experience with highly sophisticated rhetoric, and he considered himself competent to judge both the merits of an argument and the style in which it was delivered. In the Mytilenean debate (Thuc. 3. 38. 2–7) Cleon berates the assemblymen for regarding themselves as connoisseurs of rhetoric and acting as if they were listening to the haggling of sophists, rather than acting like men involved in making serious decisions that would affect the fate of the *polis*. This taste for fine rhetoric certainly continued into the fourth century. Although few public speakers attained Demosthenes' level of skill, the corpus of Attic orators is testimony both to the high standard that deliberative and forensic rhetoric achieved in the period and to the Athenian public's appreciation for fine speaking.[8] In general, we may assume that the common citizen could appreciate many of the fine points of poetry, performing arts, history, and rhetoric, although he would probably not have made the distinctions between these fields that his more highly and formally educated elite fellow citizen might have been taught to do.

(I. 2) Practical Education in Politics

In a famous passage in the Funeral Oration (Thuc. 2. 41. 1) Pericles praised the city of Athens as an education to her citizens and to all of

---

[7] For a critical review of the evidence for Herodotus' public readings at Athens, see Podlecki 1977: 247; cf. Starr 1968: 132–3.

[8] This is not to say that public rhetoric was ornate to the exclusion of meaning; cf. Ober 1989: 121–5. Aristotle (*Rh.* 1404a25–8) notes with scorn that most uneducated people still think the poetic style of rhetoric developed by Gorgias to be the finest, but this is surely a reference to epideictic rhetoric.

Hellas. The education provided by the *polis* was not, by any means, limited to literary culture and its popular by-products. A major part of the citizen's education came through performance of his political role.[9] The citizen's first formal experience with democratic government was in his deme, when he was presented to the demesmen and they voted to grant him citizenship. The political organization of the deme was modelled, both in theory and practice, on the *polis* government. The deme assemblies were training-grounds for citizens in what Whitehead has called the 'cardinal principles' of 'communal decision-making and responsibility'.[10] Members of different demes learned how to cooperate with residents from elsewhere in Attica in the tribal assemblies and, especially, on the council, which gave the citizen an extended and intimate look at many aspects of the government.[11] Service in other magistracies—in addition to the 500 *bouleutai*, some 700 other offices were filled each year (Hansen 1980)—might give the citizen further experience in dealing with different elements in his state and society. Military service, too, offered valuable education, by helping to instill a sense of common purpose and the necessity of cooperation in those who marched in the phalanx or rowed the triremes (Ridley 1979; Ober 1989: 82–4). At least in the last third of the fourth century, and perhaps earlier, the state provided the ephebes, citizens aged 18 and 19, with two years of moral, religious, and formal military training.[12] Finally, the experience of service as a juror and as an assemblyman was of primary importance in the practical political education of the citizen.

[9] See e.g. Finley 1973: 29–31; 1983: 27–9; Loraux 1986: 144–5.

[10] Whitehead 1986: 120; cf. 92–6, 313–15; Raaflaub 1980: 41–3. Hopper 1957: 13–19, overstates the case, as Whitehead demonstrates (pp. 315–24).

[11] Cf. Ober 1989: 76–82. Tribal assemblies: Hopper 1957: 14–16. Council: Gomme 1951; Woodhead 1967: 133–5; Finley 1983: 71–4. For the numbers of citizens who served on the council, see Ober 1989: 138–41.

[12] There is a voluminous literature on the *ephebia*, but Pélékidis 1962 is still the most useful summary. I argued in *Fortress Attica* (1985), 90–5, that specialized military training for the ephebes dates back to the second quarter of the 4th century, but the specifically educational aspects of the institution may be late 4th-century developments. Ruschenbusch 1979: 173–6 argued that *all* 18- and 19-year-olds (not only those of the hoplite class) were ephebes, which I believe is quite likely; cf. Ober 1989: 140 with n. 93.

(I. 3) Normative Function of State Institutions

The educational function of the polis was not limited to the 'practical' training in the political process offered to the individual citizen. Perhaps more telling, in both popular ideology and elite political theory, was the normative role of the ethos of the *polis*, expressed through the organization and actions of governmental institutions. The convictions that a good life can only be lived in a good *polis*, that therefore the moral duty of the citizen is to improve the ethos of the *polis*, and that the ethos of a good state will be exemplified and maintained by its institutions are central to the political thought of Plato and Aristotle.[13] Isocrates completely agreed; his ideal *paideia* stressed not only the formal education of children but the moral education which good institutions would inculcate in the mature citizens.[14] The differences of opinion between Isocrates and Plato, as between elite political theory and mass ideology, were not over whether the state and its institutions should be a reflection of moral good.[15] The disputes rather concerned how the good should be defined, who was capable of achieving goodness, and whether goodness could be taught. The Athenian masses, unlike the elite theorists, tended to assume that the existing state was good and, if imperfect, capable of improvement. The institutions of the state were therefore also essentially good and could justly be expected to perform a major educational and normative role in improving the citizens (cf. Plato, *Ap.* 24d–25a). Given the directness of the democracy—the lack of a government interposed between people and state—this meant not only that the laws must be as just and democratic as possible, but that the decisions reached in the assembly and in the courts had an important didactic role. Good decisions would improve the citizenry; poor decisions might worsen it. Thus Demosthenes, for example,

---

[13] Esp. Plato, *Apology* and *Crito*; Arist. *Pol.* Books 3 and 6. Cf. Jaeger 1944: ii. 150; iii. 67.

[14] Esp. Isoc. 7. 37, 48–50; cf. Jaeger 1944: iii. 119–22.

[15] It is often assumed (e.g. Adkins 1978: 145–7) that the similarities between ideas in 'popular' literature and elite literature may be traced to a 'trickle-down' of ideas of elite thinkers to mass culture. But one might rather chose to regard some of the ideas of elite writers as formalizations and elaborations of the popular ideology of the society in which they lived. Cf. Ober 1989: 336–9.

could argue (19. 343) that a failure to convict Aeschines and his
cronies would result in the worsening of every citizen, since all
would see that traitors received wealth and honours, while just
persons who spent their personal fortunes for the public good were
ill-treated. Citizens who performed significant political functions
were an important focus of normative decision-making. Demosthenes (22. 37) urged that if the present *bouleutai* lost their honorific
crown as punishment for having been misled by a rhetor, future
councilmen would be encouraged to perform diligently and to reject
attempts by political experts to dominate the proceedings. The
didactic example of judicial decisions was not, however, limited to
the political behaviour of male citizens. Apollodorus ([Dem.] 59. 113)
argued that acquittal of the prostitute Neaera would encourage poorer
female citizens to become prostitutes in order to earn money for their
dowries.

Of vital importance was the education of the youth of the city in the
political values and ideological precepts that enabled the democracy
to function. Aeschines (3. 246) argued that the wrestling grounds
(*palaistrai*), formal educational institutions (*didaskaleia*), and lyric
poetry (*mousikē*) do not, by themselves, educate (*paideuei*) the youth
of the city; more important were the decisions of the demos (*ta
dēmosia kērugmata*). Lycurgus (1. 10) claimed that the jurors knew
perfectly well that their votes must be an incentive to the young, since
the education of the youth consisted of the punishment of wrong and
the rewarding of the virtuous by the state. Isocrates (20. 21) urged the
jurors not to wrong themselves collectively, nor to teach the youth
to despise the mass of the citizens (*kataphronein tou plēthous tōn
politōn*), by acquital of a rich man accused of hubris.

Isocrates' comment on the youth and the hubristic rich and
Demosthenes' comments on the *bouleutai* and the political experts
suggest that the normative function of mass decisions was especially
important in light of existing sociopolitical inequities. Lysias' client
(30. 24) noted that the punishment of those unable to speak well was
not useful as an example but that meting out justice to powerful
speakers (*dunamenoi legein*; cf. Ober 1989: 105–8) was a fine example
(*paradeigma*) to others (cf. Lys. 14. 12; 27. 5). And Demosthenes (21.
183) exhorted the jurors in the trial of Meidias not to create an
example (*deigma*) of forgiveness of the rich man, when they had

formerly convicted without pity a man who was moderate (*metrios*) and who conformed to democratic values (*dēmotikos*; cf. Ober 1989: 230–47). The decisions of juries could, furthermore, be regarded as a means of forcing elite citizens to conform to the norms established by the masses. Lysias (14. 45) urged that the conviction of Alcibiades the Younger would be a good example to his friends (*philoi*) who were planning on becoming demagogues themselves. Demosthenes (51. 22) urged the jurors not to allow the honorable ambitiousness (*philotimia*) of those who were willing to contribute materially to the state to depend on the persuasion of expert speakers, lest the Athenians teach the rich to pay as little as possible to the state and to hire many rhetores to defend them in court. On a more positive note, Aeschines (2.183) states that if the jury saves him from Demosthenes, they will find that many others will be ready to work for the collective good of the *polis*.

Ecclesiastic decrees and dicastic judgements had for the Athenians a significance that transcended the particular case at issue and went beyond the establishment of formal constitutional or legal precedents. The democracy depended upon the maintenance of an ideological consensus among the citizen population. Lacking a state-run system of formal education, the demos itself, through the assembly and the courts, took on a large part of the task of instilling social values in the citizens. The young who were not yet fully socialized and the elites who might be influenced by value systems antithetical to democratic government were the particular groups at which much of the normative education through legislation and legal judgement was aimed. But all citizens were educated, for good or ill, by the right and wrong decisions of the assembly and juries, as well as by the laws of the state (cf. Aeschin. 1. 192–95).

(I. 4) Wisdom of the Masses

The educational function of the assembly and courts made reaching right decisions all the more important. The various decision-making bodies were composed of citizens who possessed high native intelligence (or so the Athenians liked to believe), were at least basically literate, had collectively a good grasp of literary culture, and had a high degree of practical experience in the mechanics of government and in cooperation toward a common end. But these factors do not adequately account for the strength of Athenian faith in group decision-making. Rather, that faith was grounded in the assumption that the collective wisdom of a large group was inherently greater than the wisdom of any of its parts. This conviction is one of the central egalitarian tenets of Athenian political ideology. It is implicit in both the structure of the decision-making process and the emphasis the Athenians were willing to place upon 'common report' as an index of an individual's character and behaviour, since what 'everybody knows'—or everybody believed—was deemed likely to be right (Ober 1989: 148–51).

The assumption that groups composed of individuals lacking specialized skills or education tended to produce wise decisions was explicitly, emphatically, and repeatedly rejected by Plato and some-times by other authors of elite texts as well.[16] But some elite writers were willing to consider the concept of collective wisdom seriously. In his essay attacking the 'sophists', Isocrates (13. 8) notes that those who rely on opinions (*doxai*) tend to agree with one another more (*mallon homonoountas*) and are more often correct than those who profess to have exact knowledge (*epistēmē*), and that, therefore, *idiōtai* have good reason to despise specialized studies. This passage was written in the context of an intra-elite debate over higher education and is not necessarily representative of Isocrates' general beliefs, but it shows that he was willing and able to use the *topoi* of popular ideology for polemical purposes (cf. Jaeger 1944: iii. 58–9) More striking, perhaps, is Aristotle's (*Pol.* 1281a39–b9) treatment of the issue. In the context of his discussion of the merits of democracy, he raises the possibility that the mass (*plēthos*), rather than the excellent few, should be master (*kurios*) of the good state. He argued that although the individuals who compose the mass are not worthy gentlemen (*spoudaioi andres*), they may be better collectively than the few persons who were. Hence, he points out, the mass, by common consent, was the best judge of music, of poetry, and other fields: with its many senses, it becomes like a single human being with respect to its characteristics (*ta ēthē*) and decision-making ability (*dianoia*).

---

[16] e.g. Plato *Crito* 47a–48a; *Prt.* 317a; [Xen.] *Ath. Pol.* 1. 5–10; Eur. *Andr.* 470–85.

While noting that there were some objections to this point of view, Aristotle continues (1281b9–1282a41) by pointing out that the sum of individually inferior parts is indeed very great, and so the courts, council, and assembly should be left in charge of important affairs.[17]

If Isocrates and Aristotle were willing at least to consider the idea of collective wisdom, it is hardly surprising that the political orators typically took it for granted. The elitist attack on mass decision-making was specifically refuted in the Thucydidean speech of Athenagoras of Syracuse (Thuc. 6. 39. 1). He attacked the argument that democracy was neither wise nor truly egalitarian by asserting that the many (*hoi polloi*), having listened to the deliberations of wise men (*xunetous*, meaning popular speakers like himself), were the best judges of what was right and productive of equality.[18] Demosthenes (*Ex.* 44. 1) stated that he would not have come before the assembly if the Athenians all held the same opinions on the matter at hand, even if his own opinion were different, since 'I, being one, would be more likely to be mistaken than all of you'. And again (*Ex.* 45), when arguing that making a good speech and choosing sound policies were not the same, he stated that the former was the work of the rhetor, the second of a man possessing intelligence (*nous*). Therefore, he continued, 'you, the many', are not expected to speak as well as the orators, but 'you, especially the older ones of you, are expected to have intelligence equal or better than that of the speakers, since it is experiences and having seen much that makes for intelligence'. The appeal to the older citizen is obvious, but the passage also affirms the

---

[17] Cf. *Pol.* 1284a30–4, 1286a25–35. Ultimately, in the discussion of the ideal state in Books 7 and 8 of the *Politics*, Aristotle rejects the wisdom of the masses in favour of a narrowly elitist aristocracy, due at least in part to his inability to solve the problem of how to create a just form of proportional equality (Ober 1989: 293–5). Aristotle's willingness to consider the possibility of mass wisdom may also be exemplified by the assumption in the *Rhetoric* that common opinions manifest at least a partial grasp of truth and so can be used in the formulation of enthymemes which are legitimately part of rational political discourse; for the rationality of enthymemes and the reasonableness of arguing from common opinions, see Arnhart 1981, esp. 5–7, 28–32, 183–8.

[18] A. Jones 1957: 43 notes that the 'Sicilian' speeches, which refer to democratic principles, are probably modelled on Athenian prototypes. The same general idea—that simple people deciding together are wiser than clever individuals—crops up in an extreme form in Cleon's Mytilene speech (Thuc. 3. 37. 3–5).

conviction that collective judgement by the many was superior to individual perception and more important than mere speech. Even when berating the jurors for their inconsistency, Demosthenes (23. 145–6) emphasized their good judgement and claimed that everyone (*hapantes*) quite correctly agreed that bribe-taking politicians were the worst men in the state.

The rhetor's appeal to the mass wisdom of the particular group he was addressing was based on the generalized faith the Athenians had in the collective knowledge, experiences, and judgement of the citizen body as a whole. Hyperides (1. 14) supported an argument for the validity of a legal defence that was based on a man's whole life by reference to the assumption that no one in the *polis* can deceive 'the mass of you'. Dinarchus (1. 33; cf. 2. 2) notes that 'you [jurors] see and know' the facts of Demosthenes' life 'much better than I do'. Since Dinarchus proceeded to relate Demosthenes' crimes in considerable detail, he cannot have expected his audience to believe that all the jurors or even any individual juror *actually* knew more about Demosthenes' life than he himself did. Rather, he was expressing his solidarity with an ideology that stressed group over individual knowledge. Athenagoras, Demosthenes, Hyperides, and Dinarchus all leave a place in the decision-making process for the expert politician, but each affirms that the collective wisdom of the masses must be the final arbiter.[19]

The Athenians' belief in their collective wisdom as a group need not be seen as contravening their faith in the wisdom of their laws. The laws were a highly esteemed expression and 'concretization' of mass wisdom. Laws had been, in some cases at least, affirmed by several generations of Athenians and thus represented the epitome of the masses' collective wisdom over time (cf. Ober 1989: 299–306). The laws need not be seen as external to, or as a check upon, the judgement of the demos, but rather as a partial expression of some of its most cherished and time-tested ideals.

[19] Humphreys 1988: 476 notes that in speech 23 Demosthenes uses non-technical language and a sense of 'what you all know' in reference to homicide law, and she contrasts this with the practice of Lysias. Cf. Dem. 24. 123; Ant. 2. 4.1.

II. DANGERS OF RHETORIC

The Athenian emphasis upon group decisions is the context in which we must view the forensic orator's strategy of attempting to persuade the jurors that their collective wisdom, knowledge, and experience were being challenged by the duplicitous arguments of his opponent. The jury was cast in the role of a unified body of citizens confronted by an individual (the opponent) who was perversely attempting to oppose the group's will. The orator who succeeded in generating in his audience a group-versus-individual state of mind had won the day, since by definition the group must prevail over the individual in a direct democracy of the Athenian model. This is Demosthenes' strategy (19. 297) when he reminds the jurors that in the courts 'no one has ever been greater than you, or the laws, or your oaths' and urges the jurors not to let Aeschines become greater than themselves. Of course, the elite of trained and able speakers were the most likely to try to oppose the will of the jury; Demosthenes' client (39. 14) asserts that 'you jurors' know how to keep control over even the most clever folk (*tous panu deinous*) when they overreach themselves. Lycurgus (1. 20) confidently asserts that 'you jurors' are not ignorant of the advance preparations (*paraskeuas*) used by the defendants.

(II. 1)   Rhetoric Versus Mass Wisdom

Yet, despite the general Athenian faith in mass wisdom, doubts persisted. The adversarial nature of public trials and of many assembly debates forced the voters to choose between two speakers (or potentially more, in the assembly), only one of whom could be urging the best decision. There was a very real possibility that the jurors or assemblymen would be taken in by the more clever speaker and would reject the less clever, even if the latter was in the right. This was potentially a serious political problem, especially in light of the normative role the Athenians attributed to the decisions of the assembly and courts. Consequently, Athenian jurors were often warned by orator A to beware of orator B's eloquence. Aeschines urged the jurors to watch out for Demosthenes' rhetorical tricks: 'Just as in gymnastic contests you see boxers contending with one another for position, so, for the sake of the polis, you [jurors] must do battle with him all day long for position in regard to his speech' and watch out for his evasive tactics (3. 206).

The perception that rhetorical skill represented a potential threat to the validity of the democratic decision-making process put the expert speaker in a difficult position. An orator who attempted to use his power of speech to deceive a mass audience into voting against its collective interests was obviously setting himself up as superior to the masses, a situation the demos must regard as anathema. Why then, if rhetoric involved deception, should expert rhetores be allowed to speak to the demos in the first place? In *On the Crown* (18. 280) Demosthenes lays out what, according to his considered opinion, comprised the worth of the rhetor. After accusing Aeschines of beginning a prosecution merely to make a public display of his fine voice and rhetorical ability, Demosthenes proclaims: 'But it is not the speech (*logos*) of a rhetor, Aeschines, or the power of his voice which are his worth, but it lies rather in his preference for the same things as the many and in his hating and loving the same things as his homeland. Having such a disposition (*psuchē*), everything a man says will be patriotic (*ep' eunoiai*).' This passage, taken literally, leaves no room for legitimate political or legal debate. The worthy orator prefers the same things as the many, and therefore, when speaking in public, he simply vocalizes the desires of the majority of his listeners. Because the wisdom of the group is superior to that of the individual, the desires of the majority are right desires, and the orator who voices these desires is therefore advocating the right decision. Since his opponent urges a different decision, his opponent must be wrong and consciously opposing the preferences of the people.

Demosthenes' dictum, by eliminating legitimate difference of opinion as a basis of political debate, allows—even requires—the orator to ascribe the worst possible motives to any speaker who advocated a position significantly different from his own. Since there was no legitimate reason for adopting a viewpoint at variance with the wishes of the majority, anyone who persisted in doing so must have been motivated by illegitimate and selfish personal interests. Thus a common ploy for the orator was to suggest that his opponent and his opponent's supporters were bribed or hired to say the things they did, and in either case they clearly preferred making money to speaking the truth. The bribe-taker who decided that his personal enrichment was of greater value than agreeing with the masses obviously had no love for the democracy (cf. Ober 1989: 329–32). Indeed, one might safely suggest that he hated the democracy and was probably willing to support a revolution that would destroy the power of the people (e.g. Lys. 25. 26–7). The presumption that to agree with the masses was to be in the right easily led to the implication that one's opponent must be regarded as a traitor. The savage tenor of Athenian political invective must be seen in the light of this progression.

Demosthenes' dictum on agreeing with the masses was an extreme position, and, as we will see, he suggests a very different interpretation of the orator's role later in *On the Crown*. His dictum assumes that the speaker is precisely aware of the preferences of the people. On some issues, and in broad terms, no doubt the orator did know what the majority was likely to prefer. But if the will of the masses had actually been as self-evident as Demosthenes implied, there would be no need for *isēgoria,* and the Athenians would not have had to bother listening to lengthy arguments or even with voting; all decisions would be by consensus and could be announced by acclamation. The structure of assembly meetings and jury trials was, however, predicated on the assumption that there were issues upon which debate was both legitimate and necessary. Demosthenes' dictum helps to define one end of the ideological spectrum on the subject of the relations between speaker and audience. It represents an ideal of decision-making by universal consensus which could seldom be achieved in practice. However, the ideal of a polity based on consensus survived into the fourth century (for its origins, see Ober 1989: 68–75) and buttressed the notion that the orator should be simply the mouthpiece of unspoken mass will. This constellation of ideas was an important aspect of Athenian political ideology and provided the rationale for very extreme statements by the orators regarding one-another's ulterior motives.

In the normal course of events, the preference of the people remained at least formally latent, and debate could therefore be regarded as legitimate, until the vote was taken. The vote of the assembly or jury was, however, an unambiguous statement of the people's will. After any vote that had been preceded by debate, the demos knew that at least one speaker had been arguing against the position that later turned out to be the correct one, the one that expressed the will of the majority. No rhetor could hope to win every vote. The expert politician who, by definition, engaged frequently in public trials and spoke often in the assembly must lose occasionally, and when he lost he was in the uncomfortable position of having publicly opposed the group. How was the orator to explain his failure and justify his willingness to continue advocating a policy that the masses had rejected? Demosthenes (9. 54) tried suggesting that some evil demon was driving the Athenians to prefer the purchased minions of Philip to himself, but this is not an argument one wanted to use very often.[20] Much more common was the suggestion that despite their collective wisdom, the people had been (or might be) misled by the clever and superficially convincing, but evil and deceptive, speeches of one's opponent.

Therefore, at least in part in order to create a justification for their own failures to convince the demos and for the successes of their opponents, the orators acknowledged the power of rhetoric to lead the assembly, the jury, and the state as a whole into error. Demosthenes (51.20), for example, stated that because of the speeches (*demēgoriai*) of the rhetores, many matters in the state were going from bad to worse.[21] This tendency might be exacerbated in periods of financial difficulty. Lysias (30. 22) noted that in such times the council was led to accept *eisangeliai* and to confiscate the property of citizens, being persuaded by the rascally advice of the rhetores. But the citizens themselves, as *idiōtai* and collectively as the demos, suffered in the end. Aeschines (3. 233) claimed that the juror who voted for Demosthenes would make himself weak and the rhetor strong, while the correct situation in the democratic

---

[20] Aeschin. 3. 117 (something demonic perhaps led a rude fellow to interrupt his speech to the Amphictionic council); Andoc. 1. 130–1. Mikalson 1983: 19, 59–60, notes that the attribution of an event's outcome to a god, demon, or Fortune seems to depend on how the speaker is affected by the event. Dover, in his review of Mikalson (1984: 197–8), stresses the importance of this conclusion, while noting that there are some apparent exceptions.

[21] Cf. Lys. 18. 16; 27. 4–6; 28. 11; Aeschin. 3. 168, 228; Hyp. 4. 36.

polis was for the *idiōtēs* to rule (*basileuei*) through the law and the vote.[22]

The orator who could deceive the people into voting wrongly was a manifest danger to all other citizens.[23] Hyperides (5. 25–6, cf. 4. 27) warned that if any member of the jury were on trial, as an inexperienced *idiōtēs*, he would be overpowered by the rhetorical skill (*k[atarhē]toreutheis*) of Demosthenes and his co-defendants and subsequently, though innocent, that hapless juror would be convicted and either executed or banished. The orator who set great store by his speaking ability was not merely unseemingly vain but threatened the whole state.[24] He set himself above the decrees of the assembly (e.g. Dem. 51. 22) and believed that his ability to speak well gave him immunity from prosecution (Arist. *Rh.*1372a11–17). According to Aeschines (3. 253), Demosthenes' eloquence allowed him to sail on a ship of words over the *politeia*. While taking for himself the name of protector of the democracy, which should be common to all, Demosthenes was in fact the furthest from being a true democrat (Aeschin. 3. 248). Demosthenes (19. 120), on the other hand, claimed that Aeschines took up a prosecution as easily as a dramatic role and that his ability to convict his opponents within the time-limit and without the use of witnesses was evidence for his cleverness at speaking.

There can be little doubt that, although the Athenians delighted in rhetorical displays, they remained suspicious of the expert orators and their verbal skills. The orator involved in a political fight might exploit the popular distrust of the *rhetores* against an opponent, despite the obvious danger of being tarred with his own brush. Dinarchus (1. 98) reminded the jurors of oracles that he suggested warned the Athenians against *rhetores*. Hyperides (fr. 80 Jensen = B. 19. 5 Burtt) claimed that all *rhetores* were like snakes and therefore hateful. Some, he says, were adders who were harmful to men, while others took the role of the adder-eating brown snake. Presumably, Hyperides hoped his audience would think of his opponents in the former category and

[22] Cf. Lys. 28. 9; 29. 6; Dem. 23. 184, 201; 51. 1–2; Aeschin. 3. 220; Lyc. 1. 138.

[23] This concern provides at least a partial context for the attacks upon *rhetores* in Attic comedy, for which see Ehrenberg 1962: 350–3.

[24] e.g. Isoc. 18. 21; Aeschin. 2. 22; 3. 228; Din. 1. 113.

of himself in the latter. His listeners might, however, legitimately ask themselves why snakes should be tolerated at all. The orators used the demos' fear of being misled by rhetoric to discredit their opponents, and the power of rhetoric provided a convenient excuse for a politician to explain why his policies were sometimes rejected by the people. The central question of why expert politicians should have been allowed to practice in Athens' political arenas remains to be answered. Indeed, the arguments of the orators cited above might seem to provide material for a strong case in favour of excluding experts in rhetoric from the democratic decision-making process.

(II.2)   Evils of Rhetorical Education: Sophists and Sycophants

The orator's power to deceive his audience into voting wrongly lay in his speaking ability, which was typically at least partially the product of a specialized education. Education in rhetoric was a potential focus of popular suspicion; at worst it could be characterized as a corrupting and destructive influence in the state. In the speech *Against Lacritus* (35. 40–3) Demosthenes' client played upon the jurors' distrust of rhetorical training. He asserted that, while he did not himself hold a grudge against anyone who desired to become a sophist and so paid Isocrates a stiff fee to that end, he did not think that such people had the right to look down upon others (*kataphronountas*) or, thinking themselves clever (*deinous*) and trusting in their speeches (*tōi logōi pisteuontas*), to cheat other citizens. These, he said, were the attitudes and actions of the perfidious (*ponēros*) sophist who believed he could lead jurors astray with his tricky harangues. The defendant, Lacritus, considered himself a master at deceiving juries and collected money from others for teaching them to do likewise. The prosecutor acknowledged, however, that he would have to admit that his opponent was indeed the greatest of sophists (*sophōtatos*) if Lacritus, who put his faith in his eloquence and in the 1,000 drachmas he had paid Isocrates, was able to fool the present jury.

The passage is very neatly constructed. Beginning with a claim of neutrality on the topic of rhetorical education, the prosecutor shows how the defendant's training in rhetoric had made him both arrogant and dangerous. This leads inevitably to the conclusion that if the jurors acquitted the defendant, they would acquiesce in the methods of vicious sophists who thought themselves superior to the masses and safe from conviction by virtue of their special training. Since Lacritus was not only a student of Isocrates but also a teacher of rhetoric in his own right, his acquittal would presumably encourage others to study his methods of jury subversion. Seen in this light, a school of rhetoric was, to borrow Hyperides' imagery, a nest of vipers which poisoned the entire state. The jury's didactic function of establishing and enforcing models of correct social behaviour was perverted into one of helping the sophist prove to potential students the persuasive power of his rhetoric.[25]

Isocrates himself discovered that he was much less popular among the Athenians than he had imagined, when his enemies succeeded in having him saddled with a liturgy. According to Isocrates' account of the matter (15. 4–5), his opponents at his property-exchange trial played upon the jury's distrust of his power of speech (*tēn tōn logōn tōn emōn dunamin*) and emphasized the large number of his students. Furthermore (15. 30), they stressed that among these students were not only *idiōtai* but rhetores and generals, as well as kings and tyrants.[26]

The execution of Socrates was an exceptional case, carried out in exceptional historical circumstances, but to be labelled a sophist and teacher of dangerous men was never good in Athens.[27] In the speech *Against Timarchus* (1. 173) Aeschines uses the cudgel of popular

[25] For a close parallel, see Ant. 5. 80: you jurors must help me by refusing to teach the evil sycophant to be greater than yourselves (*meizon humōn autōn dunasthai*), because if they succeed in this trial it will be a lesson to their victims, who will be more likely to knuckle under and pay them. But if the sycophants are shown in court to be evil men, 'you' will enjoy the honour and the power (*dunamis*) that is your right.

[26] On the unpopularity of 'sophists' of various stripes, cf. Thuc. 8. 68.1; Isoc. 13. 1, with Jaeger 1944: iii. 56; Arist. *Rh.* 1399a11–18. For scorn for the profession of logographer, cf. Ober 1989: 270–2.

[27] For the political background to the trial of Socrates, see Finley 1977: 60–73; Vlastos 1983: 485–516 (with discussion, pp. 495–6, of Aeschin. 1. 173). For Socrates' views on democracy, the lively and polemical account of Stone 1988 may be balanced by the more philosophically nuanced discussion of Kraut 1984, esp. 194–244. Finley 1973: 96 notes that after the trial of Socrates the 'baleful atmosphere' of anti-intellectualism thinned markedly, and that indeed orators (e.g., Aeschin. 3. 257) could use the term *philosophos* in reference to such revered figures as Solon. See also Dover 1976.

mistrust of higher education against Demosthenes: 'Oh Athenians, did you not execute Socrates the sophist for being the teacher of Critias, one of the Thirty who put down the democracy?...Then shall Demosthenes snatch his cronies (*hetairoi*) from your hands—he who takes vengeance upon *idiōtai* and friends of the people (*dēmotikoi*) for their *isēgoria*?' Aeschines then mentions (1. 173) that some of Demosthenes' students were at the trial, having come for a lesson in clever speaking. He urges (1. 175) the jurors not to furnish 'Demosthenes the sophist' with a source of laughter and a teaching example (*diatribē*) at their own expense. 'Imagine,' Aeschines (1. 175) goes on to say, 'when he is at home with his pupils, how he will brag that he stole the case away from the jurors' by his cunning speech.

This passage strikes a number of themes, each one calculated to arouse the jurymen's ire. Demosthenes is a sophist, like Socrates. The Athenians had justly executed Socrates for his role in teaching the arts of subversion to Critias, one of the Thirty Tyrants. Since Demosthenes himself teaches students, the jury could presume that he is teaching his students the same sort of thing Socrates had taught Critias, and Demosthenes therefore deserves a similar fate. Inversely, if Demosthenes is innocent, though a sophistic teacher, then Socrates had been innocent, and the current jury would be implicated in an unjust execution. This had occurred over fifty years previously, but we may note Aeschines' use of the second-person plural for those who had executed Socrates. Worse yet, Demosthenes' power of speech limits the *isēgoria* of common citizens; his oratorical skill therefore undercuts a basic principle of the democracy. If the jurors acquit the defendant, they, like the jurors in the trial of Lacritus, acquiesce in helping to teach rhetoric. Aeschines makes the insidiousness of this acquiescence explicit by claiming that the trial was being used as a lesson by Demosthenes. Furthermore, adding insult to injury, Demosthenes' students will laugh at the jurors' gullibility in the privacy of his house—obviously *they* do not view the Athenians as naturally astute—and Demosthenes will become even more vain and dangerous than before.[28]

---

[28] Aeschin. 2. 148, with Dover 1976: 50–1.

Demosthenes could hardly let this sort of abuse go unanswered, and in *On the False Embassy* he turns the tables on his opponent. Aeschines, he says (19. 246–8), calls other men logographers and sophists as an insult but is himself open to the same reproach. Demosthenes sets about proving this by pointing out that in the course of his speech Aeschines quoted from Euripides' *Phoenix*, which he had never performed on stage himself. Yet Aeschines never quoted from Sophocles' *Antigone*, which he had acted many times. So: 'Oh Aeschines, are you not a sophist... are you not a logographer... since you hunted up (*zetēsas*) a verse which you never spoke on stage to use to trick the citizens?' (19. 250). The argument that underlies Demosthenes' rejoinder says a good deal about Athenian attitudes toward specialized education. According to Demosthenes, Aeschines is a sophist because he 'hunts up' quotes from a play with which he had no reason to be familiar in order to strengthen his argument. Clearly the average Athenian would not be in a position to search out quotes when he wanted them; if the ordinary citizen ever wanted to quote poetry he would rely on verses he had memorized, perhaps from plays he had seen performed in the theatre. Demosthenes implies that the contents of an individual's memory and his general knowledge learned from experience were perfectly democratic and egalitarian; specialized research undertaken to support an argument in court, on the other hand, was sophistic and elitist. What Aeschines should have done (and, as Demosthenes implies, *would* have done were he not a sophist) was to quote the plays that he had memorized. Since he ignored the play he knew and quoted poetry from a play he did not know, he was proved to possess a sophist's training which he used to trick the average citizens on the jury. The orator who displayed evidence of special knowledge left himself open to the charge of using his elite education to deceive the audience.[29]

Popular mistrust of rhetorical ability and the skilled speakers who misused it is demonstrated by the eagerness of private trial litigants to portray their opponents as slick speakers who were using their

[29] For other passages emphasizing the wrongfulness of orators' use of formal training, practice, and advance preparation, see Dover 1974: 25–8; Kindstrand 1982: 18–19; cf. Ostwald 1986: 256–7, 273.

rhetorical ability to evil ends. One of Isaeus' clients (10. 1) said that he was unequal to his opponents, who were powerful speakers (*legein deinoi*) and well prepared (*paraskeuasasthai hikanoi*); the plaintiff himself claimed to have had no practice in speaking in court, while his opponents were experienced litigants. Another of Isaeus' clients (9. 35) cried: 'Help me, jurors. If [my opponent] Cleon is a better speaker than I (*legein emou dunatai... mallon*), do not allow this fact to be stronger than law and justice.'

The notion of the wrongfulness of advance preparation, which Demosthenes used against Aeschines in regard to poetic quotation, was used by other litigants whose opponents were castigated for having 'prepared their rhetores' against an innocent *idiōtēs*.[30] Those who used their rhetorical skills to destroy other citizens in court were often identified by their opponents as sycophants, trained speakers and experienced litigants who engaged in prosecutions solely for pecuniary gain. The sycophant was similar to the bribed politician. Both used the political apparatus of the state for illegitimate personal advantage, but, while the bribed politician sold his convictions for pay, the sycophant had no convictions in the first place. The sycophant was consequently regarded as a leech on society, who had no regard for truth or the rights of a case but was a master of slander (e.g. Dem. 57. 34).

Worst of all, the sycophants were an uncontrolled element in the democracy. They grew rich from perverting the state's legal machinery to their private ends, but they had no personal stake in their prosecutions. The sycophant made his living primarily by extorting money from victims who preferred to pay up rather than to face the uncertainties of a jury trial, at which they would be outmatched rhetorically. Thus, unlike the politician who, even if bribed, sincerely desired the jury to vote in his favour, the sycophant did not necessarily care personally about getting a conviction when he was forced by his victim's intransigence to go to trial.[31] For this reason, sycophants did not feel a proper sense of gratitude to the Athenian demos when they won their cases (e.g. Dem. 58. 63). The sycophants hence

[30] e.g. Isae. 1. 7; fr. 1.1 Forster; Dem. 44. 15.
[31] See e.g. Ant. 5. 80; Isoc. 21. 8; Dem. 55. 33; 58. 33; Hyp. 1. 2. For sycophancy in comedy, see Ehrenberg 1962: 343–7.

represented the least attractive element of the educated elite. The expert politician, who spent much of his life giving speeches, ran the risk of being branded a mere sycophant, motivated by lust for personal gain rather than by a patriotic desire to serve the polis. The line between the sycophant and the politician was somewhat vague; Lycurgus (1. 31) anticipated that Leocrates would attempt to portray himself as an *idiōtēs* who had fallen prey to 'a rhetor and a most terrible sycophant'.[32]

(II.3)   Innocence, Ignorance, and Dramatic Fictions

The logical corollary to the topos of 'my opponent is a skilled speaker' was the claim by the speaker to be unskilled and inexperienced in public speech. A client of Lysias (19. 2), for example, assured the court that everyone who knew him was aware of his inability to speak well (*apeiria*). Another of Lysias' clients (17. 1) was concerned that some of the jurors might have the idea that because he was ambitious, he could also speak better than other people (*eipein... mallon heterou dunasthai*). This, he assured them, was not true. Indeed, he was unable to speak well on his own behalf, much less in regard to the affairs of others.[33]

Some fairly obvious hypocrisy is involved with these professions of lack of ability, and Demosthenes (21.141–2) trusted that his jury would be aware that the claim that one could not speak properly (*mē dunasthai legein*) was among the myriad excuses by which individuals rationalized their failure to defend themselves in court. The

---

[32] Cf. Aeschin. 2. 145, who defines sycophantism as when one man insinuates a false impression of another into the minds of the people by calumniating him in all the assemblies and in the council; Hyp. 1. 19; 4. 13. Osborne 1985*b*: 44–8 points out that the existence of potentially remunerative public actions did not actually lead directly to sycophantism.

[33] Cf. Lys. 31. 2, 4; fr. 24.1.4 Gernet-Bizos; Dem. 55. 2, 7; Hyp. 1. 19–20; 4. 11; Aeschin. 3. 229; Plato, *Apology* 17a–d. On the related *topos* of the *apragmōn* citizen who does not get much involved in public affairs, see Hansen 1983: 43–4; Lateiner 1982: 1–12; and esp. Carter 1986: 105–10. The *apragmōn topos* must be read in the contexts of related *topoi*, the distinction between rhetor and *idiōtēs* and the general distrust of the wealthy. It does not, in my opinion, constitute clear evidence of the rejection of the 'world of the citizen' by either Athenians in general or the elite in particular.

Josiah Ober

extant speeches were preserved because of their quality as rhetorical literature. Some speeches are better examples of the orator's art than others. Some are artfully composed to give an impression of artlessness. But no speech in the corpus could possibly be construed to be the spontaneous creation of a semi-educated man 'unfamiliar with speaking' (cf. Ober 1989: 43–9). Hence, even if the actual litigant who delivered the speech in question was *not* an experienced speaker, in the case of the preserved speeches, at least, the 'I am ignorant of rhetorical ability or training' *topos* describes a fiction. As we have seen, however, the Athenian citizens had some pretensions to connoisseurship in rhetoric, and many of the jurors no doubt recognized the product of the logographer's pen when they heard it. But, since logography apparently continued to flourish through the fourth century, we must conclude that the *topos* passed muster with the jurors, and so we may suppose that the fiction it depended upon was agreeable to them.[34] The very transparency of the fiction is indicative of its importance to the participants and reveals the deep distrust of rhetoric which coexisted with the aesthetic appreciation the jurors felt for a well-composed oration. The courts, like the assembly, ran on a fuel of sophisticated rhetoric which the Athenians recognized was potentially corrosive to the machinery of the state. Thus the illusion was maintained of the simple man relating the unvarnished truth to the representatives of the demos, who would apply their collective intelligence in arriving at a just verdict. The whole process had much in common with a theatrical performance, and it may best be understood in light of the jurors' willingness to suspend their disbelief when to do so would benefit themselves and the state (Ober 1989: 152–5).

The interplay between the jurors' tendency to be swept away by rhetorical skill and their mistrust of rhetoric is particularly well elaborated in two speeches in the Demosthenic corpus. In *Against Theocrines* (Dem. 58) Epichares urges the jurors to:

aid me, caring nothing for the fact that it is not Demosthenes who is the prosecutor, but a mere boy. Nor should you consider the laws more binding when someone presents them to you carefully in rhetorical language (*eu tis*

[34] On the concept of accepted fictions and social order, cf. the discussions of Mills 1951: 33–59; Morgan 1988, esp. 152–73.

tois onomasi sumplexas) than when they are recited in the speech of everday (*tōn hopōs etuchen legontōn*)... You should all the more readily give aid to the inexperienced and the young, since they are less likely to lead you astray. (58. 41)

And again, in the peroration:

Since we are engaged in so unequal a contest, we beg you to come to our aid and to make it clear to all men that whether a boy or an old man, or one of any age, comes before you in accordance with the laws he will obtain complete justice. The honourable course for you, men of the jury, is not to put the laws or your own selves in the power of the expert speakers but to keep the speakers in your own power and to make a distinction between those who speak well and lucidly (*eu kai saphōs*) and those who speak what is just; for it is concerning justice that you have sworn to cast your votes. (58. 61)

In Demosthenes' masterful speech *Against Aristocrates* (23. 4–5) the prosecutor Euthycles begs for the attention of the jury by saying that 'I am neither one of the orators who annoy you (*tōn enochlountōn*) nor am I one of the politicians who are trusted by you (*tōn politeuomenōn kai pisteuomenōn*)'. But if the jurymen will listen with goodwill, they will help to overcome the natural reluctance of 'one of those of us' who desires to do the state a good turn, but who fears that it is a difficult thing to present a speech in public. As it is, he continues, many citizens who are poorer speakers, but better men than the eloquent ones, live in such terror of court proceedings that they never take part in public trials.

In each of the three passages cited above, the speaker contrasts himself, young/inexperienced/fearful, with his experienced and silver-tongued opponents who were used to misleading juries. The speaker professes to be genuinely apprehensive that the jurors will prefer the polished and misleading rhetoric of his opponents to his own clumsy but true account.[35] The speaker puts himself in the

---

[35] Cf. Aeschin. 1. 30–1: the lawmaker who established the procedure of *dokimasia rhētorōn* thought that a speech by a good man, even if it were said clumsily and simply, was likely to be useful to listeners and that the words of evil men, even if spoken well, would be of no benefit. Ant. 3. 2. 1–2 is a sophisticated play on the 'unskilled speaker' *topos*. In Ant. 5. 1–7 the defendant emphasizes his youth and lack of skill in speaking; he notes that many inarticulate litigants have formerly been unjustly convicted, while glib ones get off; he begs the jurors to forgive his errors in speaking and hopes they will not consider it to be cleverness if he should happen to speak well.

position of attempting to break the seductive hold that rhetoric currently exerts upon the jurors in order to win them back to the side of the average citizen and the law. This is supposed to be for the good not only of the speaker but of the jurymen themselves and of the state as a whole.[36] The speaker's acknowledgment of the jury's tendency to be seduced by rhetorical display may seem a dangerous tactic, but it actually strengthens his case. By magnifying the persuasive power of his opponent and stressing his own inarticulateness, the speaker predisposes his jury to distrust any argument made against him, no matter how convincing, and to believe his own arguments, no matter how incoherent. Of course, in each case the author of the 'inexperienced' speaker's oration was a master rhetorician. The ploy could succeed only if the jurymen, who were aware of and worried about the danger of allowing rhetoric to pervert justice, were also willing to maintain the fiction that those who warned them of the danger were as innocent of rhetorical skill and preparation as they claimed to be.

III. RHETORES' USE OF POETRY AND HISTORY

The highly ambivalent attitude of the demos toward the entire subject of rhetoric, rhetorical ability, and rhetorical education made the role of the rhetores more complex and problematic. When a well-known political orator stood up to speak in the assembly or in a lawcourt, his audience was aware of his reputation for skill at public speaking. They were both fearful of his power to sway them and eager to be entertained and instructed by a master of a highly competitive and

---

[36] The *topos* of the innocent individual saving the decision-maker from being fooled by the clever speech of a third party precedes the 4th century; e.g. Herodotus' story (5. 51) of Cleomenes' daughter and Aristagoras. Perhaps the speech of Sthenelaidas at Sparta in 432 (Thuc. 1. 86) might be seen in the same light. Cf. Cleon's comments in the Mytilenean debate (Thuc. 3. 38. 2–7). Aristotle's comment (*Rh.* 1395b20–1396a4) to the effect that the uneducated (*apaideutoi*) speak more pleasingly to the masses because they tend to speak more directly of what they know (the specific) and what concerns the audience (the general) seems inadequately to fully explain the 'unskilled speaker' *topos*.

refined art. They might distrust him if he revealed too obviously the extent of his skill, but they would be disappointed if the show was not up to their expectations. For his part, the expert speaker knew that his political career depended upon neither alienating nor disappointing his listeners. The Athenian orator who hoped to capture and hold the attention of his audience might have spent hours or days composing his speech so that the argument would be tight, the style engaging, and the delivery smooth.[37] But he was expected to maintain the fiction that his eloquence was born of conviction and the passion of righteous indignation, rather than preparation. Demosthenes' opponents mocked his speeches for having the 'stink of midnight oil' (Plut. *Dem.* 7. 3, 8, 11), and Demosthenes, who had the reputation (rightly or wrongly) of being poor at extemporaneous speaking, had to overcome the opprobrium of working too hard at his speechwriting.[38] The Athenians demanded a very high standard of oratory from their politicians, but they did not necessarily like to be frequently reminded that the orator was an educated expert who possessed abilities and training that set him above the average citizens.

The difficulties faced by the orator who had to put on a good show, but avoid giving offence, are well illustrated by politicians' use of poetry and historical examples. Quotations of poetry and citations of historical precedent could enliven a speech and help to buttress the argument by the inspired wisdom of the poet and the authority of past practice. The technique held a certain risk for the speaker, however. As we have seen (above, following n. 28), Demosthenes attacked Aeschines for 'hunting up' a quote which he had no good reason to have memorized. The orator also had to be very careful to avoid giving the impression that he disdained the educational level of his audience. The orator's role was, in its essence, a didactic one: he attempted to instruct his listeners in the facts of the matter under discussion and in the correctness of his own interpretation of those

---

[37] Isocrates (4. 14) claimed to have spent years perfecting his showpiece speeches.

[38] Dorjahn argued, in a series of articles (e.g. 1952), that Demosthenes did in fact have the ability to speak off the cuff; cf. Kennedy 1963: 210 with n. 113. For a detailed attack by a rhetorician on prepared speeches, see Alcidamas, fr. 6 Sauppe; cf. Jaeger 1944: iii. 60. Bryant 1950: 172 notes that 'there has always been a certain fondness in the public and in speakers for the impression of spontaneous eloquence …'.

facts. But when using poetic and historical examples, the orator must avoid taking on the appearance of a well-educated man giving lessons in culture to the ignorant masses.

A passage in Aeschines' speech *Against Timarchus* that precedes a series of poetic quotations makes clear the pitfalls the orator faced in citing poetry.

> But since you [my opponents] bring up Achilles and Patroclus, and Homer and the other poets as if the jurors are without education (*anēkoōn paideias*), and you, yourselves, on the other hand, are superior types (*euschēmones tines*) who far surpass (*periphronountes*) the demos in learning (*historia*)—in order to show you that we too (*kai hēmeis*) have listened carefully and have learned a little something, we shall say a few words about these matters. (1. 141)

Aeschines justifies his intention to use poetic quotations by referring to his opponents' plan to cite poetry against him. He characterizes his opponents as educated snobs who imagine themselves to be in possession of a grasp of literary culture that is superior to that of the demos. Aeschines uses the first-person plural to suggest that he is one with the demos whose knowledge of the poets has been impugned. He suggests that 'we'—Aeschines and, at least by implication, the people—have listened to the poets, not that he himself has made a special study of literature. Thus Aeschines makes himself a spokesman for the demos, called upon to defend the jurors against the scurrilous implication that they are ill-educated. The jurors are therefore prepared to listen sympathetically to the series of quotes that Aeschines will recite in order to disprove the elitist claims he has imputed to his opponents. Aeschines' elaborate justification appears worthwhile only if he believes the quotes will help to convince the jurors, but at the same time he is worried that they could construe his poetic excursus as exactly the sort of intellectual snobbery he accuses his opponents of indulging in.[39]

In another speech (3. 231) Aeschines notes that if a tragedian represented Thersites as crowned by the Greeks, 'no one of you [jurors] would allow it', since Homer says that Thersites was a coward and a sycophant. Here Aeschines grants his audience a fairly detailed

---

[39] Cf. North 1952: 27; Plato, *Apology* 26d.

knowledge of, and respect for, Homer's poem. His chosen example is particularly interesting, since Thersites was the commoner who dared speak up in the assembly of Achaean warriors and was trounced by the aristocratic Odysseus for his effrontery (*Iliad* 2. 211–78). Aeschines seems oddly unconcerned about the possibility that the unegalitarian nature of the Thersites story might undercut the sympathy his audience would feel for the poetic example.[40] Perhaps he trusted that his audience would remember that Thersites was labelled a coward and not pay much attention to the part social status played in the incident. But this would seem to be a considerable and unnecessary risk if Aeschines assumed that the ideology to which he was expected to conform was straightforward egalitarianism. We will have reason to return to this passage below (§ V).

Demosthenes also used quotations from poetry in his speeches against Aeschines, although he employed poetic quotations more rarely, and he invariably justified himself by Aeschines' prior citations. Typically, he simply throws back at Aeschines the passages his opponent had previously quoted and so carefully avoids suggesting that his own knowledge of poetry is superior to that of his audience.[41] Demosthenes (19. 247) assumes that his audience is composed of theatregoers: mocking Aeschines' career as a tragic actor, he says that 'you [jurors] know perfectly well' that it is the privilege of bit-players (*tritagōnistai*) like Aeschines to play the role of the tyrant. The orator thus uses the 'everyone knows' *topos* to avoid the impression of having a greater knowledge of theatrical performance than that of his audience.

Lycurgus made extensive use of poetic quotations in his only preserved oration. He introduced a passage from Tyrtaeus by asking hypothetically, 'Who does not know' that the Spartans took Tyrtaeus from Athens to train their youths in virtue (1. 106). He comes to this example after a long quote from Euripides, concluding (1.101–2)

---

[40] Notably Xenophon (*Mem.*1.2.58) states that one of Socrates' 'accusers' (presumably Polycrates, in a pamphlet) cited the philosopher's partiality for this section of the *Iliad* as evidence for his anti-democratic attitudes; cf. the comments of Stone 1988: 28–38. For a succinct discussion of the unequal social relationships implied by the scene, see Raaflaub 1980: 25; cf. Donlan 1980: 21–2.

[41] e.g. Dem. 19. 243, 245. Cf. North 1952: 24–5; Perlman 1964, esp. 156–7, 172. Cf. Ober 1989: 270–2 (on servile occupations), and 148–51 (on 'everyone knows').

that 'these verses, gentlemen, educated (*epaideue*) your ancestors' (*pateras*). He then (1.102) recommended Homer to the jurors, whom 'your ancestors' thought alone of the poets worthy of recitation at the Panathenaic festival. The potentially elitist thrust of Lycurgus' hortatory comments is thus deflected by the speaker's emphasis on the traditional Athenian respect for the poets and his reference to the value of poetry being proved by its inclusion in the public festival.

The orators used a similar approach in citing examples from history or myth. Demosthenes usually introduced his historical excursus with a prefatory 'I am sure you all know…', thereby avoiding giving the impression that he knew more about the past than the average citizen.[42] In a similar vein, his client (Dem. 40. 24–5) discussed the career of the demagogue Cleon who, 'they say', captured many Lacedaemonians and had great repute in the polis. Aeschines (2. 76) cited the example of Cleophon 'the lyremaker', whom 'many remember' as a slave in fetters. One did not want to claim a specialized knowledge of history, but an appeal to the memories of the Athenian elders was acceptable. In discussing exiles during the Corinthian War, for example, Demosthenes (20. 52, cf. 19. 249) mentioned events he had heard about from 'the older citizens among you'. Aeschines suggested (2. 150) that the older demesmen of Paiania would be able to confirm that his father-in-law had helped to get young Demosthenes enrolled as a citizen. He also (2. 77–8, 3. 191–2) recounted how his own father, who lived to be 95 and had shared in the great struggles that followed the Peloponnesian War, had many times told his son the story of the disasters of the war and of the virtuous conduct and strict standards of jurors in the post-war years.[43] Allusions to the memory of the older citizens or of one's own ancestors allowed the orator to avoid assuming the role of an educated man instructing his inferiors. There was clearly

---

[42] See Pearson 1941: 217–19, for a list of examples. On the orators' use of history generally, cf. Perlman 1961; Nouhaud 1982, noting in passing that the orators normally assume their audiences have no formal knowledge of history apart from what they tell them (354) and that it took about twenty years for an event to pass from current politics to the realm of history (369).

[43] Cf. Ant. 5. 70–1: the defendant discusses the wrongful execution of nine *hellēnotamiai* and concludes, 'the older ones among you remember, I suppose, and the younger ones have learned of it, just as I have'; Lys. 19. 45, 'I have heard from my father and other older men that you were … [often] deceived about men's fortunes'.

an appeal to authority involved in the references to elders, but notably the elders were the only subset of the demos to possess clearly defined legal and political privileges.

The Athenians' demonstrated concern with native intelligence, their distrust of elite education, and their respect for the authority of the elders are parodied by Aristophanes, who mimics rhetorical topoi in the speech of Lysistrata, the female demagogue:

> Listen to my words.
> I am a woman, but I'm smart enough.
> Indeed, my mind's not bad at all.
> Having listened to my father's discourses
> And those of the older men, I'm not ill-educated.
>
> (*Lysistrata* 1123–7)

IV. RHETORES ON THE ADVANTAGES OF ELITE EDUCATION

The average citizen's belief in the potential power of rhetoric to corrupt the democratic processes of the state helps to explain why both private litigants and expert political orators depict their opponents as clever speakers, wily sophists, and unscrupulous sycophants, whose persuasiveness was matched only by their venality and traitorous willingness to subvert the people's will. It also explains why *idiōtai* depicted themselves as innocent of rhetorical ability or training. The private litigant was seldom eager to complicate the basic scenario: he, an average citizen without experience or skill in public speaking, was opposed by a trained and experienced speaker who threatened both the individual and the state.

The Athenian politician's portrayal of his own and his opponent's relationship to rhetoric and education was considerably more complex. In a searing passage from *On the Crown*, Demosthenes questions Aeschines' right to appeal to virtue, intelligence, and education:

You filth, what have you or your family to do with virtue? How do you distinguish between good common report and slander? Where and how do you qualify as a moralist? Where do you get your right to talk about education? No truly educated man would use such language about himself, but would blush to hear it from others. But people like you, who make stupid pretensions to a culture of which they are utterly destitute, succeed in disgusting everybody whenever they open their lips, but never in making the sort of impression they desire. (18. 128)

This passage is the very antithesis of the *topos* of depicting one's opponent as an articulate, well-trained orator. Aeschines is characterized as a lout so ill-educated that he is completely unable to impress his audience. How, then, could he be a dangerous rhetor whose eloquence was likely to trick the jurors into voting against justice and their own interests?

Demosthenes' attack on Aeschines' lack of education is no isolated instance; in fact, political orators quite commonly claimed that their opponents were stupid, ignorant, and boorish. Demosthenes (22. 75) calls the politician Androtion so dull-witted (*skaios*) as to be unable to tell the difference between symbols of virtue and mere wealth. In describing an Amphictionic meeting, Aeschines (3. 117) notes how an Amphissan who attacked him was clearly without education (*oudemias paideias*). This might be explained as an example of contrasting the cultivated Athenians with the rest of the Greeks, but Aeschines elsewhere (1.166) claims that, in addition to his other undesirable traits, Demosthenes was uncouth (*amousos*) and uneducated (*apaideutos*). By their arrogant self-praise, he argues (3. 241), Demosthenes and his ally Ctesiphon show their lack of education (*apaideusia*). A client of Lysias (20. 12) attempts to undercut the argument that his father was a childhood friend of the oligarch Phrynichus by claiming that the latter had spent his impoverished childhood in the country tending sheep, while the plaintiff's father was being properly educated in the city (*en tōi astei epaideueto*). The claim that one's political opponent was an undereducated knave could be directly associated with the seemingly incongruous claim that he was an adroit speaker. Lysias (20. 12) goes on to suggest that after spending his childhood in the fields with the sheep, Phrynichus came to the city to be a sycophant, while his own father retired to the life of a gentleman farmer in the countryside. Among the insults he lavished on Aeschines, Demosthenes (18. 242) calls him a 'country bumpkin tragedy-king' (*arouraios Oinomaos*) and a counterfeit rhetor whose cleverness (*deinotēs*) is useless to the state. These passages are difficult to reconcile with the view that the Athenians regarded simplicity as an unalloyed virtue in a speaker (cf. Arist. *Rh.* 1418b23–5, on insult and envy).

Perhaps even more surprisingly, the politician sometimes took it upon himself to praise his own upbringing and education. Demosthenes (18. 257) makes a point of contrasting Aeschines' lack of education with his own impeccable upbringing: 'In my boyhood, Aeschines, I had the advantage of attending respectable schools (*phoitan eis ta prosēkonta didaskaleia*), and my resources were such that I was not required to engage in shameful activities through need.' This is in contrast to Aeschines who, we are told (Dem. 18. 258), spent his boyhood as a servile ink-grinder and floor-sweeper in his father's disreputable schoolroom. The entire section of the speech in which Demosthenes praises himself and mocks Aeschines (18. 256–67) is written in highly poetic language; the rhetorical structure of the passage as well as its content displays the speaker's pride in the quality of his upbringing and formal education.[44]

Demosthenes claims to be reticent about saying too much about the advantages 'in which I take some pride' (18. 258), and he prefaces his remarks (18. 256) with a plea to his audience to forgive him for seeming immodest, but the appeal to an elitist sensibility is unmistakable. Here Demosthenes is at one with Isocrates who, in his pamphlet addressed to Philip of Macedon (5. 81–2), says that 'although someone will say it is boorish (*agroikoteron*) for me to say it, I do lay claim to judgement and fine education (*phronein eu pepaideusthai kalōs*), and in comparison with others I would count myself not among the last, but among the foremost'. In an unassigned, possibly epideictic fragment (fr. XV 5 Conomis=E 6 Burtt, preserved only in Latin translation), Lycurgus says that it did not surprise him to find a man of great diligence who had risen so high, since a strong-willed individual is likely to be industrious. This quality would lead him to knowledge, from which comes the oratorical ability that results naturally in true renown. It is in the context of the pride an orator felt in his abilities and education that we must view Aeschines'

---

peroration to his speech *Against Ctesiphon* (the passage to which Demosthenes objected so vigorously): 'I, O Earth and Sun and Virtue and Intelligence (*sunesis*) and Education (*paideia*) by which we make distinction between what is good and what is shameful, I have aided [the state] and I have spoken' (3. 260).[45]

There is, of course, no reason why the skilled orator should not have harboured a personal pride in his education and speaking abilities. Aristotle (*Rh.*1378b35–1379a4) maintains that all men feel that they have the right to be esteemed by their inferiors according to whatever respect in which they excel. He includes among his illustrative examples the rhetorician (*ho rhētorikos*), who naturally feels superior to the man who is unable to speak well (*adunatos legein*). If, however, we are correct in supposing that an orator's public remarks were circumscribed by a close and generally accurate reading of popular ideology (Ober 1989: 43–9), we must assume that in certain instances, at least, the rhetores felt that the Athenian public would willingly countenance their praise of their own education as well as their sneers at their opponent's lack of educational attainments.

How are we to reconcile the egalitarian attack on the dangers of oratory and appeals to the virtue innate in simplicity with the elitist attacks on ill-educated politicians and praise for elite education? Certainly *paideia*, construed broadly, could mean much *more* than formal rhetorical training.[46] *Paideia* was associated with the virtuous leaders of Athens' past. Isocrates, in the *Panathenaicus* (12.198), praised the leadership of the 'well-born, well-raised, well-educated' Athenians of the Persian War generation. These comments might be attributed to Isocrates' elitist point of view, but Aeschines (3. 208) remarks that, more recently, the 'men from Phyle', who put down the

---

[45] Kennedy 1963: 239 suggests that Aeschines 'has about him some of the self-satisfaction of Cicero and other self-made men. They are inordinately fond of quoting themselves and proud of their education.' This characterization may be true enough; yet since it is no less true of Demosthenes it misses the general point: the speaker's pride in sharing the educational values of his audience is part of his rhetorical strategy.

[46] See esp. Jaeger 1944, a brilliant and voluminous, if not always convincing attempt to 'examine the whole development of Greek *paideia* and to study the complexities and antagonisms inherent in its problems and its meaning' (iii. 47).

dictatorship of the Thirty Tyrants, were led by their *paideia* to promote the amnesty of 403 as the best policy for the *polis*.

There was, however, more to the orator's self-praise than a general notion that *paideia* was a good thing when viewed abstractly or in a historical context. The Athenians, despite their distrust of the power of rhetoric did, after all, continue to listen willingly, even eagerly, to the speeches of trained orators both in the assembly and in the courts. Had they so desired, the Athenians could have passed laws against training in rhetoric, or they could simply have refused to listen to anyone whose speeches smacked of rhetorical sophistication. As noted above (II. 1), the orators' own attacks on the potential evils of rhetoric might have been taken as providing the basis for excluding expert speakers from the decision-making process.

Yet the Athenians did not banish the rhetores. On the contrary, they often granted them public honours and respect. Two of the greatest speeches in the corpus (Aeschin.3, Dem.18) concern whether or not Demosthenes had legitimately been granted the honour of a public crown. And Lysias' ambitious young client Mantitheus (16. 20–1) was eager to speak to the people in the assembly (*legein en tōi dēmōi*), because he saw that the only men the Athenians considered truly worthy (*axioi*) were those who participated actively in politics. Since the Athenians held this opinion (*gnōmē*), he asks, who would not be stimulated to act and speak out for the good of the *polis*? How, he wonders, could the Athenians ever be annoyed at the politicians, since they themselves were their judges? More experienced speakers made even bolder statements. Lycurgus (1. 3) suggested that it was a privilege (*ōphelimon*) for the *polis* to have at hand persons willing to engage in public trials. He felt that 'the many' should feel a suitable sense of *philanthrōpia* toward the prosecutor, rather than be irritated at him and regard him as a busybody (*philopragmōn*). When Dinarchus (1.102) attacked Demosthenes for his failure to indict his former associate Demades on charges of treason, he asked: 'Wherein do we see [in Demosthenes] evidence of the orator's protective power?' The implication seems to be that the orator's speaking ability could and should serve as a positive benefit to the state (cf. Ober 1989: 316–24).

The orators were occasionally willing to make explicit the didactic role which was always latent in their speechmaking. Hyperides (5.21–2) hints at this when he says that the younger orators should be educated (*paideuesthai*) by Demosthenes and the older generation of speakers, but as it turned out the young served as trainers (*sophronizousin*) for their elders. Again, Lycurgus (1. 124) is more daring when he says that he will describe to the jury the stele in the *bouleutērion* inscribed with a law concerning traitors, 'for my instruction (*didaskein*) backed up by many examples (*paradeigmata*), makes your decision an easy one' (cf. Dem. 21. 143).

In a passage cited above (II. 1) from *On the Crown* (18. 280), Demosthenes defined the orator's worth as consisting of his preference for the same things as the majority of the people. Clearly, however, Demosthenes' dictum was an inadequate justification for the political role of the rhetor and represented an ideological extreme. Later in the same speech, Demosthenes suggests a very different interpretation of his own role in the state: 'When the *polis* was free to choose the best policy, when there was a competition for patriotic behaviour which was open to all, I revealed myself to be the best speaker (*egō kratista legōn ephainomēn*), and all business was conducted according to my decrees, my laws, and my diplomatic delegations...' (18. 320). Albeit Demosthenes is contrasting himself with his do-nothing political opponents, and he mentions that his superiority coincided with the *polis'* freedom to choose between different policies, the extreme egotism and vainglory that his words imply cannot be fitted into the context of a purely egalitarian ideology. Demosthenes comes close to advertising himself as the man who ran the state, and he makes no attempt to hide the fact that his ascendancy depended upon his superior speaking ability. In another important passage earlier in the speech, Demosthenes (18.172) discusses his unique qualifications to advise the people at the moment of crisis in autumn of 339 BC, when Philip arrived at Elatea. At that time, the 'voice of the country' had called for someone who was not merely wealthy and patriotic but who had 'closely studied events from the beginning' and 'had rightly fathomed Philip's intentions and decisions'. Among all the Athenians, only Demosthenes fitted the bill, because only he had conducted adequate personal research on Philip and his motives. This research might be seen as comparable to the literary researches he attacks Aeschines for having undertaken (above, II. 2).[47] But Demosthenes is evidently unconcerned about that; he advertises himself as having been the man of the hour, because of his preparation and his speaking ability. In sharp contrast to his suggestion that the orator should be the mouthpiece of the people, in these two passages Demosthenes indicates that the orator must be an expert, an adviser, and even a leader of the state.

The political orators' suggestions that the Athenians should be grateful to them for their services, as well as their willingness to praise their own educational attainments while denigrating the education of opponents, imply that they believed that they should be granted a special position in the state. Furthermore, they felt that this special position was justified in part by their special abilities and elite education. The orators saw themselves, and expected their audience to regard them, as defenders, advisers, and leaders of the *polis*. Speaking ability and education in rhetoric were basic to their ability to perform these various roles. Hence, rhetorical education might be viewed as useful to the democratic government at least as long as educated speakers were patriotic citizens who kept the best interests of the state in mind when they addressed mass audiences. Throughout the period of the democracy, the Athenians continued to listen to, and often followed the advice of, the expert speakers, which suggests that the demos was in fact willing to grant the elite of ability and education certain tacit privileges within the framework of the democratic government. The masses seem to have accepted the propositions that individual Athenians could be granted political privileges and that these privileges were legitimated by those individuals' personal attainments.

V. AMBIVALENCE AND BALANCE

The expert speaker's privileged position was always a tenuous one, however, because of the strong undercurrent of distrust for rhetoric with which he had to contend. In *Against Ctesiphon* Aeschines

---

[47] Given that information on which major decisions were made was generally public property in Athens, the ancient orator could not often support his position by reference to secret sources, a common tactic of modern politicians who in fact have access to much information that is not available to their constituencies. I owe this point to John Jacob.

underlines the political orator's special place in the state, but the
speech also demonstrates that he is aware of the suspicion under
which politicians operated.

'If you jurors pay attention to the pleasing sound of his [Demos-
thenes'] speech, you will be deceived, just as you have been in the
past; but if you pay attention to his character (*phusis*) and to the
truth, you will not be deceived.... With your help I will reckon up
the necessary characteristics of the friend of the people (*dēmotikos*)
and the orderly individual' (3. 168). Aeschines suggests that the
dēmotikos must be freeborn, must inherit a love of democracy from
his ancestors (cf. Ober 1989: 261–6), must live a moderate sort of life,
and 'fourthly, he should be a man of good judgement (*eugnōmon*)
and a good speaker (*dunatos eipein*), for it is well that his discern-
ment (*dianoia*) should prefer the best things and also that his training in rhetoric and eloquence (*tēn de paideian tēn tou rhetoros kai tōn
logōn*) should persuade his listeners. But if he cannot have both, good
judgement is always to be preferred over eloquence' (3. 170). Here
Aeschines concludes that the good politician should be brave so that
he will not desert the demos.

Aeschines then proceeds to test Demosthenes against the criteria
he has just established and, not surprisingly, finds his opponent sadly
wanting. He first relates a highly coloured story of Demosthenes'
dubious antecedents and his family's willingness to intermarry with
barbarian stock for the sake of gain. Then, as for Demosthenes
himself: 'From the trierarch there suddenly appeared the logographer ... but he earned a reputation of being untrustworthy even
at this job, for he showed his speeches to his clients' opponents...'
But what about good judgement and power of speech? 'A skilful
speaker, but one who has lived an evil life.... His words are pretty
sounding (*logoi kaloi*) but his actions worthless.' And he is a coward
to boot (3. 173–5).

Aeschines begins this section of his speech with a warning to the
jurors not to be misled, as they had been in the past, by Demosthenes'
eloquence. Having invoked the aid of his listeners, he then lists the
background and character proper to the *dēmotikos*; notably, the list
includes formal education in rhetoric. Rhetorical training and eloquence are praised as perfectly suitable to the *dēmotikos*, but the
praise is qualified: eloquence must always be subsidiary to good

judgement and is useless unless the individual in question has lived a good life. The passage is structured to put Demosthenes in the worst possible light, but Aeschines must have assumed that the individual elements of his definition of the good politician's attributes would be unexceptionable to the majority of his audience. Both the positive aspects of rhetorical education and eloquence as a benefit for the demos and the need to limit the power of eloquence—by permitting it to be used only by the discerning and the moderate citizen—are implicit in Aeschines' definition.[48]

Aeschines' discussion of the *dēmotikos* provides a basis for analysing the relationship between the two seemingly antithetical attitudes toward rhetoric and rhetorical education that are evident in many speeches in the corpus. On the one hand, education in the arts of persuasion is dangerous to the state, since it threatens to undermine the validity of democratic institutions by destroying the ability of mass assemblies and juries to come to the right decisions. This in turn threatens the fabric of society, since the decisions of the assembly and courts, along with the laws, served a normative function and were especially important in educating the young and restraining the elite. On the other hand, the Athenians recognized that skilled orators could be useful. Expert speakers participated in many facets of Athenian decision-making; notably, they proposed decrees and initiated public trials. The nature of democratic decision-making and the constitutional organization of the Athenian state required a great deal of public debate, and the rhetores were enjoyable, as well as instructive, to listen to.

The dissonance between the Athenian distrust for oratory and the recognition that the orators performed a useful function is inextricably bound up in an ideological conflict intrinsic to the structure and functioning of the democracy. Egalitarian ideology stressed the native intelligence of the average Athenian, the wisdom of group decisions, the need to ensure that individuals would abide by the decisions of the majority, and the evil potential of those who possessed special abilities and training. Elitist ideology emphasized that some men did possess extraordinary skills and that these skills, which

---

[48] Cf. Thuc. 3. 42. 5–6 (speech of Diodotus); Ober 1989: 318–24. On the term *dēmotikos*, esp. in Aristotle, see Ste Croix 1954: 22–6.

could be refined by advanced education, were useful to the state. Therefore, the elite of ability and education deserved a privileged position in society and in the political organization of the state. The considerable space devoted by public speakers to passages that refer to each of these ideologies suggests that the two ideologies coexisted within the democratic ethos.

In this context, the double thrust of Aeschines' reference to the impossibility of the Athenians allowing a tragedian to depict the crowning of Thersites (3. 231; above, § III) becomes clear. The assumption that the Athenians were sufficiently cultured to disallow a scene that makes hash of Homer is a play to egalitarian sentiments. The choice of Thersites, the commoner whom Homer depicts as unworthy of speaking to the assembled Achaeans not only because of his 'cowardice' but also because of his low status, makes a statement about the elite privileges that the current speaker considers his due and denies to his opponent. This impression is reinforced shortly thereafter when Aeschines (3. 237) tells Ctesiphon that by crowning Demosthenes he deceives the ignorant (*agnoountas*) and commits violence (*hubris*) against the knowledgeable and well informed (*eidotas kai aisthanomenous*), and he gives to Demosthenes the credit that belongs to the *polis*, thinking that 'we' do not recognize this. Again there is an elitist stratum (the deception of the ignorant contrasted with the offense to the knowledgeable) and an egalitarian stratum (the credit belongs to the *polis*, not to an individual). 'We' may refer to Aeschines, to Aeschines and the 'well-informed' people in the audience, or to 'all we Athenians'. The ambiguity must be intentional.

The coexistence of the contradictory ideologies created a tension between the elite claims of the educated speaker and the sensibilities of his mass audience. This tension was, to some degree, mediated by the elaborate 'dramatic fictions' that orator and audience conspired to maintain: the private individual who delivered an ornate speech that he had purchased from a logographer presented himself in the guise of a simple man who begged the jury to forgive his lack of eloquence. The expert political orator, who had painstakingly prepared his speech down to the last nuance, was a concerned citizen who spoke spontaneously out of conviction and the passion of the moment. The orator who had spent considerable time and money acquiring rhetorical training professed to be no more familiar with poetry and history than the average citizens of his audience; like them, he learned poetry in the theatre and history from his elders. These fictions are quite transparent to us, and we need not assume that the Athenians were fooled by them either. Rather, the members of the mass audience suspended their disbelief in order to smooth over the ideological dissonance.

The dramatic fictions created a *modus vivendi* between elite rhetor and mass audience. By helping to mediate the power inequities that differing levels of speaking ability inevitably introduced into a society politically dependent upon oral discourse, the fictions helped to maintain the ideological equilibrium necessary to the continued existence of direct democracy at Athens. When they addressed the demos, or a fraction of it, the members of the educated elite participated in a drama in which they were required to play the roles of common men and to voice their solidarity with egalitarian ideals. This drama served as a mechanism of social control over the political ambitions of the elite. Only if they played their demotic roles well were the elite political orators allowed to 'step out of character' and assert their claims to special consideration. Thus the Athenians reaped the benefit of having educated men serve in advisory roles of the state. At the same time the Athenians kept their well-educated advisers on a tight leash and restrained the tendency of the educated elite to evolve into a ruling oligarchy.

12

Lady Chatterley's Lover and the Attic Orators:
The Social Composition of the Athenian Jury

S. C. Todd

HOW NOT TO DO IT

The starting-point of this paper is one of the most disastrous pieces of advocacy in modern legal history.[1] In October 1960, Penguin Books were prosecuted under Section 2 of the 1959 Obscene Publications Act for publishing an unexpurgated edition of *Lady Chatterley's Lover*. On the first day of the trial, Mr Mervyn Griffith-Jones, Senior Treasury Counsel (i.e. Crown Prosecutor), did his best to wreck his case on the strength of one remark. He had previously tried to show that he was himself a man of the world: 'Let me emphasize this on behalf of the prosecution: do not approach this matter in any priggish, high-minded, super-correct, mid-Victorian

[1] Successive versions of this paper were delivered to seminars at the Universities of Cambridge and of Keele. I would like to express my thanks to the chairman on each occasion (Prof. Keith Hopkins at Cambridge and Mr Richard Wallace at Keele) and to the other members of the seminars for the discussion which followed; to Dr Paul Cartledge, Dr Nick Fisher, Dr Mogens Hansen, Dr Paul Millett, Dr Robin Osborne, Prof. Peter Rhodes, Prof. Anthony Snodgrass, Prof. Gerhard Thür, and Mr Thomas Wiedemann, who sent me various additional suggestions, ideas, and corrections; to Prof. Tony Bottoms, who supplied me with some very useful bibliographical advice on criminology, and who did his best to correct many of my misconceptions about

manner.'[2] He now proceeded to work this out in practice: 'Would you approve of your young sons, young daughters—because girls can read as well as boys—reading this book? Is it a book that you would have lying around in your own house? Is it even a book that you would wish your wife or your servants to read?' (Rolph 1961: 17).

We cannot of course be certain how many of the jury did or did not employ servants. The property qualification for jury-service still had another dozen years to run,[3] and Lord Devlin in a memorable phrase had recently described the typical juror as 'male, middle-aged, middle-minded, and middle-class' (Devlin 1956: 20). It may, however, be significant in terms of education and possibly also of class that five of the jurors had had difficulty reading the oath (Rolph 1961: 6).

It is very unlikely that every juror employed servants. It is even less likely that every juror had a wife, since three of them were women (Rolph 1961: 6). But what is more important is that most even of those who did have wives or servants regarded Griffith-Jones' paternalism as outdated:[4] Mr Gerald Gardiner, the defence counsel, capitalized on this, citing the remark twice in the course of his summing-up to suggest that not only the prosecutor but the entire prosecution was an anachronism (Rolph 1961: 195,203). Griffith-Jones' remark became sufficiently notorious to earn a throwaway reference in the House of Lords debate on [147] the book held later in the year,[5] and prosecutors in subsequent obscenity trials seem to

the modern jury; and to the successive editors and the anonymous referees of *JHS*. None of the above, however, are to be blamed for any views or errors expressed in this paper. [The reference-style of this volume has enabled the elimination of many footnotes, and I have taken the opportunity to make minor changes of wording also. More substantial afterthoughts are summarized in a 2005 retrospective at the end of the paper.]

[2] Rolph 1961 (a transcript of the trial with comments by the editor): 16. Sir Allen Lane's private edition of this work contains also a report of the debate on the book held by the House of Lords on 14 Dec. 1960 (see n. 5 below.)

[3] It was abolished by the Criminal Justice Act of 1972 (Baldwin and McConville 1979: 94).

[4] The remark had 'a visible—and risible—effect on the jury' (Rolph 1961: 17), and when Gardiner cited the remark for the second time, the editor adds, 'And the jury smiled' (Rolph 1961: 203).

[5] Viscount Gage quoted a (suspiciously unnamed) peer who, on being asked whether he objected to his young daughter reading *Lady Chatterley's Lover*, replied that he had 'no such objections, but he had the strongest objections to the book being read by his gamekeeper' (Rolph 1961: 264).

have learnt their lesson: Mr Brian Leary, prosecuting counsel in the Oz trial in 1971, was considerably more circumspect in the way that he worded an argument very similar in substance to that of Griffith-Jones (for details, see Robertson 1979: 299–300).

It is a cardinal error for an advocate to profess (even implicitly) a set of social values which will alienate the jury. This is an obvious point, but in the study of the modern jury it has received surprisingly little attention. I was informed by a recently qualified barrister that appealing to a jury had played no part in her formal training: she was expected to pick it up by observation or by intuition. One reason for this neglect may be that her teachers (themselves barristers) were unwilling to recognize the part that non-legal factors, like social acumen, play in their pleading. Moreover, appealing to a modern jury is almost entirely of negative significance: you do not notice it until a Senior Treasury Counsel gets it wrong. There are certainly no textbooks available on the subject, and the biographical and anecdotal material[6] concentrates instead on the relationship between the barrister and the witnesses.

Barristers have, however, become interested in the jury challenge (particularly, for procedural reasons, in the United States, but also in this country): for instance, it is common for the defence to try to achieve an all-male jury in cases of rape or of drunken driving (Cornish 1968: 49–50). The emphasis of the barrister is on getting the right jury, rather than on what to do with them when you have got them.

Academic study of the modern jury is restricted, because in the United Kingdom it is illegal to record and analyse a jury deliberating, and it is probably contempt to interview them afterwards in order to study the process of reaching a verdict (Cornish 1968: 21–5). Two methods of research have therefore been attempted. One is to play

---

[6] Biographies of great advocates are common: two of the most notable are Campbell 1983 (on F. E. Smith, later Lord Birkenhead) and Hyde 1953 (on Sir Edward Carson). Similarly common are memoirs or books of anecdotes by or about great barristers: see e.g. Fordham 1951 (on cross-examination) and more generally Hastings 1956. Perhaps the most interesting study of the barrister's profession, however, is du Cann 1964: as its title, *The Art of the Advocate*, suggests, this is a book written for the newcomer and the outsider, and it does much to strip away the mystique with which the profession frequently surrounds itself. What du Cann discusses (and what he fails to discuss) provides a useful index of what barristers themselves think is important about their job, at least at the time of writing.

the film or tape of a trial to a simulated jury. This has the advantage of experimental control, in that you can play the same case to a series of 'juries', and you can include or exclude a given piece of evidence, such as the criminal record of the accused. But the unreality of the setting causes considerable distortion, because a jury may not act like a jury when nothing depends on it.[7] The second method has proved more fruitful: that is, to interview the other participants in the trial and to discover what they believe most influenced the jury. Some interesting results have been obtained:[8] ironically, the best and most recent study, that of Baldwin [148] and McConville, concludes that jury-challenging is 'an ineffective means of obtaining a noticeably sympathetic jury' (1979: 93).

One of the factors raised by Baldwin and McConville (1979: 28) was the 'general weakness of the prosecution [or defence] case', but they made no attempt to discuss this further, for instance by differentiating between weakness of facts and weakness of presentation. There has been no attempt by barristers or by criminologists to examine the way in which the change from middle-class to socially mixed juries since 1972 has influenced pleading.

THE ATHENIAN JURY

Neither barristers nor criminologists, therefore, are particularly concerned with how to appeal to a jury. This is significant, because it suggests that mistakes such as that of Griffith-Jones are rare. Any advocate even of moderate ability knows instinctively what not to say.

---

[7] McCabe and Purves 1974 attempt to avoid this problem: instead of playing a recording to a simulated jury, they put an unofficial 'jury' in the public gallery, took them out when the jury retired, and asked them to imagine that they were the real jury. This obviously gains something—although it is hard to say how much—in immediacy; equally, it loses the advantage of the 'control' experiment.

[8] The pioneering work was that of Kalven and Zeisel (1966), based on interviews with Chicago judges. A more sophisticated study was undertaken by Baldwin and McConville (1979), who made use of questionnaires completed by judges, prosecuting and defending solicitors, and police in Birmingham and London: the Bar, however, refused permission for its members to participate, and the Law Society severely restricted the questions which could be put to solicitors.

In the study of the Athenian jury, the question has received considerably more attention, but from the opposite perspective. Instead of using the social values of the jury to examine the craft of the advocate, scholars have (of necessity) used the advocate to examine the jury. We possess approximately 100 court-speeches, and twenty more delivered to the assembly: they span very roughly the period for which we are generally best informed, the century or so from the start of the Peloponnesian War in 431 BC to the Macedonian conquest and the destruction of the democracy in 322. If gaffes are rare today, then *a fortiori* they will be rarer in the orators: unlike a Treasury Counsel, an ancient speechwriter was a freelance agent who needed to display competence to win his next brief.[9] It ought therefore to be feasible to determine the social values on which the orator relied, and this has been the more influential of the two possible ways of discovering who made up the jury. If, for instance, the speeches would consistently have alienated either the taxpayers[10] or the poor, then this implies that that group did not at least form the backbone of the jury.

The second possible approach concerns the economics of jury-pay: was this enough to attract those who had to work for their living, or conversely was it set at a level that would interest only those incapable of more remunerative work? This paper will discuss the question on

[9] 'Published' versions of lawcourt speeches (most of our texts are of this kind) should be distinguished from literary pamphlets in speech-form (e.g. Isocrates' speeches 1–15). Both genres are intended to be read, presumably by the elite. We possess no transcripts of trials, and we cannot tell how far speeches in the first group have been revised for 'publication', which could distort the social values they profess. But Isocrates in his pamphlets puts forward reactionary political views which could hardly have been expressed in court (see n. 34 below), and it is striking that we do not find views like this expressed in the published lawcourt speeches: their authors are presumably more keen to retain the illusion of a lawcourt. Revision would of course provide every incentive to suppress any notorious gaffes like that of Griffith-Jones, which ironically makes them more reliable for the purpose of this paper.

[10] The two most important forms of taxation at Athens were the *eisphora* and the 'liturgy' (*leitourgia*). The former was a direct capital tax levied at irregular intervals when required (usually in time of war): the level of the *eisphora* would be set by the assembly as a percentage of the total capital assets of those required to pay. A liturgy, however, was not a formal tax; instead, those liable were obliged to fund a particular public project, such as the production of a play or the commissioning of a warship. Both forms of taxation, and especially liturgies, affected only the rich: roughly half the citizen population served as hoplites (heavy-armed soldiers, who had to supply their own armour), but the *eisphora* seems to have affected perhaps 10–15%, and fewer than 5% were apparently liable for liturgies.

the level both of pay and of values, and it is my contention that both values and pay lead to a consistent and significant series of conclusions. [149] Two words of explanation should be offered at this point. In the first place, the subject of this paper is class structure, not class struggle: when the term 'class' is used, it is to be understood in a popular rather than a technical sense, defined not in terms of 'relationship to the means of production', but to mean a group (always in this paper of citizens) with a corporate identity and common values or attitudes. Secondly, this is a paper about Athenian juries. The composition of the Athenian assembly is a parallel and closely related issue, but one which raises a number of different problems. This paper therefore concentrates primarily on lawcourt speeches and on jury-pay, but evidence concerning the assembly is used where appropriate for comparative purposes, and the composition of the assembly itself is discussed briefly in an appendix.

JONES AND THE 'MIDDLE-CLASS' JURY

The fundamental study of the Athenian jury is that of A. H. M. Jones (1957). He was not, indeed, the first scholar to be aware of the problem, but he was the first to discuss it in detail. Cornford (1907), Pickard-Cambridge (1914), Glotz (1929), Bonner and Smith (1930–8), Ehrenberg (1951), and Hignett (1952) had each raised the question, but they had mostly been content to make a passing reference to Aristophanes' *Wasps*, in which the typical juror is satirized as old and poor. Thus Ehrenberg emphasizes both halves of this picture,[11] while Bonner and Smith[12] concentrate on the age of

---

[11] Ehrenberg 1951: 53–4 and 161, on age (Aristophanes' picture exaggerated but otherwise valid) and on poverty ('the majority ... poor men') respectively. He applies the same argument on poverty to the assembly (see at n. 107 below).

[12] Bonner and Smith (1930: 231–3) focus on age, and try at length to reconcile *Wasps* with occasional references in the orators to 'younger men' among the jury (e.g. Ant. 5. 71) and the assumed needs of military service. They later note (1930: 366–7) that in the 4th century there was no longer available a pool of unemployed refugees, forced from the countryside into the city, as there had been during the Spartan occupation of Decelea in 413–404; but the question of poverty does not bulk large in their thinking.

the jurors, and Pickard-Cambridge[13] and Hignett[14] on their poverty. At first sight, Cornford and Glotz appear to break new ground, in that they are interested not in poverty or age so much as in social background, but Cornford's thinking on this point is influenced by his hidden agenda,[15] and Glotz relies on an a priori assumption rather than on argument.[16]

Jones, however, offered a far more sophisticated analysis than any of his predecessors, and it is his analysis that has dominated subsequent thinking. His argument has provoked both agreement and disagreement, in roughly equal proportions. But even for Jones' opponents, it is his analysis which has created the framework for discussing the [150] problem: later scholars may have disliked his answers, but they have felt constrained to ask his questions. This is true even of the most recent and the most thorough alternative interpretation, that of Markle (discussed in the fourth section of this paper), who has recently attacked Jones by using his method but inverting his conclusions. For this reason we are justified in speaking of Jones' interpretation as 'orthodoxy', and the response of Jones' opponents and particularly of Markle as 'heterodoxy'. The burden of this paper is that the method used both by Jones and by Markle is an oversimplification, and that other factors require greater attention.

Jones' book is a collection of papers, and he therefore restates his argument several times[17] in slightly different terms. The resulting subtlety or ambiguity (see n. 18 below), however, has generally been ignored by

[13] Pickard-Cambridge, who describes the jurors as 'the aged and infirm, the poor and the idle' (1914: 89–90), is one of the few scholars to differentiate between jurors and members of the assembly (see below at n. 106).

[14] Hignett 1952: 221, citing *Ath. Pol.* 27. 4 (for which see further at n. 33 below), concludes that the poorer citizens formed a majority in the court.

[15] Cornford (1907: 15–24 *passim*) argues that the jury consisted of artisans and tradesmen, and that the country farmers were hardly represented. The thesis of this book was that the outbreak of the Peloponnesian War should be read as the result of pressure by the Athenian mercantile classes (who in Cornford's opinion dominated policy-making) to break the stranglehold of Corinth over the trade route through the Corinthian Gulf. There is no evidence for this, and the modernizing view of ancient economic history which underlies it has generally and rightly been rejected.

[16] Glotz (1929: 241) suggests that the jury are basically middle- and lower-class town-dwellers; his unstated premise is that of physical proximity. See, however, the discussion of Athenian topography at n. 79 below.

[17] A. Jones 1957: 35–7, 50, 124. Much the same interpretation is applied by Jones (p. 109) to the assembly (on which see the appendix to this paper, at n. 107 below).

both his followers and his opponents, and since it does not really affect the argument of this paper, the following simplified version will suffice.

Jones begins where his predecessors stopped, with Aristophanes' *Wasps*: he agrees that in the late fifth century the typical juror was old and poor (1957: 124). By the mid-fourth century, however, Demosthenes is taking a highly sympathetic view of the rich and particularly of the taxpayer: he appeals to his audience to 'tax yourselves' and never to 'soak the rich' (1957: 35–7; the tax in question is the *eisphora*); moreover, when he has to produce in court a really poor man, the arbitrator Straton (Dem. 21.95), he is embarrassed. Consequently, according to Jones, the juries by this date have become 'predominantly middle or upper class' (1957: 124). He further suggests a reason for this change: jury-pay had reached 3 obols in 425, but remained static thereafter, although wages approximately doubled in the next century. Three obols is not enough for 'a working man' (in Jones' words, 1957: 37) to feed a family, especially when even unskilled casual labour could fetch three times as much.[18] Lastly, Jones uses this change from a poor to a progressively more prosperous jury to explain the change in the political temperature of Athens during this period. He rightly sees that Athens in the mid-fourth century was in reality far less democratic than it had been in the late fifth century, and he speaks of the 'increasingly bourgeois tone' of the democracy (1957: 10). His explanation for this political change is a change in the social balance of the electorate (i.e. the jury): the poor could not afford to come and vote.

Jones' interpretation of the Athenian jury has met with a wide variety of responses, but until recently, scholars have responded more to his conclusions than to the arguments on which he based them. A number of historians have cited Jones explicitly and with unqualified

---

[18] The added subtlety of Jones' case is his argument that the rich were particularly dominant in public (i.e. major political) trials: he believes that this was the result of deliberate jury-packing (A. Jones 1957: 36–7), but this presupposes a surprising level of conscious party organization. This argument has apparently been ignored both by his followers and by his opponents. Jones' most notable ambiguity concerns the position of those unable to earn a full day's wage: in the late 5th century, he believes (p. 124) that 3 obols would have been enough to attract them (but not the able-bodied) into jury service; in the 4th century, however, the real value of 3 obols dropped, but Jones (p. 37) leaves it unclear whether 3 obols continued so to attract them. Jones' followers have developed his argument here in different directions (see following note).

approval, thus apparently accepting the full implications of his case.[19] Others have been selective, mentioning only those individual conclusions which [151] meet with their approval.[20] Other scholars have been still more tentative, and have summarized Jones' case without making their own position wholly clear.[21] Perhaps the majority have indicated varying degrees of doubt: some of these have in effect side-stepped Jones' work, and have continued to speak of the typical juror as old and/or poor;[22] others have summarized Jones' case, but have expressed individual reservations;[23] a few have ignored Jones' concentration on wealth and poverty, and have attempted (though with limited success) to revert to the approaches taken by previous scholars.[24]

[19] Harrison (1971: 49, n. 2) sees the 4th-century jury as consisting only of the well-off, whereas Carey and Reid (1985: 1 and n. 2) see it as comprising the unemployable as well. Both cite Jones as authority for their views (cf. previous note). Carey and Reid make a tantalizing passing reference to 'those whose work was seasonal', but this group plays no further part in their analysis.

[20] e.g. J. Davies 1978: 109, and Fisher 1976: 31–2, both canvassing a number of alternative explanations, among them Dover's suggestion (below) that a poor jury might wish to be treated as if they were prosperous.

[21] Perlman 1963: 327 is non-committal, but in his later paper (1967: 165–6) he more clearly aligns himself with Jones' position. Finley (1985*a*: 117–18) claims against Jones that the very poor were disproportionately represented on the jury, but contrast Finley's views expressed elsewhere on the composition of the assembly (1985*a*: 52).

[22] Thus Wolff (1968 [Ch. 6 in this collection]: 7, n. 13), without reference to Jones. Ste Croix (1972: 376; 1981: 289) similarly insists against Jones that the poor made up a substantial proportion of the jury, whereas MacDowell (1978: 33–5) sees the jurors as predominantly elderly.

[23] Isager and Hansen (1975: 122) suggest that pay was intended to cover only the juror's individual needs and not those of his family (for Hansen's later views on assembly pay, see at n. 106 below). Adkins (1972: 120) sees jury-pay as a form of poor-relief, and argues that the rich will not have wanted the stigma associated with receiving it. (Social values in the lawcourts and assembly form the subject also of ch. 10 in Adkins 1960, but this concentrates on the orators' appeals to the often rival claims of justice and expediency.)

[24] Burford (1972: 154) claims that the assembly (and presumably also the jury) will have consisted primarily of poor craftsmen, rather than peasants, because they were the people who lived in Athens and Piraeus (cf. Cornford 1907 and Glotz 1929, as cited nn. 15–16 above); Harding (1981: 43, n. 20) rejects this proposition. Both arguments, however, are weakened by hidden assumptions: Burford is eager to find a significant role for her craftsmen to play in Athenian life, and Harding is trying to prove that the vaunted dichotomy between radical town-dwellers and conservative country-dwellers is a myth. Harding's argument is probably overstated (see below, p. 339 at n. 78), but I suspect that his picture is closer to reality than that of Burford.

There has, however, been surprisingly little detailed analysis of Jones' arguments. A few of Jones' supporters have developed additional evidence to support his model: Dover, for instance, stresses the way that Demosthenes attacks Aeschines for his family and upbringing, especially Demosthenes' patronizing and 'supercilious' attack on 'schoolmasters, clerks and decorators'.[25] Some of Jones' critics have sought to interpret differently the level of jury-pay, and others have outlined alternative reconstructions of the social values reflected in the speeches. Thus Rhodes[26] emphasizes the attractions of [152] 3 obols to the very poor even more than to the rich, while Mossé[27] and Strauss[28] both provide alternative explanations of Demosthenes' pleas to his hearers to 'tax yourselves' rather than to 'soak the rich'.

An original and at first sight promising approach is taken by Kroll in his study of dikastic *pinakia*;[29] he seeks to resolve the problem by means of non-literary (in this case archaeological) evidence. *Pinakia* were bronze disks, issued to every juror apparently for the purpose of identification, and retained for life. In some cases, indeed, an Athenian citizen was so devoted to his *pinakion* that it was even buried with him, and a study of these graves might be expected to provide useful

[25] Dover 1974: 34, on Dem. 19. 237. Dover's suggestion that a jury of poor men might wish to be treated as if they were prosperous is discussed in the fifth section of this paper.

[26] Rhodes, *CAAP* 691: in addition to *Wasps*, Rhodes uses *Ath. Pol.* 27. 4 and Isoc. 7. 54 (discussed at nn. 32–3 below) to support his case. The possibility that jury-pay might have attracted the very poor was of course latent within Jones' analysis (see n. 18 above), but Rhodes develops this possibility to the extent of explicitly repudiating Jones' model.

[27] Mossé 1962: 266: after twenty years of war-exhaustion, the tax was unpopular with everyone. She further argues that several statements by e.g. Isocrates are incomprehensible unless the jury consisted basically of the poor and unemployed (citing Isoc. 7. 83; clearer perhaps would be Isoc. 7. 54 and 8. 130: both passages are discussed at n. 32 below).

[28] Strauss (1979: 12, n. 18) argues that Demosthenes was trying to create an impression of unity, and to 'soak the rich' would underscore the divisions in Athenian society. He suggests here that the poor made up the largest group in the jury, even though the well-to-do formed a significant minority. In the published version of this dissertation (1987: 171), Strauss appears in another context to accept Jones' thesis that the poor became for demographic reasons a progressively less significant force during the 4th century, but he does not develop the implications of this for the composition of the jury.

[29] Kroll 1972, esp. 71–83 and 261–7. In addition to the criticisms expressed here, see the perceptive comments of Sinclair (1988: 130, n. 94 and 135, n. 118).

statistical evidence. As Kroll admits, however, the samples are at present small (a few dozen at most), and the evidence of the *pinakia* therefore inconclusive. Although he himself tends to believe that the graves in question are mainly those of the needy or of the city poor,[30] he can only sustain this conclusion by marshalling afresh the fourth-century literary evidence. And here Kroll is on weaker ground: making no direct attempt to refute Jones' argument from the social values to which Demosthenes appeals, he instead collects passages which refer to poor men serving as jurors. He finds two references in Demosthenes[31] to state-debtors (by definition poor) on the jury, two passages of Isocrates[32] which speak of citizens serving as jurors to obtain the necessities of life, and one passage in the *Athēnaiōn Politeia*.[33] criticizing the social or moral decline among the juries since the introduction of jury-pay around 450 BC. Kroll himself describes Isocrates and the *Ath. Pol.* as 'anti-democratic but probably accurate'; in other words, they can only be used to support an argument that is already accepted on other grounds. But the problems go deeper than this. The state-debtors of the two Demosthenes passages are not ordinary paupers but broken members of the elite, and although Demosthenes conjures up a tear-jerking picture of a man so destitute that he was forced to run the risk of jury service, Pyrrhos' action may well have been as much political as economic, in that a state-debtor was automatically disfranchised, and for such a man to exercise civic rights is a statement of intent. Isocrates is a

---

[30] There is, however, a further problem here, not faced by Kroll: the very poor man has more reason for pride in his status as a citizen of a democracy, and perhaps therefore more reason to want his *pinakion* buried with him.

[31] Dem 21. 182 (the aristocratic Pyrrhos was executed for this), and Dem. 24. 123 (ordinary citizens who commit this offence are severely punished, but the Athenians are far too lenient towards orators).

[32] Isoc. 7. 54 asks rhetorically, 'who can but feel aggrieved when he sees many of our citizens drawing lots [i.e. in the daily allocation of jurors to courts] in front of the lawcourts for the necessities of life, whether he is to have them or not'; and Isoc. 8. 130 criticizes 'those who live off the lawcourts' (clearly in context jurors rather than prosecutors). Other passages of Isocrates could perhaps be cited to the same purpose, e.g. Isoc. 15. 152, referring to 'those who are compelled to get their livelihood from the city' (presumably from state-pay); but Isoc. 7. 83 is less direct, referring simply to 'those who are destitute', without any specific mention of public pay (cf. n. 27 above).

[33] *Ath. Pol.* 27. 4: 'some people claim that the juries have become *cheirō* [either 'lower class' or 'morally degenerate', or more probably both] as a result of jury-pay.'

closet [153] oligarch with an obsession: the good old days of 'real democracy' (i.e. oligarchy), contrasted with the degeneracy of the present day. He is determined to find social problems everywhere, and looks in particular for unemployment and/or mercenaries, problems which he can 'solve' by advocating an invasion of Persia. So it is a grave mistake to take him seriously as evidence for Athenian social conditions.[34] As for *Ath. Pol.* 27. 4, it is hardly evidence for the fourth-century jury, and its use of language is significant: 'some people say' is a form of words used by the author of this text to introduce a statement found in his sources which is so naive or so tendentious that even he is unwilling to let it appear under his own pen (cf. *Ath. Pol.* 6. 2–3; 9. 2).

MARKLE AND THE JURY OF 'POOR' MEN

The most thorough attack on Jones, however, is contained in the paper by Markle (1985). Perhaps, indeed, this could be described as the only full-scale attack: whereas previous scholars had either ignored Jones' theory or rejected it in general terms or offered individual objections, Markle by contrast has devoted an entire article to the subject, and he is the first scholar to have worked out in detail an alternative interpretation both to Jones' theory and to those of his predecessors. Moreover, his views seem likely to be more influential than those of any previous writer on the subject since Jones himself: discussions of the social composition of the Athenian jury since Markle's paper appeared have broadly supported his conclusions.[35] His argument is that both the jury and the assembly alike were for the most part manned not by those who were rich enough not to worry about the level of pay (Jones' view), nor by those who were unemployed or destitute and for whom any pay was better than nothing (that of Jones' predecessors), but by those who had to work for their living.

---

[34] It is important to note that the Isocrates passages in question (see last-but-one note) come from political pamphlets rather than from lawcourt speeches. He could hardly have said this in a democratic court (cf. n. 9 above).

[35] Sinclair 1988, Hansen 1987, and Powell 1988: for details, see n. 62 below. There is no reference to Markle's views in the brief incidental discussion by Garner (1987: 65).

After a brief introduction (1985: 265–6), Markle's paper falls into three parts. Most of his fire is directed against Jones and his followers, on the level both of pay (pp. 271–81, supported by an appendix at pp. 293–7) and of values (pp. 281–92). But he is concerned first to guard his rear against the argument advanced both by Jones' predecessors and by some of his more recent opponents that the bulk of the jurors were destitute (pp. 267–71).

It is in this first section of his paper that Markle is at his strongest. There are two possible reasons for believing in a destitute jury—the impression given by Aristophanes' *Wasps*, and a confusion of terms over the Greek words for poverty—and Markle exposes the weakness of both arguments. It is notoriously dangerous to base broad conclusions in social history on the unsupported evidence of a comic poet like Aristophanes,[36] since comedy relies on such techniques as exaggeration and fantasy, and its apparent realism can be insidious; moreover, Aristophanes, like other Greek authors, is a member of the elite, and he shares its prejudices. When, therefore, the chorus-leader declares that he has to buy [154] barley and wood for his whole family out of his jury-pay, and that he faces starvation if for some reason the court does not sit today (*Wasps* 300–11), the joke may be simply an 'aristocratic sneer' (Markle 1985: 267): members of the elite like Aristophanes did not approve of the institution of jury-pay, if it enabled those who would not have been able to afford the time without compensation to sit in court; the easiest way to parody such an institution was to suggest that it filled the courts with idle and vindictive layabouts.[37] It is in this direction that Aristophanes will have tended to exaggerate the poverty of the jurors.[38]

---

[36] This point is well made by Ehrenberg (1951: 37–42). It would be equally dangerous to infer from the chorus-leader's rambling remark, 'the crops need rain' (*Wasps* 253–65), that the 'typical juror' is therefore a countryman rather than a town-dweller (rightly, MacDowell 1971: 168); I have therefore made no use of this passage support my own reconstructions in the fifth section of this paper.

[37] The same attitude of distaste towards the institution of jury-pay ('it made the Athenians lazy') is found in Plato, *Gorgias* 515e2–7, on which see Markle (1985: 272).

[38] Markle further argues that the archetypal juror Philokleon (the protagonist of the *Wasps*) is really a rich man who is only pretending to be poor, and that the same therefore is true of the chorus also, but it is doubtful whether this would serve any comic purpose. Admittedly Philokleon's son Bdelykleon is rich, but we should not therefore conclude (as Markle 1985: 267) that 'clearly the family had property'. Aristophanes is often more interested in the joke of the moment than in consistency

Markle's discussion of the Greek words for poverty is equally judicious. He develops in detail a distinction previously outlined both by Austin and Vidal-Naquet and by Ste Croix,[39] that those who have little or no leisure (*hoi penētes*) are different from the destitute (*hoi ptōchoi*); Markle insists that the bulk of the jury belong to the former and not to the latter category. Various ancient authors[40] suggest that the 'poor' sat on the jury, but this is not evidence that these men were destitute; it means that they normally had to work for their living.

The bulk of Markle's attention, however, is directed towards Jones and his jury of the better-off. His argument here is conducted on the two planes of pay and of values, but neither is wholly satisfactory.

Markle approaches the question of pay from two directions: external literary evidence (i.e. outside the speeches themselves, 1985: 271–7), and a statistical survey of the Athenian cost of living (pp. 277–81, 293–7). From the literary evidence, Markle seeks to demonstrate the 'effectiveness' of pay, which (he claims) achieved its aim of enabling the *penētes* to serve on juries (and, from the 390s, in the assembly). There is a risk of circular argument here, since it is dangerous to infer the purpose of a law or of an institution from its results.[41] According to Markle, however, the bitterness towards state-pay of reactionary authors such as Isocrates and Plato, together with the readiness of oligarchic activists to abolish it whenever possible,[42] implies that at least the opponents of democracy believed that jury-pay was effective.

of character: the extreme poverty of the jurors is the running joke throughout the first half of the play, and Philokleon's attempt to come to terms with high society throughout the second half, but the connection between the two propositions is not emphasized.

[39] Markle (1985: 267–71), including also a discussion of the term *aporoi* (ignored in my simplified summary, though see following note); Austin and Vidal-Naquet (1977: 16); Ste Croix (1981: 431).

[40] For instance Aristotle in the *Politics* (1279b18–20, discussed by Markle 1985: 268) defines democracy as that government where the state is controlled by the *aporoi* (a term which in Aristotle's thought, according to Markle, is equivalent to the *penētes*).

[41] To what extent was the introduction and raising of state-pay intended to encourage participation in public life and break the hold of the rich on the juries, to distribute the wealth of the community among its members (and perhaps thereby to limit the need for aristocratic patronage: see Millett 1989), or as a bid for popularity on the part of the politician proposing the increase? See further below at n. 53.

[42] As in the briefly successful oligarchic revolution of 411 (Markle 1985: 271–2).

Markle himself, however, admits that Isocrates and Plato are too 'tendentious' to be trustworthy evidence here (1985: 272), and he attaches much more importance to two less partial [155] authors, Aristotle and Aristophanes. He regards Aristotle's *Politics* as reliable, both as political theory and as political history, because it was based on the type of careful historical research that we see in the *Ath. Pol.* The onus therefore, according to Markle (pp. 272–4), rests on the sceptic to discredit Aristotle's authority—a principle of interpretation which he applies to fifth-century politics as well as to that of Aristotle's own date. But the extraordinary mixture of valuable information and tendentious rubbish which we find in the *Ath. Pol.* does not exactly create confidence in the work's 'careful research', whether we regard it as the work of Aristotle himself or of a pupil. The *Politics* is a vastly better work in terms both of accuracy and of analysis, but it is difficult to decode.[43] Aristotle tends to allow his political theory to determine his selection, and perhaps his interpretation, of facts; and it is often difficult to decide how far he is talking about real and how far about theoretical constitutions. In Book 4 of the *Politics* he distinguishes between four types of democracy; and it is his analysis of the fourth of these, described by Aristotle himself as 'final' or 'complete' and by modern scholars as 'radical' democracy, which supplies the evidence for Markle's argument. But how far is Aristotle here discussing Athens, and how far is he hypothesizing the results of democracy taken to what in his view would be its logical conclusion? Markle appears to regard state-pay as the central characteristic of 'final' democracy, and he therefore deduces that Aristotle here is analysing contemporary Athens.[44] But when Aristotle himself introduces his fourfold division, he defines 'final' democracy in terms of the sovereignty of the immediate popular will expressed in decrees without the constitutional restraint of law; the question of state-pay

[43] When Aristotle makes an empirical statement ('in city *x* they do *y*'), this can usually be taken at face value; when, however, he makes a theoretical statement, frequently cast in indefinite form ('when *x* conditions obtain …' or 'when there is a democracy of *x* type …'), these have to be interpreted much more cautiously. The quotations on which Markle (1985: 273–4) bases his argument are of the theoretical rather than the empirical kind.

[44] Markle (1985: 273): 'he must be describing not only the Athenian constitution but other Greek democracies which enabled the poor to participate by offering pay.'

is introduced later, as a characteristic property rather than a necessary criterion of this form of democracy.[45] And judged against Aristotle's own criterion (the subordination of law to the popular will), fourth-century Athens was not an example of 'final' democracy.[46] Aristotle's analysis may therefore contain ideas based on his observation of Athenian politics, but it is not a formal critique of contemporary Athens.[47] The point can be taken further: if Aristotle here is discussing not Athens but an 'ideally bad' democracy, then we have to allow for the results of wishful thinking, both negative and positive.[48] Aristotle, like Isocrates and Plato, is a member of the elite and shares its prejudices.

Although Markle himself doubted the inferences commonly drawn from Aristophanes' *Wasps*, he is nevertheless happy to use Aristophanes' *Ecclesiazusae* in his own support (1985: 274–6).[49] His argument here concerns the introduction and rapid raising of assembly-pay. Jury-pay had been introduced at 2 obols in the 450s, and raised to 3 obols in 425, remaining static thereafter until the fall of the democracy in 322. Assembly-pay was a later invention. It was introduced at some stage in the 390s at 1 obol, and raised [156] very rapidly to 2 and then 3 obols; it had recently been raised to 3 obols when the *Ecclesiazusae* was produced, probably in 392/1 or 391/0.[50] Now in the *Ecclesiazusae* there is frequent reference to the recent rises in assembly-pay from 1 to 2 to 3 obols: in particular, there is a running

---

[45] Arist. *Pol.* 1292a4–7 (decree and law) and 1293a3–7 (state-pay, cited by Markle 1985: 273).

[46] In the 4th century (although not the 5th) decrees at Athens were strictly subordinated to laws: see Hansen 1983*b*: 161–77 and 179–206.

[47] My reading of the *Politics* here is by no means uncontested: for a contrary view, see e.g. Hansen 1987: 10.

[48] Positive wishful thinking is to be found in *Politics* 1292b25–9: Aristotle approves the type of democracy where farmers and those who possess a 'moderate' amount of property are in charge of the state, because they will be too busy farming to play an active part in politics. (Whenever Aristotle mentions the word 'moderate'—*mesos* or, as here, *metrios*—he is usually idealizing.) Presumably he is envisaging a situation without any state-pay, although given ancient conditions of farming (cf. the discussion of marginal returns and of leisure preference at nn. 100–1 below) it is difficult to take him very seriously here.

[49] A similar argument is developed by Ehrenberg (1951: 84, 227) and by Hansen (1983*b*: 27).

[50] Of the later development of assembly-pay we know nothing, except that by the time of the *Ath. Pol.*, written probably during the 320s, it had reached 6 obols for an ordinary and 9 for an extraordinary meeting: see A. Jones 1957: 136–7; Markle 1985: 265, n. 1.

joke that when assembly-pay was 1 obol the assembly was empty, but now that it is 3 obols the assembly is packed (*Eccles.* 300–10); indeed, it is now so full that unless you arrive very early you will not get paid (282–92, 376–82). Markle infers that 3 obols was the crucial level of pay: anything below this was too low, but 3 obols was just enough to attract the *penētes* to attend the assembly in large numbers; consequently, he concludes, 3 obols will have been enough to attract them onto the juries as well.[51]

Markle's use of Aristophanes invites the charge of inconsistency, in that he rejects the *Wasps* but is happy to use the *Ecclesiazusae*. He seeks to deflect this charge by suggesting that either the joke about assembly-pay is a fantasy and the increase made no difference whatever to the numbers attending, or alternatively it made all the difference and Aristophanes' picture of a packed house is literally correct. But this is a false dichotomy. Any increase in pay is bound to attract at least some potential attenders. Every individual remotely interested in attending will construct his personal equation for every meeting. On the positive side: public spirit, plus intrinsic interest of the meeting, plus (perhaps) self-importance, plus level of pay. On the negative side: apathy, plus potential tedium, plus distance and trouble necessary to attend, plus loss of income (thus Sinclair 1988: 119–35). For some at least, the next increase in the level of pay will be just what is needed to tip the balance towards attending. But how many will fall into this category in any given situation? We do not know, and Aristophanes cannot tell us. Any increase in pay is bound to provoke some increase in attendance. Any increase in attendance would be enough to provoke Aristophanes into making the sort of jokes that he makes here.[52] Indeed, we cannot even safely assume that

[51] Markle assumes (1985: 274) that 3 obols was the standard level of assembly-pay. I am inclined (for reasons discussed in the appendix to this paper) to believe that he may be correct in concluding that the jump from 3 to 6 and 9 obols was both late and sudden. But his use of logic is dangerous, because on the one hand he does not himself put forward any real argument to support this assumption, and on the other hand the assumption is itself necessary to his case: unless 3 obols was adequate for the assembly, it will not have been enough for the jury. (For Markle's suggested 'non-economic reasons' for the rise to 6 and 9 obols (1985: 285), see the third paragraph of my appendix.)

[52] It is precisely jokes on the theme 'arrive early or you will not get paid' that seem most likely to be exaggeration born of fantasy; we cannot deduce from this that the change to 3 obols produced a full house. Still less can we simply compare the jokes

assembly-pay was raised from 2 to 3 obols because numbers attending the assembly were perceived to be unacceptably low: *Ath. Pol.* 41. 3 states that it was introduced by Agyrrhius, raised to 2 obols by Heracleides, and raised to 3 obols by Agyrrhius again.[53] It is tempting to interpret at least the final increase as an attempted bid for patronage by a political leader (see above at n. 41).

The rest of Markle's discussion of pay is based on a statistical study of incomes and prices. Whereas Jones had suggested that 3 obols was too low to feed a family, Markle [157] argues that this is incorrect, and that even a family of four could in fact be fed on 2½ obols (1985: 277–81, 293–7). This is an elaborate and interesting discussion, and it contains several points of general validity: for instance, it is probable that annual wages were lower than scholars have sometimes assumed,[54] and the diet of most Athenians may have been less expensive than has often been suggested. Nevertheless, the argument has weaknesses both in method and in conclusion. There is at least one small but elementary (and therefore revealing) statistical error in Markle's calculations (p. 280).[55] More significantly, because Markle believes that the 3 obols was a subsistence-allowance, his argument requires that his figures for the price of food must be accurate throughout the century during which jury-pay remained static at 3 obols, but many of his calculations are based on figures which, as he admits, belong to the late fifth century.[56] To defend himself, Markle states nonchalantly in his appendix that the price of basic foodstuffs such as grain remained static during the century in question, 'except for temporary fluctuations in prices caused by bad harvests, wars, piracy and perhaps seasonal shortages'

---

about the red rope, used in *Acharn.* 21–2 (produced in 425) to force people in to the assembly and in *Eccles.* 378–9 (produced in the late 390s) to exclude latecomers, and deduce that patterns of attendance had changed. The two are separate jokes, directed against separate (but in Aristophanes' opinion typical) facets of the Athenian national character: their irresponsibility in the *Acharnians*, and their officiousness and willingness to do anything for money in the *Ecclesiazusae*.

[53] On the political rivalry of the 390s, see Strauss 1987.

[54] Markle (1985: 296–7): our only reliable figures concern the daily pay of artisans, and Markle sounds a proper caution against simply multiplying such figures by 350 without allowing for (e.g.) festivals and days laid off.

[55] 1.0 should represent a 30% contraction not of 1.3 but of 1.43.

[56] Markle 1985: 277, 'the cost of living in late fifth-century Athens' (introducing the statistical survey); 280, 'the other kinds of food ... at the end of the fifth century BC'.

(1985: 293). This is a somewhat cavalier assertion, because there is so little evidence available that any extant figures may derive from an abnormal year, and almost any pattern can be discerned or imposed at will. But it is certainly difficult a priori to accept that the price of foodstuffs really remained static during a century in which (as Markle admits) wages had more than doubled.

Even more important, however, is the weakness implicit in Markle's conclusion. Clearly the value of money will have changed during the period in question, but there is no evidence that the Athenians themselves were consciously aware of this change. Certainly they lacked the economic theory to sustain the concept of a retail price index; I doubt if they would even have conceptualized 'you can't buy anything with 3 obols at today's prices', because this seems to imply too conscious a view of historical change. But if Markle is correct, and the 3 obols were essentially a subsistence-payment, then the declining value of money will have been brought to their attention not theoretically but practically: it will have become increasingly difficult to fill an assembly or to man a jury.[57] The fact that jury-pay was never raised after 425 will therefore lead necessarily to one of two conclusions: either (following Jones) the personnel of the jury changed increasingly over the next century; or else (if Markle is right) the jurors must have progressively tightened their belts.[58] But if so, why did the Athenians not raise the level of pay for the jury? Admittedly during the period 380–350 BC there may have been a good reason for this: Athens was chronically short of cash throughout these

[57] A minimum of 6,000 volunteers was required for jury-service each year, and without this number the system of allocation to courts would have broken down. Concerning the assembly we are less well informed, but 6,000 was a necessary quorum for certain types of fairly routine business (e.g. grants of citizenship). Hansen indeed has recently, and I believe correctly, argued that 6,000 was perceived as the proper attendance for a normal assembly (1983*b*: 1–23): see at n. 114 below.

[58] Markle does admit in passing that jury-pay even in the late 5th century will have entailed a loss of income (1985: 281, 'about half their wages'), and that jurors will therefore presumably have required considerable motivation to attend; but he nowhere mentions the ever-increasing need for tightened belts which his model implies. Sinclair (1988: 127–33) supports Markle's model by suggesting various reasons for the continuing attractiveness of the jury as compared with the assembly, but this does not really get to the heart of the problem: if, as Markle accepts, the value of 3 obols in comparison with wages was steadily declining, he needs to establish not simply a continuing but an increasing attractiveness, in order to compensate for the decline in value.

years. But [158] after this period the situation changed: probably at this time, and certainly at some time in the fourth century, the Athenians were able and willing to raise assembly-pay to 6 and 9 obols.[59]

If we dismiss as inconclusive the arguments from statistics and from the indirect literary material, we are left with only the evidence on which Jones relied: the tone of the speeches themselves, and the social values implicit in them. But it is here that Markle's critique of Jones is least convincing (1985: 281–92). He begins from the same assumption as his opponent, that the crucial question is one of income, and the crucial distinction is that between those who do and those who do not have to work for their living. He then assembles every piece of evidence which had led Jones and his followers to argue for a prosperous jury, and he asserts, one by one, that these have been misrepresented. Sometimes he is successful: for instance, he rightly notes that it is not really Straton's poverty which embarrasses Demosthenes.[60] Sometimes his arguments are less attractive: he relies heavily on the orators' frequent use of the phrase *to plēthos to humeteron*, used to describe the democracy (*plēthos* is a virtual synonym for *dēmos*)—a phrase which he translates as 'the majority of you' or 'the mass of you',[61] arguing that the majority of jurors present must therefore have been members of the 'common people'. But in Athenian political thought the court is a part of the democracy and is therefore necessarily democratic, whatever the personal opinions of individual jurors may have been, and the phrase is therefore a commonplace in the orators to describe 'your democracy'.

On some individual points therefore Markle is probably correct; on others he is less convincing. But even though his work has in general been favourably received by subsequent scholars,[62] I find his overall approach here unsatisfactory. When he is unable to explain

---

[59] The other possible explanation of the failure to raise jury-pay is that it was not primarily a subsistence allowance (see the final section of this paper at n. 101 below.)

[60] Markle 1985: 287, n. 40 (anticipated by Dover 1974: 34, n. 1) against A. Jones 1957: 36. For Straton, see Dem. 21. 95.

[61] Markle 1985: 282 and 285, on Lys. 28. 1 and Ant. 5. 8 respectively.

[62] Powell (1988: 302) calls Jones' social values 'inconclusive', and accepts Markle's arguments about the level of pay. Hansen (1987: 47–8), discussing the assembly, agrees with Markle (cited with approval at 1987: 48, n. 326) that the crucial factor determining the attractiveness of pay is its purchasing power (*sc.* as a subsistence-allowance). Sinclair (1988: 124–7) makes clear in passing (p. 127) his support

any of Jones' passages, he gets round the problem by lumping all Jones' evidence together and dismissing it collectively as 'flattery and entertainment' (Markle 1985: 281), intended to keep the jury interested. This is, to say the least, high-handed, and the problem comes to a head when Markle discusses Dover's point about Demosthenes' remarks concerning schoolmasters, clerks, and decorators, which he seeks to discount by saying that Demosthenes' opponent Aeschines started the insults (pp. 283). This may be true, but it raises two further questions: first, why did Aeschines bring up the question of family background, and secondly, why did Demosthenes choose to respond in these terms? Any schoolmasters, clerks, and decorators among the jury can hardly have found it terribly flattering, let alone entertaining.

REINTERPRETING THE ATHENIAN JURY

Perhaps the greatest difficulty in the theories of both Jones and Markle lies in their assumptions about Athenian class-structure. In the case of Jones, who was a British scholar, the class-structure assumed is that of Britain in the 1950s: he speaks of the [159] 'middle class' (1967: 124) and of the 'working man' (p. 37), in terms which suggest the existence of a working class with a separate culture, and separate values and attitudes from those of the middle class; it is interesting to note that Richard Hoggart's pioneering study of British working-class culture was published in the same year as Jones' book (1957). Jones' terminology therefore invites comparisons with modern Britain which are the more inappropriate for being subconscious.

Markle, on the other hand, is an American scholar, and for a social historian this is to some extent an advantage: social status in the United States is defined in terms not of class but of income, and inequality of income has existed throughout history. Surely, therefore, it is unobjectionable when Markle speaks of 'the poor' and (by implication) 'the rich'? On further examination, however, Markle's terminology

for Markle, but focuses on the attitudes taken towards taxpayers in Lysias' speeches 28 (delivered to the assembly) and 29 (a court-speech), in an attempt to determine their relative importance within these two bodies; this is an interesting and important discussion, but with so few assembly speeches extant it must remain speculative.

contains its own hidden assumptions, as misleading as those of his opponent; and paradoxically, it is the clarity of his analysis which has created its own problems. For his distinction between 'rich' and 'poor' to be analytically useful, Markle places a sharp division at the level of income above which a man need no longer work for his living. But the very sharpness of this division leads him into two undefended but unavoidable assumptions. In the first place, Markle's groups are internally homogeneous: that is, the only important social distinction lies between those who do and those who do not have to work for their living, and the values of, for instance, a poor farmer are identical to those of a poor craftsman. Secondly the groups are wholly discrete: peasant and richer farmer perceive themselves as being on opposite sides of the great divide, and there is no continuity, either in personnel or—more importantly—in attitudes, between the two groups.

The assumption that Athens can safely be analysed according to a bipartite division, whether of class or of income, has been challenged by several scholars. Finley (1985*b*: 38) indeed argues that there can be no such thing as a successful class ideology, because to be successful an ideology must appeal across social divisions: he notes that every social group in antiquity approved of the acquisition of wealth. Few scholars would accept without qualification the full implications of this theoretical argument, but a number of social historians have argued on empirical grounds that there was at Athens only one social class, one set of values in which the whole citizen body concurred.

Adkins, for instance, is interested in the terminology used in Greek to describe moral values, and is struck by the conservatism which allowed the rich to set the linguistic agenda for the rest of the community to follow:[63] terms of praise such as *agathoi* ('the good') are used by both rich and poor to refer to the rich, and the poor are described by such pejorative terms as *kakoi* or *ponēroi* ('base' or 'evil'). Adkins perhaps takes this argument too far, particularly when he argues (1972: 119–26) that Athenian juries placed more emphasis on a litigant's *agatha* (previous benefactions) than on his *dikaia* (the justice of his case); if the jury were really this deferential, then we would expect the rhetorical theorists to have placed far more

---

[63] See in general Adkins 1960, esp. 195–214, who applies the theory in more detail to political behaviour in Adkins 1972.

stress than they do on the relating of benefactions.[64] Nevertheless, Adkins' general conclusion is important: the conservatism of this linguistic agenda meant that there was no alternative set of values to which the poor could aspire.

Similar conclusions have been reached from a different perspective by Ehrenberg (1951: 143–5). Greek has a number of terms meaning 'trader', and earlier scholars had generally assumed that the distinction between *emporos* and *kapēlos* was one of scale; they therefore spoke of separate classes of wholesale and of retail traders, with all the social distinctions [160] that this would imply. Ehrenberg objected, however, that the terms are not used in this way: there is no real social distinction between the two types of trader; they form a single 'middle class', perhaps with a higher and a lower section, but a single social unit. He further argued that this single social unit included not just traders but craftsmen and farmers as well: all had the same political interests and social ambitions.

Dover has applied a similar argument, but only tentatively, to the question of the jury. Following Ehrenberg, he argues at one point (1974: 37–41) that there may have been no Athenian working class; elsewhere (p. 34) he suggests as a possible explanation for the social values assumed by the orators that those members of the jury who were not prosperous may have liked to be treated as if they were. But he does not connect the two ideas, and he prefers to withdraw his second suggestion in favour of a jury which was largely composed of prosperous men.

These arguments can be extended, and applied to the jury. Traders, as Ehrenberg noted, form a single social class, but the same can be said of farmers. The vast majority of Athenian citizens seem to have been farmers,[65] and of these, the vast majority can be described as peasants or subsistence farmers. 'Peasant' here is applied in a popular

---

[64] Aristotle's *Rhetoric* only mentions liturgies once (2. 23. 17), and they are not in context benefactions.

[65] Isager and Hansen (1975: 50–2) believe that more than half the population of Attica made a living as artisans or traders rather than as farmers. This estimate is in my opinion substantially exaggerated, and relies on a belief (which I would reject) that Athens had a developed market economy, but even its authors assume that a substantial majority of Athenian citizens were farmers: most of their artisans and traders are metics (resident aliens) or slaves. See further n. 103 below.

rather than a technical anthropological sense,[66] and the use of 'subsistence farmer' is not intended to suggest that the Athenian peasant never bought or sold any foodstuffs: rather, that he aimed to produce all the food which he required to feed his household. If he had a surplus of any one article, he could sell it; if a shortage, he would need to buy; but the aim was *autarkeia* (self-sufficiency),[67] rather than specialization in cash crops.

The majority of Athenian citizens were peasants in this sense, but it is significant that there is no convenient Greek word for 'peasant'.[68] An *autourgos*, 'one who works [the land] himself', appears as a major character in Euripides' *Electra*, and a speech made off-stage by another is reported in the same author's *Orestes* (917–30), but the word is not common in Greek.[69] Normally, a peasant will have been described as a *geōrgos*, a farmer. But *geōrgos* does not mean simply 'peasant': a subsistence farmer was a *geōrgos*, but so was a rich landowner like Ischomachos, the hero of Xenophon's *Oeconomicus*. This is a lexical point, but it has obvious ideological significance: if you are a subsistence farmer, you will tend to see your interests as being the same as those of the gentleman farmer. Consequently, the vast majority of the citizen body (and citizens, after all, were the only group entitled to sit on the jury) will have tended to share the same values and aspirations.

This conclusion is reinforced if we consider the effect of slavery on Athenian society. Many scholars have discussed the social implications of ancient slavery, but much of the [161] attention has focused on the Roman world. There has been particular interest in the effect of slavery at the lower end of Roman society. Did non-slave-owning citizens see themselves as natural allies of the slaves or of the

[66] Anthropologists would tend to restrict the term 'peasant' to members of a subculture which feels itself to be economically or politically dependant on a larger society. Osborne (1985a: 183–9, cf. 142) rightly emphasizes that it is the absence of a sharp distinction between town and country that makes Athens so exceptional; if 'peasant' is used in a strict sense, there were no peasants in classical Attica. See, however, Millett 1984: 84–115 (esp. 90–3), who argues for a broader use of the term.

[67] The Athenian literary elite appear to have retained the peasant outlook, and this may be significant as an instance of shared values: the peasant virtue of self-sufficiency or *autarkeia* forms the philosophical basis of much of Aristotle's social and economic theory.

[68] I owe this point to Prof. Anthony Snodgrass.

[69] Carter 1986: 76–98 translates 'the peasant farmer' back into Greek consistently as the '*autourgos*', without recognizing the rarity of the Greek word in our sources.

slave-owners? Debate has centred on the case of Pedanius Secundus, the prefect of the City of Rome (Tacitus, *Ann.* 14. 42–5); when all his slaves were executed for failing to prevent him being murdered, the *plebs urbana*, or city poor, rioted on behalf of the slaves, from which W. L. Westermann (1955: 114) deduced a 'community of interest' between free poor and slaves. De Ste Croix (1981: 372) stresses, however, that this is our only evidence; but Finley (1980: 102–3), though hesitating to follow Westermann all the way, nevertheless accepts that 'he was looking in the right place', and he emphasizes that many of the free poor of Rome were themselves ex-slaves or their descendants.

None of these scholars distinguishes here between Roman and Athenian slavery.[70] But two important factors, one probable and one certain, should make us pause before equating the two. In the first place, it seems probable that Athenian masters were less ready to free their slaves than were their Roman counterparts. This is the type of assertion which cannot be proved, for lack of quantifiable evidence, but Augustus was certainly concerned to reduce the scale of manumission in contemporary Rome, whereas no Greek author speaks of it as an Athenian social problem.[71] The second point is more clear-cut: freed slaves at Athens became metics (resident aliens), whereas freed slaves at Rome became citizens.[72] This suggests, therefore, that we should expect to find at Athens a far more rigid juridical divide between the poor citizens and slaves than is suggested for Rome by the case of Pedanius Secundus.[73] Obviously there are

[70] Jones 1957: 19 suggests, on the basis of two acts of enfranchisement, that a similar 'sense of fellow-feeling' existed between Athenian slaves and poor citizens, but his evidence is not convincing. In the first of these acts, it is only the *Ath. Pol.* who tells us tendentiously that Thrasybulus' intended beneficiaries in 403/2 were 'mostly slaves' (40.2). The second is the mass liberation and enfranchisement of the slaves who fought in the battle of Arginusae in 406, but this is the exception which breaks all the rules, and serves to indicate the strength of the immediate crisis; even after the battle of Chaeronea in 338, Hyperides proposed freedom and not enfranchisement.

[71] Suet. *Augustus* 40. 3–4; for details of the laws, see Gaius, *Institutes* 1. 38, 42. Athenian social critics do not speak of too many slaves being freed, but of slaves being 'too free' (see the examples cited in the following paragraph of this paper).

[72] Admittedly the citizen rights of a *libertus* (freed slave) at Rome were restricted, but any child born to him after manumission was *ingenuus* (free born) with the full rights of citizenship.

[73] Dover (1974: 34) does suggest that the existence of slavery allowed every Athenian to feel in some sense part of an elite, but he does not acknowledge the importance of Athens' failure to manumit and enfranchise.

exceptions to this rule, but most of these exceptions fall into a few groups, and were numerically few enough to be of little social or ideological significance.[74] Public slaves were in a class of their own, as in the case of Pittalakos, who clearly had the capacity to sue in his own name. *Chōris oikountes* formed another special group; this was the term used to describe slaves permitted by their owners to work independently, paying a flat rental (*apophora*) to the master and keeping any further profits of their labour. Slaves in managerial positions seem to have been similarly privileged: it is at least possible that Lampis the shipowner's agent was still a slave when he was allowed to witness before an arbitrator;[75] and we [162] know of two slave bank managers, Pasion and later Phormion (*APF* 427–32), who not only gained their freedom but became so rich that their state-benefactions won them the citizenship. But these exceptions are important precisely as exceptions.

At times, of course, it suited the Athenian self-image to claim that democracy was notable for the mild way in which it treated slaves. Opponents of the democracy make this a criticism: the Old Oligarch[76] complains that at Athens you cannot hit a slave (*sc.* belonging to somebody else), and explains that this is because poor citizens are so badly dressed that they would risk being struck in error; Plato (*Rep.* 563b4–d1) sarcastically claims that not only the slaves but even the domestic animals in a democracy enjoy (*sc.* excessive) liberty. But this is the viewpoint of the rich; a poor citizen might have expressed himself differently. It was admittedly true—indeed notorious—that Athenian law protected slaves as well as free men against *hubris* (gross assault). The orators found this surprising, and Demosthenes uses it

[74] Ehrenberg (1951: 173–5), Austin and Vidal-Naquet (1977: 101–3, on *chōris oikountes*). The case of Pittalakos is described by Aeschines 1. 54–62.

[75] In Dem. 34.18, Lampis is permitted to witness before the arbitrator. It is not clear whether he can do this because he is a particularly privileged type of slave (*chōris oikōn*), or because he is involved in a particularly flexible type of legal procedure (*dikē emporikē*), and the latter alternative was proposed by Gernet (1955a: 162–3). It is indeed possible that Lampis is not really a slave: he is described as an *oiketēs*, the normal term for a slave (34. 5), but this may simply mean that he is an ex-slave, or that the term is being used loosely to describe a servant; certainly it is difficult to see how a slave could be described as a *nauklēros* (shipowner) in his own right, as at 34. 6.

[76] [Xen.] *Ath. Pol.* 1. 10–12: we may wonder why he is so disappointed at not being permitted to do this.

to demonstrate the mildness of Athenian law, but his flamboyant argument here rapidly discredits itself.[77] It seems more likely that this provision served to protect the owner as much as the slave, in that to dishonour a slave is to dishonour his master (Fisher 1990; Murray 1990). Certainly the law seems to have afforded the slave little protection in practice: a story told by Apollodoros implies that tying and beating an intruder would only constitute *hubris* if he were free (Dem. 53.16). Most revealing perhaps is the brutal frankness of Demosthenes himself in another context: a citizen cannot be struck, but a slave is answerable in his body for any offence (Dem. 22. 55, a statement made precisely in defence of the rights of free citizens). This distinction was indeed institutionalized in Athenian court practice: a slave could not be a witness, and if his evidence was required, it could be received only if it was obtained under torture—thus emphasizing to the juror his privileged position. The juridical divide between slave and citizen suggests that in this respect it is Athens and not Rome which was most like the American South, and in the South it was the non-slave-owners who manned the slave patrols (Genovese 1974: 22). In the words of a pro-slavery pamphlet, 'African slavery... makes every white man in some sense a lord' (Stampp 1956: 104, quoting a successful appeal by slave-owners to poor whites).

Any society in which the entire citizen body perceives itself as a privileged class will tend to define its social values in terms of the defence of privilege; and ideology and social attitudes within the citizen body of such a society will tend to be unifying rather than divisive factors. That is not to say that social values will necessarily be consistent, and there are clear contradictions within the values esteemed at Athens. Carter has devoted a recent book (1986) to a study of Athenian *apragmosunē* or 'quietism'; and *apragmosunē*, as Carter rightly sees, is the ideological contradiction of the traditional 'democratic' virtue of active participation in politics. But Carter then assumes that different social values must necessarily be espoused by different social groups, and he locates three homes for *apragmosunē*: 'noble youths', 'rich quietists', and above all peasants. But this is

---

[77] Dem. 21. 47–50 claims that 'the barbarians' will be so impressed at this that they will all queue up to register the Athenians collectively as their protectors (*proxenoi*). Aeschin. 1. 17 gives a different rationalization.

surely a false assumption, and it is more likely that the tension [163] between political participation and *apragmosunē* will have gone on within each individual. Much of Carter's evidence for *apragmosunē* comes from the speeches of litigants, where the purpose is clear: to plead *apragmosunē* is to avoid accusations that you are politically active for what you can get out of it.

There is no need here to follow Harding (1981), who seems ready to deny the very existence of *apragmosunē* as a political virtue, but he is surely correct to argue that it was not vested in any particular social group. Harding is attacking traditional attempts to interpret Athenian politics in terms of the so-called *nautikos ochlos* ('naval mob'): according to this model, foreign policy was dominated by a radical mob of unemployed would-be rowers from the port of Piraeus who packed out the assembly and voted for war, while the industrious peasantry stayed on their farms and suffered. By the standards of other Greek *poleis*, Attica (the sovereign territory of Athens) certainly covered a large area: inhabitants of the most distant demes,[78] such as Oenoe, Rhamnus, and Sunium, lived some 20–5 miles from the city, and can only have visited Athens occasionally. But by no means every Athenian citizen lived so far away from power.

It is now generally agreed that the Athenian demes, which Cleisthenes in 508/7 had made the basis of representation in the *boulē* or council, were and continued to be centres of population and not just of administration (Osborne 1985: 47–63; Whitehead 1986: 352–8, 233–4). If this is correct, then representation on the *boulē* can be used as a rough index of population distribution, because *bouleutai* (members of the *boulē*) were returned on a regional basis, with each deme having a fixed quota in proportion to its size. Examination of the map of Attica suggests, as Hansen has observed, that roughly one-third of the citizen body lived within 6 miles of the city as the crow flies, and a further third lived within a further 6 miles.[79] Some

[78] Athenian demes were local communities, but unlike English villages, they had important constitutional roles. For instance, a man's citizen-rights depended on his being a member of a deme: see generally Osborne 1985*a* and Whitehead 1986.

[79] Hansen 1987: 8–12 (cf. previously 1983*c*: 235–7). For the locations of the Athenian demes, see Traill 1975: 14–23 and tables I–X (bouleutic quota), 37–54 with map 1 (location), and 133–4 (addenda). [For the effect of post-507 migration on the argument here, see the 2005 retrospective, below.]

of the conclusions which Hansen draws from this should perhaps be treated with caution,[80] but this central observation is sound. Piraeus is some 5 miles from the city, and nearly one-third of the population had better access to power than the putative 'naval mob'. The massive deme of Acharnae, home of farmers and of charcoal-burners, is only 7 miles from Athens; and it is Acharnae and not Piraeus which Aristophanes, in his first extant play, selects as the home of his chorus of warmongers. Above all, there were several periods, for instance 413–404, during which the peasants were driven from their farms and immured in the city by ravaging Spartan armies. If the *nautikos ochlos* theory were correct, therefore, Athens during these periods would have had a 'quietist' foreign policy, but there is no sign of this. It might, of course, be objected that war-patriotism has prevailed in this instance over class-interest, but that will not salvage the theory: it is precisely Athenian foreign policy during the war that the theory was intended to explain.[81]

[164] SOCIAL VALUES, THE ORATORS, AND THE ATHENIAN CLASS STRUCTURE

Apragmosunē, therefore, should be seen not as the distinctive ideal of a particular social class, but as one of a number of ideals held simultaneously by Athenians in general. And examination of the speeches confirms this impression that social values at Athens were a matter of consensus rather than of conflict. The speeches repeatedly display what to us would be 'middle-class values', but none of these are values that would exclude the peasant. A brief selection will be sufficient to illustrate the most significant attitudes. Education is

[80] Hansen (1987: 10–11) appears to confuse two senses of the term *thētes*, as census-class and as occupation. But those who are too poor to serve as hoplites (cf. n. 10 above) are not necessarily all hired labourers; and even though he himself notes that many city-dwellers were themselves farmers walking out to their fields, the way that his argument is developed (1987: 8–11) tends to identify city-dwellers with artisans and labourers.

[81] Most recently by Carter (1986: 97, 194), who suggests that the peace proposals of 429 and 411 (though unsuccessful) were made because the peasants held a temporary majority in the assembly.

consistently a good thing: Aeschines (2. 141, 166–7) accuses Demosthenes of speaking about Homer as if the jury were uneducated; Demosthenes responds (18. 127, esp. 257–62) by contrasting his own (expensive) education with Aeschines' early career as a Dickensian Smike. It needs to be emphasized that this attitude to education is not confined to the later orators, as Jones' theory requires: already in the fifth century, a speaker claims that his father was expensively educated whereas an opponent was not (Lys. 20. 11). Indeed, there is no evidence for any significant change in social values between the early and the later orators.[82] Lack of *paideia* (education) is shameful: Aeschines expects the jury to approve his vituperative description of a foreign envoy as 'shameful and uneducated' (3. 117, 130). Words such as *kosmios* and *sōphrōn*, which denote respectability, are always used in a favourable sense: Lysias attacks various opponents for their failure in this regard (14. 41–5; 26. 3). The respectability of one's female relatives is particularly important: Lysias (3. 6) and Demosthenes (40. 57) relate at length how the opponent's behaviour has shamed or shocked their client's womenfolk, and they clearly expect this plea to arouse the anger of the jury. Also favourable is family pedigree: Andocides' final plea to the jury is that to convict him would be to wipe out one of the oldest families in Athens (1. 146–50), and to marry into a good family can be better (or at least more creditable) than to marry money (Lys. 19. 14–15).

It is important to remember that even a humbly born citizen is still *autochthōn* ('born of the soil of Attica'), unlike metics or slaves. So the frequent attacks on opponents for servile or alien birth (e.g. Lys. 13. 8; 30. 2; Aeschin. 2. 79) will not have irritated the poor men among the jury; in fact quite the reverse. The majority of our literary sources reflect the viewpoint of the large landowner, from whose perspective the peasant is the next thing up from a slave;[83] but from the peasant's point of view, he is the next thing down from a large landowner.

On the other hand, money is a good thing, and there is no shame involved in having it—at least in moderation (see below at n. 87).

---

[82] There are changes in political values—for instance the charge of oligarchy has a far greater use and a far more specific meaning in 403–*c*.380 (being connected not with present disposition but with a single past action, behaviour during the oligarchy of 404/3)—but that is a different matter.

[83] The most notable, if admittedly tendentious, examples are Plato, *Rep.* 563b4–7 and [Xen.] *Ath. Pol.* 1. 10–12.

The self-made man is occasionally a figure of suspicion,[84] but nobody is ashamed of inherited wealth: the typical client of Isaeus is a rich man who is trying to become still richer by inheritance, at times from very distant relatives indeed (esp. Isae. 11); and Demosthenes devotes five speeches to his own attempt to recover his patrimony (Dem. 27–31). The poorer liturgy-payer, who must presumably be reasonably well off but can be depicted as burdened by heavy taxes, is a figure to whom Demosthenes [165] expects the jury to be sympathetic rather than hostile (Dem. 22. 65); and it is even claimed that an estate worth 45 *mnai*, or three-quarters of a talent, is 'not easy to live off'.[85] This may be economically realistic: the property is the patrimony of two brothers, and Demosthenes is (perhaps deliberately) ambiguous as to whether this means 45 *mnai* each, or 45 *mnai* shared; if the latter, an estate worth 23 *mnai* is only just sufficient to qualify its owner for service as a hoplite or heavy-infantryman (see n. 10 above). It is nonetheless significant that the *rentier* mentality can be so safely paraded before a jury. Similarly, owning slaves (and living off the proceeds of their labour) is everyone's ambition: the crippled pensioner of Lysias 24 is probably richer than he admits, but it is not apparently inconsistent with his persona of abject poverty to say, 'I am so poor that I cannot even afford a slave to take over the work for me'.[86] Crucially, however, there is no hostility to poor men as such. There is hostility to certain types of poor men (for instance, Dover's schoolmasters, clerks, and decorators), but that is another matter.

At first sight, this may not seem a particularly extensive catalogue of values, but many of the attitudes are illustrated repeatedly, and the list I have given is enough to support three important conclusions. First, the attitudes displayed are those which we would describe as 'middle-class values', and it is these that make Markle's case untenable: it is not enough to describe them as 'light relief'. But secondly,

---

[84] Lys. 27. 9–11 and 30. 27 attacks (politically active) opponents for their sudden rise from poverty to wealth. The implication here is that they have become rich through embezzlement or receipt of bribes; but Dem. 57. 30–1 and esp. 57. 52 suggests that the speaker is acutely embarrassed about the fact that he is rich whereas his parents had been poor.

[85] Dem. 42. 22: *zēn* here presumably means 'to live off (*sc.* without having to labour with one's own hands)'.

[86] Lys. 24. 6: for discussion of the speaker's financial status, see Bizos 1967: 130.

there is no sign of any change in values, and thirdly, there is no hostility to the poor; and both of these facts cast doubt on Jones' argument. The problem recedes, however, if we regard peasant and rich farmer as members of the same class, such that 'middle-class values' become a matter of consensus throughout citizen society.

To illustrate how this model might be developed, let us examine a famous remark about the role of women in Athenian society: 'we keep *hetairai* [courtesans] for pleasure, *pallakai* [mistresses] for our daily physical needs, and wives to bear us citizen children and to be the guardians of what is inside [*sc.* our households]' ([Dem.] 59. 122). Now of course a peasant could not afford a *hetaira* or *pallakē*; he would have to be content with *pornai* (cheap tarts). Jones' response would be, 'a prosperous jury'; Markle would have to reply, 'light relief'. But whether you can afford a thing does not necessarily determine your attitude to it. Griffith-Jones' mistake was not that his jury did not have servants, but that they did not share his paternalistic view of the proper relationship between employer and servant. Similarly, this remark need not have alienated the Athenian peasant, provided he aspired to the same view of the role of women in society: 'if only I had the money, that would be what I would do.'

This leaves open the question of whether any class-divisions between citizens can be identified, and here we are on more dangerous ground. I would tentatively identify two such divisions, but I would emphasize that these divisions seem to have been subordinate to the general consensus of society. One is a gulf between 'everybody else' and 'the very rich indeed' or 'the aristocracy'. Normally this division is latent, but it is exploited several times in cases of *hubris* (see at n. 77 above). As Jones noticed, this is what is happening in Demosthenes' attack on Meidias, where the distinction is stressed between the 'filthy rich' and 'the rest of us', and it is also the position adopted by Isocrates against Lochites.[87] But there is another, more interesting case where it seems that the same potential class divide is being opened up. This is Aeschines' prosecution of Timarchus. The charge here was [166] of homosexual prostitution; Dover (1978: 22–4) rightly notes that it is prostitution rather than homosexuality that

[87] Meidias: Dem. 21, as interpreted by A. Jones 1957: 36, followed by Dover 1974: 34 and n. 1. Lochites: Isoc. 20. esp. 11, 15, 19.

was legally the offence, and on this basis suggests that it was not homosexuality but its commercialization that was socially unacceptable. But Aeschines' tactics seem to be more elaborate than this: as Dover points out, he deliberately confuses propensity with prostitution. He does not attack homosexuality directly: it would be difficult for any member of the political elite wholly to repudiate a traditionally aristocratic practice (cf. Ehrenberg 1951: 100–2); and he is careful to admit that he has himself at least dabbled in it (Aeschin. 1. 136), partly because his opponents are threatening to read out his (*sc.* homoerotic) love-poems in open court, but perhaps also to make clear that he is not a fanatic. But the thrust of his case is that homosexuality as allegedly committed by Timarchus is itself prostitution, and the tone of his argument is revealing. With a titillated sense of outrage, he adopts the characteristic middle-class pose of 'Disgusted, Tunbridge Wells' against the characteristically aristocratic pattern of social behaviour in which homosexuality played such a part.[88] It may also be in an attempt to arouse class prejudice that Aeschines charges Timarchus with squandering his inheritance. It is not fully clear what Timarchus was doing, but it seems likely that he had been converting his estates into liquid capital to facilitate tax-evasion. Tax-evasion is the characteristic behaviour of a very few extremely wealthy Athenians (such as the elder Demosthenes): behaviour to which poor and medium-rich farmers are not going to be sympathetic, and which Timarchus therefore could not afford to admit.[89]

The second possible class-division is to be found between those who obtain their living directly from the land and everybody else: on the one hand farmers, and on the other hand artisans, shopkeepers, and traders. This is a contrast commonly drawn by Greek philosophers, and it may have been an attitude shared by society as a whole. Xenophon is very clear that farming and warfare are proper occupations for a gentleman, and that these are completely different

[88] For the significance of homosexuality as it developed in the archaic period within the nexus of gymnasium, symposium, hunting, and courtship that together made up aristocratic culture, see Murray 1980: 203–4.

[89] Aeschin. 1. 97–100. According to Aeschines, the process had already been started by Timarchus' father Arizelos (1. 101). The tax here is the liturgy, to which only the richest were liable (n. 10 above).

from the *banausikai technai* or 'vulgar trades' which spoil both body and soul (*Oeconomicus* 4, *passim*). The passage is analysed by Vernant (1983: 252–3), who observes that for Xenophon 'trades' depend on training and expertise, whereas success in both farming and warfare is a gift of the gods; in Xenophon's eyes farming is not really a 'trade'. This ties in closely with a common argument in the political theory of both Plato and Aristotle:[90] politics is a *technē* (craft or trade), but no man should have two trades, because he will not be able to do them properly, so 'tradesmen' should play no part in politics; this should be confined to gentlemen, whose expertise is in household management (*oikonomia*: not, of course, a 'trade'), and who therefore will be well qualified to run the household of the state. But is farming a 'trade' within the meaning of this argument, or is it a part of 'household management'? Plato is not fully certain: in the *Republic* he does at times say that his guardian class (who are to govern the state) are not to be farmers, but he is far more interested in emphasizing that they are not to be artisans;[91] in the *Laws*, where there is no longer a class of guardians, his citizens are to be [167] farmers rather than tradesman (842e6–850d2, esp. 846d2–3). For Aristotle, moreover, farming is a natural occupation, and therefore good; trade is unnatural and improper (*Pol.* 1256a40–b2, cf. 1256b40–1257a5). Certainly to ban farmers from politics completely would be difficult for a Greek to conceive, because it would rule out not simply the peasantry but the vast bulk of the landowning aristocracy. It is, of course, difficult to say how far the statements of the philosophers accord with popular social theories; if anything, it is likely that the views of an amateur like Xenophon may be a more reliable index than those of Plato. This hypothesis is supported by an anecdote told twice by Plutarch about the Spartan Agesilaus, which seems to indicate that for Plutarch, at least, farming was not a trade.[92] This may, therefore, be an instance where the ambiguity of the term 'farmer' tells in favour of the peasant: if the

[90] Plato, *Rep.* 370b4–c6; *Laws* 846d1–847b6; Arist. *Pol.* 1252b1–5.

[91] Guardians are not to be farmers or artisans: *Rep.* 420e1–421a9 (implicit), 468a5–7. Guardians are distinguished only from artisans: *Rep.* 406e4–407a6 (with 406e1), 434a2–b8, 434c7–10, 440e10–441a2, 456d8–10, cf. also 495c8–e2.

[92] Plut. *Agesilaus* 26. 5, repeated in *Moralia* 213f–214b: to prove that only the Spartans were 'proper' soldiers, Agesilaus separated Spartans from allies and ordered all the 'potters, smiths, builders, and those who followed any other *technē*' to stand;

landowning aristocracy believe that the proper way to exercise power is not through the *technē* of an artisan but through the *oikonomia* of a gentleman farmer, then the subsistence farmer also should share this role. Presumably this is the explanation for Demosthenes' offensive remarks about schoolmasters, clerks, and decorators: subsistence farmers do not see themselves primarily as poor men, but as farmers.

There are, admittedly, two passages which speak of the assembly as if it consisted largely of artisans, but in each case the speaker has an axe to grind. Plato takes it as the height of depravity that the assembly is prepared to listen to artisans and traders, and Xenophon's Socrates attempts to encourage a nervous young aristocratic would-be politician with the argument, 'are you afraid of them?'[93] More significant I think is the description of the assembly in the *Ecclesiazusae*, where a crowd of people assumed on account of their pale faces to be shoemakers is treated as unusual (they are in fact women in disguise); these pale-faced shoemakers are opposed in debate by the men from the country, and the speaker is surprised that the latter were in a minority.[94]

THE IMPLICATIONS OF JURY-PAY

This brings us back to the problem of pay. A full treatment of jury-pay would need to cover a large number of aspects: the rate of pay; the age of the jurors; their occupation; the extent to which work done by slaves or women created additional leisure for the would-be juror; the distance which the potential juror had to travel; the status of jurors; and the ideology of jury-service. This is not the place for a

virtually all the allies stood, but none of the Spartans. If this story has any basis in reality, the allied contingents would presumably have included many peasants, whereas Spartans did not farm their land in person. But the list is significant as evidence that farmers, in Plutarch's view, are not tradesmen.

[93] Plato, *Protagoras* 319c8–d6; Xen. *Memorabilia* 3. 7. 6: I owe this point to Dr Paul Millett. Xenophon does, incidentally, include farmers (presumably peasants) as one of his despised groups; cf. Plato's uncertainty over the status of peasants, above at n. 91.

[94] Ar. *Eccles.* 385–7, 431–4. Shoemakers were notoriously pale (schol. Ar. *Peace* 1310: I owe this reference to Dr Mogens Hansen), but Xen. *Oec.* 4. 2–3 regards pallor as the occupational hazard not merely of shoemakers but of all artisans.

full discussion of each of these topics: some have been discussed at varying stages during this paper; others will be ignored, because they neither confirm nor refute the model which I am [168] trying to construct.[95] Here I wish simply to emphasize one point, because it has previously been neglected; and this neglect has seriously weakened the argument both of Jones and particularly of Markle.[96]

The point here is an obvious one, which has frequently been made about the modern jury. Cornish notes the unfairness of the system today (1968: 58–9): if you are paid a daily or a weekly wage, your employer will normally dock it when you are absent on jury-service; if you are paid a monthly or quarterly salary, he will not. Consequently, the importance of the 3 obols is not simply its purchasing power, but how it compares with what you would have got instead. Jury-pay is likely, therefore, to have been much more attractive to the peasant than to the wage-labourer or artisan or shopkeeper, for two reasons. First, if a shopkeeper or artisan takes a day off, he stands in theory to lose 1/365 of his potential annual income; if a peasant does so, he will (except at the busiest times of year) lose little if anything of his crop-yield. Secondly, even if a peasant's yield is reduced, he does not see that loss on a daily basis, so the 3 obols is perceived as a bonus.

Obviously the contrast is crude. It assumes that the typical shopkeeper is an artisan producing and selling his own wares—an assumption which is likely to have been broadly correct.[97] More dangerous, it assumes that the typical artisan-cum-shopkeeper could sell enough of his wares to justify full production; but to the extent that demand was inadequate for this, he could afford to leave his wife or slave in charge of the shop and take the day off for jury-service: the work performed by slaves and

[95] I have not discussed in this paper the question of age. The impression of elderly jurors given by Aristophanes' *Wasps* may well have some truth in it: if 3 obols was attractive to peasants because they had a low marginal return for additional work, it would have been particularly attractive to those who were past their physical prime. On the other hand, the minimum age for jury-service was 30, whereas any adult citizen over 18 could attend the assembly. This will have had a significant effect on the age of the jury: using the model life table recommended by Hansen (1985: 11–13), it would mean that 37.2% of potential assembly-members were too young for jury-service. This may be part of the reason for Aristophanes' caricature of the elderly juror.

[96] Markle's statistical argument (above, pp. 329–30) depends on the assumption that jury-pay is essentially a subsistence payment.

[97] Ehrenberg 1951: 120–1, notes that the 'demagogues', whom modern scholars usually describe as 'manufacturers', are portrayed in comedy as 'sellers'.

women must be borne in mind. It ignores the existence of other forms of seasonal work apart from farming: during the winter, for instance, when maritime traders will have been laid up, they too may have found jury-service attractive. Furthermore, it ignores the extent to which farmers may have diversified into additional wage-labour: a peasant who can get part-time work, such as carting wood for instance, is less likely to be attracted onto the jury.

Nevertheless, the general contrast remains valid. It takes account of the different nature of the peasant economy from that of the artisan: to those living outside the cash economy, 3 obols is likely to have been more attractive than it was to those who conceive their normal earnings in cash terms.[98] It takes account also of the different nature of production in agriculture and manufacturing: if as an artisan you put in double the effort, you stand to produce double the goods; but it is characteristic of subsistence agriculture that there is a low marginal return for additional work,[99] and consequently what anthropologists have called a 'leisure-preference'.[100] We should not be misled by [169] the wishful thinking of Aristotle, who suggests that peasants ought to be too busy working on their farms to interfere in politics (*Pol.* 1292b25–9; see at n. 48 above). Clark and Haswell (1970: 142) show that in the eighteenth century the typical French peasant worked rather less than 200 days per year on his farm, and that during the same period the average working week in rural England was four days. Subsistence farming is highly labour-intensive at certain periods of the year, but even the workaholic Hesiod has to admit that in midwinter nobody but himself expects to work, and that in high summer even he is prepared to relax (cf. M. West 1978: 253).

The argument here, it should be emphasized, is not that no artisan or trader was ever to be found sitting on a jury: merely that jury-pay would have tended to be more attractive to the farmers, and that this confirms the impression given by our analysis of the social values which the orators appeal to. 'Farmers' in this context includes subsistence farmers.

[98] I owe this point to Prof. Keith Hopkins.

[99] I am not wholly convinced by the arguments of Jameson 1977 that Athenian agriculture was labour-intensive; given the low marginal return, some farmers may have preferred to combine a slightly lower yield with more days spent earning jury-pay: see further at n. 102 below.

[100] e.g. Clark and Haswell 1970: 112, and Grigg 1982: 98–9.

Presumably these would be the peasants and farmers living either in the city itself or within Hansen's radius of six or even twelve miles (above at n. 79). Pay was set at a level too low to be really attractive to the artisan or shopkeeper, and this may indeed have been deliberate. It was not a subsistence-payment, but a bonus, and so it continued to attract farmers even though it stayed static at 3 obols; it could afford to stay static, because it was still attracting them in sufficient numbers.[101]

One additional inference may perhaps be drawn. A peasant who is receiving regular injections of cash into his household budget can presumably afford to live on land that would otherwise be too small to sustain his family, while continuing to regard himself as a subsistence farmer. This may have demographic implications. Other things being equal, you might risk rearing an additional son, and therefore splitting your holding into smaller units. More significantly, we may need to revise our calculations of how many peasants the soil of Attica could support,[102] and I cannot agree with Hansen that the scale of Athenian grain imports disproves the existence of a subsistence economy.[103]

CONCLUSIONS

The conclusions of this paper are as follows. In the field of social history, the values and aspirations of Athenian citizens were a matter of consensus rather than of division. There may have been two separate classes, both small, set against the mass of the peasants and farmers: the very rich and the aristocracy, and the artisans and shopkeepers. In general, however, it would be impossible to write a study of Athenian working-class culture, partly because we lack the sources, but chiefly because there was no such separate culture.

---

[101] We therefore avoid the problem implicit in Markle's theory: see at n. 59 above.

[102] Contrast the calculations of e.g. Jameson 1977: 131.

[103] Hansen (1987: 12, n. 88) draws on the calculations of Garnsey (1985: 62–75) that Athens in a good year had to import half the grain consumed by the population of Attica, from which he infers that 'at least half the citizens (*sic*) ... had to buy their daily bread in the market'. But this is to assume that everybody buys either all or nothing, and that anybody who buys any has moved entirely from subsistence to cash economy. Compare the comments on *autarkeia* as an ideal, at n. 67 above.

In the field of political history, the bulk of the jury (and probably also of the assembly) was composed not of rich nor of poor, but of farmers (including peasants). Since these formed one class, we have no way of telling what proportion of these were very poor, fairly poor, fairly well off, or rich. These were the people who exercised passive political rights: that is not to say that they were the political leaders—a far more restricted circle—but they were the people who voted.

[170] More difficult to tie down is the relationship between social and political history. Athens certainly was constitutionally less democratic in the mid-fourth century.[104] Jones explained this shift in terms of a change in the social balance of the electorate (i.e. the jury), but as we have seen, the evidence is against such a change. There does, however, seem to have been a change in the social composition of the elite, and I hope to argue elsewhere that this is the real explanation for the change in the political temperature of Athens. But that is too large a question to raise at this stage in an article.[105]

APPENDIX: THE COMPOSITION OF THE ASSEMBLY

The subject of this paper has been the jury, but the assembly deserves separate notice, even if only in an appendix. A few scholars, such as Pickard-Cambridge and more recently Hansen and Sinclair, have drawn attention to the separate problems concerning the social composition of the assembly;[106] many,

---

[104] Note the increasing powers (*apophasis* is only the most striking) given during the 4th century to the Areopagus, and the movement from the middle of the century to reorganize Athenian finance towards efficiency and away from the use of the lot in appointments (cf. Rhodes 1980: 319–20, 309–15).

[105] I had hoped in a forthcoming paper to argue that by the mid-4th century what was left of the old aristocracy had combined with those who in the 5th century would have been 'demagogues' to work the system together, such that no one was left to supply the 'radical democrat' leadership. [See, however, the final paragraph of my 2005 retrospective, below.]

[106] Pickard-Cambridge (1914: 89–90) disliked the popular juries, and therefore contrasted them unfavourably with the assembly. Hansen (1983*b*: 137; 1987: 32–4, 47) suggests that 6 obols of assembly-pay provided full compensation for broken time, because the assembly sat for only part of the day (the 9 obols for 'special'

however, have simply applied the same arguments as to the jury.[107]

The most difficult question here concerns the level of pay, and in particular the changing relationship between jury-pay and assembly-pay. Jury-pay, it will be remembered, was introduced in *c.*450 at 2 obols, and raised to 3 obols in 425; it remained at 3 obols throughout the next century. Assembly-pay did not exist in the fifth century; it was introduced in the 390s at 1 obol, and raised to 2 and then to 3 obols by the end of the decade; we do not know anything about its level between 390 and *c.*330, when we hear that its value was at 6 obols, and 9 obols for a 'special' assembly (Jones 1957: 136–7; Markle 1985: 265, n. 1). The pattern is indeed difficult to explain, and it is complicated by lack of evidence. We possess roughly 100 court-speeches, but only twenty delivered to the assembly, and these twenty speeches (all relatively short) supply insufficient material for an analysis of their implicit social values; for the assembly, therefore, arguments based on pay can receive no support from this quarter (despite impressive attempts by Sinclair 1988: 119–27). But even pay raises further problems, both of evidence and of motive. When did the change from 3 to 6 and 9 obols occur? Was it a single increase, or did it take place in stages? Was the level of pay increased for economic or for political reasons?[108]

[171] Several patterns could be proposed to explain the relationship. Jones (1957: 37) suggested that the assembly was a boring place, making routine decisions which the courts could be expected to overthrow; consequently the level of pay had to be higher, in order to attract a reasonable quorum. Markle (1985: 285) similarly looks for an explanation in the boring nature of assembly-meetings; his

---

assemblies is therefore explained by the somewhat greater length of these meetings); there is an implicit but undeveloped contrast here with Hansen's earlier views on jury-pay, which apparently provided only partial compensation (Isager and Hansen 1975: 122, discussed at n. 23 above). Sinclair (1988: 114–35) rightly emphasizes the difference between the assembly and the courts, but his discussion (pp. 127–35) of the relative attractiveness of the two bodies to a potential voter relies heavily on his belief that consistently different attitudes towards taxpayers are displayed in assembly- and in court-speeches (pp. 119–27); as is noted in the following paragraph, however, the surviving assembly-speeches are too few and too short for such analysis to be secure.

[107] Ehrenberg 1951: 161; A. Jones 1957: 109; Markle 1985: 274, 285.

[108] These questions are discussed in the fourth section of this paper, esp. at nn. 41 and 51 above.

assumption that the economically necessary level of pay was 3 obols requires him to find non-economic reasons for the rise to 6 and 9 obols. It is probably true that the loss of an independent foreign policy after the defeat by Macedon in 338 BC had a more detrimental effect on the assembly than on the courts: the adversarial setting of a court, and its power instantly to determine the fate of even the greatest of political leaders, will have tended to sustain a sense of drama. But Hansen has shown that a typical meeting of the assembly was far shorter than the average court-sitting (1983*b*: 137; 1987: 32–4) and it is hard to imagine that the assembly was boring enough to justify double the pay for half the work.

Other possible explanations would involve the comparative size of the two bodies or the comparative frequency of their meetings (cf. above n. 106). Court-sittings were far more frequent than assembly-meetings,[109] and we might be tempted to suggest that the Athenians felt they could afford to pay more for a less frequent event. This argument is not persuasive, however, because the assembly required a much greater attendance than would be needed to man a single court. At the start of each year, a jury-panel of 6,000 was sworn in: individual juries would be manned by a selection of those members of the panel who volunteered on the day of the trial. We do hear of one jury manned by the full panel of 6,000, but the normal size for a jury appears to have been 500 (occasionally more) for a public case, and either 200 or 400 for a private one.[110] For an assembly, on the other hand, an attendance of 6,000 seems to have been required. Since we cannot tell how many juries will have been required on any particular day, a precise annual cost for the juries cannot be calculated; but it can be seen that even at 3 obols, a meeting of the assembly was already expensive.

It might, on the other hand, be suggested that assembly-pay had to be raised precisely because of the quorum: you did not need to get all 6,000 jurors to man a court, but an assembly meeting attended by only 5,000 could not perform certain essential activities. But this

[109] Hansen (1983*b*: 35–72 and 1987: 20–4) argues that after *c*.355 BC assembly-meetings were legally restricted to forty per year; the precise figure is disputed, but nobody would deny that it is in the right order of magnitude. The courts however appear to have sat on 150–200 days per year: Hansen 1979: 243–6.

[110] On jury size, Rhodes gives full references: *CAAP* 728–9. On assemblies, see above n. 57 and below at nn. 113–14.

argument, too, is open to challenge. It is easier to get people to attend a meeting that is less frequent (such as the assembly), and the pool of potential jurors is already much more restricted than is that for the assembly. Only members of the year's sworn panel of 6,000 could serve on a jury, and membership of this panel was restricted to those over the age of 30, whereas the assembly was open to any adult male citizen.

Hansen himself has not proposed any formal alternative model,[111] but a possible hypothesis may be pieced together from several passages in one of his earliest books.[112] Here Hansen suggests that in the fifth century the assembly was probably the supreme [172] organ of government, but that in the fourth century it lost this ultimate sovereignty to the courts; this was a move away from radical democracy, because the assembly was perceived as a radical institution, whereas the courts were a moderate and 'Solonic' safeguard; so to safeguard them from radical domination by the poor, assembly-pay was made financially more attractive than jury-service. This hypothesis, however, raises several problems. I am not attracted by the argument that the courts were perceived as 'moderate' institutions, but even if this were correct, it seems an odd process to introduce assembly-pay (thereby in Greek eyes raising the prestige of the assembly) as a way of defending the court.

Perhaps the wisest conclusion is that of Dover, who describes the relationship between jury-pay and assembly-pay as 'obscure' (1974: 34–5).

Nevertheless, some progress may be possible. Let us take as a starting-point the size of the Pnyx, the auditorium where the assembly met. The Pnyx was redesigned on several occasions, but its size throughout the late fifth and much of the fourth centuries remained approximately constant.[113] Hansen has argued that this corresponds

---

[111] Hansen's more recent and broader work on the subject has concentrated on the cost of assembly-pay to the state (1987: 48), which he does explicitly contrast with the cost of the juries (1987: 119); and on the value of assembly pay to the individual (1987: 47), where he does not raise the question.

[112] Hansen (1974: 12 and 59–61). It is not certain, however, that Hansen would still hold the views expressed here in quite this form; certainly in more recent work (1987: 94–107) he specifically repudiates use of the term 'sovereignty', preferring to speak in terms of the Greek adjective *kurios* ('authoritative').

[113] Pnyx I (until *c.*400 BC), *c.*2,400 m^2; Pnyx II (from *c.*400 to (at least) *c.*345 BC), *c.*2,600 m^2. The big expansion comes with Pnyx III, *c.*5,500 m^2: the date of this final rebuilding is discussed immediately below. For the dimensions, see Hansen 1983*b*: 16.

to a capacity of approximately 6,000; he points out that 6,000 was the quorum for certain types of routine business, and he argues that this was also the number who could regularly be expected to attend (1983*b*: 1–23; 1987: 14–19). I suspect that his conclusion here is probably correct; his interpretation of the literary and epigraphic evidence is persuasive, although arguments based on crowd-density are always difficult to interpret.[114]

At some date, however, the capacity of the Pnyx was substantially increased; Hansen (1983*b*: 16–18; 1987: 14–19) calculates that Pnyx III could comfortably hold 13,800 people. The date of this rebuilding is unfortunately not certain. The archaeologists have suggested a variety of dates, and it may well be that some of the work is Roman, but it is generally conceded that the project was at least begun in the third quarter of the fourth century BC; it may not have been completed then, but the increase in size is of fourth-century date.[115] If this is correct, then the project may plausibly be connected with the financial administration of Eubulus or more probably of Lycurgus, who were said to have increased the revenues of Athens from 130 to 400 talents (Eubulus, between *c.*355 and the mid-340s) and then from 400 to 1,200 talents (Lycurgus, from the mid-330s to the mid-320s).[116] Lycurgus in particular is known to have used the newly increased revenues to fund a massive programme of public building.[117]

If, however, Hansen is correct to argue that the reason why the Pnyx before 340 could accommodate 6,000 is that this was the

---

[114] The point is well made by Sinclair 1988: 118. It should be noted that the House of Commons can seat only some two-thirds of its 650 members, and it is easier to tell when a space looks empty than whether it is 'full' or 'over-full'.

[115] The changing views of the archaeologists are clearly summarized by Hansen (1983*b*: 23; cf. 1987: 12, n. 96). Hansen himself (1987: 14, n. 104) now dates the rebuilding at '*c.*340'. [On this question, see now my 2005 retrospective at n. 121 below.]

[116] For the dates of Eubulus, see Cawkwell 1963: 47–9. Lycurgus is said to have been in charge of Athenian revenues for 'three periods of four years' ([Plut.] *Moralia* 841b–c): if this means the four-year periods between successive Panathenaic festivals, it can only refer to 338–326; but it may not, and Rhodes (1980: 313) prefers the more cautious figure I have given. The revenue-figures derive from Dem. 10. 37–8 and Theopompus fr. 166 (Eubulus), and a combination of [Plut.] *Moralia* 841b–c and 842f (Lycurgus).

[117] For Lycurgus' building programme, see [Plut.] *Moralia* 841c–d, listing a series of projects but not mentioning the Pnyx. Given the nature of this text, however, such a silence is by no means indicative.

number who could be expected to attend, then this suggests a significant corollary: if you double the size of the Pnyx, then you [173] must be expecting to fill it with double the number of citizens.[118] But as we have seen, the level of pay seems to have been determined not by conscious index-linking, but as a response to the perception of need: it was increased if the numbers coming were thought to be too low (cf. above at n. 52). Consequently, the rebuilding of the Pnyx may supply a suitable context for a one-off increase in assembly-pay, perhaps even the whole increase from 3 to 6 and 9 obols.

The chronological sequence within this process is unclear. Perhaps the Pnyx was rebuilt in grander fashion, but was then perceived to be empty, and pay was increased to rectify this. Perhaps pay was increased until the assembly was bursting at the seams, and this led to calls to rebuild the Pnyx. It does not matter, because the two halves of the process, according to this hypothesis, are logically interconnected. Clearly, however, the process has a twofold significance. On the one hand, it reveals the Athenian attitude to public finance: because the money is now available, you look at once for ways to distribute it among the citizen-body.[119] On the other hand, you are making an interesting ideological statement about your democracy: by raising the level of assembly-pay above jury-pay, you are hinting in no uncertain terms, 'we are an assembly-based rather than a court-based democracy'.[120]

RETROSPECTIVE (2005)

In the fifteen years since this paper was written, a Lycurgan rather than a Hadrianic date for Pnyx III (cf. n. 115 above) has been

[118] Hansen (1987: 19; cf. previously 1986: 93–7) suggests that admission (and therefore pay) in the period of Pnyx II was restricted to the first 6,000, but that the restriction no longer applied after the construction of Pnyx III. He does not, however, draw the corollary that is proposed here.

[119] Hansen's view that the institution of four meetings of the assembly per prytany did not occur until after 355 might support this hypothesis (see above n. 109).

[120] It is striking that we have no hint of such a conscious policy in any of the speeches of the later orators, but this may be simply a statement about the lacunose nature of our sources for this period. We have, after all, no direct literary evidence for the construction of Pnyx III.

conclusively established by Rotroff and Camp (1996: 263–94),[121] whose re-examination of the results of the 1930–1 excavations has led to a redating of the Roman material as third rather than second century AD. Major rebuilding of the Pnyx itself is inconceivable at this period, and they explain the substantial but isolated nature of the Roman deposits as the result either of intrusion by natural drainage or of disruption caused by a putative attempt to acquire building-stone for late-Roman fortifications such as the Valerian Wall. To my knowledge, nobody has explored further the question raised at n. 118 of my paper, whether Pnyx III represents an expectation that attendance was to increase in parallel with its vastly increased size.

One or two gaps in the details of my argument should be noted. In particular, the comments about UK juries in the first section of the paper were already slightly out-of-date in 1990 (I failed to note that the right of peremptory challenge had been abolished by the Criminal Justice Act of 1988),[122] and the Department of Constitutional Affairs has recently (21 January 2005) issued a consultation paper proposing some relaxation of the rules restricting academic research on jury deliberations (http://www.dca.gov.uk/consult/2005.htm). Similarly, I should have made explicit (at nn. 79–80 above) the fact that Athenian deme-membership was hereditary in the male line, and for later periods is therefore evidence only for ancestral residence. But since the net impact of post-507 migration is likely to have been towards rather than away from the city, this would if anything have strengthened rather than weakened my case against *nautikos ochlos* theories of Athenian democracy.

My use of the term 'peasant' was avowedly contentious (cf. n. 66 above), and has since been criticized by V. D. Hanson in an appendix on Athenian farming terminology.[123] Of the alternatives that he suggests, I would have reservations about 'intensive farmer' (for reasons put forward at n. 99 above) or 'homestead farmer' (which

---

[121] Their findings are accepted e.g. by Hansen 1997, as thesis 4 on p. 218, with discussion in an appendix on pp. 245–6 (repr. in Hansen 1999: 331 and 353–4 respectively).

[122] It is still possible to challenge on certain specified grounds (Buxton 1990), but this remains unusual: English law, unlike that of the USA, does not permit potential jurors to be cross-examined before trial.

[123] Hanson 1995: 435 (quotation and criticism), 438 (alternative terms).

presupposes a particular answer to the still-vexed question of agricultural residence). I would, however, be happy with his 'small farmer' or 'yeoman farmer', both of which are compatible with my contention that those based in a non-monetized system of agriculture will tend to view 3 obols as a cash-injection rather than a substitute for lost earnings.

The balance between peasants and traders in Athenian juries and assemblies was discussed in a follow-up paper by Markle himself (1990), which unfortunately appeared too late for me to take into account (and vice versa): I would agree with many, though not all, of his interpretations of individual passages in ancient authors, but would wish to put greater emphasis on the issue of leisure-preference (which he mentions only briefly) and particularly the significance of the non-monetized economy

Evidence for Athenian wages has been comprehensively collected by Loomis (1998), who argues that market forces such as supply and demand can best explain the fact that rates of pay seem to have increased significantly during the century leading up to the 320s for construction workers on public building projects, and for some holders of public office (in which category he includes the receipt of assembly-pay), but not for soldiers or jurors. Some criticisms of this argument, and of the book's methodology, are put forward by R. G. Osborne (2000).

The study of Athenian sexuality has seen huge increases in sophistication over recent years, and my analysis of Aeschines 1 (at n. 88) has been rightly criticized in Fisher's recent commentary (2001: 59), on the grounds that I failed to take sufficient account of the complexity of the value-system that Aeschines claims to share with his opponents.

Addresses to the jury in the Attic Orators are discussed in a recent article by Wolpert (2003), who focuses particularly on how they are represented in ways that deny the presence of awkward groups like former supporters of the 404/3 oligarchy. But the work which I most regret not having had access to until after I had completed my paper was the magisterial study by Ober (1989), which took as its starting-point the elitist tone of Athenian political oratory, but developed this in very different ways, as the basis of a far-reaching analysis of ideological compromise mediated between the individual power of the litigant/orator and the collective power of the *dēmos*. Ober discusses questions of jury-composition only briefly (1989: 142–4); but although I still believe in two of the phenomena noted in my final paragraph (that Athens was constitutionally less democratic in the mid-fourth century than in the late fifth, and that there had during this period been a change in the social composition of the elite), he has succeeded in persuading me that the link between the two is less clear than I had thought.

13

Arguments from Precedent in Attic Oratory*

Lene Rubinstein

In the year 345 BC Aeschines brought a *dokimasia rhētorōn* against Timarchus the son of Arizelos of Sphettos. His prosecution was based on the charge that Timarchus had broken the law that barred male prostitutes from addressing the Assembly as well as exercising other citizen's privileges (1. 1–3). According to Aeschines, the trial of Timarchus was important, not only because its immediate aim was to prevent Timarchus from continuing his allegedly unlawful activities, but also because a verdict against Timarchus would serve to deter other citizens from engaging in similar illegal conduct:

You must be well aware—and do pay attention to what I am about to say— that if Timarchus pays the penalty for his activities you will provide the foundation for orderly conduct in our city. But if he is acquitted, it would have been better if this trial had never taken place. For before Timarchus was brought to trial, the law and the name of the courts did cause some men to fear. But if this very notorious man who is a champion in disgusting

* This article began life as a paper delivered at the American Philological Association meeting in Washington, DC in 1993. It was subsequently published in a slightly revised form in Danish as 'Precedensargumenter i de attiske retstaler' (1995). In the version presented here, I have expanded the footnotes; however, I have not attempted to incorporate more recent scholarship on this question. Nor have I made extensive revisions to the text so as to reflect my subsequent work over the past ten years on other generic differences between private and public speeches. Unlike more recent studies, this study is based not only upon speeches delivered in the ordinary *dikastēria* but also upon speeches delivered in trials heard by the Areopagus and by other homicide courts (Ant. 1 and 6; Lys. 1, 3, 4, and 7) as well as by the assembly (Lys. 28). However, I have not included speeches delivered before the council of 500 (Lys. 16, 24, 26, and 31, Dem. 51).

behaviour should escape from this court action unharmed, this will induce many others to commit offences, and in the end it will not be speeches but the critical situation that will arouse your anger. (1. 192)

Aeschines claims that the response of his present audience of *dikastai* will influence the future behaviour of other citizens of a disposition similar to that of Timarchus. His argument is based upon the assumption that potential lawbreakers will seek to predict the likely reaction of the courts to a particular type of crime, before they set out to commit it. Their prediction and risk-assessment will, according to this line of reasoning, be informed by their observation of the communal attitude to a particular type of crime as expressed through the judges' verdict in the concrete case against Timarchus.

This type of argumentation is used very frequently in Athenian lawcourt speeches. Many litigants maintain that the decision reached by the judges will establish a precedent, and that their verdict therefore is of significance not only for the particular case currently under consideration but also for the extent to which the laws will be respected and even enforced in the future. Some prosecutors assert that an acquittal of the present defendant will create *adeia* ('amnesty' or 'immunity') for others intent on committing similar crimes in the future.[1] The plaintiff who delivered Isoc. 20 in a private action for violent assault (*dikē aikeias*) against Lochites even goes as far as to claim (20. 21) that individuals who share the defendant's oligarchic disposition 'all hold the established laws in contempt, but, as for the decisions reached in your court, those they respect as laws'.[2]

In spite of the frequency with which the *topos* was employed by Athenian litigants, it was arguably based upon a fiction. This may be one reason why modern research on the Athenian administration of justice has largely passed over this type of argumentation in silence, in spite of its prominence in Athenian forensic oratory. There was no method by which the Athenians could ensure, in practice, that the decision reached by one panel of *dikastai* would inform the decisions

---

[1] Lys. 1. 36, 49; 12. 85; 22. 19; 30. 23, 34; Dem. 19. 272, 289; 23. 94; 54. 21.

[2] A very similar remark is made in Lys. 1. 36. Here the speaker argues that if he is convicted of unlawful murder of the lover of his wife, all thieves caught in the act will in future claim to have broken into other people's houses in order to commit adultery: 'for they will all know that they need not give a hoot about the laws on adultery, whereas they need to fear your vote.'

reached by future panels in the hearing of comparable cases. What is a central concept in modern administration of justice, namely, the predictability and consistency exercised by the courts in the application of statutes to individual cases, was impossible to achieve in practice in the context of the Athenian *dikastēria*, for several reasons.

First, there were no established legal experts who might have influenced court practice and contributed to creating consistency in the way successive panels of *dikastai* responded to particular offences (for a comprehensive discussion, see above all Wolff 1964). Second, there was neither the time nor the opportunity for the Athenian *dikastai* to study decisions reached in similar cases by previous panels before casting their votes. The decision-making process itself, which took the form of a secret ballot of panels of hundreds of citizens (and sometimes thousands in certain types of important public actions), allowed no collective pronouncement as to what had moved the majority to cast their votes in a particular way. It has been debated whether there was ever any systematic attempt to record, even in the most cursory fashion, decisions reached by the courts in such a way as to enable future consultation by individual litigants. But even in those cases where the court's decision was published, it seems safe to assume with Thür (1987) that the published text of a verdict did not go beyond the reproduction of the wording of the *enklēma* ('writ'), the penalty, the name of the court, the number of votes for conviction and acquittal, and a note of whether or not the parties had been present at the trial.[3] Third, and perhaps more important than any of the practical obstacles outlined so far, the Athenians seem to have insisted that any individual panel of *dikastai* (chosen by lot from among citizens over 30 years of age) was fully capable of reaching a decision in each individual case on the basis of the laws alone, sometimes in combination with the judges' own *gnōmē dikaiotatē*.[4]

---

[3] Thür 1987 offers a comprehensive survey of epigraphically attested verdicts. He notes an important difference between the publication of verdicts passed by the courts in the *poleis* themselves and those pronounced by judges and arbitrators in inter-*polis* disputes. While the latter show a growing tendency towards the inclusion of the judges' reasons for reaching a particular decision, the former do not go beyond a very simple rejection or acceptance of the charge made in the *enklēma*.

[4] See esp. Dem. 22. 5–7, where the speaker anticipates that Androtion, the defendant in the present action for unlawful decree proposal (*graphē paranomōn*), will refer to previous aprobouleumatic decrees that have been upheld. The prosecutor

Since the predictability of the Athenian courts regarding the application of statutes to individual cases was a fiction, at least from a modern point of view, it may be regarded as entirely justified to dismiss the *topos* employed in Aeschines 1. 192 as 'pure rhetoric'. Yet, the fiction itself seems to have been of immense importance for the way in which the Athenians themselves represented their administration of justice and the actual operation of their courts. In addition to Aeschines 1 no fewer than forty-six of the ninety-nine preserved lawcourt speeches contain this type of argument.[5] In the *Rhetorica ad Alexandrum* 4. 6 (1427a14–21) the author provides a detailed example of the *topos* to be deployed by prosecutors in contexts where the defendant claims to have been acting from mistake or by accident: 'You must also say that *if the judges accept this line of argument from the defendant they will be landed with numerous people who will commit*

dismisses this line of argument as follows: 'Yet if this has indeed taken place, while the law prescribes the opposite, it is not a valid reason for unlawful behaviour now that such transgressions have often taken place in the past. Quite the contrary: we should start forcing people to conduct such matters as the law prescribes, starting with you, Androtion.' The argument is found also in Aeschin. 3. 193 and Dem. 23. 95–9, where similar appeals to precedents (i.e. acquittals in parallel cases) are anticipated from the defendants. A parallel concern with the use of precedent as coming into conflict with the authority of the highest legal institution within a particular jurisdiction is highlighted by Jensen (1990: 441) in relation to the absolute monarchy that prevailed in Denmark from 1660 to 1849: 'As mentioned in the article on the workings of the Danish Supreme Court... it was not permitted for the court to append its *ratio decidendi* to its verdicts in the period from 1674 to 1856. This prohibition, which did not extend to other courts in the land, *was founded on the then prevailing absolutist state theories, which had as their centre the monarch as the formal president of the court.* The result was that neither the opposing parties nor the general public were in a position to ascertain what had caused the quashing of a verdict that had been appealed, or whether the confirmation of a decision reached by a lower court had been based on the same or different legal considerations.' (My translation and emphasis.)

[5] Public prosecution speeches: Lys. 6. 8; 12. 35, 85; 14. 4, 11–12; 15. 9; 22. 16–21; 27. 5–7; 28. 10–11, 16; 29. 13; 30. 24–5, 35; Dem. 19. 232, 270, 289, 342–3; 20 *passim*; 21. 7–8, 37, 76, 100, 227; 22. 19, 37, 46; 23. 93–4, 99; 24. 101, 130, 153; 25. 6–7, [26]. 2; [53]. 29; [59]. 77, 111–13; Aeschin. 1. 36, 90–1, 177–9, 185–7, 192, 195; 3. 5–8, 177, 180, 193, 233–5, 245–6; Lyc. 1. 7–8, 9, 27, 67, 78, 110, 116, 145, 150; Hyp. 4 *Phil.* 5; Din.1. 3, 15, 16, 22–3, 27, 46, 67, 88, 107, 113; 2. 21–3; 3. 21 (total 26); public defence speeches: Ant. 5. 80; Andoc. 1. 103–5, Lys. 5. 5; 18. 23; [20]. 31–2; 25. 33–4; Isaeus. 11. 32 (total 7); private prosecution speeches: Isoc. 18. 21–2, 26, 33–4, 42–4; 20. 12, 18; 21. 18; Dem. 36. 58; 37. 60; 38. 22; 45. 87; 50. 1, 64, 66; 54. 43, 56. 48–50 (total 10); private defence speeches: Lys. 1. 34–6, 47–9; Dem. 34. 51–2; 35. 56 (total 3); *diadikasia*: Dem. 42. 15 (total 1).

crimes deliberately. For if such people succeed they will have accomplished what they want, while, if they fail, they will escape punishment by claiming that they have made a transgression out of ignorance.' In practice, too, this type of argumentation seems to have been used predominantly by prosecutors: it is found in thirty-six prosecution speeches but only in ten speeches delivered by or on behalf of defendants. However, what is even more important is that the argument appears to have belonged first and foremost in the context of public actions. The frequency with which the argument is deployed in public prosecution speeches suggests an awareness of different genres of forensic oratory among its practitioners, and that the representation of the role and duties of the courts advanced by a given litigant depended to some extent on whether his case had been launched under the heading of a public procedure or as a private suit, as well as the nature of the complaint itself that had given rise to the legal action in question.

For modern scholars it has proved very difficult indeed to produce a precise, let alone simple, definition of the differences between Athenian public and private actions. To be sure, certain formal criteria varied according to whether a case was heard as a public or as a private suit: the dicastic panels were larger in public actions than in private ones, and the parties in the former had considerably longer speaking time at their disposal (*Ath. Pol.* 67. 1–2). Once the *dikastai* had pronounced their verdict, its execution depended on the type of procedure that had been employed by the prosecutor: the winner of a private action was himself responsible for the implementation of the court's decision, while this was not the case for public actions.[6]

Another possible distinction is the standing of the prosecutor in relation to the case as either directly affected or as a third party: while public actions could be initiated by any citizen who wished to do so (*ho boulomenos*), private actions could in principle be launched only by the victim in person (Isoc. 20. 2), or, if the victim was a male under 18 years of age or a female, by his or her *kyrios.* This distinction should not be pressed too hard, however, for many volunteer prosecutors in public actions whose speeches have survived justify their intervention with the claim that they themselves were victims of

---

[6] The most comprehensive treatment on the execution of verdicts in private and public actions respectively remains that of Lipsius, *AR* 942–52.

the defendant's criminal behaviour (though not necessarily of the particular crime with which he was presently being charged).[7]

Equally problematic is a distinction based upon the identity of the victim as either a named individual or the *polis* collectively: although offences perceived to have been committed against the community as a collectivity were typically brought before the court under the procedural heading of a public action, there were also certain public procedures that could be employed in cases where the victim concerned was indisputably a single individual.[8] What complicates matters further is that, in certain areas of the Athenian administration of justice, the injured party would be in a position to choose between a range of public and private actions as an instrument by which he could take the offender to court. That the line separating public actions from private suits was indeed blurred is also indicated by the fact that plaintiffs involved in private actions sometimes tried to represent the entire *polis* as a direct fellow victim of the defendant's illegal actions, rather than presenting their case as a matter that affected only the two opposing parties.[9]

It is thus tempting to assume that it would be open to any litigant to represent any injustice committed against an individual citizen as an injustice that ultimately affected the entire Athenian community as a collectivity, and, consequently, that any litigant appearing in an Athenian court would be able to claim that the verdict in his own particular case would be likely to influence future court practice as well as future community behaviour. However, the evidence of the extant speeches suggests that the scope for deployment of this particular type of argument was limited, and that its limitations were to some extent imposed by the nature of the matter under dispute.

---

[7] The following public speeches were delivered by prosecutors who all referred to their personal enmity towards the defendants, often (but not always) combined with the claim that they had themselves been victims of the defendant's behaviour: Lys. 12. 1–34, 13 *passim*; 14. 1–2; 15. 12; Aeschin. 1. 1–3, 20; Dem. 19. 17; 21. 77–8; 22. 1–3; 24. 6–16; 25. 37; [53]. 4–18; [58]. 1–4; [59]. 4–8.

[8] Many of these actions appear to have offered legal protection, through the intervention of a third party, to individuals such as orphans and *epiklēroi*, who were unable to defend their own interests in person, or citizens who had wrongfully been registered as state-debtors and whose *atimia* prevented them from challenging their registration. But other actions, such as the *graphē hubreōs* for example, could in principle be brought on behalf of an adult male citizen in possession of full legal competence.

[9] Isoc. 20. 21; Isae. 6. 4, Dem. [50]. 65–6; 56. 44, 47.

There is a significant disparity between public and private cases: out of fifty-one public speeches, the *topos* occurs in thirty-three, almost two-thirds of the total; in private speeches the argument is employed in only fourteen out of fifty-two, little more than a quarter.[10] Bearing in mind that the *topos* is a typical prosecution argument, it is important to note that in the surviving material there is an even distribution of prosecution speeches in the public and private categories.[11] We are fortunate that the source material is so evenly balanced that a comparison is possible. Moreover, it is clear from Isocrates 18. 33 that the apparent difference between public and private speeches cannot be ascribed to mere coincidence.

Isocrates 18 was delivered in a private suit, a *paragraphē*, and this speech is one of the fourteen private speeches in which the litigant claims that the verdict passed in the present lawsuit will have a wider effect on the shaping not only of future court practice, but also of community behaviour in general. The speaker breaks off this line of argument by inserting the following apologetic note: 'And let no one think that I exaggerate or am speaking out of proportion (*meizō legein*), because I, a defendant in a private suit (*dikēn idian*), have spoken in this fashion.' The speaker is anticipating a possible negative reaction on the part of his audience to his claim that their verdict will have general effect that goes far beyond the issue under dispute in the present case. He is clearly aware that he is crossing the boundaries of genre, that he is somehow breaking recognized court etiquette by employing an argument normally expected in public speeches only. The question that needs to be addressed is why Athenian litigants apparently observed such limitations on the deployability of the argument in certain types of legal action. Part of the explanation may lie with the purposes that the *topos* was supposed to serve.

---

[10] As listed above, n. 5: among public speeches, 26 for the prosecution, 7 for the defence; among private speeches, 10 for the prosecution, 3 for the defence, one in a *diadikasia* in connection with an *antidosis*.

[11] Public prosecution speeches: Lys. 6, 12, 13, 14, 15, 22, 25, 27, 28, 29, 30; Dem. 19, 20, 21, 22, 23, 24, 25, [26], [53], 58, [59]; Aesch. 1, 3; Lyc. 1; Hyp. 1 (*Dem.*), 4 (*Phil*); Din. 1, 2, 3 (total 30). Private prosecution speeches: Lys. 10, 23; Isoc. 17, 18, 20, 21; Isaeus 3, 5, 6; Dem. 27, 28, 30, 31, 32, 33, 37, 38, 39, 40, 41, 36, [44], 45, [46], 47, 48, [49], [50], 54, 56; Hyp. 5 *Ath.* (total 31).

The *topos* serves to define the role of the audience, the judges. Just as each litigant defines rhetorically his own role and that of his opponent (for example by means of the argument 'my opponent ought to say or demonstrate *x*, *y*, or *z*; not *a*, *b*, or *c*', or 'my opponent must cite the law that warrants his behaviour'), part of the game is to inform the judges of their role in the concrete case: the speaker will tell them how they ought to respond and why they ought to react in the way that he is suggesting. That kind of argumentation is often linked with more general attempts to define the function and role of the court itself.

When a litigant refers to the wider consequences of the judges' decision in his own case, he is in effect inviting his audience to turn their attention towards the future, and by engaging in that line of argumentation he is crossing the line between the dicastic and the symbouleutic genres as defined by Aristotle (*Rh.* 1358b2–20).[12] Indeed, some speakers go as far as to invite the judges to think of themselves not just as *dikastai* but also as *nomothetai*, that is, lawgivers.[13]

When the judges are told that they are now 'legislating for the future', the audience addressed by the speaker is not the specific panel of judges, the individuals sitting as *dikastai* at this particular trial, as much as it is *hoi aei dikazontes*, the institution of the popular court sitting at any and all times. In the same way as the individuals making up any particular panel in a public suit are but contributing to the constant flow of *dikastai*, the verdict they pass also forms part of a continuum, extending to both future and past. And thus the orators do not confine themselves entirely to arguments concerning the

[12] See esp. 11358b13–20: 'The time-orientation of each: for the deliberator the future (for it is about what is to be that he deliberates, whether urging or dissuading), and for the litigant the past (for both prosecution and defence make claims about what has happened), while for the display orator the present is most important (for it is on the basis of how things are that all men accord praise or blame), though they often make additional use of historical recollection or anticipatory conjecture.' Note that a similar awareness of crossing the lines between different genres of oratory is expressed also by Lycurgus (1. 46), when he is about to embark on themes that clearly belong to epideictic speeches: 'On these matters, judges, I shall elaborate a little more, and I ask you to listen and not to regard such arguments as out of place (*allotrioi*) in the context of public trials (*hoi dēmosioi agōnes*).'

[13] The following passages instruct the judges to think of themselves as *nomothetai*: Isoc. 21. 18; Lys. 14. 4; Dem. 19. 232; 56. 48; Lyc. 1. 9. Note that Lys. 15. 9 (delivered in the same trial as Lys. 14), also on the side of the prosecution, explicitly instructs the judges that they must *not* think of themselves as *nomothetai*.

future effects of the judges' decision in the present case: in a number of cases the judges are instructed to let previous court decisions influence their verdict. The argument from previous decisions appears to have served a purpose similar to that of the future-oriented argument that the court is now about to set a precedent: when a speaker claims that the judges must pass their verdict that is consistent with previous practice, he is in effect reminding them that they form part of a tradition, and that they themselves are participating in shaping and perpetuating that tradition.

The exhortation to the judges to ensure that their present verdict will conform to verdicts passed by previous panels are much rarer than the assertion that the present verdict will influence the decisions reached by future panels; but it still occurs in no fewer than twenty different speeches.[14] Like its future-oriented counterpart, it belongs predominantly in the context of speeches delivered by prosecutors in public actions, and this argument, too, receives treatment in *Rhetorica ad Alexandrum* 1.19 (1422b12–16), where the author offers a suggestion as to how to argue on the basis of past verdicts (*ek tōn kekrimenōn*): 'And it is not only I who assert that the lawgiver enacted this statute for those reasons; but also on a previous occasion, when Lysitheides instructed the judges using arguments that are very similar to the ones that I am now presenting, they voted for the same decision in regard to this statute.' The notion that past verdicts ought to influence current court practice, and that the decision reached by the courts ought to show a high level of consistency in

---

[14] Ant. 5. 59–70 (conviction of Hellenotamiai); Lys. 6. 17 (Diagoras of Melos), 54 (unnamed Megarian); 12. 36 (trial of generals after Arginusae); 13. 55–7 (Menekrates); 27. 4 (Onomasas); Dem. 18. 222–3 (acquittal of Demomeles and Hyperides, proposers of motions similar to that of Ctesiphon); 19. 180 (Ergophilos, Kephisodotos, Timomachos, Ergokles, Dionysios), 270–1 (Arthmios of Zeleia), 273–9 (Epikrates), 19. 280–1 (Thrasyboulos Thrasyboulou); 21.73–5 (Euaion), 143–7 (Alkibiades), 175–80 (Euandros, unnamed paredros of archon, Ktesikles); 24. 138 (Eudemos of Kydathenaion, Philippos Philippou); 34. 50 (unnamed general); [59]. 116–17 (Archias); Aeschin. 1. 113 (Socrates); 3. 195 (Thrasyboulos of Steiria), 252 (reference to Lycurgus' prosecution of Leocrates, Lyc. 1); Lyc. 1. 52–4 (Autolykos), 112–15 (Phrynichos), 117–18 (Hipparchos), 122–3 (unnamed individual); Hyp. 1 *Dem.* 27 (Konon of Paiania); 3 *Eux* 1 (Timomachos, Leosthenes, Kallistratos, Philon, Timotheos), 3 (Diognides, Antidoros, Agasikles); Din. 1. 13–14 (Timotheos), 23 (Menon, Themistios of Aphidna, Euthymachos), 55–6 (acquittals of individuals in *apophaseis*), 57–9 (acquittal of Polyeuktos in *apophasis*); 2. 24–5 (Arthmios of Zeleia); 3. 17 (Timotheos).

regard to the application of the law in parallel cases, is of supreme importance in modern jurisprudence, not only in administrations of justice that operate with a principle of binding precedent, but also in legal systems such as the Danish one, in which precedent, though not binding, nevertheless constitutes an important source of law.[15] Apparently, this notion was not entirely alien to the Athenians, although it must be emphasized again that the very structure of the Athenian administration of justice made any systematic use of precedents as a source of law impossible in practice. In this connection it is also important to note that arguments from precedent are rarely supported by documentary proof in the way that discussions of the wording of individual statutes or witness statements are accompanied by and based upon documents that were read out by the court attendant. Only on seven occasions is an indictment and/or verdict read out in a way similar to the formal presentation of laws, decrees, and witness testimony.[16]

As noted above, the argument from precedent (both its future-oriented and its past-oriented variants) occurs more rarely in speeches composed for delivery in private actions. In most private actions the speakers tend to emphasize that the most important task of the judges is to reach the most just decision in the case at hand, and that their role is primarily that of choosing between two accounts of the present case as presented by the two opposing parties. Only in fourteen private speeches out of fifty-two do the litigants claim that the judges' decision in the present case will have wider repercussions, because the verdict will contribute to the shaping of future court practice and thus also to the shaping of the future behaviour of other individuals.

[15] Jensen (1990) provides a brief historical survey of the attitudes to and use of precedent as a source of law in Denmark, in which he notes that: 'the fact that a verdict or decision in principle only decides on a concrete legal question in relation to the two opposing parties, on the basis of the production of concrete evidence . . . has not prevented—in spite of restrictive clauses in various Supreme Court instructions on the interpretative competence of the courts—that large areas of legal theory as well as the day-to-day operation of the courts have built and still build upon guidelines extrapolated from previous decisions made by the courts, and by the Supreme Court in particular.' (p. 441, my translation).

[16] Decrees recording charges and verdicts against offenders are read out by the court attendant in Dem. 19. 170 (decree concerning the trial of Arthmios of Zeleia) and 19. 276 (decree concerning trial of Epikrates and other ambassadors), Lyc. 1. 114 (decree concerning trial of Phrynichos) 117–18 (decree concerning trial of Hipparchos), and 122–3 (decree concerning 'man in Salamis'); Din. 1. 13–14 (decree concerning trial of Timotheos); 2. 24–5 (decree concerning Arthmios of Zeleia).

One of these speeches is Lysias 1, delivered in an action for homicide (*dikē phonou*) heard by the Delphinion. However, it must be noted that the argument concerning the setting of a precedent was probably less of a fiction in the context of the Athenian homicide courts than in the context of the large *dikastēria* that were composed from citizens randomly selected by lot. The Athenian *dikai phonou* were heard by members of the council of the Areopagus (when the victim of intentional homicide or attempted homicide was an Athenian citizen) or by the *ephetai* in other types of murder trials (for instance, accidental or lawful killing of an Athenian or the murder of non-citizens). Although it is not known who exactly the *ephetai* were, there is a broad consensus that they were not selected from the annual pool of ordinary *dikastai*.[17] It is therefore fair to assume that *dikai phonou* were heard by experienced judges, whose experience would most likely contribute to the creation of more continuity and consistency in their decisions than would have been the case in the ordinary courts.

Of the remaining thirteen private speeches that contain the *topos* on precedent, nine share the common feature that the matter under dispute was *by definition* a matter of general public concern. Two of these speeches were delivered in legal actions concerned with liturgies (Dem. 42 and 50); one was concerned with the general application of the ban on litigation that was enacted after the civil war of 404/3 (Isoc. 18); one was delivered in a dispute over silver-mining (Dem. 37); three disputes concerned grain trade (Dem. 34, 35, and 56); and two were delivered in actions for violent assault, *dikē aikeias* (Isoc. 20, Dem. 54). In these last two it is striking that the speakers from the very outset attempt to define their complaint as an accusation of *hubris* (Isoc. 20. 1–2; Dem. 54. 1), for cases of *hubris* were of the kind that could be brought before the court under the heading of a public action, a *graphē*. Indeed, the strategy of instructing the judges not to think of the present action as a *dikē idia* is employed in no fewer than five of the fourteen private speeches in which the *topos* on precedent occurs.[18]

It may, of course, be asked if such a redefinition by individual litigants of their private dispute as a matter of general public concern is not what should in fact be expected. It is perfectly conceivable that

---

[17] See e.g. MacDowell 1963, 48–67; Rhodes, *CAAP* 646–8; Carawan 1991.

[18] Lys. 1. 47; Isoc. 18. 33; Dem. [50]. 1; 54. 1, 42; 56. 50.

every plaintiff (or indeed defendant) in a private action might want
to attempt an amplification of his case by exaggerating its significance for the community as a whole, and that he might achieve this
aim by emphasizing how an adverse decision was likely to affect not
only himself personally but also other citizens who might find
themselves in a similar position in the future.

However, the corpus of surviving forensic speeches suggests that
not all types of legal dispute permitted this kind of amplification.
Most importantly, the twenty-four speeches delivered in inheritance
disputes and other strictly *oikos*-related matters do not employ the
topos on precedent at all. Given the notorious difficulties in applying
the Solonian laws on adoption and wills, it is especially striking to the
modern observer that no litigants involved in such disputes ever cite
previous examples of wills or adoptions that have been respected or
rejected by the courts in order to lend support to their own positions
and their own interpretations of the laws.[19] Nor do such litigants
attempt to persuade the judges that a wrong decision may encourage
numerous forgers of wills in the future—or, if the speech was delivered by the beneficiary of a will or adoption, that a rejection of his
claim would encourage other callous relatives to ride roughshod over
the last wishes of their deceased kin. The general tendency is that
litigants in such private actions refrain from placing their case in a
broader context of general law-enforcement, and their audiences are
not encouraged to think of themselves as lawgivers whose decision
will contribute directly to the shaping of future court-practice or
influence the social behaviour of other members of the community.

In that respect, the speeches delivered in private actions correspond more closely to Aristotle's definition (*Rhetoric* 1358b10–20) of
the *logos dikanikos* as a genre than do the speeches composed for
delivery in high-profile public actions: the emphasis in the private
speeches is overwhelmingly on the past, the focus is on the representation of past events and on the question whether or not the past
actions of the two opposing parties were in accordance with the laws
as well as general norms for acceptable behaviour. The role of the
judges as it is represented in the private speeches is first and foremost
defined as that of providing compensation to the injured party,

---

[19] See e.g. Rubinstein 1993: 62 and *passim*.

sometimes combined with the imposition of an additional penalty, and to provide an appropriate decision in the dispute between the two parties. Only rarely do such speakers attempt to claim that the wider interests of the community are also at stake.

To sum up: The kind of argumentation which is based on the expectation that decisions reached by a particular dicastic panel should conform to past decisions in comparable cases, and that the panel's decision will inform future verdicts as well as future community behaviour, is clearly linked with public legal procedures. It is sometimes employed by litigants in private actions, but predominantly in such disputes as had arisen in contexts that were clearly of recognized public interest rather than in those concerned with the behaviour of individuals towards each other in the *oikos* sphere. Arguably, in this respect, the role of the courts themselves is represented differently according to whether the trial in question was public or private. A verdict pronounced at the end of a public action could be interpreted as an expression of the collective attitude of the Athenian people to a particular breach of the law, which, partly through the choice of procedure, was defined as a matter that concerned the community as a whole. In theory, at least, that attitude ought to be immutable and consistent, and, hence, the same legal transgressions should ideally be met with the same penal response by the community. And thus the representation of the Athenian courts as a political institution, as the voice of the Athenian people, is most pronounced in public actions, while in private actions the emphasis is on the courts as an institution through which individual conflicts could be settled decisively in favour of one of the contending parties.

Aeschines' claim that, if Timarchus is acquitted, many Athenian citizens will be tempted to break the law in the future, because they no longer fear the response from the courts, is based upon the assumption that an acquittal will be interpreted as a collective expression of Athenian indifference towards the kind of crime that Timarchus has committed, and that future criminals will expect similar transgression to be met with a similarly mild response and indifference. Thus, the *topos* on precedent reflects the political function of the Athenian courts in public actions, where the judges in effect act as the mouthpiece of the entire Athenian *dēmos*, much more than it reflects a genuinely jurisprudential principle.

14

Politics as Literature: Demosthenes and the Burden of the Athenian Past

Harvey Yunis

In a lawcourt in Athens in the year 330 BC Demosthenes delivered a speech in which he successfully defended his career against a bitter adversary. That speech, known as *On the Crown*, has had a history that illustrates many of the vicissitudes, ancient and modern, of both classical literature and its study. At one time the speech was considered one of the greatest literary and rhetorical masterpieces and determined how the fourth-century struggle between Greece and Macedon was understood. Recently the speech has fallen on hard times: while students of rhetoric still admire it, few pay much attention to it; students of literature ignore it entirely; and students of history use it where they can but are openly scornful of it as a historical source. In my view, the speech needs to be looked at again, not for the sake of restoring lustre to an outmoded classic, but because, by combining perspectives that in the modern era have diverged, the speech can instruct us about both politics in classical Athens and the nature of classical literature.

First, some background. The dispute that came to trial in 330 BC between Aeschines and Demosthenes had formally been set in motion six years earlier, though the roots of the dispute lay even further back. Athens had been at war with Philip II of Macedon since the mid-350s. In 338 a showdown occurred when Philip's Macedonian army faced combined Athenian and allied Greek forces at Chaeronea, a town in southern central Greece roughly midway between Thebes and Delphi. As a result of his overwhelming victory, Philip gained control over all the states of the Greek mainland, including Athens. After Philip's assassination in 336, Macedonian control was extended by Philip's son and successor, Alexander, whose conquest of the Persian empire inaugurated a new era in which Athens was permanently deprived of the ability to function as a major power on the world scene. Demosthenes had been the architect and foremost proponent of the policy that brought the Athenians to Chaeronea, which, for Athens, had the sorry consequences just mentioned.

Two years after Chaeronea, in the spring of 336, a political associate of Demosthenes named Ctesiphon moved a proposal that the Athenians should bestow on Demosthenes a golden crown in a formal public ceremony in the theatre of Dionysus. This was the customary procedure by which the community conferred its highest honour on individual citizens. Ctesiphon's motion was approved by the council, but Aeschines, using the *graphē paranomōn*, or the indictment of a decree in conflict with statute law, halted consideration of Ctesiphon's motion in the assembly and moved the issue into the courts. However, the case languished amid the uncertainty arising from epoch-making events; it finally came to trial in the fall of 330.

Although several points of law ostensibly bore on the case, the brunt of it was explicitly political: the court had to decide whether Demosthenes' record was such that he *deserved* the public honour proposed by Ctesiphon. The arguments range widely, but nevertheless focus on one issue: did Demosthenes do well or ill by leading the Athenians to Chaeronea? That was precisely the issue that would have confronted the assembly had the motion been allowed to proceed there, back in 336; but the situation had changed by 330—a point to which I will return later. There is no direct evidence to indicate the reason why the case was revived after it had been dormant for six years. Nevertheless, if Aeschines sought an opportunity to unleash the anger and disaffection of the Athenian *dēmos* against his old enemy, this was the moment: at precisely that time the consequences of Chaeronea appeared more dire and unalterable than ever before. Yet Demosthenes defeated his opponent soundly, taking more than four-fifths of the votes of the citizens sitting as judges. The clear-cut victory allowed Demosthenes to continue his political career and ended that of Aeschines.

Within a hundred years of the trial, the reception of *On the Crown* was underway as the burgeoning literary culture of the Hellenistic world incorporated Demosthenes' speeches into the body of prized and closely studied literary documents of classical Athens (Lossau 1964). Since then, *On the Crown* has been understood primarily as a work of literature. By that I mean not merely that readers of the speech tended to focus on the artistry and to neglect political and historical questions. I mean also that few readers were in a position to subject the speech to the kind of scrutiny that we would call historical scrutiny. Indeed, the quarrel between Aeschines and Demosthenes and the Macedonian conquest of Greece were well known. But only within the past century-and-a-half have students of classical literature possessed an understanding of fourth-century history and politics sufficient even to begin to assess the speech as a historical document.[1]

For example, by the second century AD the discipline of rhetoric and the social, political, and artistic uses to which rhetorical expertise was put had grown so tremendously that Demosthenes had become one of the most popular and extensively studied of the classical authors, and the single most popular author of Greek prose.[2] In this environment of literary reverence, it was bound to be the case that Demosthenes' political role was viewed through the lens of the very speeches that he himself wrote and that won him his extraordinary reputation.[3] This

---

[1] Even insofar as ancient readers were interested in the political matters raised by the speech (cf. Polybius 18. 1 4), historical ignorance and the prevailing habits of literary interpretation conspired to make the text's own presentation of the political situation so overpowering as to prevent any independent view of it from emerging; cf. Drerup 1923. On the Alexandrian scholar Didymus, who cites earlier historians but possessed an extremely poor and confused understanding of the historical issues in Demosthenes' speeches, see S. West 1970; Harris 1989. The first work of critical history on Demosthenes was Schäfer 1885–7, *Demosthenes und seine Zeit* (1st edn. 1856–8).

[2] Cf. *On Sublimity* 12 .4; Dion. Hal. *Dem.* 22; Drerup 1923: 144–66; Bompaire 1984. Demosthenes became known as 'the orator', in correspondence with Homer, 'the poet'; cf. Rutherford 1998: 61–3. Among the literary papyri that have been recovered from the ancient world, Demosthenes is the best-represented prose author and, among all authors, second only to Homer; cf. Willis 1968: 212. Although Willis's raw numbers are out of date, the proportions have not changed.

[3] Though Aeschines' speeches against Demosthenes also survived, Demosthenes' superiority as a rhetorical artist ensured that his perspective dominated. This rule, so to speak, of Demosthenic reception—that Demosthenes' speeches eventually determined how he was viewed as a historical figure—is confirmed by the one exception of which I am aware, the black mark on Demosthenes' reputation earned from his role in the Harpalus

phenomenon reached its purest manifestation in a work entitled *Encomium of Demosthenes* by Lucian of Samosata, the sophist and writer of satirical dialogues of the second century AD.[4] The encomium is unconventional in that it celebrates Demosthenes the political leader to the virtual exclusion of Demosthenes the rhetorical artist; but it does so by creating a conspicuous literary fiction woven from Demosthenes' speeches. The heroic champion of Greek freedom praised by Lucian's Antipater and Philip is cobbled together from Demosthenes' own thoughts, phrases, notions, and arguments in his political speeches, which the educated reader of the dialogue is surely expected to recognize. Among examples concerning treachery (*Enc. Dem.* 33), the heroes of Marathon (36, 49, 50), Athenian demagogues (31, 41), and steadfast adherence to duty (44), consider 'Philip's' view of his victory at Chaeronea (38):

On the topic of Chaeronea, not even after his great victory there would [Philip] stop telling us into what great danger Demosthenes had brought us. 'For', he would say, 'even if against expectation, we won a victory thanks to the cowardice of their generals, the lack of discipline in their troops, and the unbelievable way that fortune... veered to us, yet on this one day he made me risk losing my kingdom and my life, since he had united the best cities, collected together the whole might of Greece, compelled not only the Athenians but also Thebans and all the other Boeotians, Corinthians, Euboeans, Megarians, and all the mightiest powers in Greece to brave the hazard of battle, and had not even allowed me to cross into Attic soil.' (Macleod tr. 1967)

'Philip' has just summed up the major points of Demosthenes' argument in *On the Crown*: the creation of the Greek alliance,

---

affair: in 323, one year before his death, Demosthenes was accused of corruption, suffered a severe political setback, and went into exile. None of Demosthenes' speeches delivered during this episode was ever preserved (Hansen 1984); hence the post-classical tradition never heard his side of this story and was forced to rely entirely on his opponents, the prosecutors, whose speeches were preserved (Hyp. 5, Din. 1).

[4] Plutarch's *Life of Demosthenes*, which portrays the man as a tragic hero, is the other main example of the post-classical tendency to view Demosthenes' life in literary terms. The authenticity of Lucian's *Encomium* has been challenged, though one of the main reasons alleged for denying authenticity, that the satire is too inept for it to be accepted as a genuine effort of the great satirist, is mistaken; see Baldwin 1969; Pernot 1993: 572–7. But the question of authenticity is not germane to the current argument; the dialogue is a genuine work of imperial Greek rhetorical culture, and the only point at issue here is how the work treats Demosthenes.

including the Thebans, Athens' traditional enemy; the incompetence of the generals in the field; the preservation of Attica; and, above all, the role of chance, which according to Demosthenes gave Philip victory.

This post-classical, heroic Demosthenes, in which the historical figure is constructed on the basis of the speeches, continued to surface into the early decades of the twentieth century, as evidenced in works on Demosthenes by Georges Clemenceau (1926), the French statesman, and Werner Jaeger (1938), the author of *Paideia*.[5] But this Demosthenes was already doomed, and deservedly so, when the rise of the discipline of critical history in nineteenth-century Germany created a new approach to ancient documents such as the Demosthenic speeches;[6] that is, the speeches began to be scrutinized not for their artistry or literary interest, but specifically for their reliability as evidence for historical events. It is clear that once this trend became established, Demosthenes would be completely re-evaluated: while he constantly speaks about and refers to historical events, it is of the very essence of his art to shape the view of those events in a self-serving way. Out of this large historical movement, I would like to mention just one example, the Oxford historian George Cawkwell, who produced in the 1960s and 1970s a formidable body of work that completely reversed the traditional assessment of Demosthenes. There are other scholars whose work on Demosthenes is in the same vein as Cawkwell's, but it suffices here to focus on him as the most prominent among them.[7] (The ensuing discussion takes full account of recent work on Demosthenes, but Cawkwell serves as the point of departure because his work sharpened the dilemma that currently affects the study of Demosthenes.)

A critical review of the events and policies of the 340s and 330s leads Cawkwell to conclude, in common with Aeschines, that Demosthenes' policy was a total disaster. In an article entitled 'The Crowning of Demosthenes' (1969), Cawkwell revisits the issue

---

[5] Pickard-Cambridge 1914 presents a similarly idealizing account. On Jaeger's Demosthenes, cf. Badian 1992: 289–315.

[6] Cf. Schäfer 1885–7, with Julius Beloch, Paul Wendland, and Ulrich Kahrstedt as cited by Drerup 1923: 6.

[7] Cawkwell's approach to Demosthenes is followed by J. Ellis 1976 and Griffith 1979. Cawkwell's views on the subject are summed up in *Philip of Macedon* (1978), which also contains full bibliography.

addressed at the original trial; but he wants to consider the question while avoiding the rhetoric, lies, flattery, and distortion that he finds in the speeches of both Aeschines and Demosthenes and that had been tacitly accepted by readers for more than two millennia. Now, Cawkwell understands very well that an advocate will, indeed must, say anything to win his case; thus his complaint is not so much against Demosthenes as against those who failed to see through Demosthenes' rhetoric, which includes the original audience. While Cawkwell concedes that Demosthenes' rhetoric is 'brilliant', by which he means that Demosthenes has the ability to make lies sound convincing and a bad situation look good, he does not excuse the Athenians. In Cawkwell's view, Demosthenes' victory in court is 'less a defence of Demosthenes than the disclosure of a melancholy fact about Athens'; the votes cast in support of Demosthenes were cast 'at the same moment in condemnation of Athens' (1969: 165, 180, 180). For Cawkwell, Demosthenes' speech *On the Crown* is nothing but a fraud which the Athenians were too blind or stupid to penetrate.

It is not my concern to contest Cawkwell's evaluation of Demosthenes' original policy. I am concerned to explain the success of Demosthenes' speech, which Cawkwell's account fails to do. The historian's attempt to evaluate the claims and arguments of *On the Crown* strictly in terms of their truth or falsity is to misjudge the nature of the appeal that Demosthenes makes to his audience and therefore to misunderstand the nature of the interaction between *rhētōr* and *dēmos*. The error is the reverse of that exemplified in Lucian's satirical dialogue. Whereas the post-classical world viewed fourth-century Greek history in terms of its literary representation, and therefore had a distorted view of both history and the political literature, now, even though we have a much better view of fourth-century history, fourth-century political literature has been effectively reduced to a sub-literary sphere of historical evidence, and this, I contend, is a distortion of both that literature and the historical situation that produced it. It is necessary to express this dilemma explicitly, because students of ancient rhetoric have failed to respond adequately to the historicization of Demosthenes' political rhetoric. On the one hand, they have simply perpetuated the old literary model while labelling Cawkwell an extremist and so ignoring his argument (Schindel 1987: 1–26; Carlier 1990); on the other hand, they have

failed to perceive that the work of Cawkwell and other historians has
rendered the old literary model of Demosthenic rhetoric obsolete.

Therefore, I would like to look again at how Demosthenes conveys his
message, that is, at the artistry of the speech, in order to try to answer one
of the historical questions raised by Cawkwell and others: how could the
Athenians, eight years after the defeat at Chaeronea, when Macedonian
hegemony seemed more secure than ever, have endorsed the policy that
brought them to that miserable state of affairs? At that time they had less
freedom of action and were more vulnerable than they had been eight
years after their defeat in the Peloponnesian War two generations earlier.
A further historical consideration, not mentioned by Cawkwell, makes
the problem even sharper. It was a regular part of the Athenian system of
law and politics for the *dēmos* to use the courts to repudiate and punish
political leaders whose policies had failed.[8] This was possible because
judicial decision-making in Athens was in no way limited by the concerns
of the law proper, but was traditionally used to enable the community to
seek and exert its interests without constraints. The list of Athenian
politicians and generals who at some time failed in their tasks and were
punished for it is a long one, containing many of the famous names of
Athenian history.[9] Todd sums up the situation thus (1993: 306): 'Athenian public discourse rests on a success-oriented model of politics in
which incompetence is criminal.'

The success-oriented model made Demosthenes' situation extremely
precarious. Aeschines was a clever, experienced opponent, capable of
exploiting all the elements of this situation. The legal weapon that he
used to attack Demosthenes—the *graphē paranomōn*—gave him ample
latitude to present precisely the kind of case that would most likely
provoke the ire of the judges.[10] He did not omit any of the arguments

---

[8] Politicians were personally liable for their public 'promises' and were identified
with particular policies. They were often accused and convicted of treachery rather
than incompetence. The tendency of the Athenian *dēmos* to punish their leaders
harshly is castigated by ancient historians as irrational, and noted by modern political
scientists as contributing to the stability of democratic rule; cf. J. Roberts 1982.

[9] e.g. Miltiades, Cimon, Pericles, the historian Thucydides, Alcibiades, Cleophon,
Thrasybulus. Generals were punished after the battle of Arginusae (406), the
Corinthian War (395–2), the campaign in Oropus (366), the naval battle in the
Hellespont in the Social War (356), and the battle of Chaeronea (338).

[10] On the *graphē paranomōn* and the arguments used in such cases, see Wolff 1970,
Hansen 1974, Yunis 1988.

that were customary in such cases: he argues that Ctesiphon's decree violates the letter and spirit of specific Athenian statutes; he portrays Demosthenes as a corrupt, ill-fated rogue in the employ of Philip or the Persians, wrecking Athenian interests in pursuit of personal gain at every opportunity; he disparages Demosthenes' competence as a politician and diplomat; and he manipulates democratic ideology in many ways, for instance, by suggesting that Athenian democracy cannot endure if such corrupt politicians are honoured.

But Aeschines' strongest argument by far was the one based on the simple, undeniable facts, the one, in fact, endorsed by Cawkwell: it would be criminal and utterly disgraceful for Athens to bestow the highest public honour on the citizen most responsible for the disaster at Chaeronea and undisputed Macedonian hegemony (Aeschin. 3. 49, 125–7, 130–1, 152–8, 243–7). This argument, placed in the centre of the speech, is supported by a detailed account of Demosthenes' role in the events leading up to Chaeronea. And it is driven home by an emotional passage that is the rhetorical high point of the entire speech (152–8). Anticipating the scene prescribed by Ctesiphon's decree, Aeschines imagines the Athenians convened in their sacred theatre, evocative of Athens' glorious past when crowns were rightly bestowed for successful actions that bolstered the community. In contrast, the present case would be an abomination: with fellow Greeks looking on, the herald would grandly proclaim a golden crown not for a victorious, self-sacrificing hero, but for the man who profited by leading Athens to defeat, by putting Athenians and other Greeks in their graves, by turning young Athenians into orphans. Aeschines gives vent to the outrage that would be done to the dead of Chaeronea. The shame would be overwhelming, Athens disgraced.[11] Aeschines clearly intended the judges to respond vindictively to the politician whose policy turned out so badly.

Had he wished to, Demosthenes could have fashioned a response that denies or in some way extenuates his responsibility for the failed policy. For instance, in an earlier trial between him and Aeschines concerning the second embassy to Philip in 346, it was agreed by both prosecution and defence that the policy at issue had failed; argument raged over who had actually instigated the failed policy,

---

[11] The dramatic force of this passage is discussed by Wilson 1996: 322–3.

with each side accusing the other. In that case (represented by Dem. 19 and Aeschin. 2) Aeschines successfully defended himself by shifting the blame onto others, viz. onto Demosthenes and Philocrates, the Athenian politician who lately had been discredited. Thus, in the trial on the crown Demosthenes could have composed a similar kind of argument; that is, he could have denied or shifted responsibility for the failed policy; he could also have minimized both the extent to which the Chaeronea policy exemplified his career and the degree to which the defeat at Chaeronea led to Macedonian domination. He does none of these things, but adopts a completely different strategy. While he hardly refrains from blaming Aeschines and a multitude of other people for a multitude of sins and failures, he also does not distance himself from the failed policy; in fact, he embraces it even in retrospect and insists on his responsibility for it. Then, in the course of the speech he rejects the standard of evaluation that Aeschines, following Athenian legal and political custom, applied to him, and that Cawkwell, in his historical judgement, applies to him; that is, he rejects the success-oriented model of public discourse and portrays himself as a hero deserving public honour, even though the policy, his policy, failed.

In principle, an argument of this kind need not be particularly difficult to understand; it would depend on how and to whom the argument is made. However, Demosthenes was faced with the problem of making the argument compelling to a mass audience in a context where it would be unexpected and clash with convention. In theory, he could try either of two strategies. He could, in the manner of a moral philosopher or sophist, attempt to instruct the audience on why success should be rejected as the prevailing measure of worth and some other measure substituted instead. But this strategy, as we know from Plato's Socrates and elsewhere, would leave his popular audience cold. The other strategy, which he did adopt, also stems from an extra-legal context, viz., the heritage of Homeric and tragic poetry. These models offered the great advantage of being familiar to the mass of citizens, indeed of being well accepted and even cherished by them. In these literary genres it often occurs that events and human actions are presented and evaluated as admirable or contemptible, noble or base, good or bad, without regard for their success or failure on a scale of advantage and disadvantage. The primary example, of course, is Achilles, whose furious pursuit of his friend's killer would inevitably lead, as he well knew, to his own death. Antigone's costly piety towards her brother's corpse is another example, Theseus' recovery of the bodies of the Argive attackers of Thebes yet another. Further examples are easily recalled. This is the raw material, as it were, of tragic poetry, which is based on ties of family or community or the deepest friendship, and which produces in average people a gut reaction far more intense than does the abstract reasoning of the moral philosopher. I will consider below why this strategy may have been appropriate for the occasion. Before I do that, let me briefly discuss three basic respects in which it functions in the speech.

First, Demosthenes avoids any kind of debate about the merits of the policy that led to Chaeronea. The policy is presented as the *only* alternative to either collaboration with Philip or outright surrender (18. 60–72). Instead of debate about the merits of the policy, Demosthenes offers vivid description of the decision to adopt it, making it seem as if the events and decisions that led to it were inevitable. This narrative reaches a rhetorical crescendo in the famous passage describing the reaction to the news that Philip had seized the Phocian city of Elatea, the act that placed Athens in grave and immediate danger (18. 169–79). As Demosthenes describes it, at first the city was frantic, but then, in an assembly convened early the next morning, the citizens were hushed as they awaited the one speaker who would rise to save them. After summarizing the speech he delivered on that occasion, in which the policy to ally with Thebes and confront Philip is set out, Demosthenes concludes as follows (18. 179):

Having spoken these words and others to the same effect, I stepped down. Everyone approved and no one said a word in opposition. I did not deliver the speech without moving a proposal, nor did I move a proposal without serving as envoy, nor did I serve as envoy without winning over the Thebans. I persevered from beginning to end and for your sake applied myself entirely to the dangers encircling the city.[12]

There was no debate, no opposition in the Athenian assembly!—a statement that rightly strains a historian's credulity. The fact of the matter is beyond our reach, but the rhetorical intent is clear: Demosthenes wants to claim sole responsibility for the Chaeronea

---

[12] Translations of Demosthenes are mine.

policy, in both conception and execution. This enables him to make Chaeronea simultaneously the natural culmination of Athens' history and the defining act of his career.

Second, Demosthenes distinguishes between incompetence and failure. He argues that, even in hindsight, his anti-Philip policy was perfect and ought by every measure of such things to have succeeded: he formed an accurate assessment of the danger posed by Philip to Athens and Athenian interests; he implemented it flawlessly and proved it correct in the years leading up to Chaeronea, when Athens made significant gains at Philip's expense;[13] and he had the unwavering support of the *dēmos*, who were enabled to understand and undertake the policy because of Demosthenes' public eloquence (18. 88, 94, 172–3, 179, 219–21, 246, 276–81). Far from being incompetent, his policy and political behaviour were flawless. How then did the defeat at Chaeronea and Athens' subjection to Macedon come to pass? By the best human reckoning, Demosthenes argues, success ought to have followed, as until then it had under his leadership; but the Athenians were opposed either by the gods or by inscrutable chance (18. 192–210, 270–5). In constructing this explanation for the defeat at Chaeronea, which was emphasized by Lucian's 'Philip', Demosthenes evokes the awe associated with tragedy and thereby encourages the audience to see in him the stature of a tragic hero. In the following passage, which recalls Solon's homily on the fickleness of fortune as told by Herodotus (1. 30–2), Demosthenes dignifies his plight in response to Aeschines' attempt to belittle it (18. 252): 'It makes no sense at all for one human being to scoff at another human being because of his fortune. A man may suppose that he enjoys the utmost prosperity and believe that he possesses unsurpassed good fortune, but he does not know if he shall still have it that evening. How then is one to speak about it? How is one to reproach another?'[14]

Bernard Williams recently observed that this perspective on human action, derived primarily from epic and tragic poetry, can also be used to explain our world, the world of affairs:

Greek tragedy precisely refuses to present human beings who are ideally in harmony with their world, and has no room for a world that, if it were

---

[13] In Euboea, the Chersonese, and Byzantium in the late 340s (Dem. 18. 79–94).

[14] Dem. 18. 303–5 revisits this point.

understood well enough, could instruct us how to be in harmony with it. There is a gap between what the tragic character is, concretely and contingently, and the ways in which the world acts upon him. In some cases, that gap is comprehensible, in terms of conflicting human purposes. In other cases, it is not fully comprehensible and not under control. *That may be as true of social reality as of a world that contains supernatural necessities. The interaction of character or individual project with forces, structures, or circumstances that can destroy them can retain its significance without the presence of gods or oracles.* (1993: 164–5; emphasis added)

The third respect in which Demosthenes adopts a tragic way of thinking is by explicitly rejecting outcome—that is, the standard applied, in their distinct ways, by both Aeschines and Cawkwell—and by insisting on his intentions as the proper measure of his record (18. 199–200):

Since Aeschines insists vehemently on how things have turned out, I wish to say something rather paradoxical. Do not, by Zeus and the gods, be astonished at the outrageousness of my argument... If what was going to happen was clear to all in advance and all knew in advance... not even in those circumstances should the city have abandoned its policy, *if indeed it valued its reputation or its forebears or the future.* True, the city seems to have failed in its objectives, which is the common lot of all mankind when god so decides. But if it claimed to be the leader of the rest of Greece and then retired before Philip, it would have been guilty of betraying all Greeks.

The pivotal phrase is the one I have emphasized: if the city 'valued its reputation or its forebears or the future'; this phrase reveals the thread of reasoning that Demosthenes uses to make the claim about his intentions compelling. Earlier in the speech Demosthenes argued that as an *Athenian* politician, one conscious of Athens' heritage as the defender of Greek freedom against barbarian tyranny, he had no choice but to recommend the aggressive policy against Philip; likewise the *dēmos*, who were reminded of this heritage daily by numerous civic monuments and patriotic occasions, also had no choice but to adopt it (18. 66–8).

The claim made by the burden of the past receives its most potent formulation in what is the most famous passage of the speech, the oath by the fighters of Marathon (18. 208):

But you were not wrong, Athenians, no, you were not wrong to take on danger for the sake of the safety and freedom of all—I swear it by your forefathers who led the fight at Marathon, by those who stood in the line at

Plataea, by those who fought on ship at Salamis and Artemisium, and by the many other brave citizens lying in the public tombs, all of whom the city buried, deeming them all equally worthy of the same honour, Aeschines, not just those among them who were successful or victorious.

Aeschines' outrage over the dead of Chaeronea derived its force from the premise that useful and beloved lives were wasted in criminally misguided policy. Demosthenes attempts to defuse the notion that they were criminally misguided by making the audience, as the author of *On Sublimity* says (16.2), 'as proud of the battle with Philip as of the triumphs of Marathon and Salamis'. Marathon and Salamis, of course, were kept alive in Athenian funeral orations and public monumental art as the touchstones of Athenian valour.[15] How could Demosthenes' policy have been criminally misguided if the dead of Chaeronea were emulating these ancestors? No matter that the Athenians *lost* the battle with Philip: the civic impulse was one and the same in both triumph and defeat, a principle that the Athenians already implicitly recognize when they bestow public burial on all Athenian soldiers who die in battle, regardless of whether they won or were defeated.

The burden of the Athenian past—that is, the necessity to confront Philip at Chaeronea in order to remain true to their heritage and therefore to themselves—is clearly not a political argument in the sense that it considers advantage and disadvantage. But, like the response of Thucydides' Melians who spurn the 'reasonable' offer of the plain-speaking Athenian invaders, it is a political argument in that it affects communal action while rejecting the question of advantage. Beyond the practical circumstances that, at the time, may have conduced to make the Chaeronea policy desirable or even necessary, an issue that Demosthenes does not omit, he adds this further layer of explanation that has nothing to do with utilitarian considerations, but which creates in the audience an emotionally resonant awareness of the rightness of the action. Again, this is a recognizable feature of Greek tragedy, in which action—such as Ajax's suicide, Achilles' generosity towards Priam, or Medea's murder of her children—is expressive of character and constitutes the chief vehicle through which character asserts its moral claims.

---

[15] On funeral orations, cf. Loraux 1986: 155–71; on public art, Hölscher 1998.

This anti-utilitarian perspective on action was considered by Stuart Hampshire (a former colleague of Williams). Hampshire (1978) views it as the assertion of a moral imperative not because of any moral injunction, rational principle, or utilitarian consideration, but as the expression of a way of life, an ideal way of life, that will not be abandoned or sacrificed. Like Williams, Hampshire specifically rejects divine or supernatural associations as a necessary component. For instance, one can readily imagine a mundane context for such utterances as 'I cannot leave him now: it would be impossible'; or 'Surely you understand that I *must* help him' (1978: 9). More germane to the present case might be Hector's decision that he *must* go out and fight, even though he will surely die and thereby hasten the destruction of family and city; or that of Eteocles, that he *must* fight at the seventh gate, even though he will thereby kill his brother. In both cases the decision to act is taken in the name of a way of life which the agent finds it impossible to renounce. In Hampshire's words, these are

judgments of unconditional necessity, in the sense that they imply that what must be done is not necessary because it is a means to some independently valued end, but because the action is a necessary part of a way of life and ideal of conduct. The necessity resides in the nature of the action itself, as specified in the fully explicit moral judgment. The principal and proximate grounds for claiming that the action must, or must not, be performed are to be found in the characterisation of the action . . . *and then a whole way of life will have to be described.* (1978: 13; emphasis added)

The Athenian past, as Demosthenes describes it in *On the Crown*, is this whole way of life, this ideal of conduct, that constrained the Athenians' choice of action. Demosthenes' account of the inexorable march towards Chaeronea functions as the characterization of the action. Together, this description of the Athenian way of life and this characterization of the essential Athenian action create the impression of an unconditional necessity that the Athenians should meet Philip on the field at Chaeronea. This rhetorical move presents Demosthenes' intentions, his decisive fidelity to Athenian tradition at a moment of crisis, as his lasting, successful contribution to Athens. Thus Demosthenes does not argue for exoneration on the basis of law or justice. Rather, in typical Athenian fashion he argues that it is the very superior interests of the community that should encourage the jurors to exonerate him, as a public statement that in Athens questions of self-interest are still subordinated to questions of honour, as they always have been in the Athenian tradition.

Consider a final, crucial question: how was it that Demosthenes' argument regarding the defeat at Chaeronea, his adaptation of what I have called a tragic mode of thinking,[16] was successful with the audience? Although the various arenas of public discourse in Athens each possessed their own defining conventions and settings, there was considerable overlap among them of both the people involved and the topics discussed. This is especially true of the theatre and the political institutions. Artistic exchange passing over the bounds of the genres took place and it did so in various forms. In political or judicial rhetoric, for instance, speakers might quote epic or tragic poetry in order to use the prestige of the poet to bolster a particular argument. So, for instance, Demosthenes quotes Sophocles' *Antigone* to illustrate Aeschines' failure to place the community's interests over personal ones, or Lycurgus quotes at length Praxithea's speech from Euripides' *Erechtheus* to illustrate the virtue of self-sacrifice.[17] This sort of thing could be done on almost any occasion.[18] Only the right bit of poetry had to be found to suit the point at hand, much as American politicians and lawyers of an earlier day used suitable passages of the Bible to support whatever case they were arguing at the moment.

Nevertheless, the artistic borrowing described in this paper is different in kind from merely incorporating a passage of poetry into a prose speech. It is, rather, the borrowing of a way of thinking and reasoning that is typical in one genre and adapting it for use in the other genre, as for instance, to return to the American analogy, political figures of the civil rights movement incorporated into their public reasoning a biblical notion of redemption, which was most evident in the speeches of Martin Luther King, Jr. Demosthenes' task, however, presented a particular challenge: there was a fundamental

[16] Not *the* tragic mode of thinking, which would assert too much. Clearly, Greek tragic poetry is not so monolithic as to be characterized by a single mode of thinking.

[17] Dem. 19. 246–50, Lyc. *Leoc.* 98–102; cf. also Aeschin. 1. 141–54. According to Arist. *Rh.* 1. 15. 13, Cleophon quoted Solon's elegies in a speech against Critias. Cf. also Plutarch's report (*Phoc.* 17.1) that Phocion quoted the *Odyssey* against Demosthenes.

[18] See Wilson 1996: 312–15; Ford 1999; Perlman 1964, esp. 162–5.

divide, seldom bridged, between the pessimism of Athenian tragic poetry and the optimism of Athenian political and legal speeches. Demosthenes could hardly make an explicit appeal to his audience to adopt a tragic point of view in a forum where that would be out of place.[19] Further, language in the grand style of the tragic stage sounded bombastic in an Athenian court, as Demosthenes derisively reminds Aeschines, the former tragic actor.[20] Thus, while attempting to endow himself with attributes of a tragic hero, Demosthenes had to do so surreptitiously and generally had to avoid an overt display of tragic style.

Recall the consequences of a borrowing across the same genres that went in the reverse direction, when Euripides learned from the *rhētores* and sophists of the fifth century and seamlessly incorporated rhetorical and political ways of reasoning and speaking into tragic diction. He produced new kinds of tragic characters and tragic plots, or, as Aristophanes and Nietzsche claimed, by dragging political reality onto the tragic stage he brought tragedy to an end (cf. Goldhill 1997). When viewed in retrospect, this kind of artistic innovation may seem to express the mood of the times, a mood that otherwise may have been latent and unconscious. But that is a pat answer that begs the question: what were the circumstances in which *On the Crown* was delivered and what was it in those circumstances that made Demosthenes' use of a tragic mode compelling to his audience?

In 330 BC, as Cawkwell argued (1969), Athens had virtually no prospect of emerging from its subjugation to Macedon.[21] Alexander had recently delivered the decisive blow to Darius, the Persian king, at the battle of Gaugamela; and the revolt against Macedonian hegemony led by Agis of Sparta, which Athens had not joined, had recently been crushed.[22] Thus Athens could no longer hope for assistance from either Persia or Sparta, the only remaining potential allies. On the other hand, these grim facts do not tell the whole story: after Chaeronea the Athenians rebuilt their fortifications, reformed

[19] Parker 1997, esp. 155–6; Strasburger 1958: 17–40. In the surviving corpus of classical Greek oratory, including the funeral orations, Dem. 18 is the only instance in which the pessimistic, tragic mode takes on a central role in persuasion.

[20] Dem. 18. 13, 127, 242, 313; cf. Ar. *Peace* 136; Easterling 1999.

[21] On Athens' political situation during this period, cf. Habicht 1997: 23–35.

[22] The date of the defeat of Agis has been contested, some arguing for fall of 331; cf. Habicht 1997: 21, arguing for the spring of 330.

the military training of their youth (*ephēbeia*), enlarged their armada, and improved their armaments.²³ As is shown by the speech *On the Treaty with Alexander*, which stems from the late 330s and was preserved in the Demosthenic corpus ([Dem.] 17), anti-Macedonian feeling in Athens was strong enough to lead some to advocate open revolt.²⁴ The attitude in Athens in the years after Chaeronea can be seen most clearly, perhaps, in the startling events of 323: when Alexander died suddenly, the Athenians revolted immediately and with massive force, putting at sea the largest fleet ever in their history. They had been waiting and preparing for the moment, but having had no battle experience in sixteen years, they were no match for the battle-tested Macedonians (Habicht 1997: 36–42).

Thus, in 330 the Athenians were weak, subjugated, in no position to revolt, yet somehow unwilling to accept defeat. I would add that the memory of the panic of 335—the sense of disaster barely averted—was still fresh, as was a lesson which Demosthenes may have learned on that occasion. In that year a rumour of Alexander's death soon after his accession had emboldened the Thebans to rise in revolt (Arrian, *Anab.* 1. 7. 2–3; Justin, *Epit.* 11. 2. 8). The Athenians, led by Demosthenes, gave some material aid to the revolt, and were in the midst of considering whether to join it when it was quickly and brutally crushed: Alexander, with the aid of some Greeks, razed Thebes to the ground and killed or sold into slavery all the inhabitants. The Athenians were stunned. From time immemorial Thebes had always been there, but, as Aeschines put it (3. 133), 'Thebes, Thebes, our neighbour city, has in one day been snatched from the midst of Greece'. As the largest state and recent head of resistance to Macedon, the Athenians now stood exposed to the ultimate danger. The city was thrown into utter panic; for the first and, so far as we know, only time, the celebration of the Eleusinian Mysteries was broken off after it had begun.²⁵

---

²³ On the reform of the *ephēbeia*, the two-year military training given to all Athenian men as young adults, cf. Arist. *Ath. Pol.* 42; Habicht 1997: 16; Bosworth 1988: 209–10. On the strengthening of the navy, cf. ibid. 208–9. On Lycurgus' programme rebuilding the fortifications, cf. Engels 1992: 15–17.

²⁴ On the date of [Dem.] 17, cf. Will 1983: 67–70.

²⁵ Arrian, *Anab.* 1. 10. 3. On the interruption of the Mysteries, cf. Mylonas 1961: 257.

In fact, Alexander held his hand, but he demanded several prominent Athenians, Demosthenes among them, to be handed over as hostages to assure Athenian loyalty. The assembly in which the matter was debated is reported by two sources, which agree on the basic facts, including the gist of a speech by Demosthenes.[26] In the midst of heated debate, Phocion urged that the hostages should indeed be handed over; for, he said, they should be glad to have the opportunity to die for their city. But Demosthenes, who naturally had a different view, prevailed upon the *dēmos* to reject the demand. As Diodorus reports it (17. 15. 2–3): 'The people drove [Phocion] from the platform in an uproar and rejected his advice. And when Demosthenes delivered a carefully prepared speech, they were carried away with sympathy for the men and clearly wished to save them' (Welles tr. 1963, adapted).

Ultimately the hostages were not handed over and Phocion and Demades negotiated another method of placating Alexander. The Athenians managed to escape Alexander's wrath while gesturing towards the independence that they prized and, one must believe, longed for. But thereafter Athens remained a quiescent subject state of Macedon for as long as Alexander reigned. Though Chaeronea was the decisive military event in which power was shifted out of Athenian hands, the quick and utter destruction of Thebes was, I suggest, the decisive event for Athenian public consciousness. Demosthenes may have learned from the panic of 335 and the consequent debate on the hostages that even though the *dēmos* were thoroughly cowed and would not do anything actually to provoke Alexander, they felt the need to make a gesture of independence, which the practical, busy Alexander was inclined to tolerate (Habicht 1997: 13, 15). This is what Demosthenes enabled them to do in 330, by allowing them to crown him in the name of their glorious, ancestral tradition. And—equally important—he did so without openly inciting them to revolt.

It does not matter that the burden of the Athenian past may have played no role at all in the formulation of the original policy. In 330, when anticipation had taken the place of resistance and any designs to free Athens from Macedonian hegemony had to be indefinitely

---

[26] Plut. *Dem.* 23. 4–6, Diod. Sic. 17. 15. 2–3. The quotations in Plutarch's account, attributed to Aristobulus of Cassandreia (*FGrH* 139 F 3), are fictitious.

postponed, it was a question of artistically contrived reminiscence or, to put it bluntly, wishful remembering. At the time of the trial, the events under discussion were relatively recent, but no longer fresh. Most of the jurors would themselves have been participants in the events, and they would have been encumbered by memories, gaps, and prejudices that both advocates had to account for. The audience was as little prepared to accept or recognize an objective account as the advocates were inclined to offer one. To judge from the outcome of the trial, the audience found Demosthenes' version of the past more compelling, which obviously does not imply that Demosthenes' version was closer to the truth. If it implies anything, it is that Demosthenes' version was closer to the way the jurors wished to recollect the past. The *dēmos* had, after all, followed Demosthenes step by step down the road to Chaeronea; they held the power of decision; they adopted Demosthenes' policy. Had they wished to, the jurors could have accepted Aeschines' version of the past, which, while making Demosthenes into an inveterate cheat, would have made them into dupes.

Demosthenes, however, offered his audience a noble version of their reasons for adopting his advice, reasons that were compelling in the face of a failure which they were forced to reckon with but not prepared to accept as final. While presenting himself as a hero, Demosthenes takes meticulous care to present his audience simultaneously as demotic Athenian heroes like the fighters of Marathon. If he was heroic and true to Athenian tradition for leading them to Chaeronea, they were equally heroic and true to that tradition for choosing to follow him there (18. 206–8, 215–16, 293). Even though they were defeated, Demosthenes gave them reason both to think well of themselves for having resisted Philip as best they could and to bide their time until the next opportunity. If they could not defeat Philip, at least they could save their reputation and their purpose, which is what Demosthenes managed for them while preserving his career. He offered them the moral confidence amid a changing, collapsing world that is a mark of Greek epic and tragic poetry, indeed of heroic fiction in general. Post-classical students of classical literature correctly sensed the power of this artistry; they were also correct to feel that in its way it rivals Homer. They were simply not in a position to understand it critically in its historical context.

A Glossary of Greek and Latin Terms

for Rhetoric and Law (as used in this volume)

actio, pl. *actiones*: in Roman procedure, a legal 'action' or lawsuit, esp. a remedy specific to the offence (e.g. *actio doli*, 'suit for fraud'); see *legis actiones*

agōn, pl. *agōnes*: (1) 'contest', trial; (2) 'argument' in the proof-section of the speech

akribeia: precision, esp. in choice of words or details

Amphictiony: a league of states committed to preserve a religious centre (the members were Amphictiones, 'neighbours'); esp. the league for defence of Apollo's shrine at Delphi

anakrisis: preliminary hearing before the archon

antidosis: a legal challenge for exchange of property, issued by a plaintiff who contends that a more wealthy adversary should take over his burden of 'liturgies'; if the adversary refuses, the court decides whether he must assume the liturgy

apagōgē: 'summary arrest', seizing a wrongdoer in clearly incriminating circumstances

aphesis: formal 'release' from debt or liability, often paired with *apallagē*, discharge or 'quittance' (esp. involving payment or exchange)

apodeixis: (1) exposition or outline (esp. of the argument); (2) argument or demonstration in the proof-section of the speech.

apographē: listing of property for confiscation, or the suit to seize the listed property of a state debtor

apologia: speech for the defence

apophasis: a fourth-century procedure against corruption and official wrongdoing: a preliminary investigation was held before the Areopagus council; they handed down an indictment which was reviewed by the assembly before issuing a decree for trial

apragmosunē (or *apragmosynē*): 'quietism', avoiding involvement in lawsuits and public business (as opposed to *polypragmosunē*, excessive involvement)

aprobouleumatic: referring to a decree lacking the council's preliminary authorization (*probouleuma*)

archon: an executive officer (lit. 'leader, ruler'), esp. in his role as magistrate (though the term is sometimes used of any public office). Among the nine executives were the Archon Basileus (homicide and religious matters) and the six Thesmothetae

Areopagus (or Areiopagos): the hill just west of the Acropolis, or the council of former archons who convened there for murder trials and other procedures (see *apophasis*)

astynomos: 'city supervisor'; an official of the late fourth century, esp. in charge of streets and public buildings

atechnos pistis, pl. *atechnoi pisteis*: 'artless proof'(without *technē*). By the fourth century these were documentary sources of argumentation: affidavits of witnesses, challenges to oath or to torture; texts of laws or contracts

atimia: disfranchisement (lit. 'dishonour' or 'rightlessness'): being denied citizen rights, esp. the right to legal redress. Those affected are *atimoi*

basanos: generally a test of truth ('touchstone'). In the speeches this term usually refers to the 'interrogation' of slaves under torture or the challenge to submit a question to slaves under torture

boulē: council: at Athens the deliberative body of 500 (fifty chosen by lot from each tribe) whose duties included preparing the agenda for the assembly, 'scrutiny', and accountings of public officials (see *dokimasia* and *euthuna*)

bouleutēs, pl. *bouleutai*: member of council (*boulē*)

captatio benevolentiae: securing the goodwill of the audience (a standard feature of the prologue)

chorēgia: the public duty (liturgy) of producing a 'chorus', choral performance, or drama

cleruch (*klērouchos*): 'colonist'; an Athenian citizen sent out to take possession of property in subjugated states within the empire

de cuius: lit. 'from (or concerning) whose (estate)'; the person (deceased) whose property is at issue

deinōtēs: powerful or arresting effect; the rhetorical style or skill producing that effect

deme (one sense of *demos*): one of the 139 villages or precincts of Attica; the basic unit of political life, with its own assembly and executive officer (demarch)

dēmēgorikos: 'addressing the people', esp. a speech addressing the assembly

deme judges: originally circuit judges who travelled to the demes, deciding minor cases; replaced in the fourth century by a board of Forty, four assigned to each tribe

dēmos: the people, esp. the assembly as sovereign body of the people

diabolē: (1) generally 'slander'; (2) the rhetorical strategy of discrediting the adversary by rousing the suspicion and resentment of the audience

diadikasia: disposition by magistrate or court of a contested estate

diaita: arbitration; the arbitrator is *diaitētēs*

diamarturia: a peremptory statement, often sufficient to decide claims to property

dianoia: rational conception or 'decision-making ability' (as opposed to 'character', *ēthos*)

dicanic: having to do with the courts, 'forensic' (as opposed to 'symbouleutic')

dicast (or dikast): see *dikastēs*

dikastai kata dēmous: see 'deme judges'

dikastērion, pl. *dikastēria*: court; esp. the ordinary court manned by a citizen jury

dikastēs, pl. *dikastai*: the judge or 'juror' in Athenian courts; often Anglicized as 'dicast'

dikē, pl. *dikai*: (1) lawsuit, esp. civil litigation; (2) 'justice' in the abstract

dikē dēmosia or *idia*: distinguished as 'public or private'

Distinguished by nature of the offence:

aikeias: 'for assault', esp. involving physical violence

blabēs: 'for damage', including losses in business

emporikē: 'commercial suit', esp. involving maritime trade

exoulēs: for unlawfully barring the owner from his property (esp. when a plaintiff has won the right to seize property in payment or penalty)

kakēgorias: 'for slander'

lipomarturiou: for failing to appear for testimony, after summons (*klēteusis*)

metallikē: 'mining suit', involving mines leased from the polis

phonou: 'for homicide' (prosecuted by kinsmen of the deceased)

pseudomarturiōn: 'for false testimony'; sometimes rendered 'perjury', as witnesses were under oath for *dikē phonou* and in other cases they could be challenged to swear if they refused testimony

diēgēsis: 'narrative', the portion of a speech relating the sequence of events in the case

digressio: digression = *parekbasis*

divisio, pl. *divisiones*: conventional division of the speech into parts with designated functions

dokimasia: examination (or 'confirmation hearing'), of incoming officers by the council or of candidates for citizenship in the deme, sometimes leading to court trial

dokimasia rhētorōn: a trial procedure to disqualify and penalize speakers active in the assembly (esp. those who proposed decrees)

drachma: standard unit of Athenian money; 6 obols make a drachma; see also *mna*

echinos: the jar for evidence (sealed) in cases on appeal from a public arbitrator

eikos, pl. *eikota*: 'likeness' or 'likelihood', esp. argument from 'probability'

eisangelia: lit. a 'report', esp. to the council or assembly, denouncing a public official for corruption or misconduct (= 'impeachment'). The same term is used of complaints to the archon for mistreatment or defrauding of orphans or *epiklēroi*

eisphora: a tax on property assessed in times of need

elenchos: refutation; a test or challenge that forces a confession or contradiction

embateusis: lit. 'entering' a property to take possession of it (as an inheritance or in payment of a debt)

enklēma: the formal charge, written out in particular wording consistent with the relevant law (hence 'writ'), which the presiding magistrate would read (along with the defendant's statement) at the commencement of the trial

entechnos pistis: 'artful proof'; argument crafted by rhetorical technique, using circumstantial considerations (as opposed to documentary material in *atechnos pistis*)

enthymeme (enthumēma): an argument or sequence of reasoning; esp. rhetorical syllogism, in which the premises are 'probabilities' (see *eikos*)

ephebe, ephēbēs: the young man newly come of age for citizenship and military service

ephēbeia (or *ephēbia*): the transition to manhood. In the fourth century this term describes a compulsory period of military training

ephetai: the jury of fifty-one who sat in judgement of homicides other than intentional murder, esp. at the Palladium and Delphinium courts (for unintentional and 'justifiable' killing, respectively)

epieikeia: 'equity' or fairness, esp. as a consideration weighing against the letter of the law

epiklēros: often glossed as 'heiress', the surviving daughter of a man who died without sons. Her father's property would go with her (in trust) to the kinsman she married, to be inherited by the grandson

erōtikos (pl. *-oi*) or *eroticus*: amorous essay or plea

ēthopoeia: the technique of character portrayal

ēthos: 'character' as a persuasive element, esp. through portrayal of motives and emotions

euthuna (or *euthyna*): accounting of public officials

exagōgē: 'removal', claiming rightful ownership and formally dislodging the holder of a property

exceptio doli: in Roman procedure, an objection or plea to bar a claim because of fraud (esp. in contract disputes)

exordium: the beginning of a speech (cf. *captatio benevolentiae*)

exō tou pragmatos: 'outside the matter', irrelevant to the issue in dispute

gelōtopoeia: technique aimed at humorous effect, lit. 'causing laughter'

genos, pl. *genē*: a group claiming common descent, esp. a subgroup of the phratry. Members are *gennētai*

gnōmē dikaiotatē: the jury's 'most just opinion', invoked where the law is not definitive

grammateus: scribe or recorder: (1) the clerk of court who reads out the documents; (2) the secretary to the council (*boulē*) charged with publishing decrees

graphē: 'public suit' (as roughly opposed to 'private' *dikē*). Distinguished by charge:

    hubreōs: for *hubris* or 'violation', esp. sexual or otherwise humiliating assault

    paranomōn: for proposing an unconstitutional measure

gunē, pl. *gunaikes*: woman or wife, usually of citizen status (whose children are legitimate)

hēgemōn: 'leader' or governing authority; esp. the presiding magistrate in court

heliasts, heliastic court: the ordinary juries of the people, so called from the combined body of all jury-panels, the Heliaea

hetaira: female 'companion' or 'courtesan'

ho boulomenos: 'the one willing': any 'concerned citizen' who took it upon himself to bring a public action (*graphē, eisangelia*, etc.)

horos (pl. -*oi*): boundary stone or pillar (1) to bar *atimoi* from the agora and other prohibited areas; (2) inscribed to indicate mortgaged property

hubris (or hybris): violent assault or violation

idiōtēs, pl. *idiōtai*: private person, as opposed to one active in public business

idiōtismos (pl. -*oi*): peculiarities (of speech)

isēgoria: equal rights in speaking, esp. the right to address the assembly

kakourgos, pl. -*oi*: malefactor or 'felon', subject to 'summary arrest' (*apagōgē*), esp. when taken in the act of robbery or assault

katastasis: (1) 'setting up', an outline or 'arrangement' of topics in a speech, as preface to narrative and argument (as in 'Anaximenes'); see *prokatastasis*; (2) sometimes equivalent to the 'narrative', *diēgēsis* (as used by Isocrates)

katēgoria: speech for the prosecution

charis: grace or charm, as a feature of style

klepsudra: water-clock, used to measure out the allotted time for speeches in the courts

klēteusis: summoning a witness (under threat of *dikē lipomarturiou* if he fails to appear)

kurios (or *kyrios*): the 'master' exercizing authority over a household (typically husband or father). In legal matters women, children, slaves, and other dependents, had to be represented by their male *kurios*. It is sometimes extended to other settings: thus the law, the court, or the demos is sometimes called *kurios* ('supreme' if not 'sovereign')

legis actiones: in early Roman procedure, formalistic remedies prescribed by statute (*lex*), in which the complaint should strictly adhere to the wording of the statute

liturgy, *leitourgia*: a public duty, such as producing a drama or outfitting a warship, assigned to wealthy individuals or groups

loci communes: rhetorical 'commonplaces', stock passages adapted for use in different speeches

logographos: 'speechwriter', who scripted speeches for others to deliver (esp. at trial)

logopoios: (1) 'story-writer', esp. historian; (2) in later usage, a synonym for *logographos*

marturia: testimony (from *martus*, witness)

metic, metoikos: resident alien. Ineligible for most offices, these registered foreigners were entitled to legal protections (relying on a citizen representative, *prostatēs*) and were liable for taxes and liturgies

mna, pl. *mnai* (minae or minas): a unit of money equal to 100 drachmas, 1/60th of a talent

moichos, pl. -*oi*: 'adulterer' or seducer of a woman under another man's protection

nomothetai: lit. 'lawgivers'. In the fourth century a special panel of dicasts convened for the ratification of new laws (as distinct from decrees of the assembly)

oikos: 'house(hold)'; esp. the family (with slaves and dependents) as a group connected by property rights and personal obligations

paideia: 'education', both formal training and formative cultural experience

pallakē: concubine or mistress; a woman kept for sexual relations (whose offspring were freeborn)

paragraphē: 'special plea' to bar a lawsuit, esp. on grounds of some previous settlement, statute of limitations, improper jurisdiction, or other procedural obstacle

paraskeuē, pl. -*ai*: 'preparation', prepared speech

paredros: coadjutor; one who assists or acts on behalf of a magistrate, esp. for the archons

parekbasis: digression

peristatika: circumstances or relevant details (esp. the 'where, when, who, why, and how')

phasis: 'denunciation' of illegal goods (or the suit initiated in this way)

phatry: lit. 'brotherhood' or 'fraternity'; a tribal subgroup. Admission to the phratry generally preceded citizenship (cf. 'deme'). Members are *phratores* or *phrateres*

pinakion, pl. *-ia*: (1) the bronze disk that served as a juror's identification; (2) more commonly, a plaque giving notice of lawsuits or legal decisions

pistis, pl. *pisteis*: lit. 'trust', used of evidence in which once places trust; (1) often glossed as 'proof' (esp. as a section of the speech); (2) more strictly, 'evidentiary material'

Piraeus (or Peiraieus): the main harbour of Athens, to the south

Pnyx: the low hill just west of the Areopagus, where the Athenian assembly convened

pornē: prostitute

praeteritio: rhetorical 'bypass'. The speaker alludes to a topic which (he suggests) he might pursue to great advantage, but which (for now) he leaves aside

proem or proeme (*prooimion*, pl. *prooimia*): prologue or preface, the first part of the speech

prokatalēpsis: pre-emptive 'anticipation' of arguments from the opposition

prokatastasis: the section of a speech (in more complex arrangements) preliminary to the layout of topics, *katastasis*

proklēsis: a challenge to decide certain legal issues by mutual agreement, esp. by oath or slave torture (*basanos*)—not to be confused with *prosklēsis*, 'summons'

proparaskeuē: 'advance preparation'; the part of a speech (esp. for court cases) laying groundwork for the argument

prostatēs, pl. *prostatai*: generally a 'protector' (lit. 'one who stands in front'); esp. the citizen patron of a metic

proxenos, pl. *-oi*: an official representative of Athenian interests abroad or of other communities at Athens. Such officials were often honoured with special privileges and protections

prytany: the presiding committee of council and assembly, or the time-period of their presidency. Each of the ten tribes was represented in council by a committee of fifty members which held the prytany in rotation. A member of the presiding committee was a *prytanis* (pl. *prytaneis*)

psēphos: vote or ballot. The court ballot was a bronze disk with a shaft in the middle, either hollow (a vote for the first speaker) or solid (for the second). See cover illustration

ratio decidendi: the rationale for a court decision—the Athenian courts gave none

rhētōr, pl. *rhetores*: (1) generally 'speaker', 'orator'; (2) expert in rhetoric (author of a rhetorical treatise); (3) as a term of law a *rhētor* is one who proposed decrees in the assembly and is legally accountable for those proposals

rhētorikē (sc. *technē*): 'rhetoric' as an art or discipline (a term perhaps coined by Plato)

stasis, pl. *staseis*: (1) 'issue'; the essential matter in dispute. Rhetorical theory (as early as Aristotle) distinguished between such issues as fact, law, and 'definition'; (2) faction, civil conflict

sub iudice: lit. 'under a judge', referring to the magistrate's handling of the suit before it can be brought before the jury

sukophantia: predatory litigation. The extent of the abuse is open to question. By the popular model, *sukophants* robbed their victims through frivolous lawsuits and extortion

sumbolaion (or *symbolaion*): contractual obligation or debt owing on a transaction

sumbouleutikos, symbouleutic: deliberative, esp. in the role of councillor or addressed to the council

sumboulos: consultant, adviser

sunagōgē (or *synagōgē*): ' collection', esp. in reference to the 'Collection of Rhetorical Handbooks', *Synagōgē Technōn*, of Aristotle

sunēgoros (or *synēgoros*), pl. *-oi*: supporting speaker

sungraphē: written contract (the document apparently required in *dikai emporikai*); from *sungraphein* = to draft a contract

sunthēkē, pl. *sunthēkai*: 'contract' or treaty, esp. a particular clause of a written agreement

technē. pl. *-ai*: lit. 'craft' or 'technique'; esp. the written exposition of rhetoric as a technique

tetralogy: a set of four speeches on one case (thesis and rebuttal for each side), as in the *Tetralogies* attibuted to Antiphon

thēs, pl. *thētes*: a member of the lowest property class at Athens (originally landless)

thesmothetēs, pl. *thesmothetai* or Thesmothetae: among the chief executives of Athenian government (the archons); the six *thesmothetai* served esp. as magistrates, conducting preliminary hearings and presiding at trial

thiasos, pl. *-oi*: a group devoted to a particular cult (esp. maintaining the shrine and conducting observances). Members are *thiasōtai*

topos: lit. 'a place' or 'passage'; esp. a 'commonplace' or 'common topic' in the sense of a conventional argument or theme

trierarch: a citizen charged with outfitting a trireme, one of the most costly 'liturgies'

trireme: an Athenian warship with three levels of oarsmen

trittys, pl. *trittyes*: a set of demes constituting the 'third-part' of a tribe. By the reforms of Cleisthenes (508 BC) citizens were grouped in ten tribes, each with a trittys from each of three geographical regions in Attica

vis maior: 'superior force' (*force majeur*); a plea that defendant is not liable as the damage was due to natural cause or necessity

References

ADKINS, A. W. H. (1960), *Merit and Responsibility*, Oxford.

—— (1972), *Moral Values and Political Behaviour in Ancient Greece*, London.

—— (1978), 'Problems in Greek Popular Morality', review of Dover 1974, *CP* 73: 143–58.

ALBINI, U. (1952), 'Lisia narratore', *Maia*, 5: 182–90.

—— (1958), 'Antifone logografo', *Maia*, 10: 38–65, 132–45.

ALLEN, D. S. (2000), *The World of Prometheus: The Politics of Punishing in Democratic Athens*, Princeton.

AMPOLO, C. (1981), 'Tra finanza e politica: carriera e affari del signor Moirokles', *Rivista di filologia*, 109: 187–204.

ANASTASSIOU, A., and IRMER, D. (1977) (eds.), *Kleinere Attische Redner*, Wege der Forschung, 127, Darmstadt.

ANDERSON, B. (1991), *Imagined Communities: Reflections on the Origin and Spread of Nationalism*, revised edn., London.

ANDRESEN, C., BARTELS, K., and HUBER, L. (1965) (eds.), *Lexikon der Alten Welt*, Zurich.

ANDREWES, A. (1961), 'Philochoros on Phratries', *JHS* 81: 1–15.

ARANGIO-RUIZ, V. (1946), *Rariora*, Rome.

ARMSTRONG, A. M. (1950), 'Trial by Combat Among the Greeks', *G&R* 19: 73–9.

ARNHART, L. (1981), *Aristotle on Political Reasoning: A Commentary on the 'Rhetoric'*, Dekalb, Ill.

AUSTIN, M. M., and VIDAL-NAQUET, P. (1977), *Economic and Social History of Ancient Greece: An Introduction*, London (French original, Paris 1972).

AVERY, H. C. (1991), 'Was Eratosthenes the Oligarch Eratosthenes the Adulterer?', *Hermes*, 119: 380–4.

AVEZZÙ, G. (1982) (ed.), *Alcidamante: Orazioni e frammenti*, Rome.

BADER, B. (1971), 'The *Psophos* of the House-Door in Greek New Comedy', *Antichthon* 5: 35–48.

BADIAN, E. (1992), 'Jaeger's *Demosthenes*: An Essay in Anti-History', in W. M. Calder III (ed.), *Werner Jaeger Reconsidered*, Atlanta, Ga.: 289–315.

BAITER, J. G., and SAUPPE, H. (1845–50) (eds.), *Oratores Attici: Pars Posterior. Scholia, Fragmenta, Indices*, Zurich.

BALDWIN, B. (1969), 'The Authorship and Purpose of Lucian's *Demosthenis Encomium*', *Antichthon*, 3: 54–62.

BALDWIN, J., and McCONVILLE, M. (1979), *Jury Trials*, Oxford.

BALL, M. S. (1975), 'The Play's the Thing: An Unscientific Reflection on Courts under the Rubric of Theater', *Stanford Law Review*, 28: 81–115.

BARABINO, G. (1967) (ed.), P. *Rutili Lupi schemata dianoeas et lexeos*, Genoa.

BARWICK, K. (1963), 'Das Problem der isokrateischen Techne', *Philologus*, 107: 43–60.

BEARZOT, C. (1990), 'Sul significato del divieto di *exō tou pragmatos legein* in sede areopagitica', *Aevum*, 64: 47–55.

BEAUCHET, L. (1897), *Histoire du droit privé de la République athénienne*, 4 vols. Paris, repr. New York, 1976.

BECHTLE, G. (1995), 'The Adultery-Tales in the Ninth Book of Apuleius' *Metamorphoses*', *Hermes*, 123: 106–16.

BENNETT, W. L., and FELDMAN, M. S. (1981), *Reconstructing Reality in the Courtroom*, New Brunswick, NJ.

BERNEKER, E. (1968), *Zur Griechischen Rechtsgeschichte*, Wege der Forschung, 45, Darmstadt.

BERS, V. (1994), 'Tragedy and Rhetoric', in Worthington 1994: 176–95.

BISCARDI, A. (1970), 'La "*gnomē dikaiotatē*" et l'interprétation des lois dans la Grèce ancienne', *RIDA* 17: 219–32.

BIZOS, M. (1967) (ed.), *Lysias: Quatre discours*, Érasme, 12, Paris.

BLUNDELL, J. (1980), *Menander and the Monologue*, Hypomnemata, 59, Göttingen.

BOEGEHOLD, A. L., and SCAFURO, A. C. (1994) (eds.), *Athenian Identity and Civic Ideology*, Baltimore.

BOGAERT, R. (1968), *Banques et banquiers dans les cités grecques*, Leiden.

BOHANNAN, P. (1957), *Justice and Judgment Among the Tiv*, London.

BOLTANSKI, L. (1990), *L'Amour et la justice comme compétences*, Paris.

BOMPAIRE, J. (1984), 'L'Apothéose de Démosthène, de sa mort jusqu'à l'époque de la IIᵉ Sophistique,' *Bulletin de l'association Guillaume Budé*: 14–26.

BOSWORTH, A. B. (1988), *Conquest and Empire: The Reign of Alexander the Great*, Cambridge.

BONADEO, A. (1981), 'Marriage and Adultery in the *Decameron*', *PQ* 60: 287–303.

BONNER, R. J. (1905), *Evidence in Athenian Courts*, Chicago.

—— (1916), 'The Institution of Athenian Arbitrators', *CP* 11: 191–5.

—— (1927), *Lawyers and Litigants in Ancient Athens: The Genesis of the Legal Profession*, Chicago

—— (1938), *The Administration of Justice from Homer to Aristotle*, II, Chicago.

—— and SMITH, G. (1930), *The Administration of Justice from Homer to Aristotle*, I, Chicago.

BOSSUET, J. B. (1975), *Sermons*, P. Sellier (ed.), Paris.

BOURDIEU, P. (1977), *Outline of a Theory of Practice*, Cambridge (1st edn. Geneva, 1972).

BROWN, H. L. (1914), *Extemporary Speech in Antiquity*, Chicago.

BROWN, P. G. M. (1993), 'Love and Marriage in Greek New Comedy', *CQ* 43: 189–205.

BROWN, P. R. L. (1975), 'Society and the Supernatural: A Medieval Change', *Daedalus*, 104.2: 133–51 (reprinted in Brown 1982).

—— (1982), *Society and the Holy in Late Antiquity*, Berkeley and Los Angeles.

BRUCK, E. F. (1909), *Die Schenkung auf den Todesfall im griechischen und römischen Recht, Zugleich ein Beitrag zur Geschichte des Testaments*, Aalen.

BRYANT, D. (1950), 'Aspects of the Rhetorical Tradition, I (The Intellectual Foundation)', *Quarterly Journal of Speech*, 36: 169–76.

BRUNS, I. (1896), *Das Literarische Porträt der Griechen*, Berlin.

BURFORD, A. (1972), *Craftsmen in Greek and Roman Society*, London.

BURKHARDT, J. (1956–7), *Griechische Kulturgeschichte*, Basel and Stuttgart.

BURNS, A. (1981), 'Athenian Literacy in the Fifth Century B.C.', *Journal of the History of Ideas*, 42: 371–87.

BUSOLT, G. (1920), *Griechische Staatskunde*, I, *Handbuch der Altertumswissenschaft*, 4.1.1, Munich.

—— and SWOBODA, H. (1926), *Griechische Staatskunde*, II: *Darstellung einzelner Staaten und der zwischenstaatlichen Beziehungen*, *Handbuch der Altertumswissenschaft*, 4.1.2, Munich.

BUXTON, R. (1990), 'Challenging and Discharging Jurors', *Criminal Law Review*, 37.4: 225–35 and 37.5: 284–91.

CALHOUN, G. M. (1913), *The Athenian Clubs in Politics and Litigation*, New York, repr. 1970.

—— (1914), 'Documentary Frauds in Litigation at Athens', *CP* 9: 134–44.

—— (1918), '*Diamarturia, paragraphē*, and the Law of Archinus', *CP* 13: 169–85.

—— (1919a), 'Oral and Written Pleading in Athenian Courts', *TAPA* 50: 177–193.

—— (1919b), 'Athenian Magistrates and Special Pleas', *CP* 14: 338–50.

—— (1927), *The Growth of Criminal Law in Ancient Greece*, Berkeley.

CAMPBELL, J. (1983), *F. E. Smith, First Earl of Birkenhead*, London.

CANFORA, L. (1974) (ed.), *Discorsi e lettere di Demostene*, I, Turin.

CANTARELLA, E. (1972), ' "Moicheia" e omicidio legittimo in diritto attico', *Labeo*, 18: 78–88.

CARAWAN, E. (1991): '*Ephetai* and Athenian Courts for Homicide', *CP* 86: 1–16.

—— (1998), *Rhetoric and the Law of Draco*, Oxford.

—— (2001), 'What the Laws Have Prejudged: *Paragraphē* and Early Issue Theory', in C. Wooten (ed.), *The Orator in Action and Theory in Greece and Rome*, Leiden.

—— (2002), 'The Athenian Amnesty and the "Scrutiny of the Laws" ', *JHS* 122: 1–23.

—— (2006), 'Amnesty and Accountings for the Thirty', *CQ* 56: 57–76.

CAREY, C. (1989) (ed.), *Lysias: Selected Speeches*, Cambridge.

—— (1992) *Greek Orators, VI. Apollodorus Against Neaira, [Demosthenes] 59*, Warminster.

—— (1993), 'Return of the Radish *or* Just when you thought it was safe to go back into the Kitchen', *LCM* 18: 53–5.

—— (1994), ' "Artless" Proofs in Aristotle and the Orators', *BICS* 39: 95–106 (Ch. 9 in this collection).

—— (1995), 'Rape and Adultery in Athenian Law', *CQ* 45: 407–17.

—— (1996), '*Nomos* in Rhetoric and Oratory', *JHS* 116: 33–46.

—— and REID, R. A. (1985), *Demosthenes: Selected Private Speeches*, Cambridge.

CARLIER, P. (1990), *Démosthène*, Paris.

CARTER, L. B. (1986), *The Quiet Athenian*, Oxford.

CARSON, A. (1990), 'Putting Her in Her Place: Woman, Dirt, and Desire', in D. M. Halperin, J. J. Winkler, and F. I. Zeitlin (eds.), *Before Sexuality: The Construction of Erotic Experience in the Ancient Greek World*, Princeton: 135–69.

CARTLEDGE, P. A., and HARVEY, F. D. (1985) (eds.), *Crux: Essays Presented to G. E. M. de Ste. Croix on his 75th Birthday*, Exeter.

—— MILLETT, P. C., and TODD, S. C. (1990) (eds.), *NOMOS: Essays in Athenian Law, Politics and Society*, Cambridge.

—— —— and REDEN, S. VON (1998) (eds.), *Kosmos: Essays in Order, Conflict, and Community in Classical Athens*, Cambridge.

CAWKWELL, G. L. (1963), 'Eubulus', *JHS* 83: 47–67.

—— (1978), *Philip of Macedon*, London.

—— (1969), 'The Crowning of Demosthenes', *CQ*² 19: 163–80.

CARRITHERS, M., COLLINS, S., and LUKES, S. (1985) (eds.), *The Category of the Person: Anthropology, Philosophy, History*, Cambridge.

CHALMERS, A. F. (1976), *What is this Thing called Science?* St. Lucia, Queensland, repr. Indianapolis, 1994.

CHAMBRY, E. (1964) (tr.), Platon, *Le Banquet; Phèdre*, Paris.

CHANIOTIS, A. (1996), 'Conflicting Authorities: Asylia Between Secular and Divine Law in the Classical and Hellenistic Poleis', *Kernos*, 9: 65–86.

—— (2004), 'Under the Watchful Eyes of the Gods: Divine Justice in Hellenistic and Roman Asia Minor', *YCS* 31: 1–43.

CLARK, C., and HASWELL, M. (1970), *The Economics of Subsistence Agriculture*, 4th edn., London.

CLARK, W. P. (1929), 'Private and Public Benefactions in Athenian Litigation', *CW* 23: 33–5.

CLEMENCEAU, G. (1926), *Démosthène*, Paris.

COHEN, D. (1983), *Theft in Athenian Law*, Munich.

—— (1991*a*), *Law, Sexuality, and Society: The Enforcement of Morals in Classical Athens*, Cambridge.

—— (1991*b*), 'Sexuality, Violence, and the Athenian Law of Hubris', *G&R* 38: 171–88.

—— (1995), *Law, Violence, and Community in Classical Athens*, Cambridge.

—— (2003), 'Writing, Law, and Legal Practice in the Athenian Courts', in H. Yunis (ed.), *Written Texts and the Rise of Literate Culture in Ancient Greece*, Cambridge: 78–96.

—— and MÜLLER-LUCKNER, E. (2002) (eds.), *Demokratie, Recht und soziale Kontrolle im klassischen Athen*, Munich.

COHEN, E. E. (1973), *Ancient Athenian Maritime Courts*, Princeton.

—— (1992), *Athenian Economy and Society: A Banking Perspective*, Princeton.

COHEN, J. A. (1968), *The Criminal Process in the People's Republic of China 1949–1963: An Introduction*, Cambridge, Mass.

COHN-HAFT, L. (1956), *The Public Physicians of Ancient Greece*, Northampton, Mass.

—— (1995), 'Divorce in Classical Athens', *JHS* 115: 1–14.

COLE, S. G. (1981), 'Could Greek Women Read and Write?', in H. P. Foley (ed.), *Reflections of Women in Antiquity*, New York: 219–45.

—— (1984), 'Greek Sanctions Against Sexual Assault', *CP* 79: 97–113.

COLE, T. (1991*a*), 'Who Was Corax?', *Illinois Classical Studies*, 16: 65–84 (Ch. 3 in this collection).

—— (1991*b*), *The Origins of Rhetoric in Ancient Greece*, Baltimore.

COLLARD, C. (2004) (ed.), 'Euripides, *Palamedes*', in C. Collard, M. J. Cropp, and J. Gibert (eds.), *Euripides: Selected Fragmentary Plays*, II, Warminster: 92–103.

CONN, S., and HIPPLER, A. E. (1974), 'Conciliation and Arbitration in the Native Village and the Urban Ghetto', *Judicature*, 58: 228–35.

CONNOR, W. R. (1971), *The New Politicians of Fifth-Century Athens*, Princeton.

—— (1984), *Thucydides*, Princeton.

CORNFORD, F. M. (1907), *Thucydides Mythistoricus*, London.

CORNISH, W. R. (1968), *The Jury*, London.

CROISSANT, F., and SALVIAT, F. (1966), 'Aphrodite guardienne des magistrats: gynéconomes de Thasos et polémarques de Thèbes', *Bulletin de Correspondance Hellénique*, 90: 460–71.

Cunha, M. C. da (1985), 'Silences of the Law: Customary Law and Positive Law on the Manumission of Slaves in 19th century Brazil', in Humphreys 1985: 427–43.

Dalby, A. (2002), 'Levels of Concealment: The Dress of *Hetairai* and *Pornai* in Greek Texts', in L. Llewellyn-Jones (ed.), *Women's Dress in the Ancient Greek World*, London: 111–24.

Dareste de la Chavanne, R. (1875), *Les Plaidoyers civils de Démosthène*, Paris.

Darkow, A. C. (1917), 'The Spurious Speeches of the Lysianic Corpus', diss. Bryn Mawr.

Davidson, J. N. (2000), '*Gnesippus Paigniagraphos:* The Comic Poets and the Erotic Mime', in D. Harvey and J. Wilkins (eds.), *The Rivals of Aristophanes: Studies in Athenian Old Comedy*, London: 41–64.

Davies, J. K. (1978), 'Athenian Citizenship: The Descent Group and the Alternatives', *CJ* 73: 105–21.

Davies, W. (1985), 'Disputes, their Conduct and their Settlement in the Village Communities of Eastern Brittany in the Ninth Century', in Humphreys 1985: 289–312.

Davison, J. A. (1962), 'Literature and Literacy in Ancient Greece', *Phoenix*, 16: 141–56, 219–33.

Deacy, S., and Pierce, K. F. (1997) (eds.), *Rape in Antiquity*, London.

De Brauw, M. (2001–2), ' "Listen to the Laws Themselves": Citations of Laws and Portrayal of Character in Attic Oratory', *CJ* 97: 161–76.

Desbordes, F. (1990), 'L'Argumentation dans la rhétorique antique: une introduction', *LALIES* 8: 81–110.

Detienne, M. (1979), 'Violentes "eugénies". En pleines Thesmophories: des femmes couvertes de sang', in M. Detienne and J.-P. Vernant (eds.), *La Cuisine du sacrifice en pays grec*, Paris: 183–214.

Devlin, P. (1956), *Trial by Jury*, London.

Devries, W. L. (1892), *Ethopoiia: A Rhetorical Study of the Types of Character in the Orations of Lysias*, Baltimore.

Dies, A. (1927), *Autour de Platon: essai de critique et d'homme*, 2 vols., Paris.

Dimock, G. E. (1952), '*Alla* in Lysias and Plato's *Phaedrus*', *AJP* 73: 381–96.

Domingo-Forasté, D. (1994) (ed.), *Lysias on the Murder of Eratosthenes*, CANE Instructional Material, Amherst, Md.

Donlan, W. (1980), *The Aristocratic Ideal in Ancient Greece: Attitudes of Superiority from Homer to the End of the Fifth Century*, Lawrence, Kan.

Doo, L.-W. (1973), 'Dispute Settlement in Chinese-American Communities', *American Journal of Comparative Law*, 21.4: 627–63.

Dorjahn, A. (1935), 'Anticipation of Arguments in Athenian Oratory', *TAPA* 66: 274–95.

DORJAHN, A (1941), 'On the Athenian Anakrisis', *CP* 36: 182–5.

—— (1947), 'On Demosthenes' Ability to Speak Extemporaneously', *TAPA* 78: 69–76.

—— (1950), 'A Further Study on Demonsthenes' Ability to Speak Extemporaneously', *CP* 45: 9–16.

—— (1952), 'A Third Study on Demosthenes' Ability to Speak Extemporaneously', *TAPA* 83: 164–71.

—— (1955), 'A Fourth Study on Demosthenes' Ability to Speak Extemporaneously', *CP* 50: 191–3.

—— and CRONIN, J. F. (1938), 'Outside Influence on Athenian Courts', *Philological Quarterly* (Iowa State University), 17: 18–25.

DOUGLAS, A. E. (1955), 'The Aristotelian *Synagōgē Technōn* after Cicero *Brutus* 46–48', *Latomus*, 14: 536–9.

DOVER, K. J. (1950), 'The Chronology of Antiphon's Speeches', *CQ* 44: 44–60.

—— (1968), *Lysias and the Corpus Lysiacum*, Sather Classical Lectures 39, Berkeley.

—— (1971) (ed.), *Theocritus: Select Poems*, London.

—— (1974), *Greek Popular Morality in the Time of Plato and Aristotle*, Oxford.

—— (1976), 'The Freedom of the Intellectual in Greek Society', *Talanta*, 7: 24–54.

—— (1978), *Greek Homosexuality*, London.

—— (1984), review of Mikalson, *Athenian Popular Religion* (1983), *Phoenix*, 38: 197–8.

—— (1994), *Marginal Comment: A Memoir*, London.

DRERUP, E. (1898), 'Über die bei den attischen Rednern eingelegten Urkunden', *Jahrbuch für Philologie*, Suppl. 24: 221–366.

—— (1899), 'Antike Demosthenesausgaben', *Philologus*, Suppl. 7: 533–88.

—— (1923), *Demosthenes im Urteile des Altertums*, Würzburg.

DU CANN, R. (1964), *The Art of the Advocate*, London.

DUE, B. (1980), *Antiphon: A Study in Argumentation*, Copenhagen.

DURBACH, F. (1932), *Lycurge, 'Contre Léocrate'*, Paris.

EASTERLING, P. E. (1999), 'Actors and Voices: Reading Between the Lines in Aeschines and Demosthenes', in Goldhill and Osborne 1999: 154–66.

EDELSTEIN, L. (1956), 'The Professional Ethics of the Greek Physician', *Bulletin of the History of Medicine*, 30: 391–419 (repr. in Edelstein 1967: 319–48).

—— (1967), *Ancient Medicine*, Baltimore.

EDWARDS, M. J. (1995) (ed.), *Greek Orators, IV: Andocides*, Warminster.

—— (1999) (ed.), *Lysias: Five Speeches. Speeches 1, 12, 19, 22, 30*, London.

—— and USHER, S. (1985) (eds.), *Greek Orators*, I: *Antiphon and Lysias*, Warminster and Chicago.

EHRENBERG, V. (1921), *Die Rechtsidee im frühen Griechentum*, Leipzig, repr. Darmstadt, 1966.

—— (1962), *The People of Aristophanes: A Sociology of Old Attic Comedy*, 3rd edn. New York (2nd edn., Oxford, 1951).

ELLIS, J. R. (1976), *Philip II and Macedonian Imperialism*, London.

ELLIS, L. (1989), *Theories of Rape: Inquiries into the Causes of Sexual Aggression*, New York.

ENGELS, J. (1992), 'Zur Stellung Lykurgs und zur Aussagekraft seines Militär- und Bauprogramms für die Demokratie vor 322 v. Chr.', *Anc. Soc.* 23: 5–29.

ERBSE, H. (1958), 'Lysias-Interpretationen', in H. Diller and H. Erbse (eds.), *Festschrift Ernst Kapp zum 70. Geburtstag am 21. Januar 1958*, Hamburg: 51–66.

ERDMANN, W. (1934), *Die Ehe im alten Griechenland*, Münchener Beiträge zur Papyrusforschung und antiken Rechtsgeschichte, 20, Munich, repr. New York, 1979.

ERLANGER, H. S. (1970), 'Jury Research in America: Its Past and Future', *Law and Society Review*, 4: 345–70.

FALLERS, L. A. (1969), *Law Without Precedent*, Chicago.

FANTHAM, E. (1986), '*Zelotypia*: A Brief Excursion into Sex, Violence, and Literary History', *Phoenix*, 40: 45–57.

FARAONE, C. (1999), 'Curses and Social Control in the Law Courts of Classical Athens', *Dike*, 2: 99–121 (revised in D. Cohen and Müller-Luckner 2002: 77–92).

FARENGA, V. (1979), 'Periphrasis on the Origin of Rhetoric', *Modern Language Notes*, 94: 1033–53.

FEIFER, G. (1964), *Justice in Moscow*, London.

FILIPPO BALESTRAZZI, E. DI (1984), 'Apollon Agyieus', *LIMC* 2.1.327–32 and 2.2.279–83.

FINLEY, M. I. (1952), *Studies in Land and Credit in Ancient Athens, 500–200 B.C.: The Horos Inscriptions*, New Brunswick, repr. 1985.

—— (1973), *Democracy Ancient and Modern*, New Brunswick, NJ.

—— (1977), *Aspects of Antiquity*, New York.

—— (1980), *Ancient Slavery and Modern Ideology*, London.

—— (1982), *Authority and Legitimacy in the Classical Greek City-State*, Copenhagen.

—— (1983), *Politics in the Ancient World*, Cambridge.

—— (1985a), *Democracy Ancient and Modern*, rev. edn. London.

FINLEY, M. I. (1985*b*), *The Ancient Economy*, 2nd edn. London (1st edn. Berkeley (Sather Classical Lecture 43), 1973).

FINNEGAN, R. J. (1992), 'Women in Herodian Mime', *Hermathena*, 152: 21–37.

FISHER, N. R. E. (1976), *Social Values in Classical Athens*, London and Toronto.

—— (1990), 'The Law of *Hubris* in Athens', in Cartledge *et al.* 1990: 123–38.

—— (1992), *Hybris: A Study in the Values of Honour and Shame in Ancient Greece*, Warminster.

—— (2001), *Aeschines, 'Against Timarchos', with Introduction, Translation and Commentary*, Oxford.

FORD, A. (1999), 'Reading Homer from the Rostrum: Poems and Laws in Aeschines, *Against Timarchus*', in Goldhill and Osborne 1999: 231–56.

FORDHAM, E. W. (1951), *Notable Cross-examinations*, London, Toronto, and Cape Town.

FOXHALL, L., and LEWIS, A. D. E. (1996) (eds.), *Greek Law in its Political Setting: Justifications Not Justice*, Oxford.

FOWLER, R. L. (1996), 'How the *Lysistrata* Works', *EMC* 40: 245–9.

FRÄNKEL, H. (1960), *Wege und Formen frühgriechischen Denkens*, 2nd edn., Munich.

FUMAROLA, V. (1965), 'Il problema storico, civile e letterario di Lisia', *A&R* 10: 49–65.

GAGARIN, M. (1984), 'The Testimony of Witnesses in the Gortyn Laws', *GRBS* 25: 345–9.

—— (1986), *Early Greek Law*, Berkeley and Los Angeles.

—— (1989*a*), 'The Function of Witnesses at Gortyn', in G. Thür (ed.), *Symposion 1985* (Cologne): 29–54.

—— (1989*b*), *The Murder of Herodes*, Studien zur klassischen Philologie, 45, Frankfurt.

—— (1990), 'The Nature of Proofs in Antiphon', *CP* 85: 22–32 (Ch. 8 in this collection).

—— (1996), 'The Torture of Slaves in Athenian Law', *CP* 91: 1–18.

—— (1997), 'Oaths and Oath-Challenges in Greek Law', in G. Thur and J. Vélissaropoulos-Karakostas (eds.), *Symposion 1995* (Cologne), 125–34.

—— (2002), *Antiphon the Athenian: Oratory, Law, and Justice in the Age of the Sophists*, Austin, Tex.

—— (2003), 'Telling Stories in Athenian Law', *TAPA* 133: 197–207.

—— and COHEN, D. (2005) (eds.), *The Cambridge Companion to Ancient Greek Law*, Cambridge.

GARDNER, J. F. (1989), 'Aristophanes and Male Anxiety—The Defence of the *Oikos*', *G&R* 36: 51–62.

GARNER, R. (1987), *Law and Society in Classical Athens*, New York and London.

GARNSEY, P. D. A. (1985), 'Grain for Athens', in Cartledge and Harvey 1985: 62–75.

GASTALDI, S. (1981), *Discorso della città e discorso della scuola*, Florence.

GAUTHIER, P. (1972), *Symbola. Les Étrangers et la justice dans les cités grecques*, Nancy.

GENOVESE, E. D. (1974), *Roll, Jordan, Roll: The World the Slaves Made*, New York.

GENTILI, B. (1988), *Poetry and its Public in Ancient Greece: From Homer to the Fifth Century*, T. Cole (tr.), Baltimore.

GERCKE, A. (1897), 'Die alte *Technē Rhetorikē* und ihre Gegner', *Hermes*, 32: 341–81.

GERNET, L. (1917), *Recherches sur le développement de la pensée juridique et morale en Grèce*, Paris (repr., with preface by E. Cantarella, 2001).

—— (1926) (ed.), *Lysias, Discours*, II, Paris.

—— (1962–4) (ed.), *Lysias, Discours*, 2 vols., 5th edn., Paris.

—— and BIZOS, M. (1924) (eds.), Lysias, *Discours*, I, 1st edn., Paris.

—— (1927), 'La Diamartyrie, procédure archaïque du droit athénien', *Revue Historique de Droit Français et Étranger*, ser. 4.6: 5–37 (repr. in Gernet 1955*a*: 83–102).

—— (1938), 'Sur les actions commerciales en droit athénien', *REG* 51: 1–44 (repr. in Gernet 1955*a*: 173–200).

—— (1939), 'L'Institution des arbitres publics à Athènes', *REG* 52: 389–414.

—— (1948), 'Jeux et droit', *Revue Historique de Droit Français et Étranger*, 26: 177–88 (repr. in Gernet 1955*a*: 9–18).

—— (1950), 'Aspects du droit athénien de l'esclavage', *Archives d'Histoire du Droit Oriental*, 5: 159–87 (repr. in Gernet 1955*a*: 151–72).

—— (1951), 'Droit et prédroit en Grèce ancienne', *L'Année Sociologique*, 1948–9: 21–119 (reprinted in Gernet 1968: 175–260).

—— (1954) (ed.), *Démosthène. Plaidoyers civils*, I, París.

—— (1955*a*), *Droit et société dans la Grèce ancienne*, Paris.

—— (1955*b*), 'Le Droit de vente et la notion du contrat en Grèce d'apres Pringsheim', *Revue Historique de Droit Français et Étranger*, 29: 560–84.

—— (1954–60) (ed.), *Démosthène, plaidoyers civils*, 4 vols., Paris.

—— (1956), 'Le Temps dans les formes archaiques du droit', *Journal de Psychologie*, 53: 379–406 (repr. in Gernet 1968: 261–87).

—— (1957) (ed.), *Démosthène. Plaidoyers civils*, II, Paris.

—— (1959), 'Note sur la notion de délit privé en droit grec', in *Droits de l'antiquité et sociologie juridique, Mélanges H. Lévy-Bruhl*, Paris: 393–405.

—— (1960) (ed.), *Démosthène. Plaidoyers civils*, IV, Paris.

GERNET, L. (1965) (ed.), *Antiphon*, Paris (1st edn. 1923).

—— (1968), *Anthropologie de la Grèce antique*, Paris (= *The Anthropology of Ancient Greece*, tr. J. Hamilton and B. Nagy, Baltimore, 1981).

GILES, H., and ST. CLAIR, R. N. (1979) (eds.), *Language and Social Personality*, Oxford.

GLOTZ, G. (1904*a*), *La Solidarité de la famille dans le droit crimine en Grèce*, Paris.

—— (1904*b*), *L'Ordalie dans la Grèce primitive*, Paris.

—— (1929), *The Greek City and its Institutions*, London (French original, Paris, 1928).

GLUCKMAN, M. (1955), *The Judicial Process Among the Barotse of Northern Rhodesia*, Manchester.

GOEBEL, G. (1983), 'Early Greek Rhetorical Theory and Practice: Proof and Arrangement in the Speeches of Antiphon and Euripides', diss. Madison, Wisc.

GOLDEN, M. (1990), *Children and Childhood in Classical Athens*, Baltimore.

GOLDHILL, S. (1994), 'Representing Democracy: Women at the Great Dionysia', in R. Osborne and S. Hornblower (eds.), *Ritual, Finance, Politics: Athenian Democratic Accounts Presented to David Lewis*, Oxford and New York: 347–69.

—— (1997), 'The Language of Tragedy: Rhetoric and Communication', in P. E. Easterling (ed.), *The Cambridge Companion to Greek Tragedy*, Cambridge: 127–50.

—— and OSBORNE, R. (1999) (eds.), *Performance Culture and Athenian Democracy*, Cambridge.

GOMME, A. W. (1933), *The Population of Athens in the Fifth and Fourth Centuries B.C.*, Oxford.

—— (1951), 'The Working of the Athenian Democracy', *History*, 36: 12–28.

—— and SANDBACH, F. H. (1973), *Menander: A Commentary*, Oxford.

GREGORIO, L. DI (1995), 'La Figura di Metriche nel primo mimiambo di Eronda', in L. Belloni, G. Milanese, and A. Porro (eds.), *Studia classica Iohanni Tarditi oblata*, Milan: i. 675–94.

GREENE, F. (1962), *The Wall has Two Sides*, London.

GRIFFITH, G. W. (1979), 'The Reign of Philip the Second', part II of N. G. L. Hammond and G. T. Griffith, *A History of Macedonia*, vol. II, *550–336 B.C.*, Oxford.

GRIGG, D. (1982), *The Dynamics of Agricultural Change: The Historical Experience*, London.

GRIMALDI, W. M. A., SJ (1980), *Aristotle, 'Rhetoric' I: A Commentary*, New York.

GULLIVER, P. H. (1963), *Social Control in an African Society*, London.

—— (1969), 'Dispute Settlement Without Courts: The Ndendeuli of Southern Tanzania', in L. Nader (ed.), *Law in Culture and Society*, Chicago (repr. Berkeley, 1997): 24–68.

GUTHRIE, W. K. C. (1969), *A History of Greek Philosophy*, III: *The Fifth-Century Enlightenment*, Cambridge.

HABICHT, C. (1997), *Athens from Alexander to Antony*, tr. D. L. Schneider, Cambridge, Mass.

HACKING, I. (1995), *Rewriting the Soul*, Princeton.

HALLERAN, M. R. (1995) (ed.), *Euripides: Hippolytus*, Warminster.

HALPERIN, D. M. (1990), *One Hundred Years of Homosexuality and Other Essays on Greek Love*, New York.

HAMBERGER, P. (1914), *Die rednerische Disposition in der alten* technē rhētorikē *(Korax, Gorgias, Antiphon)*, Rhetorische Studien, 2, Paderborn.

HAMNETT, I. (1977) (ed.), *Social Anthropology and Law*, London.

HAMPSHIRE, S. (1978), *Public and Private Morality*, Cambridge.

HANSEN, M. H. (1974), *The Sovereignty of the People's Court in Athens in the Fourth Century B.C. and the Public Action against Unconstitutional Proposals*, Odense.

—— (1976), *Apagoge, Endeixis and Ephegesis against Kakourgoi, Atimoi and Pheugontes*, Odense.

—— (1979), 'How Often Did the Athenian *Dikastēria* Meet?', *GRBS* 20: 243–6.

—— (1980), 'Seven Hundred *Archai* in Classical Athens', *GRBS* 21: 151–73.

—— (1982) (ed.), *Lysias' taler (1, 3, 10, 13, 24, 30)*, Copenhagen.

—— (1983*a*), 'The Athenian "Politicians", 403–322 B.C.', *GRBS* 24: 33–55.

—— (1983*b*), *The Athenian Ecclesia: A Collection of Articles 1976–1983*, Copenhagen.

—— (1983*c*), 'Political Activity and the Organization of Attica in the Fourth Century B.C.', *GRBS* 24: 227–38.

—— (1984), 'Two Notes on Demosthenes' Symbouleutic Speeches', *C&M* 35: 57–70.

—— (1985), *Demography and Democracy: The Number of Athenian Citizens in the Fourth Century B.C.*, Herning.

—— (1986), 'The Construction of Pnyx II and the Introduction of Assembly Pay', *C&M* 37: 89–98.

—— (1987), *The Athenian Assembly in the Age of Demosthenes*, Oxford.

—— (1997), 'One Hundred and Sixty Theses about Athenian Democracy', *C&M* 48: 205–65.

—— (1999), *The Athenian Democracy in the Age of Demosthenes*, 2nd edn., Bristol (1st edn., Oxford, 1991).

HANSON, V. D. (1995), *The Other Greeks: The Family Farm and the Agrarian Roots of Western Civilisation*, New York.

HARDING, P. E. (1981), 'In Search of a Polypragmatist', in G. S. Shrimpton and D. J. McCargar (eds.), *Classical Contributions: Studies in Honour of Malcolm Francis MacGregor*, Locust Valley, NY.

HARRELL, H. C. (1936), *Public Arbitration in Athenian Law*, Columbia, Mo.

HARRIS, E. M. (1989), 'More Chalcenteric Negligence', *CP* 84: 36–44.

—— (1990), 'Did the Athenians Regard Seduction as a Worse Crime than Rape?', *CQ* 40: 370–7.

—— (1994), 'Law and Oratory', in Worthington 1994: 130–50.

—— and RUBINSTEIN L. (2004) (eds.), *The Law and the Courts in Ancient Greece*, London.

HARRISON, A. R. W. (1968), *The Law of Athens*, I: *The Family and Property*, Oxford.

—— (1971), *The Law of Athens*, II: *Procedure*, Oxford.

HARVEY, F. D. (1966), 'Literacy in the Athenian Democracy', *REG* 79: 585–635.

HASTINGS, P. (1956), *Famous and Infamous Cases*, London.

HAUSSOULLIER, B. (1883), *La Vie municipale en Attique*, Paris.

—— and MATHIEU, G. (1941) (eds.), *Aristote, 'Constitution d' Athénes'*, Paris (1st edn. 1922).

HAVELOCK, E. A. (1982), *The Literate Revolution in Greece and its Cultural Consequences*, Princeton.

HEADLAM, J. W. (1892–3), 'The Procedure of the Gortynian Inscription', *JHS* 13: 48–69.

—— (1893), 'On the *proklēsis eis basanon* in Attic Law', *CR* 7: 1–5.

—— (1894), 'Slave Torture in Athens', *CR* 8: 136–7.

HEADLAM, W. G. (1922), *Herodas: The Mimes and Fragments*, ed. A. D. Knox, Cambridge.

HENDERSON, J. (1991), *The Maculate Muse: Obscene Language in Attic Comedy*, 2nd edn., New York.

HENSE, O. (1900), 'Zum zweiten Mimiamb des Herodas', *RhM* 55: 222–31.

HERMAN, G. (1993), 'Tribal and Civic Codes of Behaviour in Lysias 1', *CQ* 43: 406–19.

HIGNETT, C. (1952), *A History of the Athenian Constitution*, Oxford.

HINKS, D. A. G. (1940), 'Tisias and Corax and the Invention of Rhetoric', *CQ* 34: 61–9.

HIRZEL, R. (1900), *Agraphos Nomos*, Lepzig, repr. Hildesheim, 1979.

—— (1907), *Themis, Dike und Verwandtes; ein Beitrag zur Geschichte der Rechtsidee bei den Griechen*, Leipzig.

HITZIG, H. F. (1897), 'Zum griechisch-attischen Rechte', *ZRG* 18: 146–96.

—— (1907), 'Der griechische Fremdenproß im Licht der neueren Inschriftenfunde', *ZRG* 28: 211–53.

HOFFMANN, G. (1990), *Le Châtiment des amants dans la Grèce classique*, Paris.

HOGGART, R. (1957), *The Uses of Literacy*, London.

HÖLSCHER, T. (1998), 'Images and Political Identity: The Case of Athens', in D. Boedeker and K. Raaflaub (eds.), *Democracy, Empire, and the Arts in Fifth-Century Athens*, Cambridge, Mass.: 153–83.

HOPPER, R. J. (1957), *The Basis of the Athenian Democracy*, University of Sheffield Inaugural Lecture, Sheffield.

HUDSON-WILLIAMS, H. L. (1949a), 'Impromptu Speaking', *G&R* 18: 28–31.

—— (1949b), 'Isocrates and Recitations', *CQ* 43: 65–68.

—— (1951), 'Political Speeches in Athens', *CQ²* 1: 68–73.

HUMPHREYS, S. C. (1978), *Anthropology and the Greeks*, London.

—— (1983a), *The Family, Women and Death: Comparative Studies*, London.

—— (1983b), 'The Date of Hagnias' Death', *CP* 78: 219–25.

—— (1983c), 'The Evolution of Legal Process in Attica', in E. Gabba (ed.), *Tria Corda, studi in onore di Arnaldo Momigliano*, Como: 229–56.

—— (1985) (ed.), *The Discourse of Law*, London (*History and Anthropology*,1.2).

—— (1986), 'Kinship Patterns in the Athenian Courts', *GRBS* 27: 57–91.

—— (1988), 'The Discourse of Law in Archaic and Classical Greece', *Law and History Review*, 6: 465–93.

—— (1989), 'Family Quarrels', *JHS* 109: 182–5.

—— (1998), 'Gender and Social Relationships', *Kodai*, 8.9: 53–6.

—— (2002), '*Bindung*: A Processual Approach', in Y. Elkana *et al.* (eds.), *Unraveling Ties*, Frankfurt a.M.: 312–30.

HUNTER, R. (1995), 'Plautus and Herodas', in L. Benz, E. Stärk, and G. Vogt-Spira (eds.), *Plautus und die Tradition des Stegreifspiels. Festgabe für Eckard Lefèvre zum 60. Geburtstag*, Tübingen: 155–69.

HUNTER, V. J. (1994), *Policing Athens: Social Control in the Attic Lawsuits, 420–320 B.C.*, Princeton.

HYDE, H. M. (1953), *Carson: The Life of Sir Edward Carson, Lord Carson of Duncairn*, London.

IMMERWAHR, H. R. (1990), *Attic Script: A Survey*, Oxford.

ISAGER, S., and HANSEN, M. H. (1975), *Aspects of Athenian Society in the Fourth Century BC: A Historical Introduction and Commentary on the 'Paragraphe', Speeches and 'Against Dionysodorus' in the Corpus Demosthenicum*, Odense.

JAEGER, W. (1938), *Demosthenes: The Origin and Growth of his Policies*, Sather Classical Lecture, 13, tr. E. S. Robinson, Berkeley.

—— (1939), *Demosthenes: der Staatsmann und sein Werden*, Berlin.

JAEGER, W. (1944), *Paideia: The Ideals of Greek Culture*, 3 vols., tr. G. Highet, New York.

JAMESON, M. H. (1977), 'Agriculture and Slavery in Classical Athens', *CJ* 73: 122–45

JANKO, R. (1982), *Homer, Hesiod and the Hymns*, Cambridge.

JEBB, R. C. (1893), *The Attic Orators from Antiphon to Isaeus*, 2nd edn., London, repr. New York, 1962.

JENSEN, T. (1990), 'Domstolenes retsskabende, retsudfyldende og responderende virksomhed', *Ugeskrift for Retsvæsen*, 124 Afd. b: 441–8.

JOHNSON, R. (1959), 'Isocrates' Methods of Teaching', *AJP* 80: 25–36.

JOHNSTONE, S. (1999), *Disputes and Democracy: The Consequences of Litigation in Ancient Athens*, Austin, Tex.

JONES, A. H. M. (1957), *Athenian Democracy*, Oxford.

JONES, J. (1962), *On Aristotle and Greek Tragedy*, London, repr. Stanford, 1980.

JONES, J. W. (1956), *The Law and Legal Theory of the Greeks*, Oxford.

JOUAN, F., and VAN LOOY, H. (2000) (eds.), *Euripide*, tome 8, *Fragments*, 2ᵉ partie: *Béllérophon—Protésilas*, Paris.

JUST, R. (1989), *Women in Athenian Law and Life*, London and New York.

KALVEN, H., and ZEISEL, H. (1966), *The American Jury*, Boston.

KAPPARIS, K. (1993), 'Is Eratosthenes in Lys.1 the Same Person as Eratosthenes in Lys. 12?', *Hermes*, 121: 364–5.

—— (1995), 'When Were the Athenian Adultery Laws Introduced?', *RIDA* 42: 97–122.

KEHOE, P. K. (1984), 'The Adultery Mime Reconsidered', in D. F. Bright and E. S. Ramage (eds.), *Classical Texts and their Traditions: Studies in Honor of C. R. Trahman*, Chico, Calif.: 89–106.

KENNEDY, G. A. (1957), 'The Ancient Dispute over Rhetoric in Homer,' *AJP* 78: 23–35.

—— (1958), 'The Oratory of Andocides', *AJP* 79: 32–43.

—— (1963), *The Art of Persuasion in Greece*, Princeton.

—— (1968), 'The Rhetoric of Advocacy in Greece and Rome', *AJP* 89: 419–36.

—— (1980), *Classical Rhetoric and its Christian and Secular Tradition from Ancient to Modern Times*, Chapel Hill, NC.

—— (1991) *Aristotle 'On Rhetoric': A Theory of Civic Discourse*, Oxford and New York (2nd edn. 2006).

KEULS, E. C. (1985), *The Reign of the Phallus: Sexual Politics in Ancient Athens*, New York.

KHARKHORDIN, O. (1999), *The Collective and the Individual in Russia: A Study of Practices*, Berkeley.

KILMER, M. F. (1993), *Greek Erotica on Attic Red-Figure Vases*, London.

—— (1997), ' "Rape" in Early Red-Figure Pottery: Violence and Threat in Homo-erotic and Hetero-erotic Contexts', in Deacy and Pierce 1997: 123–41.

KINDSTRAND, J. F. (1982), *The Stylistic Evaluation of Aeschines in Antiquity,* Upsala.

KNOX, B. M. W., and EASTERLING, P. E. (1986) (eds.), *The Cambridge History of Classical Literature,* vol. 1: *Greek Literature,* Cambridge.

KOCH, H.-A. (1970), *Homo Mensura: Studien zu Protagoras und Gorgias,* Tübingen.

KOHLER, J., and ZIEBARTH, E. (1912), *Das Stadtrecht von Gortyn,* Göttingen, repr. Hildesheim, 1972.

KONSTAN, D. (1994), 'Premarital Sex, Illegitimacy, and Male Anxiety in Menander and Athens', in Boegehold and Scafuro 1994: 217–35.

KOWALSKI, G. (1933), *De artis rhetoricae originibus,* Lwow.

—— (1937) *De arte rhetorica,* Lwow.

KRASTEV, I. (2003), 'When "Should" Does Not Imply "Can": The Making of the Washington Consensus on Corruption', in W. Lepenies (ed.), *Entangled Histories and Negotiated Universals,* Frankfurt a.M.: 105–26.

KRAUT, R. (1984), *Socrates and the State,* Princeton.

KRENTZ, P. (1984), 'Was Eratosthenes Responsible for the Death of Polemarchos?', *PP* 39: 23–32.

KROLL, J. H. (1972), *Athenian Bronze Allottment Plates,* Cambridge, Mass.

KÜBLER, B. G. A. (1934), 'Griechische Einflüsse auf die Entwicklung der römischen Rechtswissenschaft gegen Ende der republikanischen Zeit', in *Atti del Congresso Internazionale di Diritto Romano (Bologna e Roma, xvii–xxvii aprile, MCMXXXIII), Roma* (= part 2), Pavia: i. 79–98.

KUHN, T. S. (1962), *The Structure of Scientific Revolutions,* Chicago.

KUNKEL, W. (1928), review of Maschke, *Willenslehre* (1926), *ZRG* 48: 709–22.

—— and WOLFF, H. J. (1954) (eds.), *Festschrift für Ernst Rabel,* II: *Geschichte der antiken Rechte und allgemeine Rechtslehre,* Tübingen.

KURCZEWSKI, J., and FRIESKE, K. (1978), 'The Social Conciliatory Commissions in Poland', in M. Cappeletti (ed.), *Access to Justice,* vol. II: *Promising Institutions,* Milan: 153–427.

LABARBE, J. (1953), 'L'Age correspondant au sacrifice du *koureion* et les données historiques du sixième discours d'Isée', *Academie Royale de Belgique, Bulletin de la classe des lettres et des sciences morales et politiques,* sér. 5.39: 358–94.

LACEY, W. K. (1968), *The Family in Classical Greece,* London.

LÄMMLI, F. (1938), *Das attische Prozessverfahren in seiner Wirkung auf die Gerichtsrede,* Rhetorische Studien, 20, Paderborn.

416   *References*

LANNI, A. M. (2000), 'The Homicide Courts and the *Dikasteria:* A Paradigm not Followed', *GRBS* 41: 311–30.

—— (2004), 'Arguing from "Precedent": Modern Perspectives on Athenian Practice', in Harris and Rubinstein 2004: 159–71.

—— (2006), *Law and Justice in the Courts of Classical Athens*, Cambridge.

LANZA, D. (1979), *Lingua e discorso nell'Atene delle professioni*, Naples.

LAPE, S. (2004), *Reproducing Athens*, Princeton.

LATEINER, D. (1982), ' "The Man Who Does Not Meddle in Politics": A *Topos* in Lysias', *CW* 76: 1–12.

—— (2000), 'Marriage and the Return of Spouses in Apuleius' *Metamorphoses*', *CJ* 95: 313–32.

LATTE, K. (1920), *Heiliges Recht. Untersuchungen zur Geschichte der sakralen Rechtsformen in Griechenland*, Tübingen.

LAVENCY, M. (1964), *Aspects de la logographie judiciaire attique*, Université de Louvain Recueil de Travaux d' Histoire et de Philologie, 4. 32, Leuven.

LEACH, E. R. (1954), *Political Systems of Highland Burma*, London.

LEISI, E. (1908), *Der Zeuge im attischen Recht*, Frauenfeld, repr. New York, 1979.

LEIST, G. (1896), 'Der attische Eigentumsstreit im System der Diadikasien', diss. Jena.

LESKY, A. (1963), *Geschichte der griechischen Literatur*, Bern.

LEWIS, D. M. (1955), 'Notes on Attic Inscriptions (II)', *Annual of the British School at Athens*, 50: 1–36.

—— (1959), 'Attic Manumissions', *Hesperia*, 28: 208–38.

LEWIS, G. C. (1849), *An Essay on the Influence of Authority in Matters of Opinion*, London.

—— (1852), *A Treatise on the Methods of Observation and Reasoning in Politics*, London.

LIND, E. A., and O'BARR, W. M. (1979), 'The Social Significance of Speech in the Courtroom', in Giles and St. Clair 1979: 66–87.

LIPSIUS, J. H. (1886), *Quaestiones logographicae*, Leipzig.

—— (1916), '*Dikē exoulēs*', *ZRG* 37: 1–14

—— (1918), 'Nochmals zur *dike exoulēs*', *ZRG* 39: 36–51.

LLOYD-BOSTOCK, S., and CLIFFORD, B. R. (1983) (eds.), *Evaluating Witness Evidence*, New York.

LLOYD-JONES, H. (1975), *Females of the Species: Semonides on Women*, London and Park Ridge.

LOENING, T. C. (1987), *The Reconciliation Agreement of 403/402 in Athens: Its Content and Application*, Hermes Einzelschr., 53, Stuttgart.

LOOMIS, W. T. (1998), *Wages, Welfare Costs, and Inflation in Classical Athens*, Ann Arbor, Mich.

LORAUX, N. (1986), *The Invention of Athens: The Funeral Oration in the Classical City*, tr. A. Sheridan, Cambridge, Mass.

LOSSAU, M. J. (1964), *Untersuchungen zur antiken Demosthenesexegese*, Bad Homburg.

LUHMANN, N. (1982), *Liebe als Passion: zur Codierung von Intimität*, Frankfurt a.M. (Eng. tr., *Love as Passion*, Oxford, 1986, repr. Stanford, 1998).

McBARNET, D. J. (1981), *Conviction: Law, the State and the Construction of Justice*, London.

McCABE, S., and PURVES, R. (1974), *The Shadow Jury at Work*, Oxford.

McCORMICK, C. T. (1972), *McCormick's Handbook of the Law of Evidence*, 2nd edn., ed. E. R. Cleary, St Paul, Minn.

MacDOWELL, D. M. (1963), *Athenian Homicide Law in the Age of the Orators*, Manchester.

—— (1971), *Aristophanes 'Wasps'*, Oxford.

—— (1978), *The Law in Classical Athens*, London and Ithaca.

—— (1985), 'The Length of the Speeches on the Assessment of the Penalty in Athenian Courts', *CQ* 35: 525–6.

McKEOWN, J. C. (1979), 'Augustan Elegy and Mime', *PCPS* 25: 71–84.

MacLEOD, M. D. (1967) (tr.), *Lucian*, VIII, Cambridge, Mass.

MAFFI, A. (2001), 'Hans Julius Wolff e gli studi di diritto greco a trent' anni dal I Symposion', *Dike*, 4: 269–91.

MALINOWSKI, B. (1913), *The Family Among the Australian Aborigines*, London.

MANTHE, U. (2000), 'Die Tötung des Ehebrechers', in L. A. Burckhardt und J. von Ungern-Sternberg (eds.), *Grosse Prozesse im antiken Athen*, Munich: 219–33.

MANNZMANN, A. (1962), *Griechische Stiftungsurkunden*, Münster.

MARGER, M. N. (1981), *Elites and Masses: An Introduction to Political Sociology*, New York.

MARKLE, M. M. (1985), 'Jury Pay and Assembly Pay at Athens', in Cartledge and Harvey 1985: 265–97, (repr. in Rhodes 2004*b*: 95–131).

—— (1990), 'Participation of Farmers in Athenian Juries and Assemblies', *Anc. Soc.* 21: 149–65.

MARROU, H. I. (1964), *A History of Education in Antiquity*, tr. G. Lamb, New York.

MASCHKE, R. (1926), *Die Willenslehre im griechischen Recht*, Berlin, repr. New York, 1979.

MASSA POSITANO, L. (1971), *Eroda: Mimiambo*, II, Naples.

MASTROMARCO, G. (1990). 'Eine alexandrinische Kupplerin', *WJA* 6: 87–99.

MASTRONARDE, D. J. (1994) (ed.), *Euripides: Phoenissae*, Cambridge Classical Texts and Commentaries, 29, Cambridge and New York.

MATHIEU, G. (1947) (ed.), *Démosthène. Plaidoyers politiques*, IV, Paris.

MATHIEU, G., and BRÉMOND, E. (1950–62) (eds.), *Isocrate. Discours*, 4 vols., 2nd edn. Paris.

MATTIACCI, S. (1996) (ed.), *Le novelle dell'adulterio: Apuleio, Metamorfosi 9*, Florence.

MAUET, T. A. (1980), *Fundamentals of Trial Technique*, Boston.

MEIER, M. H., and SCHÖMANN, G. F. (1883–7), *Der attische Prozeß*, ed. J. H. Lipsius (4 books in 2 vols.), Berlin.

MEISTER, R. M. E. (1908), 'Eideshelfer im griechischen Rechte', *RhM* 63: 559–86.

MENSCHING, E. (1963), 'Zu Demosthenes' 54. Rede', *RhM* 106: 307–12.

MESSICK, B. (1993), *The Calligraphic State: Textual Domination and History in a Muslim Society*, Berkeley.

MEYER-LAURIN, H. (1965), *Gesetz und Billigkeit im attischen Prozess*, Graezistische Abh. 1, Weimar.

MICHELAKES, E., (1953), *Platons Lehre von der Anwendung des Gesetzes und der Begriff der Billigkeit bei Aristoteles*, Munich.

MICHELS, R. (1915), *Political Parties: A Sociological Study of the Oligarchic Tendencies of Modern Democracy*, tr. E. and C. Paul, Glencoe, Ill., repr. New York, 1962.

MIKALSON, J. (1983), *Athenian Popular Religion*, Chapel Hill, NC.

MILLETT, P. C. (1989), 'Patronage and its Avoidance in Classical Athens', in A. F. Wallace-Hadrill (ed.), *Patronage in Ancient Society*, London and New York: 15–47.

—— (1984) 'Hesiod and his World', *PCPS* 30: 84–115.

MILLS, C. W. (1951), *White Collar: The American Middle Classes*, New York.

—— (1956), *The Power Elite*, New York.

MIRHADY, D. C. (1991*a*), 'The Oath-Challenge in Athens', *CQ* 41: 78–83.

—— (1991*b*), 'Non-Technical *Pisteis* in Aristotle and Anaximenes', *AJP* 112: 5–28.

—— (1996), 'Torture and Rhetoric in Athens', *JHS* 116: 119–31 (Ch. 10 in this collection).

—— (2001), 'The Athenian Rationale for Torture', in V. Hunter and J. Edmondson (eds.), *Law and Social Status in Classical Athens*, Oxford: 53–74.

—— and TOO, Y. L. (2000), *Isocrates*, I, Austin, Tex.

MITTEIS, L. (1902), 'Romanistische Papyrusstudien', *ZRG* 23: 274–314.

MODRZEJEWSKI, J., and LIEBS, D. (1982) (eds.), *Symposion 1977*, Cologne.

MOMIGLIANO, A. (1964), 'Le conseguenze del rinnovamento della storia dei diritti antichi', *RSI* 76: 133–49 (repr. in id., *Terzo Contributo* (Rome, 1966): 285–302).

MOORE, S. F. (1977), 'Individual Interests and Organisational Structures: Dispute Settlements as "Events of Articulation"', in Hamnett 1977: 159–88.

—— (1978), *Law as Process: An Anthropological Approach*, London.

—— (1981), 'Chagga "Customary" Law and the Property of the Dead', in S. C. Humphreys and H. King (eds.), *Mortality and Immortality*, London: 225–48.

MORGAN, E. S. (1988), *Inventing the People: The Rise of Popular Sovereignty in England and America*, New York.

MORROW, G. R. (1939), *Plato's Law of Slavery in its Relation to Greek Law*, Illinois Studies in Language and Literature, 25.3, Urbana, Ill., repr. New York, 1976.

—— (1960), *Plato's Cretan City*, Princeton.

MOSSÉ, C. (1962), *La Fin de la démocratie athénienne*, Paris.

MUIR, J. V. (2001) (ed.), *Alcidamas: The Works and Fragments*, London.

MURPHY, C. T. (1972), 'Popular Comedy in Aristophanes', *AJP* 93: 169–89.

MURRAY, O. (1980), *Early Greece*, London.

—— (1990), 'The Solonian Law of *Hubris*', in Cartledge *et al.* 1990: 139–45.

MUTSCHMANN, H. (1918), 'Die älteste Definition der Rhetorik', *Hermes*, 53: 440–3.

MYLONAS, G. E. (1961), *Eleusis and the Eleusinian Mysteries*, Princeton.

NANETTI, O. (1941), 'Ricerche sui medici e sulla medicina nei papiri', *Aegyptus*, 21: 301–14.

NAVARRE, O. (1900), *Essai sur la rhétorique grecque avant Aristote*, Paris.

NEDELSKY, J. (1990), 'Law, Boundaries, and the Bounded Self', *Representations*, 30: 162–89.

NOCK, A. D. (1933), *Conversion*, London.

NORTH, H. (1952), 'The Use of Poetry in the Training of the Ancient Orator', *Traditio*, 8: 1–33.

NOUHAUD, M. (1982), *L'Utilisation de l'histoire par les orateurs attiques*, Paris.

OBER, J. (1985), *Fortress Attica, Defense of the Athenian Land Frontier, 404–322 B.C.*, Mnemosyne Suppl., 84, Leiden.

—— (1989), *Mass and Elite in Democratic Athens: Rhetoric, Ideology, and the Power of the People*, Princeton.

OGDEN, D. (1996), *Greek Bastardy in the Classical and Hellenistic Periods*, Oxford and New York.

—— (1997), 'Rape, Adultery, and the Protection of Bloodlines in Classical Athens', in Deacy and Pierce 1997: 25–41.

OLIVIERI, A. (1946–7) (ed.), *Frammenti della commedia greca e del mimo nella Sicilia e nella Magna Grecia*, II: *Frammenti della commedia fliacica*, 2nd edn., Naples.

OMITOWOJU, R. (1997), 'Regulating Rape: Soap Operas and Self-Interest in the Athenian Courts', in Deacy and Pierce 1997: 1–24.

OSBORNE, M. J., and BYRNE, S. G. (1994) (eds.), *A Lexicon of Greek Personal Names*, II: *Attica*, Oxford and New York.

OSBORNE, R. G. (1985*a*), *Demos: The Discovery of Classical Attika*, Cambridge.

—— (1985*b*), 'Law in Action in Classical Athens', *JHS* 105: 40–58.

—— (2000), review of Loomis, *Wages* (1998), in *CR* 50: 185–7.

OSTWALD, M. (1986), *From Popular Sovereignty to the Sovereignty of Law: Law, Society, and Politics in Fifth-Century Athens*, Berkeley.

O'SULLIVAN, N. (1992), *Alcidamas, Aristophanes and the Beginnings of Greek Stylistic Theory*, Hermes Einzelschr., 60, Stuttgart.

PANAYOTAKIS, C. (1995), *Theatrum Arbitri: Theatrical Elements in the Satyrica of Petronius*, Mnemosyne Suppl., 146, Leiden and New York.

PAOLI, U. E. (1933), *Studi sul Processo attico*, Padua.

—— (1950), 'Il reato di adulterio (*MOICHEIA*) in diritto attico', *SDHI* 16: 123–82 (repr. in id., *Altri studi di diritto greco e romano*, Milan, 1976: 251–307).

PARKER, R. (1997), 'Gods Cruel and Kind: Tragic and Civic Theology', in C. Pelling (ed.), *Greek Tragedy and History*, Oxford.

—— (2005), 'Law and Religion', in Gagarin and Cohen (eds.), *The Cambridge Companion to Ancient Greek Law*, Cambridge: 61–81.

PARTSCH, J. (1909), *Griechisches Bürgschaftsrecht*, Leipzig.

PATTERSON, C. (1990), 'Those Athenian Bastards', *Classical Antiquity*, 9: 40–73.

PEACOCK, J. L. (1968), *Rites of Modernization: Symbolic and Social Aspects of Indonesian Proletarian Drama*, Chicago.

PEARSON, L. (1941), 'Historical Allusions in the Attic Orators', *CP* 36: 209–29.

—— (1976), *The Art of Demosthenes*, Beiträge zur klassischen Philologie, 68, Meisenheim am Glan, repr. Chico, Calif., 1981.

PÉLÉKIDIS, C. (1962), *Histoire de l' éphébie attique, des origines à 31 av. J.-C.*, Paris.

PERLMAN, S. (1961), 'The Historical Example, Its Use and Importance as Political Propaganda in the Attic Orators', *Scripta Hierosolymitana*, 7: 150–66.

—— (1963), 'The Politicians in the Athenian Democracy of the Fourth Century BC', *Athenaeum*, 41: 327–55.

—— (1964), 'Quotations from Poetry in Attic Orators of the Fourth Century B.C.', *AJP* 85: 155–72.

—— (1967), 'Political Leadership in Athens in the Fourth Century BC', *Parola del Passato*, 22: 161–76.

PERNOT, L. (1993), *La Rhétorique de l'éloge dans le monde gréco-romain*, Paris.

PEROTTI, P. A. (1989–90), 'La I orazione di Lisia fu mai pronunciata?', *Sandalion*, 12–13: 43–8.

PERRY, J. A. G. (1977), 'Law-codes and Brokerage in a Lesotho Village', in Hamnett 1977: 189–228.

PHOTIADES, P. S. (1925), 'Nomikē hermeneia tēs Demosthenous pros Zēnothemin paragraphēs', *Athena*, 36: 109–32.

PICKARD-CAMBRIDGE, A. W. (1914), *Demosthenes and the Last Days of Greek Freedom*, London and New York.

PIÉRART, M. (1971), 'Les *euthynoi* athéniens', *Ant. Class.* 40: 526–73.

PODLECKI, A. J. (1977), 'Herodotus in Athens?', in K. H. Kinzl (ed.), *Greece and the Eastern Mediterranean in Ancient History and Prehistory: Studies presented to F. Schachermeyer*, Berlin: 246–65.

POLJAKOV, F. M. (1989) (ed.), *Die Inschriften von Tralles und Nysa*, Inschriften griechischen Städten aus Kleinasien, 36.1, Vienna.

PORTER, J. R. (1994), *Studies in Euripides' Orestes*, Mnemosyne Suppl., 128, Leiden and New York.

—— (1997), 'Adultery by the Book: Lysias 1 (*On the Murder of Eratosthenes*) and Comic *Diegesis*', *EMC* 40 (NS 16): 421–53 (Ch. 4 in this collection).

—— (2003), 'Nicolaus Reads Euphiletus: A Note on the *Nachleben* of Lysias 1', *AN* 3: 82–7.

PORTER, R. (1986), 'Rape—Does it have a Historical Meaning?', in S. Tomaselli and R. Porter (eds.), *Rape: An Historical and Social Enquiry*, Oxford and New York: 216–36.

POWELL, C. A. (1988), *Athens and Sparta: Concerning Greek Political and Social History from 478 B.C.*, London.

PRÉAUX, C. (1964), 'La Preuve à l'époque hellénistique, principalement dans l'Égypte grecque', *Recueils de la Société Jean Bodin*, 16: 161–222.

PRINGSHEIM, F. (1916), *Der Kauf mit fremdem Geld: Studien über die Bedeutung der Preiszahlung für den Eigentumserwerb nach griechischen und römischen Recht*, Leipzig, repr. New York, 1979.

—— (1949), 'The Greek Law of Sale by Auction', in *Scritti Ferrini*, 4 (Milan): 284–343 (German tr. in Pringsheim 1961: ii. 262–329).

—— (1950), *The Greek Law of Sale*, Weimar.

—— (1951), 'Le Témoignage dans la Grèce et Rome archaique', *RIDA* 6:161–75 (repr. in Pringsheim 1961: ii. 330–8).

—— (1955), 'The Transition from Witnessed to Written Transactions in Athens', in *Aequitas und Bona Fides: Festgabe zum 70. Geburtstag von August Simonius*, Basel: 287–97 (repr. in Pringsheim 1961: ii. 401–9).

—— (1961) *Gesammelte Abhandlungen*, 2 vols., Heidelberg.

RAAFLAUB, K. (1980), 'Des freien Bürgers Recht der freien Rede: Ein Beitrag zur Begriffs- und Sozialgeschichte der athenischen Demokratie', in W. Eck (ed.), *Studien zur Antiken Sozialgeschichte: Festschrift F. Vittinghoff,* Cologne.

RABEL, E. (1915), '*Dikē exoulēs* und *verwandtes*', *ZRG* 36: 340–90.

—— (1917), 'Zur *dikē exoulēs*', *ZRG* 38: 296–316.

RADERMACHER, L. (1897) 'Studien zur Geschichte der griechischen Rhetorik', *RhM* 52: 412–24.

RANDAZZO, R. (1974), *Lisia: Per l'uccisione di Eratostene,* Milan (first publ. 1966).

RAWLS, J. (2001), *Justice as Fairness: A Restatement,* Cambridge, Mass.

REA, J., *et al.* (1962) (eds.), *The Oxyrhynchus Papyri,* 27, London.

REDFIELD, J. M. (1975), *Nature and Culture in the Iliad: The Tragedy of Hector,* Chicago.

REDONDO MOYANO, E. (1994), 'Bátaro, un *pornoboskos* ante los tribunales (*Mimo* II de Herodas)', in F. R. Adrados (ed.), *Actas del VIII congreso español de estudios clásicos,* Madrid: ii. 361–7.

REYNOLDS, R. W. (1946), 'The Adultery Mime', *CQ* 40: 77–84.

REVILLOUT, E. (1892), 'Une importante découverte', *Revue Égyptologique,* 7.1: 1–21.

RHEINSTEIN, M. (1954) (ed.), *Max Weber on Law in Economy and Society,* Cambridge, Mass., repr. New York, 1967.

RHODES, P. J (1972), *The Athenian Boule,* Oxford.

—— (1980), 'Athenian Democracy after 403 B.C.', *CJ* 75: 305–23.

—— (1998), 'Enmity in Classical Athens', in Cartledge *et al.* 1998: 144–61.

—— (2004a), 'Keeping to the Point', in Harris and Rubinstein 2004: 137–58.

—— (2004b) (ed.), *Athenian Democracy,* Edinburgh, New York, and Oxford.

RICHTER, D. C. (1971), 'The Position of Women in Classical Athens', *CJ* 67: 1–8.

RIDLEY, R. T. (1979), 'The Hoplite as Citizen: Athenian Military Institutions in their Social Context', *Ant. Class.* 48: 508–48.

ROBERTS, J. T. (1982), *Accountability in Athenian Government,* Madison, Wisc.

ROBERTS, W. R. (1904), 'The New Rhetorical Fragment (*Oxyrhynchus Papyri,* III., pp. 27–30) in Relation to the Sicilian Rhetoric of Corax and Tisias', *CR* 18: 18–21

ROBERTSON, G. (1979), *Obscenity: An Account of Censorship Laws and their Enforcement in England and Wales,* London.

ROBIN, L. (1926) (ed.), *Platon, '*Phèdre', Platon, *Oeuvres complétes,* IV.3, Paris.

ROLPH, C. H. (1961) (ed.), *The Trial of Lady Chatterley,* London.

ROMILLY, J. DE (1985), *A Short History of Greek Literature,* tr. L. Doherty, Chicago.

ROSEN, R. M. (1988), 'Hipponax, Boupalos, and the Conventions of the *Psogos',* *TAPA* 118: 29–41.

ROTROFF, S. I., and CAMP, J. M. (1996), 'The Date of the Third Period of the Pnyx', *Hesperia,* 65.3: 263–94.

ROY, J. (1997), 'An Alternative Sexual Morality for Classical Athens', *G&R* 44: 11–22.

RUBINSTEIN, L. (1993), *Adoption in IV. Century Athens,* Copenhagen.

—— (1995), 'Precedensargumenter i de attiske retstaler', in G. Tortzen and T. Heine Nielsen (eds.), *Gammel Dansk: Studier til ære for M.H. Hansen,* Copenhagen: 80–4 (tr. and revised as Ch. 13 in this collection).

—— (2000), *Litigation and Cooperation: Supporting Speakers in the Courts of Classical Athens,* Historia Einzelschr., 147, Stuttgart.

RUSCHENBUSCH, E. (1961), 'Ephesis', *ZRG* 78: 386–90.

—— (1968), *Untersuchungen zur Geschichte des athenischen Strafrechts,* Cologne and Graz.

—— (1979), 'Die soziales Herkunft der Epheben um 330', *ZPE* 35: 173–6.

—— (1982), 'Der Ursprung des gerichtlichen Rechtsstreits bei den Griechen', in Modrzejewski and Liebs 1982: 1–8.

RUSSELL, D. A. (1983), *Greek Declamation,* Cambridge.

—— (1990), 'Ethos in Oratory and Rhetoric', in C. Pelling (ed.), *Characterization and Individuality in Greek Literature,* Oxford: 197–212.

RUTHERFORD, I. (1998), *Canons of Style in the Antonine Age,* Oxford.

RYDBERG-COX, J. A. (2003) (ed.), *Selected Speeches of Lysias: 1, 2, 3, 4, and 24,* Newburyport.

STE CROIX, G. M. E. DE, (1954), 'The Character of the Athenian Empire', *Historia,* 3: 1–41.

—— (1972), *The Origins of the Peloponnesian War,* London.

—— (1981), *The Class Struggle in the Ancient Greek World,* London.

SAKS, M. J., and HASTIE, R. (1978), *Social Psychology in Court,* New York.

SANDER, F. E. A., and SNYDER, F. E. (1979), *Alternative Methods of Dispute Settlement: A Selected Bibliography,* Washington, DC (American Bar Association, Committee on Resolution of Minor Disputes).

SANDYS, J. E., and PALEY, F. A. (1896), *Select Private Orations of Demosthenes,* II, 3rd. edn., Cambridge (1st edn. 1875).

SAUTEL, G. (1964), 'Les Preuves dans le droit grec archaïque', *Recueils de la Société Jean Bodin,* 16: 117–60.

SCAFURO, A. C. (1997), *The Forensic Stage: Settling Disputes in Graeco-Roman New Comedy*, Cambridge.

SCHÄFER, A. (1858), *Demosthenes und seine Zeit*, III.2: *Beilagen*, Leipzig.

—— (1885–7), *Demosthenes und seine Zeit*, 2nd edn. Leipzig (1st edn. 1856–8).

SCHAPS, D. (1977), 'The Woman Least Mentioned: Etiquette and Women's Names', *CQ* 27: 323–30.

SCHEPPELE, K. L. (1990), 'Facing Facts in Legal Interpretation', *Representations*, 30: 42–77.

SCHERER, K. R. (1979), 'Voice and Speech Correlates of Perceived Social Influence in Simulated Juries', in Giles and St. Clair 1979: 88–120.

SCHIAPPA, E. (1990), 'Did Plato Coin *Rhētorikē*?', *AJP* 111: 457–70.

—— (1993), 'The Beginnings of Greek Rhetorical Theory', in D. Zarefsky (ed.), *Rhetorical Movement: Essays in Honor of Leland M. Griffin*, Evanston, Ill.

—— (1994) (ed.), *Landmark Essays on Classical Greek Rhetoric*, Davis, Calif.

—— (1999), *The Beginnings of Rhetorical Theory in Classical Greece*, New Haven.

SCHINDEL, U. (1987) (ed.), *Demosthenes*, Wege der Forschung, 350, Darmstadt.

SCHMITZ, W. (1997), 'Der Nomos Moicheias: Das athenische Gesetz über den Ehebruch', *ZRG* 114: 45–140.

SCHÖLL, R. (1871), review of F. Blass (ed.) *Antiphon* (1st edn. Leipzig, 1871), *Jahrbücher für classische Philologie* (A. Fleckeisen, ed.), 103: 297–309.

SCHOTTLÄNDER, R. (1967), 'Der römische Redner und sein Publikum', *Wiener Studien*[2], 1: 125–46.

SCHWARTZ, S. (2000–1), 'Clitophon the *Moichos*: Achilles Tatius and the Trial Scene in the Greek Novel', *AN* 1: 93–113.

SCHWEIZER, A. (1936), *Die 13. Rede des Lysias: eine rhetorische Analyse*, Leipzig.

SCODEL, R. (1980), *The Trojan Trilogy of Euripides*, Hypomnemata, 60, Göttingen.

—— (1986) (ed.), *Lysias: Orations 1, 3*, Bryn Mawr.

—— (1993), 'Meditations on Lysias 1 and Athenian Adultery', *Electronic Antiquity*, 1.2.

SEALEY, R. (1960), 'Who Was Aristogeiton?', *BICS* 7: 33–43.

—— (1967), 'Pseudo-Demosthenes XIII and XXV', *REG* 80: 250–5.

—— (1984), 'The *Tetralogies* Ascribed to Antiphon', *TAPA* 114: 71–85.

—— (1990), *Women and Law in Classical Greece*, Chapel Hill, NC.

SEELIGER, K. (1876), 'Zur Charakteristik des Isaios', *Jahrbücher für classische Philologie* (A. Fleckeisen, ed.), 113: 637–79.

SEGAL, C. (1985), 'Space, Time and Imagination in Theocritus' Second *Idyll*', *Cl. Ant.* 4: 103–19.

SHACK, W. A. (1979), 'Collective Oath: Compurgation in Anglo-Saxon England and African States', *Archives Européennes de Sociologie*, 20: 1–18.

SHAPLAND, J. (1981), *Between Conviction and Sentencing: The Process of Mitigation*, London.

SHEPHERD, J. W., ELLIS, H. D., and DAVIES, G. A. (1982) (eds.), *Identification Evidence*, Aberdeen.

SHOREY, P. (1933), 'On the Eroticus of Lysias in Plato's *Phaedrus*', *CP* 28: 131–2.

SIEVEKING, H. (1893), *Das Seedarlehen des Altertums*, Leipzig.

SIMON, R. J. (1967), *The Jury and the Defense of Insanity*, Boston.

—— (1975), *The Jury System in America: A Critical Overview*, London.

—— (1980), *The Jury: Its Role in American Society*, Lexington, Mass.

SINCLAIR, R. K. (1988), *Democracy and Participation in Athens*, Cambridge.

SLATER, W. J. (1995), 'The Theatricality of Justice', *CB* 71: 143–57.

SMITH, E. H. (1944), 'Some Things About Witnesses', *Kentucky State Bar Journal*, 8: 37–44.

SMITH, R. W. (1974), *The Art of Rhetoric in Alexandria*, The Hague.

SMOTRYTSCH, A. P. (1966), 'Die Vorgänger des Herondas', *AAntHung* 14: 1–75.

SOLMSEN, F. (1931), *Antiphonstudien*, Neue Philologische Untersuchungen, 8, Berlin, repr. Hildesheim, 2004.

—— (1954), review of Radermacher, *AS*, in *Gnomon*, 26: 213–19.

SOUBIE, A. (1973–4), 'Les Preuves dans les plaidoyers des orateurs attiques', *RIDA* 20: 171–253; 21: 77–134.

SPENGEL, L. (1828) *Artium scriptores*, Stuttgart.

SPRAGUE, R. K. (1972) (ed.), *The Older Sophists*, Columbia, SC.

STAMPP, K. M. (1956), *The Peculiar Institution: Slavery in the Ante-bellum South*, New York.

STARR, C. G. (1968), *The Awakening of the Greek Historical Spirit*, New York.

STEINWENTER, A. (1925), *Die Streitbeendigung durch Urteil, Schiedsspruch und Vergleich nach griechischem Recht*, Münchener Beiträge zur Papyrusforschung und antiken Rechtsgeschichte, 8, Munich.

—— (1934), review of Paoli, *Studi sul processo attico* (1933), *ZRG* 54: 382–7.

STOFFELS, P. (1954), 'Billijkheid in het Oud-Griekse recht', diss. Amsterdam.

STONE, I. F. (1988), *The Trial of Socrates*, Boston.

STRASBURGER, H. (1958), 'Thukydides und die politische Selbstdarstellung der Athener', *Hermes*, 86: 17–40.

STRAUSS, B. S. (1979), 'Division and Conquest: Athens 403–386 BC', diss. Yale (pub. as Strauss 1987).

STRAUSS, B. S. (1987), *Athens After the Peloponnesian War: Class, Faction, and Policy 403–386 BC*, London and Sydney.

SÜSS, W. (1910), *Ethos: Studien zur älteren griechischen Rhetorik*, Leipzig and Berlin.

TALAMANCA, M. (1975), 'La legge di Dem. "or." 21, 94', *Bulletino dell' Istituto di Diritto Romano*, 17: 93–159.

THOMAS, Y. (1984), *Mommsen et l'"isolierung" du droit (Rome, l'Allemagne et l'État)*, Paris.

THOMPSON, C. V. (1894), 'Slave Torture in Athens', *CR* 8: 134–5.

THOMPSON, W. E. (1968), 'An Oratorical Fragment. POxy. 2538', *Rivista di filologia*, 96: 149–50.

—— (1971*a*), 'The Prosopography of Demosthenes LVII', *AJP* 92: 89–91.

—— (1971*b*), 'The Deme in Kleisthenes' Reforms', *Symb. Osl.* 46: 72–9.

—— (1974), 'Tot Atheniensibus Idem Nomen Erat...', in D. W. Bradeen and M. F. McGregor (eds.), *Phoros: Tribute to Benjamin Dean Merritt*, Locust Valley: 144–9.

—— (1981), 'Athenian Attitudes to Wills', *Prudentia*, 13: 13–24.

THÜR, G. (1977), *Beweisführung vor den Schwurgerichtshöfen Athens: Die Proklesis zur Basanos*, Sitz. Wien, 317, Vienna.

—— (1987): 'Neuere Untersuchungen zum Prozeßrecht der griechischen Poleis: Formen des Urteils', in D. Simon (ed.) *Ius Commune. Akten des 26. Deutschen Rechtshistorikertages, Sonderhefte 30.* Frankfurt a.M.: 467–84.

—— (1996*a*), 'Oaths and Dispute Settlement in Ancient Greek Law', in Foxhall and Lewis 1996: 57–72.

—— (1996*b*), 'Reply to D. C. Mirhady: Torture and Rhetoric in Athens', *JHS* 116: 132–4.

TODD, S. C. (1990*a*), 'The Purpose of Evidence in Athenian Courts', in Cartledge *et al.* 1990: 19–39.

—— (1990*b*), '*Lady Chatterley's Lover* and the Attic Orators: The Social Composition of the Athenian Jury', *JHS* 110: 146–73 (Ch. 12 in this collection).

—— (2000) (tr.), *Lysias*, Austin, Tex.

TORTZEN, G., and HEINE NIELSEN, T. (1995) (eds.), *Gammel Dansk: Studier til ære for M. H. Hansen*, Copenhagen.

TRAILL, J. S. (1975), *The Political Organization of Attica: A Study of the Demes, Trittyes and Phylai, and their Representation in the Athenian Council*, Hesperia Suppl., 14, Princeton.

TRENKNER, S. (1958), *The Greek Novella in the Classical Period*, Cambridge.

TREVES, P. (1936), 'Apocrifi Demostenici', *Athenaeum*, 14: 233–66.

—— (1940), 'Les Documents apocryphes du "Pro Corona" ', *Les Études Classiques*, 9: 138–74.

TREVETT, J. (1992), *Apollodoros, the Son of Pasion*, Oxford.

TURNER, E. G. (1952), *Athenian Books in the Fifth and Fourth Centuries B.C.*, London.

TWINING, W. (1983), 'Identification and Misidentification in Legal Processes: Redefining the Problem', in Lloyd-Bostock and Clifford 1983: 255–83.

—— (1984), 'Evidence and Legal Theory', *Modern Law Review*, 47: 261–83.

UDOVITCH, A. (1985), 'Islamic Law and the Social Context of Exchange in the Medieval Middle East', in Humphreys 1985: 445–65.

USHER, S. (1965), 'Individual Characterisation in Lysias', *Eranos*, 63: 99–119.

—— (1976), 'Lysias and his Clients', *GRBS* 17: 31–40 (Ch. 2 this collection).

—— (1985) (tr.), *Dionysius of Halicarnassus: Critical Essays*, II, Cambridge, Mass.

—— (1999), *Greek Oratory: Tradition and Originality*, Oxford.

—— and NAJOCK, D. (1982), 'A Statistical Study of Authorship in the Corpus Lysiacum', *CHum* 16: 85–105.

USSHER, R. G. (1985), 'The Mimic Tradition of "Character" in Herodas', *QUCC* 50: 45–68.

VAHLEN, J. (1903), 'Über die Rede des Lysias in Platos Phaedrus', *Sitzungsberichte der Berliner Akademie* 2: 788–816, repr. in id., *Gesammelte Philologische Schriften*, II (Leipzig, 1923): 675–707.

VAN GULIK, R. (1956), *T'ang-yin-pi-shih, 'Parallel Cases from under the Peartree': A Thirteenth Century Manual of Legal Jurisprudence*, Leiden.

VAN VELSEN, J. (1969), 'Procedural Informality, Reconciliation and False Comparisons', in M. Gluckman (ed.), *Ideas and Procedures in African Customary Law*, London: 137–50.

VANDERPOOL, E. (1966), 'Some Attic Inscriptions', *Hesperia*, 66: 274–83.

VENEZIS, E. (1931), *To Noumero 31328*, Athens.

VERNANT, J.-P. (1983), *Myth and Thought among the Greeks*, London (French original, Paris, 1965).

VERRALL, A. W. (1889*a*), '*TOPOS, TOPÊ (?)*, and *TOPAÔ*', *Journal of Philology*, 9: 126–63.

—— (1889*b*), 'Korax and Tisias', *Journal of Philology*, 9: 197–210.

VERSNEL, H. (1991), 'Beyond Cursing: The Appeal to Justice in Judicial Prayers', in C. A. Faraone and D. Obbink (eds.), *Magika Hiera: Ancient Greek Magic and Religion*, New York.

VIANELLO DE CÓRDOVA, P. (1980) (ed.), *Lisias: Sobre el asesinato de Eratóstenes, Defensa*, Cuadernos del Centro de Estudios Clásicos, 11, Mexico City.

VINOGRADOFF, P. (1922), *Outlines of Historical Jurisprudence*, 2 vols., Oxford; repr. New York, 1971.

VINOGRADOFF, P. (1928), *The Collected Papers of Paul Vinogradoff with a Memoir by the Right Hon. H. A. L. Fisher*, 2 vols. Oxford; repr. London, 1963.

VOLLMER, G. (1958), 'Studien zum Beweis antiphontischer Reden', diss. Hamburg.

WALLACE, R. W. (2000), review of Carawan, *Rhetoric and the Law of Draco* (1998), in *BMCR* 02.05.2000. (http://ccat.sas.upenn.edu/bmcr/2000/2000–5–02.html).

WEINSTOCK, H. (1912), *De Erotico Lysiaco*, Westfalen.

WEISS, E. (1923), *Griechisches Privatrecht auf rechtsvergleichender Grundlage*, I, Leipzig.

WEIßENBERGER, M. (1993), 'Die erste Rede des Lysias', *AU* 36.3: 55–71.

WELLES, C. B. (1963) (tr.), *Diodorus of Sicily* VIII *(Books XVI. 66–95 and XVII)*, Cambridge, Mass.

WEST, M. L. (1978), *Hesiod, Works and Days*, Oxford.

WEST, S. (1970), 'Chalcenteric Negligence', *CQ* 20: 288–96.

WESTERMANN, A. (1850), 'Untersuchungen über die in die attischen Redner eingelegten Urkunden. II. Prüfung sammtlicher in die attischen Redner eingelegten Zeugenaussagen', *Abhandlungen der philologisch-historischen Classe der Königlich Sächsischen Gesellschaft der Wissenschaften*, 1: 61–136.

WESTERMANN, W. L. (1955), *The Slave Systems of Greek and Roman Antiquity*, Philadelphia.

WHITE, J. B. (1990), *Justice as Translation: An Essay in Cultural and Legal Criticism*, Chicago.

WHITEHEAD, D. (1977), *The Ideology of the Athenian Metic*, Philological Society Suppl., 4, Cambridge.

—— (1980), 'The Tribes of the Thirty Tyrants', *JHS* 100: 208–13.

—— (1986), *The Demes of Attica 508/7–c. 250 BC: A Political and Social Study*, Princeton.

WIEAEKER, F. (1965), *Cicero als Advokat*, Vortrag gehalten vor der Berliner Juristischen Gesellschafte am 29. April 1964, Berlin, Schriftenreihe der Juristischen Gesellschaft e. V. Berlin, Heft 20.

WIEMKEN, H. (1972), *Der griechische Mimus: Dokumente zur Geschichte des antiken Volkstheaters*, Bremen.

WILAMOWITZ-MOELLENDORFF, U. VON (1923*a*), 'Lesefrüchte CLXXI', *Hermes*, 58: 57–61.

—— (1923*b*) 'Lesefrüchte CLXXII', *Hermes*, 58: 61–9.

WILCOX, S. (1943), 'Corax and the "Prolegomena" ', *AJP* 64: 1–23.

WILES, D. (1989), 'Marriage and Prostitution in Classical New Comedy', in J. Redmond (ed.), *Themes in Drama*, 11: *Women in Theatre*, Cambridge: 31–48.

WILL, W. (1983), *Athen und Alexander. Untersuchungen zur Geschichte der Stadt von 338 bis 322 v. Chr.*, Munich.

WILLETTS, R. F. (1967), *The Law Code of Gortyn, Kadmos* Suppl., 1, Berlin.

WILLIAMS, B. (1993), *Shame and Necessity*, Berkeley.

WILLIAMS, D. (1983), 'Women on Athenian Vases: Problems of Interpretation', in A. Cameron and A. Kuhrt (eds.), *Images of Women in Antiquity*, London and Detroit: 92–106.

WILLIS, W. H. (1968), 'A Census of the Literary Papyri from Egypt', *GRBS* 9: 205–41.

WILSON, P. J. (1996), 'Tragic Rhetoric: The Use of Tragedy and the Tragic in the Fourth Century', in M. S. Silk (ed.), *Tragedy and the Tragic: Greek Theatre and Beyond*, Oxford: 310–31.

WÖHRLE, G. (1995) (ed.), *Lysias: Drei ausgewählte Reden*, Stuttgart.

WOLF, E. (1950–68), *Griechisches Rechtsdenken*, 4 vols., Frankfurt a.M.

—— (1954), *Griechisches Rechtsdenken*, III, pt. 1: *Rechtsphilosophie der Sokratik und Rechtsdichtung der alten Komödie*, Frankfurt a.M.

—— (1956), *Griechisches Rechtsdenken*, III, pt. 2: *Die Umformung des Rechtsgedankens durch Historik und Rhetorik*, Frankfurt a.M.

WOLFF, H. J. (1946), 'The Origin of Judicial Litigation among the Greeks', *Traditio*, 4: 31–87.

—— (1954), 'Das attische Apotimema', in Kunkel and Wolff 1954: 293–333.

—— (1957), 'Die Grundlage des griechischen Vertragsrechts', *ZRG* 74: 26–7.

—— (1961), *Beiträge zur Rechtsgeschichte Altgriechenlands und des hellenistisch-römischen Ägypten*, Weimar.

—— (1962) 'Gewohnheitsrecht and Gesetzesrecht in der griechischen Rechtsauffassung', in *Deutsche Landesreferate zum VI. Internationalen Kongreß für Rechtsvergleichung in Hamburg 1962*, Berlin and Tubingen: 3–18 (repr. in Berneker 1968: 99–120).

—— (1963), 'Verjährung von Ansprüchen nach attischem Recht', in *Eranion für G. S. Maridakis*, Athens: i. 87–109.

—— (1964), 'Rechtsexperten in der griechischen Antike', *Festschrift zum 45. Deutschen Juristentag*, Karlsruhe: 1–22.

—— (1966) *Die attische 'Paragraphe': ein Beitrag zum Problem der Auflockerung archaischer Prozessformen*, Weimar.

—— (1968), *Demosthenes als Advokat: Funktionen und Methoden des Prozeßpraktikers im klassischen Athen*, Vortrag gehalten vor der Berliner Juristischen Gesellschaft am 30. Juni 1967, Berlin (tr. as Ch. 5 in this collection).

—— (1970), *'Normenkontrolle' und Gesetzesbegriff in der attischen Demokratie*, Heidelberg.

WOLFF, H. J. (1971), 'Methodische Grundfragen der rechtsgeschichtlichen Verwendung attischer Gerichtsreden', in *La Critica del Testo: Atti del II. Congresso Internazionale della Società Italiana di Storia del Diritto (Venezia 18–22 Sett. 1967)*, Florence: ii. 1123–35 (repr. in Wolff 1974: 27–39).

—— (1974), *Opuscula Dispersa*, ed. J. G. Wolf and F. Wieacker, Amsterdam.

—— (1978–2002), *Das Recht der griechischen Papyri Ägyptens in der Zeit der Ptolemäer und des Prinzipats*, Handbuch der Altertumswissenschaft, 10.5, ed. H.-A. Rupprecht, 2 vols., Munich.

WOLPERT, A. O. (2001), 'Lysias 1 and the Politics of the Oikos', *CJ* 96: 415–24.

—— (2002), *Remembering Defeat: Civil War and Civic Memory in Ancient Athens*, Baltimore and London.

—— (2003), 'Addresses to the Jury in Attic Orators', *AJP* 124.4: 537–55.

WORTHINGTON, I. (1992), *A Historical Commentary on Dinarchus: Rhetoric and Conspiracy in Later Fourth-Century Athens*, Ann Arbor, Mich.

—— (1994) (ed.), *Persuasion: Greek Rhetoric in Action*, London and New York.

WYSE, W. (1904), *The Speeches of Isaeus*, Cambridge.

XANTHAKIS-KARAMANOS, G. (1979), 'The Influence of Rhetoric on Fourth-Century Tragedy', *CQ* 29: 66–76.

—— (1980), *Studies in Fourth-Century Tragedy*, Athens.

YAFFE, J. (1972), *So Sue Me! Story of a Community Court*, New York.

YUNIS, H. (1988), 'Law, Politics, and the *Graphê Paranomôn* in Fourth-Century Athens', *GRBS* 29: 361–82.

—— (2000), 'Politics as Literature: Demosthenes and the Burden of the Athenian Past', *Arion*, 8: 97–118 (Ch. 14 in this collection).

—— (2001) (ed.), *Demosthenes On the Crown*, Cambridge.

ZAGAGI, N. (1995), *The Comedy of Menander: Convention, Variation, and Originality*, Bloomington, Ind.

ZOGRAPHOU-LYRA, G. (1991), 'Gorgia 'Hyper Palamēdous Apologia', Alkidamanta 'Odysseus kata Palamēdous Prodosias': Sygkritikē Meletē', Dodone, 20: 9–59.

ZUNTZ, G. (1947), 'Once Again the Antiphontean Tetralogies', *MH* 6: 100–3.

Acknowledgements

Permission to reprint the following items is gratefully acknowledged.

Marius Lavency, 'The Written Plea of the Logographer', tr. from 'Le Plaidoyer écrit du logographe', in *Aspects de la logographie judiciaire attique*, Université de Louvain, Recueil de Travaux d'Histoire et de Philologie, 4.32 (Louvain 1964), 124–51 (tr. George Kennedy).

S. Usher, 'Lysias and his Clients', *Greek Roman and Byzantine Studies*, 17 (1976), 31–40.

Thomas Cole, 'Who Was Corax?', *Illinois Classical Studies*, 16 (1991), 65–84.

John R. Porter, 'Adultery by the Book: Lysias 1 (*On the Murder of Eratosthenes*) and Comic Diegesis', *Echos du Monde Classique*, 40 (1997), 421–53.

Hans Julius Wolff, 'Demosthenes as Advocate', tr. from *Demosthenes als Advokat: Funktionen und Methoden des Prozesspraktikers in klassischen Athen* (Berlin: Walter de Gruyter & Co., 1969) (tr. Jess Miner in collaboration with Gerhard Thür).

Harald Meyer-Laurin, 'Law and Equity in the Attic Trial', tr. from *Gesetz und Billigkeit im attischen Prozess*, Graezistische Abhandlungen, 1 (Weimar, 1965), 1–31 (tr. David Mirhady).

S. C. Humphreys, 'Social Relations on Stage: Witnesses in Classical Athens', in Sally Humphreys (ed.), *The Discourse of Law* (*History and Anthropology*, 1.2) (London, 1985).

Michael Gagarin, 'The Nature of Proofs in Antiphon', *Classical Philology*, 85 (1990), 22–32.

Christopher Carey, '"Artless Proofs" in Aristotle and the Orators', *Bulletin of the Institute of Classical Studies*, 39 (1994), 95–106.

David Mirhady, 'Torture and Rhetoric in Athens', *Journal of Hellenic Studies*, 116 (1996), 119–31.

Josiah Ober, 'Ability and Education: The Power of Persuasion', from *Mass and Elite in Democratic Athens: Rhetoric, Ideology, and the Power of the People* (Princeton: Princeton University Press, 1989), 156–91.

Stephen Todd, '*Lady Chatterley's Lover* and the Attic Orators', *Journal of Hellenic Studies*, 110 (1990), 146–73.

Lene Rubinstein, 'Arguments from Precedent in the Attic Orators', tr. from 'Praecedensargumenter i de attiske retstaler', in Chr. Gorm. Tortzen and Thomas Heine Nielsen (eds.), *Gammel Dansk. studiere et alia til ære for Mogens Herman Hansen på hans 55-års fødselsdag 20. august 1995* (Copenhagen, 1995), 80–4.

Harvey Yunis, 'Politics as Literature: Demosthenes and the Burden of the Athenian Past', *Arion*, 8 (2000), 97–118.

Index of Passages Discussed